MKT 111

Principles of Marketing

Charles W. Lamb | Joseph F. Hair | Carl McDaniel

CENGAGE
Learning™

Australia • Brazil • Japan • Korea • Mexico • Singapore • Spain • United Kingdom • United States

CENGAGE
Learning™

MKT 111: Principles of Marketing

Essentials of Marketing, 7th Edition
Charles W. Lamb | Joseph F. Hair | Carl McDaniel
© 2012, 2009 South-Western Cengage Learning. All rights reserved.

MKTG, 5th Edition
Charles W. Lamb | Joseph F. Hair | Carl McDaniel
© 2012, 2011 South-Western, Cengage Learning. All rights reserved.

Executive Editors:
Maureen Staudt
Michael Stranz

Senior Project Development Manager:
Linda deStefano

Marketing Specialist:
Courtney Sheldon

Senior Production/Manufacturing Manager:
Donna M. Brown

PreMedia Manager:
Joel Brennecke

Sr. Rights Acquisition Account Manager:
Todd Osborne

Cover Image:
Getty Images*

*Unless otherwise noted, all cover images used by Custom
Solutions, a part of Cengage Learning, have been supplied
courtesy of Getty Images with the exception of the Earthview
cover image, which has been supplied by the National
Aeronautics and Space Administration (NASA).

For product information and technology assistance, contact us at
Cengage Learning Customer & Sales Support, 1-800-354-9706

For permission to use material from this text or product,
submit all requests online at **cengage.com/permissions**
Further permissions questions can be emailed to
permissionrequest@cengage.com

This book contains select works from existing Cengage Learning resources and
was produced by Cengage Learning Custom Solutions for collegiate use. As such,
those adopting and/or contributing to this work are responsible for editorial
content accuracy, continuity and completeness.

Compilation © 2011 Cengage Learning
ISBN-13: 978-1-133-27067-6

ISBN-10: 1-133-27067-0

Cengage Learning
5191 Natorp Boulevard
Mason, Ohio 45040
USA

Cengage Learning is a leading provider of customized learning solutions with
office locations around the globe, including Singapore, the United Kingdom,
Australia, Mexico, Brazil, and Japan. Locate your local office at:
international.cengage.com/region.
Cengage Learning products are represented in Canada by Nelson Education, Ltd.
For your lifelong learning solutions, visit **www.cengage.com/custom.**
Visit our corporate website at **www.cengage.com.**

Printed in the United States of America

Table of Contents

From Essentials of Marketing, 7th Edition

Chapter 1   An Overview of Marketing 2
Chapter 2   Strategic Planning for Competitive Advantage 34
Chapter 3   Ethics and Social Responsibility 72
Chapter 4   The Marketing Environment... 102
Chapter 6   Consumer Decision Making 188
Chapter 8   Segmenting and Targeting Markets 258
Chapter 9   Decision Support Systems and Marketing Research 290
Chapter 10   Product Concepts 332
Chapter 12   Marketing Channels and Supply Chain Management 388
Chapter 14   Marketing Communications and Advertising.................... 470
Chapter 15   Public Relations, Sales Promotion, and Personal Selling 524

Glossary 602
Endnotes 612
Indexes 625

From MKTG, 5e

Chapter 22   Social Media and Marketing 350

The World of Marketing

PART 1

WHAT'S INSIDE

An Overview
of Marketing 2

Strategic Planning for
Competitive Advantage 34

Ethics and Social
Responsibility 72

The Marketing
Environment 102

Developing a
Global Vision 142

An Overview of Marketing

LEARNING OUTCOMES

1 Define the term *marketing*

2 Describe four marketing management philosophies

3 Discuss the differences between sales and market orientations

4 Describe several reasons for studying marketing

WHAT IS MARKETING?

What does the term *marketing* mean to you? Many people think it means the same as personal selling. Others think marketing is the same as personal selling and advertising. Still others believe marketing has something to do with making products available in stores, arranging displays, and maintaining inventories of products for future sales. Actually, marketing includes all of these activities and more.

Marketing has two facets. First, it is a philosophy, an attitude, a perspective, or a management orientation that stresses customer satisfaction. Second, marketing is activities and processes used to implement this philosophy.

The American Marketing Association's definition of marketing focuses on the second facet. Marketing is the activity, set of institutions, and processes for creating, communicating, delivering, and exchanging offerings that have value for customers, clients, partners, and society at large.[1]

Marketing involves more than just activities performed by a group of people in a defined area or department. In the often-quoted words of David Packard, cofounder of Hewlett-Packard, "Marketing is too important to be left only to the marketing department." Marketing entails processes that focus on delivering value and benefits to customers, not just selling goods, services, and/or ideas. It uses communication, distribution, and pricing strategies to provide customers and other stakeholders with the goods, services, ideas, values, and benefits they desire when and where they want them. It involves building long-term, mutually rewarding relationships when these benefit all parties concerned. Marketing also entails an understanding that organizations have many connected stakeholder "partners," including employees, suppliers, stockholders, distributors, and society at large.

Research shows that companies that reward employees with incentives and recognition on a consistent basis are those that perform best.[2] Home Depot CEO Frank Blake rejects the notion that you should pay employees as little as you can and get as much work out of them as possible.[3] The motto of Wegmans Food Markets, the Rochester-based grocery chain that has been ranked by *Fortune* magazine as the best company to work for in America, states, "Employees first, customers second." The rationale is that if employees are happy, customers will be too.[4]

> *Marketing is too important to be left only to the marketing department.*

One desired outcome of marketing is an exchange; people giving up something to receive something they would rather have. Normally, we think of money as the medium of exchange. We "give up" money to "get" the goods and services we want. Exchange does not require money, however. Two persons may barter or trade such items as baseball cards or oil paintings. An exchange can take place only if the following five conditions exist:

1. There must be at least two parties.

2. Each party has something that might be of value to the other party.

Please note your opinion on each of the following questions.

Think about where you buy cosmetics or personal care products. Using the following scale, enter the number that indicates how likely you are to:

1	2	3	4	5	6
Not likely at all					Extremely likely

___ Say positive things about the company to other people.

___ Recommend the company to someone who seeks your advice.

___ Encourage friends and relatives to do business with the company.

___ Consider the company your first choice to buy cosmetics or personal care products.

___ Do more business with the company in the next few years.

Now, total your score. Read the chapter to find out what your score means at the end.

marketing
The activity, set of institutions, and processes for creating, communicating, delivering, and exchanging offerings that have value for customers, clients, partners, and society at large.

exchange
People giving up something to receive something they would rather have.

Each party is capable of communication and delivery.

4. Each party is free to accept or reject the exchange offer.

5. Each party believes it is appropriate or desirable to deal with the other party.[5]

Exchange will not necessarily take place even if all these conditions exist. They are, however, necessary for exchange to be possible. For example, you may place an advertisement in your local newspaper stating that your used automobile is for sale at a certain price. Several people may call you to ask about the car, some may test-drive it, and one or more may even make you an offer. All five conditions are necessary for an exchange to exist. But unless you reach an agreement with a buyer and actually sell the car, an exchange will not take place. Notice that marketing can occur even if an exchange does not occur. In the example just discussed, you would have engaged in marketing even if no one bought your used automobile.

production orientation
A philosophy that focuses on the internal capabilities of the firm rather than on the desires and needs of the marketplace.

sales orientation
The idea that people will buy more goods and services if aggressive sales techniques are used and that high sales result in high profits.

REVIEW LEARNING OUTCOME

LO① Define the term *marketing*

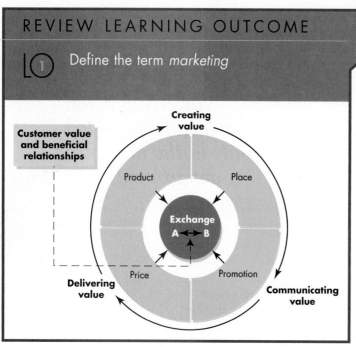

LO②
MARKETING MANAGEMENT PHILOSOPHIES

Four competing philosophies strongly influence an organization's marketing processes. These philosophies are commonly referred to as production, sales, market, and societal marketing orientations.

Production Orientation

A *production orientation* is a philosophy that focuses on the internal capabilities of the firm rather than on the desires and needs of the marketplace. A production orientation means that management assesses its resources and asks these questions: "What can we do best?" "What can our engineers design?" "What is easy to produce, given our equipment?" In the case of a service organization, managers ask, "What services are most convenient for the firm to offer?" and "Where do our talents lie?" Some have referred to this orientation as a *Field of Dreams* orientation, from the movie's well-known line, "If we build it, they will come." The furniture industry is infamous for its disregard of customers and for its slow cycle times. This has always been a production-oriented industry.

There is nothing wrong with assessing a firm's capabilities; in fact, such assessments are major considerations in strategic marketing planning (see Chapter 2). A production orientation falls short because it does not consider whether the goods and services that the firm produces most efficiently also meet the needs of the marketplace. Sometimes what a firm can best produce is exactly what the market wants. For example, the research and development department of 3M's commercial tape division developed and patented the adhesive component of Post-It Notes a year before a commercial application was identified. In other situations, as when competition is weak or demand exceeds supply, a production-oriented firm can survive and even prosper. More often, however, firms that succeed in competitive markets have a clear understanding that they must first determine what customers want and then produce it, rather than focusing on what company management thinks should be produced.

Sales Orientation

A *sales orientation* is based on the ideas that people will buy more goods and services if aggressive sales techniques are used and that high sales result in high profits. Not only are sales to the final buyer emphasized, but intermediaries are also encouraged to push manufacturers' products more aggressively. To sales-oriented firms, marketing means selling things and collecting money.

The fundamental problem with a sales orientation, as with a production orientation, is a lack of understanding of the needs and wants of the marketplace. Sales-oriented companies often find that, despite the quality of their sales force, they cannot convince people to buy goods or services that are neither wanted nor needed.

Some sales-oriented firms simply fail to understand what is important to their customers. Many so-called dot-com businesses that came into existence in the late 1990s are no longer around because they focused on the technology rather than the customer.

Market Orientation

The marketing concept is a simple and intuitively appealing philosophy that articulates a market orientation. It states that the social and economic justification for an organization's existence is the satisfaction of customer wants and needs while meeting organizational objectives. It is based on an understanding that a sale does not depend on an aggressive sales force, but rather on a customer's decision to purchase a product. What a business thinks it produces is not of primary importance to its success. Instead, what customers think they are buying—the perceived value—defines a business. The marketing concept includes the following:

© CARL D. WALSH/AURORA PHOTOS

1. Focusing on customer wants and needs so that the organization can distinguish its product(s) from competitors' offerings

2. Integrating all the organization's activities, including production, to satisfy these wants

3. Achieving long-term goals for the organization by satisfying customer wants and needs legally and responsibly

The recipe for success is to consistently deliver a unique experience that your competitors cannot match and that satisfies the intentions and preferences of your target buyers.[6] This requires a thorough understanding of your customers and distinctive capabilities that enable your company to execute plans on the basis of this customer understanding, and delivering the desired experience using and integrating all of the resources of the firm.[7]

Firms that adopt and implement the marketing concept are said to be market oriented. Achieving a market orientation involves obtaining information about customers, competitors, and markets; examining the information from a total business perspective; determining how to deliver superior customer value; and implementing actions to provide value to customers.

What are the names of some firms known for delivering superior customer value and satisfaction? The third annual National Retail Federation/American Express Customer Service Survey listed L.L. Bean, Zappos.com, Amazon.com, Overstock.com, and Blair as the top five U.S. retailers for customer service.[8] *BusinessWeek* listed USAA, L.L. Bean, Fairmont Hotels, Lexus, and Trader Joe's as its best-in-class Customer Service Champs.[9]

Understanding your competitive arena and competitors' strengths and weaknesses is a critical component of a market orientation. This includes assessing what existing or potential competitors might be intending to do tomorrow as well as what they are doing today. Western Union failed to define its competitive arena as telecommunications, concentrating instead on telegraph services, and was eventually outflanked by fax technology. Had Western Union been a market-oriented company, its management might have better understood the changes taking place, seen the competitive threat, and developed strategies to counter the threat.

marketing concept
The idea that the social and economic justification for an organization's existence is the satisfaction of customer wants and needs while meeting organizational objectives.

market orientation
A philosophy that assumes that a sale does not depend on an aggressive sales force but rather on a customer's decision to purchase a product. It is synonymous with the marketing concept.

"Have we met before?"
Recycling a single aluminum can
saves enough energy to power
a TV for three hours.

© AP IMAGES/PRNEWSFOTO/PEPSI-COLA COMPANY

Societal Marketing Orientation

The societal marketing orientation extends the marketing concept by acknowledging that some products that customers want may not really be in their best interests or the best interests of society as a whole. This philosophy states that an organization exists not only to satisfy customer wants and needs and to meet organizational objectives, but also to preserve or enhance individuals' and society's long-term best interests. Marketing products and containers that are less toxic than normal, are more durable, contain reusable materials, or are made of recyclable materials is consistent with a societal marketing orientation. The American Marketing Association's definition of marketing recognizes the importance of a societal marketing orientation by including "society at large" as one of the constituencies for which marketing seeks to provide value.

Although the societal marketing concept has been discussed for over 30 years, it did not receive widespread support until the early 2000s. Concerns such as climate change, the depleting ozone layer, fuel shortages, pollution, and raised health concerns have caused consumers and legislators to be more aware of the need for companies and consumers to adopt measures that conserve resources and cause less damage to the environment.

Studies reporting consumers' attitudes toward, and intentions to buy, more environmentally friendly products show widely varying results. One study that helps explain some of this contradiction found that 44 percent of consumers were "theoretically" interested in buying environmentally friendly products, but the proportion doing so was much less.[10] The three top reasons customers gave for not following through by purchasing and using these more environmentally friendly products were doubts about effectiveness, expense, and lack of availability at convenient outlets.[11] Another study generally confirmed the notion that many consumers have favorable attitudes regarding environmentally friendly products but are not willing to accept trade-offs. Specifically, 50 to 75 percent of consumers reported that environmental issues are important, but they are not willing to make trade-offs for higher costs or lower performance. Only 5 to 10 percent are willing to accept trade-offs to buy environmentally friendly products.[12]

Some believe that many consumers want to "go green" but don't know where to start.[13] One study found that while half of its respondents thought a company's environmental record was important, only 7 percent could name an environmentally friendly product they had purchased.[14]

Many marketers have made substantial commitments to either produce products using more environmentally friendly processes or making more environmentally friendly products. Coca-Cola has committed to spending $44 million to build the world's largest plastic-bottle-to-bottle recycling plant.[15] The company has also set a goal of returning to communities and nature an equivalent amount of water as used in its beverages and their production.[16] Home Depot, UPS, and Wal-Mart are also among the business leaders in the so-called "eco-friendly" movement.[17]

What will the future bring? The current trends are that more customers are becoming concerned about the environment each year, more customers are trying to buy environmentally friendly products and support more environmentally friendly companies, and more companies are

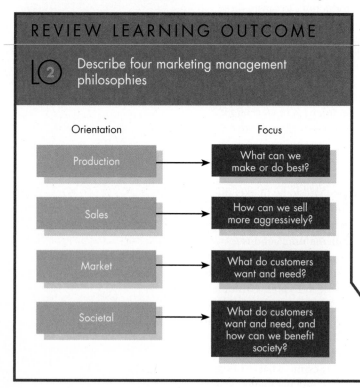

REVIEW LEARNING OUTCOME

LO 2   Describe four marketing management philosophies

Orientation	Focus
Production	What can we make or do best?
Sales	How can we sell more aggressively?
Market	What do customers want and need?
Societal	What do customers want and need, and how can we benefit society?

joining the movement by developing processes and products that do less damage to the environment than in the past. The number of "green" products released in the U.S. more than doubled from 2005 to 2007, and even more were introduced in 2008.[18] Adopting a societal marketing orientation and clearly communicating this decision and the actions that support it helps firms differentiate themselves from competitors and strengthens their positioning.

DIFFERENCES BETWEEN SALES AND MARKET ORIENTATIONS

The differences between sales and market orientations are substantial. The two orientations can be compared in terms of five characteristics: the organization's focus, the firm's business, those to whom the product is directed, the firm's primary goal, and the tools used to achieve those goals.

The Organization's Focus

Personnel in sales-oriented firms tend to be "inward looking," focusing on selling what the organization makes rather than making what the market wants. Many of the historic sources of competitive advantage—technology, innovation, economies of scale—allowed companies to focus their efforts internally and prosper. Today, many successful firms derive their competitive advantage from an external, market-oriented focus. A market orientation has helped companies such as the Royal Bank of Canada and Southwest Airlines outperform their competitors. These companies put customers at the center of their business in ways most companies do poorly or not at all.

A sales orientation has led to the demise of many firms including Streamline.com, the Digital Entertainment Network, and Urban Box Office. As one technology industry analyst put it, "No one has ever gone to a Web site because they heard there was great Java running."[19]

Customer Value Customer value is the relationship between benefits and the sacrifice necessary to obtain those benefits. Customer value is not simply a matter of high quality. A high-quality product that is available only at a high price will not be perceived as a good value, nor will

COURTESY OF SOUTHWEST AIRLINES

Southwest Airlines was recently named one of *BusinessWeek* "Customer Service Champs," and has ranked in as one of "America's Top Ten" most admired corporations by *Fortune* magazine for 11 consecutive years.

bare-bones service or low-quality goods selling for a low price. Instead, customers value goods and services that are of the quality they expect and that are sold at prices they are willing to pay. Value can be used to sell a Mercedes-Benz as well as a Tyson frozen chicken dinner.

Lower-income consumers are price sensitive, but they will pay for products if they deliver a benefit that is worth the money.[20] The Global Perspectives box in this chapter illustrates that point.

The automobile industry provides another illustration of the importance of creating customer value. To penetrate the fiercely competitive luxury automobile market, Lexus adopted a customer-driven approach, with particular emphasis on service. Lexus stresses product quality with a standard of zero defects in manufacturing. The service quality goal is to treat each customer as one would treat a guest in one's home, to pursue the

societal marketing orientation
The idea that an organization exists not only to satisfy customer wants and needs and to meet organizational objectives, but also to preserve or enhance individuals' and society's long-term best interests.

customer value
The relationship between benefits and the sacrifice necessary to obtain those benefits.

P&G in Mexico

In the early 2000s the Mexican market share for Downy fabric softener was low and stagnant. Proctor & Gamble (P&G) wasn't sure what could be done about it, since the assumption was that people who didn't have modern washing machines didn't use softener. Not wanting to compromise the Downy brand by dropping the price too much, P&G decided to try to come up with something specific to the needs of the lower-income consumer.

One of the things P&G people noticed was the problem of water. Millions of rural women still lug buckets back from wells or communal pumps. In the cities, many have running water for only a few hours a day. Most homes do not have fully automatic washing machines; even fewer have dryers. All this makes doing the laundry a seriously draining chore.

At the same time, lower-income Mexican women take laundry very, very seriously. They cannot afford to buy many new clothes, but they take great pride in ensuring that their family is dressed well. Sending your children to school in clean, ironed clothing is a visible sign of being a good mother. P&G found that Mexican women spend more time on laundry than on the rest of their housework combined. More than 90 percent use softener, even women who do some or all of their laundry by hand.

"By spending time with women, we learned that the softening process is really demanding," recalls Antonio Hidalgo, P&G brand manager for Downy Single Rinse at the time of its debut in March 2004. A typical load of laundry went through the following six-step process: wash; rinse; rinse; add softener; rinse; rinse. No problem if all this is just a matter of pressing a button every once in a while. But it's no joke if you are doing the wash by hand or have to walk half a mile to get water. Even semiautomatic machines require that water be added and extracted manually. And if you get the timing wrong, the water supply might run out in the middle. "The big aha!" says a P&G executive, was discovering how valuable water was to lower-income Mexicans. "And we only got that by experiencing how they live their life."

Putting it all together, P&G knew that Mexican women liked to use softener; they had high standards for performance; and doing the laundry was arduous and time consuming, and required large amounts of water.

Having identified a problem (making laundry easier and less water-intensive), P&G turned to its labs for an answer. Their solution: Downy Single Rinse (DSR). Instead of a six-step process, DSR reduced it to three—wash, add softener, rinse—saving enormous time, effort, and water. The product was launched in 2004 and became an immediate hit.[21]

What lessons can other consumer goods manufacturers learn from P&G's experience? Explain why value is more important than price in marketing to lower-income households.

perfect person-to-person relationship, and to strive to improve continually. This pursuit has enabled Lexus to establish a clear, high-quality image and capture a significant share of the luxury car market.

Marketers interested in customer value:

☛ *Offer products that perform:* This is the bare minimum requirement. The example discussed in the Global Perspectives box in this chapter illustrates the importance of listening to customers to determine the performance characteristics that are most important to them.

☛ *Earn trust:* A stable base of loyal customers enhances a firm's ability to grow and prosper. About 80 percent of Starbucks' revenues come from customers who visit the store an average of 18 times per month.[22]

☛ *Avoid unrealistic pricing:* E-marketers are leveraging Internet technology to redefine how prices are set and negotiated. With lower costs, e-marketers can often offer lower prices than their brick-and-mortar counterparts. The enormous popularity of auction sites such as eBay and Amazon.com and the customer-bid model used by Priceline illustrates that online customers are interested in bargain prices. Many are not willing to pay a premium for the convenience of examining the merchandise and taking it home with them. Others will gladly pay a premium for an experience that is not only functionally rewarding, but emotionally rewarding as well. Executives at Starwood Hotels and Resorts' "W" chain believe that they are able to make an emotional connection when customers walk through the door of their hotel room and see the bed with clean-looking, sumptuous linens and other amenities.[23]

☞ *Give the buyer facts:* Today's sophisticated consumer wants informative advertising and knowledgeable salespeople. It is becoming very difficult for business marketers to differentiate themselves from competitors. Rather than trying to sell products, salespeople need to find out what the customer needs, which is usually a combination of products, services, and thought leadership.[24] In other words, salespeople need to start with the needs of the customer and work toward the solution.

☞ *Offer organization-wide commitment in service and after-sales support:* According to Gartner Research vice president Michael Maoz, organizations should incorporate customer service as a wide-ranging business strategy in order to keep up with customer expectations. "In the past, customer service was a department, the place that you called for specific redress of a grievance or information about your bill. Right now, rather than a function in that department, it is an enterprise strategy. That transition has profound implications on how we design all our processes across all our different communications channels."[25]

☞ *Co-Creation:* Some companies and products allow customers to help create their own experience. For example, TiVo allows people to watch chosen TV shows on their own schedules.

Customer Satisfaction Customer satisfaction is the customer's evaluation of a good or service in terms of whether that good or service has met the customer's needs and expectations. Failure to meet needs and expectations results in dissatisfaction with the good or service. Some companies, in their passion to drive down costs, have damaged their relationships with customers. Dell Computers, Home Depot, and Northwest Airlines are examples of companies where executives lost track of the delicate balance between efficiency and service.[26] Each has realized change is needed and has implemented improvements. Firms that have a reputation for delivering high levels of customer satisfaction do things differently from their competitors. Top management is obsessed with customer satisfaction, and employees throughout the organization understand the link between their job and satisfied customers. The culture of the organization is to focus on delighting customers rather than on selling products.

Nordstrom's impeccable reputation for customer service comes not from its executives or its marketing team, but from the customers themselves. The retail giant is willing to take risks, do unusual and often expensive favors for shoppers, and reportedly even accept returns on items not purchased there. Still, they keep improving. The company recently installed a new database enabling salespeople to assist customers in locating items in inventory somewhere in the chain, but not in a particular store. Customers can then purchase these items online.[27]

© DAN LAMONT/CORBIS

Building Relationships Attracting new customers to a business is only the beginning. The best companies view new-customer attraction as the launching point for developing and enhancing a long-term relationship. Companies can expand market share in three ways: attracting new customers, increasing business with existing customers, and retaining current customers. Building relationships with existing customers directly addresses two of the three possibilities and indirectly addresses the other.

The Customer Experience box in this chapter provides more information about providing customers with rewarding experiences that lead to long-term relationships.

customer satisfaction
Customers' evaluation of a good or service in terms of whether it has met their needs and expectations.

The Essence of Marketing

When one strips away all of the functions, plans, and strategies of marketing and asks the simple question, "What is this all about?" the answer is the customer experience. Think about it—whether you buy something a second or third time or become loyal to a brand depends on the experience that you had while purchasing and consuming the product or service. Most products need to be sold to a customer more than once in order for the company to start making money. Coca-Cola, for example, would have real problems if people bought just one can of Coke and then never purchased a Coke again.

A theme that you will find running throughout this text is the critical importance of providing a good customer experience. In each chapter you will find a box entitled, "Customer Experience" that links the chapter material to the customer experience. Quality is the key driver that can make the customer experience a good one. When we speak of quality we aren't simply referring to product quality or service quality. We are talking about having the highest-quality personnel operations, financial operations, sales activities, and anything else with which the organization is involved. General Electric is the pioneer of a concept called "Six Sigma." A company that adheres to Six Sigma will have only 3.4 defects per 1 million opportunities to experience failure! Thus, purchasers almost never receive a defective product, which is the beginning of a good customer experience.

A good customer experience can lead to customer satisfaction, which, in turn, can lead to loyalty. Satisfaction and loyalty are related but different. Customers are satisfied when their needs and expectations are met. Customers are loyal when they buy again due to rational and emotional ties to the product or service. While satisfaction is necessary for loyalty, it is not sufficient for true loyalty.

You would think that all companies would strive to create a great customer experience. However, a recent study showed that this is not the case. A study of executives conducted nationwide found that 80 percent strongly agree that customer strategies are more important to a company's success than ever before, but many companies fail to design and deliver those strategies and, as such, lose customer commitment and loyalty.[28]

Why do you think that some companies don't have policies to maximize the customer experience? Why is there not a perfect one-to-one relationship between satisfaction and loyalty? That is, if you are satisfied, why might you not be loyal?

---

relationship marketing
A strategy that focuses on keeping and improving relationships with current customers.

Relationship marketing is a strategy that focuses on keeping and improving relationships with current customers. It assumes that many consumers and business customers prefer to have an ongoing relationship with one organization than to switch continually among providers in their search for value. USAA is a good example of a company focused on building long-term relationships with customers. In 2007, a *BusinessWeek/* J.D. Powers & Associates survey ranked USAA as the top provider of customer service among U.S. firms.[29] Customer retention was a core value of the company long before customer loyalty became a popular business concept. USAA believes so strongly in the importance of customer retention that managers' and executives' bonuses are based, in part, on this dimension.

Most successful relationship marketing strategies depend on customer-oriented personnel, effective training programs, employees with authority to make decisions and solve problems, and teamwork.

Customer-Oriented Personnel For an organization to be focused on building relationships with customers, employees' attitudes and actions must be customer oriented. An employee may be the only contact a particular customer has with the firm. In that customer's eyes, the employee is the firm. Any person, department, or division that is not customer-oriented weakens the positive image of the entire organization. For example, a potential customer who is greeted discourteously may well assume that the employee's attitude represents the whole firm.

Isadore Sharp, founder, chair, and CEO of the Four Seasons hotel chain, says that "personal service is not something you can dictate as a policy. It comes from the culture. How you treat your employees is how you expect them to treat the customer."[30]

Some companies, such as Coca-Cola, Delta Air Lines, Hershey Company, Kellogg's, Nautilus, and Sears, have appointed chief customer officers (CCOs). These customer advocates provide an executive voice for customers and report directly to the CEO. Their responsibilities include ensuring that the company maintains a customer-centric culture and that all company employees remain focused on delivering customer value.

The Role of Training Leading marketers recognize the role of employee training in customer service and relationship building. Sales staff at The Container Store receive over 240 hours of training and generous benefits compared to an industry average of 8 hours training and modest benefits.

Empowerment In addition to training, many market-oriented firms are giving employees more authority to solve customer problems on the spot. The term used to describe this delegation of authority is empowerment. Employees develop ownership attitudes when they are treated like part-owners of the business and are expected to act the part. These employees manage themselves, are more likely to work hard, account for their own performance and the company's, and take prudent risks to build a stronger business and sustain the company's success. FedEx customer service representatives are trained and empowered to resolve customer problems. Although the average FedEx transaction costs only $16, the customer service representatives are empowered to spend up to $100 to resolve a customer problem.

Employees at Ritz-Carlton hotels are encouraged to take whatever steps they feel are necessary to ensure that guests enjoy their visits. Any employee can spend up to $2,000—without seeking permission from management—to solve a problem for guests. One Ritz-Carlton chef in Bali had special eggs and milk imported from Singapore and personally delivered by plane so that he could cook for a young guest with food allergies.[31]

Empowerment gives customers the feeling that their concerns are being addressed and gives employees the feeling that their expertise matters. The result is greater satisfaction for both customers and employees.

Teamwork Many organizations that are frequently noted for delivering superior customer value and providing high levels of customer satisfaction, such as Southwest Airlines and Walt Disney World, assign employees to teams and teach them team-building skills. Teamwork entails collaborative efforts of people to accomplish common objectives. Job performance, company performance, product value, and customer satisfaction all improve when people in the same department or work group begin supporting and assisting each other and emphasize cooperation instead of competition. Performance is also enhanced when cross-functional teams align their jobs with customer needs. For example, if a team of telecommunications service representatives is working to improve interaction with customers, back-office people such as computer technicians or training personnel can become part of the team with the ultimate goal of delivering superior customer value and satisfaction.

The Firm's Business

A sales-oriented firm defines its business (or mission) in terms of goods and services. A market-oriented firm defines its business in terms of the benefits its customers seek. People who spend their money, time, and energy expect to receive benefits, not just goods and services. This distinction has enormous implications. As a senior executive of the Coca-Cola Co. noted, Coke is in the hydration business.[32]

empowerment
Delegation of authority to solve customers' problems quickly—usually by the first person that the customer notifies regarding a problem.

teamwork
Collaborative efforts of people to accomplish common objectives.

Because of the limited way it defines its business, a sales-oriented firm often misses opportunities to serve customers whose wants can be met through a wide range of product offerings instead of specific products. For example, in 1989, 220-year-old Britannica had estimated revenues of $650 million and a worldwide sales force of 7,500. Just five years later, after three consecutive years of losses, the sales force had collapsed to as few as 280 representatives. How did this respected company sink so low? Britannica managers saw that competitors were beginning to use CD-ROMs to store huge masses of information, but chose to ignore the new computer technology, as well as an offer to team up with Microsoft.

It's not hard to see why parents would rather give their children an encyclopedia on a compact disc instead of a printed one. The CD-ROM versions were either given away or sold by other publishers for under $400. A full 32-volume set of *Encyclopaedia Britannica* weighs about 120 pounds, costs a minimum of $1,500, and takes up four and one-half feet of shelf space. If Britannica had defined its business as providing information instead of publishing books, it might not have suffered such a precipitous fall.

Adopting a "better late than never" philosophy, Britannica has made its complete 32-volume set available free on the Internet. The company no longer sells door-to-door and hopes to return to profitability by selling advertising on its Web site.

Answering the question, "What is this firm's business?" in terms of the benefits customers seek, instead of goods and services, offers at least three important advantages:

☛ It ensures that the firm keeps focusing on customers and avoids becoming preoccupied with goods, services, or the organization's internal needs.

☛ It encourages innovation and creativity by reminding people that there are many ways to satisfy customer wants.

☛ It stimulates an awareness of changes in customer desires and preferences so that product offerings are more likely to remain relevant.

Having a market orientation and focusing on customer wants do not mean that customers will always receive everything they want. It is not possible, for example, to profitably manufacture and market automobile tires that will last for 100,000 miles for $25. Furthermore, customers' preferences must be mediated by sound professional judgment as to how to deliver the benefits they seek. As Henry Ford once said, "If I had listened to the marketplace, I would have built a faster, cheaper horse."[33] Consumers have a limited set of experiences. They are unlikely to request anything beyond those experiences because they are not aware of benefits they may gain from other potential offerings. For example, before the Internet, many people thought that shopping for some products was boring and time consuming, but could not express their need for electronic shopping.

Those to Whom the Product is Directed

A sales-oriented organization targets its products at "everybody" or "the average customer." A market-oriented organization aims at specific groups of people. The fallacy of developing products directed at the average user is that relatively few average users

L'ORÉAL
PARiS

My perfect weapon to fight
dry and **brittle** hair

ELVIVE
ANTI-BREAKAGE
WITH NUTRI-CERAMIDE

PROVEN RESULTS
UP TO
-60%
LESS BREAKAGE
FROM BRUSHING

Blow-drying and brushing can take its toll on your hair. **ELVIVE Nutri-Ceramide** targets the damaged areas of the hair to help repair it.

► Discover self-defence for your hair.
► The unique Nutri-Ceramide formula helps to transform dry, brittle hair, making it **soft** and **smooth**.
► Elvive Nutri-Ceramide can even help to **prevent split ends**, and leave your hair stronger* than before. The proof: Up to 60 % **less breakage** from brushing.**

BECAUSE YOU'RE WORTH IT.

New ELVIVE Anti-Breakage program with Nutri-Ceramide
A 3 step hair rescue plan. A daily shampoo and conditioner routine with an intensive masque; specially designed to give you stronger,* beautiful hair.

L'ORÉAL
PARIS

www.lorealparis.com

actually exist. Typically, populations are characterized by diversity. An average is simply a midpoint in some set of characteristics. Because most potential customers are not "average," they are not likely to be attracted to an average product marketed to the average customer. Consider the market for shampoo as one simple example. There are shampoos for oily hair, dry hair, and dandruff. Some shampoos remove the gray or color hair. Special shampoos are marketed for infants and elderly people. There is even shampoo for people with average or normal hair (whatever that is), but this is a fairly small portion of the total market for shampoo.

A market-oriented organization recognizes that different customer groups want different features or benefits. It may therefore need to develop different goods, services, and promotional appeals. A market-oriented organization carefully analyzes the market and divides it into groups of people who are fairly similar in terms of selected characteristics. Then the organization develops marketing programs that will bring about mutually satisfying exchanges with one or more of those groups.

Paying attention to the customer isn't exactly a new concept. Back in the 1920s, General Motors began designing cars for every lifestyle and pocketbook. This was a breakthrough for an industry that had been largely driven by production needs ever since Henry Ford promised any color as long as it was black. Chapter 8 thoroughly explores the topic of analyzing markets and selecting those that appear to be most promising to the firm.

The Firm's Primary Goal

A sales-oriented organization seeks to achieve profitability through sales volume and tries to convince potential customers to buy, even if the seller knows that the customer and product are mismatched. Sales-oriented organizations place a higher premium on making a sale than on developing a long-term relationship with a customer. In contrast, the ultimate goal of most market-oriented organizations is to make a profit by creating customer value, providing customer satisfaction, and building long-term relationships with customers. The exception is so-called nonprofit organizations that exist to achieve goals other than profits. Nonprofit organizations can and should adopt a market orientation.

Tools the Organization Uses to Achieve Its Goals

Sales-oriented organizations seek to generate sales volume through intensive promotional activities, mainly personal selling and advertising. In contrast, market-oriented organizations recognize that promotion decisions are only one of four basic marketing mix decisions that have to be made: product decisions, place (or distribution) decisions, promotion decisions, and pricing decisions. A market-oriented organization recognizes that each of these four components is important. Furthermore, market-oriented organizations recognize that marketing is not just a responsibility of the marketing department. Interfunctional coordination means that skills and resources throughout the organization are needed to create, communicate, and deliver superior customer service and value.

A Word of Caution

This comparison of sales and market orientations is not meant to belittle the role of promotion, especially personal selling, in the marketing mix. Promotion is the means by which organizations communicate with present and prospective customers about the merits and characteristics of their organization and products. Effective promotion is an essential part of effective marketing. Salespeople who work for market-oriented organizations are generally perceived by their customers to be problem solvers and important links to supply sources and new products. Chapter 15 examines the nature of personal selling in more detail.

REVIEW LEARNING OUTCOME

LO 3 Discuss the differences between sales and market orientations

	What is the organization's focus?	What business are you in?	To whom is the product directed?	What is your primary goal?	How do you seek to achieve your goal?
Sales Orientation	Inward, on the organization's needs	Selling goods and services	Everybody	Profit through maximum sales volume	Primarily through intensive promotion
Market Orientation	Outward, on the wants and preferences of customers	Satisfying customer wants and needs and delivering superior value	Specific groups of people	Profit through customer satisfaction	Through coordinated marketing and interfunctional activities

---

WHY STUDY MARKETING?

Now that you understand the meaning of the term *marketing*, why it is important to adopt a marketing orientation, how organizations implement this philosophy, and how one-to-one marketing is evolving, you may be asking, "What's in it for me?" or "Why should I study marketing?" These are important questions, whether you are majoring in a business field other than marketing (such as accounting, finance, or management information systems) or a nonbusiness field (such as journalism, economics, or agriculture). There are several important reasons to study marketing: Marketing plays an important role in society, marketing is important to businesses, marketing offers outstanding career opportunities, and marketing affects your life every day.

Marketing Plays an Important Role in Society

The total population of the United States exceeds 300 million people.[34] Think about how many transactions are needed each day to feed, clothe, and shelter a population of this size. The number is huge. And yet it all works quite well, partly because the well-developed U.S. economic system efficiently distributes the output of farms and factories. A typical U.S. family, for example, consumes 2.5 tons of food a year. Marketing makes food available when we want it, in desired quantities, at accessible locations, and in sanitary and convenient packages and forms (such as instant and frozen foods).

Marketing Is Important to Business

The fundamental objectives of most businesses are survival, profits, and growth. Marketing contributes directly to achieving these objectives. Marketing includes the following activities, which are vital to business organizations: assessing the wants and satisfactions of present and potential customers, designing and managing product offerings, determining prices and pricing policies, developing distribution strategies, and communicating with present and potential customers.

All businesspeople, regardless of specialization or area of responsibility, need to be familiar with the terminology and fundamentals of accounting, finance, management, and marketing. People in all business areas need to be able to communicate with specialists in other areas. Furthermore, marketing is not just a job done by people in a marketing department. Marketing is a part of the job of everyone in the organization. Therefore, a basic understanding of marketing is important to all businesspeople.

Marketing Offers Outstanding Career Opportunities

Between a fourth and a third of the entire civilian workforce in the United States performs marketing activities. Marketing offers great career opportunities in such areas as professional selling, marketing research, advertising, retail buying, distribution management, product management, product development, and wholesaling. Marketing career opportunities also exist in a variety of nonbusiness organizations, including hospitals, museums, universities, the armed forces, and various government and social service agencies.

As the global marketplace becomes more challenging, companies all over the world and of all sizes have to become better marketers. For a comprehensive look at career opportunities in marketing and a variety of other useful information about careers, read the Career Appendix at the end of this chapter and visit our Web site at **http://www.cengagebrain.com**.

Marketing Affects Your Life Every Day

Marketing plays a major role in your everyday life. You participate in the marketing process as a consumer of

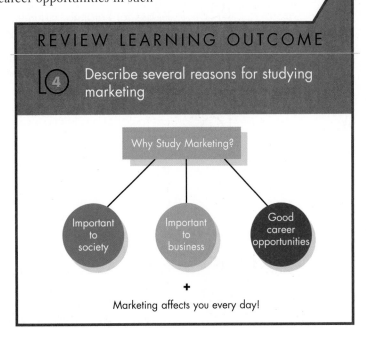

REVIEW LEARNING OUTCOME

LO 4 Describe several reasons for studying marketing

Why Study Marketing?

Important to society

Important to business

Good career opportunities

+

Marketing affects you every day!

goods and services. About half of every dollar you spend pays for marketing costs, such as marketing research, product development, packaging, transportation, storage, advertising, and sales expenses. By developing a better understanding of marketing, you will become a better-informed consumer. You will better understand the buying process and be able to negotiate more effectively with sellers. Moreover, you will be better prepared to demand satisfaction when the goods and services you buy do not meet the standards promised by the manufacturer or the marketer.

Number of competing marketing philosophies (or orientations) that influence an organization's marketing processes ▶ **4**

Number of sales staff training hours/year retail industry average ▶ **8**

The dollar amount FedEx customer service reps are empowered to spend to resolve a customer problem ▶ **100**

240 ◀ Number of training hours/year for The Container Store sales staff

16 ◀ The dollar cost of the average FedEx transaction

2.5 ◀ Tons of food a typical U.S. family consumes each year

REVIEW AND APPLICATIONS

Define the term *marketing*. Marketing is the activity, set of institutions, and processes for creating, communicating, delivering, and exchanging offerings that have value for customers, clients, partners, and society at large.

1.1 What is the AMA? What does it do? How do its services benefit marketers? **www.marketingpower.com**

Describe four marketing management philosophies. The role of marketing and the character of marketing activities within an organization are strongly influenced by its philosophy and orientation. A production-oriented organization focuses on the internal capabilities of the firm rather than on the desires and needs of the marketplace. A sales orientation is based on the beliefs that people will buy more products if aggressive sales techniques are used and that high sales volumes produce high profits. A market-oriented organization focuses on satisfying customer wants and needs while meeting organizational objectives. A societal marketing orientation goes beyond a market orientation to include the preservation or enhancement of individuals' and society's long-term best interests.

2.1 Your company president has decided to restructure the firm to make it more market oriented. She is going to announce the changes at an upcoming meeting. She has asked you to prepare a short speech outlining the general reasons for the new company orientation.

2.2   Donald E. Petersen, former chairman of the board of Ford Motor Company, remarked, "If we aren't customer driven, our cars won't be either." Explain how this statement reflects the marketing concept.

2.3   Give an example of a company that might be successfully following a production orientation. Why might a firm in this industry be successful following such an orientation?

Discuss the differences between sales and market orientations. First, sales-oriented firms focus on their own needs; market-oriented firms focus on customers' needs and preferences. Second, sales-oriented companies consider themselves to be deliverers of goods and services, whereas market-oriented companies view themselves as satisfiers of customers. Third, sales-oriented firms direct their products to everyone; market-oriented firms aim at specific segments of the population. Fourth, although the primary goal of both types of firms is profit, sales-oriented businesses pursue maximum sales volume through intensive promotion, whereas market-oriented businesses pursue customer satisfaction through coordinated activities.

3.1   A friend of yours agrees with the adage "People don't know what they want—they only want what they know." Write your friend a letter expressing the extent to which you think marketers shape consumer wants.

3.2   Your local supermarket's slogan is "It's your store." However, when you asked one of the stock people to help you find a bag of chips, he told you it was not his job and that you should look a littler harder. On your way out, you noticed a sign with an address for complaints. Draft a letter explaining why the supermarket's slogan will never be credible unless the employees carry it out.

3.3   How does Philip Morris handle the sensitive issues associated with marketing tobacco? What kind of information does its Web site at **www.philipmorris .com/** provide about smoking and its negative effects on health? How do you think Philip Morris is able to justify such marketing tactics? After checking around the site, do you think that approach makes the company more or less trustworthy?

Describe several reasons for studying marketing. First, marketing affects the allocation of goods and services that influence a nation's economy and standard of living. Second, an understanding of marketing is crucial to understanding most businesses. Third, career opportunities in marketing are diverse, profitable, and expected to increase significantly during the coming decade. Fourth, understanding marketing makes consumers more informed.

4.1   Write a letter to a friend or family member explaining why you think that a course in marketing will help you in your career in some field other than marketing.

KEY TERMS

customer satisfaction	9	marketing	3	relationship marketing	10
customer value	7	marketing concept	5	sales orientation	4
empowerment	11	market orientation	5	societal marketing orientation	6
exchange	3	production orientation	4	teamwork	11

EXERCISES

APPLICATION EXERCISE

Understanding the differences among the various marketing management philosophies is the starting point for understanding the fundamentals of marketing.[35] From reading the chapter, you may be convinced that the market orientation is the most appealing philosophy and the one best suited to creating a competitive advantage. Not all companies, however, use the market orientation. And even companies that follow it may not execute well in all areas.

Activities

1. Visit your local grocery store and go through the cereal, snack-food, and dental hygiene aisles. Go up and down each aisle slowly, noticing how many different products are available and how they are organized on the shelves.

2. Count the varieties of product in each product category. For example, how many different kinds of cereal are on the shelves? How many different sizes? Do the same for snack food and toothpaste.

3. Now try to find a type of product in the grocery store that does not exhibit such variety. There may not be many. Why do you think there are enough kinds of cereals to fill an entire aisle (and then some), but only a few different types of, say, peanut butter? Can this difference be explained in terms of marketing management philosophy (peanut butter manufacturers do not follow the marketing concept) or by something else entirely?

4. Have you ever wanted to see a particular kind of cereal or snack food on the shelf? Think of product varietals (like grapefruit-flavored toothpaste or peanut butter-covered popcorn) that you have never seen on the shelf but would be interested in trying if someone would make it. Write a letter or send an e-mail to an appropriate company, suggesting that it add your concept to its current product line.

ETHICS EXERCISE

In today's business environment, ethics are extremely important. In recent years, there have been numerous scandals and trials that stem from a lack of ethical judgment. For this reason, we are including an ethical exercise in every chapter. A brief scenario will present you with a situation in which the right thing to do may or may not be crystal clear, and you will need to decide the ethical way out of the dilemma.

Rani Pharmaceuticals is the maker of several popular drugs used to treat high blood pressure and arthritis. Over time, the company has developed a positive relationship with many of the patients who use its medications through a quarterly newsletter that offers all the latest information on new medical research findings and general health and fitness articles. The company has just been acquired by a group of investors who also own Soothing Waters Hot Tubs and Spas. The marketing director for Soothing Waters would like to use Rani's mailing list for a direct-mail promotion.

Questions

1. What should Rani Pharmaceuticals do?

2. Do you think it is ethical to use customer information across multiple divisions of the same company? Explain.

3. To which marketing management philosophy do you think the marketing director for Soothing Waters subscribes? Explain.

MARKETING PLAN EXERCISE

You can use many of the basic concepts of marketing introduced in this book to get the career you want by marketing yourself to a prospective employer. This exercise and the Career Appendix at the end of this chapter can help you plan that particular marketing campaign. Build a marketing plan for yourself in a one-page document or table with these elements:

1. *What is your mission?* Are you looking for part-time or temporary experience to enhance your résumé, a career stepping-stone, or a full-time, long-term career choice? (This mission will help you set the stage for the rest of your plan.)

2. *What are your strengths and weaknesses?* Make an honest self-assessment, because these issues often come up during job interviews. What about opportunities and threats in the marketplace? Who are your competitors? Do you have a competitive advantage? List any special leadership skills, international travel, computer experience, team projects, communications efforts, and other attributes. (Any competitive advantages you possess should be noted in the cover letter of your résumé and in your job interview.)

3. *What are your objectives?* Do you need to find a job within the next thirty days, or are you more flexible? Are there specific job activities that you would like to perform? (These job activities could be stated in the objectives portion of your résumé. Be sure the objectives are very specific: general objectives are of little use to you or an employer.)

4. *What is your target market?* Are you looking only for jobs with big, established organizations or small entrepreneurial firms? Are you looking at companies in a particular industry? Do you have any geographic preferences? When you figure out your target, compile a list of firms that meet your requirements and describe them. (The more you know about your target-market potential employers, the more prepared you will be in an interview.)

5. You are the product. *How can you best present yourself?* Think of your own packaging with regard to dress, appearance, mannerisms, and speech.

6. What about place? *Are you willing to travel or relocate?* Or do you need an employer close to home? How will you travel to the employer? Is telecommuting an option?

7. *How will you promote yourself?* A carefully constructed cover letter, résumé, business card, and personal Web site can all help communicate your skills to a potential employer.

8. Think carefully about pricing issues, including salary, commission, bonuses, overtime, flexible time, insurance, and other benefits. *What is a fair price for you?* What is a normal price for a company of that size in that industry to offer?

9. And finally, *how will you implement your plan?* That is, what is your plan for applying to companies? How will you contact them for potential interviews? How will you prepare your wardrobe and work on your interviewing skills? When job offers come in, how will you evaluate them? If job offers don't come in, can you find out why and control for these aspects?

The Appendix at the end of this chapter introduces various aspects of a career in marketing, such as types of marketing jobs, pay scales, preparation for interviewing, and what to expect the first year on the job.

© SHNS PHOTO COURTESY ACTIVISION/ NEWSCOM

CASE STUDY: HARMONIX

EMBRACE YOUR INNER ROCK STAR

Little more than three years ago you had probably never heard of Harmonix. In 2005 the video game design studio released Guitar Hero, which subsequently became the fastest video game in history to top $1 billion in North American sales. The game concept focuses around a plastic guitar-shaped controller. Players press colored buttons along the guitar neck to match a series of dots that scroll down the TV in time with music from a famous rock tune, such as the Ramones' "I Wanna Be Sedated" and Deep Purple's "Smoke on the Water." Players score points based on their accuracy. In November 2007, Harmonix released Rock Band, adding drums, vocals, and bass guitar options to the game. Rock Band has sold over 3.5 million units with a $169 price tag (most video games retail at $50–60). In 2006 Harmonix's founders sold the company to Viacom for $175 million, maintaining their operational autonomy while providing them greater budgets for product development and licensing music for their games. Harmonix's success, however, did not come overnight.

The company was originally founded by Alex Rigopulos and Eran Egozy in 1995, focused around some demo software they had created in grad school and a company vision of providing a way for people without much musical training or talent to experience the joy of playing and creating music. The founders believed that if people had the opportunity to create their own music, they would jump at the chance. Their software, which they eventually dubbed The Axe, provided basic music composition tutorials and allowed participants to use a joystick to improvise solos along to popular music tracks. They attempted to market their creation through an interface with Japanese karaoke machines, a demo package deal with Intel, and even in an exhibition at Disney's Epcot. And while the software always proved technically impressive, people generally expressed little initial interest in trying it out, or else it just didn't seem like they were having much fun.

In 2000, Rigopulos and Egozy hit on a concept that would engage consumers, and Harmonix became a video game company. Where The Axe software provided an improvisation program with no set goal, most video games were designed with a purpose and offered competition, which helped engage, direct, and motivate players. At the time, the market for music-based games had not fully developed, but especially in Japan, rhythm-based games, in which players would tap different combinations of buttons in time with a beat or a tune, were becoming increasingly more popular. Harmonix created two games, Frequency and Amplitude, in which players hit buttons along with a beat, unlocking tracks for different layers of instruments in a song. Neither of the games proved especially successful, however, as both were very complex and the expense of generating initial interest proved too high for their publisher, Sony, to continue funding them.

Harmonix finally found some measure of success in its 2004 release of Karaoki Revolution, in which players would use a microphone or headset peripheral to score points singing along to pop songs. In a way, it allowed gamers to play the role and be a part of the music. In 2005, when Red Octane, a company that had found success making peripheral video game controllers, contacted Harmonix about creating Guitar Hero, their philosophy for attracting gamers was based off a similar concept.

Guitar Hero put players in the role of the lead guitarist in a rock band, climbing its way to stardom. The game soundtrack, filled with remixes of classic American rock 'n' roll hits, would appeal to a broader musical audience and the guitar controller put the iconic instrument of American rock 'n' roll directly in the player's hands. The game was released in November of that year, and when retailers set up in-store demo kiosks, game sales went through the roof.

After the success of the first game, even real rock stars began to pick it up, demonstrating its broad appeal. Music labels started to jump on the bandwagon, allowing the licensing of actual songs rather than just composition rights. Rock Band 2, which came out in September 2008, includes songs by AC/DC and Bob Dylan. Gamers can also download additional songs, like The Who's greatest hits, onto their Xbox 360s and Playstation 3s at $1.99 per song, only a dollar more than purchasing a song from Apple's iTunes music store. Licenses for Rock Band have even been secured for songs by the Beatles, which have yet to be licensed to iTunes or other electronic media stores. As the market for music video games has matured, sales are now expanding beyond the traditional gamers to first-time gamers and even families. The Rock Band franchise has sold over 5 million units since its release in 2007, and with the release of Rock Band 2, the hits just keep on coming.[36]

Questions

1. What marketing management philosophy did Harmonix use at first and how did their philosophy change?

2. As a firm, how do you think Harmonix would describe its business?

3. To whom was Harmonix's product directed and how did they create a product that would appeal to that audience?

COMPANY CLIPS

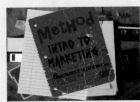

© NKP MEDIA, INC./ CENGAGE

METHOD—LIVE CLEAN

Method, the innovative branding concept in household cleaning, was conceived by roommates Eric Ryan and Adam Lowry during their drive to a ski lodge. Eric had been thinking of ways to introduce design to the home care industry (i.e., cleaning products) and began talking about his vision to Adam. A chemical engineer from Stanford University with a degree in environmental science, Adam was the perfect sounding board. He soon realized that he could use his expertise to create naturally derived, biodegradable formulas for the beautiful products Eric had in mind.

Questions

1. Is method best described as having a market orientation or a societal-marketing orientation?

2. How does method implement the marketing concept?

Marketing & You Results

The higher your score, the more likely you are to do business with the company you thought of and recommend it to others. That is, you have a commitment to the organization and are likely a loyal customer. As you read in Chapter 1, building relationships is a central part of the market orientation!

Career Appendix

One of the most important decisions in your life is choosing a career. Not only will your career choice affect your income and lifestyle, but it also will have a major impact on your happiness and self-fulfillment.

You can use many of the basic concepts of marketing introduced in this book to get the career you want by marketing yourself. The purpose of marketing is to create exchanges that satisfy individual as well as organizational objectives, and a career is certainly an exchange situation for both you and an organization. The purpose of this appendix is to help you market yourself to prospective employers by providing some helpful tools and information.

AVAILABLE CAREERS

Marketing careers have a bright outlook into the next decade. The U.S. Bureau of Labor Statistics estimates that employment in marketing fields will grow between 21 and 35 percent through 2012. Many of these increases will be in the areas of sales, public relations, retailing, advertising, marketing research, product management, and marketing management.

- **Sales:** There are more opportunities in sales than in any other area of marketing. Sales positions vary greatly among companies. Some selling positions focus more on providing information; others emphasize locating potential customers, making presentations to committees, and closing the sale. Because compensation is often in the form of salary plus commission, there are few limits on the amount of money a person can make and therefore great potential. Sales positions can be found in many organizations, including manufacturing, wholesaling, retailing, insurance, real estate, financial services, and many other service businesses.

- **Public relations:** Public relations firms help create an image or a message for an individual or organization and communicate it effectively to a desired audience. All types of firms, profit and nonprofit organizations, individuals, and even countries employ public relations specialists. Communication skills, both written and oral, are critical for success in public relations.

- **Retailing:** Retail careers require many skills. Retail personnel may manage a sales force or other personnel,

select and order merchandise, and be responsible for promotional activities, inventory control, store security, and accounting. Large retail stores have a variety of positions, including store or department manager, buyer, display designer, and catalog manager.

- **Advertising:** Many organizations employ advertising specialists. Advertising agencies are the largest employers; however, manufacturers, retailers, banks, radio and television stations, hospitals, and insurance agencies all have advertising departments. Creativity, artistic talent, and communication skills are a few of the attributes needed for a successful career in advertising. Account executives serve as a liaison between the advertising agency and the client. Account executives must have a good knowledge of business practices and possess excellent sales skills.

- **Marketing management:** Marketing managers develop the firm's detailed marketing strategy. With the help of subordinates, including market research managers and product development managers, they determine the demand for products and services offered by the firm and its competitors. In addition, they identify potential markets—for example, business firms, wholesalers, retailers, government, or the general public. Marketing managers develop pricing strategy with an eye toward maximizing the firm's share of the market and its profits while ensuring that the firm's customers are satisfied. In collaboration with sales, product development, and other managers, they monitor trends that indicate the need for new products and services and oversee product development. Marketing managers work with advertising and promotion managers to promote the firm's products and services and to attract potential users.

- **Marketing research:** The most rapid growth in marketing careers is in marketing research. Marketing research firms, advertising agencies, universities, private firms, nonprofit organizations, and governments provide growing opportunities in marketing research. Researchers conduct industry research, advertising research, pricing and packaging research, new-product testing, and test marketing. Researchers are involved in one or more stages of the research process, depending on the size of the organization conducting the research. Marketing research requires knowledge of

EXHIBIT 1

The FAB Matrix

Need of Employer This job requires . . .	Feature of Job Applicant I have . . .	Advantage of Feature This feature means that . . .	Benefit to Employer You will . . .
• Frequent sales presentations to individuals and groups.	• Taken 10 classes that required presentations.	• I require limited or no training in making presentations.	• Save on the cost of training and have an employee with the ability and confidence to be productive early.
• Knowledge of personal computers, software, and applications.	• Taken a personal computer course and used Lotus in most upper-level classes.	• I can already use Word, Excel, dBase, SAS, SPSS, and other software.	• Save time and money on training.
• A person with management potential.	• Been president of a student marketing group and social fraternity president for two years.	• I have experience leading people.	• Save time because I am capable of stepping into a leadership position as needed.

statistics, data processing and analysis, psychology, and communication.

- *Product management:* Product managers coordinate all or most of the activities required to market a product. Thus, they need a general knowledge of all aspects of marketing. Product managers are responsible for the successes and failures of a product and are compensated well for this responsibility. Most product managers have previous sales experience and skills in communication. The position of product manager is a major step in the career path of top-level marketing executives.

Starting in a marketing job is also one of the *best routes to the top* of any organization. More CEOs come from sales and marketing backgrounds than from any other field. As examples, Lee Iacocca (Chrysler), Phil Lippincott (Scott Paper), John Akers (IBM), John Sparks (Whirlpool), and Bruno Bich (Bic Pen) came up through sales and marketing. Typically, a college graduate enters the marketing field in a sales position, then moves to sales supervisor, and next sales manager at the district, regional, and national levels. Individuals who prefer to advance through the ranks of marketing management can usually make a career move into product or brand management or another marketing headquarters job after serving for a couple of years in the initial sales position.

Probably the most difficult part of job hunting is deciding exactly what type of work you would like. Many students have had no working experience other than summer jobs, so they are not sure what career to pursue. Too often, college students and their parents rush toward occupational fields that seem to offer the highest monetary payoff or are currently "hot," instead of looking at the long run over a 40- to 50-year working life. One straightforward approach to deciding what type of job to undertake is to do a "self-analysis." This involves honestly asking yourself what your skills, abilities, and interests really are and then identifying occupational fields that match up well with your personality profile. Some students prefer to take various vocational aptitude tests to help identify their interests and abilities. Your college's placement office or psychology department can inform you about the availability of these tests. You may find it useful to develop a FAB (feature–advantage–benefit) matrix that shows what your skills are, why they offer an advantage, and how they would benefit an employer. Exhibit 1 shows an example.

YOUR FIRST MARKETING ASSIGNMENT

Marketing yourself to a prospective employer will usually be your first big marketing assignment. With your services (as represented by your qualifications, education, training, and personal characteristics) as the product, you must convince prospective employers that they should buy your services over those of many other candidates for the job. All the steps of the marketing and sales process apply: identifying opportunities, developing yourself as a product, prospecting for potential employers, planning your approach to them, approaching with a résumé and cover letter, making your sales presentation and demonstrating your qualifications in a personal interview, dealing with objections or giving reasons why the employer should hire you over other candidates, attempting to close the sale by enthusiastically asking for the job and employing appropriate closing techniques, and following up by thanking the prospective employer for the interview and reinforcing a positive impression.

Prospecting for a Potential Employer

After you have determined what you're selling (your skills, abilities, interests, and so forth) and identified the type of job you think you would like, you might begin your personal selling process by looking at the *College Placement Annual* at your college placement office. The *College Placement Annual* provides a variety of information about prospective employers and lists the organizations according to the types of jobs they have available—for example, advertising, banking, marketing research, and sales. Another very important source is an online search on the Internet. Other sources of information about prospective employers include directories such as those published by Dun and Bradstreet, Standard & Poor's, and trade associations; the annual American Marketing Association membership directory (company listings); the Yellow Pages of telephone books in cities where you would like to live and work; and classified sections of *The Wall Street Journal* or city newspapers. Before contacting a particular company, look up its annual report and stock evaluation (from *Value Line* or various other sources) in your college library to learn as much as possible about the company and its prospects for the future. You might also obtain a list of articles on the company from the *Business Periodicals Index* (*BPI*).

College Placement Office

Use your college placement office to find out which companies are going to be interviewing on campus on what dates; then sign up for interviews with those companies that seem to best match your job skills and requirements. Usually, the college placement office has books, pamphlets, or files that will give you leads on other prospective employers that may not be interviewing on campus that term.

Job-Hunting Expenses

Although campus interviews are convenient, students seldom get a job without follow-up interviews with more senior managers—usually at company headquarters. These additional interviews generally take a full day and may involve long-distance trips. You should be forewarned that job hunting can be expensive. Printing your résumé, typing cover letters, buying envelopes and stamps, making long-distance telephone calls, incurring travel expenses, and buying new clothing will require a sizable outlay of money. Even though most companies eventually reimburse you for expenses incurred on a company visit, they seldom pay in advance. Reimbursement can take several weeks, so you may encounter some cash-flow problems over the short run.

The Internet

The Internet is the fastest-growing medium for job searching today. Many companies are using the Internet to assist

them in their recruiting efforts. Some companies are even conducting initial interviews online via videoconferencing. Just as some companies post jobs on a bulletin board, companies can list job opportunities on job posting Web sites. Some of the more popular job search Web sites are listed in Exhibit 2. These sites also contain information about résumé writing and interviewing, as well as tips that you can use to secure the job that you want.

Employment Agencies

Although many employment agencies receive fees from employers for providing good job candidates, others charge job seekers huge fees (sometimes thousands of dollars) for helping them find jobs. Therefore, make sure you fully understand the fee arrangement before signing up with an employment agency. Some employment agencies may not be worth your time and/or money because they use a programmed approach to helping you write your résumé and cover letter and prospect for potential employers. Potential employers have seen these "canned" formats and approaches so many times that your personal advertisement (your résumé and cover letter) will be almost indistinguishable from others.

The Hidden Job Market

It has been estimated that nearly 90 percent of available jobs are never advertised and never reach employment agency files, so creative resourcefulness often pays off in finding the best jobs. Consider every reasonable source for leads. Sometimes your professors, deans, or college administrators can give you names and contact persons at companies that have hired recent graduates.

Do not be bashful about letting other people know that you are looking for work. Classmates, friends, and business associates of your family may be of help not only directly but also indirectly, acting as extra pairs of eyes and ears alert to job opportunities for you.

Planning Your Approach (The Preapproach)

After conducting your self-analysis and identifying potential employers looking for people with your abilities and interests, you need to prepare your résumé (or personal advertisement). Your résumé should focus on your achievements to date, your educational background, your work experience, and your special abilities and interests. Some students make the mistake of merely listing their assigned responsibilities on different jobs without indicating what they accomplished on the job. If you achieved something on the job, say it—for example, "Helped computerize office files," "Increased sales in my territory by 10 percent," "Received a 15 percent raise after three months on the job," or "Promoted to assistant store manager after four months." When looking for a job, remember that employers are looking for a track record of achievement, so you must distinguish yourself from those who may have had the same assigned job responsibilities as you did but performed poorly. If your work experience is minimal, consider a "skills" résumé, in which you emphasize your particular abilities, such as organizing, programming, or leadership skills, and give supporting evidence whenever you can. Examples of various types of résumés can be found in the *College Placement Annual* and in various other job-hunting publications. (Ask your college business reference librarian to direct you.) Exhibit 2 lists some Web sites where you can learn about résumé formats.

Remember that there is no one correct format for your résumé. A little tasteful creativity can help differentiate your résumé from countless look-alike résumés. If you are a young college graduate, your résumé will usually be only one page long, but do not worry about going to a second page if you have something important to present. One student so blindly followed the one-page résumé rule that he left out having served in the military—service that is usually viewed very positively by prospective employers, especially if it involved significant leadership responsibilities or work experience.

If you know what job you want, you may want to put your job objective near the top of your résumé. If you are not sure what job you want or want to send out the same résumé for several different jobs, then you can describe your job objective in your cover letter. A key element in the cover letter is convincing the prospective employer to grant you an interview. Thus, you must talk in terms of the employer's interests, not just your own. You are answering the question: "Why should we hire you?" You may need to send a letter with your résumé enclosed to a hundred or more companies to obtain five to ten interviews, so do not be discouraged if you get replies from only a few companies or are told by many companies that they have no job opportunities at present. You will probably need only a few interviews and just one job offer to get your career started.

Review some of the publications and sources mentioned in the previous section on prospecting (e.g., *College Placement Annual*, Dun and Bradstreet directories, and annual reports) to learn as much as you can about your prospective employer so that you can tailor your cover letter. Remember, the employer is thinking in terms of the company's needs, not yours. For one example of a résumé, see Exhibit 3. A cover letter is illustrated in Exhibit 4.

EXHIBIT 3

Sample Résumé

RACHEL E. SANFORD
2935 Mountain View Road
Ellington, PA 19401
(216) 567-0000

JOB OBJECTIVE	Sales representative for a consumer-products company
EDUCATION	Graduated *cum laude* with BS in Marketing Management (June 2006), University of Southern Pennsylvania. Career-related courses included Selling and Sales Management, Public Speaking, Business Writing, Public Relations, Marketing Research, Computer Programming, and Multivariate Data Analysis.
ACTIVITIES AND HONORS	President, Student Marketing Association; Vice president, Chi Omega Sorority; Captain, women's varsity tennis team; sportswriter for the *Campus View* student newspaper. Named to Who's Who among American College Students, 2004–2005. On Dean's List all four years. Overall grade point average = 3.65.

WORK EXPERIENCE

Summer 2005	*Sales representative*, Peabody Manufacturing Company. Sold women's blouses to boutiques and small department stores in southeastern Pennsylvania. Exceeded assigned sales quota by 20 percent; named "outstanding" summer employee for 2005.
Summer 2004	*Buyer*, Hamm's Department Stores, Inc., Midway, Pa. Developed purchase plan, initiated purchase orders, monitored and controlled expenditures for nearly $2 million worth of women's clothing. Made monthly progress reports (written and oral) to Hamm's Executive Committee. Received 15 percent bonus as #2 buyer in the six stores of the Hamm's chain in special "Back to School" purchasing competition.
Summer 2003	*Retail clerk*, Hamm's Department Stores, Inc., Midway, Pa. After 3 months, received 10 percent pay raise and promotion to evening salesclerk supervisor over seven part-time salesclerks. Devised new inventory control system for handbags and accessories that cut costs over $50,000 annually.
Summer 2002	*Cosmetics salesperson*, Heavenly Charm, Inc., Midway, Pa. Sold $63,000 worth of Heavenly Charm cosmetics door to door. Named #1 salesperson in the sales region. Offered full-time job as sales supervisor.
INTERESTS	Tennis, golf, public speaking, short story writing, and reading biographies.

EXHIBIT 4

Sample Cover Letter

Rachel E. Sanford
2935 Mountain View Road
Ellington, PA 19401

Mr. Samuel Abramson
District Sales Manager
Hixson Appliance Company
Philadelphia, PA 19103

Dear Mr. Abramson:

Hixson has been a familiar name to me ever since I was barely able to see over my mother's kitchen counter. Virtually every appliance we had was a Hixson, so I know firsthand what fine quality products you sell. My career interest is in sales, and there is no company that I would rather work with than Hixson Appliance.

I will be graduating this June from Southern Pennsylvania University with a BS in marketing management, and I would like you to consider me for a job as a sales representative with your company. As you can see in my enclosed résumé, I have successfully worked in sales jobs during three of the last four summers. My college course electives (e.g., public speaking, business writing, and public relations) have been carefully selected with my career objective in mind. Even my extracurricular activities in sports and campus organizations have helped prepare me for working with a variety of people and competitive challenges.

Will you please grant me an interview so that I can convince you that I'm someone you should hire for your sales team? I'll call you next Thursday afternoon to arrange an appointment at your convenience.

Look forward to meeting you soon.

Sincerely,

Rachel E. Sanford

Enclosure

Making Your Approach

Prospective employers can be approached by mail, telephone, the Internet, or personal contact. Personal contact is best, but this usually requires that you know someone with influence who can arrange an interview for you. Of course, a few enterprising students have devised elaborate and sometimes successful schemes to get job interviews. For example, we know of one young man who simply went to the headquarters of the company he wanted to work for and asked to see the president. Told that the president of the company could not see him, the student said that he was willing to wait until the president had time. This audacious individual went back three different days until the president finally agreed to see him, perhaps mainly out of curiosity about what sort of young man would be so outrageous in his job search.

Fortunately for this young man, he had a lot to offer and was able to communicate this to the president, so he was hired. This unorthodox approach shows how far people have gone to impress potential employers, and if you feel comfortable doing it, then go ahead. A personal contact within the company certainly can win you some special attention and enable you to avoid competing head-on with the large number of other candidates looking for a job. Most students, however, start their approach in the traditional way by mailing their résumé and cover letter to the recruiting department of the company. More recently, students have begun to e-mail their résumés, and some companies are requiring this as a means of screening out applicants who are not computer literate. Unless your résumé matches a particular need at that time, it will probably be filed away for possible future reference or merely discarded. To try to get around the system, some students send their letter by express mail or mailgram or address it to a key executive, with "Personal" written on the envelope. These students believe that bypassing the company's personnel office will increase the likelihood that their cover letter and résumé will be read by someone with authority to hire. Other students send their résumé on a CD or DVD, and one student in Louisiana sent a King Cake to the recipient of the résumé, while another sent a packet of Louisiana spices. Using gimmicks, no matter how creative, to get a job interview will offend some executives and thus cause you to be rejected from consideration for a job. But you can probably also be sure that a few executives will admire your efforts and grant you an interview.

Only you know how comfortable you feel with different approaches to obtaining a job interview. We advise you not to use an approach that is out of character for you and thus will make you feel awkward and embarrassed.

Making Your Sales Presentation

Your personal sales presentation will come during the interview with the prospective employer's recruiters or interviewers. Like any presentation, it requires thorough preparation and an effective follow-up, as well as a solid performance during the interview itself.

Pre-Interview Considerations

Preparing for the interview is crucial. You will already have gathered information on the company, as suggested in the preceding sections; you should review it now. Exhibit 5 shows a pre-interview checklist that can help you prepare. In addition, the self-assessment test in Exhibit 6 can help you determine if you're ready for the interview.

Keep the following in mind in preparing for your interview:

- Find out the exact place and time of the interview.

- Be certain you know the interviewer's name and how to pronounce it if it looks difficult.

- Do some research on the company with which you are interviewing—talk to people and read the company literature to know what its products or services are, where its offices are located, what its growth has been, and how its prospects look for the future.

- Think of two or three good questions that you would like to ask during your interview.

- Plan to arrive at the designated place for your interview a little early so that you will not feel rushed and worried about being on time.

- Plan to dress in a manner appropriate to the job for which you are interviewing.

A guide for the interview conversation itself is to prepare nine positive thoughts before you go in for the interview:

- Three reasons why you selected the employer to interview

- Three reasons you particularly like the employer

- Three assets you have that should interest the employer

EXHIBIT 5

Before the Interview

- **Practice**
  - ✓ Questions you may be asked
  - ✓ Questions you want to ask about the position and organization
  - ✓ Role-playing an interview
- **Self-assessment**
  - ✓ Goals
  - ✓ Skills, abilities, accomplishments
  - ✓ Work values (important factors you look for in a job)
  - ✓ Experiences
  - ✓ Personality
- **Research**
  - ✓ Obtain company literature
  - ✓ Write or visit the organization
  - ✓ Talk to people familiar with the organization
- **Obtain references**
- **Plan ahead**
  - ✓ Attire to be worn to the interview
  - ✓ Directions to the interview site
  - ✓ Time of arrival (get there with at least 5–10 minutes to spare)

EXHIBIT 6

Self-Assessment Test

How assertive are you (or will you be) as you interview for a position? Listed below are questions that will help you to evaluate yourself: answer yes or no to the questions, being honest with yourself. If you have five or fewer yes answers, you still have some work to do. A good score is seven or more yes answers.

Yes   No

____ ____ Have you made an effort to research the company before the interview?

____ ____ Have you prepared several questions that you want to ask?

____ ____ If an interviewer asks a personal question unrelated to the job, will you be able to tactfully call this to his attention?

____ ____ If an interviewer gives you a hypothetical job-related problem, do you have confidence in your ability to respond in a timely and succinct manner?

____ ____ If the interviewer seems distracted or uninterested during your interview, will you be able to steer the interview back on track and gain her attention?

____ ____ When you meet the interviewer, will you be the first to introduce yourself and begin the conversation?

____ ____ If the interviewer continually interrupts when you are responding to questions or giving information about yourself, can you politely handle this?

____ ____ If the interviewer never gives you the opportunity to talk about yourself and you have only five minutes remaining in the interview, have you thought about phrases or ways to redirect the interview and regain control of the process?

____ ____ When the interviewer is beginning to close the interview, are you prepared to ask questions about how you stand, what the determining factors are for candidate selection, and by what date you will have an answer?

Try to make a positive impression on everyone you encounter in the company, even while waiting in the lobby for your interview. Sometimes managers will ask their receptionists and secretaries for an opinion of you, and your friendliness, courtesy, professional demeanor, personal habits, and the like will all be used to judge you. Even the magazines you choose to read while waiting can be a positive or negative factor. For instance, it will probably be less impressive if you leaf through a popular magazine like *People* or *Sports Illustrated* than if you read something more professional such as *BusinessWeek* or *The Wall Street Journal*.

During the Interview

During the interview, do not be merely a passive respondent to the interviewer's questions. Being graciously assertive by asking reasonable questions of your own will indicate to the interviewer that you are alert, energetic, and sincerely interested in the job. The personal interview is your opportunity to persuade the prospective employer that you should be hired. To use a show business analogy, you will be onstage for only a short time (during the personal interview), so try to present an honest but positive image of yourself. Perhaps it will help you to be alert and

EXHIBIT 7

Some Questions Frequently Asked During a Job Interview

- Of the jobs you've had to date, which one did you like best? Why?
- Why do you want to work for our company?
- Tell me what you know about our company.
- Do any of your relatives or friends work for our company? If so, in what jobs?
- Tell me about yourself, your strengths, weaknesses, career goals, and so forth.
- Is any member of your family a professional marketer? If so, what area of marketing?
- Why do you want to start your career in marketing?
- Persuade me that we should hire you.
- What extracurricular activities did you participate in at college? What leadership positions did you have in any of these activities?
- What benefits have you derived from participation in extracurricular activities that will help you in your career?
- Where do you see yourself within our company in five years? In ten years? Twenty years?
- What is your ultimate career goal?
- What do you consider your greatest achievement to date?
- What is your biggest failure to date?
- What is (was) your favorite subject in school? Why?
- Are you willing to travel and possibly relocate?
- How would the people who know you describe you?
- How would you describe yourself?
- What do you like most about marketing?
- What do you like least about marketing?
- If we hire you, how soon could you start work?
- What is the minimum we would have to offer you to come with us?
- What goals have you set for yourself? How are you planning to achieve them?
- Who or what has had the greatest influence on the development of your career interests?
- What factors did you consider in choosing your major?
- Why are you interested in our organization?
- What can you tell me about yourself?
- What two or three things are most important to you in a position?
- What kind of work do you want to do?
- What can you tell me about a project you initiated?
- What are your expectations of your future employer?
- What is your GPA? How do you feel about it? Does it reflect your ability?
- How do you resolve conflicts?
- What do you feel are your strengths? Your weaknesses? How do you evaluate yourself?
- What work experience has been the most valuable to you and why?
- What was the most useful criticism you ever received, and who was it from?
- Can you give an example of a problem you have solved and the process you used?
- Can you describe the project or situation that best demonstrates your analytical skills?
- What has been your greatest challenge?

EXHIBIT 7

Some Questions Frequently Asked During a Job Interview (continued)

- Can you describe a situation where you had a conflict with another individual and explain how you dealt with it?
- What are the biggest problems you encountered in college? How did you handle them? What did you learn from them?
- What are your team-player qualities? Give examples.
- Can you describe your leadership style?
- What interests or concerns you about the position or the company?
- In a particular leadership role you had, what was the greatest challenge?
- What idea have you developed and implemented that was particularly creative or innovative?
- What characteristics do you think are important for this position?
- How have your educational and work experiences prepared you for this position?
- Can you take me through a project where you demonstrated skills?
- How do you think you have changed personally since you started college?
- Can you tell me about a team project that you are particularly proud of and discuss your contribution?
- How do you motivate people?
- Why did you choose the extracurricular activities you did? What did you gain? What did you contribute?
- What types of situations put you under pressure, and how do you deal with the pressure?
- Can you tell me about a difficult decision you have made?
- Can you give an example of a situation in which you failed and explain how you handled it?
- Can you tell me about a situation when you had to persuade another person of your point of view?
- What frustrates you the most?
- Knowing what you know now about your college experience, would you make the same decisions?
- What can you contribute to this company?
- How would you react to having your credibility questioned?
- What characteristics are important in a good manager? How have you displayed one of these characteristics?
- What challenges are you looking for in a position?
- What two or three accomplishments have given you the most satisfaction?
- Can you describe a leadership role of yours and tell why you committed your time to it?
- How are you conducting your job search, and how will you make your decision?
- What is the most important lesson you have learned in or out of school?
- Can you describe a situation where you had to work with someone who was difficult? How was the person difficult, and how did you handle it?
- We are looking at a lot of great candidates; why are you the best person for this position?
- How would your friends describe you? Your professors?
- What else should I know about you?

enthusiastic if you imagine that you are being interviewed on television. Exhibit 7 lists a number of questions that are frequently asked during interviews.

Sometimes prospective employers will ask you to demonstrate certain abilities by having you write a timed essay about some part of your life, sell something (such as a desk calculator) to the interviewer, or respond to hostile questions. Be calm and confident during any such unorthodox interviewing approaches and you will make a good impression. Remember, most employers want you to perform well because they are looking for the best people they can find in a given time frame for the money they have to offer.

If you are given intelligence, aptitude, or psychological tests, you should try to be honest so that you do not create unrealistic expectations that you will not be able to fulfill. It is just as important that you do not create a false impression and begin with a company that is not right for you as it is to secure employment in the first place. Many

experts say that it is not very difficult to "cheat" on aptitude or psychological tests if you are able to "play the role" and provide the answers that you know the company wants to read. Usually, the so-called safe approach in most personality and preference (interest) tests is to not take extreme positions on anything that is not clearly associated with the job you are applying for. For sales jobs, it is probably safe to come across as highly extroverted and interested in group activities, but it may not be safe to appear to be overly interested in literature, music, art, or any solitary activity. In addition, the "right" answers tend to indicate a conservative, goal-oriented, money-motivated, and gregarious personality.

Dealing with Objections Sometimes interviewers will bluntly ask, "Why should we hire you?" This requires that you think in terms of the employer's needs and present in concise form all your major "selling points." Also, sometimes the interviewer may bring up reasons why you are not the ideal candidate. For example, he or she may say: (1) "We're really looking for someone with a little more experience"; (2) "We'd like to get someone with a more technical educational background"; or (3) "We need someone to start work within two weeks." These kinds of statements are similar to objections or requests for additional information. In other words, the interviewer is saying, "Convince me that I shouldn't rule you out for this reason." To overcome such objections, you might respond to each, respectively, along the following lines:

(1) "I've had over a year's experience working with two different companies during my summer vacations, and I've worked part-time with a third company all during college. I'm a fast learner, and I've adapted well to each of the three companies, so I feel that my working experience is equivalent to that of someone who has had three or four years' experience with the same company."

(2) "Although I didn't choose to earn a technical undergraduate degree, I've taken several technical courses in college, including basic engineering courses, chemistry, physics, and two years of math. I'm very confident that I can quickly learn whatever is necessary technically to do the job, and my real strength is that my education has been a blend of technical and managerial courses."

(3) "Well, I do have one more term of school, so I couldn't start full-time work in two weeks, but perhaps we could work out an arrangement in which I could work part-time—maybe Friday, Saturday, and Sunday or on weekends until I graduate."

Good "salespeople" do not allow an objection to block a sale. Providing reasonable solutions or alternative perspectives can often overcome objections or, at least, allow room for further negotiation toward a compromise solution.

How to Act during the Interview The following can help you behave appropriately during the interview:

- Think positive. Be enthusiastic, interested, knowledgeable, and confident.

- Take few notes. It is acceptable to take notes during the interview, but limit them to things that are essential to remember. You want to focus more on listening and observing rather than writing.

- Relate to the interviewer. Build positive rapport with the interviewer. Listen and observe; relate yourself to the employer or position.

- Watch your body language. Be aware of nervousness (fidgeting, shaking leg, tapping, etc.). Project confidence (eye contact, firm handshake, upright posture).

- Be aware of the questions the employer asks. Answer with information relevant to the position. Provide a direct answer; avoid being long-winded.

- Think about the questions you ask. They should indicate that you know something about the job. Avoid questions that could easily be answered elsewhere (through research). Obtain information you need to know to be satisfied with the job (interviewing is a two-way process). Salary and benefit questions should be asked after the job is offered.

- Achieve effective closure. Ask when the employer expects to make a decision. Restate your interest and ability to perform the job. Show confidence and enthusiasm (smile, end with a firm handshake). Obtain the employer's business card, if possible (it may be useful when writing a thank-you letter).

Interview Questions Too many employment applicants spend all their time preparing for the questions employers will ask them. Too often, they fail to ask vital questions that would help them learn if a job is right for them. Failing to ask important questions during the interview often leads to jobs that offer neither interest nor challenge. Too often, uninformed applicants accept positions hoping that they will develop into something more meaningful and rewarding later. Exhibit 8 suggests questions that you may want to ask.

Closing the Sale

Although it is not likely that a prospective employer will offer you a job immediately after the job interview, you should nevertheless let the interviewer know that you definitely want the job and are confident that you will do an excellent job for the employer. You will need to use your best judgment on how to best do this.

In each stage of the personal selling process, you should be looking for feedback from the interviewer's body language and voice inflections or tone.

Following Up the Interview

Within a few days after any job interview, whether you want the job or not, it is business courtesy to write thank-you letters to interviewers. In these letters you can reinforce the positive impression you made in the interview and again express your keen interest in working for the company. If you do not hear from the company within a few weeks, it may be appropriate to write another letter expressing your continuing interest in the job and asking for a decision so that you can consider other options if necessary. As a possible reason for this follow-up letter, you might mention an additional personal achievement since the interview, give a more detailed answer to one of the interviewer's questions, or perhaps send a newspaper or magazine article of interest. A neat, well-written, courteous follow-up letter gives you a chance not only to make a stronger impression on the interviewer but also to exhibit positive qualities such as initiative, energy,

EXHIBIT 8

Sample Interview Questions to Be Asked by Job Candidates

- Where is the organization going? What plans or projects are being developed to maintain or increase its market share? Have many new product lines been decided upon recently? Is the sales growth in the new product line sustainable?
- Who are the people with whom I will be working? May I speak with some of them?
- May I have a copy of the job description?
- What might be a typical first assignment?
- Do you have a performance appraisal system? How is it structured? How frequently will I be evaluated?
- What is the potential for promotion in the organization? In promotions, are employees ever transferred between functional fields? What is the average time to get to _____ level in the career path? Is your policy to promote from within, or are many senior jobs filled by experienced people from outside? Do you have a job posting system?
- What type of training will I receive? When does the training program begin? Is it possible to move through your program faster? About how many individuals go through your internship program?
- What is the normal routine of a (an) _____ like? Can I progress at my own pace, or is it structured? Do employees normally work overtime?
- How much travel is normally expected? Is a car provided to traveling personnel?
- How much freedom is given to new people? How much discipline is required? How much input does the new person have? How much decision-making authority is given to new personnel?
- How frequently do you relocate employees? Is it possible to transfer from one division to another?
- What is the housing market for a single person in _____ (city)? Is public transportation adequate?
- How much contact with and exposure to management is there?
- How soon should I expect to report to work?

sensitivity to others' feelings, and awareness of business protocol.

Many applicants fail to write a thank-you letter after an interview, yet many employers say that the deciding factor between several similar job candidates is often the thank-you note. The thank-you letter should be typewritten. If the interviewer is a very technology-driven person, a thank-you e-mail may also be appropriate. However, the personal touch of a typewritten and hand-signed letter leaves a better impression.

Be sure to write a follow-up letter in all of the following situations:

- After two or three weeks of no reply.

- When a job has been refused. Express your regret that no job is available and ask if you might be considered in the future. Also, ask how you could improve yourself to better fit what the company is looking for.

- After an interview. Express your thanks for the interviewer's time and courtesy. Answer any unanswered questions and clarify any misconceptions.

- To accept a job (even if previously done in person or on the phone). State your acceptance. Reiterate the agreement, the time for beginning work, and the like. Do not start asking for favors.

- To refuse a job offer. Graciously decline the offer. Be warm and interested and indicate that you appreciate the offer.

Follow-up letters are also appropriate after you have received replies to both solicited and unsolicited letters of inquiry. Always make certain that your letters possess the attitude, quality, and skill of a professional.

ON THE JOB
Working Conditions

Advertising, marketing, promotions, public relations, and sales managers work in offices close to those of top managers. Long hours, including evenings and weekends, are common. About 44 percent of advertising, marketing, and public relations managers work more than 40 hours per week. Substantial travel may also be involved. For example, attendance at meetings sponsored by associations or industries is often mandatory. Sales managers travel to local, regional, and national offices and to various dealers and distributors. Advertising and promotions managers may travel to meet with clients or representatives of communications media. At times, public relations managers travel to meet with special interest groups or government officials. Job transfers between headquarters and regional offices are common, particularly among sales managers.

Moving Up the Ladder

Most advertising, marketing, promotions, public relations, and sales management positions are filled by promoting experienced staff or related professional personnel. For example, many managers are former sales representatives, purchasing agents, buyers, or product, advertising,

31

promotions, or public relations specialists. In small firms, where the number of positions is limited, advancement to a management position usually comes slowly. In large firms, promotion may occur more quickly.

Although experience, ability, and leadership are emphasized for promotion, advancement can be accelerated by participation in management training programs conducted by many large firms. Many firms also provide their employees with continuing education opportunities, either in-house or at local colleges and universities, and encourage employee participation in seminars and conferences, often provided by professional societies. In collaboration with colleges and universities, numerous marketing and related associations sponsor national or local management training programs. Staying abreast of what is happening in your industry and getting involved in related industry associations can be important for your career advancement.

YOUR EARLY WORKING CAREER

Even though you want to choose a company that you will stay with throughout your working life, it is realistic to recognize that you will probably work for three, four, or more companies during your career. If you are not fully satisfied with your job or company during the first few years of your full-time working life, remember that you are building experience and knowledge that will increase your marketability for future job opportunities. Keep a positive outlook and do the best you can in all job assignments—and your chance for new opportunities will come. Do not be too discouraged by mistakes that you may make in your career; nearly every successful person has made and continues to make many mistakes. View these mistakes largely as learning experiences, and they will not be too traumatic or damaging to your confidence.

Good luck in your marketing career!

Essentials of Marketing

7e

Lamb ▪ Hair ▪ McDaniel

2

Strategic Planning for Competitive Advantage

LEARNING OUTCOMES

LO 1   Understand the importance of strategic marketing and know a basic outline for a marketing plan

LO 2   Develop an appropriate business mission statement

LO 3   Describe the components of a situation analysis

LO 4   Explain the criteria for stating good marketing objectives

LO 5   Identify sources of competitive advantage

LO 6   Identify strategic alternatives

LO 7   Discuss target market strategies

LO 8   Describe the elements of the marketing mix

LO 9   Explain why implementation, evaluation, and control of the marketing plan are necessary

LO 10   Identify several techniques that help make strategic planning effective

THE NATURE OF STRATEGIC PLANNING

Strategic planning is the managerial process of creating and maintaining a fit between the organization's objectives and resources and the evolving market opportunities. The goal of strategic planning is long-run profitability and growth. Thus, strategic decisions require long-term commitments of resources.

A strategic error can threaten a firm's survival. On the other hand, a good strategic plan can help protect and grow the firm's resources. For instance, if the March of Dimes had decided to focus on fighting polio, the organization would no longer exist. Most of us view polio as a conquered disease. The March of Dimes survived by making the strategic decision to switch to fighting birth defects.

Strategic marketing management addresses two questions: What is the organization's main activity at a particular time? How will it reach its goals? Here are some examples of strategic decisions:

☛ General Electric Company has initiated an effort called "Ecomagination," which will shift its focus to being an environmentally conscious company that is working to solve some of the planet's most critical environmental issues. This effort represents a complete transformation in strategy for GE that is changing the way it develops products, sells to customers, and enters emerging markets.[1]

☛ Toys"R"Us has suffered as younger and younger children abandon traditional toys for electronic entertainment and because parents tend to buy toys during weekly trips to one-stop shops like Wal-Mart. The company responded by expanding its infant line, Babies"R"Us, and is using it to lure parents of older children into their toy selections.[2]

☛ McDonald's decision to offer more healthful foods by focusing on fresh fruits and vegetables with its new line of premium salads.[3]

☛ SC Johnson's introduction of Shout Color Catchers, a laundry sheet for the washer that collects loose dyes and prevents clothes from bleeding color onto other laundry items.

All these decisions have affected or will affect each organization's long-run course, its allocation of resources, and ultimately its financial success. In contrast, an operating decision, such as changing the package design for Post's cornflakes or altering the sweetness of a Kraft salad dressing, probably won't have a big impact on the long-run profitability of the company.

Marketing & You

What do you think about planning? Enter your answers on the lines provided.

Describes my style

1	2	3	4	5	6	7
Not at all						Perfectly

__ I start my work without spending too much time on planning.*

__ I list the steps necessary for completing a task before starting it.

__ I think about strategies I will fall back on if problems arise.

__ Because so many aspects of my work are unpredictable, planning is not useful.*

__ I keep good records of the projects I'm working on.

__ I set personal goals for myself.

__ Each week I make a plan for what I need to do.

__ I do not waste time thinking about what I should do.*

__ I am careful to work on the highest-priority tasks first.

__ Planning is a waste of time.*

__ Planning is an excuse for not working.*

__ I don't need to develop a strategy for completing my assignments.*

Now, total your score, reversing your score for items with asterisks—that is, if you put a 2, put a 6, and vice versa. Read the chapter, and see what your score means at the end.

strategic planning
The managerial process of creating and maintaining a fit between the organization's objectives and resources and evolving market opportunities.

How do companies go about strategic marketing planning? How do employees know how to implement the long-term goals of the firm? The answer is a marketing plan.

What is a Marketing Plan?

Planning is the process of anticipating future events and determining strategies to achieve organizational objectives in the future. Marketing planning involves designing activities relating to marketing objectives and the changing marketing environment. Marketing planning is the basis for all marketing strategies and decisions. Issues such as product lines, distribution channels, marketing communications, and pricing are all delineated in the marketing plan. The marketing plan is a written document that acts as a guidebook of marketing activities for the marketing manager. In this chapter, you will learn the importance of writing a marketing plan and the types of information contained in a marketing plan.

Why Write a Marketing Plan? By specifying objectives and defining the actions required to attain them, you can provide in a marketing plan the basis by which actual and expected performance can be compared. Marketing can be one of the most expensive and complicated business activities, but it is also one of the most important. The written marketing plan provides clearly stated activities that help employees and managers understand and work toward common goals.

Writing a marketing plan allows you to examine the marketing environment in conjunction with the inner workings of the business. Once the marketing plan is written, it serves as a reference point for the success of future activities. Finally, the marketing plan allows the marketing manager to enter the marketplace with an awareness of possibilities and problems.

Marketing Plan Elements Marketing plans can be presented in many different ways. Most businesses need a written marketing plan because a marketing plan is large and can be complex. Details about tasks and activity assignments may be lost if communicated orally. Regardless of the way a marketing plan is presented, some elements are common to all marketing plans. These include defining the business mission, performing a situation analysis, defining objectives, delineating a target market, and establishing components of the marketing mix. Exhibit 2.1 shows these elements, which are also described further below. Other elements that may be included in a plan are budgets, implementation timetables, required marketing research efforts, or elements of advanced strategic planning. A marketing planning outline and an example of a marketing plan appear in the appendices to this chapter.

Selecting which alternative to pursue depends on the overall company philosophy and culture. The choice also depends on the tool used to make the decision. Companies generally have one of two philosophies about when they expect profits. They either pursue profits right away or first seek to increase market share and then pursue profits. In the long run, market share and profitability are compatible goals. Many companies have long followed this credo: Build market share, and profits will surely follow. Michelin, the tire producer, consistently sacrifices short-term profits to achieve market share. On the other hand, IBM stresses profitability and stock valuation over market share, quality, and customer service. As you can see, the same strategic alternative may be viewed entirely differently by different firms.

A number of tools exist to help managers select a strategic alternative. The most common of these tools are in matrix form. The portfolio matrix is described here in more detail.

EXHIBIT 2.1

Elements of a Marketing Plan

Writing the Marketing Plan

The creation and implementation of a complete marketing plan will allow the organization to achieve marketing objectives and succeed. However, the marketing plan is only as good as the information it contains and the effort, creativity, and thought that went into its creation. Having a good marketing information system and a wealth of competitive intelligence (covered in Chapter 9) is critical to a thorough and accurate situation analysis. The role of managerial intuition is also important in the creation and selection of marketing strategies. Managers must weigh any information against its accuracy and their own judgment when making a marketing decision.

Note that the overall structure of the marketing plan (Exhibit 2.1) should not be viewed as a series of sequential planning steps. Many of the marketing plan elements are decided on simultaneously and in conjunction with one another. Further, every marketing plan has a different content, depending on the organization, its mission, objectives, targets, and marketing mix components. The example of a marketing plan in Appendix I of this chapter should not be regarded as the only correct format for a marketing plan. Many organizations have their own distinctive format or terminology for creating a marketing plan. Every marketing plan should be unique to the firm for which it was created. Remember, however, that although the format and order of presentation should be flexible, the same types of questions and topic areas should be covered in any marketing plan. As you can see by the extent of the marketing planning outline and the example of the e-motion software marketing plan in Appendix II, creating a complete marketing plan is not a simple or quick effort.

REVIEW LEARNING OUTCOME

 Understand the importance of strategic marketing and know a basic outline for a marketing plan

What	→	Strategic planning
Why	→	Long term profitability and growth
How	→	Write a marketing plan

LO 2

DEFINING THE BUSINESS MISSION

The foundation of any marketing plan is the firm's mission statement, which answers the question, "What business are we in?" The way a firm defines its business mission profoundly affects the firm's long-run resource allocation, profitability, and survival. The mission statement is based on a careful analysis of benefits sought by present and potential customers and an analysis of existing and anticipated environmental conditions. The firm's mission statement establishes boundaries for all subsequent decisions, objectives, and strategies. The Southwest Airlines mission statement is shown in Exhibit 2.2.

A mission statement should focus on the market or markets the organization is attempting to serve rather than on the good or service offered. Otherwise, a new technology may quickly make the good or service obsolete and the mission statement irrelevant to company functions. Business mission statements that are stated too narrowly suffer from marketing myopia—defining a business in terms of goods and services rather than in terms of the benefits customers seek. In this context, *myopia* means narrow, short-term thinking. For example, Frito-Lay defines its mission as being in the snack-food business rather than in the corn chip business. The mission of sports teams is not just to play games but to serve the interests of the fans.

© DAVID YOUNG WOLF/PHOTOEDIT

mission statement
A statement of the firm's business based on a careful analysis of benefits sought by present and potential customers and an analysis of existing and anticipated environmental conditions.

marketing myopia
Defining a business in terms of goods and services rather than in terms of the benefits that customers seek.

EXHIBIT 2.2

Southwest Airlines Mission Statement

The mission of Southwest Airlines is dedication to the highest quality of Customer Service delivered with a sense of warmth, friendliness, individual pride, and Company Spirit.

To Our Employees

We are committed to provide our Employees a stable work environment with equal opportunity for learning and personal growth. Creativity and innovation are encouraged for improving the effectiveness of Southwest Airlines. Above all, Employees will be provided the same concern, respect, and caring attitude within the organization that they are expected to share externally with every Southwest Customer.

Source: http://www.southwestairlines.com/about_swa/mission

REVIEW LEARNING OUTCOME

 2 Develop an appropriate business mission statement

Q: What business are we in?

A: Business mission statement

- Too narrow ——→ marketing myopia
- Too broad ——→ no direction
- Just right ——→ focus on markets served and benefits customers seek

strategic business unit (SBU)
A subgroup of a single business or a collection of related businesses within the larger organization.

SWOT analysis
Identifying internal strengths (S) and weaknesses (W) and also examining external opportunities (O) and threats (T).

Alternatively, business missions may be stated too broadly. "To provide products of superior quality and value that improve the lives of the world's consumers" is probably too broad a mission statement for any firm except Procter & Gamble. Care must be taken when stating what business a firm is in. For example, the mission of Ben & Jerry's centers on three important aspects of its ice cream business: (1) Product: "To make, distribute, and sell the finest quality all natural ice cream and related products in a wide variety of innovative flavors made from Vermont Dairy products"; (2) Economic: "To operate the company on a sound financial basis of profitable growth, increasing value for our shareholders, and creating career opportunities and financial rewards for our employees"; and (3) Social: "To operate the company in a way that actively recognizes the central role that business plays in the structure of society by initiating innovative ways to improve the quality of life of a broad community—local, national, and international."[4] By correctly stating the business mission in terms of the benefits that customers seek, the foundation for the marketing plan is set. Many companies are focusing on designing more appropriate mission statements because these statements are frequently displayed on the company's Web sites.

The organization may need to define a mission statement and objectives for a strategic business unit (SBU), which is a subgroup of a single business or a collection of related businesses within the larger organization. A properly defined SBU should have a distinct mission and specific target market, control over its resources, its own competitors, and plans independent of the other SBUs in the organization. Thus, a large firm such as Kraft Foods may have marketing plans for each of its SBUs, which include breakfast foods, desserts, pet foods, and beverages.

LO 3

CONDUCTING A SITUATION ANALYSIS

Marketers must understand the current and potential environment that the product or service will be marketed in. A situation analysis is sometimes referred to as a SWOT analysis; that is, the firm should identify its internal strengths (S) and weaknesses (W) and also examine external opportunities (O) and threats (T).

When examining internal strengths and weaknesses, the marketing manager should focus on organizational resources such as production costs, marketing skills, financial resources, company or brand image, employee capabilities, and available technology. For example, a potential weakness for AirTran Airways (formerly ValuJet) is the age of its airplane fleet, which could project an image of danger or low quality. Other weaknesses include high labor turnover rates and limited flights. A potential strength is the airline's low operating costs, which translate into lower prices for consumers. Another issue to consider in this section of the marketing plan is the historical background of the firm—its sales and profit history.

When examining external opportunities and threats, marketing managers must analyze aspects of the marketing environment. This process is called environmental scanning—the collection and interpretation of information about forces, events, and relationships in the external environment that may affect the future of the organization or the implementation of the marketing plan. Environmental scanning helps identify market opportunities and threats and provides guidelines for the design of marketing strategy. The six most often studied macroenvironmental forces are social, demographic, economic, technological, political and legal, and competitive. These forces are examined in detail in Chapter 3. Rising gas prices and a weakening dollar have created a complex, but possibly advantageous, environment for McDonald's. While increased gas costs may discourage some consumers from visiting its drive-through windows, the fast-food giant hopes that its widespread availability, its inexpensive prices, and its new gourmet-style coffee offerings will attract consumers trying to save money by downgrading from Starbucks and other pricy venues. McDonald's marketers are even taking advantage of gas price increases by running commercials in which teenagers decide not to fill their empty gas tank and buy $1 double cheeseburgers to fill their stomachs instead.[5]

REVIEW LEARNING OUTCOME

LO 3 Describe the components of a situation analysis

INTERNAL	Strengths	EXTERNAL	Opportunities
	• production costs		• social
	• marketing skills		• demographic
	• financial resources		• economic
	• image		• technological
	• technology		• political/legal
			• competitive
	Weaknesses		**Threats**

LO 4

SETTING MARKETING PLAN OBJECTIVES

Before the details of a marketing plan can be developed, objectives for the plan must be stated. Without objectives, there is no basis for measuring the success of marketing plan activities.

A marketing objective is a statement of what is to be accomplished through marketing activities. To be useful, stated objectives should meet several criteria:

McDonald's marketers are taking advantage of gas price increases by running commercials in which teenagers decide not to fill their empty gas tank and buy $1 double cheeseburgers to fill their stomachs instead.

© AP IMAGES/PAUL SAKUMA

☛ *Realistic*: Managers should develop objectives that have a chance of being met. For example, it may be unrealistic for start-up firms or new products to command dominant market share, given other competitors in the marketplace.

☛ *Measurable*: Managers need to be able to quantitatively measure whether or not an objective has been met. For example, it would be difficult to determine success for an objective that states "To increase sales of cat food." If the company sells 1 percent more cat food, does that mean the objective was met? Instead, a specific number should be stated, "To increase sales of Purina brand cat food from $300 million to $345 million."

☛ *Time-specific*: By what time should the objective be met? "To increase sales of Purina brand cat food between January 1, 2010 and December 31, 2010."

☛ *Compared to a benchmark*: If the objective is to increase sales by 15 percent, it is important to know the baseline against which the objective will be measured. Will it be current sales? Last year's sales? For example, "To increase sales of Purina brand cat food by 15 percent over 2010 sales of $300 million."

environmental scanning
Collection and interpretation of information about forces, events, and relationships in the external environment that may affect the future of the organization or the implementation of the marketing plan.

marketing objective
A statement of what is to be accomplished through marketing activities.

Realistic, measurable, and time-specific objectives consistent with the firm's objectives:

1. Communicate marketing management philosophy

2. Provide management direction

3. Motivate employees

4. Force executives to think clearly

5. Allow for better evaluation of results

Objectives must also be consistent with and indicate the priorities of the organization. Specifically, objectives flow from the business mission statement to the rest of the marketing plan. Exhibit 2.3 shows some well-stated and some poorly stated objectives. Notice how well they do or do not meet the aforementioned criteria.

Carefully specified objectives serve several functions. First, they communicate marketing management philosophies and provide direction for lower-level marketing managers so that marketing efforts are integrated and pointed in a consistent direction. Objectives also serve as motivators by creating something for employees to strive for. When objectives are attainable and challenging, they motivate those charged with achieving the objectives. Additionally, the process of writing specific objectives forces executives to clarify their thinking. Finally, objectives form a basis for control; the effectiveness of a plan can be gauged in light of the stated objectives.

COMPETITIVE ADVANTAGE

Performing a SWOT analysis allows firms to identify their competitive advantage. A **competitive advantage** is a set of unique features of a company and its products that are perceived by the target market as significant and superior to the competition. It is the factor or factors that cause customers to patronize a firm and not the competition. There are three types of competitive advantages: cost, product/service differentiation, and niche strategies.

Cost Competitive Advantage

Cost leadership can result from obtaining inexpensive raw materials, creating an efficient scale of plant operations, designing products for ease of manufacture, controlling overhead costs, and avoiding marginal customers. DuPont, for example, has an exceptional cost competitive advantage in the production of titanium dioxide. Technicians created a production process using low-cost feedstock, giving DuPont a 20 percent cost advantage over its competitors. The cheaper feedstock technology is complex and can be duplicated only by investing about $100 million and several years of testing time.

competitive advantage
The set of unique features of a company and its products that are perceived by the target market as significant and superior to the competition.

EXHIBIT 2.3

Examples of Marketing Objectives

Poorly Stated Objectives	Well-Stated Objectives
Our objective is to maximize profits.	Our objective is to achieve a 10 percent return on investment from January 1, 2009 until December 31, 2009, with a payback on new investments of no longer than December 31, 2013.
Our objective is to better serve customers.	Our objective is to obtain customer satisfaction ratings of 90 percent on the 2009 annual customer satisfaction survey, and to retain 85 percent of our 2009 customers as repeat purchasers in 2010.
Our objective is to be the best that we can be.	Our objective is to increase market share from 30 percent in 2009 to 40 percent in 2010 by increasing promotional expenditures by 14 percent over 2009 levels from January 1, 2010 to December 31, 2010.

Having a cost competitive advantage means being the low-cost competitor in an industry while maintaining satisfactory profit margins.

A cost competitive advantage enables a firm to deliver superior customer value. Wal-Mart, the world's leading low-cost general merchandise store, offers good value to customers because it focuses on providing a large selection of merchandise at low prices and good customer service. Wal-Mart is able to keep its prices down because it has strong buying power in its relationships with suppliers.

Costs can be reduced in a variety of ways.

☞ *Experience curves:* Experience curves tell us that costs decline at a predictable rate as experience with a product increases. The experience curve effect encompasses a broad range of manufacturing, marketing, and administrative costs. Experience curves reflect learning by doing, technological advances, and economies of scale. Firms like Boeing use historical experience curves as a basis for predicting and setting prices. Experience curves allow management to forecast costs and set prices based on anticipated costs as opposed to current costs.

☞ *Efficient labor:* Labor costs can be an important component of total costs in low-skill, labor-intensive industries such as product assembly and apparel manufacturing. Many U.S. manufacturers such as Nike, Levi Strauss, and Liz Claiborne have gone offshore to achieve cheaper manufacturing costs. Many American companies are also outsourcing activities such as data entry and other labor-intensive jobs.

☞ *No-frills goods and services:* Marketers can lower costs by removing frills and options from a product or service. Southwest Airlines, for example, offers low fares but no seat assignments or meals. Low costs give Southwest a higher load factor and greater economies of scale, which, in turn, mean lower prices for consumers.

☞ *Government subsidies:* Governments may provide grants and interest-free loans to target industries. Such government assistance enabled Japanese semiconductor manufacturers to become global leaders.

☞ *Product design:* Cutting-edge design technology can help offset high labor costs. BMW is a world leader in designing cars for ease of manufacture and assembly. Reverse engineering—the process of disassembling a product piece by piece to learn its components and obtain clues as to the manufacturing process—can also mean savings. Reverse engineering a low-cost competitor's product can save research and design costs. Japanese engineers have reverse engineered many products, such as computer chips coming out of Silicon Valley.

☞ *Reengineering:* Reengineering entails fundamental rethinking and redesign of business processes to achieve dramatic improvements in critical measures of performance. It often involves reorganizing from functional departments such as sales, engineering, and production to cross-disciplinary teams.

☞ *Production innovations:* Production innovations such as new technology and simplified production techniques help lower the average cost of production. Technologies such as computer-aided design and computer-aided manufacturing (CAD/CAM) and increasingly sophisticated robots help companies like Boeing, Ford, and General Electric reduce their manufacturing costs.

☞ *New methods of service delivery:* Medical expenses have been substantially lowered by the use of outpatient surgery and walk-in clinics. Airlines, such as Delta, are lowering reservation and ticketing costs by encouraging passengers to use the Internet to book flights and by providing self-check-in kiosks at the airport.

Product/Service Differentiation Competitive Advantage

Because cost competitive advantages are subject to continual erosion, product/service differentiation tends to provide a longer lasting competitive advantage. The durability of this strategy tends to make it more attractive to many top managers. A product/service differentiation competitive advantage exists when a firm provides something

cost competitive advantage
Being the low-cost competitor in an industry while maintaining satisfactory profit margins.

experience curves
Curves that show costs declining at a predictable rate as experience with a product increases.

product/service differentiation competitive advantage
The provision of something that is unique and valuable to buyers beyond simply offering a lower price than the competition's.

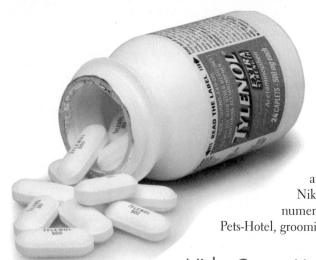

© DANIEL HURST/EDITORIAL/ALAMY

unique that is valuable to buyers beyond simply offering a low price. Examples include brand names (Lexus), a strong dealer network (Caterpillar Tractor for construction work), product reliability (Maytag appliances), image (Neiman Marcus in retailing), or service (FedEx). A great example of a company that has a strong product/service competitive advantage is Nike. Nike's advantage is built around one simple idea—product innovation. The company's goal is to think of something that nobody has thought of before or improve something that already exists. Nike Air, ACG, Nike Swift, and Nike Shox are examples of innovative shoes introduced by Nike.[6] Another example is PetSmart. Not only does PetSmart offer numerous products for all types of pets; it also offers services such as Pets-Hotel, grooming, and training.

Niche Competitive Advantage

A niche competitive advantage seeks to target and effectively serve a single segment of the market (see Chapter 8). For small companies with limited resources that potentially face giant competitors, niche targeting may be the only viable option. A market segment that has good growth potential but is not crucial to the success of major competitors is a good candidate for developing a niche strategy.

Many companies using a niche strategy serve only a limited geographic market. Buddy Freddy's is a very successful restaurant chain, but is found only in Florida. Migros is the dominant grocery chain in Switzerland. It has no stores outside that small country.

Block Drug Company uses niche targeting by focusing its product line on tooth products. It markets Polident to clean false teeth, Poligrip to hold false teeth, and Sensodyne toothpaste for persons with sensitive teeth. The Orvis Company manufactures and sells everything that anyone might ever need for fly-fishing. Orvis is a very successful niche marketer.

Building Sustainable Competitive Advantage

The key to having a competitive advantage is the ability to sustain that advantage. A sustainable competitive advantage is one that cannot be copied by the competition. Nike, discussed earlier, is a good example of a company that has a sustainable competitive advantage. Others include Rolex (high-quality watches), Nordstrom department stores (service), and Southwest Airlines (low price). In contrast, when Datril was introduced into the pain-reliever market, it was touted as being exactly like Tylenol, only cheaper. Tylenol responded by lowering its price, thus destroying Datril's competitive advantage and ability to remain on the market. In this case, low price was not a sustainable competitive advantage. Without a competitive advantage, target customers don't perceive any reason to patronize an organization instead of its competitors.

The notion of competitive advantage means that a successful firm will stake out a position unique in some manner from its rivals. Imitation of competitors indicates a lack of competitive advantage and almost ensures mediocre performance. Moreover, competitors rarely stand still, so it is not surprising that imitation causes managers to feel trapped in a seemingly endless game of catch-up. They are regularly surprised by the new accomplishments of their rivals.

niche competitive advantage
The advantage achieved when a firm seeks to target and effectively serve a small segment of the market.

sustainable competitive advantage
An advantage that cannot be copied by the competition.

REVIEW LEARNING OUTCOME

LO 5 Identify sources of competitive advantage

To create sustainable competitive advantage, don't copy someone else; build your own:

Sources of Competitive Advantage

- Cost $
- Product/ Service Differentiation A vs. B vs. C
- Niche Strategies

CUSTOMER Experience

Retail Entertainment

Bass Pro Shops was named the "Outdoor Retailer of the Year" in 2007 by the *Sporting Goods Business* magazine. This honor is due, in part, to the fact that the company understands how to offer the customer a quality experience by entertaining them while they shop. This experiential aspect of Bass Pro Shops provides them with a strong competitive advantage.

They operate almost 50 stores throughout the United States, about 30 of which are designed to showcase the characteristics of the area where they are located. These stores bring in elements of a natural-history museum, an art gallery, and an aquarium. Taxidermy mounts on the walls are animals native to the each area, and stores have an indoor water feature that contains indigenous fish species. For example, a Florida store features the hull of a sunken ship, while a Massachusetts store has a 30-foot-long blue whale on display.

In some of the aquariums, professional fishermen and store staff hold demonstrations that show customers how to use artificial bait. Classes are offered at the stores, ranging from fly-casting, Dutch-oven cooking, archery hunting, and GPS navigation. Most stores also offer full service restaurants on site. The Las Vegas store is connected to a casino and cabin-themed resort.

The design details of the stores are a unique feature that enhances the customer experience. Bass Pro has their own shop that builds the pine and cedar log buildings, and 55 artisans that include coppersmiths, blacksmiths, carvers, and painters who hand-make the lighting fixtures, wood carvings, and iron work that is used throughout the store. Artists paint large murals on the walls and ceilings that incorporate mounted animals.

Stores receive up to 3 million visitors every year. In fact, Bass Pro Shops have assumed the status of a tourist destination. Some people spend their vacations driving from store to store.[7]

How might the concept of retail entertainment be applied to other types of retail stores or shopping areas/malls? Either think of examples you have experienced or create a new idea for using this concept.

Companies need to build their own competitive advantages rather than copy a competitor. The sources of tomorrow's competitive advantages are the skills and assets of the organization. Assets include patents, copyrights, locations, equipment, and technology that are superior to those of the competition. Skills are functions such as customer service that the firm performs better than its competitors. Netflix, for example, created and remains dominant in the market for renting movies by mail. Marketing managers should continually focus the firm's skills and assets on sustaining and creating competitive advantages.

Remember, a sustainable competitive advantage is a function of the speed with which competitors can imitate a leading company's strategy and plans. Imitation requires a competitor to identify the leader's competitive advantage, determine how it is achieved, and then learn how to duplicate it.

STRATEGIC DIRECTIONS

The end result of the SWOT analysis and identification of a competitive advantage is to evaluate the strategic direction of the firm. Selecting a strategic alternative is the next step in marketing planning.

Strategic Alternatives

To discover a marketing opportunity, management must know how to identify the alternatives. One method for developing alternatives is Ansoff's strategic opportunity matrix (see Exhibit 2.4), which matches products with markets. Firms can explore these four options:

market penetration
A marketing strategy that tries to increase market share among existing customers.

market development
A marketing strategy that entails attracting new customers to existing products.

product development
A marketing strategy that entails the creation of new products for current customers.

diversification
A strategy of increasing sales by introducing new products into new markets.

☞ *Market penetration:* A firm using the market penetration alternative would try to increase market share among existing customers. If Kraft Foods started a major campaign for Maxwell House coffee, with aggressive advertising and cents-off coupons to existing customers, it would be following a penetration strategy. McDonald's sold the most Happy Meals in history with a promotion that included Ty's Teeny Beanie Babies. Customer databases, discussed in Chapter 9, helped managers implement this strategy.

☞ *Market development:* Market development means attracting new customers to existing products. Ideally, new uses for old products stimulate additional sales among existing customers while also bringing in new buyers. McDonald's, for example, has opened restaurants in Russia, China, and Italy and is eagerly expanding into Eastern European countries. Sara Lee is entering the market for meals on the go by introducing Hillshire Farm Salad Entrees, kits that contain meat and other ingredients that the company already makes, to be added to lettuce.[8] In the nonprofit area, the growing emphasis on continuing education and executive development by colleges and universities is a market development strategy.

☞ *Product development:* A product development strategy entails the creation of new products for present markets. McDonalds introduced yogurt parfaits, entrée salads, and fruit to offer their current customers more healthy options. Managers following the product development strategy can rely on their extensive knowledge of the target audience. They usually have a good feel for what customers like and dislike about current products and what existing needs are not being met. In addition, managers can rely on established distribution channels.

☞ *Diversification:* Diversification is a strategy of increasing sales by introducing new products into new markets. For example, Ralph Lauren developed a new brand of clothing called Rugby to appeal to young people from 14 to 29.[9] Sony practiced

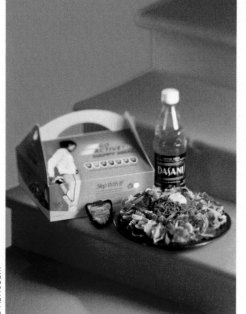

© NEWSCOM

a diversification strategy when it acquired Columbia Pictures; although motion pictures are not a new product in the marketplace, they were a new product for Sony. Coca-Cola manufactures and markets water-treatment and water-conditioning equipment, which has been a very challenging task for the traditional soft drink company. A diversification strategy can be risky when a firm is entering unfamiliar markets. On the other hand, it can be very profitable when a firm is entering markets with little or no competition.

Selecting a Strategic Alternative

Portfolio Matrix Recall that large organizations engaged in strategic planning may create strategic business units. Each SBU has its own rate of return on investment, growth potential, and associated risk. Management must find a balance among the SBUs that yields the overall organization's desired growth and profits with an acceptable level of risk. Some SBUs generate large amounts of cash, and others need cash to foster growth. The challenge is to balance the organization's "portfolio" of SBUs for the best long-term performance.

To determine the future cash contributions and cash requirements expected for each SBU, managers can use the Boston Consulting Group

EXHIBIT 2.4

Ansoff's Strategic Opportunity Matrix

	Present Product	New Product
Present Market	**Market penetration:** McDonald's sells more Happy Meals with Disney movie promotions.	**Product development:** McDonald's introduces premium salads and McWater.
New Market	**Market development:** McDonald's opens restaurants in China.	**Diversification:** McDonald's introduces line of children's clothing.

(BCG) portfolio matrix. The portfolio matrix classifies each SBU by its present or forecast growth and market share. The underlying assumption is that market share and profitability are strongly linked. The measure of market share used in the portfolio approach is *relative market share*, the ratio between the company's share and the share of the largest competitor. For example, if firm A has a 50 percent share and the competitor has 5 percent, the ratio is 10 to 1. If firm A has a 10 percent market share and the largest competitor has 20 percent, the ratio is 0.5 to 1.

Exhibit 2.5 is a hypothetical portfolio matrix for a large computer manufacturer. The size of the circle in each cell of the matrix represents dollar sales of the SBU relative to dollar sales of the company's other SBUs. The following categories are used in the matrix:

☛ *Stars:* A star is a market leader and growing fast. For example, computer manufacturers have identified notebook and handheld models as stars. Star SBUs usually have large profits but need a lot of cash to finance rapid growth. The best marketing tactic is to protect existing market share by reinvesting earnings in product improvement, better distribution, more promotion, and production efficiency. Management must strive to capture most of the new users as they enter the market.

☛ *Cash cows:* A cash cow is an SBU that usually generates more cash than it needs to maintain its market share. It is in a low-growth market, but the product has a dominant market share. Personal computers and laptops are categorized as cash cows in Exhibit 2.5. The basic strategy for a cash cow is to maintain market dominance by being the price leader and making technological improvements in the product. Managers should resist pressure to extend the basic line unless they can dramatically increase demand. Instead, they should allocate excess cash to the product categories where growth prospects are the greatest. For instance, the Clorox Company owns Kingsford charcoal; the Glad brand of products; Fresh Step, Scoop Away, and other pet litters; Brita water filtration systems; and K. C. Masterpiece barbecue sauce, among others. Traditionally, the company's cash cow has been Clorox bleach, which owns the lion's share of a low-growth market. The Clorox Company has been highly successful in stretching the Clorox line to include scented chlorine bleach as well as Clorox 2, chlorine-free bleach for colored clothing. Another example is Heinz, which has two cash cows: ketchup and Weight Watchers frozen dinners.

☛ *Problem children:* A problem child, also called a question mark, shows rapid growth but poor profit margins. It has a low market share in a high-growth industry. Problem children need a great deal of cash. Without cash support, they eventually become dogs. The strategy options are to invest heavily to gain better market share, acquire competitors to get the necessary market share, or drop the SBU. Sometimes a firm can reposition the products of the SBU to move them into the star category. Zima brand beer, targeted at Generation X, was a problem child for Adolph Coors Company. The company ultimately withdrew its heavy marketing investment in Zima and positioned it as a niche product.

☛ *Dogs:* A dog has low growth potential and a small market share. Most dogs eventually leave the marketplace. In the computer manufacturer example, the mainframe computer has become a dog. Other examples include Warner-Lambert's Reef mouthwash and Campbell's Red Kettle soups. Frito-Lay has produced several dogs, including Stuffers cheese-filled snacks, Rumbles granola nuggets, and Toppels cheese-topped crackers—a trio irreverently known as Stumbles, Tumbles, and Twofers. The strategy options for dogs are to harvest or divest.

EXHIBIT 2.5

Portfolio Matrix for a Large Computer Manufacturer

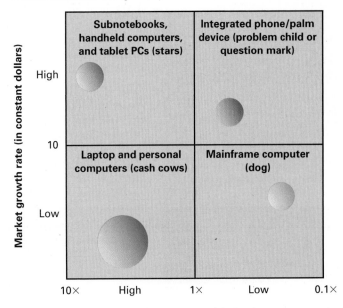

Market growth rate (in constant dollars)

High | 10 | Low

Subnotebooks, handheld computers, and tablet PCs (stars)

Integrated phone/palm device (problem child or question mark)

Laptop and personal computers (cash cows)

Mainframe computer (dog)

10× High   1× Low   0.1×

Market share dominance (share relative to largest competitor)

Note: The size of the circle represents the dollar sales relative to sales of other SBUs on the matrix—for example, 10x means sales are ten times greater than those of the next largest competitor.

portfolio matrix
A tool for allocating resources among products or strategic business units on the basis of relative market share and market growth rate.

star
In the portfolio matrix, a business unit that is a fast-growing market leader.

cash cow
In the portfolio matrix, a business unit that usually generates more cash than it needs to maintain its market share.

problem child (question mark)
In the portfolio matrix, a business unit that shows rapid growth but poor profit margins.

dog
In the portfolio matrix, a business unit that has low growth potential and a small market share.

After classifying the company's SBUs in the matrix, the next step is to allocate future resources for each. The four basic strategies are to:

- *Build:* If an organization has an SBU that it believes has the potential to be a star (probably a problem child at present), building would be an appropriate goal. The organization may decide to give up short-term profits and use its financial resources to achieve this goal. Procter & Gamble built Pringles from a money loser into a record profit maker.

- *Hold:* If an SBU is a very successful cash cow, a key goal would surely be to hold or preserve market share so that the organization can take advantage of the very positive cash flow. Bisquick has been a prosperous cash cow for General Mills for over two decades.

- *Harvest:* This strategy is appropriate for all SBUs except those classified as stars. The basic goal is to increase the short-term cash return without too much concern for the long-run impact. It is especially worthwhile when more cash is needed from a cash cow with long-run prospects that are unfavorable because of low market growth rate. For instance, Lever Brothers has been harvesting Lifebuoy soap for a number of years with little promotional backing.

- *Divest:* Getting rid of SBUs with low shares of low-growth markets is often appropriate. Problem children and dogs are most suitable for this strategy. Procter & Gamble dropped Cincaprin, a coated aspirin, because of its low growth potential.

REVIEW LEARNING OUTCOME

 LO6 Identify strategic alternatives

Market development = ↑ customers
Market penetration = ↑ share
Product development = ↑ products
Diversification = ↑ New Products + ↑ New Markets

LO7

DESCRIBING THE TARGET MARKET

Marketing strategy involves the activities of selecting and describing one or more target markets and developing and maintaining a marketing mix that will produce mutually satisfying exchanges with target markets.

Target Market Strategy

A market segment is a group of individuals or organizations that share one or more characteristics. They therefore may have relatively similar product needs. For example, parents of newborn babies need products such as formula, diapers, and special foods. The target market strategy identifies the market segment or segments on which to focus. This process begins with a market opportunity analysis (MOA)—the description and estimation of the size and sales potential of market segments that are of interest to the firm and the assessment of key competitors in these market segments. After the firm describes the market segments, it may target one or more of them. There are three general strategies for selecting target markets. Target market(s) can be selected by appealing to the entire market with one marketing mix, concentrating on one segment, or appealing to multiple market segments using multiple marketing mixes. The characteristics, advantages, and disadvantages of each strategic option are examined in Chapter 8. Target markets could be smokers who are concerned about white teeth (the target of Topol toothpaste), people concerned about sugar and calories in their soft drinks (Diet Pepsi), or college students needing inexpensive about-town transportation (Yamaha Razz scooter).

Any market segment that is targeted must be fully described. Demographics, psychographics, and buyer behavior should be assessed. Buyer behavior is covered in Chapters 6 and 7. If segments are differentiated by ethnicity, multicultural aspects of the marketing mix should be examined. If the target market is international, it is especially important to describe differences in culture, economic and technological development, and political structure that may affect the marketing plan. Global marketing is covered in more detail in Chapter 5.

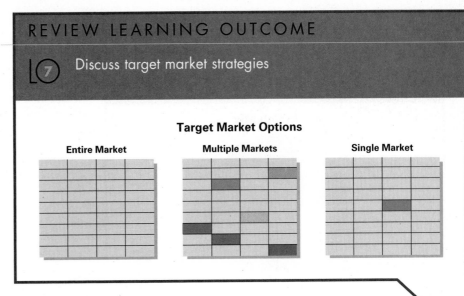

REVIEW LEARNING OUTCOME

LO 7   Discuss target market strategies

Target Market Options

| Entire Market | Multiple Markets | Single Market |

THE MARKETING MIX

The term marketing mix refers to a unique blend of product, place (distribution), promotion, and pricing strategies (often referred to as the four Ps) designed to produce mutually satisfying exchanges with a target market. The marketing manager can control each component of the marketing mix, but the strategies for all four components must be blended to achieve optimal results. Any marketing mix is only as good as its weakest component. For example, the first pump toothpastes were distributed over cosmetic counters and failed. Not until pump toothpastes were distributed the same way as tube toothpastes did the products succeed. The best promotion and the lowest price cannot save a poor product. Similarly, excellent products with poor placement, pricing, or promotion will likely fail.

Successful marketing mixes have been carefully designed to satisfy target markets. At first glance, McDonald's and Wendy's may appear to have roughly identical marketing mixes because they are both in the fast-food hamburger business. However, McDonald's has been most successful at targeting parents with young children for lunchtime meals, whereas Wendy's targets the adult crowd for lunches and dinner. McDonald's has playgrounds, Ronald McDonald the clown, and children's Happy Meals. Wendy's has salad bars, carpeted restaurants, and no playgrounds.

Variations in marketing mixes do not occur by chance. Astute marketing managers devise marketing strategies to gain advantages over competitors and best serve the needs and wants of a particular target market segment. By manipulating elements of the marketing mix, marketing managers can fine-tune the customer offering and achieve competitive success.

> *Strategic planning should be an ongoing process.*

Product Strategies

Typically, the marketing mix starts with the product "P." The heart of the marketing mix, the starting point, is the product offering and product strategy. It is hard to design a place strategy, decide on a promotion campaign, or set a price without knowing the product to be marketed.

The product includes not only the physical unit but also its package, warranty, after-sale service, brand name, company image, value, and many other factors. A Godiva chocolate has many product elements: the chocolate itself, a fancy gold wrapper, a customer satisfaction guarantee, and the prestige of the Godiva brand name. We

marketing mix
A unique blend of product, place, promotion, and pricing strategies designed to produce mutually satisfying exchanges with a target market.

four Ps
Product, place, promotion, and price, which together make up the marketing mix.

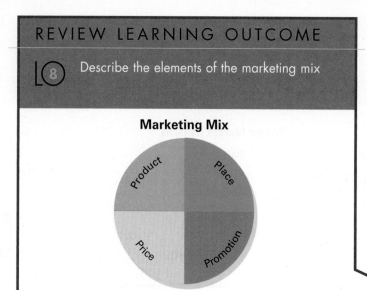

buy things not only for what they do (benefits) but also for what they mean to us (status, quality, or reputation).

Products can be tangible goods such as computers, ideas like those offered by a consultant, or services such as medical care. Products should also offer customer value. Product decisions are covered in Chapters 10 and 11.

Place (Distribution) Strategies

Place, or distribution, strategies are concerned with making products available when and where customers want them. Would you rather buy a kiwi fruit at the 24-hour grocery store within walking distance or fly to Australia to pick your own? A part of this place "P" is physical distribution, which involves all the business activities concerned with storing and transporting raw materials or finished products. The goal is to make sure products arrive in usable condition at designated places when needed. Place strategies are covered in Chapter 12.

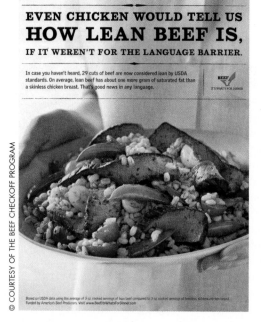

EVEN CHICKEN WOULD TELL US HOW LEAN BEEF IS, IF IT WEREN'T FOR THE LANGUAGE BARRIER.

In case you haven't heard, 29 cuts of beef are now considered lean by USDA standards. On average, lean beef has about one more gram of saturated fat than a skinless chicken breast. That's good news in any language.

BEEF
IT'S WHAT'S FOR DINNER

Based on USDA data using the average of 3 oz. cooked servings of lean beef compared to 3 oz. cooked servings of boneless, skinless chicken breast.
Funded by America's Beef Producers. Visit www.BeefItsWhatsForDinner.com

© COURTESY OF THE BEEF CHECKOFF PROGRAM

Promotion Strategies

Promotion includes advertising, public relations, sales promotion, and personal selling. Promotion's role in the marketing mix is to bring about mutually satisfying exchanges with target markets by informing, educating, persuading, and reminding them of the benefits of an organization or a product. A good promotion strategy, like using the Dilbert character in a national promotion strategy for Office Depot, can dramatically increase sales. Each element of the promotion "P" is coordinated and managed with the others to create a promotional blend or mix. These integrated marketing communications activities are described in Chapters 14 and 15.

implementation
The process that turns a marketing plan into action assignments and ensures that these assignments are executed in a way that accomplishes the plan's objectives.

Pricing Strategies

Price is what a buyer must give up to obtain a product. It is often the most flexible of the four marketing mix elements—the quickest element to change. Marketers can raise or lower prices more frequently and easily than they can change other marketing mix variables. Price is an important competitive weapon and is very important to the organization because price multiplied by the number of units sold equals total revenue for the firm. Pricing decisions are covered in Chapter 16.

LO 9

FOLLOWING UP ON THE MARKETING PLAN

Implementation

Implementation is the process that turns a marketing plan into action assignments and ensures that these assignments are executed in a way that accomplishes the

Surrogate Ads

Indian law prohibits companies from advertising tobacco and liquor. However, companies that sell these products are among the largest advertisers in the country. They accomplish this by using what are known as "surrogate advertisements," which instead of featuring cigarettes and alcoholic beverages, focus on unrelated, cheap-to-make products that they also produce. Surrogate products include CDs, playing cards, and bottled water that all have the same brand name as the companies' spirits and smokes. These ads have been blamed for luring India's young people (10–14 years old) to take up smoking. One study showed that current use of tobacco was five times lower among students who had not watched surrogate promotions. The companies say that they buy ads for the actual products advertised and deny that they use surrogate advertising.

India's Health Minister has asked the Information and Broadcasting Ministry to take action against the companies that are showing surrogate ads. The government has asked that broadcasters stop airing ads from tobacco and liquor companies for products with brand names that are the same as their tobacco and liquor brands, regardless of the product being advertised. If broadcasters comply, they could experience an estimated $50 million loss of advertising revenue, and even more if the government extends the ban on surrogate ads to other forms of media.

Government actions against surrogate ads are causing the liquor and tobacco companies to use sponsorships of sporting events, concerts, and other entertainment venues as an alternative to promoting their products. For example, the chairman of the UB Group, which markets Kingfisher beer and Royal Challenge whiskey, bought a professional cricket team. The team was named the "Royal Challengers" and the colors and logos of the team are the same as those of the whiskey brand. Bacardi Martini India sells a line of music CDs with the brand name Bacardi Blast, which is also the branding used for high-profile events.[10] Is it ethical for India's tobacco and liquor companies to use surrogate advertising to get their brand names in front of customers? Take a stand and defend your answer.

---

plan's objectives. Implementation activities may involve detailed job assignments, activity descriptions, timelines, budgets, and lots of communication. Although implementation is essentially "doing what you said you were going to do," many organizations repeatedly experience failures in strategy implementation. Brilliant marketing plans are doomed to fail if they are not properly implemented. These detailed communications may or may not be part of the written marketing plan. If they are not part of the plan, they should be specified elsewhere as soon as the plan has been communicated.

Evaluation and Control

After a marketing plan is implemented, it should be evaluated. Evaluation entails gauging the extent to which marketing objectives have been achieved during the specified time. Four common reasons for failing to achieve a marketing objective are unrealistic marketing objectives, inappropriate marketing strategies in the plan, poor implementation, and changes in the environment after the objective was specified and the strategy was implemented.

Once a plan is chosen and implemented, its effectiveness must be monitored. Control provides the mechanisms for evaluating marketing results in light of the plan's objectives and for correcting actions that do not help the organization reach those objectives within budget guidelines. Firms need to establish formal and informal control programs to make the entire operation more efficient.

evaluation
Gauging the extent to which the marketing objectives have been achieved during the specified time period.

control
Provides the mechanisms for evaluating marketing results in light of the plan's objectives and for correcting actions that do not help the organization reach those objectives within budget guidelines.

REVIEW LEARNING OUTCOME

LO 9 Explain why implementation, evaluation, and control of the marketing plan are necessary

Perhaps the broadest control device available to marketing managers is the marketing audit—a thorough, systematic, periodic evaluation of the objectives, strategies, structure, and performance of the marketing organization. A marketing audit helps management allocate marketing resources efficiently. It has four characteristics:

☛ *Comprehensive:* The marketing audit covers all the major marketing issues facing an organization and not just trouble spots.

☛ *Systematic:* The marketing audit takes place in an orderly sequence and covers the organization's marketing environment, internal marketing system, and specific marketing activities. The diagnosis is followed by an action plan with both short-run and long-run proposals for improving overall marketing effectiveness.

☛ *Independent:* The marketing audit is normally conducted by an inside or outside party who is independent enough to have top management's confidence and to be objective.

marketing audit
A thorough, systematic, periodic evaluation of the objectives, strategies, structure, and performance of the marketing organization.

☛ *Periodic:* The marketing audit should be carried out on a regular schedule instead of only in a crisis. Whether it seems successful or is in deep trouble, any organization can benefit greatly from such an audit.

Although the main purpose of the marketing audit is to develop a full profile of the organization's marketing effort and to provide a basis for developing and revising the marketing plan, it is also an excellent way to improve communication and raise the level of marketing consciousness within the organization. It is a useful vehicle for selling the philosophy and techniques of strategic marketing to other members of the organization.

REVIEW LEARNING OUTCOME

LO 10 Identify several techniques that help make strategic planning effective

LO 10

EFFECTIVE STRATEGIC PLANNING

Effective strategic planning requires continual attention, creativity, and management commitment. Strategic planning should not be an annual exercise in which managers go through the motions and forget about strategic planning until the next year. It should be an ongoing process because the environment is continually changing and the firm's resources and capabilities are continually evolving.

Sound strategic planning is based on creativity. Managers should challenge assumptions about the firm and the environment and establish new strategies. For example, major oil companies developed the concept of the gasoline service station in an age when cars needed frequent and rather elaborate servicing. They held on to the full-service approach, but independents were quick to respond to new realities and moved to lower-cost self-service and convenience-store operations. The majors took several decades to catch up.

Perhaps the most critical element in successful strategic planning is top management's support and participation. For example, Michael Anthony, CEO of Brookstone, Inc., and the Brookstone buying team earn hundreds of thousands of frequent-flyer miles searching the world for manufacturers and inventors of unique products that can be carried in its retail stores, catalogs, and Internet site. Anthony has codeveloped some of these products and has also been active in remodeling efforts for Brookstone's 250 permanent and seasonal stores.

3 ◄ Types of competitive advantages

Macroenvironmental forces affecting marketing ► **6**

Debut of the Boston Consulting Group (BCG) portfolio matrix ► **1996**

4 ◄ Elements of the marketing mix; quadrants in the Boston Consulting Group (BCG) portfolio matrix

3 million ▲ Visitors to Bass Pro Shops each year

REVIEW AND APPLICATIONS

Understand the importance of strategic marketing and know a basic outline for a marketing plan. Strategic marketing planning is the basis for all marketing strategies and decisions. The marketing plan is a written document that acts as a guidebook of marketing activities for the marketing manager. A marketing plan provides the basis by which actual and expected performance can be compared.

Although there is no set formula or a single correct outline, a marketing plan should include basic elements such as stating the business mission, setting objectives, performing a situation analysis of internal and external environmental forces, selecting target market(s), delineating a marketing mix (product, place, promotion, and price), and establishing ways to implement, evaluate, and control the plan.

1.1 Your cousin wants to start his own business, but he has decided not to write a marketing plan because he thinks that preparing one would take too long. He says he doesn't need a formal proposal because he has already received funding from your uncle. Explain why it is important for him to write a plan anyway.

1.2 After graduation, you decide to take a position as the marketing manager for a small snack-food manufacturer. The company, Shur Snak, is growing, and this is the first time that the company has ever employed a marketing manager. Consequently, there is no marketing plan in place for you to follow. Outline a basic marketing plan for your boss to give her an idea of the direction you want to take the company.

1.3 How are Coke and Pepsi using their Web sites, **www.coca-cola.com** and **www.pepsi.com**, to promote their newest product offerings? Do you see hints of any future strategies the companies might implement? Where?

LO 2 Develop an appropriate business mission statement. The mission statement is based on a careful analysis of benefits sought by present and potential customers and an analysis of existing and anticipated environmental conditions. The firm's mission statement establishes boundaries for all subsequent decisions, objectives, and strategies. A mission statement should focus on the market or markets the organization is attempting to serve rather than on the good or service offered.

2.1 Thinking back to question 1.2, write a business mission statement for Shur Snak. What elements should you include? Evaluate the mission statement you wrote against some of those you can find online.

LO 3 Describe the components of a situation analysis. In the situation (or SWOT) analysis, the firm should identify its internal strengths (S) and weaknesses (W) and also examine external opportunities (O) and threats (T). When examining external opportunities and threats, marketing managers must analyze aspects of the marketing environment in a process called environmental scanning. The six most often studied macroenvironmental forces are social, demographic, economic, technological, political and legal, and competitive.

3.1 Competition in the private courier sector is fierce. UPS and FedEx dominate, but other companies, such as DHL and even the United States Postal Service (USPS), still have a decent chunk of the express package delivery market. Perform a mini-situation analysis on one of the companies listed below by stating one strength, one weakness, one opportunity, and one threat. You may want to consult the following Web sites as you build your grid:

UPS	**www.ups.com**	DHL	**www.dhl-usa.com**
FedEx	**www.fedex.com**	USPS	**www.usps.com**

LO 4 Explain the criteria for stating good marketing objectives. Objectives should be realistic, measurable, and time specific. Objectives must also be consistent and indicate the priorities of the organization.

4.1 Building on the Shur Snak example, imagine that your boss has stated that the marketing objective of the company is to do the best job of satisfying the needs and wants of the customer. Explain that although this objective is admirable, it does not meet the criteria for good objectives. What are these criteria? What is a specific example of a better objective for Shur Snak?

LO 5 Identify sources of competitive advantage. A competitive advantage is a set of unique features of a company and its products that are perceived by the target market as significant and superior to the competition. There are three types of competitive advantages: cost, product/service differentiation, and niche strategies. Sources of cost competitive advantages include experience curves, efficient labor, no-frills goods and services, government subsidies, product design, reengineering, product innovations, and new methods of service delivery. A product/ service differentiation competitive advantage exists when a firm provides something unique that is valuable to buyers beyond just low price. Niche competitive advantages come from targeting unique segments with specific needs and wants. The goal of all these sources of competitive advantage is to be sustainable.

5.1 Break into small groups and discuss examples (at least two per person) of the last few products you have purchased. What specific strategies were used to achieve competitive advantage? Is that competitive advantage sustainable against the competitors?

LO 6 Identify strategic alternatives. The strategic opportunity matrix can be used to help management develop strategic alternatives. The four options are market penetration, product development, market development, and diversification. In selecting a strategic alternative, managers may use a portfolio matrix, which classifies strategic business units as stars, cash cows, problem children, or dogs, depending on their present or projected growth and market share.

6.1 Based on your SWOT analysis, decide what the strategic growth options are for the company you chose in question 3.1.

Discuss target market strategies. The target market strategy identifies which market segment or segments to focus on. This process begins with a market opportunity analysis (MOA), which describes and estimates the size and sales potential of market segments that are of interest to the firm. In addition, an assessment of key competitors in these market segments is performed. After the market segments are described, one or more may be targeted by the firm. The three strategies for selecting target markets are appealing to the entire market with one marketing mix, concentrating on one segment, or appealing to multiple market segments using multiple marketing mixes.

7.1 You are given the task of deciding the marketing strategy for a transportation company. How do the marketing mix elements change when the target market is (a) low-income workers without personal transportation, (b) corporate international business travelers, or (c) companies with urgent documents or perishable materials to be delivered to customers?

Describe the elements of the marketing mix. The marketing mix (or four Ps) is a blend of product, place, promotion, and pricing strategies designed to produce mutually satisfying exchanges with a target market. The starting point of the marketing mix is the product offering. Products can be tangible goods, ideas, or services. Place (distribution) strategies are concerned with making products available when and where customers want them. Promotion includes advertising, public relations, sales promotion, and personal selling. Price is what a buyer must give up to obtain a product and is often the easiest to change of the four marketing mix elements.

8.1 Choose three or four other students and make up a team. Create a marketing plan to increase enrollment in your school. Describe the four marketing mix elements that make up the plan.

Explain why implementation, evaluation, and control of the marketing plan are necessary. Before a marketing plan can work, it must be implemented; that is, people must perform the actions in the plan. The plan should also be evaluated to see if it has achieved its objectives. Poor implementation can be a major factor in a plan's failure. Control provides the mechanisms for evaluating marketing results in light of the plan's objectives and for correcting actions that do not help the organization reach those objectives within budget guidelines.

9.1 Have your school enrollment marketing plan team (from question 8.1) develop a plan to implement, evaluate, and control the marketing strategy.

Identify several techniques that help make strategic planning effective. First, management must realize that strategic planning is an ongoing process and not a once-a-year exercise. Second, good strategic planning involves a high level of creativity. The last requirement is top management's support and cooperation.

10.1 What techniques can make your school enrollment marketing plan more effective?

KEY TERMS

cash cow	45	market development	44	planning	36
competitive advantage	40	marketing mix	47	portfolio matrix	45
control	49	marketing myopia	37	problem child (question mark)	45
cost competitive advantage	41	marketing objective	39	product development	44
diversification	44	market opportunity analysis		product/service differentiation	
dog	45	(MOA)	46	competitive advantage	41
environmental scanning	39	market penetration	44	star	45
evaluation	49	marketing plan	35	strategic business unit (SBU)	38
experience curves	41	marketing planning	35	strategic planning	35
four Ps	47	marketing strategy	46	sustainable competitive	
implementation	48	mission statement	37	advantage	42
marketing audit	50	niche competitive advantage	42	SWOT analysis	38

EXERCISES

APPLICATION EXERCISE

As you now know from reading the chapter, an important part of the strategy-making process involves scanning the environment for changes that affect your marketing efforts. This exercise is designed to introduce you to the business press and to help you make the connection between the concepts you learn in the classroom and real-world marketing activities.

Activities

1. Find a current article of substance in the business press (*The Wall Street Journal, The Financial Times, Fortune, BusinessWeek, Inc.,* etc.) that discusses topics you have covered in this course. Although this is only Chapter 2, you will be surprised by the amount of terminology you have already learned. If you are having trouble finding an article, read through the table of contents at the beginning of the book to familiarize yourself with the names of concepts that will be presented later in the course. Read your article carefully, making notes about relevant content.

2. Write a one-paragraph summary of the key points in your article; then, write a list of the terms or concepts critical to understanding the article. Provide definitions of those terms. If you are unfamiliar with a term or concept that is central to the article, do some research in your textbook or see your professor during office hours. Relate these key points to the concepts in your text by citing page numbers.

3. Explain the environments that are relevant to the situation presented in the article. (Chapter 4 contains a full list of environmental factors.)

ETHICS EXERCISE

Abercrombie & Fitch, a retail clothing chain based in New Albany, Ohio, launched a line of thong underwear for preteen girls. Words like "eye candy" and "wink wink" were printed on the front of the skimpy underwear that some argued would fit girls aged 5 to 10. Abercrombie is known for its provocative ads and sexually oriented catalogs. Supporters of the strategy claim that producing thong-style underwear for 10- to 16-year-olds is a good move; critics think that the line is tasteless and that marketing it to young girls is contemptuous.

Questions

1. Is marketing adult-styled undergarments to a younger audience unethical? Why or why not?

2. Would Abercrombie have been in the spotlight had the sexy words been omitted from the product? Explain your answer.

MARKETING PLAN EXERCISE

Throughout the rest of this book, these end-of-chapter marketing plan exercises will help you build a strategic marketing plan for a company of your choosing. The company you choose should be one that interests you, such as the manufacturer of your favorite product, a local business where you would like to work, or even a business you would like to start yourself to satisfy an unmet need or want. Once you've completed the marketing plan exercise for each chapter in Part 1 of this textbook, you can complete the Part 1 Marketing Planning Worksheet on your companion Web site at **www.cengage.com/marketing/lamb**. Use the following exercises to guide you through the first part of your strategic marketing plan:

Questions

1. Describe your chosen company. How long has it been in business, or when will it start business? Who are the key players? Is the company small or large? Does it offer a good or service?

2. Write the mission statement of your company, keeping in mind the benefits offered to customers rather than the product or service sold. If you are starting the online arm of a traditional store, should you make any changes to the company's overall mission statement?

3. List at least three specific, measurable objectives for your company. Be sure these objectives relate to the mission statement and include a time frame.

4. Begin a SWOT analysis by determining the primary strength of your company by asking, "What is the key differential or competitive advantage of my firm?" What are other keys to the potential success of your company? What other strengths can your firm capitalize on?

5. Continue the SWOT analysis by taking an honest look at the weaknesses of your firm. How can you overcome them?

CASE STUDY: DISNEY

THE HAPPIEST BRAND ON EARTH

In 2006, Disney's Pixar released the hit movie *Cars*, which grossed $462 million worldwide. Since then, *Cars* merchandise has generated over $2 billion in sales each year. Pixar has since created a series of *Cars* shorts to be aired on the Disney Channel with a subsequent DVD release. A *Cars* sequel is in the works for 2011, and an online virtual gaming world was released in 2009. In 2012, Disney's California Adventure theme park will open its 12-acre Cars Land attraction.

At Disney, the brand is the name of the game, and cross-platform success of the *Cars* franchise is by no means the exception to the rule. Disney also has the Jonas Brothers, *Hannah Montana*, *High School Musical*, the Disney Princesses, *Pirates of the Caribbean*, and the list goes on and on. The man behind the magic is Disney's CEO, Bob Iger, who has lead a dramatic revitalization of the Disney brand since succeeding longtime head Michael Eisner in 2005. When he first took the post, his strategy shifted Disney's focus around its stable of "franchises." These franchises are distributed across Disney's multiple company platforms and divisions, such as Disney's various television broadcasts platforms (the Disney Channel, ABC, ESPN), its consumer products business, theme parks, Disney's Hollywood Records music label, and Disney's publishing arm in Hyperion just to name a few.

Iger's franchise strategy has been supported by the other major move he made upon first becoming CEO. On his first day on the job, Iger told the board that revitalizing Disney's animation business was a top priority, which would be improved through the purchase of Pixar. As part of Iger's franchise strategy the deal made perfect sense, as many of Disney's latest TV shows, Disneyland rides, and merchandise was based of Pixar characters.

Finding a new market to push the Disney franchise became a priority as well. With the Disney brand growing flat, it was becoming evident that Disney had missed some opportunities for broader success due to a narrowing of its target market, which was at the time largely associated with younger children.

Iger's first move was to broaden Disney's viewership by moving the Disney Channel from premium to basic cable and launching local versions in key global markets. Then, Disney began pushing franchises to capture the rapidly growing tween market. Putting its support behind the Disney channel's *High School Musical* and *Hannah Montana* and the Jonas Brothers who were emerging out of Disney's music label, Disney quickly generated a series of franchise juggernauts in the tween-girl market.

Though Disney's focus has remained on family-friendly fair, Iger has shown a new willingness to look to even broader markets, if it fits with the Disney brand. Disney's *Pirates of the Caribbean*, the first Disney film with a PG-13 rating, played a major role in refocusing the brand, being based off the classic theme park ride, and it also helped expand the Disney appeal older kids and even adults. The *Pirates* and *Cars* franchises also provided preliminary steps for Disney's latest endeavors to crack the tween boy market, age 6 to 14, one traditionally difficult for media companies to sustainably capture. Their efforts focus around the new Disney XD channel, with a broad range of offerings, such as potential new franchises like the science fiction action-adventure show *Aaron Stone* and showcases of new musical talent. Disney will also be able to leverage ESPN to create original sports-based programming. The channel is accompanied by a Disney XD Web site, which promotes the channel's programs, as well as offers games and original videos, social networking, and online community opportunities.

As it continues to expand and provide new franchise offerings, Disney looks to have relatively strong momentum, even in the midst of rising economic challenges. As Jobs puts it, "Family is a renewable resource," and right now, Disney is making the most of it.[11]

Questions

1. Do a brief market opportunity analysis for Disney, identifying the major markets that Disney has expanded into.

2. How does Disney's cross-platform franchising help create sustainable competitive advantage?

3. Describe the marketing mix for one of Disney's franchises.

4. Describe the major components of Bob Iger's strategic plan.

COMPANY CLIPS

© NKP MEDIA, INC./CENGAGE

METHOD—HEALTHY HOME

Cash-strapped start-up companies generally do not spend a great deal of time and money on planning. Founders are so busy with the rudiments of business—finding customers and creating, manufacturing, and delivering the product—that they may even forget important things, like invoicing. Eric Lowry reinforces this notion in the opening of the second method video segment. Nonetheless, strategic planning is an important part of successful marketing. Listen closely to the segment, which introduces method's CEO, Alastair Dorward, and gauge for yourself how much planning you think this innovative start-up did before launching its brand.

Questions

1. Based on what you heard in the video, does method have a marketing plan?

2. Explain the elements that make up method's competitive advantage. Is it sustainable?

3. What are the elements in method's marketing mix?

4. What are method's target market strategies and how does it use them in its operations?

Marketing & You Results

The higher your score, the greater importance you place on planning. You also develop plans more often and devote more energy to the planning process. High scores also indicate a motivation to work "smart" and efficiently. If your score was low, you are less inclined to spend energy planning and, as a result, may have lower performance.

Marketing Plan Outline

Appendix I

I BUSINESS MISSION

II SITUATION ANALYSIS
(SWOT ANALYSIS)

A. Internal Strengths and Weaknesses

B. External Opportunities and Threats

III OBJECTIVES

IV MARKETING STRATEGY

A. Target Market Strategy

B. Marketing Mix

1. Product

2. Place/Distribution

3. Promotion

4. Price

V IMPLEMENTATION, EVALUATION,
AND CONTROL

As you read in Chapter 2, there is more than one correct format for a marketing plan. Many organizations have their own distinctive format or terminology for creating a marketing plan, and every marketing plan should be unique to the firm for which it was created. The format and order of presentation, therefore, must be flexible.

This appendix presents only one way to organize a marketing plan. The outline is meant to give you a more detailed look at what you need to include, topics you need to cover, and the types of questions you must answer in any marketing plan. But, depending on the product or service for which you are drafting a plan, this set of questions may only be the starting point for more industry-specific issues you need to address.

An actual marketing plan from e-motion software follows this outline. The e-motion marketing plan includes annotations that tie each part of the plan to the material throughout the book. You'll see the correlation between chapter concepts and the elements of a professional marketing plan for a real company.

If you are assigned a marketing plan as a course requirement, this appendix can help you organize your work. In addition, worksheets that guide you through the process of marketing planning are available on your textbook's companion site. The worksheets can be completed electronically or printed out and filled in by hand.

I BUSINESS MISSION

- What is the mission of the firm? What business is it in? How well is its mission understood throughout the organization? Five years from now, what business does it wish to be in?

- Does the firm define its business in terms of benefits its customers want rather than in terms of goods and services?

II SITUATION ANALYSIS (SWOT ANALYSIS)

- Has one or more competitive advantages been identified in the SWOT analysis?

- Are these advantages sustainable against the competition?

A. Internal Strengths and Weaknesses

- What is the history of the firm, including sales, profits, and organizational philosophies?

- What is the nature of the firm and its current situation?

- What are the firm's resources (financial, human, time, experience, asset, skill)?

- What policies inhibit the achievement of the firm's objectives with respect to organization, resource allocation, operations, hiring, training, and so on?

B. External Opportunities and Threats

- *Social*: What major social and lifestyle trends will have an impact on the firm? What action has the firm been taking in response to these trends?

- *Demographics*: What impact will forecasted trends in the size, age, profile, and distribution of population have on the firm? How will the changing nature of the family, the increase in the proportion of women in the workforce, and changes in the ethnic composition of the population affect the firm? What action has the firm taken in response to these developments and trends? Has the firm reevaluated its traditional products and expanded the range of specialized offerings to respond to these changes?

- *Economic*: What major trends in taxation and income sources will have an impact on the firm? What action has the firm taken in response to these trends?

- *Political, Legal, and Financial*: What laws are now being proposed at international, federal, state, and local levels that could affect marketing strategy and tactics? What recent changes in regulations and court decisions affect the firm? What political changes are taking place at each government level? What action has the firm taken in response to these legal and political changes?

- *Competition*: Which organizations are competing with the firm directly by offering a similar product? Which organizations are competing with the firm indirectly by securing its prime prospects' time, money, energy, or commitment? What new competitive trends seem likely to emerge? How effective is the competition? What benefits do competitors offer that the firm does not? Is it appropriate for the firm to compete?

- *Technological*: What major technological changes are occurring that affect the firm?

- *Ecological*: What is the outlook for the cost and availability of natural resources and energy needed by the firm? Are the firm's products, services, and operations environmentally friendly?

III OBJECTIVES

- Is the firm's mission statement able to be translated into operational terms regarding the firm's objectives?

- What are the stated objectives of the organization? Are they formally written down? Do they lead logically to clearly stated marketing objectives? Are objectives based on sales, profits, or customers?

- Are the organization's marketing objectives stated in hierarchical order? Are they specific so that progress toward achievement can be measured? Are the objectives reasonable in light of the organization's resources? Are the objectives ambiguous? Do the objectives specify a time frame?

- Is the firm's main objective to maximize customer satisfaction or to get as many customers as possible?

IV MARKETING STRATEGY

A. Target Market Strategy

- Are the members of each market homogeneous or heterogeneous with respect to geographic, socio-demographic, and behavioral characteristics?

- What are the size, growth rate, and national and regional trends in each of the organization's market segments?

- Is the size of each market segment sufficiently large or important to warrant a unique marketing mix?

- Are market segments measurable and accessible to distribution and communication efforts?

- Which are the high- or low-opportunity segments?

- What are the evolving needs and satisfactions being sought by target markets?

- What benefits does the organization offer to each segment? How do these benefits compare with benefits offered by competitors?

- Is the firm positioning itself with a unique product? Is the product needed?

- How much of the firm's business is repeat versus new business? What percentage of the public can be classified as nonusers, light users, or heavy users?

- How do current target markets rate the firm and its competitors with respect to reputation, quality, and price? What is the firm's image with the specific market segments it seeks to serve?

- Does the firm try to direct its products only to specific groups of people or to everybody?

- Who buys the firm's products? How does a potential customer find out about the organization? When and how does a person become a customer?

- What are the major objections given by potential customers as to why they do not buy the firm's products?

- How do customers find out about and decide to purchase the product? When and where?

- Should the firm seek to expand, contract, or change the emphasis of its selected target markets? If so, in which target markets, and how vigorously?

- Could the firm more usefully withdraw from some areas where there are alternative suppliers and use its resources to serve new, unserved customer groups?

- What publics other than target markets (financial, media, government, citizen, local, general, and internal) represent opportunities or problems for the firm?

B. Marketing Mix

- Does the firm seek to achieve its objective chiefly through coordinated use of marketing activities (product, place, promotion, and pricing) or only through intensive promotion?

- Are the objectives and roles of each element of the marketing mix clearly specified?

  1. Product

  - What are the major product/service offerings of the firm? Do they complement each other, or is there unnecessary duplication?

  - What are the features and benefits of each product offering?

  - Where are the firm and each major product in the life cycle?

  - What are the pressures among various target markets to increase or decrease the range and quality of products?

  - What are the major weaknesses in each product area? What are the major complaints? What goes wrong most often?

  - Is the product name easy to pronounce? Spell? Recall? Is it descriptive, and does

it communicate the benefits the product offers? Does the name distinguish the firm or product from all others?

- What warranties are offered with the product? Are there other ways to guarantee customer satisfaction?

- Does the product offer good customer value?

- How is customer service handled? How is service quality assessed?

  2. Place/Distribution

  - Should the firm try to deliver its offerings directly to customers, or can it better deliver selected offerings by involving other organizations? What channel(s) should be used in distributing product offerings?

  - What physical distribution facilities should be used? Where should they be located? What should be their major characteristics?

  - Are members of the target market willing and able to travel some distance to buy the product?

  - How good is access to facilities? Can access be improved? Which facilities need priority attention in these areas?

  - How are facility locations chosen? Is the site accessible to the target markets? Is it visible to the target markets?

  - What are the location and atmosphere of retail establishments? Do these retailers satisfy customers?

  - When are products made available to users (season of year, day of week, time of day)? Are these times most appropriate?

  3. Promotion

  - How does a typical customer find out about the firm's products?

  - Does the message the firm delivers gain the attention of the intended target audience? Does it address the wants and needs of the target market, and does it suggest benefits or a means for satisfying these wants? Is the message appropriately positioned?

  - Does the promotion effort effectively inform, persuade, educate, and remind customers about the firm's products?

- Does the firm establish budgets and measure effectiveness of promotional efforts?

  a. Advertising

    - Which media are currently being used? Has the firm chosen the types of media that will best reach its target markets?

    - Are the types of media used the most cost-effective, and do they contribute positively to the firm's image?

    - Are the dates and times the ads will appear the most appropriate? Has the firm prepared several versions of its advertisements?

    - Does the organization use an outside advertising agency? What functions does the ad agency perform for the organization?

    - What system is used to handle consumer inquiries resulting from advertising and promotions? What follow-up is done?

  b. Public Relations

    - Is there a well-conceived public relations and publicity program? Does the program have the ability to respond to bad publicity?

    - How is public relations normally handled by the firm? By whom? Have those responsible nurtured working relationships with media outlets?

    - Is the firm using all available public relations avenues? Is an effort made to understand each of the publicity outlet's needs and to provide each with story types that will appeal to its audience in readily usable forms?

    - What does the annual report say about the firm and its products? Who is being effectively reached by this vehicle? Does the benefit of the publication justify the cost?

  c. Personal Selling

    - How much of a typical salesperson's time is spent soliciting new customers as compared to serving existing customers?

    - How does the sales force determine which prospect will be called on and by whom? How is the frequency of contacts determined?

    - How is the sales force compensated? Are there incentives for encouraging more business?

    - How is the sales force organized and managed?

    - Has the sales force prepared an approach tailored to each prospect?

    - Has the firm matched sales personnel with the target market characteristics?

    - Is there appropriate follow-up to the initial personal selling effort? Are customers made to feel appreciated?

    - Can database or direct marketing be used to replace or supplement the sales force?

  d. Sales Promotion

    - What is the specific purpose of each sales promotion activity? Why is it offered? What does it try to achieve?

    - What categories of sales promotion are being used? Is sales promotion directed to the trade, the final consumer, or both?

    - Is the effort directed at all the firm's key publics or restricted to only potential customers?

4. Price

- What levels of pricing and specific prices should be used?

- What mechanisms does the firm have to ensure that the prices charged are acceptable to customers?

- How price sensitive are customers?

- If a price change is put into effect, how will the number of customers change? Will total revenue increase or decrease?

- Which method is used for establishing a price: going rate, demand oriented, or cost based?

- What discounts are offered, and with what rationale?

- Has the firm considered the psychological dimensions of price?

- Have price increases kept pace with cost increases, inflation, or competitive levels?

- How are price promotions used?

- Do interested prospects have opportunities to sample products at an introductory price?

- What methods of payment are accepted? Is it in the firm's best interest to use these various payment methods?

V IMPLEMENTATION, EVALUATION, AND CONTROL

- Is the marketing organization structured appropriately to implement the marketing plan?

- What specific activities must take place? Who is responsible for these activities?

- What is the implementation timetable?

- What other marketing research is necessary?

- What will be the financial impact of this plan on a one-year projected income statement? How does projected income compare with expected revenue if the plan is not implemented?

- What are the performance standards?

- What monitoring procedures (audits) will take place and when?

- Does the firm seem to be trying to do too much or not enough?

- Are the core marketing strategies for achieving objectives sound? Are the objectives being met, and are the objectives appropriate?

- Are enough resources (or too many resources) budgeted to accomplish the marketing objectives?

The E-Motion Software Marketing Plan

Appendix II

I COMPANY DESCRIPTION

II BUSINESS MISSION

III SITUATION ANALYSIS

Industry Analysis

SWOT Analysis

Trends

Competitors

Consumer Profile

Technology

Strengths

Weakness

Opportunities

Threats

IV MARKETING OBJECTIVE

V MARKETING STRATEGY

Target Marketing Strategy

Marketing Mix

Product

Place/Distribution

Promotion

Price

VI IMPLEMENTATION, EVALUATION, AND CONTROL

Marketing Research

Organizational Structure and Plan

Financial Projections

Implementation Timetable

VII SUMMARY

e*motion*software
we keep the business of business moving

I COMPANY DESCRIPTION

Scott Keohane and a partner founded e-motion software in 2003 and established its worldwide headquarters in Austin, Texas. They envisioned software solutions that conformed to a particular business, not the other way around, with products designed to (1) improve operating efficiency, (2) empower users, (3) enhance security, (4) improve ROI, and (5) streamline business processes. [Chapter 1: Market Orientation—focusing upon customer needs and integrating all activities to readily provide customer satisfaction, while achieving long-term company goals.] Ultimately, however, Keohane's partner did not want to remain with the company. Keohane converted the partner's shares into a note, according to the partnership agreement the two had in place.

The origins of the company were based in Keohane's 10 years of entrepreneurial endeavors, with 4 years of this time spent as an independent consultant in the Oracle applications marketplace. Oracle is the world's largest enterprise software company. According to Oracle's Web site, the company's business is information—how to manage it, use it, share it, and protect it. Commercial enterprise information management software systems, such as those offered by Oracle, promised seamless integration of all information flowing through a company.

In a global marketplace in which external company collaborations are driving business efforts and internal cross-functional integration is critical for timely decision making, enterprise systems could help position companies in a highly competitive environment. [Chapter 7: Business Marketing—E-motion software operates as a business marketer since it provides good and services to organizations for purposes other than personal consumption.] Enterprise systems, such as the Oracle E-Business Suite, provided a simplified, unifying corporate technology platform. This type of platform enabled companies to utilize high-quality internal and external information both strategically and tactically. There were numerous product families in the E-Business Suite (e.g., advanced procurement, contracts, performance management, customer data/relationship management, financial, human resource management, logistics, manufacturing, marketing, order management, projects, sales, service, and supply chain management). [Chapter 9: E-Business is one product line in Oracle's product mix width. There are numerous product items in this product line.]

As an independent consultant, Keohane was continually asked to customize existing Oracle technology or create one-off applications to meet common requirements. The need for third-party products that would withstand upgrades to the underlying Oracle architecture was identified and e-motion software was formed. The overall business concept was to utilize the Oracle E-Business Suite as the underlying framework for customization to fit a particular customer's needs. Soon after incorporation, e-motion software became a member of the Oracle Partner Network. By joining the Oracle Partner Network, e-motion software gained access to Oracle Software Licenses, technical training, marketing funds, and co-marketing opportunities. [Chapter 7: Strategic Partnership—E-motion software partnered with Oracle so as to improve the offerings to its customers.]

II BUSINESS MISSION

[Chapter 2: The foundation of any marketing plan is the firm's mission statement.]

E-motion software is committed to the Oracle E-Business Suite of Applications and will provide a level of support that is unmatched in the industry. The company's goals are to make Oracle Applications more reliable, to enhance the Applications' functionality, and to make the Suite's use more efficient. [Chapter 2: What business is e-motion software in?] The company's products offer an attractive alternative to in-house development and support. E-motion software customers will be utilizing functional products that are self-funding. That is, the savings achieved through a more efficient workforce and security enhances will far exceed the cost of the company's products. The company's commitment extends from the methods used to build e-motion software products to the company's simple installation procedures to the post-installation service. E-motion software products run on multiple server platforms, require no customization, and are fully compatible with existing hardware and software warranties. [Chapter 2: E-motion software is focused on markets served and benefits sought by its customers.]

III SITUATION ANALYSIS

[Chapter 2: Marketers must understand the current and potential environment before defining marketing tactics.]

Industry Analysis [Chapter 2: Environmental scanning is the collection and interpretation of information about forces, events, and relationships in the external environment that may affect the future of the organization or the implementation of the marketing plan.]

Trends The Enterprise Resource Planning (ERP) community has undergone a radical change since the turn of the century. Historically, applications were designed for the professional user or technology expert. Today's marketplace, however, has shifted from the professional user to employee users. That is, employees in all functional areas have access to and utilize information from the ERP application. Thus, ERP providers have shifted to developing applications intended for individual employee use instead of releasing bigger applications designed for the professional user. These self-service, employee-based applications have fundamentally changed the way ERP applications are sold, implemented, and administered. Professional users are no longer the keepers of the data, manually entering and updating data from forms and memos. They have now become administrators in charge of ensuring data integrity. The promise of turning departments, such as HR and benefits, from manual intensive data entry shops to proactive reporting shops has shifted the marketplace to self-service suite applications. This emerging trend has prompted the development of self-service applications that enable employees to utilize systems within their individual realms of expertise, yet systems that are integrated across the firm.

Competitors E-motion software represents a new voice within the Oracle community. The company is creating a new niche in the marketplace and, as such, competition comes from a variety of sources. There are currently no head-to-head competitors. Competition can be split into three very distinct groups: Oracle, consulting firms, and in-house development centers.

Apart from being the company that created the ERP industry, *Oracle* has resources that dwarf every other company in the ERP marketplace. The availability of capital and the size of the development group infer that Oracle can simply reallocate a small development team to work on competing products. Oracle has, however, repeatedly released products that were little more than advanced betas, resulting in weeks of downtime for companies implementing the new products. By building applications that require no customization to Oracle code, e-motion software can confidently assure its customers that its products will work.

Consulting firms could advise the client to include the cost of custom application development into the total cost of the consulting engagement. This is standard protocol for competing consultancies and would effectively stop e-motion software from entering into a client site. Most consultancies, however, do not have a support and development center to handle ongoing system management. E-motion software will compete directly with consultancies by providing superior service at an affordable price.

The *In-House Development Center* (IHDC) poses a tricky problem for e-motion software. If a company has an IHDC, it is usually a trusted source that knows the company, its standards, and its software. Additionally, the IHDC is usually considered a "no-cost" center since salaries are already included in the company's budget. Thus, program development and implementation is considered just another project with no additional cost. On the positive side, information technology (IT) budgets were slashed and IT departments scaled down over the past few years. While IT spending has begun to trend upward again, the creation of IHDC units has lagged this spending trend. E-motion software plans to capitalize on this lag in IHDC unit development and upward spending trend.

Customer Profile The marketplace has moved from professional users to employee users. Basically, professional users are now babysitters, ensuring that employees do not enter incorrect information into the system. This poses quite a quandary. Professional users must maintain the integrity of the system while releasing control of it at the same time. This often forces the professional user to become a reactive unit, rushing to fix things when they break down. Employee users do not generally know the idiosyncrasies of the ERP system, of which there are many. Thus to maintain system integrity and ensure data reliability, professional users are often double-checking employee's data entry and also answering help desk calls regarding how to use the system. This is not, however, what a self-service ERP solution is designed to deliver. E-motion software proposes to enter the self-service arena with a broad range of products designed to regain the efficiencies promised by self-service applications.

Technology The costs of developing and maintaining an ERP solution require that the underlying technology be relevant for several years after product purchase and installation. The rapid emergence of Internet-based transactions (e.g., banking, loan applications, etc.) brought self-service applications to the forefront of business opportunity. Initially, Oracle attempted to use a mix of PL/SQL and DHTML code in the self-service offerings. This mix, however, did not provide the best-looking applications, had little functionality, and were difficult to implement. Oracle then switched to using Java Server Pages (JSP) as its self-service foundation, with PL/SQL and HTML as the accessory languages. Products with the JSP foundation were well received in the marketplace. E-motion software plans to adhere to Oracle's decision to use JSP, especially since JSP offers e-motion software some key benefits: (1) JSP is robust and flexible allowing all applications to use the same coding techniques, (2) JSP is recyclable

which means that e-motion software can leverage existing code across new applications, (3) JSP is accessible since Java is one of the most well-known programming languages, (4) JSP is portable, allowing e-motion software to easily enter other ERP markets, and (5) the use of JSP means that e-motion software will always comply with Oracle approved practices.

SWOT Analysis

The strengths, weaknesses, opportunities, and threats (SWOT) analysis provides a snapshot of e-motion software's internal strengths and weaknesses and external opportunities and threats. [Chapter 2: Performing a SWOT analysis allows firms to identify their competitive advantage.]

Strengths [Chapter 2: Strengths are *internal* to the firm.]

- Founder—Scott Keohane is not only extremely knowledgeable about the third-party marketplace; he is also personally and financially dedicated to making the business a success.
- Active and committed advisory council
- Reliable products and product support
- Member of Oracle Partner Network

Weaknesses [Chapter 2: Weaknesses are *internal* to the firm.]

- A one-person company that has to supplement the company with independent consulting services
- Not enough time dedicated to company development
- While considerable anecdotal information, the company is lacking in marketing research.
- Financial resources

Opportunities [Chapter 2: Opportunities are *external* to the firm.]

- Changing marketplace that coincides with e-motion software's product development
- The move toward employee users instead of professional users
- Growth market
- Technological changes
- Refocus on IT applications
- Persistent threat of security breaches
- Growing focus on cross-functional interactions in the business press

- New entries into the workforce (e.g., recent college graduates) are trained to use computers in decision making and thus expect companies to have data programs in place.

Threats [Chapter 2: Threats are *external* to the firm.]

- Competitors—all three groups of competitors likely have deeper pockets than e-motion software

- Offerings can be duplicated by knowledgeable experts.

- Limited market access across the United States

- Economies of scale in larger companies such as Oracle

- IT departments do not have unlimited budgets.

IV MARKETING OBJECTIVE

The marketing objective is to establish the company as an expert in the third-party marketplace. [Chapter 2: The marketing objective statement provides a look at what the company seeks to accomplish. It is consistent with the priorities of the organization.] The third-party product market for functions that are specifically designed for integration with Oracle Applications is in its infancy. E-motion software has to establish itself as a leader in this new marketplace. To accomplish this objective, customers must see that e-motion software products are safe and secure and that they do not affect existing Oracle functionality or their Oracle warranty.

Objective Metric: Three major Oracle clients by the end of 2005 [Chapter 2: Stated objectives must be measurable and time specific.]

To accomplish this marketing objective, e-motion software must obtain three major Oracle clients by the end of 2005. These clients will serve as reference sites for the company. These clients will enable e-motion software to demonstrate the gains achieved by using e-motion software products. As such, the clients need to be vocal and create viral marketing within the industry.

Objective Metric: One client in each region of the United States by the end of 2006 [Chapter 2: Stated objectives must be measurable and time specific.]

Given the close-knit nature of Oracle clients through organizations such as the Oracle Application User's Group (OAUG), e-motion software needs to gain clients within each of the major geographic areas in the United States: Northeast, Mid-Atlantic, Southeast, Midwest, Northwest, and West Coast.

V MARKETING STRATEGY
Target Market Strategy

E-motion software's sales plan is based on the company's understanding of the marketplace and on how it will resolve inefficiencies with the use of the Oracle E-Business Suite of Applications. From his consulting experience in helping potential clients install and maintain their individualized suite of applications, Keohane has considerable understanding of users' needs. To obtain clients, e-motion software, will rely on continuing relationships with prospective clients, maintaining ongoing relationships with other consulting firms with an ongoing relationship, and reaching new clients via marketing and sales initiatives.

Geographically, e-motion software will direct its marketing and sales efforts within the contiguous United States. [Chapter 8: Geographic segmentation refers to segmenting markets by region of a country or the world, market size, market density, or climate.] Though global operations are potential clients, the current size of e-motion software suggests that the U.S. marketplace is more viable at this time. [Chapter 8: Accessibility—the firm must be able to reach members of the targeted segment.] Within this marketplace, e-motion software will focus upon companies that have between 500 and 10,000 employees. These are the small to midsize companies that utilize the Oracle E-Business Suite of Applications. Companies of this size are unlikely to have their own development staffs in place or have the desire to develop and/or support homegrown applications. [Chapter 8: Responsiveness—the targeted market must respond to the marketing mix offered by the company.] Within these small to midsize companies, the individual target customer varies by the product offering. For example, a database administrator will be targeted for the company's system administrator products, and the IT director will be targeted for the functional line of product offerings.

Marketing Mix
[Chapter 2: Marketing mix (the four Ps) refers to the unique blend of product, place (distribution), promotion, and pricing strategies.]

Product [Chapter 6: E-motion software provides a business service to its customers.]

E-motion software develops applications specifically for the Oracle E-Business Suite. For clients of Oracle Applications who desire greater efficiency and an increase in ROI on their installed ERP systems, e-motion software will offer a line of products designed specifically to improve performance of the existing Oracle Application installation. Clients that have in-house development staff will be able to lower the total cost of ownership of a product by having e-motion software upgrade their Oracle installation. [Chapter 7: The buying center includes all persons in an organization who become involved in the purchase decision. In-house development staff will play a critical role in the buying process.] Clients without in-house staff, however, are more likely to benefit from e-motion software installations because they will now be able to perform a greater number of tasks that are not offered by Oracle. [Chapter 7: In this instance, the members of the buying center are different than a company with an in-house development staff.]

As a product-based company, e-motion software cannot ignore the importance of product marketing. The three product attributes that will drive the business are level of service, usability, and clear return on purchase price. [Chapter 7: Quality, service, and price are important evaluative criteria in a purchase decision involving software products.] The reluctance of some customers to install relatively new third-party products into their ERP systems is an obstacle to overcome via product marketing. [Chapter 7: This is often a new buy for the customer.] The company has to deliver on the promise of the products—that promise being that "E-motion software products make the business process of our customers more efficient, while easily understanding the upgrades to the underlying Oracle Application." E-motion must remain focused on this promise during both the product development and the product delivery process. [Chapter 7: Keeping current customers satisfied is just as important as attracting new ones.]

E-motion software's product line consists of functions that respond to inefficiencies identified from years of experience with Oracle ERP systems. Because the product portfolio is built expressly for the Oracle Applications E-Business Suite, the products are updated continually to maintain compatibility as well as to take advantage of new technologies and capabilities released by Oracle. [Chapter 10: Quality and functional modifications keep e-motion software's products up-to-date with ongoing technological changes.] All products enjoy the following characteristics: tight integration with Oracle, intuitive design, compatible architecture, and streamlined interfaces. Product offerings are iPraise, Responsibility Management, Password Reset, and Global Directory. [Chapter 10: E-motion software's product mix width is composed of one product—enterprise software. This product line is comprised of four product items.]

iPraise. [Chapter 10: iPraise is an individual brand.] The employee appraisal system developed by e-motion software is the most dynamic appraisal system available to Oracle customers. Combining e-motion software's commitment to streamlined application interfaces with the vast functionality available to Oracle E-Business Suite customers, iPraise represents the next generation of appraisal

systems. The system is flexible, allowing it to be configured to meet the specific needs of the organization. Using the appraisal configuration engine, the customer can choose to include or omit several aspects of the appraisal process and even determine in which order they are to be constructed. Thus, iPraise is a complete solution for Oracle customers. Customers can opt to integrate other modules of Oracle that have been configured previously with the E-Business Suite. Installing iPraise is fast and easy.

Responsibility Management. [Chapter 10: Responsibility Management is an individual brand.] Responsibility Management solves one of the most important questions faced by all Oracle system administrators: "Who has access to which data?" Using Responsibility Management, a system administrator or database administrator can quickly, easily, and accurately identify who has access to which data in real-time. Responsibility Management can inform the administrator of the following:

- Employees with particular responsibility
- Employees without a single responsibility
- User names that are not attached to any employee
- User names that are attached to more than one employee
- User accounts that are expiring in x number of days
- User accounts created in x days prior
- All users that have been given y responsibilities in x days prior

Results are displayed in a simple table that can be arranged and sorted. The table can also be exported to Excel for further investigation.

In addition to the query capabilities, Responsibility Management enables the system administrator to make changes to the user account, such as

- End-date a responsibility
- User account expiration update for a particular responsibility
- Bulk assignment of responsibilities (by organization, job, location, etc.)
- Bulk end-dating of responsibilities (by organization, job, location, etc.)

Overall, Responsibility Management enables system administrators to enforce security policies by providing a simple, easy-to-use function to identify who has what responsibility. Each day that a person has access not identified with his or her position is unnecessary and insecure.

Password Reset. [Chapter 10: Password Reset is an individual brand.] Forgotten passwords are the single largest end-user issue. Every day, help desks are bombarded with calls from end-users who have forgotten their passwords.

The standard Oracle log-in link does not provide a solution for this problem; thus, end-users are forced to call the help desk to reset the password. E-motion software's Password Reset function is the solution.

Password Reset is modeled after the standard password reset functionality available on most Web sites. Even if the user is using Password Reset for the first time, all the components will seem familiar and the user will know where to go next without receiving complex instructions or training. Password Reset functions as a part of the Oracle Applications. There are not outside Web sites to access or other applications to open. The user simply clicks on a link from the login page, enters the required information, and the password is reset. The user can then login immediately with the new password. Password Reset validates a user's identity by going directly to the Oracle database and running queries against it. This tight integration ensures reliability.

Global Directory. [Chapter 10: Global Directory is an individual brand.] Most companies utilize a separate system for their corporate directory. This requires entering and maintaining all employee information in Oracle and then reentering that information into a separate system. Worse yet, they print the company directory from a separate system. Not only is this extremely inefficient, but there is a greater chance for error. In today's fast-changing world, employee information can change on a weekly basis. As a result, the "other" system is often neglected and its data are unreliable. Global Directory solves this issue by "going to source" and gathering data directly from the Oracle database; thus, Global Directory has up-to-the-minute validity. Global Directory allows users to query the database for a wide variety of information. The results can be customized to give your employees the depth of knowledge they require.

Global Directory functions as a part of the Oracle Applications. There are no outside Web sites to access or other applications to open. Using the export function, users can transfer results into Excel, XML, or CSV, making it possible to utilize the information for such items as contact lists, distribution forms, and mailing labels.

Place/Distribution

E-motion software is now headquartered in Bedford, Massachusetts. However, home office location has little to do with the actual distribution of e-motion software's products since the products are installed and implemented at the client company. E-motion software will perform its own marketing channel functions (e.g., transactional, logistical, and facilitating) and does not foresee the need for any intermediaries in this process. [Chapter 12: Channel members facilitate the exchange between buyer and seller. E-motion software is the only channel member engaged in getting its product to the customer. Thus, it uses a direct channel.] However, e-motion software is a strong supporter of industry

groups, such as the Oracle Applications User Group, and related industry events. Such support allows the company to become recognized as a vendor among Oracle Applications clients.

E-motion software does offer a partner program for companies that wish to resell or refer e-motion software products to Oracle ERP clients. The program is segmented into two separate categories. The Alliance Partner Referral Program is tailored for businesses that have customer relationships with companies in specific industries or with businesses or IT needs that e-motion software programs can uniquely address. An Alliance Partner will identify e-motion software customers and refer them to e-motion software for a revenue share of the revenue from the referred account. As part of the program, Alliance Partner members receive all the training and materials needed to promote e-motion software solutions to their client base. The Alliance Solution Provider Program is designed for qualified Oracle-focused consultancies with a strong track record for providing top-notch service to their clients. Partner program members are trained and certified by e-motion software. Once certified, implementation partners can then configure and implement e-motion software products with unparalleled service and support. [Chapter 12: This is a form of a strategic channel alliance for e-motion software.]

Promotion [Chapter 14: E-motion software strives for integrated marketing communications.]

As a third party purveyor of products for Oracle, it is important for e-motion software to convey, clearly and succinctly, its "reason for being." Company material will have the heading: "e-motion software: we keep the business of business moving." [Chapter 13: This is the company's unique selling proposition.] We will emphasize the Oracle connection with the following statement on documents, as appropriate: "Oracle clients around the country are realizing true gains in productivity and efficiency by taking every day tasks and putting them in *motion*."

E-motion software will adhere to mainstream thinking regarding the promotion of third-party products for ERP solutions. [Chapter 14: As a complex buying decision, personal selling and strong print are effective methods for reaching potential customers.]

- A cohesive, easy-to-maneuver, and user-friendly Web site (www.e-motionsoftware.com) [Chapter 13: Company Web sites can be used to introduce new products, promote existing products, obtain consumer feedback, post news releases, etc.]

- Recorded demos on the company Web site (requires users to register for a demo user account) [Chapter 16: Registration is important for customer relationship management.]

	License Price	Software Update & Support	Licensing Metric	Minimum
Application Infrastructure:				
Password Reset	$15,000	$2,700/year	Enterprise	N/A
Responsibility Management	$6	18 percent/year	User	2,000
User Application:				
iPraise	$10	18 percent/year	User	2,000
Corporate Information:				
Global Directory	$2	18 percent/year	User	2,000

- Press releases as a member of the Certified Oracle Partner Network [Chapter 15: Public relations is an important element of the promotional mix. Press releases can place positive information in the news media to attract attention to e-motion software.]

- Demonstrations presented at trade shows and events [Chapter 15: Trade promotions push a product through the distribution channel and are popular among business marketers. Trade shows and events are an important aspect of sales promotions.]

- Word-of-mouth and reference sites [Chapter 15: Referrals are a good source for leads in the personal selling process.]

- The Internet via Google AdWords campaigns to drive potential clients to the company Web site [Chapter 14: The Internet has changed the advertising industry. Popular Internet sites sell advertising space to marketers, and search engine advertising is a popular approach.]

- Product datasheets that provide pertinent product data, features, and benefits of installation (available on the company Web site or via hard copy) [Chapter 14: Product information is critical in the sales process.]

Importantly, e-motion software is a company that relies heavily on direct selling to reach potential customers. [Chapter 15: Producers of most business goods rely more heavily on personal selling than advertising. Informative personal selling is common for installations such as those offered by e-motion software.] This promotional method requires a large amount of cold calling. [Chapter 15: Personal selling is important when product has high value and is technically complex. Relationship selling, or consultative selling, builds long-term relationships with clients.] E-motion software purchases the names of potential customers from marketing services that collect such information from customers of Oracle ERP products. [Chapter 15: Generating leads is the first step in the selling process.]

Price E-motion software prices its products to sufficiently cover the costs associated with development, sales, and support and to provide cash flow for future growth and development. [Chapter 16: As a new company, e-motion software is very concerned about covering its costs and having money left over for investment into the business. While not stated exactly, it appears that the company has a profit-oriented pricing objective.] The table above provides the company's standard price list. These list prices can vary, however, as there is a trickle-down effect in the industry. Essentially, pricing starts with Oracle, trickles through the consulting firm, and then down to e-motion products.

Prices are based on industry standards for classification. [Chapter 16: Status quo pricing is when a company meets the competition or going rate pricing. It appears that e-motion software is using status quo logic in its price setting.] For example, Password Reset, as an enterprise system product, has a total purchase price of $15,000, with a $2,700 software update and support fee. [Chapter 16: Two-part pricing is when the company charges two separate amounts for the product. In this instance, the buyer pays the $15,000 for the enterprise system product and then pays another $2,700 for the update and fee.] Responsibility Management, iPraise, and Global Directory are priced on a per employee (user) basis with a minimum purchase per number of employees. For example, Global Directory is $2 per employee with a minimum purchase of 2,000 employees. Thus, the least amount a company could purchase this product for is $4,000. The 18 percent annual maintenance fee is the industry standard. [Chapter 16: This shows the two-part, status quo pricing.]

	2006	2007	2008	2009	2010
Revenues:					
iPraise	$50,000	$100,000	$600,000	$2,250,000	$5,500,000
Responsibility Mgt	$60,000	$80,000	$160,000	$420,000	$700,000
Password Reset	$225,000	$180,000	$180,000	$150,000	$75,000
Global Directory	$45,000	$75,000	$180,000	$300,000	465,000
Cost of Goods Sold	0	0	0	0	0
General & Administrative	$350,000	$765,000	$1,600,000	$2,165,000	$2,600,000

VI IMPLEMENTATION, EVALUATION, AND CONTROL

Marketing Research

The company needs to keep abreast of two distinct segments in the marketplace: its client needs and Oracle's direction. E-motion software needs to understand its clients and their ongoing needs. [Chapter 9: E-motion software captures customer data, storing and integrating it into a customer database.] This includes meeting current needs and forecasting future needs as the Oracle Application Suite continues to evolve. E-motion software must also maintain up-to-date and accurate intelligence on both current Oracle offerings and planned initiatives. [Chapter 8: Ongoing marketing research will help the company keep abreast of what is happening in the marketplace.] By doing this, it will be able to introduce products that complement new Oracle functions and will be less likely to offer products that compete for functions that are included at no charge in an Oracle license. Additionally, this will present opportunities to introduce products that complement new Oracle functionality.

Organizational Structure and Plan

As a start-up company, e-motion software currently has only one member on its staff, Scott Keohane. As e-motion software matures into a stable, profitable organization, the need for employees will grow. The first foreseeable employee need is in the area of sales. The plan is to hire a salesperson in early 2006 to allow Mr. Keohane can continue his consulting on a regular basis, while at the same time ensuring a steady supply of funds for continued development efforts. To obtain the financial flexibility it needs to manage its cash flow successfully, the company has made contractors a significant component of its workforce. Contractors are used in the following areas: application development, database administration, and marketing. Current contractors have been associated with e-motion software almost since the company's inception and are largely credited with its early successes.

To provide a management resource from which Keohane can receive regular advice and guidance, e-motion software has assembled a nonvoting, nonbinding advisory council to assist in decision making, overall strategy, and execution. The advisory council is composed of four outside members who have made a commitment to provide their expertise and experience, free of charge, to e-motion software. Advisory members interact quarterly via teleconference.

Financial Projections

[Chapter 2: Evaluation and control are important mechanisms for monitoring the effectiveness of the marketing plan. Financial objectives are a common measure of success/failure.]

The financial objective is to be financially solvent within the first two years of operation.

Objective Metric: Sales of $250,000 by the end of 2005
Sales of $2 million by the end of 2007
Gross margin higher than 80 percent
Positive cash flow yearly

[Chapter 2: Stated objectives must be measurable and time specific.]

The five-year financial projection plan (in U.S. dollars) for e-motion software can be reviewed in the table above.

Implementation Timetable

[Chapter 2: Implementation is the process that turns a marketing plan into action assignments and ensures that these assignments are executed appropriately.]

2005

- The company plans to have three major Oracle clients by the end of 2005.

2006

- The company plans to have secured at least one client in each region of the United States by the end of 2006. This would mean at least one customer in the Northeast, the Mid-Atlantic, the Southeast, the Midwest, the Northwest, and the West Coast.

- Keohane plans to hire one full-time salesperson.

VII SUMMARY

E-motion software continually monitors activities with current and potential clients. As a consultant in the industry, Keohane is always on the lookout for potential clients. He has set quarterly and yearly sales targets, and actual sales will be compared to these quarterly plans. Additionally, Keohane will continue in his efforts to enlist at least one client in each of the major geographic regions of the United States. However, it may take a qualified salesperson to devote the time necessary to acquire new customers. Additionally, by not being restricted to Keohane's current consultancies, a dedicated salesperson could more readily identify potential e-motion software clients by not being restricted to current consultancies that Keohane is involved with. Of major concern is that the current financial strategy of supporting the new business by personal funds from consulting may prove to be too onerous for Keohane.

Ultimately, the goal is to "make it big." The hope is that, over the next five years, the small products that e-motion software has developed will hopefully generate cash sufficient to build a larger module that one of the larger ERP companies (e.g., Oracle) will want to acquire.

MR. PARSONS MR. O'NEAL MR. FINNEGAN MR. MOZILO

3

Ethics
and Social
Responsibility

LEARNING OUTCOMES

LO1 Explain the determinants of a civil society

LO2 Explain the concept of ethical behavior

LO3 Describe ethical behavior in business

LO4 Discuss corporate social responsibility

LO5 Describe the arguments for and against social responsibility

LO6 Explain cause-related marketing

John Mackey, CEO of the Whole Foods Market, went online using the screen name "rahodeb" (a scramble of Deborah, his wife's name) and attacked competitor Wild Oats Markets on Yahoo! He said the smaller company was "mediocre with a terrible track record." William Swanson, Chairman and CEO of Raytheon, wrote a book titled *Swanson's Unwritten Rules of Management.* It was later discovered the book contained passages that exactly mirrored a 1944 book by an engineering professor. David Edmondson, former CEO of RadioShack, claimed to have degrees in theology and psychology, but completed only two semesters of course work.[1] And the list could go on.

The activities of these top managers were clearly wrong. Yet for several thousand years, religious teaching and secular ethics have sought to encourage socially beneficial behavior. The literature of virtually every religious tradition, as well as Eastern and Western philosophy, are full of examples, rules, and guidance regarding what constitutes right and wrong.

LO 1

DETERMINANTS OF A CIVIL SOCIETY[2]

Have you ever stopped and thought about the social glue that binds society together? That is, what factors are in place that keep people and organizations from running amuck and doing harm, and what factors create order in a society like ours as opposed to chaos. The six modes of social control are listed below:

1. *Ethics:* The first is ethical rules and guidelines along with customs and traditions that provide principles of right action.

2. *Laws:* Often rules and guidelines are codified into law. Laws created by governments are then enforced by governmental authority. Thus, the dictum, "Thou shall not steal," is part of formal law throughout the land. Law, however, is not a perfect mechanism for ensuring good corporate and employee behavior. This is because laws often address the lowest common denominator of socially acceptable behavior. In other words, just because something is not illegal doesn't mean that it is right.

   For example, an individual goes to Barnes and Noble every day and spends the afternoon reading books and magazines in the store. The store has big comfortable chairs and the clerks never bother him or ask him to leave. He even takes his own lunch if he plans to spend the day there. He does this at least 20 days per month. The bookstore allows this practice and it is not against the law. It is, however, not ethical. If everyone who bought books followed this individual's behavior, Barnes and Noble would soon be bankrupt!

3. *Formal and Informal Groups:* Businesses, professional organizations (such as the American Marketing Association), clubs (e.g., Shriners or Ducks Unlimited), and professional associations (e.g., American Medical Association) all have codes of conduct. These codes prescribe acceptable and desired behaviors of their members.

Marketing & You

Using the following scale, enter the numbers that reflect your opinions.

1 2 3 4 5 6 7 8 9

Completely disagree   Completely agree

__ The ethics and social responsibility of a firm are essential to its long-term profitability.

__ Business ethics and social responsibility are critical to the survival of a business enterprise.

__ The overall effectiveness of a business can be determined to a great extent by the degree to which it is ethical and socially responsible.

__ Good ethics is often good business.

__ Business has a social responsibility beyond making a profit.

__ Corporate planning and goal-setting sessions should include discussions of ethics and social responsibility.

__ Social responsibility and profitability can be compatible.

Now, total your score. Find out what it means after you read the chapter.

1 Explain the determinants of a civilized society

The "social glue" that holds a society together is composed of six factors: ethics, laws, formal and informal groups, self regulation, the media, and an active civil society.

4. *Self regulation*: Self regulation involves the voluntary acceptance of standards established by nongovernmental entities such as the American Association of Advertising Agencies (AAAA) or the American Manufacturers Association. The AAAA has a self-regulation arm that deals with deceptive advertising. Other associations have regulations relating to child labor, environmental issues, conservation, and a host of other issues.

5. *The Media*: In an open, democratic society, the media play a key role in informing the public about actions of individuals and organizations. These stories sometimes praise, such as the media coverage of Wal-Mart's efforts to help people and reopen stores after Hurricane Katrina. Or, they shine the spotlight on unscrupulous behavior, such as those of Enron and Worldcom. Business firms dislike negative publicity, which can lead to lost sales, damage to corporate reputations, government actions, and legal liability. Conversely, favorable publicity stimulates sales and builds the firm's reputation. An example of investigative reporting comes from *Smart Money* magazine. When millions of Americans have problems with a product or service, they often call the Better Business Bureau (BBB). *Smart Money* raises the question, "Is the BBB too cozy with the firms it monitors?" For example, a woman in Shreveport, Louisiana, had a problem with Cingular (now AT&T) over her cell phone. The BBB has an online complaint form, which is about ten pages long, that the Shreveport resident carefully filled out. What she didn't know was that the BBB had been asking for extra information from unhappy cell phone customers, then giving or selling the data to some of the firms themselves.[3] Cingular, in fact, paid the BBB $50,000 for its customer-driven intelligence. Rick Weirick, product development officer of the BBB's national council, said that the fee was just to defray costs.[4]

6. *An Active Civil Society*: An informed and engaged society can help shape and mold individual and corporate behavior. The last state in the union to get a Wal-Mart store was Vermont. Citizen campaigns against the big-box retailer were deciding factors in management's decision to avoid the state. When pro football player Michael Vick was convicted of dog fighting, a grass roots campaign sprang up to boycott Nike. Vick had an endorsement contract with the shoe manufacturer.

All six factors above individually and in combination are critical to achieving a socially coherent, vibrant, civilized society. These six factors (the social glue) are more important today than ever before due to the increasing complexity of the global economy and the melding of customs and traditions within societies.

2

THE CONCEPT OF ETHICAL BEHAVIOR

It has been said that ethics is something everyone likes to talk about but nobody knows exactly what it is. Others have noted that defining ethics is like trying to "nail Jell-O to the wall." You begin to think that you've got it, but that's when it starts slipping out between your fingers.

Ethics refers to the moral principles or values that generally govern the conduct of an individual or a group. Ethics also can be viewed as the standard of behavior by which conduct is judged. As noted above, standards that are legal may not always be ethical, and vice versa. Laws are the values and standards enforceable by the courts. Ethics, then, consists of personal moral principles. For example, there is no legal statute that makes it a crime for someone to "cut in line." If someone doesn't want to wait in line and cuts to the front, it often makes others very angry. We sneer at drivers who sneak along the side of the road to get around a line of traffic as we sit and wait our turn.

If you have ever resented a line-cutter, then you understand ethics and have applied ethical standards in life. Waiting your turn in line is an expectation society has. "Waiting your turn" is not an ordinance, a statute, or even a federal regulation. "Waiting your turn" is an age-old principle developed because it was fair to proceed with first-in-time, first to be served. "Waiting your turn" exists because when there are large groups waiting for the same road, theater tickets, or fast food at noon in a busy downtown area, we found that lines ensured order and that waiting your turn was a just way of allocating the limited space and time allotted for the movie tickets, the traffic, or the food. "Waiting your turn" is an expected but unwritten behavior that plays a critical role in an orderly society.[5]

So it is with ethics. Ethics consists of those unwritten rules we have developed for our interactions with each other. These unwritten rules govern us when we are sharing resources or honoring contracts. "Waiting your turn" is a higher standard than the laws that are passed to maintain order. Those laws apply when physical force or threats are used to push to the front of the line. Assault, battery, and threats are forms of criminal conduct for which the offender can be prosecuted. But the law does not apply to the stealthy line-cutter who simply sneaks to the front, perhaps using a friend and a conversation as a decoy for edging into the front. No laws are broken, but the notions of fairness and justice are offended by one individual putting himself above others and taking advantage of others' time and position.

When you say to yourself, "That's unjust!" or "That's unfair!" you have just defined ethics for yourself. Ethics is not just about standards of behavior; ethics is about honesty, justice, and fairness. This is true for both personal and business behavior.

Ethical questions range from practical, narrowly defined issues, such as a business person's obligation to be honest with his customers, to broader social and philosophical questions, such as a company's responsibility to preserve the environment and protect employee rights. Many ethical conflicts develop from conflicts between the differing interests of company owners and their workers, customers, and surrounding community. Managers must balance the ideal against the practical—the need to produce a reasonable profit for the company's shareholders with honesty in business practices, and larger environmental and social issues.

> *Ethics is something everyone likes to talk about but nobody knows exactly what it is.*

© COMSTOCK IMAGES/JUPITERIMAGES

Ethical Theories

People usually base their individual choice of ethical theory on their life experiences. The following are some of the ethical theories that apply to marketing.[6]

Deontology The deontological theory states that people should adhere to their obligations and duties when analyzing an ethical dilemma. This means that a person will follow his or her obligations to another individual or society because upholding one's duty is what is considered ethically correct. For instance, a deontologist will always keep his promises to a friend and will follow the law. A person who follows this theory will produce very consistent decisions because they will be based on the individual's set duties. Note that this theory is not necessarily concerned with the welfare of others. Say, for example, a salesperson has decided that it's his ethical duty (and very practical!) to always be on time to meetings with clients. Today he is running late. How is he supposed to drive? Is the deontologist supposed to speed, breaking the law to uphold his

utilitarian ethical theory
A theory that holds that the choice that yields the greatest benefit to the most people is the choice that is ethically correct.

casuist ethical theory
A theory that compares a current ethical dilemma with examples of similar ethical dilemmas and their outcomes.

Aristotle and Plato taught that solving ethical dilemmas requires training, that individuals solve ethical dilemmas when they develop and nurture a set of virtues.

© KUTTIG-TRAVEL/ALAMY

duty to society, or is the deontologist supposed to arrive at his meeting late, breaking his duty to be on time? This scenario of conflicting obligations does not lead us to a clear, ethically correct resolution, nor does it protect the welfare of others from the deontologist's decision.

Utilitarianism The utilitarian ethical theory is founded on the ability to predict the consequences of an action. To a utilitarian, the choice that yields the greatest benefit to the most people is the choice that is ethically correct. One benefit of this ethical theory is that the utilitarian can compare similar predicted solutions and use a point system to determine which choice is more beneficial for more people. This point system provides a logical and rational argument for each decision and allows a person to use it on a case-by-case context.

There are two types of utilitarianism: act utilitarianism and rule utilitarianism. *Act utilitarianism* adheres exactly to the definition of utilitarianism as described in the above section. In act utilitarianism, a person performs the acts that benefit the most people, regardless of personal feelings or the societal constraints such as laws. *Rule utilitarianism*, however, takes into account the law and is concerned with fairness. A rule utilitarian seeks to benefit the most people but through the fairest and most just means available. Therefore, added benefits of rule utilitarianism are that it values justice and doing good at the same time.

As is true of all ethical theories, however, both act and rule utilitarianism contain numerous flaws. Inherent in both are the flaws associated with predicting the future. Although people can use their life experiences to attempt to predict outcomes, no human being can be certain that his predictions will be true. This uncertainty can lead to unexpected results, making the utilitarian look unethical as time passes because his choice did not benefit the most people as he predicted.

Another assumption that a utilitarian must make is that he has the ability to compare the various types of consequences against each other on a similar scale. However, comparing material gains such as money against intangible gains such as happiness is impossible because their qualities differ so greatly.

Casuist The casuist ethical theory compares a current ethical dilemma with examples of similar ethical dilemmas and their outcomes. This allows one to determine the severity of the situation and to create the best possible solution according to others' experiences. Usually, one will find examples that represent the extremes of the situation so that a compromise can be reached that will hopefully include the wisdom gained from the previous situations.

One drawback to this ethical theory is that there may not be a set of similar examples for a given ethical dilemma. Perhaps that which is controversial and ethically questionable is new and unexpected. Along the same line of thinking, this theory assumes that the results of the current ethical dilemma will be similar to results in the examples. This may not be necessarily true and would greatly hinder the effectiveness of applying this ethical theory.

Moral Relativists[7] Moral relativists believe in time-and-place ethics; that is, ethical truths depend on the individuals and groups holding them. Arson is not always wrong in their book. If you live in a neighborhood in which drug dealers are operating a crystal meth lab or crack house, arson is ethically justified. If you are a parent and your child is starving, stealing a loaf of bread is ethically correct. The proper resolution to ethical dilemmas is based upon weighing the competing factors at the moment and then

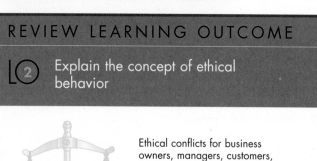

REVIEW LEARNING OUTCOME

LO 2 Explain the concept of ethical behavior

Ethical conflicts for business owners, managers, customers, workers, and the communities can sometimes be resolved through the reliance on ethical theories such as deontology, utilitarianism, casuist, moral relativism, and virtue ethics.

EXHIBIT 3.1

Standards for Being Virtuous

Virtue Standard	Definition	Virtue Standard	Definition
Ability	being dependable and competent	Humility	giving proper credit
Acceptance	making the best of a bad situation	Humor	bringing relief; making the world better
Amiability	fostering agreeable social contexts	Independence	getting things done despite bureaucracy
Articulateness	ability to make and defend one's case	Integrity	being a model of trustworthiness
Attentiveness	listening and understanding	Justice	treating others fairly
Autonomy	having a personal identity	Loyalty	working for the well-being of an organization
Caring	worrying about the well-being of others despite power	Pride	being admired by others
Charisma	inspiring others	Prudence	minimizing company and personal losses
Compassion	sympathetic	Responsibility	doing what it takes to do the right thing
Coolheadedness	retaining control and reasonableness in heated situations	Saintliness	approaching the ideal in behavior
Courage	doing the right thing despite the cost	Shame (capable of)	regaining acceptance after wrong behavior
Determination	seeing a task through to completion	Spirit	appreciating a larger picture in situations
Fairness	giving others their due; creating harmony	Toughness	maintaining one's position
Generosity	sharing, enhancing others' well-being	Trust	dependable
Graciousness	establishing a congenial environment	Trustworthiness	fulfilling one's responsibilities
Gratitude	giving proper credit	Wittiness	lightening the conversation when warranted
Heroism	doing the right thing despite the consequences	Zeal	getting the job done right; enthusiasm
Honesty	telling the truth; not lying		

Source: From Robert C. Solomon, *A Better Way to Think About Business: How Personal Integrity Leads to Corporate Success* (New York: Oxford University Press, 2003), 18. Used by permission of Oxford University Press, Inc.

making a determination to take the lesser of the evils as the resolution. Moral relativists do not believe in absolute rules. Their beliefs center on the pressure of the moment and whether the pressure justifies the action taken.

Virtue Ethics[8] Aristotle and Plato taught that solving ethical dilemmas requires training, that individuals solve ethical dilemmas when they develop and nurture a set of virtues. A virtue is a character trait valued as being good. Aristotle taught the importance of cultivating virtue in his students and then had them solve ethical dilemmas using those virtues once they had become an integral part of their being through their virtue training.

Some modern philosophers have embraced this notion of virtue and have developed lists of what constitutes a virtuous business person. Exhibit 3.1 reveals a list of virtuous standards.

moral relativists
Persons who believe that ethical truths depend on the individuals and groups holding them.

virtue
A character trait valued as being good.

LO③

ETHICAL BEHAVIOR IN BUSINESS

Depending upon which, if any, ethical theory a businessperson has accepted and uses in his or her daily conduct, the action taken may vary. For example, faced with bribing a foreign official to get a critically needed contract or shutting down a factory and laying off a thousand workers, a person following a deontology strategy would not pay the bribe. Why? A deontologist always follows the law. However, a moral relativist will probably pay the bribe.

While the boundaries of what is legal and what is not are often fairly clear (e.g., don't run a red light, don't steal money from a bank, and don't kill someone), the boundaries of ethical decision making are predicated on which ethical theory one is following. The law typically relies on juries to determine if an act is legal or illegal. Society determines whether an action is ethical or unethical. Sometimes society decides that a person acted unethically—recall the O.J. Simpson murder trial—but a jury may decide that no illegal act was committed. The jury in Simpson's most recent trial for armed robbery and kidnapping found him guilty (and obviously unethical). In a business-related case, a jury recently found Richard Scrushy, charged with a $1.4 billion fraud at HealthSouth Corporation, innocent on all counts. On the other hand, Bernard Ebbers, former CEO of WorldCom, was found guilty of securities fraud and filing false documents and was sentenced to 25 years in prison.

Morals are the rules people develop as a result of cultural values and norms. Culture is a socializing force that dictates what is right and wrong. Moral standards may also reflect the laws and regulations that affect social and economic behavior. Thus, morals can be considered a foundation of ethical behavior.

Morals are usually characterized as good or bad. "Good" and "bad" have different connotations, including "effective" and "ineffective." A good salesperson makes or exceeds the assigned quota. If the salesperson sells a new stereo or television set to a disadvantaged consumer—knowing full well that the person can't keep up the monthly payments—is the salesperson still a good one? What if the sale enables the salesperson to exceed his or her quota?

"Good" and "bad" can also refer to "conforming" and "deviant" behaviors. A doctor who runs large ads offering discounts on open-heart surgery would be considered bad, or unprofessional, in the sense of not conforming to the norms of the medical profession. "Bad" and "good" are also used to express the distinction between criminal and law-abiding behavior. And finally, different religions define "good" and "bad" in markedly different ways. A Muslim who eats pork would be considered bad, as would a fundamentalist Christian who drinks whiskey.

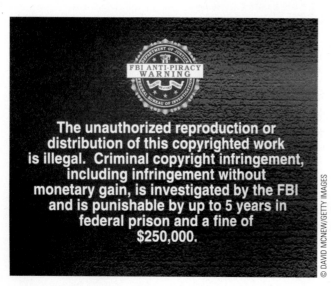

Morality and Business Ethics

Today's business ethics actually consist of a subset of major life values learned since birth. The values businesspeople use to make decisions have been acquired through family, educational, and religious institutions.

Ethical values are situation specific and time oriented. Nevertheless, everyone must have an ethical base that applies to conduct in the business world and in personal life. One approach to developing a personal set of ethics is to examine the consequences of a particular act. Who is helped or hurt? How long lasting are the consequences? What actions produce the greatest good for the greatest number of people? A second approach stresses the importance of rules. Rules come in the form of customs, laws, professional standards, and common sense. Consider these examples of rules:

- Always treat others as you would like to be treated.
- Copying copyrighted computer software is against the law.
- It is wrong to lie, bribe, or exploit.

Another approach emphasizes the development of moral character within individuals. Ethical development can be thought of as having three levels[9]:

- *Preconventional morality*, the most basic level, is childlike. It is calculating, self-centered, and even selfish, based on what will be immediately punished or rewarded. Fortunately, most businesspeople have progressed beyond the self-centered and manipulative actions of preconventional morality.

- *Conventional morality* moves from an egocentric viewpoint toward the expectations of society. Loyalty and obedience to the organization (or society) become paramount. At the level of conventional morality, a marketing decision maker would be concerned only with whether the proposed action is legal and how it will be viewed by others. This type of morality could be likened to the adage "When in Rome, do as the Romans do."

- *Postconventional morality* represents the morality of the mature adult. At this level, people are less concerned about how others might see them and more concerned about how they see and judge themselves over the long run. A marketing decision maker who has attained a postconventional level of morality might ask, "Even though it is legal and will increase company profits, is it right in the long run? Might it do more harm than good in the end?"

EXHIBIT 3.2

Unethical Practices Marketing Managers May Have to Deal With

- Entertainment and gift giving
- False or misleading advertising
- Misrepresentation of goods, services, or company capabilities
- Lying to customers in order to get the sale
- Manipulation of data (falsifying or misusing statistics or information)
- Misleading product or service warranties
- Unfair manipulation of customers
- Exploitation of children or disadvantaged groups
- Stereotypical portrayals of women, minority groups, or senior citizens
- Invasion of customer privacy
- Sexually oriented advertising appeals
- Product or service deception
- Unsafe products or services
- Price deception
- Price discrimination
- Unfair or inaccurate statements about competitors
- Smaller amounts of product in the same-size packages

Ethical Decision Making

How do businesspeople make ethical decisions? There is no cut-and-dried answer. Some of the ethical issues managers face are shown in Exhibit 3.2. Studies show that the following factors tend to influence ethical decision making and judgments[10]:

- *Extent of ethical problems within the organization:* Marketing professionals who perceive fewer ethical problems in their organizations tend to disapprove more strongly of "unethical" or questionable practices than those who perceive more ethical problems. Apparently, the healthier the ethical environment, the more likely that marketers will take a strong stand against questionable practices.

- *Top-management actions on ethics:* Top managers can influence the behavior of marketing professionals by encouraging ethical behavior and discouraging unethical behavior. Research found that 13 percent of large-company top executives thought that having strong ethical traits was the most important leadership trait of CEOs. That is down from 20 percent in 2003.[11] The most important trait to the majority of respondents was the ability to inspire others (37 percent).[12] Other research found three ethics-related actions by managers have the greatest impact on employee ethics. These are setting a good example, keeping promises and commitments, and supporting others in adhering to ethics standards.[13]

- *Potential magnitude of the consequences:* The greater the harm done to victims, the more likely that marketing professionals will recognize a problem as unethical.

- *Social consensus:* The greater the degree of agreement among managerial peers that an action is harmful, the more likely that marketers will recognize a problem as unethical.

☞ *Probability of a harmful outcome:* The greater the likelihood that an action will result in a harmful outcome, the more likely that marketers will recognize a problem as unethical.

☞ *Length of time between the decision and the onset of consequences:* The shorter the length of time between the action and the onset of negative consequences, the more likely that marketers will perceive a problem as unethical.

☞ *Number of people to be affected:* The greater the number of persons affected by a negative outcome, the more likely that marketers will recognize a problem as unethical.

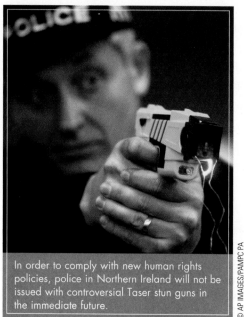

In order to comply with new human rights policies, police in Northern Ireland will not be issued with controversial Taser stun guns in the immediate future.

© AP IMAGES/PAMPC PA

As you can see, many factors determine the nature of ethical decision making. An example is Taser International Inc., the world's largest maker of stun guns. Management talks tough when the subject turns to people who've sued the company for injuries or deaths allegedly inflicted by electric shock from its weapons. The word has gotten out: Taser doesn't settle. Taser general counsel Doug Klint said, "Anyone who sues us is in for a fight." Taser's stun gun, sold mainly to police departments, fires two insulated conductive wires with barbs at the end as far as 35 feet, delivering a 50,000-volt jolt that temporarily paralyzes the target. Taser's refusal to settle personal-injury or wrongful-death claims has resulted in fewer lawsuits being filed, Klint said. While about 50 suits are still pending, Taser has seen a "significant decline" in the rate of new litigation. "There was a lot of controversy in 2005, a lot of concerns about the safety of the product, but I think after 52 consecutive wins in court, we've laid the concerns to rest," Chief executive officer Rick Smith said in an interview. When asked whether the company considers settling, he said, "We like to litigate every one that we can."[14] Lawyers for alleged Taser victims say the company overstates its legal scoreboard to discourage lawsuits and boost its stock price. "They're trying to deter other litigants while making themselves look good to investors," said Las Vegas attorney E. Brent Bryson, who represents plaintiffs in two cases over Taser-related deaths.[15]

Ethical Guidelines and Training

Many organizations have become more interested in ethical issues. One sign of this interest is the increase in the number of large companies that appoint ethics officers—from virtually none a few years ago to almost 33 percent of large corporations now. More and more companies are providing ethics resources for their employees. Today over 70 percent of employees in the United States can seek advice on ethics questions via telephone, e-mail, Web, or in-person. (See **www.ethics.org** for more information.) In addition, many companies of various sizes have developed a code of ethics as a guideline to help marketing managers and other employees make better decisions. Some of the most highly praised codes of ethics are those of Intel, IBM, Starbucks, and Costco.

Creating ethics guidelines has several advantages:

☞ The guidelines help employees identify what their firm recognizes as acceptable business practices.

☞ A code of ethics can be an effective internal control on behavior, which is more desirable than external controls like government regulation.

☞ A written code helps employees avoid confusion when determining whether their decisions are ethical.

☞ The process of formulating the code of ethics facilitates discussion among employees about what is right and wrong and ultimately leads to better decisions.

An example of a basic code of ethics is shown in Exhibit 3.3.

EXHIBIT 3.3

General Mills Code of Ethics

Times may change, but our values have endured. Honesty. Integrity. Trust. Our values are the source of our strength. They remain the heart of who we are and what we do.

For more than 130 years — since John S. Pillsbury and Cadwallader C. Washburn first began building their competing businesses along the Mississippi River — we have held our company and ourselves to the highest standards of ethical conduct and personal integrity.

We set very high expectations for ourselves — and for the integrity of our company. We will not compromise those standards.

- We strive for the highest quality in our products, services, and relationships.
- We set and maintain the highest standards for all aspects of our work.
- We advance and grow our businesses honestly and ethically, taking no shortcuts that might compromise our high standards.
- We comply with local laws in every nation where we operate. We recognize and respect the cultures, customs, and practices of our consumers and customers in nations around the world.
- We steer clear of conflicts of interest, and work to avoid even the perception of conflict.
- We deliver on our promises.
- We are ever mindful of the trust our consumers, customers, partners, and employees place in General Mills. We will never knowingly or willfully undermine that trust.

Source: General Mills

Businesses, however, must be careful not to make their code of ethics too vague or too detailed. Codes that are too vague give little or no guidance to employees in their day-to-day activities. Codes that are too detailed encourage employees to substitute rules for judgment. For instance, if employees are involved in questionable behavior, they may use the absence of a written rule as a reason to continue behaving that way, even though their conscience may be saying no. The checklist in Exhibit 3.4 is an example of a simple but helpful set of ethical guidelines. Following the checklist will not guarantee the "rightness" of a decision, but it will improve the chances that the decision will be ethical. Although many companies have issued policies on ethical behavior, marketing managers must still put the policies into effect. They must address the classic "matter of degree" issue. For example, marketing researchers must often resort to deception to obtain unbiased answers to their research questions. Asking for a few minutes of a respondent's time is dishonest if the researcher knows the interview

EXHIBIT 3.4

Ethics Checklist

- Does the decision benefit one person or group but hurt or not benefit other individuals or groups? In other words, is my decision fair to all concerned?
- Would individuals or groups, particularly customers, be upset if they knew about my decision?
- Has important information been overlooked because my decision was made without input from other knowledgeable individuals or groups?
- Does my decision presume that my company is an exception to a common practice in this industry and that I therefore have the authority to break a rule?
- Would my decision offend or upset qualified job applicants?
- Will my decision create conflict between individuals or groups within the company?
- Will I have to pull rank or use coercion to implement my decision?
- Would I prefer to avoid the consequences of my decision?
- Did I avoid truthfully answering any of the above questions by telling myself that the risks of getting caught are low or that I could get away with the potentially unethical behavior?

will last 45 minutes. Not only must management post a code of ethics, but it must also give examples of what is ethical and unethical for each item in the code. Moreover, top management must stress to all employees the importance of adhering to the company's code of ethics. Without a detailed code of ethics and top management's support, creating ethical guidelines becomes an empty exercise.

Ethics Training Ethics training is a good way to help employees put good ethics into practice. Because of the numerous corporate scandals in the past decade, such as Enron, Tyco, Worldcom, Hewlett-Packard, and Adelphia Communications Corporation, more and more companies are offering ethics training to their employees. Today, about 70 percent of all large employers (over 500 employees) provide ethics training.[16] Simply giving employees a long list of "dos and don'ts" is a start, but doesn't really help navigate the gray areas. What is needed then is a more contextual approach to ethics training.

Lockheed Martin is one firm that has moved to contextual ethics training. Recently, Manny Zulueta met with seven colleagues to watch a DVD. In one scene, a worker complained to his manager's boss after the manager yelled at her workers. The manager apologized, but the worker soon felt that the manager was retaliating by giving him lousy assignments, nitpicking his work, and reprimanding him for arriving late. Mr. Zulueta, Lockheed Martin's senior vice president of shared services, then led what he says was a "nuanced" discussion about the ethical issues involved in that scene. Zuelueta's colleagues rightly noted that they needed more information—they needed to put the scene in context—to discern whether the manager's actions were retaliatory.[17] Understanding the context of an ethical problem helps employees navigate the gray areas.

Do ethics training programs work? While there are exceptions depending on the quality of the program, the general answer is yes.[18] In addition to Lockheed Martin, another company that does a good job with ethics training is the accounting and consulting firm Ernst & Young (E&Y). Michael Hamilton, chief learning and development officer for the Americas, said undeniable ethics is the foundation of why people hire the firm. To help provide employees with an ethical foundation, E&Y implemented a formal ethics curriculum, including a mandatory two-hour Web-based course titled "Living Our Core Values." The first 45 minutes of the course set forth the ethical foundation and values for the firm. The remaining bulk of the learning is experiential, applying E&Y standards or the firm's collective wisdom regarding those values to real-life situations.

"We put employees in situations and ask them to take the firm's values and ethics to solve problems at the firm itself," Hamilton said. "It's the only way you can give them that experience. You can talk at them all day, but when it comes to making tough calls and essentially interpreting between the lines, you have to let people have an emotional connection that says, 'This is what I feel, in my heart, is right, based on the firm's values.' You can't expect people to exercise the right answers unless you give them a chance to apply them to real-life situations."[19]

The Most Ethical Companies Each year, *Ethisphere* magazine (targeted toward top management and focused on ethical leadership) examines over 5,000 companies in 30 separate industries seeking the world's most ethical companies. It then lists the top 100. The magazine uses a rigorous format to identify true ethical leadership. A few of the selected winners are shown in Exhibit 3.5.

Forcing Ethical Standards on Others A company such as Wal-Mart has a huge amount of power over its suppliers. As the world's largest seller of toys, Wal-Mart ordered its suppliers to meet a new set of children's-product safety requirements by the fall of 2008 that goes far beyond existing government regulations. The standards include strict limits for lead and a broad array of other heavy metals and chemicals that have been linked to various medical and developmental problems in children.

EXHIBIT 3.5

Selected Winners of the World's Most Ethical Companies Award

ALCOA

Perry Minis, Director of Global Ethics & Compliance

Perry Minis is the Director of Global Ethics & Compliance for Alcoa, a metals and mining company with over 120,000 employees in 44 countries. Minnis, who started with Alcoa in finance 39 years ago, runs the Global Ethics & Compliance department to track metrics and determine if the company has a positive impact on the community. According to Minnis, "Our management has a very strong focus on safety. Alcoa is considered to be one of the safest corporations in the world." The company's Ethics and Compliance Council, which includes the CEO, vice presidents, and department directors, was formed in order to notify all executives of the latest in operations. The Council presents findings to the Board on a quarterly basis.

Minnis notes that Alcoa's Code of Conduct has been condensed to apply to specific roles and translated into different languages in order to make it an effective tool for all employees. The Code is also provided to suppliers, so they understand Alcoa's expectations and policies. "If a vendor's values or policies differ drastically from Alcoa, chances are they won't be doing business with us," emphasizes Minnis. He continues, "The most important thing is our values. We have a set of values and policies that is consistent across the company, and we train all employees to adhere to and uphold those values."

EATON

Sandy Cutler, CEO

Sandy Cutler, CEO of Eaton Corporation, spoke in great detail about the basic beliefs that make Eaton a value-based company. These core values have allowed Eaton to maintain a strong foundation and sense of stability during recent internal changes and mergers. Rather than approaching ethics as a compliance issue, Cutler believes, "It's about doing business right through internal philosophies and customer commitments. We'll lose business before we will compromise our values."

Eaton employs 61,000 people in 125 countries, and almost all of their products are targeted at helping people and companies to effectively use energy. For example, Eaton developed a technology with the EPA for UPS that allowed the shipping company to save 70 percent in fuel economy. Additionally, Eaton developed a hybrid electric bus technology for possible use during the Beijing Olympics.

Eaton places high value on contributions in the workplace and community, believing they are key components for doing business right. "People will work where the company and the community involvement values reflect their own," insists Cutler. Every employee at Eaton has the opportunity to raise questions if they believe their personal morals are at risk. If a company is committed to doing business ethically, "you can cut the top off and the bottom would keep working," maintains Cutler.

JOHN DEERE

James R. Jenkins, Senior Vice President and General Counsel

In business for 170 years, John Deere prides itself on enabling "human flourishing." With core values of integrity, quality, innovation, and commitment, the company provides advanced products and services for agriculture, forestry, construction, and landscaping, as well as manufacturing engines for use in heavy equipment. James R. Jenkins, Senior VP and General Counsel for Deere & Company, said, "John Deere fully recognizes the need to conduct business with integrity. Our broad approach to citizenship, coupled with market leadership, helps us improve the world while growing a business."

Deere believes in creating and distributing service in ways that respect the earth's limited resources while providing commitment to helping find policy solutions that benefit the environment. "We believe that effective policy to address global climate change must include development and support of renewable energy sources including agricultural, forestry, wind, and bio-technologies, as well as processing and distribution improvements," says Jenkins.

With a passionate commitment to doing what is right and operating ethically, John Deere makes their conduct guidelines transparent to employees, customers, and suppliers. Acting out of principled, long-term self-interest, Deere contributes to the greater good by supporting the quality of life in their communities, protecting the environment, and preserving precious resources. According to Jenkins, "We believe that exceptional performance will not be sustainable if it is at the expense of our values."

Source: Ethisphere.com (August 28, 2007).

The initiative also encourages suppliers to mark children's products with "traceability information," including the factory in which the goods were made. About 80 percent of the toys sold in the United States, including those marketed by U.S.-based toy makers, are manufactured in China.

Wal-Mart's action, and similar moves by rivals such as Target Corp. and Toys"R"Us Inc., follow the discovery of high lead levels in children's products, the recall of about 25 million toys in 2007, and toy-related deaths. The new Wal-Mart standards are estimated to increase toy manufacturing costs by 5 to 7 percent.[20]

Wal-Mart also has implemented strict new quality, environmental, and safety standards for its Chinese suppliers. It also began requiring specific levels of energy efficiency for its Chinese suppliers in 2009. Wal-Mart feels that the new standards will help because in some factories up to 20 percent of the goods produced were rejected as not up to quality standards. This resulted in a lot of waste. Wal-Mart hopes to eliminate customer returns due to defective merchandise by 2012.[21]

The ultimate question many ask is, "Does being ethical pay?" We explore this issue in the "Customer Experience" box below.

Cultural Differences in Ethics

Studies suggest that ethical beliefs vary only a little from culture to culture. Certain practices, however, such as the use of illegal payments and bribes, are far more acceptable in some places than in others. Some countries have a dual standard concerning illegal payments. For example, German businesspeople typically treat bribes as tax-deductible business expenses. In Russia, bribes and connections in the government are essential for doing business. For instance, bribing a public official is the fastest method for accomplishing bureaucratic tasks such as registering a business. What we call bribery is a natural way of doing business in some other cultures. Do these widespread practices suggest that global marketers should adopt a "When in Rome, do as the Romans do" mentality?

Yet another example of cultural differences is the Japanese reluctance to enforce their antitrust laws. Everyday business practices, from retail pricing to business structuring, ignore antitrust regulations against restraint of trade, monopolies, and price discrimination. Not surprisingly, the Japanese are tolerant of scandals involving antitrust violations, favoritism, price fixing, bribery, and other activities considered unethical in the United States.

Concern about U.S. corporations' use of illegal payments and bribes in international business dealings led to passage of the Foreign Corrupt Practices Act. This act prohibits U.S. corporations from making illegal payments to public officials of foreign governments to obtain business rights or to enhance their business dealings in those countries. The act has been criticized for putting U.S. businesses at a competitive disadvantage. Many contend that bribery is an unpleasant but necessary part of international business.

CUSTOMER Experience

Will Consumers Pay More for an Ethical Company's Products?

In a perfect world, consumers would pay more for good companies' products than unethical companies' products if the product were relatively homogenous. But does this really happen? To find out, researchers conducted a series of experiments. They showed consumers the same products—coffee and T-shirts—but told one group the items had been made using high ethical standards and another group that low standards had been used. A control group got no information. In all of the tests, consumers were willing to pay a slight premium for the ethically made goods. But they went much further in the other direction: they would buy unethically made products only at a steep discount. What's more, consumer attitudes played a big part in shaping those results. People with high standards for corporate behavior rewarded the ethical companies with bigger premiums and punished the unethical ones with bigger discounts.[22]

Other research has found that there is a positive relationship between a firm's ethical ideals and practices and profitability. High ethical standards tended to inspire and motivate employees. It also gave them a feeling of well-being. Strong corporate ethics tend to build a high level of internal trust that enables the firm to retain good employees. This, in turn, can lower costs and lead to higher profits.[23]

Do you think that high ethical standards pay off for businesses? Why or why not? Are you willing to pay more for essentially the same product if it is sold by a company with high ethical standards? Why or why not?

Ethical Dilemmas Related to Developing Countries

For companies, the benefits of seeking international growth are several. A company that cannot grow further in its domestic market may reap increased sales and economies of scale not only by exporting its product but also by producing it abroad. A company may also wish to diversify its political and economic risks by spreading its operations across several nations.

Expanding into developing countries offers multinational companies the benefits of low-cost labor and natural resources. But many multinational firms have been criticized for exploiting developing countries. Although the firms' business practices may be legal, many business ethicists argue that they are unethical. The problem is compounded by the intense competition among developing countries for industrial development. Ethical standards are often overlooked by governments hungry for jobs or tax revenues.

Take the tobacco industry, for instance. With tobacco sales decreasing and regulations stiffening in the United States and Western Europe, tobacco companies have come to believe that their future lies elsewhere: in China, Asia, Africa, Eastern Europe, and Russia. Despite the known health risks of their product, the large tobacco companies are pushing their way into markets that typically have few marketing or health-labeling controls. In Hungary, Marlboro cigarettes are sometimes handed out to young fans at pop concerts. In the last 10 years, cigarette advertising on Japanese television has soared from 40th to 2nd place in air time and value; it appears even during children's shows.

Interestingly, at a time when smoking is being discouraged in the United States, U.S. trade representatives are talking to developing countries like China and Thailand about lowering their tariffs on foreign cigarettes. Japan, Taiwan, and South Korea have already given in to the threats. Entering these developing countries, the tobacco companies and trade representatives insist, will help U.S. tobacco manufacturers make up for losses in their home market. Worldwide, tobacco causes nearly 5 million deaths per year. It is expected to rise to 10 million by 2020.[24] Is it ethical for tobacco executives to promote and export this product?

© AP IMAGES/ANDY WONG

In the face of the rising number of smokers in their country, the Malaysian government has banned the advertising of tobacco products. However, many firms in the tobacco industry skirt the law by sponsoring sports and entertainment events, such as this motorsport event, or by advertising their brands without referring to cigarettes.

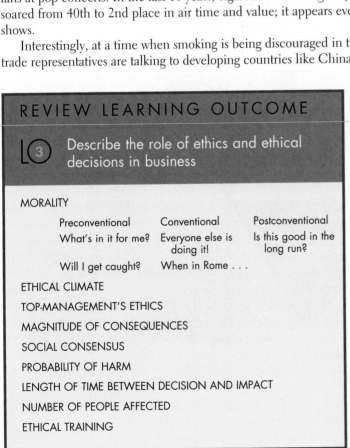

REVIEW LEARNING OUTCOME

LO 3 Describe the role of ethics and ethical decisions in business

MORALITY

Preconventional	Conventional	Postconventional
What's in it for me?	Everyone else is doing it!	Is this good in the long run?
Will I get caught?	When in Rome . . .	

ETHICAL CLIMATE

TOP-MANAGEMENT'S ETHICS

MAGNITUDE OF CONSEQUENCES

SOCIAL CONSENSUS

PROBABILITY OF HARM

LENGTH OF TIME BETWEEN DECISION AND IMPACT

NUMBER OF PEOPLE AFFECTED

ETHICAL TRAINING

corporate social responsibility
Business's concern for society's welfare.

sustainability
The idea that socially responsible companies will outperform their peers by focusing on the world's social problems and viewing them as opportunities to build profits and help the world at the same time.

Environmental issues are another example. As U.S. environmental laws and regulations gain strength, many companies are moving their operations to developing countries, where it is often less expensive to operate. These countries generally enforce minimal or no clean-air and waste-disposal regulations. For example, an increasing number of U.S. companies have located manufacturing plants called *maquiladoras* in Mexico, along the U.S.–Mexican border. Many blame the *maquiladoras* for "not putting back into the border area what they have been taking out," referring to the region's inadequate sewers and water-treatment plants.

Because Mexico has been eager to attract foreign employers, *maquiladoras* pay little in taxes, which would normally go toward improving the country's infrastructure. Cuidad Juárez, a populous and polluted *maquiladora* city bordering El Paso, Texas, generates millions of gallons of sewage a day and has no sewage system at all.

CORPORATE SOCIAL RESPONSIBILITY

Corporate social responsibility is a business's concern for society's welfare. This concern is demonstrated by managers who consider both the long-range best interests of the company and the company's relationship to the society within which it operates. The newest theory in social responsibility is called sustainability. This refers to the idea

EXHIBIT 3.6

Stakeholders in a Typical Corporation

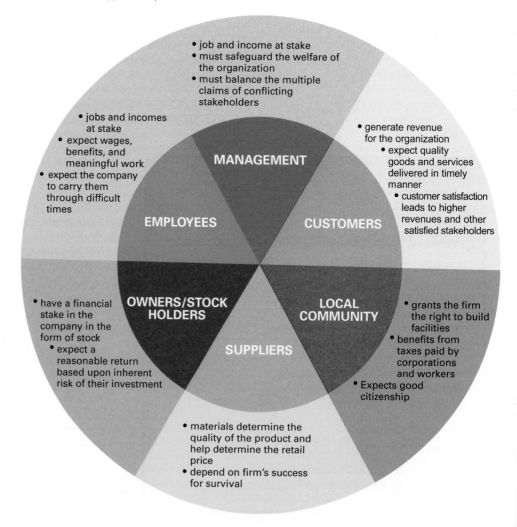

that socially responsible companies will outperform their peers by focusing on the world's social problems and viewing them as opportunities to build profits and help the world at the same time. It is also the notion that companies cannot thrive for long (i.e., lack sustainability) in a world where billions of people are suffering and are desperately poor. Thus, it is in business's interest to find ways to attack society's ills. Only business organizations have the talent, creativity, and executive ability to do the job.

Stakeholders and Social Responsibility

A second approach to social responsibility is known as the stakeholder theory. This says that social responsibility is paying attention to the interest of every affected stakeholder in every aspect of a firm's operation.[25] The stakeholders in a typical corporation are shown in Exhibit 3.6.

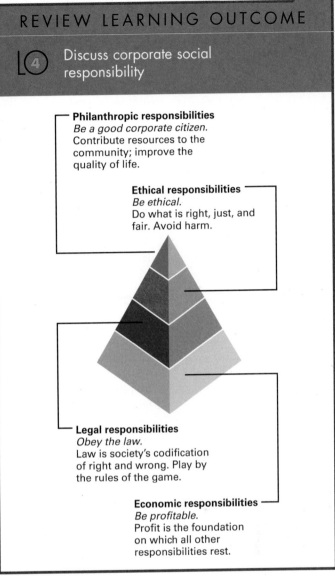

REVIEW LEARNING OUTCOME

LO 4 Discuss corporate social responsibility

Philanthropic responsibilities
Be a good corporate citizen.
Contribute resources to the community; improve the quality of life.

Ethical responsibilities
Be ethical.
Do what is right, just, and fair. Avoid harm.

Legal responsibilities
Obey the law.
Law is society's codification of right and wrong. Play by the rules of the game.

Economic responsibilities
Be profitable.
Profit is the foundation on which all other responsibilities rest.

- ☛ *Employees* have their jobs and incomes at stake. If the firm moves or closes, employees often face a severe hardship. In return for their labor, employees expect wages, benefits, and meaningful work. In return for their loyalty, workers expect the company to carry them through difficult times.

- ☛ *Management* plays a special role, as they also have a stake in the corporation. Part of their stake is like that of the employees. On the other hand, management must safeguard the welfare of the organization. Sometimes this means balancing the multiple claims of conflicting stakeholders. For example, stockholders want higher return and perhaps lower costs by moving factories overseas. This naturally conflicts with employees, the local community, and perhaps suppliers.

- ☛ *Customers* generate the revenue for the organization. In exchange, they expect high-quality goods and services delivered in a timely manner. Customer satisfaction leads to higher revenues and the ability to enhance the satisfaction of other stakeholders.

- ☛ *The local community*, through its government, grants the firm the right to build facilities. In turn, it benefits directly from local taxes paid by the corporation and indirectly by property and sales taxes paid by the workers. The firm is expected to be a good citizen by paying a fair wage, not polluting the environment, and so forth.

- ☛ *Suppliers* are vital to the success of the firm. If a critical part, for example, is not available for an assembly line, then production grinds to a halt. The materials supplied determine the quality of the product produced and create a cost floor, which helps determine the retail price. In turn, the firm is the customer of the supplier and is therefore vital to the success and survival of the supplier. Small firms who sold most of their production to Wal-Mart and were subsequently dropped by Wal-Mart have sometimes gone bankrupt.

- ☛ *Owners* have a financial stake in the form of stock in a corporation. They expect a reasonable return based upon the amount of inherent risk on their investment. Often managers and employees have a portion of their retirement funds in company stock. In the case of Enron's bankruptcy, many workers lost their entire retirement savings.

stakeholder theory
A theory that holds that social responsibility is paying attention to the interest of every affected stakeholder in every aspect of a firm's operation.

One theorist suggests that total corporate social responsibility has four components: economic, legal, ethical, and philanthropic. The pyramid of corporate social responsibility portrays economic performance as the foundation for the other three responsibilities. At the same time that it pursues profits (economic responsibility), however, a business is expected to obey the law (legal responsibility); to do what is right, just, and fair (ethical responsibilities); and to be a good corporate citizen (philanthropic responsibility). These four components are distinct but together constitute the whole. Still, if the company doesn't make a profit, then the other three responsibilities are moot.

pyramid of corporate social responsibility
A model that suggests corporate social responsibility is composed of economic, legal, ethical, and philanthropic responsibilities and that the firm's economic performance supports the entire structure.

ARGUMENTS AGAINST AND FOR CORPORATE SOCIAL RESPONSIBILITY (CSR)

Today very few managers are against social responsibility initiatives. The debate, instead, is the degree and kinds of social responsibility that an organization should pursue.

Arguments Against CSR

Skeptics say business should focus on making a profit and leave social and environmental problems to nonprofit organizations (like the World Wildlife Federation or the Sierra Club) and government. The late economist Milton Friedman believed that the free market, not companies, should decide what is best for the world. He asked, "If businesspeople do have a social responsibility other than making maximum profits for stockholders, how are they to know what it is?"[26] Friedman argued that when business executives spend more money than they need to—to purchase delivery vehicles with hybrid engines or to pay higher wages in developing countries, or even to donate company funds to charity— they are spending shareholders' money to further their own agendas. It is better to pay dividends and let the shareholders give the money away, if they choose.

Another argument is that businesses are created to produce goods and services, and not to handle welfare activities. They don't have the expertise to make social decisions. And if managers take time and monies to pursue social responsibilities, it will take away from the primary goals of the firm.

A final argument is that being socially responsible might damage the company in the global marketplace. That is, cleaning up the environment, ensuring product safety, and donating money and time for social causes all raise costs. This will be reflected in the final prices of the goods and services a company sells. In countries that don't emphasize social responsibility, a company will have lower costs because it doesn't engage in activities related to social responsibility. If the American company competes with the foreign competitor in the global marketplace, it will be at an economic disadvantage.

Arguments For Social Responsibility

The most basic argument for social responsibility is that it is simply the right thing to do. Some societal problems have been brought about by corporations such as pollution and poverty-level wages; it is the responsibility of business to right these wrongs. Another position is that business has the resources, so business should be given the chance to solve social problems. For example, business can provide a fair work environment, safe products, and informative advertising.

Another, more pragmatic, reason for being socially responsible is that, if business isn't responsible, then government will create new regulations and perhaps levy fines against corporations. For example, Valero Energy was recently fined $4.25 million for pollution at three of its refineries and was required to spend an additional $232 million on new pollution controls.[27] To the extent that business polices itself with self-disciplined standards and guidelines, government intervention can be avoided.

A final argument for social responsibility is that it can be a profitable undertaking. Smart companies, they say, can prosper and build shareholder value by tackling global problems. For General Electric, selling more wind power and energy-efficient locomotives is a no-brainer. When it comes to philanthropy, or supply chain audits designed to keep GE from being linked to sweatshops, or decisions about granting domestic-partner benefits, the business case usually comes down to GE's reputation and its desire to attract and engage great people. Some years back, for example, GE decided not to sell low-end ultrasound machines in China (and to put warning labels on the high-end machines it did sell) because it did not want the machines to be used for gender screening that could lead to abortions. The potential harm to GE's image was too great to take the risk.

But applying that kind of cost-benefit analysis to decisions with moral dimensions is a tricky business. Although GE operates in more than 100 countries, it has decided not to do business in Myanmar because the government there is a notorious violator of human rights and has been spotlighted by human-rights groups—and because the business upside is limited. GE has judged that it has more to lose than gain by being there.

Wal-Mart has experienced its share of criticism for not paying a living wage, putting small independent firms out of business, and using too much energy. However, Wal-Mart has aggressively become proactive toward the environment and hopes to make money by "being green." Lee Scott, Wal-Mart's CEO, vows to use 100 percent renewable energy, drastically reduce waste through recycling, and sell "sustainable" products that are more environmentally friendly. Cutting energy use is saving money, and consumers appreciate Wal-Mart's forays into organic cotton products and coffee certified to have earned farm workers a decent wage.

Switching stores to more efficient light bulbs and adding skylights for natural light has trimmed Wal-Mart's electricity bill by 17 percent since 2002. Using less packaging on house-brand toys will save $2.4 million annually in shipping costs. Even Wal-Mart's push to slash America's electricity use—and thus greenhouse gas emissions—by selling 100 million compact fluorescent bulbs a year has a bottom-line benefit. Customers will save $3 billion and the expectation is that these savings will come back in terms of purchases at Wal-Mart.[28]

Some other companies that profit from being socially responsible are shown in Exhibit 3.7. One recent study found that, for large companies, a one percent increase in the firm's social responsibility ratings led to a $17 million increase in profits.[29]

Growth of Social Responsibility

Social responsibility of businesses is growing around the world. A recent study of social responsibility, in selected countries, asked the following: "Does your company consider social responsibility factors when making business decisions?" The percentage of firms that said "yes" were Brazil, 62 percent; Canada, 54 percent; Australia, 52 percent; America, 47 percent; India, 38 percent; China, 35 percent; Mexico, 26 percent.[30]

Another survey pointed out that 47 percent of American firms was simply not adequate. Seventy-five percent felt that United States companies needed to do more in the area of social responsibility.[31]

The UN Global Compact One way that U.S. firms can do more is join the UN's Global Compact. The United Nations Global Compact, the world's largest global corporate citizenship initiative, has seen its ranks swell over the past few years. In 2001—the first full year after its launch—just 67 companies joined, agreeing to abide by ten principles covering, among other things, human rights, labor practices, and the environment. The ten principles are shown in Exhibit 3.8. In 2008, there were more than 5,600 participants in 120 countries around the world.[32]

EXHIBIT 3.7

Doing Well by Doing Good

Automobiles

Toyota: The maker of the top-selling Prius hybrid leads in developing efficient gas-electric vehicles.

Renault: Integrates sustainability throughout organization; has fuel-efficient cars and factories.

Volkswagen: A market leader in small cars and clean diesel technologies.

Computers & Peripherals

Hewlett-Packard: Despite board turmoil, the company rates high on ecological standards and digital technology for the poor.

Toshiba: At the forefront of developing eco-efficient products, such as fuel cells for notebook PC batteries.

Dell: Among the first U.S. PC makers to take hardware back from consumers and recycle it for free.

Retail

Marks & Spencer: Buys local product to cut transit costs and fuel use; good wages and benefits help retain staff.

Home Retail Group: High overall corporate responsibility standards have led to strong consumer and staff loyalty.

Aeon: Environmental accounting has saved $5.6 million; good employee policies in China and SE Asia.

Household Durables

Philips Electronics: Top innovator of energy-saving appliances, lighting, and medical gear and goods for the developing world.

Sony: Is ahead on green issues and ensuring quality, safety, and labor standards of global suppliers.

Matsushita Electric: State-of-the-art green products; eliminated 96 percent of the most toxic substances in its global operations.

Pharmaceuticals

Roche: Committed to improving access to medicine in poor nations; invests in drug research for Third World.

Novo Nordisk: Spearheads efforts in diseases like leprosy and bird flu and is a leading player in lower-cost generics.

Glaxo-SmithKline: One of few pharmas to devote R&D to malaria and TB; first to offer AIDS drugs at cost.

Utilities

FPL: Largest U.S. solar generator; has 40 percent of wind-power capacity; strong shareholder relations.

Source: "Who's Doing Well by Doing Good," *BusinessWeek*, January 29, 2007, 53. Reprinted from the January 29, 2007, issue of *BusinessWeek* by special permission, copyright © 2007 by The McGraw-Hill Companies, Inc.

Firms are realizing that corporate social responsibility isn't easy or quick. It doesn't work without long-term strategy and effort, and coordination throughout the enterprise. It doesn't always come cheap, either. And the payoff, both to society and the business itself, isn't always immediate. Businesses say they want to be responsible citizens, but that's often not their only reason for taking action. In a recent survey, the United Nations Global Compact asked members why they had joined. "Networking opportunities" was the second-most-popular reason; "Addressing humanitarian concerns" was third. The first was to "Increase trust in company."[33]

Proactive Social Responsibility Two companies that are frequently lauded for their social responsibility are food giant H. J. Heinz and Chiquita, the banana grower. Heinz has been a leader in social responsibility from its inception. For Chiquita, its awakening came later.

H. J. Heinz[34]

Founded in 1869, H. J. Heinz Co. was socially responsible long before corporate social responsibility became a banner corporations were advised to adopt. In fact, founder Henry Heinz was one of the first advocates of pure food and corporate transparency. "Our history is captured by the pure food products label," says Ted Smyth, SVP and chief administrative officer for Heinz. "Realizing horseradish was being sold with ingredients like sawdust to fill it out, Henry Heinz used a clear bottle so the consumer could see it wasn't adulterated. It was a great success and brilliant marketing."

EXHIBIT 3.8

The Principles of the UN Global Compact

Human Rights
- Principle 1: Businesses should support and respect the protection of internationally proclaimed human rights; and
- Principle 2: make sure that they are not complicit in human rights abuses.

Labor Standards
- Principle 3: Businesses should uphold the freedom of association and the effective recognition of the right to collective bargaining;
- Principle 4: the elimination of all forms of forced and compulsory labor;
- Principle 5: the effective abolition of child labor; and
- Principle 6: the elimination of discrimination in respect of employment and occupation.

Environment
- Principle 7: Businesses should support a precautionary approach to environmental challenges;
- Principle 8: undertake initiatives to promote greater environmental responsibility; and
- Principle 9: encourage the development and diffusion of environmentally friendly technologies.

Anti-Corruption
- Principle 10: Businesses should work against corruption in all its forms, including extortion and bribery.

Source: www.unglobalcompact.org/AboutTheGC/TheTenPrinciples/index.html, accessed January 21, 2009.

These days, consumers are concerned with not only the quality, but also the nutritional content of foods. More than 70 percent of Heinz products can be classified in the health category, and incremental health improvements are planned. Ingredients such as trans fat, salt, and sugar are being removed. Organic varieties are available, and many foods are being fortified with vitamins and minerals. "We operate in fundamentally healthy categories," says Andrew Towle, VP of global marketing. "Removing ingredients of concern is a technical challenge. We cannot go backward in taste."

Established in 1951, The Heinz Co. Foundation (HCF) is funded by the company to promote health, nutrition, and well-being in communities where Heinz operates. Indeed, social responsibility is undeniably part of Heinz's DNA, yet many are unaware of it because social responsibility is standard practice. In 2002, HCF began its micronutrient program, supported by Dr. Stanley Zlotkin, creator of Sprinkles, an iron-supplement multivitamin powder. The company has used existing packaging and distribution channels to deliver the supplements to more than 1.2 million children in 15 countries. "Sixty packets can cure one child of anemia for a year," says HCF director Tammy Aupperle. "We hope to reach 10 million by 2010." In 2003, Heinz and Helen Keller International, which fights causes and consequences of blindness and malnutrition, partnered in Indonesia. They distributed more than 44 million supplement packets, benefiting more than 400,000 people. The model will be replicated in India and China.

A few additional Heinz initiatives are

- *Nutrient program:* Nutritional supplement packets have been distributed to more than 1.2 million children in Indonesia, Guyana, Mongolia, Pakistan, Haiti, Ghana, and other countries.
- *Health and wellness initiatives:* A Global Health & Wellness Task Force is addressing ingredients of concern (sodium, sugar, and others), adding more goodness to products, and adding functional benefits for consumers.

No one grows Ketchup like Heinz.

IMAGE COURTESY OF THE ADVERTISING ARCHIVES

GLOBAL Perspectives

What Good Works Can Do

In 1967, the year after Botswana gained its independence from Britain, a huge diamond deposit was discovered in a remote area called Orapa, about 400 kilometers, or 250 miles, from the capital city of Gaborone. The company that found the source was DeBeers, then, as now, the dominant seller of "rough stones" in the world. Four years and $33 million later, the mine was ready for production.

In the early years of its nationhood, Botswana was one of the poorest countries in the world, with a per capita income of about $80 a year. Today, it is among the most prosperous countries in Africa, with a real middle class and a per capita income approaching $6,000 a year. By contrast, the average citizen in Angola earns about $2,500 a year, while in the Democratic Republic of the Congo, it is a little more than $1,500, according to the World Bank.

There is no question that the discovery of the diamonds was the most important catalyst in Botswana's economic growth. Prior to the discovery, Botswana had an agricultural economy. By the early 1980s, diamond, manganese, and copper mines controlled by DeBeers accounted for fully 50 percent of the country's gross domestic product. Though the Botswana economy has since diversified, DeBeers' operations still account for around one-third of the Botswana gross domestic product. There is also no question, though, that Botswana was greatly aided by something else: DeBeers' own sense of corporate responsibility.

From the start, it entered into a 50–50 diamond mining venture with the government; about a decade ago, it also sold the government a 15 percent stake in the company. It has also built hospitals and schools in Botswana, worked to help the country deal with HIV and AIDS, assisted the government in building roads and infrastructure, and been involved in a hundred other things that have helped make Botswana an African success story. Most of the executives in the government-company venture are black Africans who have been trained by DeBeers. In 2008, the company closed its diamond sorting facility in London and opened the largest, most technologically advanced diamond sorting complex in the world in Gaborone. It employs 600 people.

"We think our approach is a competitive advantage," said Gareth Penny, the cherubic, 45-year-old South African who has been the company chief executive since 2006. It is hard to disagree. Botswana's citizens need roads, but so does DeBeers, to transport its diamonds. DeBeers needs a healthy workforce, so its emphasis on HIV awareness and treatment is clearly in its self-interest. A more prosperous Botswana helps DeBeers in every way imaginable, not least by providing a stable environment in which it can do business. "The country can now attract banks and service industries—and avoid the natural resource curse," Penny said.[36]

Do you think that DeBeers was simply acting in its own self-interest and social responsibility played no part? What else might DeBeers do in Botswana to demonstrate its social responsibility?

- ☞ *Sustainable agriculture:* Agricultural practices include hybrid seeds, water conservation and reuse, recycling waste, minimal pesticide use, and partnership with Chinese government and farmers.
- ☞ *Eco-friendly packaging:* New packaging includes reduced steel, recycled paper trays and cartons, non-bleached cartons, and reduced resin use.

Heinz is a firm that truly cares about its stakeholders.

Chiquita Cleans Up Its Act[35]

"For decades the $3.9-billion-a-year fruit giant was synonymous with the notion of the greedy multinational. Farmworkers toiled long hours in dangerous conditions, agrochemical runoff contaminated water, and tropical forests were cleared for expansion," says J. Gary Taylor, coauthor of *Smart Alliance*, a book about Chiquita.

Enter Rainforest Alliance, which had previously worked with timber companies in Indonesia to lessen the impact of logging. In 1992 the Alliance sent banana companies a list of environmental and worker-rights standards required to gain its certification. During the next two years, Dave McLaughlin, Chiquita CEO, says Chiquita spent $40,000 to overhaul the Costa Rican farms, phase out toxic pesticides, and build new warehouses to store chemicals. McLaughlin began monitoring water quality and providing workers with better safety equipment. The farms also started recycling programs.

Today all 110 of Chiquita's company-owned farms and the vast majority of its independent farms are certified by the Rainforest Alliance. Things are getting better for its Latin American employees, who can now join unions. Four recent initiatives are

☛ One hundred percent of the plastic bags and twine used on Chiquita farms is recycled.

☛ Pesticide use has been cut by 26 percent, and workers are provided with better protective gear.

☛ Working conditions have been improved by new Chiquita-built housing and schools for employees' families.

☛ Buffer zones along farm borders help prevent chemical runoff and erosion.

Chiquita is an example of a multinational firm that has taken its social responsibility very seriously. Perhaps one of the greatest impacts a firm has had on any country is DeBeers, the diamond company. The story unfolds in the Global Perspectives box.

The Cost of Ignoring Social Responsibilities[37]

In today's environment, a firm that disregards its stakeholders and its social responsibilities does so at its own peril. In the case of AOL, it didn't treat its customers (key stakeholders) as they should have been treated. A deluge of AOL customers complained that they tried to close their accounts only to be thwarted in their attempts or to discover they were still being billed for services that they thought had been canceled. Although it had long been one of the Internet's best-known companies, AOL didn't set up an online cancellation system. All cancellation requests had to be made by fax, mail, or telephone. Subscribers who phoned AOL to cancel their service sometimes were greeted by aggressive customer service representatives who were paid bonuses of up to $3,000 if they found a way to retain the business. Customers complained that AOL's incentive system created an obstructive culture that made service cancellations difficult. "Consumers who called were put on hold or transferred repeatedly until they hung up in disgust," says Connecticut Attorney General Richard Blumenthal, who described AOL's practices as "outlandish and underhanded."

These customer complaints led to a $3 million settlement with 48 states and the District of Columbia. As part of the resolution, AOL agreed to make it easier for its remaining customers to leave and to maintain an online channel for processing cancellations.

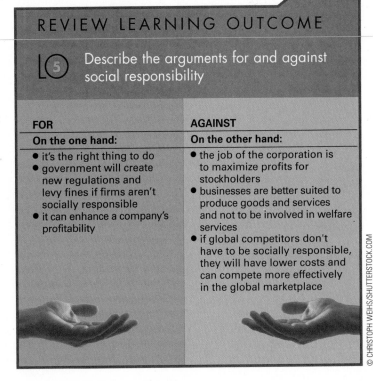

REVIEW LEARNING OUTCOME

LO 5 Describe the arguments for and against social responsibility

FOR	AGAINST
On the one hand:	On the other hand:
• it's the right thing to do • government will create new regulations and levy fines if firms aren't socially responsible • it can enhance a company's profitability	• the job of the corporation is to maximize profits for stockholders • businesses are better suited to produce goods and services and not to be involved in welfare services • if global competitors don't have to be socially responsible, they will have lower costs and can compete more effectively in the global marketplace

Green Marketing

An outgrowth of the social responsibility movement is green marketing. Green marketing is the development and marketing of products designed to minimize negative effects on the physical environment or to improve the environment.[38] Not only can a company aid the environment through green marketing, but it can often help its bottom line as well. Environmentally aware consumers tend to earn more and are willing to pay more for green products.[39] The problem, however, is that only a very small percentage of customers make their buying decisions primarily of the environmental qualities of the product.[40] Also, it may not be readily apparent how one product is better for the environment than another. Thus, the marketer may have to educate the consumer about the green product. To make the sale, the green marketer may even use a traditional non-green benefit. For example, General Electric energy-efficient CFL flood lights are good for the environment. The promotion theme is "Long life for hard to reach places." GE is selling convenience because the floodlight doesn't need replacing as often.[41]

Some green products have practical consumer benefits that are readily apparent to consumers. A few examples are: energy efficient washing machines and other appliances (cut electric bills), heat-reflective windows (cut air conditioning costs), and organic foods (no pesticides poisoning the food or planet). Each Dole organic banana has a sticker with a number. If you enter that number at **doleorganic.com,** a Google Earth application will show you the exact place where the fruit was grown.[42]

One company that has done an excellent job of going green is Waste Management, which disposes waste for 22 million customers. The company produces more renewable energy each year than the entire North American solar industry. Its Wheelabrator division combusts waste to create electricity. Waste Management has also had 33 working landfills certified as wildlife habitat preserves. The firm hopes to have 100 certified by the Wildlife Habitat Council before 2020.[43]

LO 6 CAUSE-RELATED MARKETING

A sometimes controversial subset of social responsibility is cause-related marketing. Sometimes referred to as simply "cause marketing," it is the cooperative efforts of a "for-profit" firm and a "nonprofit organization" for mutual benefit. Cause-related marketing is sometimes used as any marketing effort for social or other charitable causes. Cause marketing differs from corporate giving (philanthropy) as the latter generally involves a specific donation that is tax deductible, while cause marketing is a marketing relationship not based on a straight donation.

Cause-related marketing is very popular and is estimated to generate about $7 billion a year in revenue.[44] It creates good public relations for the firm and will often stimulate sales of the brand. Yet, the huge growth of cause-related marketing can lead to a case

As a matter of fact, the water you drink does make a difference.

- Matt Damon

Over one billion people around the world lack clean water. Join me in my partnership with Ethos Water and H2O Africa and make a difference in the world water crisis. Every time you buy a bottle of Ethos, money goes to help provide children with the access to clean water they need. So if you choose to drink bottled water, please choose to make a difference. To learn more, **visit ethoswater.com.**

H2O AFRICA

Every Bottle Makes a Difference.™

Ethos is a proud supporter of "Running The Sahara." In theaters this spring.

A donation of $0.05 is made for every bottle of Ethos sold toward the Ethos Water Fund goal of donating $10 million by 2010.

of consumer cause fatigue. A 2007 nationwide survey found that 36 percent said they bought a product in the previous 12 months after learning of its maker's commitment to social issues, down from 43 percent in 2004. Only 14 percent said they intentionally paid more for a product that supports a cause, down from 28 percent. And just 30 percent said they told a family member or friend about a product or company committed to a social issue, compared with 43 percent in 2004.[45]

Examples of cause-related marketing abound. Starwood Hotels has announced that for every Westin Heavenly Bed, Sheraton Sweet Sleeper Bed, and Four Points by Sheraton Four Comfort Bed sold through Starwood retail channels, the firm will donate $50 to the Special Olympics. Avaya recently publicized that it will donate $5 to the American Cancer Society for each pink desk phone faceplate it sells. The money is to be used to raise breast cancer awareness. Starbucks donates 5 cents of every sale of Ethos Water to help children around the world get access to clean drinking water. American Express launched a campaign to restore the Statue of Liberty and Ellis Island. The company contributes 1 cent per card transaction and $1 for every new card issued. American Express collected $1.7 million for the restoration effort.[46]

Cause-Related Marketing Controversy

Few causes have been more saturated with marketing than breast cancer awareness. Consumers can buy everything from food to toilet paper with labels that feature a pink ribbon. This generally signifies that for each product sold money is donated to breast cancer awareness. Yoplait ran a campaign that donated 10 cents to the Canadian Breast Cancer Foundation every time a consumer mailed back one of its yogurt carton lids. Aside from the fact that someone would have to eat three cartons of yogurt a day for more than three months just to raise $20, and that consumers spent more on postage than they raised with each lid, Yoplait left it to the fine print to state it was capping donations at $80,000—keeping the rest as profit.[47]

The Gap has been criticized for The Gap (Product) Red campaign. Thanks to the Gap and others, more than $25 million has been raised to fight HIV/AIDS, tuberculosis, and malaria. The Gap has stated that "50 percent of (Product) Red products" are being directed to the cause. Yet the promotional expenditures for the (Product) Red campaign were $100 million![48]

The Susan G. Komen Breast Cancer Foundation is on the receiving end of much cause-related marketing. The Foundation recently put out an information piece titled, "Five Questions to Ask before Participating in a Cause-Related Marketing Program." The questions are

1. Is this company committed? Read the product packaging and promotional materials or display and visit the company Web site to make sure the company is credible and committed to the cause.

2. How is the program structured? Transparency is key. Is the company clearly stating how the money is raised and how much will be going to charity? For example, if it's a donation per purchase, ask how much of purchase price goes to charity—is it 2 percent or 10 percent—or some other amount? If there is a minimum contribution guaranteed by the company, what is the amount? Is there a maximum donation that will be made by the company?

3. Who does the program benefit? Does it support a well-managed, reputable nonprofit or fund? Again, the Komen Foundation recommends that consumers read Web sites. The Komen

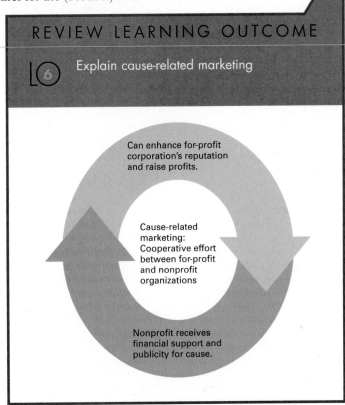

REVIEW LEARNING OUTCOME

LO 6 Explain cause-related marketing

Cause-related marketing: Cooperative effort between for-profit and nonprofit organizations

Can enhance for-profit corporation's reputation and raise profits.

Nonprofit receives financial support and publicity for cause.

Foundation makes it very clear on its site what it is, how it structures programs, and how the monies are used. The Better Business Bureau's Wise Giving Alliance is one resource for information on nonprofit organizations.

4. How will the organization that benefits use my money? It should be abundantly clear where the monies go. What organization will they support? Will the dollars generated go to research, education, community programs, or all of the above? The Komen Foundation is very specific about their programs, activities, and grants awarded to support their mission to eradicate breast cancer as a life-threatening disease. Visit **ww5.komen.org** to view the Komen Foundation's most recent Annual Report.

5. Is the program meaningful to me? Is the program supporting a cause you believe in or have been touched by? Based on the details of the program and the potential for dollars to be raised, does the program make sense to you? Selecting the right program is a personal choice based on your interests, your passions, and a cause that is important to you.[49]

---

13 ◄ percent of today's large-company top executives who report that having strong ethical traits is the most important leadership trait of CEOs

20 ◄ percent of large-company top executives in 2003 who reported that having strong ethical traits was the most important leadership trait of CEOs

37 ◄ percent of large-company top executives who report that the most important trait of CEOs is the ability to inspire others

$2.4 million ◄ shipping costs saved annually by Wal-Mart by using less packaging on house-brand toys

70 ◄ percent of large employers offer ethics training

17 ◄ percent Wal-Mart trimmed off electricity bill by switching to efficient light bulbs and adding skylights

---

REVIEW AND APPLICATIONS

Explain the determinants of a civil society. The "social glue" that holds a society together is composed of six factors. They are ethics, laws, formal and informal groups, self-regulation, the media, and an active civil society. All of these are necessary for a coherent, vibrant, and civil society. These six factors are more important in countries than ever before because of the increasing complexity of the global economy and the melding of customs and traditions within societies.

1.1 Explain how each of the six factors contributes to a civil society.

1.2 Why is a free and uncontrolled media important in a country?

1.3 Can customs and laws sometimes conflict, especially when a society experiences an influx of immigrants?

Explain the concept of ethical behavior. Ethics are the moral principles or values that generally govern the conduct of an individual or a group. Ethics can also be viewed as the standard of behavior by which conduct is judged. Ethical conflicts sometimes arise between businesses, customers, workers, and the surrounding community. Conflicts can sometimes be resolved through the reliance on ethical theories. Ethical theories that are applicable to marketing include deontology, utilitarianism, casuist, moral relativism, and virtue ethics.

2.1 It is sometimes said that ethics hold a person to higher standards than laws. Explain.

2.2 Moral relativists are basically time and place ethicists. Explain what this means.

2.3 Explain the differences between utilitarianism, casuist, and deontology theories.

Describe ethical behavior in business. The law typically relies on juries to determine whether an act is legal or illegal. Society determines whether an action is ethical or unethical. Morals are the rules that people develop as a result of cultural values and norms. More and more companies are using ethics training to help put good ethics into practice. Ethical beliefs vary a little from culture to culture. However, some ethical practices vary significantly from one culture to the next.

3.1 Explain the difference between ethics and morals and describe the relationship between the two.

3.2 What are the differences between preconventional morality, conventional morality, and postconventional morality? Give an example of each.

3.3 Give several examples of how ethical practices can vary from one culture to the next.

Discuss corporate social responsibility. Responsibility in business refers to a firm's concern for the way its decisions affect society. A second theory says that the corporation should always pay attention to the interests of its stakeholders. These are management, customers, the local community, owners/stockholders, suppliers, and employees. Social responsibility has four components: economic, legal, ethical, and philanthropic. These are intertwined, yet the most fundamental is earning a profit. If a firm does not earn a profit, the other three responsibilities are moot. Most businesspeople believe they should do more than pursue profits. Although a company must consider its economic needs first, it must also operate within the law, do what is ethical and fair, and be a good corporate citizen. The concept of sustainability is that socially responsible companies will outperform their peers by focusing on the world's social problems and viewing them as an opportunity to earn profits and help the world at the same time.

4.1 Describe at least three situations in which you would not purchase the products of a firm even though it is very socially responsible.

4.2 A firm's only responsibility to society is to earn a fair profit. Comment.

4.3 Is sustainability a viable concept for America's businesses?

4.4 Illustrate how there can be conflicts between the needs and desires of various stakeholders.

Describe the arguments for and against social responsibility. Today, virtually all managers endorse social responsibility of corporations. It is, instead, a matter of what types of responsibility and the degree of responsibility. The arguments against social responsibility are: The job of the corporation is to maximize profits for stockholders; businesses are better suited to produce goods and services and not to be involved in welfare services; if global competitors aren't socially responsible it could hurt the domestic competitor. The arguments for social responsibility are: It's the right thing to do; government will create new regulations and levy fines if firms aren't socially responsible; social responsibility can enhance a company's profitability.

5.1 Explain the relationship between the global economy and social responsibility.

5.2 Defend the proposition that the only responsibility of the firm is to make money for the stockholders.

5.3 Explain how a firm can earn additional profits by being socially responsible.

 Explain cause-related marketing. Cause-related marketing is the cooperative effort between a for-profit firm and a nonprofit organization. It is different from philanthropy, which is a specific, tax deductible donation. Cause-related marketing is very popular because it can enhance the reputation of the corporation and also make additional profit for the company. Sometimes companies have abused cause-related marketing and received much greater benefits than the nonprofit that has supposedly been helped. These cases are a small minority.

6.1 Why are more firms jumping on the cause-related marketing bandwagon?

6.2 Explain the controversy surrounding some cause-related marketing.

6.3 What are some questions that consumers should consider before participating in a cause-related campaign?

KEY TERMS

casuist ethical theory	76	ethics	75	stakeholder theory	87
cause-related marketing	94	Foreign Corrupt Practices Act	84	sustainability	86
code of ethics	80	moral relativists	76	utilitarian ethical theory	76
corporate social responsibility	86	morals	78	virtue	77
deontological ethical theory	75	pyramid of corporate social responsibility	88		

EXERCISES

APPLICATION EXERCISE

Many companies today are concerned with social responsibility. They may pursue philanthropic activities and/or strive to be ethical. Your goal for this assignment is to evaluate how firms are being socially responsible. Limit your answers to one page, and provide a printout of the Web site you visited.

Activities

1. Choose a company and find that company's Web site on the Internet. Once you get to the Web site, look for information that tells you about the firm's efforts to be socially responsible. Look for things like news releases, company information, information about community programs, and so on? Look in your textbook and your notes to help you define what might be considered

socially responsible activities. Describe what you find and explain why you think the company is involved with the activities you describe.

2. Do the activities described on the Web site seem consistent with the company's products? Why or why not? (For example, a shoe company may sponsor a race that raises money to help prevent a disease. People who participate in the race may use that company's running shoes, and therefore, the race would be consistent with the company's products.)

3. Evaluate how effective you think the information you find is in terms of how it is presented, what impact it might have and whether it will help to sell the company's products. Be sure to support any claims you make.

4. Does the information you collected during this activity improve your evaluation of the company? Would it influence your decision to buy the company's product? Why or why not?

ETHICS EXERCISE

Jane Barksdale has designed a line of clothing targeted toward Hispanic Americans. The items are sold only by catalog and on the Internet. She thinks that she can increase sales by claiming in ads that the firm is owned by a Hispanic American and all the employees are Hispanic Americans. She is not Hispanic American nor are most of the employees. She needs a high level of sales to pay her bank loan and remain in business.

Questions

1. Should Jane claim that she is Hispanic American? Explain your response.

2. Does the Federal Trade Commission address this issue? Go to **www.ftc.gov** and search for guidelines for small business advertising or e-commerce. What does Jane risk in making false claims in her ads?

MARKETING PLAN EXERCISE

These end-of-chapter marketing plan exercises are designed to help you use what you learned in the chapter to build a strategic marketing plan for a company of your choosing. Once you've completed the marketing plan exercise for each chapter in Part 1 of this textbook, you can complete the Part 1 Marketing Planning Worksheet on your companion Web site at **www.cengage.com/marketing/lamb.**

In the first part of this exercise (Chapter 2), you described your chosen company, wrote its mission statement and set its marketing objectives. Use the following exercises to guide you through the next part of your strategic marketing plan:

1. Identify any ethical issues that could impact your chosen firm. What steps should be taken to handle these issues?

2. How should your company integrate corporate social responsibility into its marketing plan?

3. In addition to suggestions for philanthropic responsibilities, write up a brief code of ethics for your firm. To see other codes of ethics, go to **www.iit .edu/libraries/csep/codes/coe.html.**

CASE STUDY: (PRODUCT) RED

CAN A T-SHIRT SAVE THE WORLD?[50]

When Oprah and Bono walked down Chicago's Magnificent Mile together in the fall of 2006, it was the shopping trip seen around the world. The famous duo attracted mobs of fans and extensive media coverage as they promoted a

© SUSAN VAN ETTEN

revolutionary new cause-marketing event called (Product) RED. Bono urged people to buy RED products, explaining that a portion of the proceeds would go to The Global Fund to fight HIV/AIDS in Africa. Oprah, wearing an "INSPI(RED)" Gap T-shirt on her talk show that day, proclaimed, "I am wearing the most important T-shirt I've ever worn in my life!"

Other companies that licensed the RED brand and created products for the charity included Apple, which sold a limited edition iPod Nano, and Motorola, which introduced a red Motorazr phone. Emporio Armani designed a special RED capsule collection for London Fashion Week, and Converse designed a line of RED shoes to be sold at Gap stores.

Oprah's shopping spree with Bono drew a reported an incredible one billion media impressions worldwide. (Product) RED set up its own Web site, **www .joinred.com**, and took over Myspace.com for the day to launch a page that now boasts over 600,000 friends. RSS (Really Simple Syndication) funneled news about RED to mobile phones and blog sites, and it quickly became a hot topic of discussion on message boards across the Internet.

(Product) RED was the brainchild of Bono and Bobby Shriver, who designed it as a commercial initiative that could change the way causes are marketed in the future. "They didn't want a one-time event," says Julia Cordua, VP of marketing. "They want five to ten years of ongoing donations."

Gap initially offered to give 100 percent of its profits to the cause, but Bono and Shriver refused to accept more than 50 percent. Shriver insists that they want companies to make money off the campaign, explaining, "We want people buying houses in the Hamptons based on this because if that happens, this thing is sustainable." As a result, Gap treats RED like a business, spending millions on marketing it. Within months of its launch, they saw sales of an estimated $71 million in revenue and donated about $2.5 million to The Global Fund.

According to the (Product) RED Web site, "Each company that becomes (RED) places its logo in this embrace and is then elevated to the power of red." You can be embraced by the RED, it suggests, by purchasing a Gap T-shirt or African-print Converse shoes. "What better way to become a good-looking Samaritan?!"

Some critics, such as Charles Kernaghan, director of the National Labor Committee for Worker and Human Rights, aren't buying it, though. "The thought of using consumer dollars made off the backs of workers held in sweatshops to help fund Bono's causes is really hypocritical—that's not the way to go," he says, referring to Gap's reputation for using factories that violate labor laws.

Since 2004 Gap has been working to combat this type of criticism by releasing Social Responsibility Reports on Gap factories in over 50 countries. Despite their efforts, however, nearly half of the factories still failed inspection as recently as 2005. When questioned, a Gap spokesperson responded by stating that Bono himself had inspected the African factory where RED products were being made, and it was "sparkling."

Some bloggers remain skeptical of the fund-raiser, however, declaring it "khaki colonialism." Michael Medved argued that it would be better to forget the overpriced T-shirts and send money directly to The Global Fund. But whether you agree with the way (Product) RED does business or not, the campaign is hard to ignore. David Hessekiel of the Cause Marketing Forum proclaimed it "the launch of the year." Stacy Palmer of *The Chronicle of Philanthropy*, wrote, "These are iconic brands that appeal to younger consumers who are very interested in buying cause-related products. (Product) RED borrows on ideas that have been used a lot, but its scale makes it different. People are getting bombarded by RED."

(Product) RED president Tamsin Smith reported on the campaign's blog that much of the merchandise was sold out within hours of the launch. Oprah's INSPI(RED) T-shirt went on to become the best-selling item in the Gap's 35-year history. Long-term success, however, depends on how well the participating brands continue to market new products. They'll have to find ways to keep socially conscious consumers interested in RED now that most of them have been there, done that, and (literally) bought the T-shirt.

Questions

1. Discuss the four components of corporate social responsibility (CSR) and how they relate to a charitable campaign such as (Product) RED. How does participation in a cause-marketing event contribute to a company's CSR? What role does sustainability play?

2. Do you think a partnership with (Product) RED can improve Gap's image? Is it a sign that they are making a commitment to corporate social responsibility or do you agree with critics who say their involvement is an attempt to spit-shine the company's image while continuing to do business as usual?

3. Describe the various types of technology that have contributed to the media coverage, marketing efforts, and public discussion of the RED campaign.

4. A year after (Product) RED's launch, *Ad Age* reported that although $100 million had been spent on marketing the campaign, only about $25 million had gone to the charity itself. Industry observers speculated that this could trigger a backlash against the campaign. Do you believe the criticism is justified? Do you think the campaign could lose supporters as a result?

COMPANY CLIPS

METHOD—PEOPLE AGAINST DIRTY

Method's first "lab" was the kitchen of founders Eric Ryan and Adam Lowry, two friends whose goal was to evolve the household cleaner from a toxic object that hid under the sink to an all-natural, biodegradable, and stylish countertop accessory. This video segment shows method through yet another lens, that of corporate social responsibility (CSR) and sustainability. Chemical engineer Adam Lowry outlines the chemical aspects of traditional cleaning products and describes how method's products are healthier. As you watch the video, keep in mind the various marketing orientations you learned in Chapter 1.

© NKP MEDIA, INC./CENGAGE

Questions

1. Does method have a societal marketing orientation, or is it just a market-oriented company that integrates a number of environmental practices into its operations? Explain.

2. How is method practicing sustainability?

3. Discuss the changing social factors that have made it possible for method to be so successful.

Marketing & You Results

The higher your score, the more important you think ethics and socially responsible behavior are to achieving corporate objectives. A high score also suggests that you are an ethical idealist, or someone who sees right and wrong as absolute, rather than an ethical relativist, or someone who sees right and wrong as situation dependent.

4

The Marketing Environment

LEARNING OUTCOMES

LO 1   Discuss the external environment of marketing, and explain how it affects a firm

LO 2   Describe the social factors that affect marketing

LO 3   Explain the importance to marketing managers of current demographic trends

LO 4   Explain the importance to marketing managers of multiculturalism and growing ethnic markets

LO 5   Identify consumer and marketer reactions to the state of the economy

LO 6   Identify the impact of technology on a firm

LO 7   Discuss the political and legal environment of marketing

LO 8   Explain the basics of foreign and domestic competition

LO ① THE EXTERNAL MARKETING ENVIRONMENT

If there is one constant in the external environment (outside the firm) where firms work and compete, it is that things are constantly changing. If the organization doesn't understand or fails to react to the changing world around it, it will soon be a follower rather than a leader. In the worst-case scenario, the firm disappears from the marketplace. Applebee's was, at one time, a hot, trendy restaurant chain. Now, the company faces falling profits and unhappy stockholders. What happened? Applebee's didn't adapt quickly enough to the changing environment. High gasoline prices resulted in many customers staying at home. More importantly, it didn't change quickly enough when competitors copied it. Newer eateries offer slick interiors in contrast with Applebee's busy walls full of photos and sports memorabilia. Menus at many newer generation restaurants stress the freshness or naturalness of the food. Applebee's still focused on the fried and breaded items.[1]

Perhaps the most important decisions a marketing manager must make relate to the creation of the marketing mix. Recall from Chapters 1 and 2 that a marketing mix is the unique combination of product, place (distribution), promotion, and price strategies. The marketing mix is, of course, under the firm's control and is designed to appeal to a specific group of potential buyers. A target market is a defined group that managers feel is most likely to buy a firm's product.

As the Applebee's example shows, managers must alter the marketing mix because of changes in the environment in which consumers live, work, and make purchasing decisions. Also, as markets mature, some new consumers become part of the target market; others drop out. Those who remain may have different tastes, needs, incomes, lifestyles, and buying habits than the original target consumers.

Although managers can control the marketing mix, they cannot control elements in the external environment that continually mold and reshape the target market. Review Learning Outcome 1 shows the controllable and uncontrollable variables that affect the target market, whether it consists of consumers or business purchasers. The uncontrollable elements in the center of the diagram continually evolve and create changes in the target market. In contrast, managers can shape and reshape the marketing mix, depicted on the left side of the diagram, to influence the target market. That is, managers react to changes in the external environment and attempt to create a more effective marketing mix.

Understanding the External Environment

Unless marketing managers understand the external environment, the firm cannot intelligently plan for the future. Thus, many organizations assemble a team of specialists to continually collect and evaluate environmental information, a process called *environmental scanning*. The goal in gathering the environmental data is to identify future market opportunities and threats.

Does environmental scanning really make a difference? The Aberdeen Group is a Boston-based research firm. It found that firms that used feedback, from the external environment, to create and modify their marketing mix had an average 26 percent increase in return on their marketing investment over the previous year.[2]

Marketing & You

Using the following scale, enter the numbers that reflect your opinions.

1	2	3	4	5	6	7
Strongly disagree						Strongly agree

___ I need more hours in the day to get my work done.

___ I *don't* have to overextend myself to find the time to get my work done.

___ I feel like I'm always "fighting fires."

___ I seldom have to take shortcuts to get my work done on time.

___ I never have enough time to think ahead.

___ I feel like I have a lot of time on my hands.

___ I feel like no matter how hard I work, I'll never get caught up.

Total your score. Read the chapter and find out what your score means at the end.

Source: From Scale #119, *Marketing Scales Handbook*, G. Bruner, K. James, H. Hensel, eds., Vol. III. © by American Marketing Association.

target market
A defined group most likely to buy a firm's product.

Companies that used environmental scanning less efficiently had only a 4 percent return. Those firms that didn't use scanning at all tended to be laggards in the marketplace. In summary, using environmental scanning to understand the ever-changing marketplace and then adapting the marketing mix accordingly are critical to long-term success of the organization.

Philips Electronics is a firm that is proactive in trying to keep a step ahead of the latest environmental trends. The firm's new strategic plan focuses on "sense and simplicity." The idea is to give consumers what they want in the way of electronic products in the health, lifestyle, and technology areas. Because Philips is dominated by engineers, it decided that if it was really going to create products that are simple to use and consumer-oriented, it needed help. The company created a four-person advisory group of opinion leaders from around the globe. The group consists of Sara Berman, a British fashion designer; Dr. Peggy Fritzsche, a California radiology professor; Gary Chang, a leading Chinese architect; and John Maeda, an MIT graphic designer. They meet several days each month in places like Paris, Rome, or New York to help Philips understand how the environment of business is changing. Their goal is to help Philips create intuitive, easy-to-use products that meet specific needs. Andrea Ragnatti, chief marketing officer for Philips, notes that it took the firm quite a while to adopt the marketing concept. She notes, "In the past we just developed the technology and hoped someone would buy it. Now we are starting from the point of discovering what exactly consumers want a product to do."[3]

Philips Electronics does a good job of understanding the ever-changing external environment. Some of the key areas that firms should monitor in the external environment are

☛ *Understanding current customers.* That is, how they buy, where they buy, what they buy, and when they buy.

☛ *Understanding what drives consumer decisions.* Successful firms know why customers buy. One study showed that

Philips Electronics is a firm that is proactive in trying to keep a step ahead of the latest environmental trends. The firm's new strategic plan focuses on "sense and simplicity."

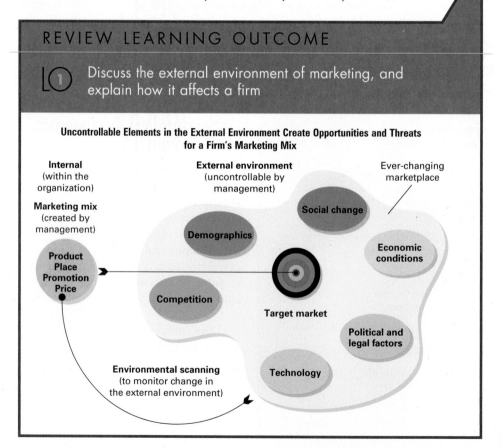

REVIEW LEARNING OUTCOME

LO 1 Discuss the external environment of marketing, and explain how it affects a firm

Uncontrollable Elements in the External Environment Create Opportunities and Threats for a Firm's Marketing Mix

Internal (within the organization)

Marketing mix (created by management)

Product Place Promotion Price

External environment (uncontrollable by management)

Ever-changing marketplace

Social change
Demographics
Economic conditions
Competition
Target market
Political and legal factors
Technology

Environmental scanning (to monitor change in the external environment)

grocery shoppers patronize 3.6 stores regularly. Why? Because distinct stores filled distinct roles in a consumer's shopping portfolio. They went to Costco for bulk items; Trader Joe's (a local chain) to find interesting and unique items; and Wal-Mart for one-stop shopping for a variety of basic goods. The local chain was losing business to niche stores to buy high-margin items like meat, seafood, and produce. Intelligence data showed that the local chain could recapture about half of these consumers by stocking more variety in organic, international foods, and signature products.[4]

☛ *Identify the most valuable customers and understand their needs.* Often 20 percent of a firm's customers produce 80 percent of the firm's revenue. An organization must understand what drives that loyalty and then take steps to ensure that those drivers are maintained and enhanced.

☛ *Understand the competition.* Successful firms know their competitors and attempt to forecast their future moves. Competitors offer both threats to a firm's market share and profitability but also may offer opportunities to our firm to capture competitors' business. During the economic downturn of 2007–2009, T.J. Maxx, the off-price retailer, noted that competitors were taking 60 to 90 days to pay their vendors. T.J. Maxx had the cash and decided to pay within 30 days. This caused the big-name fashion brands to flock to the retailer. Now, TJX, which owns T.J. Maxx, Marshalls, and HomeGoods, has a better assortment of well-known brands to sell in its stores. For the first time, T.J. Maxx is selling items like True Religion jeans for $99 (regularly $160) and Bottega Veneta sweaters for $149 (normally $750). Sales, market share, and profit are up for TJX.[5]

Environmental Management

No one business is large or powerful enough to create major change in the external environment. Thus, marketing managers are basically adapters rather than agents of change. For example, despite the huge size of firms like General Electric, Wal-Mart, Apple, and Caterpillar, they don't control social change, demographics, or other factors in the external environment.

However, just because a firm cannot fully control the external environment, it doesn't mean that it is helpless. Sometimes a firm can influence external events. For example, extensive lobbying by FedEx has enabled it to acquire virtually all of the Japanese routes that it has sought. Japan had originally opposed new cargo routes for FedEx. The favorable decision was based on months of lobbying by FedEx at the White House, at several agencies, and in Congress for help in overcoming Japanese resistance. When a company implements strategies that attempt to shape the external environment within which it operates, it is engaging in environmental management.

The factors within the external environment that are important to marketing managers can be classified as social, demographic, economic, technological, political and legal, and competitive.

SOCIAL FACTORS

Social change is perhaps the most difficult external variable for marketing managers to forecast, influence, or integrate into marketing plans. Social factors include our attitudes, values, and lifestyles. Social factors influence the products people buy, the prices paid for products, the effectiveness of specific promotions, and how, where, and when people expect to purchase products.

American Values

A *value* is a strongly held and enduring belief. During the United States' first 200 years, four basic values strongly influenced attitudes and lifestyles:

☛ *Self-sufficiency:* Every person should stand on his or her own two feet.

> **environmental management**
> When a company implements strategies that attempt to shape the external environment within which it operates.

☛ *Upward mobility:* Success would come to anyone who got an education, worked hard, and played by the rules.

☛ *Work ethic:* Hard work, dedication to family, and frugality were moral and right.

☛ *Conformity:* No one should expect to be treated differently from everybody else.

These core values still hold for a majority of Americans today. A person's values are key determinants of what is important and not important, what actions to take or not to take, and how one behaves in social situations.

People typically form values through interaction with family, friends, and other influencers such as teachers, religious leaders, and politicians. The changing environment can also play a key role in shaping one's values. For example, people born during the 1980s and 1990s tend to be more comfortable with technology and its importance in the home than persons born in the 1960s.

Values influence our buying habits. Today's consumers are demanding, inquisitive, and discriminating. No longer willing to tolerate products that break down, they are insisting on high-quality goods that save time, energy, and often calories. U.S. consumers rank the characteristics of product quality as (1) reliability, (2) durability, (3) easy maintenance, (4) ease of use, (5) a trusted brand name, and (6) a low price. Shoppers are also concerned about nutrition and want to know what's in their food, and many have environmental concerns.

Personality Traits Vary by Region[6]

Certain regional stereotypes have existed for a long time and have become clichés: the stressed and hurried New Yorker and the cool, laid-back Californian. New research, based upon 600,000 interviews, has looked at geography and personality. Even after controlling for variables such as race, income, and education levels, a state's dominant personality turns out to be strongly linked to certain outcomes. Amiable states, like Minnesota, tend to be lower in crime. Dutiful states—an eclectic bunch that includes New Mexico, North Carolina, and Utah—produce a disproportionate share of mathematicians. States that rank high in openness to new ideas are quite creative, as measured by per-capita patent production. But they're also high-crime and a bit aloof. As for high-anxiety states, that group includes not just New York and New Jersey, but also states stressed by poverty, such as West Virginia and Mississippi. As a group, these states tend to have higher rates of heart disease and lower life expectancy.

The most conscientious states were mostly in America's heartland, but also included Florida, Georgia, and North Carolina. The states highest on "openness" were along the West Coast but also included Maine. "Extraversion" was strongest in the Upper Midwest along with Georgia, Florida, and Maine. The linking of geography and personalities raises intriguing chicken-and-egg-type questions. Do states tend to nurture specific personalities because of their histories, cultures, even climates? Or do Americans, seeking kindred spirits, migrate to the states where they feel at home? Maybe both forces are at work—but in what balance? As of yet, we don't know the answer.

The Growth of Component Lifestyles

People in the United States today are piecing together component lifestyles. A lifestyle is a mode of living; it is the way people decide to live their lives. In other words, they are choosing products and services that meet diverse needs and interests rather than conforming to traditional stereotypes.

In the past, a person's profession—for instance, banker—defined his or her lifestyle. Today, a person can be a banker and also a gourmet, fitness enthusiast, dedicated single parent, and Internet guru. Each of these lifestyles is associated with different goods and services and represents a target audience. For example, for the gourmet, marketers offer cooking utensils, wines, and exotic foods through magazines such as *Bon Appétit* and *Gourmet*. The fitness enthusiast buys Adidas equipment and special jogging outfits and reads *Runner* magazine. Component lifestyles increase the complexity of consumers' buying habits. The banker may own a BMW but change the oil himself or herself. He or she may buy fast food for lunch but French wine for dinner, own sophisticated photographic equipment and a low-priced home stereo, and shop for socks at Kmart or Wal-Mart and suits or dresses at Brooks Brothers. The unique lifestyles of every consumer can require a different marketing mix.

The Changing Role of Families and Working Women

Component lifestyles have evolved because consumers can choose from a growing number of goods and services, and most have the money to exercise more options. The growth of dual-income families has resulted in increased purchasing power. Approximately 63 percent of all females between 16 and 65 years old are now in the workforce. Today, more than 10 million women-owned businesses in the United States, employing 18.2 million persons, generate $3.6 trillion in revenues.[7] The phenomenon of working women has probably had a greater effect on marketing than any other social change.

> *The growth of dual-income families has resulted in increased purchasing power.*

As women's earnings grow, so do their levels of expertise, experience, and authority. Working-age women are not the same group businesses targeted 30 years ago. They expect different things in life—from their jobs, from their spouses, and from the products and services they buy. Home improvement centers, such as Home Depot or Lowe's, know that women shoppers are vital to their success. Yet, women feel that these retailers offer an unnecessarily complex shopping process. A recent study found that women want a stress-free experience and want to feel that Lowe's and Home Depot appreciate their business. Ninety-seven percent of the women interviewed said that having one person capable of answering all of their questions was one of the most important services a home improvement retailer could provide.[8]

Single women now account for 27 percent of all first-time home buyers and 21 percent of the homebuyers overall. This is more than double the rate of 20 years ago.[9] Part of this is due to the fact that women are earning more than ever before. In big cities, such as New York, Boston, Chicago, and Dallas, women under 30 years old are earning more than their male counterparts.[10]

Single and married women are making purchase decisions and buying more products and services that were traditionally dominated by males. This has not been lost on savvy marketers, as the Customer Experience box explains.

There Is Never Enough Time

Research shows that the large percentage of people who say they never have enough time to do all that they need to do keeps inching up. It is estimated that over 80 percent of the working population is worried about having too little time.[11] With the economic downturn of 2007–2009, many stay-at-home moms are going back to work to help make ends meet. These time-constrained mothers find that they have even fewer quality hours to spend with their families.[12]

Over 31 percent of college-educated male workers are regularly working 50 or more hours a week, up from 22 percent in 1980. About 40 percent of American adults get less than seven hours of sleep on weekdays, up from 34 percent in 2001. Almost 60 percent of meals are rushed, and 34 percent of lunches are eaten on the run.[13] To manage their scarce time, about 74 percent of working adults engage in multitasking—doing

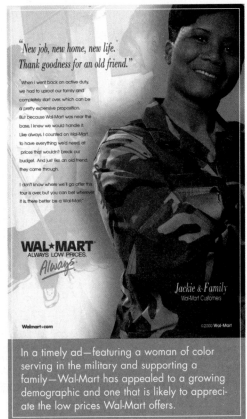

"*New job, new home, new life. Thank goodness for an old friend.*"

WAL★MART
ALWAYS LOW PRICES.
Always

Jackie & Family
Wal-Mart Customers

Walmart.com   ©2000 Wal-Mart

In a timely ad—featuring a woman of color serving in the military and supporting a family—Wal-Mart has appealed to a growing demographic and one that is likely to appreciate the low prices Wal-Mart offers.

CUSTOMER Experience

Harley-Davidson Navigates Down New Roads

Harley-Davidson Inc., based in Milwaukee, Wisconsin, is the largest motorcycle manufacturer in the United States and leads the pack in heavyweight motorcycle sales. With more than 9,000 full-time employees and more than 1,500 dealers worldwide, the century-old company sells more than $6.1 billion in motorcycles and accessories annually. A leather jacket, a weathered tan, and a rough smattering of whiskers have long been the hallmarks of a Harley-Davidson rider—but no longer. The company says the number of female Harley-Davidson owners has tripled in the past 20 years; female buyers now account for 12 percent of new Harley-Davidson purchases, up from 4 percent in 1990. For years, Harley-Davidson primarily had tailored both its product design and its marketing to a target market of 35- to 55-year-old males. Now, Harley-Davidson wants more women to move from the back of the bike onto the driver's seat. Says Leslie Prevish, Harley-Davidson's women's outreach manager: "We have marketed to women for decades and have an advertisement in our archives from 1920 that encourages women to ride, [but] we've boosted our efforts in the last five years as we've increased our overall marketing efforts to grow the sport."

The challenge for Harley-Davidson is to maintain its tough, road-tested brand identity while finding new ways to connect with female consumers—and to continue to play to its strengths rather than indulging in female stereotypes. "Women riders are diverse, so some like the black and chrome, while others prefer purples and pinks," Prevish says. "Our materials and initiatives appeal to a common personality trait of strong, independent women who enjoy taking on a challenge and feeling of adventure."

The company started by making its product more accessible to females, modifying motorcycles to fit women's smaller frames and offering an instructional manual and courses to teach women how to handle their bikes. Rider's Edge New Rider courses have become an important marketing vehicle with which Harley-Davidson can encourage women to enter the sport. "While there are some shifts in [the] emphasis of the brand as we continue to increase relevance for the women's market, we remain true to the brand," says Ken Ostermann, general manager of outreach marketing at Harley-Davidson. A financial analyst for Harley-Davidson adds, "I don't think we're going to see any pink [Harley-Davidson motorcycles] on the road.... There is a market that they're going after that is, 'I want to be free, I want to be independent, I want to be my own person,' and that person can be a guy or a girl," he says. "They don't have to add bigger mirrors so women can do their cosmetics.... They want to sell Harleys to women, and they want to sell them to women who want to ride a Harley.[15]

Do you think that targeting women will alienate its core male market? Why? Should Harley produce a motorcycle directed only to the female market?

REVIEW LEARNING OUTCOME

LO 2 Describe the social factors that affect marketing

Social Factors
- Time pressure
- Component lifestyles
- Changing role of women
- Values

more than one thing at a time.[14] They're talking on their cell phones while rushing to work or school, answering e-mails during conference calls, waking up at 4 A.M., and generally multitasking day and night.

"With Americans now spending a record-breaking 60 percent of their waking hours at work, the days of stopping by your neighbor's front porch in the afternoon to discuss current events over an iced tea are over," said Stephanie Molnar, CEO of WorkPlace Media. "These days, time-starved consumers are more likely to stop by a colleague's cubicle on their way out for an iced coffee than socialize with neighbors back at home, where household chores and family responsibilities take precedence over casual conversation."[16] On an average day (which includes all 7 days of the week), 83 percent of women and 66 percent of men spent some time doing household activities, such as housework, cooking, lawn care, or financial and other household management.[17] Recent research has found that

- With rising pump prices and busy schedules, consumers are highly likely to consolidate shopping trips, making purchases on their drive to or from work, or during their lunch break. Almost three-fourths of at-work consumers indicate they regularly or occasionally dine out or purchase groceries and beverages during the workday.

- At-work consumers research products online before purchasing, with almost half of them (47.2 percent) reporting having researched electronics online in the last 90 days during the workday before making a purchase in a store.

- Word-of-mouth is highly influential on purchases made by at-work consumers, with 95.6 percent indicating they regularly or occasionally give advice to their peers about products and services, and 92.9 percent indicating they also *seek* advice from peers before making purchases.

- Because the workplace is full of conversation among peers, it presents the perfect environment to create buzz for product introductions and new store openings. While taking a break from work, at-work consumers are likely to socialize with co-workers as 67.8 percent indicate they do so. 42.2 percent also indicate they communicate with friends and family during the workday.[18]

DEMOGRAPHIC FACTORS

Another uncontrollable variable in the external environment—also extremely important to marketing managers—is demography, the study of people's vital statistics, such as their age, race and ethnicity, and location. Demographics are significant because the basis for any market is people. Demographic characteristics are strongly related to consumer buyer behavior in the marketplace.

Population[19]

The most basic statistic of all is population because people are directly or indirectly the basis of all markets. The U.S. population is now slightly above 300 million. But it is the 400 million milestone, which the United States will reach in about 30 to 35 years, that has demographers and economists really talking. Those additional 100 million people, many of them immigrants, will replace aging baby boomers in the workforce, fill the Social Security coffers, and, in all likelihood, keep the economy vital and life interesting. But they also will further crowd cities and highways, put new strains on natural resources, end the majority status of whites, and probably widen the gulf between society's haves and have-nots.

With about 86 people per square mile nationwide now, the United States would seem to have plenty of room for more. Even after the next 100 million people are added, the United States still will have one-sixth the density of Germany, whose population is expected to stop growing within a few years. But those averages hide disparities that could prove worrying. Even as it grows, the population is increasingly concentrating in just a dozen or so states, such as Florida, Texas, North Carolina, and Colorado. North Dakota is losing population, Ohio is adding a mere 20,000 people a year, and heartland states like Kansas and Nebraska average fewer than 14 households per square mile. The economic downturn of 2007–2009 has resulted in more people staying put. The housing slump has made it harder to sell a home, so homeowners who would like to relocate will find it more difficult to do so.[20]

More than half the population lives within 50 miles of the coasts. In the next decade, an additional 25 million people—half the total population increase—will join them there. That concentration of population is likely to result in megacities of

demography
The study of people's vital statistics, such as their age, race and ethnicity, and location.

Tweens
Ages 9–14
Pop. 20 million
Spend over $21 billion/year
Heavy buying influence on parents
Biggest growth area: cell phone usage

25 million or more as people head to them for jobs. Economists predict that market forces eventually will shift some of the U.S. population back to interior states where housing is cheaper, land is more abundant, social services are less stressed, and labor is cheaper for businesses.

We turn our attention now to a closer look at age groups, their impact, and the opportunities they present for marketers. The cohorts have been given the names of tweens, Generation Y, Generation X, and baby boomers. You will find that each cohort group has its own needs, values, and consumption patterns.

Tweens

They watch cable channels designed just for them, they cruise the Net with ease, they know what they want—and often get it. They are America's tweens (today's pre- and early adolescents, ages 9 to 14), a population of more than 20 million. With attitudes, access to information, sophistication well beyond their years, and purchasing power to match, these young consumers spend over $21 billion annually. If one adds in the amount parents spend on tweens, the total spending is estimated as high as $300 billion.[21]

Tweens' styles don't reflect those of their parents. They want their own look. And parents spend about $230 per tween on back-to-school clothes to give them just that.[22] In fact, there is now a clothing line just for the girl tween called "It Chick." It Chick clothing includes sparkly tank tops, dressier tops with satin-bow detailing, and cool, retro roller-skate T-shirts. Denim skorts, leggings, and gauchos are also part of the collection. Abercrombie stores, the tween version of Abercrombie & Fitch, features loud, thumping music; blowup posters of young girls and boys; and clothing just for preteens. Clothes are not the only product area that has caught the eye of "tween marketers." Cell phone usage by tweens will be the industry's biggest growth area through 2011. This will be a financial windfall for the carriers because tweens like text messaging.[23]

Tweens overwhelmingly (92 percent) recognize television commercials for what they are—"just advertising." About three-quarters regard billboards and radio spots as paid advertising, and about half recognize promotional mediums such as product placements on television shows.[24]

What is really important to tweens? Research found the following (in order of importance): being happy, getting along with family, getting good grades, being healthy, the school he or she goes to, and being good with money. Parents of tweens had generally the same rankings, except they were much more likely than their tweens to mention "getting lots of sleep" and "eating right."[25]

Tweens are not the youngest market that is growing in importance. Pre-tweens, ages 6 to 9, are moving beyond Chuck E. Cheese. For example, every treatment chair at Peaches & Cream Spa is filled. Feet are buffed, nails meticulously polished, and shoulders massaged with hot stones as the sound of female voices fills the room with intense discussion on the issues du jour—which, at the moment, includes speculation on who among them owns the most My Little Pony toys. The clients are all pre-tweens. They are attending a "princess spa birthday party."[26]

Teens

Teens
Ages 13–19
Pop. 25 million
Spend $195 billion/year
Two-thirds go to a mall once/week.
90 percent engage in on-demand media/entertainment.

There are approximately 25 million teens in the United States, and they spend about $195 billion annually. They spend approximately 72 hours per week tuned in electronically. This includes TV, Internet, music, video games, cell phones, and text messages. Many teens participate in online social networks such as MySpace, which has 70 million unique visitors each month. Fully 68 percent of teens have created profiles on MySpace, Zanga, or Facebook.[27]

The average teen may spend 11.5 hours a week online, but not everything is more appealing to teens in an online format. When asked a series of "would you rather" questions, teens chose reality over virtual reality in many aspects of their lives. Given the choice, teens would rather have real friends (91 percent) than online friends (9 percent), date someone from school (87 percent) than someone from the Internet (13 percent), and shop in a store (82 percent) than shop online (18 percent). Even though teens prefer real stores, they do shop online (58 percent). On average, teens who make a purchase online are spending $46 per month, and 26 percent of teens are spending $50 or more. Clothes and music are the two most popular online purchases, followed by books and electronics.[28]

Recently Kohl's launched a new line of plaid skirts and printed T-shirts, but they aren't available in its 1,000 retail stores. Instead, it's selling them on Stardoll .com, a virtual community for teens and tweens where they can use "Stardollars"— purchased online at a nominal sum—to buy apparel for their online characters. Old-line retailers, including Sears, JCPenney, and Nordstrom, are enticing teens to try virtual versions of their clothes, hoping that they will buy the real thing later on. In a recent experiment, JCPenney determined that 1.5 million avatars (an icon, picture, or 3-D model or representation of a computer user in a shared virtual reality) wore its clothing in one virtual world. In the same virtual community, 5 million JCPenney outfits were tried on.[29]

For teens, shopping has become a social sport online or at the mall. Over 62 percent say that they love to shop. They patronize the big box retailers, such as Best Buy, and luxury brands, with little room for retailers in between. Teens love Armani, Gucci, and Coach. They also go to Taco Bell and drink Coke.

A few more interesting facts about teens:

- ☛ The average teen or tween earns about $30.00 per week. A substantial portion of their budget (43 percent) is spent on fashion.

- ☛ Teens are multicultural. Four in 10 children ages 5 to 9 (40 percent) are nonwhite or Hispanic, as are 38 percent of those ages 15 to 17.

- ☛ Music and entertainment are (still) critical to everyday life. Eight in 10 teens (80 percent) listen to music during their free time.

- ☛ Entertainment has to be on-demand for teens. More than 90 percent engage in on-demand media consumption.

- ☛ Life revolves around the mall. More than two-thirds of teens go to the mall at least once a week, both to shop and socialize.

- ☛ It's not all about new media. The average teen reader spends 43 minutes per day reading.[30]

Generation Y

Those designated by demographics as Generation Y were born between 1979 and 1994. They are about 73 million strong, more than three times as large as Generation X. And though Generation Y is much smaller than the baby boom, which lasted nearly 20 years and produced 78 million children, its members are plentiful enough to put their own footprints on society. Most Gen Yers are the children of baby boomers and hence are also referred to as "echo boomers," or the "millennial generation."

They already spend nearly $200 billion annually and over their lifetimes will likely spend about $10 trillion. Some have already started their careers and are making major purchasing decisions such as cars and homes; at the very least, they are buying lots of computers, MP3 players, cell phones, DVDs, and sneakers.

Researchers have found Gen Yers to be

- ☛ *Impatient:* Gen Y has grown up in a world that's always been automated, and they've had access to computers, CD-ROMs, the Internet, DVD players, chat rooms, instant messaging, and the like, for as long as they can remember, so it's no surprise that they expect things to be done *now*.

Gen Y
Born between
1979–1994
Pop. 73 million
Spend $200 billion/
year
Family-oriented, time
managers
Most ethnically
diverse generation

© RUBBERBALL/JUPITERIMAGES

Generation Y
People born between 1979 and 1994.

Gen X
Born between 1965–1978
Pop. 40 million
65 percent report no retail brand loyalty.
Want reliability and authenticity

☛ *Family-oriented*: Unlike Gen X before them, overall Gen Yers had relatively stable childhoods. They also grew up in a very family-focused time when even big companies strived to become more family- and kid-friendly. It's the generation that inspired spin-off stores like babyGap and the makeover of Las Vegas into a family vacation destination.

☛ *Inquisitive*: Knowing more than their parents about computers and technology has always been a source of pride for the echo boomers. It's led to a natural inquisitiveness that many still possess. They want to know why things happen, how things work, and what they can do next.

☛ *Opinionated*: From the time they were children, Gen Yers have been encouraged by their parents, teachers, and other authority figures to share their opinions. That's translated to a group who feel that their opinions are always needed and welcomed.

☛ *Diverse*: This is the most ethnically diverse generation the nation has ever seen, and many don't identify themselves as being only one race. Consequently, they're much more accepting overall of people who are different from themselves.

☛ *Time managers*: Their entire lives have been scheduled—from playgroups to soccer camp to Little League. So, it's no surprise that they've picked up a knack for planning along the way.

☛ *"Street Smart"*: The term isn't used in the literal sense, but simply means that these young people have seen a lot. With the Internet and 24-hour cable TV news exposing them to recounts of violence, war, and sexuality at a young age, they're not easily shocked. They're much more aware of the world around them than earlier generations were.[31]

☛ *Connected*: Fifty-four percent use social networking sites like MySpace or Facebook; 44 percent have created profiles featuring photos, hobbies, and interests.[32]

Gen Yers care about the environment. They will often seek out "green" products. They also look to brands for information about the environment. In the case of Honest Tea, many applauded the brand's decision to go to plastic after it was explained via its packaging that less fuel is used to ship plastic than the heavier glass bottles. The favorite green brands of Gen Yers are Whole Foods, Trader Joe's, Toyota, Honda, and Google.[33]

Generation X

Generation X—people born between 1965 and 1978—consists of 40 million consumers. It was the first generation of latchkey children—products of dual-career households or, in roughly half of the cases, of divorced or separated parents. Gen Xers have been bombarded by multiple media since their cradle days; thus, they are savvy and cynical consumers.

Gen Xers, now in their 30s and 40s, are reaching the age where they are sending their kids off to college. Gen Xers tend to be more protective and involved with their kids than were the baby boomer generation. They highly value the importance of education. Sixty-three percent say they began planning for their kids' college education in elementary school or earlier.[34]

Although Gen Xers are buying homes and spending money to decorate and renovate them, most companies still ignore them, focusing instead on the larger demographic groups—baby boomers and Gen Y. However, some furniture retailers, such as Williams-Sonoma's Pottery Barn and Crate & Barrel, target Gen Xers who want to mix and match different styles. Ethan Allen is now attracting Gen Xers with its new TV ads. Williams-Sonoma also appeals to more Gen Xers with West Elm, its newer furniture concept, which offers edgier designs and lower prices than those found at Pottery Barn.

Gen Xers are avid buyers of the latest clothes, technology, and recreational products. Now that they have advanced in the corporate world, they are demanding certain values from the retailers that they patronize. Gen Xers want frankness, client service, reliability, and authenticity. If retailers aren't true to their word, they quickly lose their Gen X customer.[35]

Gen Xers are careful shoppers when it comes to home furnishings. Some 31 percent of Gen Xers polled said they checked at least four stores before buying, and 65 percent held no loyalty to any retail brand (only 13 percent did) while 41 percent said they'd shop at any store "that had a good deal." Asked what furniture brands come immediately to mind, the largest bloc of respondents (35 percent) said "none," and 70 percent cited brand as the least important factor in buying.[36]

Researchers have found that a male Gen X traveler is more likely than a boomer to pick a hotel with a sports bar. But the pub must be genuine and the workout room cutting edge. So, Holiday Inn Select is adding Sporting News Grill restaurants and Fitness by Nautilus workout centers to its offerings. In-room amenities will include Wolfgang Puck coffee, Moen showerheads, and Garden Botanika bath products.

A study of over 5,000 Gen Xers in 17 countries determined that their favorite brands were Google (88 percent), Sony (76 percent), Nokia (69 percent), and BMW (66 percent).[37] Why does tailoring the merchandise to particular age groups matter? One reason is that each generation enters a life stage with its own tastes and biases, and tailoring products to what customers value is key to sales.

Baby Boomers—America's Mass Market

When Vespa motor scooters came puttering back into the U.S. market in 2000 after a 15-year absence, managers at the Italian company figured their biggest customers would be twentysomethings looking for a cheap way to get around. But executives at Piaggio, Vespa's parent company, noticed something odd as they scootered back and forth to their Manhattan offices: The most enthusiastic sidewalk gawkers were often aging baby boomers who remembered the candy-colored bikes from their youth. It turns out that boomers have lost none of their affection for Vespa. Better yet, now they can afford to buy top-of-the-line models with all the trimmings. Much to the company's surprise, consumers age 50 and older now buy a quarter of the scooters Vespa sells in the United States. In fact, the average U.S. head of household is now nearly 50 years old (49.5 years).[38] More than 80 percent of the growth in the number of households between 2008 and 2013 will be among those headed by people 55 and older.[39] The oldest region of the country is New England, and the youngest is the West Coast. Diversity drives a lower average age of a region.

There are 77 million baby boomers (persons born between 1946 and 1964), making them the largest demographic segment in the population today. The oldest have already turned 60. With average life expectancy at an all-time high of 77.4 years, more and more Americans over 50 consider middle age a new start on life. Fewer than 20 percent say they expect to stop work altogether as they age. Of those who plan to keep working at least part-time, 67 percent said they'll do so to stay mentally active, and 57 percent said to stay physically active. People now in their 50s may well work longer than any previous generation.[40] The economic downturn of 2007–2009 has resulted in baby boomers' savings and housing values declining very rapidly. As a result, boomers are postponing retirement. It is estimated that boomers lost over $2 trillion in the 2008 stock market meltdown.[41] Only 23 percent of persons over 55 years old have more than $250,000 in savings and investment.[42]

Many marketers believe that consumers' brand preferences are locked in by age 40. That might have been true for previous generations, but today's over-50 crowd is just as likely, and in some cases more likely, as everyone else to try different brands within a product category. According to Yankelovich, Inc., 33 percent of consumers older than 50 agree that it's "risky" to buy an unfamiliar brand. That's less than the 36 percent of respondents aged 16 to 34 and only a little more than the 30 percent of people aged 35 to 49 who agree with that notion.[43] In some categories such as cosmetics and electronics, older consumers are even more willing to brand-hop than younger ones.

Baby Boomers
Born between 1946–1964
Pop. 77 million
Fewer than 20 percent expect to stop working.
Heavily rely on word-of-mouth promotion
Account for 60 percent spent on consumer goods

baby boomers
People born between 1946 and 1964.

Procter & Gamble's Cover Girl brand, which depends on women older than 55 for about 20 percent of its sales, has just launched its first line of makeup aimed at older women. The name of the product, Advanced Radiance Age-Defying makeup, hints that advancing age can be pretty. And although ads still show a stunningly gorgeous face, that face belongs to an older woman—55-year-old former supermodel Christie Brinkley.

Baby boomers are not a monolithic group. A recent lifestyle study divided this huge market into four segments:

☛ *"Looking for balance" boomers:* About one-quarter of boomers (27 percent) fall into this very active and busy segment. They represent an excellent market for companies that can offer them time-saving products and services. Though money is important, saving time is equally important to this segment. Companies engaged in travel-related businesses and food-service businesses will find key opportunities here.

☛ *"Confident and living well" boomers:* Confident and living well boomers represent 23 percent of all boomers. They have the highest incomes of all the segments and relish the chance to be the first to purchase a new product or service. They are technologically oriented and care about what is stylish and trendy. They are the most active boomers, and travel is one of their favorite interests. Marketers offering luxury goods and services will find prime boomer prospects here.

☛ *"At ease" boomers:* At ease boomers represent 31 percent of all boomers. They are at peace with themselves and do not worry about the future, job security, or financial security. They express the least interest in luxury goods and services and don't travel much. They are the most home-centric and family-oriented segment of the boomers. Marketers of traditional household products and services will find this group of boomers most receptive to their offerings. New products and innovations are least likely to appeal to this group. Established and trusted brand names will resonate most strongly with this boomer segment.

☛ *"Overwhelmed" boomers:* As the smallest segment of the boomer population, overwhelmed boomers represent less than 20 percent of boomers. This group has the lowest income of all the segments. They worry about the future and their financial security. This segment is also the least active, and health is a big concern for them. They are also the least social boomers, spending little time with family and friends. These boomers are also far less accepting of technology and are well below average on using electronic, digital, and tech products.[44]

Baby boomers, because of the sheer size of the market segment, account for 60 percent of all shopping dollars spent on consumer packaged goods.[45] Baby boomers are also heavily involved in word-of-mouth promotion. When fellow boomers ask them for advice on products and services, 89 percent of them deliver it. And they are likely to seek such a recommendation approximately 90 times per year. Moreover, 93 percent of baby boomers trust their friends for information.[46] Nevertheless, marketers spend countless hours trying to create promotional messages that will resonate with boomers. Here are a few examples:

☛ *Connecting with boomers' sense of themselves as trailblazers.* At every stage of their lives, boomers have challenged the status quo. Brands that convey a totally new benefit will appeal to boomers' inherent desire to break from the norm. American Express's Ameriprise financial services division expresses it well: "You changed everything that came before you. That was you then … that's still you now."

☛ *Focusing on their lives, not their ages.* Boomers don't need to be reminded of how old they are getting. Rather than stressing their age, Centrum Silver uses advertising to reflect older consumers' passion to continue doing the things they love.

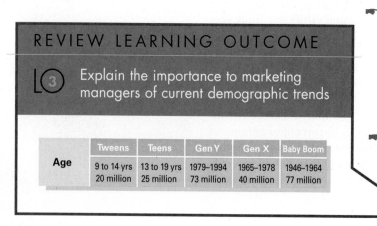

REVIEW LEARNING OUTCOME

LO 3 Explain the importance to marketing managers of current demographic trends

Age	Tweens	Teens	Gen Y	Gen X	Baby Boom
	9 to 14 yrs	13 to 19 yrs	1979–1994	1965–1978	1946–1964
	20 million	25 million	73 million	40 million	77 million

- *Linking the brand with a major life event.* Bayer Aspirin's "Do More" effort builds an emotional bond by telling the story of someone who "had a heart attack and lived"; that's why the person is committed to Bayer.

- *Knowing that boomers are jaded students of ads.* Boomers are idealists, but they grew up with TV ads and are skeptical of empty promises. The Dove campaign that shows real-looking women instead of models is not just relatable; it preempts boomers' suspicions about exaggerated beauty claims.[47]

LO 4

GROWING ETHNIC MARKETS

The minority population of the United States in 2008 reached 101 million. About one in three U.S. residents is a minority. To put this into perspective, there are more minorities here today than there were people in the United States in 1910. In fact, the minority population in the United States is larger than the total population of all but 11 countries.[48] Whites will comprise less than half of the U.S. population by 2042.[49]

The Asian population will continue to increase because of immigration and higher birthrates, and the non-Hispanic black population will increase mostly because of higher birthrates. In 2050 the share of the black population will have increased by one percentage point to 14 percent; Asians will rise to about 9 percent from 5 percent today.[50] But it is the Hispanic population that is driving minority growth. The total U.S. population is projected to grow to 439 million by 2050, and most of that growth will come from Hispanics (see Exhibit 4.1). By 2050 about one in three U.S. residents will be Hispanic. While immigration continues to be a driver of the growing Hispanic population, for the past several years most of the growth has come from births.[51]

Four states and the District of Columbia (68 percent) are majority-minority. The states are Hawaii (75 percent), New Mexico (57 percent), California (57 percent), and Texas (52 percent).[52] Counties around Denver, Las Vegas, and Orlando will all have majority-minorities by 2010.

In 2009, Hispanics wielded more than $1 trillion in spending power, an increase of 345 percent since 1990. In that same year, African Americans' spending topped $921 billion, and Asian Americans' spending power soared over 400 percent since 1990, to $526 billion—far outpacing total U.S. growth in buying power.[53]

Companies across the United States have recognized that diversity can result in bottom-line benefits. More than ever, diversity is emerging as a priority goal for visionary leaders who embrace the incontestable fact that the United States is becoming a truly multicultural society. Smart marketers increasingly are reaching out and tapping these growing markets. Recently, Pepsi attributed one percentage point of its 7.4 percent revenue growth, or about $250 million, to new products inspired by diversity efforts. Those products included guacamole-flavored Doritos chips and Gatorade Xtremo, aimed at Hispanics, and Mountain Dew Code Red, which tends to appeal to African Americans.[54]

Marketing to Hispanic Americans

The term *Hispanic* encompasses people of many different backgrounds. Nearly 60 percent of Hispanic Americans are of Mexican descent. The next largest group, Puerto Ricans, makes up just under 10 percent of Hispanics. Other groups, including Central Americans, Dominicans, South Americans, and Cubans, each account for less than 5 percent of all Hispanics.

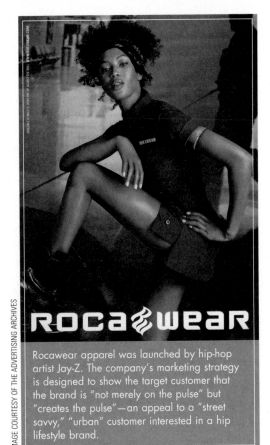

IMAGE COURTESY OF THE ADVERTISING ARCHIVES

Rocawear apparel was launched by hip-hop artist Jay-Z. The company's marketing strategy is designed to show the target customer that the brand is "not merely on the pulse" but "creates the pulse"—an appeal to a "street savvy," "urban" customer interested in a hip lifestyle brand.

EXHIBIT 4.1

U.S. Population by Race

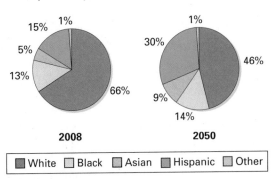

2008: 15%, 1%, 5%, 13%, 66%
2050: 30%, 1%, 46%, 9%, 14%

■ White □ Black ■ Asian ■ Hispanic □ Other

Source: U.S. Census Bureau.

The diversity of the Hispanic population and the language differences create many challenges for those trying to target this market. Hispanics, especially recent immigrants, often prefer products from their native country. Therefore, many retailers along the southern U.S. border import goods from Mexico. In New York City, more than 6,000 *bodegas* (grocery stores) sell such items as plantains, chorizo (pork sausage), and religious candles to Puerto Rican Americans. The *bodegas* also serve as neighborhood social centers. Fresh produce is usually very important to Hispanics because of the tradition of shopping every day at open-air produce markets in their native country.

In general, Hispanics tend to be very brand loyal, but they often are not aware of many mainstream U.S. brands. Instead, many Hispanics are loyal to the brands found in their homeland. If these are not available, Hispanics will choose brands that reflect their native values and culture. This preference for brands from home has helped Mexico's Jarritos become one of the fastest-growing soft drinks in the United States. Yet until recently it was *una marca desapareciendo*—a dying brand. Despite having name recognition in its homeland that rivaled that of Coca-Cola, the 55-year-old soda was losing ground to imported U.S. rivals. So parent company Novamex boldly crossed the border. In the past few years, it has moved onto the competition's turf with marketing that speaks to Mexican Americans' thirst for the good old days. Today, Jarritos's 11 flavors are sold in more than 50,000 U.S. outlets.[55]

Wal-Mart has been the largest retailer in Mexico since 2000. But until recently, it has taken a low-key approach to targeting Hispanics in the United States. Now the world's largest retailer is stepping up efforts to attract America's fastest-growing immigrant group. In 2004, Wal-Mart began printing its monthly ad circulars in English and Spanish. It also launched its own Hispanic magazine, called *Viviendo* (Living), which it distributes free at 1,300 stores heavily shopped by Hispanics. The glossy quarterly magazine features profiles of Latino leaders and celebrities next to ads highlighting Wal-Mart's expanding line of products and services geared toward Hispanics.

In another move, Wal-Mart recently teamed up with Sprint to offer a new prepaid wireless service expressly targeted to Hispanics. Wal-Mart is also stocking a line of bathroom and tabletop accessories from New York restaurateur and cookbook author Zarela Martinez, whose designs are inspired by Mexican folk art and culture. And Wal-Mart's three-year-old financial-services department offers cut-rate fees on money wire transfers, a big lure for immigrants who support family back home.[56]

Sprint recently teamed up with Juanes, a popular Columbian rocker. Sprint will sponsor concerts and provide the technological backdrop for mobile music and video, and a series of "mobisodes" featuring an exclusive behind-the-scenes look at the recording of his music video. Purchases of a Sprint Power Vision phone get a virtual backstage pass.[57] The campaign features in-store promotions in major Hispanic markets.

About 68 percent of U.S. Hispanics have home Internet access, and 42 percent shop online.[58] Hispanics who use the Internet are, on average, much younger than the general online population. Sixty-three percent of Hispanics who have Internet access use the Web to look for information, rather than to play games or hang out in chat rooms, versus 52 percent of the general population.[59] Kraft Foods has realized that the Net is a good way to connect with Hispanics. The company launched **www.comidakraft .com**, where Hispanics can share or post their recipes online, through what's called the Recipe Connection. The Recipe Connection page encourages Hispanic consumers to submit a favorite recipe containing at least one Kraft food product, "perhaps one that has been passed down in your family or an original creation from your own kitchen." Many of the recipes later appear in the magazine, *comida y familia*, a Spanish-language recipe index published by Kraft.

Marketers have found that simply having TV programs in Spanish is not sufficient to attract the target market. It must also be meaningful to their culture. Previously, MTV en Español was just that—traditional MTV in Spanish. The program today is called MTV Tr3s, which is bilingual (subtitles appear in Spanish when English is spoken) and features shows like *Quiero Mis Quinces*, about *quinceañera* (15th birthday) parties, and *Pimpeando*, about car culture.

Marketing to African Americans

Many firms are creating new and different products for the African American market. Often entrepreneurial African Americans are the first to realize unique product opportunities. For example, when Yla Eason couldn't find an African American superhero doll to buy for her son, she founded Olmec Corporation. Now this New York–based toy manufacturer is a $2 million company, marketing more than 60 kinds of African American and Hispanic dolls. Eason has a distribution partnership with Hasbro.

Several companies owned by African Americans—such as Soft Sheen, M&M Johnson, and ProLine—target the African American market for health and beauty aids. Huge corporations like Revlon, Gillette, and Alberto-Culver have either divisions or major product lines for this market as well. Alberto-Culver's hair-care line for this segment includes 75 products. In fact, hair-care items are the largest single category in the African American health and beauty aid industry. Maybelline with its Shades of You product line has the largest share (28 percent) of the African American health and beauty aid market.

Allstate has been targeting black consumers for several decades. Each year it spends more of its advertising budget to reach the African American market. Allstate offers *The Black Enterprise African American Travel Guide* and gives away Allstate-branded hand fans, extolling Allstate's aid to black families, at churches with predominantly black congregations. The African American twist Allstate adds to its "You're in good hands . . ." tagline is the connotation, "Only Allstate respects you enough to give you the insurance experience you truly deserve."[60]

There are few differences between African American and non-African American households when it comes to shopping at grocery, mass merchandisers (JCPenney, Sears), and warehouse club stores. A much larger proportion of African American consumers shop at convenience-oriented formats such as drug, dollar, and convenience/gas stores. Nearly half (46 percent) of African American households shop at beauty supply stores—almost three times the rate for non–African American households. Automotive supply stores and electronic stores follow beauty stores as the most popular alternative channels for African American consumers.[61]

African American consumers create a wide range of possibilities for marketers in various industries:

☛ *Food and Beverage:* 3.9 million black consumers spend $150 or more per week on groceries.

☛ *Health and Fitness:* 7.6 million African Americans said they exercise regularly at home, which opens up possibilities for marketers of exercise equipment.

☛ *Clothing:* African American men and women represent 22 percent and 26 percent of all suit-buyers, respectively.[62]

Black media continue to offer advertisers access to African American consumers, who nevertheless also share many of the mainstream media preferences of other American viewers and readers:

☛ Television is a top source of media consumption, with 4 in 10 households containing 4 or more televisions.

☛ Spending on magazines is 6 percent more than the national average.

☛ Radio and newspapers are less popular than the average.

☛ Internet use was 41 percent in 2008; by 2012, penetration in the African American community is expected to reach 62 percent.[63]

The promotional dollars spent on African Americans continue to rise, as does the number of black media choices. BET, the black cable TV network, has over 80 million viewers. The 40-year-old *Essence* magazine reaches one-third of all black females ages 18 to 49. But radio holds a special appeal. African Americans spend considerable time with radio (an astounding 4 hours a day versus 2.8 hours for other groups), and urban audiences have an intensely personal relationship with the medium. ABC Radio Network's Tom Joyner reaches an audience of more than 8 million in 115 markets, and Doug Banks is heard by 1.5 million listeners in 36 markets. Pepsi used radio to raise the level of Mountain Dew awareness and its market share in urban markets. Artists like Busta Rhymes personify the image of Mountain Dew and create the lyrics and the vibe that sells the product.

Coca-Cola recently used the TV program *American Idol* to target black consumers. The new ads, titled "Timeline," feature a series of milestones in black history complemented by images that illustrate the progression of the Coca-Cola contour bottle over time. "'Timeline' pays respect to the many incredible contributions that African Americans have made to culture, science, and community," said Anne Sempowski Ward, assistant vice president, African American Marketing, Coca-Cola North America. "This special salute honors the past and inspires optimism for the future, and reminds people that Coca-Cola was there to celebrate these landmark achievements."[64]

The election of President Obama has given hope and motivation to several generations of African Americans. Young people are realizing that hard work and good education can create opportunities once thought not possible. Recent research shows that more African Americans than ever before are achieving the American dream. In 2009, there were 2.4 million African Americans earning more than $75,000 annually.[65] Some of the characteristics of this group are

- ☛ Affluent African Americans most often read the newspapers *The New York Times* and *The Wall Street Journal*, as well as the magazines *BusinessWeek*, *Newsweek*, *Jet*, and *The Economist*.

- ☛ 50 percent go out for fine dining, and more than 25 percent go to clubs/bars at least once a week.

- ☛ More than 20 percent go clothes shopping at least once a week. Men focus their fashion spending on career wear, casual wear, and shoes, while women spend on purses and shoes.

- ☛ 75 percent shop in higher-end, specialty department stores, and 66 percent shop in traditional department stores. Outlets and "last chance" stores also are popular destinations, suggesting that even affluent shoppers look for bargains.

- ☛ More than 10 percent travel on business at least once a week and about one quarter shop during business travel.

- ☛ More than 70 percent have a passport and have used it on international travel in the past year. About one-third travel internationally at least three times a year and one-tenth travel internationally at least every other month.

- ☛ While more than 60 percent have gym or fitness center memberships and one-third have home gyms, nearly 40 percent wish they were doing more to stay fit.[66]

Marketing to Asian Americans

Asian Americans, who represent only 4.2 percent of the U.S. population, have the highest average family income of all groups. At $66,500, it exceeds the average U.S. household income by more than $10,000. Forty-eight percent of all Asian Americans have at least a bachelor's degree.[67]

Because Asian Americans are younger, better educated, and have higher incomes than average, they are sometimes called a "marketer's dream." Not only is their purchasing power expected to grow, but as a group, Asian Americans are more comfortable with technology than the general population is. They are far more likely to use automated teller machines, and many more of them own the latest electronic gear, such as the iPhone. Of those Asian Americans who use the Internet, 52 percent bank online.[68]

A number of products have been developed specifically for the Asian American market. For example, Kayla Beverly Hills salon draws Asian American consumers because the firm offers cosmetics formulated for them. Anheuser-Busch's agricultural products division targets the Asian American market with eight varieties of California-grown rice, each with a different label, to cover a range of nationalities and tastes.

Cultural diversity within the Asian American market complicates promotional efforts. Some of the major cultural differences among key groups of Asian Americans are the following:

☛ CHINESE

    Largest Asian American segment

    Four distinct geographic areas in Chinese category: Taiwan, Hong Kong, People's Republic of China, and Southeast Asia

    Two major dialects: Mandarin and Cantonese

    May be cautious in personal and business dealings

    Tend to be price-conscious

    Embrace idea of planning for long term

    Strong emphasis on family and education

☛ FILIPINO

    Second-largest Asian American segment

    High rate of U.S. acculturation due to English competency

    Heritage/cultural values that are similar to Hispanic culture

    Strong sense of family and community preservation

    Highly religious (predominately Roman Catholic)

☛ ASIAN INDIAN

    Third-largest Asian American segment

    Speak many different languages, and come from a variety of Indian cultural and religious backgrounds

    National heritage, culture, and values very important

    Extreme emphasis on education

    Highly price-/value-conscious

    Very loyal to strong brands

    Respond best to advertising in English, with Indian national cultural values woven in seamlessly

☛ VIETNAMESE

    Fourth-largest Asian American segment

    Large number of immigrants were refugees

    Quality-conscious and value seekers

    Strong political beliefs

    Extremely strong tendency for cultural and community preservation

    Strong emphasis on family and education

☛ KOREAN

    Fifth-largest Asian American segment

    Most homogeneous of top Asian subgroups, with the majority of Korean Americans coming from similar socioeconomic backgrounds in Korea

    Most likely of all Asian American segments to have immigrated as complete family units

    May be more emotional in decision making

    Prefer name brands to lower prices

    Strong emphasis on family and education

☛ JAPANESE

    Sixth-largest Asian American segment

    Highest percentage of U.S.-born individuals of any Asian American segment (due to waves of immigration dating back to the mid-1800s)

A critical mass of Japanese temporary residents in the United States, to establish a subculture; includes students, temporary workers and trainees, and expatriate business families

Tend to value group consensus over individual opinion

Value name brands over price

Strong emphasis on family and education[69]

Although Asian Americans embrace the values of the larger U.S. population, they also hold on to the cultural values of their particular subgroup. Consider language. Many Asian Americans, particularly Koreans and Chinese, speak their native tongue at home. Filipinos are far less likely to do so. Cultural values are also apparent in the ways different groups make big-ticket purchases. In Japanese American homes, the husband alone makes the decision on such purchases nearly half the time; the wife decides only about 6 percent of the time. In Filipino families, however, wives make these decisions a little more often than their husbands do, although by far the most decisions are made by husbands and wives jointly or with the input of other family members.[70]

Asian Americans like to shop at stores owned and managed by other Asian Americans. Small businesses such as flower shops, grocery stores, and appliance stores are often best equipped to offer the products that Asian Americans want. For example, at first glance the Ha Nam supermarket in Los Angeles's Koreatown might be any other grocery store. But next to the Kraft American singles and the State Fair corn dogs are jars of whole cabbage kimchi. A snack bar in another part of the store cooks up aromatic mung cakes, and an entire aisle is devoted to dried seafood.

One American food product held in high esteem in Asia is Hormel's canned meat product, Spam (no, not what you receive in your e-mail inbox). In South Korea, wedding couples are said to have a long and prosperous life if they receive a wedding pack of Spam. In Hawaii, Spam is sold at McDonald's restaurants, and travel agents send tours packed with Hawaiian residents on annual pilgrimages to the Spam Museum in Austin, Minnesota.[71]

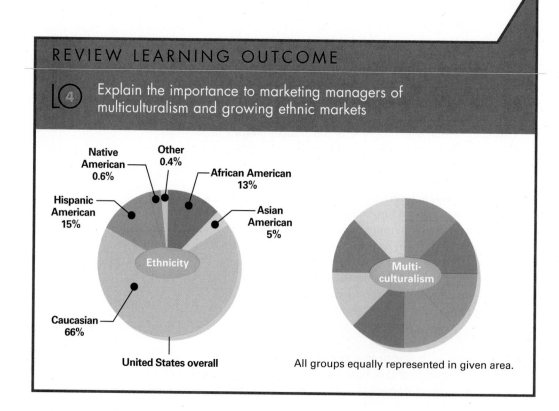

REVIEW LEARNING OUTCOME

LO 4 Explain the importance to marketing managers of multiculturalism and growing ethnic markets

Native American 0.6%
Other 0.4%
African American 13%
Hispanic American 15%
Asian American 5%
Ethnicity
Caucasian 66%
United States overall

Multi-culturalism
All groups equally represented in given area.

Ethnic and Cultural Diversity

Multiculturalism occurs when all major ethnic groups in an area—such as a city, county, or census tract—are roughly equally represented. Because of its current demographic transition, the trend in the United States is toward greater multiculturalism.

San Francisco County is the most diverse county in the nation. The proportions of major ethnic groups are closer to being equal there than anywhere else. People of many ancestries have long been attracted to the area. Elsewhere, however, a careful examination of the statistics from the latest U.S. Census Bureau reveals that the nation's minority groups, especially Hispanics and Asians, are heavily clustered in selected regions and markets. Rather than witnessing the formation of a homogeneous national melting pot, we are seeing the creation of numerous mini-melting pots, while the rest of America remains much less diverse.

In a broad swath of the country, the minority presence is still quite limited. America's racial and ethnic patterns have taken on distinctly regional dimensions. Hispanics dominate large portions of counties in a span of states stretching from California to Texas. Blacks are strongly represented in counties of the South as well as selected urban areas in the Northeast and Midwest. The Asian presence is relatively small and highly concentrated in a few scattered counties, largely in the West. And Native Americans are concentrated in select pockets in Oklahoma, the Southeast, the upper Midwest, and the West. Multiethnic counties are most prominent in California and the Southwest, with mixes of Asians and Hispanics, or Hispanics and Native Americans.

ECONOMIC FACTORS

In addition to social and demographic factors, marketing managers must understand and react to the economic environment. The three economic areas of greatest concern to most marketers are consumers' incomes, inflation, and recession.

Consumers' Incomes

As disposable (or after-tax) incomes rise, more families and individuals can afford the "good life." In recent years, however, U.S. incomes have risen at a rather slow pace. After adjustment for inflation, the median household income in the United States in 2008 was projected to be approximately $49,000. This means half of all U.S. households earned less and the other half earned more.[72]

Education is the primary determinant of a person's earning potential. For example, only 1 percent of those with only a high school education earn over $100,000 annually. By comparison, 13 percent of college-educated workers earn six figures or more.[73] Along with "willingness to buy," or "ability to buy," income is a key determinant of target markets. A marketer who knows where the money is knows where the markets are. If you are seeking a new store location for Dollar General, a retail chain that caters to lower-income consumers, you would probably concentrate on the South and Midwest because most households with annual incomes of less than $45,000 are concentrated in these areas.

The U.S. Census Bureau normally deals in very big numbers; for example, the richest 1 percent of the households (719,910 of them) have an average annual income of $364,657.[74] Sometimes, however, the Census Bureau puts the U.S. economy under a microscope. Here are a few key findings from the most current census:

☛ In ranking larger American cities, the Census Bureau found San Jose, California, and Plano, Texas, had the highest median incomes, at around $71,000, while Miami and Cleveland had the lowest, with median incomes below $25,000.

multiculturalism
When all major ethnic groups in an area—such as a city, county, or census tract—are roughly equally represented.

purchasing power
A comparison of income versus the relative cost of a set standard of goods and services in different geographic areas.

inflation
A measure of the decrease in the value of money, expressed as the percentage reduction in value since the previous year.

☛ Cleveland also had the highest poverty rate for big cities at 32.4 percent, followed closely by Detroit, two cities suffering from the downturn in the American automobile industry and manufacturing.

☛ Camden, New Jersey, a city struggling with crime, had a poverty rate of 44 percent, the highest number among small to midsize cities—but so, too, did College Station, Texas, home of Texas A&M University.

☛ Among counties with populations of more than 250,000, the three where the households had the highest median incomes were in suburban Washington, D.C.—Loudoun and Fairfax counties in Virginia and Howard County in Maryland.

☛ The ratio of single men to single women between ages 15 and 44 was highest in Nevada (120.2 per 100 women), North Dakota (120.1) and Alaska (118.9). It was lowest in the District of Columbia (93.4).[75]

Purchasing Power

Rising incomes don't necessarily mean a higher standard of living. Increased standards of living are a function of purchasing power. Purchasing power is measured by comparing income to the relative cost of a set standard of goods and services in different geographic areas, usually referred to as the cost of living. Another way to think of purchasing power is income minus the cost of living (i.e., expenses). In general, a cost of living index takes into account housing, food and groceries, transportation, utilities, health care, and miscellaneous expenses such as clothing, services, and entertainment. Homefair's salary calculator uses these metrics when it figures that the cost of living in New York City is almost three times the cost of living in Youngstown, Ohio. This means that a worker living in New York must earn nearly $279,500 to have the same standard of living as someone making $100,000 in Youngstown.

When income is high relative to the cost of living, people have more discretionary income. That means they have more money to spend on nonessential items (in other words, on wants rather than needs). This information is important to marketers for obvious reasons. Consumers with high purchasing power can afford to spend more money without jeopardizing their budget for necessities, like food, housing, and utilities. They also have the ability to purchase higher-priced necessities, for example, a more expensive car, a home in a more expensive neighborhood, or a designer handbag versus a purse from a discount store.

Inflation

Inflation is a measure of the decrease in the value of money, generally expressed as the percentage reduction in value since the previous year, which is the rate of inflation. Thus, in simple terms, an inflation rate of 5 percent means you will need 5 percent more units of money than you would have needed last year to buy the same basket of products. If inflation is 5 percent, you can expect that, on average, prices have risen by about 5 percent since the previous year. Of course, if pay raises are matching the rate of inflation, then employees will be no worse off in terms of the immediate purchasing power of their salaries.

In times of low inflation, businesses seeking to increase their profit margins can do so only by increasing their efficiency. If they significantly increase prices, no one will purchase their goods or services.

From November 2006 until November 2008, prices rose 7.8 percent. Wages and benefits did not rise as much as prices; therefore, real purchasing power fell.[76] In more inflationary times, marketers use a number of pricing strategies to cope. But in general, marketers must be aware that inflation causes consumers to either build up or diminish their brand loyalty. In one research session, a consumer panelist noted, "I used to use just Betty Crocker mixes, but now I think of either Betty Crocker or

Research

The United States excels at both basic and applied research. Basic research (or *pure research*) attempts to expand the frontiers of knowledge but is not aimed at a specific, pragmatic problem. Basic research aims to confirm an existing theory or to learn more about a concept or phenomenon. For example, basic research might focus on high-energy physics. Applied research, in contrast, attempts to develop new or improved products. The United States has dramatically improved its track record in applied research. For example, the United States leads the world in applying basic research to aircraft design and propulsion systems.

Rather than invention for the sake of invention, many firms are turning to the marketing concept to guide their research. To give its scientists guidance, Dow first interviews customers to find out their wants and needs. A wish list of products and/or technical characteristics helps the scientists create inventions with market value. Dow recently created a fiber called XLA after learning that apparel makers wanted a "soft stretch" fiber with a natural feel. Dow thinks that the product might deliver sales of $300 million within ten years.

Although developing new technology internally is a key to creating and maintaining a long-term competitive advantage, external technology is also important to managers for two reasons. First, by acquiring the technology, the firm may be able to operate more efficiently or create a better product. Second, a new technology may render your existing products obsolete.

An example of operating more efficiently by using external technology is UPS. Not so long ago, UPS drivers worked off maps, 3 × 5 note cards, and their own memory to figure out the best way to run their routes. That changed when UPS began to implement a $600 million route optimization system—think MapQuest on steroids—that each evening maps out the next day's schedule for the majority of its 56,000 drivers. So sophisticated is the software that it designs each route to minimize the number of left turns, thus reducing the time and gas that drivers waste idling at stoplights. The latest wrinkle: a new feature that, with the aid of global positioning system technology, warns drivers with a beep if they pull into the wrong driveway. It also enables UPS to send a driver more quickly after you call in a pickup because dispatchers know exactly which driver is closest. UPS now offers package-flow technology to launch a service that allows customers to reroute a package in transit to a different address.[82]

> **basic research**
> Pure research that aims to confirm an existing theory or to learn more about a concept or phenomenon.
>
> **applied research**
> An attempt to develop new or improved products.

Global Innovation

Microsoft spent $80 million to open an Advanced Technology Center outside Beijing, China. With nearly 500 engineers, PhD students, and visiting professors, it is one of Microsoft's most important facilities for developing graphics, handwriting-recognition, and voice-synthesizing technologies. The technology center illustrates how innovation is increasingly becoming a global process conducted at worldwide research and development operations. Like Microsoft, IBM has facilities around the world including major labs in China, Israel, Switzerland, Japan, and India.

General Electric has become a leader in wind energy technology by tapping into a global network. The technology for GE's new wind turbines comes from the following countries:

☞ *United States:* The main research center in Niskayuna, New York, handles basic research, while other centers in New York, Pennsylvania, South Carolina, California, and Virginia tackle other design and engineering aspects.

REVIEW LEARNING OUTCOME

LO 6 Identify the impact of technology on a firm

Basic Research → Applied Research → Technological Advances → Marketing Mix

- *Canada*: Engineers at GE Consumer & Industrial in Peterborough, Ontario, provided the manufacturing technology for the generator.
- *India*: Researchers at Bangalore have crafted a series of analytical models and turbine system design tools that affect the entire turbine.
- *China*: Researchers in Shanghai are in charge of the turbine simulator to test new products and conduct high-end tests for variable-speed power electronics.
- *Germany*: The lead experts on the gearbox work at GE Wind operations in Salzbergen. Researchers in Munich design sensors and monitor advanced controls.[83]

Innovation Carries to the Bottom Line

Innovation pays off big for creative organizations. One study found that the most innovative firms have an average profit margin growth of 3 percent higher than the typical firm.[84] Other research has found higher stock market returns among firms that spend heavily on research and development.[85] Each year, respected business journals pay tribute to the most innovative companies around the globe. *BusinessWeek's* rankings are shown in Exhibit 4.3.

EXHIBIT 4.3

The World's Most Innovative Companies

Ranking 1—Apple: Apple is a master of product and store design. Now that it's invading the cell-phone market, will it continue its winning streak?

Ranking 2—Google: It didn't invent search advertising, but lifted it to its current heights. Google's famously chaotic innovation process has plunged it into everything from radio ads to online office software.

Ranking 3—Toyota Motor: Toyota's dominance in hybrids could lead to the first plug-in electric auto. Now the No. 1 carmaker, its continuous improvement process is copied worldwide.

Ranking 4—General Electric: CEO Jeff Immelt's push for "imagination breakthroughs," or growth opportunities of $50 million to $100 million, are increasingly leading GE into emerging markets and "green" technology.

Ranking 5—Microsoft: To some, Microsoft is more fast follower than leading innovator. Still, the software giant's massive R&D budget generates creations that help ensure the popularity of Windows and Office.

Ranking 6—Procter & Gamble: After years of scouting for new products outside its walls, P&G has mapped the innovation strengths of global regions. CEO A.G. Lafley is pushing for more disruptive new ideas.

Ranking 7—3M: The legendary Post-it Note is just one of 3M's many creations, which include everything from dental fillings to roofing shingles. Next on its list: diagnostic tests for infectious diseases.

Ranking 8—Walt Disney: CEO Bob Iger is refueling Disney's creative culture. Moves such as putting ABC shows on iTunes and acquiring Pixar helped move Disney up.

Ranking 9—IBM: The tech services behemoth held an online brainstorm with 150,000 people to dream up new ideas. It hosts annual symposia with outsiders to collaborate on forecasting.

Ranking 10—Sony: This traditional tech hardware maker is devoting more resources to software. To turn its PlayStation 3 console from living-room box into virtual gateway, it created a 3-D online world.

Ranking 11—Wal-Mart Stores: Wal-Mart is struggling with growth, but its "green" actions, such as using its leverage as the world's largest retailer to cut suppliers' packaging waste, helped it make the top 20.

Ranking 12—Honda Motor: Headed by a former R&D chief, Honda has been known for its fuel-efficient cars. But its environmental approach isn't limited to autos. Next up: solar panels and a fuel-sipping jet.

Ranking 13—Nokia: To build sales in emerging markets, managers spend time in the homes of local customers. This has led to features for illiterate users such as an icon-driven handset directory.

Ranking 14—Starbucks: The coffee chain's 50-person R&D group created eight new flavors in one year. It also started its own music label and partnered with outsiders to publish books and produce movies.

Ranking 15—Target: Target stands out from its discount rivals by selling designer-inspired products. Innovative marketing, such as buying all the ads in one issue of *The New Yorker*, has also set it apart.

Ranking 16—BMW: BMW is flat, flexible, and fast-reacting. Employees are urged to "break the rules" to cut costs or push through winning ideas, such as the Z4 coupe, which higher-ups initially nixed.

Ranking 17—Samsung Electronics: Samsung stays ahead with intensive investment in new facilities and production systems. These days, it's focusing on the convergence of technologies and phone features.

Ranking 18—Virgin Group: Most of its businesses, such as credit card or mobile virtual networks, are collaborative; Virgin supplies the branding and customer service while partners put up much of the cash.

Ranking 19—Intel: The world's largest chipmaker, Intel is making a big headway in selling to the health-care market. It recently previewed its most powerful chip to date and is planning a $2.5 billion plant in China.

Ranking 20—Amazon: The online retailer is now innovating its business model, turning its backroom operations into a digital utility that rents out computer power and warehouse space to other firms.

Source: Reprinted from the May 14, 2007, issue of *BusinessWeek* by special permission, copyright © 2007 by The McGraw-Hill Companies, Inc.

ETHICS in Marketing

Maybe Technology Can Save the Planet: But Should It?

Recently, a private company proposed "fertilizing" parts of the ocean with iron, in hopes of encouraging carbon-absorbing blooms of plankton. Meanwhile, researchers elsewhere are talking about injecting chemicals into the atmosphere, launching sun-reflecting mirrors into stationary orbit above the Earth, or taking other steps to reset the thermostat of a warming planet. This technology might be useful, even lifesaving. But it would inevitably produce environmental effects impossible to predict and impossible to undo. So a growing number of experts say it is time for broad discussion of how and by whom it should be used, or if it should be tried at all.

Similar questions are being raised about nanotechnology, robotics, and other powerful emerging technologies. There are even those who suggest humanity should collectively decide to turn away from some new technologies as inherently dangerous. "The complexity of newly engineered systems, coupled with their potential impact on lives, the environment, etc., raise a set of ethical issues that engineers had not been thinking about," said William Wulf, a computer scientist.

When scientists and engineers discuss geoengineering, it is obvious they are talking about technologies with the potential to change the planet. But the issue of engineering ethics applies as well to technologies whose planet-altering potential may not emerge until it is too late. Ronald Arkin, a computer scientist that advises the U.S. Army on robotic weapons, says robotics researchers should consider not just how to make robots more capable, but also who must bear responsibility for their actions and how much human operators should remain "in the loop," particularly with machines to aid soldiers on the battlefield or the disabled in their homes. Paul Thompson, a philosopher at Michigan State and former secretary of the International Society for Environmental Ethics, said many scientists were trained to limit themselves to questions answerable in the real world, in the belief that "scientists and engineers should not be involved in these kinds of ethical questions."[86]

New technology involves many "unknown unknowns." These factors will not become obvious until the technology is put into widespread use. Should government step in and block new technology with many "unknown unknowns?" If you were going to block one technology, which one mentioned above would it be? Why?

While innovation can raise productivity and make the world a better place to live, is applying new technology always the right thing to do? We explore this issue in the Ethics in Marketing box above.

POLITICAL AND LEGAL FACTORS

Business needs government regulation to protect innovators of new technology, the interests of society in general, one business from another, and consumers. In turn, government needs business because the marketplace generates taxes that support public efforts to educate our youth, pave our roads, protect our shores, and so on. The private sector also serves as a counterweight to government. The decentralization of power inherent in a private-enterprise system supplies the limitation on government essential for the survival of a democracy.

Every aspect of the marketing mix is subject to laws and restrictions. It is the duty of marketing managers or their legal assistants to understand these laws and conform to them because failure to comply with regulations can have major consequences for a firm. Sometimes just sensing trends and taking corrective action before a government agency acts can help avoid regulation. The tobacco industry failed to do this. As a result, Joe Camel and the Marlboro Man are fading into the sunset in the United States along with other strategies used to promote tobacco products.

The challenge is not simply to keep the marketing department out of trouble, however, but to help it implement creative new programs to accomplish marketing objectives. It is all too easy for a marketing manager or sometimes a lawyer to say "no" to a marketing innovation that actually entails little risk. For example, an overly cautious lawyer could hold up sales of a desirable new product by warning that the package design could prompt a copyright infringement suit. Thus, it is important to have a thorough understanding of the laws established by the federal government, state governments, and regulatory agencies to govern marketing-related issues.

Federal Legislation

Federal laws that affect marketing fall into several categories. First, the Sherman Act, the Clayton Act, the Federal Trade Commission Act, the Celler-Kefauver Antimerger Act, and the Hart-Scott-Rodino Act were passed to regulate the competitive environment. Second, the Robinson-Patman Act was designed to regulate pricing practices. Third, the Wheeler-Lea Act was created to control false advertising. The Lanham Act protects trademarks. These key pieces of legislation are summarized in Exhibit 4.4. The primary federal laws that protect consumers are shown in Exhibit 4.5.

EXHIBIT 4.4

Primary U.S. Laws That Affect Marketing

Legislation	Impact On Marketing
Sherman Act of 1890	Makes trusts and conspiracies in restraint of trade illegal; makes monopolies and attempts to monopolize a misdemeanor.
Clayton Act of 1914	Outlaws discrimination in prices to different buyers; prohibits tying contracts (which require the buyer of one product to also buy another item in the line); makes illegal the combining of two or more competing corporations by pooling ownership of stock.
Federal Trade Commission Act of 1914	Created the Federal Trade Commission to deal with antitrust matters; outlaws unfair methods of competition.
Robinson-Patman Act of 1936	Prohibits charging different prices to different buyers of merchandise of like grade and quantity; requires sellers to make any supplementary services or allowances available to all purchasers on a proportionately equal basis.
Wheeler-Lea Amendments to FTC Act of 1938	Broadens the Federal Trade Commission's power to prohibit practices that might injure the public without affecting competition; outlaws false and deceptive advertising.
Lanham Act of 1946	Establishes protection for trademarks.
Celler-Kefauver Antimerger Act of 1950	Strengthens the Clayton Act to prevent corporate acquisitions that reduce competition.
Hart-Scott-Rodino Act of 1976	Requires large companies to notify the government of their intent to merge.

EXHIBIT 4.5

Primary U.S. Laws Protecting Consumers

Legislation	Impact On Marketing
Federal Food and Drug Act of 1906	Prohibits adulteration and misbranding of foods and drugs involved in interstate commerce; strengthened by the Food, Drug, and Cosmetic Act (1938) and the Kefauver-Harris Drug Amendment (1962).
Federal Hazardous Substances Act of 1960	Requires warning labels on hazardous household chemicals.
Kefauver-Harris Drug Amendment of 1962	Requires that manufacturers conduct tests to prove drug effectiveness and safety.
Consumer Credit Protection Act of 1968	Requires that lenders fully disclose true interest rates and all other charges to credit customers for loans and installment purchases.
Child Protection and Toy Safety Act of 1969	Prevents marketing of products so dangerous that adequate safety warnings cannot be given.
Public Health Smoking Act of 1970	Prohibits cigarette advertising on TV and radio and revises the health hazard warning on cigarette packages.
Poison Prevention Labeling Act of 1970	Requires safety packaging for products that may be harmful to children.
National Environmental Policy Act of 1970	Established the Environmental Protection Agency to deal with various types of pollution and organizations that create pollution.
Public Health Cigarette Smoking Act of 1971	Prohibits tobacco advertising on radio and television.
Consumer Product Safety Act of 1972	Created the Consumer Product Safety Commission, which has authority to specify safety standards for most products.
Child Protection Act of 1990	Regulates the number of minutes of advertising on children's television.
Children's Online Privacy Protection Act of 1998	Empowers the FTC to set rules regarding how and when marketers must obtain parental permission before asking children marketing research questions.
Aviation Security Act of 2001	Requires airlines to take extra security measures to protect passengers, including the installation of stronger cockpit doors, improved baggage screening, and increased security training for airport personnel.
Homeland Security Act of 2002	Protects consumers against terrorist acts. Created the Department of Homeland Security.
Do Not Call Law of 2003	Protects consumers against unwanted telemarketing calls.
CAN-SPAM Act of 2003	Protects consumers against unwanted e-mail, or spam.

State Laws

Legislation that affects marketing varies state by state. Oregon, for example, limits utility advertising to 0.5 percent of the company's net income. California has forced industry to improve consumer products and has enacted legislation to lower the energy consumption of refrigerators, freezers, and air conditioners. Several states, including New Mexico and Kansas, are considering levying a tax on all in-state commercial advertising.

Many states and cities are attempting to fight obesity by regulating fast-food chains and other restaurants. California has passed a law banning trans fats in restaurants and bakeries. New York City chain restaurants must now display calorie counts on menus. Boston has now banned trans fats in restaurants. And the list goes on.

Regulatory Agencies

Although some state regulatory bodies actively pursue violators of their marketing statutes, federal regulators generally have the greatest clout. The Consumer Product Safety Commission, the Federal Trade Commission, and the Food and Drug Administration are the three federal agencies most directly and actively involved in marketing affairs. These agencies, plus others, are discussed throughout the book, but a brief introduction is in order at this point.

The sole purpose of the Consumer Product Safety Commission (CPSC) is to protect the health and safety of consumers in and around their homes. The CPSC has the power to set mandatory safety standards for almost all products that consumers use (about 15,000 items). The CPSC consists of a five-member committee and about 400 staff members, including technicians, lawyers, and administrative help. The commission can fine offending firms up to $500,000 and sentence their officers to up to a year in prison. It can also ban dangerous products from the marketplace. The CPSC oversees about 400 recalls per year. The CPSC operates under rules that prohibit staff from publicizing information about product complaints until the manufacturer OK's the release. Besides handing over a lot of control to companies, this process routinely delays public disclosure of hazards. It has also been suggested that the CPSC is extremely underfunded.[87]

The Federal Trade Commission (FTC) also consists of five members, each holding office for seven years. The FTC is empowered to prevent persons or corporations from using unfair methods of competition in commerce. It is authorized to investigate the practices of business combinations and to conduct hearings on antitrust matters and deceptive advertising. The FTC has a vast array of regulatory powers (see Exhibit 4.6). Nevertheless, it is not invincible. For example, the FTC had proposed to ban all advertising to children under age 8, to ban all advertising of the sugared products that are most likely to cause tooth decay to children under age 12, and to require the food industry to pay for dental health and nutritional advertisements. Business reacted by lobbying to reduce the FTC's power. The two-year lobbying effort resulted in passage of the FTC Improvement Act of 1980. The major provisions of the act are as follows:

- ☛ It bans the use of unfairness as a standard for industry-wide rules against advertising. All the proposals concerning children's advertising were therefore suspended, because they were based almost entirely on the unfairness standard.

- ☛ It requires oversight hearings on the FTC every six months. This congressional review is designed to keep the commission accountable. Moreover, it keeps Congress aware of one of the many regulatory agencies it has created and is responsible for monitoring.

Businesses rarely band together to create change in the legal environment as they did to pass the FTC Improvement Act. Generally, marketing managers react only to legislation, regulation, and edicts. It is usually less costly to stay attuned to the regulatory environment than to fight the government. If marketers had toned down their hard-hitting advertisements to children, they might have avoided an FTC inquiry altogether. The FTC also regulates advertising on the Internet as well as Internet abuses of consumer privacy. The Food and Drug Administration (FDA), another powerful agency, is charged with enforcing regulations against selling and distributing adulterated, misbranded, or hazardous food and drug products. In the last decade it took a very aggressive stance against tobacco products and is now paying attention to the fast-food industry.

The Battle Over Consumer Privacy

The popularity of the Internet for direct marketing, for collecting consumer data, and as a repository for sensitive consumer data has alarmed privacy-minded consumers. So

EXHIBIT 4.6

Powers of the Federal Trade Commission

Remedy	Procedure
Cease-and-Desist Order	A final order is issued to cease an illegal practice—and is often challenged in the courts.
Consent Decree	A business consents to stop the questionable practice without admitting its illegality.
Affirmative Disclosure	An advertiser is required to provide additional information about products in advertisements.
Corrective Advertising	An advertiser is required to correct the past effects of misleading advertising. (For example, 25 percent of a firm's media budget must be spent on FTC-approved advertisements or FTC-specified advertising.)
Restitution	Refunds are required to be given to consumers misled by deceptive advertising. According to a 1975 court-of-appeals decision, this remedy cannot be used except for practices carried out after the issuance of a cease-and-desist order.
Counteradvertising	The FTC proposed that the Federal Communications Commission permit advertisements in broadcast media to counteract advertising claims (also that free time be provided under certain conditions).

many online users have complained about "spam," the Internet's equivalent of junk mail, that the U.S. Congress passed the CAN-SPAM Act in an attempt to regulate it. The act, which took effect on January 1, 2004, does not totally ban spam, but it does prohibit commercial e-mailers from using a false address and presenting false or misleading information. It also requires commercial e-mailers to provide a way for recipients to "opt out" of receiving further e-mail from the sender. A person opting out cannot be required to pay a fee or provide any other personally identifying information other than an email address.[88]

Another problem is that Web surfers, including children who are using the Internet, are routinely asked to divulge personal information in order to access certain screens or purchase goods or services online. Internet users who once felt fairly anonymous when using the Web are now disturbed by the amount of information marketers collect on them and their children as they visit various sites in cyberspace.

Most consumers are unaware of how technology is used to collect personal data or how the personal information is used and distributed after it is collected. The government actively sells huge amounts of personal information to list compilers. State motor vehicle bureaus sell names and addresses of individuals who get driver's licenses. Hospitals sell the names of women who just gave birth on their premises. Consumer credit databases, developed and maintained by large providers such as Equifax Marketing Services and TransUnion, are often used by credit card marketers to pre-screen targets for solicitations.

Although privacy policies for companies in the United States are largely voluntary and there are almost no regulations on the collection and use of personal data, collecting consumer data outside the United States is a different matter. Database marketers venturing into new data territories must carefully navigate foreign privacy laws. The European Union's *European Data Protection Directive*, for instance, states that any business that trades with a European organization must comply with the EU's rules for handling information about individuals or risk prosecution. This directive prohibits the export of personal data to countries not doing enough to protect privacy, in particular, the United States.

More than 50 nations have, or are developing, privacy legislation. Europe has the strictest legislation regarding the collection and use of consumer data, and other countries look to that legislation when formulating their policies. Australia, for instance, recently introduced legislation that would require private companies

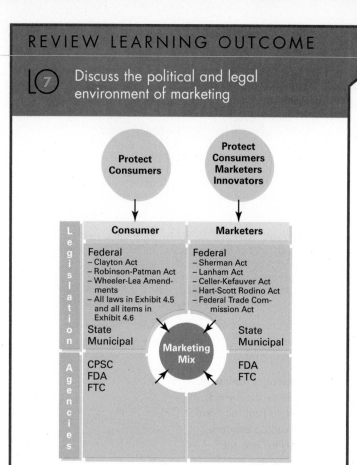

to follow a set of guidelines regarding the collection, storage, use, and transfer of personal information about individuals. Common privacy rules include obtaining data fairly and lawfully, using the information only for the original purpose specified, making sure it is accurate and up-to-date, and destroying data after the purpose for collection is completed. The EU requires that consumers be presented with an opt-out provision at the point of data collection.

Despite cries from consumer and advocacy groups for privacy legislation, to date Congress has failed to act. So far, only the states have enacted meaningful protections, with California in the lead. Now, more than 30 states have adopted laws that require notification if a customer's personal information has been improperly exposed. In 2007, The TJX Companies, which owns Marshalls, T.J. Maxx, HomeGoods, and A.J. Wright, reported that customers' credit and debit card information, along with some driver's license data, had been lifted from its computer system. When asked how many people were affected, a spokesperson for TJX replied, "substantially less than millions."[89] Others put the number of persons exposed at 45 million.[90]

Identity Theft People are right to be concerned about their personal information. Identity theft costs $55 billion per year. One company that has come under fire is ChoicePoint. Since spinning off from the credit bureau Equifax in 1997, it has been buying up databases and data-mining operations. Businesses, individuals, and even the FBI now rely on its storehouse. But its customers have also included Nigerian scammers who apparently used the data to steal people's identities.

In 1998, Congress passed the Identity Theft and Assumption Deterrence Act. This law prohibits knowingly transferring or using another person's identification with the intent to commit an unlawful activity, such as theft of funds. Guilty parties face up to 15 years in prison.

Governmental Actions Three other key laws (one a state law) have been passed to protect consumers from identity theft. The federal laws are:

- *Gramm-Leach-Bliley Act (Financial Services Modernization Act):* This act is aimed at financial companies. It requires those corporations to tell their customers how they use their personal information and to have policies that prevent fraudulent access to it. Partial compliance has been required since 2001.

- *Health Insurance Portability and Accountability Act:* This law is aimed at the healthcare industry. It limits disclosure of individuals' medical information and imposes penalties on organizations that violate privacy rules. Compliance has been required for large companies since 2003.

The state law is

- *California's Notice of Security Breach Law:* If any company or agency that has collected personal information about a California resident discovers that non-encrypted information has been taken by an unauthorized person, the company or agency must tell the resident. Compliance has been required since 2003. (Some 30 other states are considering similar laws.)

COMPETITIVE FACTORS

The competitive environment encompasses the number of competitors a firm must face, the relative size of the competitors, and the degree of interdependence within the industry. Management has little control over the competitive environment confronting a firm.

Competition for Market Share and Profits

As U.S. population growth slows, global competition increases, costs rise, and available resources tighten, firms find that they must work harder to maintain their profits and market share regardless of the form of the competitive market. Take, for example, something as basic as facial tissues. Both Kimberly-Clark and Procter & Gamble go head-to-head in this $1 billion market. Kimberly-Clark is marketing its new, 3-ply tissue as the company's biggest innovation for Kleenex Facial Tissues in four decades. The new Kleenex Facial Tissue with Lotion is softer and 17 percent stronger than its predecessor, the company claims. For P&G, it is the addition of shea butter, a moisturizer, to its Puffs Plus line of lotion tissues, plus new box designs for three of its primary Puffs products. Lotion tissues make up about 20 percent of the facial tissue category and have grown 7 percent between 2006 and 2008.[91]

Kimberly-Clark could use a boost for its Kleenex brand, which saw sales decline 5.9 percent to $495 million in 2008. P&G, meanwhile, saw its Puffs product grow 3.2 percent to $258 million, thanks in large part to its Puffs Plus tissues with lotion, aloe, and vitamin E. Puffs Plus grew 14.7 percent to $136 million.[92] The tissue battle is one of millions that goes on every day in the American marketplace.

American aircraft manufacturer Boeing still faces competition from European company Airbus, even though Airbus recently lost its edge in that $50 billion market. Airbus has been beset with problems, while Boeing's new 787 Dreamliner gave the company a much needed lift. Marketers tout the Dreamliner's features, which include large windows, mood lighting, electronic shades, wider seats and aisles, and a state-of-the-art climate control system, as providing a unique flying experience. By 2007, Boeing had sold over 500 Dreamliners, whereas the huge Airbus A350 lagged far behind. Both Boeing and Airbus have experienced delivery problems. Boeing's difficulties have been due to parts availability and a machinist strike. Airbus has experienced management and logistics problems.

Global Competition

Boeing is a very savvy international competitor conducting business throughout the world. Many foreign competitors also consider the United States to be a ripe target market. Thus, a U.S. marketing manager can no longer focus only on domestic competitors. In automobiles, textiles, watches, televisions, steel, and many other areas, foreign competition has been strong. In the past, foreign firms penetrated U.S. markets by concentrating on price, but today the emphasis has switched to product quality. Nestlé, Sony, Rolls-Royce, and Sandoz Pharmaceuticals are noted for quality, not cheap prices.

For a century, vacuuming has been synonymous with one brand, whose iconic status is such that the British and French still refer to "hoovering the carpet."

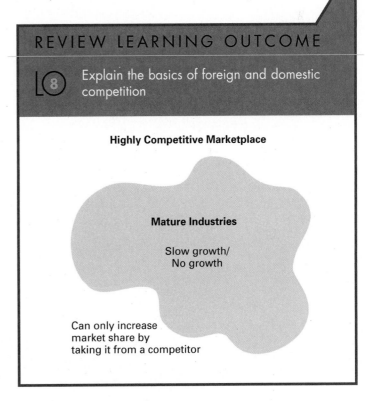

REVIEW LEARNING OUTCOME

LO 8 Explain the basics of foreign and domestic competition

Highly Competitive Marketplace

Mature Industries

Slow growth/ No growth

Can only increase market share by taking it from a competitor

But two years after launching his bagless cleaners in the United States, English inventor James Dyson's company now makes America's best-selling vacuum. Dyson has captured 21 percent of the U.S. market, leaving Canton, Ohio–based Hoover with 16 percent. Dyson's clean sweep is all the more surprising given that his product goes for $399 to $550 while an average vacuum costs $150.[93]

Not all global competitors that enter the U.S. market are successful at taking market share from American firms. In 2004, DHL entered the U.S. market determined to take market share from UPS and FedEx. DHL entered the market by purchasing Airborne, a package delivery service with a weak ground network. When DHL came into the market, it began with a mutlimillion-dollar promotion campaign. The campaign brought DHL a rush of business that it wasn't prepared to handle. As a result, DHL developed a reputation for poor service. To save money, DHL closed one of its two U.S. hubs in 2005 and shifted all traffic to its Wilmington, Ohio, hub. The transition was not smooth, resulting in long delays causing customers to defect to rivals. In late fall 2008, DHL announced that it was stopping domestic deliveries and cutting 9,500 jobs.[94]

Global competition is discussed in much more detail in Chapter 5.

6 ◀ components of the external marketing environment

$21 ◀ billion spent by tweens in 2008

percent of adult Americans who get less than 7 hours of sleep each night ▶ **40**

56,000 ◀ drivers at UPS

maximum fine the CPSC can issue for violations ▼

$500,000

REVIEW AND APPLICATIONS

Discuss the external environment of marketing and explain how it affects a firm. The external marketing environment consists of social, demographic, economic, technological, political and legal, and competitive variables. Marketers generally cannot control the elements of the external environment. Instead, they must understand how the external environment is changing and the impact of that change on the target market. Then marketing managers can create a marketing mix to effectively meet the needs of target customers.

1.1   What is the purpose of environmental scanning? Give an example.

1.2   Form six teams and make each one responsible for one of the uncontrollable elements in the marketing environment. Your boss, the company president, has asked each team to provide one-year and five-year forecasts of the major trends the firm will face. The firm is in the telecommunications equipment industry. It has no plans to become a telecommunications service provider like, for example, Verizon and AT&T. Each team should use the library, the Internet, and other data sources to make its forecasts. Each team member should examine a minimum of one data source. The team members should then pool their data and prepare a recommendation. A spokesperson for each team should present the findings to the class.

Describe the social factors that affect marketing. Within the external environment, social factors are perhaps the most difficult for marketers to anticipate. Several major social trends are currently shaping marketing strategies. First, people of all ages have a broader range of interests, defying traditional consumer profiles. Second, changing gender roles are bringing more women into the workforce and increasing the number of men who shop. Third, an increase in the number of dual-career families has created demand for time-saving goods and services.

2.1   Every country has a set of core values and beliefs. These values may vary somewhat from region to region of the nation. Identify five core values for your area of the country. Clip magazine advertisements that reflect these values and bring them to class.

2.2   Give an example of component lifestyles based on someone you know.

Explain the importance to marketing managers of current demographic trends. Today, several basic demographic patterns are influencing marketing mixes. Because the U.S. population is growing at a slower rate, marketers can no longer rely on profits from generally expanding markets. Marketers are also faced with increasingly experienced consumers among the younger generations such as tweens and teens. And because the population is also growing older, marketers are offering more products that appeal to middle-aged and older consumers.

3.1   Baby boomers in America are aging. Describe how this might affect the marketing mix for the following:

   a.   Bally's Health Clubs

   b.   McDonald's

   c.   Whirlpool Corporation

   d.   The state of Florida

   e.   Target stores

3.2   You have been asked to address a local Chamber of Commerce on the subject of "Generation Y." Prepare an outline for your talk.

3.3 How should Ford Motor Company market differently to Generation Y, Generation X, and baby boomers?

Explain the importance to marketing managers of multiculturalism and growing ethnic markets. Multiculturalism occurs when all major ethnic groups in an area are roughly equally represented. Growing multiculturalism makes the marketer's task more challenging. America is not a melting pot but numerous mini-melting pots. Hispanics are the fastest-growing segment of the population followed by African Americans. Many companies are now creating departments and product lines to effectively target multicultural market segments. Companies have quickly found that ethnic markets are not homogeneous.

4.1 Go to the library and look up a minority market such as the Hispanic market. Write a memo to your boss that details the many submarkets within this segment.

4.2 Using the library and the Internet, find examples of large companies directing marketing mixes to each major ethnic group.

Identify consumer and marketer reactions to the state of the economy. In recent years, U.S. incomes have risen at a slow pace. At the same time, the financial power of women has increased, and they are making the purchasing decisions for many products in traditionally male-dominated areas. During a time of inflation, marketers generally attempt to maintain level pricing to avoid losing customer brand loyalty. During times of recession, many marketers maintain or reduce prices to counter the effects of decreased demand; they also concentrate on increasing production efficiency and improving customer service.

5.1 Explain how consumers' buying habits may change during a recessionary period.

5.2 Periods of inflation require firms to alter their marketing mix. Suppose a recent economic forecast predicts that inflation will be almost 10 percent during the next 18 months. Your company manufactures hand tools for the home gardener. Write a memo to the company president explaining how the firm may have to alter its marketing mix.

Identify the impact of technology on a firm. Monitoring new technology is essential to keeping up with competitors in today's marketing environment. The United States excels in basic research and, in recent years, has dramatically improved its track record in applied research. Without innovation, U.S. companies can't compete in global markets. Innovation is increasingly becoming a global process.

6.1 Give three examples of how technology has benefited marketers. Also, give several examples of firms that have been hurt because they did not keep up with technological changes.

Discuss the political and legal environment of marketing. All marketing activities are subject to state and federal laws and the rulings of regulatory agencies. Marketers are responsible for remaining aware of and abiding by such regulations. Some key federal laws that affect marketing are the Sherman Act, Clayton Act, Federal Trade Commission Act, Robinson-Patman Act, Wheeler-Lea Amendments to the FTC Act, Lanham Act, Celler-Kefauver Antimerger Act, and Hart-Scott-Rodino Act. Many laws, including privacy laws, have been passed to protect the consumer as well. The Consumer Product Safety Commission, the Federal Trade Commission, and the Food and Drug Administration are the three federal agencies most involved in regulating marketing activities.

7.1 The Federal Trade Commission and other governmental agencies have been both praised and criticized for their regulation of marketing activities.

To what degree do you think the government should regulate marketing? Explain your position.

7.2 Can you think of any other areas where consumer protection laws are needed?

7.3 What topics are currently receiving attention in FDA News (**www.fdanews .com**)? What effect has the attention had on market share?

Explain the basics of foreign and domestic competition. The competitive environment encompasses the number of competitors a firm must face, the relative size of the competitors, and the degree of interdependence within the industry. Declining population growth, rising costs, and shortages of resources have heightened domestic competition.

8.1 Explain how the nature of competition is changing in America.

8.2 Might there be times when a company becomes too competitive? If so, what could be the consequences?

KEY TERMS

applied research	125	environmental management	105	Generation Y	111
baby boomers	113			inflation	122
basic research	125	Federal Trade Commission (FTC)	130	multiculturalism	121
component lifestyles	106			purchasing power	122
Consumer Product Safety Commission (CPSC)	130	Food and Drug Administration (FDA)	130	recession	123
demography	109	Generation X	112	target market	103

EXERCISES

APPLICATION EXERCISE

Demographic factors play a large role in shaping the external marketing environment. One of those demographic factors is culture. The importance of cultural understanding cannot be overstated, especially in today's global marketplace and our own multicultural country. In general, Americans tend to be ethnocentric; that is, they are quick to prejudge other cultural norms as wrong (or of less significance) because they differ from American practices.

One way to be exposed to another culture is to examine the foods typical of that culture. In this exercise, you will need to work in a team to create a guide to ethnic dining in your city or area. The finished guide will be descriptive in nature; it is not meant to be a rating guide.

Activities

1. Identify ethnic dining categories for inclusion in your guide. Once you have identified categories for your area, make a list of restaurants for each category.

2. You will need to create a data collection form so that the same information is collected from each restaurant. For example, you will want to include the name, address, and phone number for each restaurant. Think of other information that would be helpful.

3. Divide up the restaurant list your team generated in Activity 1 so that each team member is responsible for collecting information from a certain number of restaurants. Consider dividing the list geographically so that each team member can visit an assortment of ethnic restaurants. If your budget allows, eat at a few of the restaurants in addition to collecting the information. After you have all the information, meet to review and compare your findings.

4. Was there a meal or type of food that you particularly liked? Disliked? Which type of ethnic restaurant seemed most foreign to you? Why do you think that was?

ETHICS EXERCISE

Gary Caplan has developed a new "energy drink" designed to burn calories while sleeping, which he intends to market to grossly overweight consumers. According the Centers for Disease Control and Prevention, 20 percent of Americans are obese. Gary's mother, a doctor, argues that it's unethical to target the obese—that they are as vulnerable a target market as much as the elderly and children.

Questions

1. Is Gary targeting a "vulnerable" market?

2. Does the AMA Statement of Ethics address this issue? Go to **www .marketingpower.com** and review the statement. Then write a brief paragraph on what it contains that relates to Gary Caplan's marketing decision.

MARKETING PLAN EXERCISE

These end-of-chapter marketing plan exercises are designed to help you use what you learned in the chapter to build a strategic marketing plan for a company of your choosing. Once you've completed the marketing plan exercise for each chapter in Part 1 of this textbook, you can complete the Part 1 Marketing Planning Worksheet on your companion Web site at **www.cengage.com/marketing/lamb.** Now continue building your strategic marketing plan that you started in Chapter 2 by completing the following exercises:

1. Describe how your company will handle privacy concerns.

2. Scan the marketing environment. Identify opportunities and threats to your chosen company in areas such as technology, the economy, the political and legal environment, and competition. Is your competition foreign, domestic, or both? Also identify opportunities and threats based on possible market targets, including social factors, demographic factors, and multicultural issues.

3. Complete your company's SWOT analysis by identifying opportunities and threats in the external marketing environment by performing environmental scanning:

   a. List the demographic, ethnic, and social trends that could impact your firm, by investigating data from the U.S. Census Bureau at **www.census.gov.**

   b. Determine which economic factors could influence the strategies of your firm by visiting the U.S. Economic and Statistics Administration at **www.esa.doc.gov** or the Bureau of Economic Analysis at **www.bea .doc.gov.**

   c. Explore **www.lawguru.com** and report on at least three political and legal factors that could influence your marketing decisions.

d.   Investigate the Web sites of federal government agencies that regulate your firm and industry and list at least six laws that regulate your business offering. The Federal Trade Commission is at **www.ftc.gov.** The Federal Communications Commission is at **www.fcc.gov.** The Food and Drug Administration is at **www.fda.gov.** The Consumer Product Safety Commission is at **www.cpsc.gov.** The Better Business Bureau is at **www.bbb.org.** The Internal Revenue Service is at **www.irs.gov.**

e.   Identify your key competitors. A simple "yellow pages" listing of firms in the same business category can start your search. For online competitors, try **www.bizrate.com.**

f.   Competition often comes from companies that are working on the same exact market as yours. That is especially true on the Internet. After you search for your direct competition, look for and think about what other companies are positioned to execute a similar business strategy for your target market. Determine if there are any players who might be able to develop technology more quickly or reach your target customers more effectively than you.

CASE STUDY: STARBUCKS

SELLING COFFEE IN THE LAND OF TEA

Starbucks has been doing business in China since 1999 when they opened their first coffee shop in Beijing. Today, hundreds of Starbucks stores sell coffee in the land of tea, including one at the Great Wall. It has become one of the most popular brands among the country's 20- to 40-year-old upwardly mobile Chinese, or "Chuppies," as they're called, but so far China accounts for only about 10 percent of Starbucks' global sales. Nevertheless, Chairman Howard Schultz believes the country will someday be the company's largest market outside North America. "The market response," he says, "has exceeded our expectations."

This may seem surprising when you consider the fact that the majority of China's one billion-plus population are tea drinkers who didn't know what coffee was until Nestlé introduced a powdered version on store shelves in the 1980s. But Starbucks is betting that it can win the new generation over by marketing its signature product as an emblem of modern China's new sophistication.

"Coffee represents the change," says Wang Jinlong, president of Starbucks Greater China. "The disposable income is concentrated on the young people, and this is the place they want to come." Success in China could depend on how well Starbucks markets itself to what Wang calls the "little emperors." China's one-child law has spawned a generation that isn't interested in collective goals, he says. Instead, they embrace the Western belief in individuality that Starbucks embodies.

After surveying Chinese consumers, Starbucks compiled a list of the top reasons they go to cafés. Surprisingly, the number one reason was "to gather with family and friends," while "to drink coffee" lagged behind at number six. Living spaces are generally small and cramped there, making places to congregate important to the Chinese.

Da Wei Sun, manager of outlets in Beijing, believes that Starbucks found success in China because it took this idea of a place to gather and gave people in the cities a "third space" beyond work and home, making it cool to have a latte and hang out. Starbucks offers more food on the Chinese menu, including duck sandwiches, moon pies, and green-tea cheesecake, than in other countries, and more seating as well. Only 20 percent of North American customers eat and drink inside the store after ordering, but the number is close to 90 percent in China.

China remains a communist country, so a change in its one-party dictatorship could potentially affect business overnight. Schultz says the key to establishing stores there is to first find local partners who understand the changing political and business landscapes. Starbucks initially entered China by authorizing local developers to use its brand and setting up joint ventures with partners.

Industry analyst Pei Liang advised that for long-term success in the country, Starbucks would need to acquire controlling stakes in its joint ventures. This, Pei explained, would strengthen management's control and put it in position to reap more of the profits as the market grew. "Licensing or holding a minority stake is an effective tool when first stepping into a new market because it involves a small investment," says Pei. "But Starbucks, the brand's owner, receives only royalty fees from the licensee."

In late 2006, Starbucks announced that it was buying out its partner in China and taking control of 60 stores. The market had changed after Beijing entered the World Trade Organization in 2001, making it easier for foreign companies to navigate alone. "Buying out one's partner is becoming more common," says industry consultant Kent D. Kedl. "Starbucks probably feels they *sic* know better how China works now so they *sic* can go it on their own."

Chairman Howard Schultz says that Starbucks will concentrate most of its future expansion efforts in China, and Kedl predicts it will see continued success there: "It's not just a drink in China. It's a destination. It's a place to be seen and a place to show how modern one is." And with China's economy continuing to grow in double digits, the number of Chuppies willing to pay $3.63 for a Mocha Frappuccino Grande is likely to grow, too.

Source: "Starbucks Targets Growing China Market," *AsiaPulse News*, 6/13/2006; Janet Adamy, "Starbucks' Task China? Winning Over Tea Drinkers," *The Seattle Times*, 11/30/2006; Jeffrey S. Harrison, "Exporting a North American Concept to Asia", *Cornell Hotel & Restaurant Quarterly*, May 2005; Craig Harris, "Starbucks Sees China as Key to Its International Growth," *Seattle Post-Intelligencer*, 10/7/2006; Dexter Roberts, "Starbucks Caffeinates Its China Growth Plan," *Business Week Online*, 10/26/2006.

Questions

1. Many of the same environmental factors, such as cultural factors, that operate in the domestic market also exist internationally. Discuss the key cultural factors Starbucks had to consider as it expanded into China.

2. Discuss the key political and legal factors Starbucks had to consider in the Chinese marketplace. What are the risks of entering a country with these factors? What changes have occurred in China's political and legal structure to the advantage of foreign companies?

3. What demographic factors were important for Starbucks to understand in China? What were the demographics they decided to target?

4. What was the initial global-market strategy Starbucks employed to enter China? Discuss the advantages and disadvantages to this early strategy. How has their strategy changed since then and why?

COMPANY CLIPS

METHOD—ENTERING A CROWDED MARKET

Companies large and small, new and old are all participants in the market, and as such, they are all subject to the forces that act on each entity in the marketplace. The same is true of method. As you've already seen in the company clips from Chapters 2 and 3, method has been attentive to the customer, analyzed the competition, focused on social change, and identified economic factors that have affected how it does and will do business. Review the company clips from Chapters 2 and 3 to hear founders Adam Lowry and Eric Ryan and CEO Alastair Dorward describe several factors in the external environment that have influenced how method entered the market and the success the company has experienced.

Questions

1. Method's founders and CEO repeatedly reference the role of competition and consumers in their assessments of their external environment. Is there a hierarchy to the environmental factors discussed in this chapter? Explain.

2. Should other companies imitate the emphasis method gives to certain factors in its external environment? Why or why not?

3. Does method's assessment of its external environment seem to be lacking anything? What?

Marketing & You Results

A high score means you have a strong perception of time limitations for work-related task completion. Research indicates that when you perceive yourself to be working under time pressure your creativity is negatively affected. As you read in Chapter 4, time is an important social factor in the external environment that affects marketing. Understanding your own perceptions and reaction to time constraints will be helpful in planning to meet the needs of the time-constrained consumer. Your challenge as a busy marketer will be to continue thinking creatively on their behalf.

Analyzing Marketing Opportunities

PART 2

WHAT'S INSIDE

Consumer Decision Making 188

Business Marketing 230

Segmenting and Targeting Markets 258

Decision Support Systems and Marketing Research 290

Consumer Decision Making

LEARNING OUTCOMES

1 Explain why marketing managers should understand consumer behavior

2 Analyze the components of the consumer decision-making process

3 Explain the consumer's postpurchase evaluation process

4 Identify the types of consumer buying decisions and discuss the significance of consumer involvement

5 Identify and understand the cultural factors that affect consumer buying decisions

6 Identify and understand the social factors that affect consumer buying decisions

7 Identify and understand the individual factors that affect consumer buying decisions

8 Identify and understand the psychological factors that affect consumer buying decisions

THE IMPORTANCE OF UNDERSTANDING CONSUMER BEHAVIOR

Consumers' product and service preferences are constantly changing. Marketing managers must understand these desires in order to create a proper marketing mix for a well-defined market. So it is critical that marketing managers have a thorough knowledge of consumer behavior. Consumer behavior describes how consumers make purchase decisions and how they use and dispose of the purchased goods or services. The study of consumer behavior also includes the factors that influence purchase decisions and product use.

Understanding how consumers make purchase decisions can help marketing managers in several ways. For example, if a manager knows through research that gas mileage is the most important attribute for a certain target market, the manufacturer can redesign a car to meet that criterion. If the firm cannot change the design in the short run, it can use promotion in an effort to change consumers' decision-making criteria, for example, by promoting style, durability, and cargo capacity.

REVIEW LEARNING OUTCOME

LO❶ Explain why marketing managers should understand consumer behavior

Consumer behavior = HOW
- consumers make purchase decisions
- consumers use and dispose of products

LO❷ THE CONSUMER DECISION-MAKING PROCESS

When buying products, particularly new or expensive items, consumers generally follow the consumer decision-making process shown in Exhibit 6.1: (1) need recognition, (2) information search, (3) evaluation of alternatives, (4) purchase, and (5) postpurchase behavior. These five steps represent a general process that can be used as a guide for studying how consumers make decisions. It is important to note, though, that consumers' decisions do not always proceed in order through all of these steps. In fact, the consumer may end the process at any time or may not even make a purchase. The section on the types of consumer buying decisions later in the chapter discusses why a consumer's progression through these steps may vary. We begin, however, by examining the basic purchase process in greater detail.

consumer behavior
Processes a consumer uses to make purchase decisions, as well as to use and dispose of purchased goods or services; also includes factors that influence purchase decisions and product use.

consumer decision-making process
A five-step process used by consumers when buying goods or services.

189

EXHIBIT 6.1

Consumer Decision-Making
Process

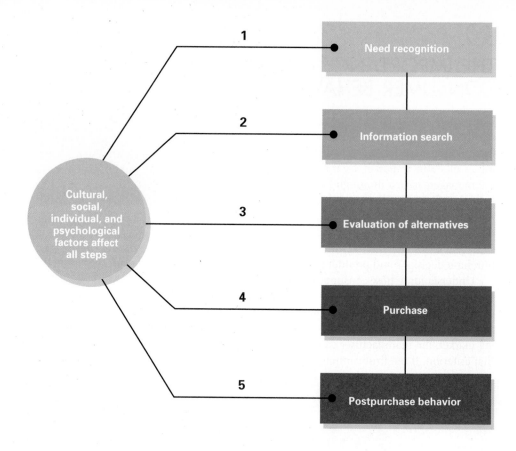

1 Need recognition

2 Information search

3 Evaluation of alternatives

4 Purchase

5 Postpurchase behavior

Cultural, social, individual, and psychological factors affect all steps

need recognition
Result of an imbalance between actual and desired states.

want
The way a consumer goes about addressing a need.

stimulus
Any unit of input affecting one or more of the five senses: sight, smell, taste, touch, hearing.

Need Recognition

The first stage in the consumer decision-making process is need recognition. Need recognition occurs when consumers are faced with an imbalance between actual and desired states that arouses and activates the consumer decision-making process. A want is the way that a consumer goes about addressing a need. For example, have you ever gotten blisters from an old running shoe? Or maybe you have seen a TV commercial for a new sports car and wanted to buy it. Need recognition is triggered when a consumer is exposed to either an internal or an external stimulus. *Internal stimuli* are occurrences you experience, such as hunger or thirst. For example, you may hear your stomach growl and then realize that you are hungry. *External stimuli* are influences from an outside source such as someone's recommendation of a new restaurant, the color of an automobile, the design of a package, a brand name mentioned by a friend, or an advertisement on television or radio.

A marketing manager's objective is to get consumers to recognize an imbalance between their present status and their preferred state. Advertising and sales promotion often provide this stimulus. Surveying buyer preferences provides marketers with information about consumer wants and needs that can be used to tailor products and services. Marketing managers can create wants on the part of the consumer. For example, when college students move in to their own apartment or dorm room, they often need to furnish it and want new furniture rather than hand-me-downs from their parents. A want can be for a specific product, or it can be for a certain attribute or feature of a product. In this example, the college students not only need home furnishings, but also want items that reflect their personal sense of style. Similarly, consumers may want ready-to-eat meals, drive-through dry-cleaning service, and Internet shopping to fill their need for convenience.

Another way marketers create new products and services to meet wants is by observing trends in the marketplace. IKEA, the home furnishing giant, watches the home decor trends and then creates affordable, trendy furniture. For example, marketers at IKEA realized that Generation Y consumers prefer furniture that is stylish, easy to clean, multifunctional, and portable. As a result, IKEA uses "bold orange, pink and green colors." The wood boasts a lacquered finish that can be wiped clean and doesn't need polish. IKEA also offers a space-saving, multifunction desk that can be converted into a dining table; it has wheels so that it can be easily moved.

Consumers recognize unfulfilled needs in various ways. The two most common occur when a current product isn't performing properly and when the consumer is about to run out of something that is generally kept on hand. Consumers may also recognize unfulfilled wants if they become aware of a product that seems superior to the one currently used. Such wants are usually created by advertising and other promotional activities. For example, aware of the popularity of MP3s and consumers' desire to take their music with them, car stereo manufacturers such as SonicBlue and Kenwood have added MP3 interfaces. Other companies, including Apple, Microsoft, RCA, and Creative Technology, are hoping to fulfill consumer desires for smaller audio and video players, referred to as portable media centers. The newest devices have wireless Internet connection capabilities providing access to downloadable movies and TV as well as music and video games. But Apple continues to lead the field with its iPod Shuffle and Nano and extensive downloadable music and TV programs.

Marketers selling their products in global markets must carefully observe the needs and wants of consumers in various regions. Unilever hit on an unrecognized need of European consumers when it introduced Persil Tablets, premeasured laundry detergent in tablet form. Though the tablets are more expensive than regular detergents, Unilever found that European consumers considered laundry a chore and wanted the process to be as simple and uncomplicated as possible. Unilever launched the tablets as a less messy and more convenient alternative. The laundry tablets were an immediate success in the United Kingdom and enabled Unilever's Persil brand to beat out rival Procter & Gamble's best-selling Ariel powder detergent.[1]

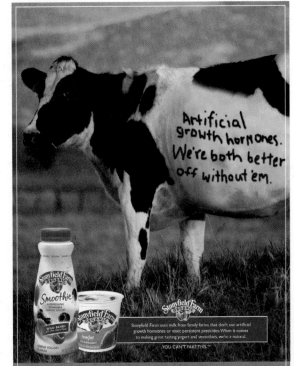

Unlike nonmarketing-controlled information, which is neutral, marketing-controlled information is biased toward a specific product. This ad from Stonyfield Farm might be doing double duty—attempting to build bias for hormone-free Stonyfield products and against its possibly growth-hormone-using competitors' products.

Information Search

After recognizing a need or want, consumers search for information about the various alternatives available to satisfy it. For example, as gasoline prices increase, many people are searching for information on vehicles that use alternatives to gasoline, such as Honda's hybrid models. An information search can occur internally, externally, or both. In an internal information search, the person recalls information stored in the memory. This stored information stems largely from previous experience with a product. For example, while traveling with your family, you encounter a hotel where you stayed during spring break earlier that year. By searching your memory, you can probably remember whether the hotel had clean rooms and friendly service.

In contrast, an external information search seeks information in the outside environment. There are two basic types of external information sources: nonmarketing controlled and marketing controlled. A nonmarketing-controlled information source is not associated with marketers promoting a product. These information sources include personal experiences (trying or observing a new product); personal sources (family, friends, acquaintances, and coworkers who may recommend a product or service); and public sources, such as Underwriters Laboratories, *Consumer Reports*, and other rating organizations that comment on products and services. For example, if you are in the mood to go to the movies, you may search your memory for past experiences at various cinemas when determining which one to go to (personal experience). To choose which movie you will see, you may rely on the recommendation of a friend or family member (personal sources). Alternatively, you may read the critical reviews in the newspaper or online (public sources). Marketers gather information on how these information sources

internal information search
The process of recalling past information stored in the memory.

external information search
The process of seeking information in the outside environment.

nonmarketing-controlled information source
A product information source that is not associated with advertising or promotion.

marketing-controlled
information source
A product information source that
originates with marketers promoting
the product.

work and use it to attract customers. For example, car manufacturers know that younger customers are likely to get information from friends and family, so they try to develop enthusiasm for their products via word of mouth.

Living in the digital age has changed the way consumers get nonmarketing-controlled information. It can be from blogs, bulletin boards, activist Web sites, Web forums, and/or consumer opinion sites like **www.consumerreview.com**, **www.triadvisor.com**, or **www.epinions.com**. The average American spends at least six hours per week online, according to many estimates. Nearly 94 percent of U.S. consumers regularly or occasionally research products online before making an offline purchase and nearly half of those consumers then share the information and advice they gleaned online with other consumers, according to Worthington, Ohio-based market research firm BIGresearch.[2]

The latest research has examined how consumers use information picked up on the Internet. For example, in Web forums the information seeker has normally never met the information provider or ever interacted with the person before. Researchers found that an information provider's response speed, the extent to which the provider's previous responses within the forum had been positively evaluated by others, and the breadth of the provider's previous responses across different but related topics affected the information seeker's judgment about the value of the information. So, for example, if other information seekers had found the provider trustworthy, then the current seeker tended to believe the information.[3]

A marketing-controlled information source is biased toward a specific product because it originates with marketers promoting that product. Marketing-controlled information sources include mass-media advertising (radio, newspaper, television, and magazine advertising), sales promotion (contests, displays, premiums, and so forth), salespeople, product labels and packaging, and the Internet. Many consumers, however, are wary of the information they receive from marketing-controlled sources, believing that most marketing campaigns stress the product's positive attributes and ignore its faults. These sentiments tend to be stronger among better educated and higher-income consumers. Some marketing-controlled information sources can shift out of marketers' control, however, when there is bad news to report. Toy maker Mattel Inc. has made headlines for its recall of toys with lead paint contamination or powerful magnets that can cause illness or even death in children who ingest them. Newspaper stories across the country, in this instance a nonmarketing-controlled information source, recounted the many toy recalls Mattel has had to make in the past. Mattel then used marketing-controlled information sources to try to combat the negative publicity. Damage control for Mattel took the form of full-page ads in *The New York Times* and *The Wall Street Journal*, as well as video coverage on its own and Yahoo's Web sites, with an apology and assurances of future safety of its products from Bob Eckert, Mattel's chairman and CEO.

The extent to which an individual conducts an external search depends on his or her perceived risk, knowledge, prior experience, and level of interest in the good or service. Generally, as the perceived risk of the purchase increases, the consumer enlarges the search and considers more alternative brands. For example, suppose that you want to purchase a surround sound system for your home stereo. The decision is relatively risky because of the expense and technical nature of the stereo system, so you are motivated to search for information about models, prices, options, compatibility with existing entertainment products, and capabilities. You may decide to compare attributes of many speaker systems because the value of the time expended finding the "right" stereo will be less than the cost of buying the wrong system.

A consumer's knowledge about the product or service will also affect the extent of an external information search. A consumer who is knowledgeable and well informed about a potential purchase is less likely to search for additional information. In addition, the more knowledgeable consumers are, the more efficiently they will conduct the search process, thereby requiring less time to search. For example, many consumers know that AirTran and other discount airlines have much lower fares, so they generally use the discounters and do not even check fares at other airlines.

The extent of a consumer's external search is also affected by confidence in one's decision-making ability. A confident consumer not only has sufficient stored information about the product, but also feels self-assured about making the right decision. People lacking this confidence will continue an information search even when they know a great deal about the product. Consumers with prior experience in buying a certain product will have less perceived risk than inexperienced consumers. Therefore, they will spend less time searching and limit the number of products that they consider.

A third factor influencing the external information search is product experience. Consumers who have had a positive prior experience with a product are more likely to limit their search to items related to the positive experience. For example, when flying, consumers are likely to choose airlines with which they have had positive experiences, such as consistent on-time arrivals. They will avoid airlines with which they had a negative experience, such as lost luggage.

Finally, the extent of the search is positively related to the amount of interest a consumer has in a product. A consumer who is more interested in a product will spend more time searching for information and alternatives. For example, suppose you are a dedicated runner who reads jogging and fitness magazines and catalogs. In searching for a new pair of running shoes, you may enjoy reading about the new brands available and spend more time and effort than other buyers in deciding on the right shoe.

The consumer's information search should yield a group of brands, sometimes called the buyer's evoked set (or consideration set), which are the consumer's most preferred alternatives. From this set, the buyer will further evaluate the alternatives and make a choice. Consumers do not consider all brands available in a product category, but they do seriously consider a much smaller set. For example, from the many brands of pizza available, consumers are likely to consider only the alternatives that fit their price range, location, take-out/delivery needs, and taste preferences. Having too many choices can, in fact, confuse consumers and cause them to delay the decision to buy or, in some instances, cause them not to buy at all.

Evaluation of Alternatives and Purchase

After getting information and constructing an evoked set of alternative products, the consumer is ready to make a decision. A consumer will use the information stored in memory and obtained from outside sources to develop a set of criteria. Recent research has shown that exposure to certain cues in your everyday environment can affect decision criteria and purchase. For example, when NASA landed the Pathfinder spacecraft on Mars, it captured media attention worldwide. The candy maker Mars also noted a rather unusual increase in sales. Although the Mars Bar takes its name from the company's founder and not the planet, consumers apparently responded to news about the planet Mars by purchasing more Mars Bars. In a recent lab experiment, participants who used an orange (green) pen chose more orange (green) products. Thus, conceptual cues or primers (the pen color) influenced product evaluations and purchase likelihood.[4]

The environment, internal information, and external information help consumers evaluate and compare alternatives. One way to begin narrowing the number of choices in the evoked set is to pick a product attribute and then exclude all products in the set that don't have that attribute. For example, assume Jane and Jill, both college sophomores, are looking for their first apartment. They need a two-bedroom apartment, reasonably priced, and located near campus. They want the apartment to have a swimming pool, washer and dryer, and covered parking. Jane and Jill begin their search with all apartments in the area and then systematically eliminate possibilities that lack the features they need. Hence, if there are 50 alternatives in the area, they may reduce their list to just 10 apartments that possess all of the desired attributes.

Another way to narrow the number of choices is to use cutoffs. Cutoffs are either minimum or maximum levels of an attribute that an alternative must pass to be considered. Suppose Jane and Jill set a maximum of $1,000 to spend on combined rent. Then all apartments with rent higher than $1,000 will be eliminated, further reducing the list of apartments from ten to eight. A final way to narrow the choices is to rank the attributes under consideration in order of importance and evaluate the products based on how well each performs on the most important attributes. To reach a final decision on one of the

evoked set (consideration set) A group of brands, resulting from an information search, from which a buyer can choose.

remaining eight apartments, Jane and Jill may decide proximity to campus is the most important attribute. As a result, they will choose to rent the apartment closest to campus.

If new brands are added to an evoked set, the consumer's evaluation of the existing brands in that set changes. As a result, certain brands in the original set may become more desirable. Suppose Jane and Jill find two apartments located equal distance from campus, one priced at $800 and the other at $750. Faced with this choice, they may decide that the $800 apartment is too expensive given that a comparable apartment is cheaper. If they add a $900 apartment to the list, however, then they may perceive the $800 apartment as more reasonable and decide to rent it.

The purchase decision process described above is a piecemeal process. That is, the evaluation is made by examining alternative advantages and disadvantages along important product attributes. A different way consumers can evaluate a product is according to a categorization process. The evaluation of an alternative depends upon the particular category to which it is assigned. Categories can be very general (motorized forms of transportation), or they can be very specific (Harley-Davidson motorcycles). Typically, these categories are associated with some degree of liking or disliking. To the extent that the product can be assigned membership to a particular category, it will receive an evaluation similar to that attached to the category. If you go to the grocery store and see a new organic food on the shelf, you may evaluate it on your liking and opinions of organic food.

So, when consumers rely on a categorization process, a product's evaluation depends on the particular category to which it is perceived as belonging. Given this, companies need to understand whether consumers are using categories that evoke the desired evaluations. Indeed, how a product is categorized can strongly influence consumer demand. For example, what products come to mind when you think about the "morning beverages" category? To the soft drink industry's dismay, far too few of us include sodas in this category. Several attempts have been made at getting soft drinks on the breakfast table, but with little success.

Brand extensions, in which a well-known and respected brand name from one product category is extended into other product categories, is one way companies employ categorization to their advantage. Brand extensions are a common business practice. Disney took a name built on cartoon characters and amusement parks and extended it to the cruise line industry. Kimberly-Clark, the maker of Huggies, the best-selling brand of disposable diapers in the United States, has extended the Huggies name to disposable washcloths and liquid soap for babies, and Huggies toiletries. Coca-Cola has Coke, Diet Coke, Coke Zero, Cherry Coke, Diet Cherry Coke, Caffeine-free Coke, and the list goes on.[5]

To Buy or Not to Buy Ultimately, the consumer has to decide whether to buy or not buy. Specifically, consumers must decide

1. Whether to buy

2. When to buy

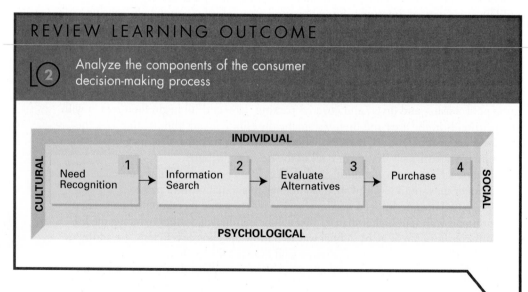

REVIEW LEARNING OUTCOME

LO2 Analyze the components of the consumer decision-making process

3. What to buy (product type and brand)

4. Where to buy (type of retailer, specific retailer, online or in-store)

5. How to pay

When a person is buying an expensive or complex item, it is often a *fully planned purchase* based upon a lot of information. People rarely buy a new home simply on impulse. Often consumers will make a *partially planned purchase* where they know the product category they want to buy (shirts, pants, reading lamp, car floor mats) but wait until they get to the store to choose a specific style or brand. Finally, there is the *unplanned purchase* where people buy on impulse. Research has found that up to 68 percent of the items bought during major shopping trips and 54 percent on smaller shopping trips are unplanned.[6]

POSTPURCHASE BEHAVIOR

When buying products, consumers expect certain outcomes from the purchase. How well these expectations are met determines whether the consumer is satisfied or dissatisfied with the purchase. For example, if a person bids on a used car stereo from eBay and wins, he may have fairly low expectations regarding performance. If the stereo's performance turns out to be of superior quality, then the person's satisfaction will be high because his expectations were exceeded. Conversely, if the person bid on a new car stereo expecting superior quality and performance, but the stereo broke within one month, he would be very dissatisfied because his expectations were not met. Price often influences the level of expectations for a product or service.

For the marketer, an important element of any postpurchase evaluation is reducing any lingering doubts that the decision was sound. When people recognize inconsistency between their values or opinions and their behavior, they tend to feel an inner tension called cognitive dissonance. For example, suppose a person who normally tans in a tanning bed decides to try a new "airbrush" tanning method, called a "Hollywood" or "mystic" tanning. Mystic tanning costs $30 to $50, significantly more than "fake tanner" or a tanning bed. Prior to spending more on the tan, the person may feel inner tension or anxiety, which is a feeling of dissonance. This feeling occurs because she knows the product has some disadvantages, such as being expensive, and some advantages, such as being free of harmful ultraviolet rays. In this case, the disadvantage of higher cost battles the advantage of no harmful UV rays.

Consumers try to reduce dissonance by justifying their decision. They may seek new information that reinforces positive ideas about the purchase, avoid information that contradicts their decision, or revoke the original decision by returning the product. To ensure satisfaction, thereby reducing dissonance, consumers using the "mystic tanning" mentioned above may ask several friends about their experiences, do online research, and talk with the tanning booth representative to obtain additional information about the

REVIEW LEARNING OUTCOME

Explain the consumer's postpurchase evaluation process

Cognitive Dissonance

?

Product or Service

To Reduce Dissonance

Consumer can
- justify decision
- seek new information
- avoid contradictory information
- return product

Marketer can
- send postpurchase thank you or letter
- display product superiority in ads
- offer guarantees

Satisfied Customer

!

Product or Service

cognitive dissonance
Inner tension that a consumer experiences after recognizing an inconsistency between behavior and values or opinions.

procedure. In some instances, people deliberately seek contrary information in order to refute it and reduce dissonance. Dissatisfied customers sometimes rely on word of mouth to reduce cognitive dissonance, by letting friends and family know they are displeased.

Marketing managers can help reduce dissonance through effective communication with purchasers. For example, a customer service manager may slip a note inside the package congratulating the buyer on making a wise decision. Postpurchase letters sent by manufacturers and dissonance-reducing statements in instruction booklets may help customers feel at ease with their purchase. Advertising that displays the product's superiority over competing brands or guarantees can also help relieve the possible dissonance of someone who has already bought the product. In the tanning example, the tanning salon may offer a 100 percent money-back guarantee. The **mystictan.com** Web site explains the procedure and even shows endorsements from various celebrities. Because the company offers this additional information and communicates effectively with its customers, its customers are more likely to understand the procedure and the expected results; hence, it is likely that the outcome will meet or exceed their expectations rather than being disappointing.

One factor that can raise or lower dissonance is service during and after the sale. The Customer Experience box explains how Zappos.com provides great customer service.

CUSTOMER Experience

At Zappos.com Service Is Always On

Zappos.com is an online retailer known originally for footwear, but also offering clothing, handbags, and accessories. Founded in 1999 and renowned for its unparalleled customer service, Zappos offers nearly 1,200 brands and about 2.7 million products, and had $1 billion in gross sales in 2008.

While Zappos is familiar to shoppers because of its wide selection of brands, styles, and sizes, the Henderson, Nevada-based company strives to position itself as the absolute online service leader. Shoppers love the company for its free shipping and returns, 365-day return policy and 24-7 customer service. But that's just the beginning of Zappos' corporate culture of service: The company and its 1,600 employees—half of whom work in its headquarters and call center, the other half in its Shepherdsville, Kentucky, warehouse—embrace ten core concepts, the first of which is to "Deliver WOW through service." Other concepts range from being open and honest and driving change to having fun. "Customer service is everything to us, and the reason we can stay focused and successful is that it's ingrained into our culture, and our brand is our culture," says Aaron Magness, who works in business development for Zappos.

Zappos' service-oriented culture starts in the hiring process. According to Magness, while half of the initial interview is dedicated to finding out if potential hires have the right technical skills for the job, the other half is about making sure they're a good cultural fit. "Getting customers excited about the service they had at Zappos has to come naturally," he says. "You can't teach it; you have to hire for it."

Once hired, all new employees, regardless of position, are required to complete a four-week customer loyalty training program in the call center to learn the history of the company, get immersed in its culture, and make sure they're a good fit. To ensure that's the case, CEO Tony Hsieh steps in during the second week of training and offers $2,000 to anyone who wants to quit. Magness says that only about 1 percent of the trainees actually take the offer.

Once Zappos wins over shoppers (roughly 75 percent of its orders are placed by repeat customers), the company works to keep them engaged through various online and social media outlets, including inviting customers to submit online reviews. It also maintains an active presence on Facebook and Twitter. "We want to let our customers speak for themselves on our site. If someone wants to say 'I really didn't like this shirt,' we want other customers to know. We're not afraid to hear good reviews and bad reviews," Magness says.

On Twitter, Hsieh has about 12,000 followers who read his posts on topics ranging from free shoe giveaways and feedback requests to where he's having dinner. According to Magness, not only does this ability to relate to the company help create a stronger relationship with shoppers, but also it provides the company with valuable consumer insight.[7]

How does Zappos' great customer service help reduce cognitive dissonance? Can a company put too much emphasis on customer service? Have you ever had poor customer service from an online vendor? If so, what did it do to your level of dissonance?

TYPES OF CONSUMER BUYING DECISIONS AND CONSUMER INVOLVEMENT

All consumer buying decisions generally fall along a continuum of three broad categories: routine response behavior, limited decision making, and extensive decision making (see Exhibit 6.2). Goods and services in these three categories can best be described in terms of five factors: level of consumer involvement, length of time to make a decision, cost of the good or service, degree of information search, and the number of alternatives considered. The level of consumer involvement is perhaps the most significant determinant in classifying buying decisions. Involvement is the amount of time and effort a buyer invests in the search, evaluation, and decision processes of consumer behavior.

Frequently purchased, low-cost goods and services are generally associated with routine response behavior. These goods and services can also be called low-involvement products because consumers spend little time on search and decision before making the purchase. Usually, buyers are familiar with several different brands in the product category but stick with one brand. For example, a person may routinely buy Tropicana orange juice. Consumers engaged in routine response behavior normally don't experience need recognition until they are exposed to advertising or see the product displayed on a store shelf. Consumers buy first and evaluate later, whereas the reverse is true for extensive decision making. A consumer who has previously purchased a whitening toothpaste and was satisfied with it will probably walk to the toothpaste aisle and select that same brand without spending 20 minutes examining all other alternatives.

Limited decision making typically occurs when a consumer has previous product experience but is unfamiliar with the current brands available. Limited decision making is also associated with lower levels of involvement (although higher than routine decisions) because consumers do expend moderate effort in searching for information or in considering various alternatives. But what happens if the consumer's usual brand of whitening toothpaste is sold out? Assuming that toothpaste is needed, the consumer will be forced to choose another brand. Before making a final decision, the consumer will likely evaluate several other brands based on their active ingredients, their promotional claims, and the consumer's prior experiences.

Consumers practice extensive decision making when buying an unfamiliar, expensive product or an infrequently bought item. This process is the most complex type of consumer buying decision and is associated with high involvement on the part of the consumer. This process resembles the model outlined in Exhibit 6.1. These consumers want to make the right decision, so they want to know as much as they can about the product category and available brands. People usually experience the most cognitive dissonance when buying high-involvement products. Buyers use several criteria for evaluating their options and spend much time seeking information. Buying a home or a car, for example, requires extensive decision making.

The type of decision making that consumers use to purchase a product does not necessarily remain constant. For instance, if a routinely purchased product no longer satisfies, consumers may practice

involvement
The amount of time and effort a buyer invests in the search, evaluation, and decision processes of consumer behavior.

routine response behavior
The type of decision making exhibited by consumers buying frequently purchased, low-cost goods and services; requires little search and decision time.

limited decision making
The type of decision making that requires a moderate amount of time for gathering information and deliberating about an unfamiliar brand in a familiar product category.

extensive decision making
The most complex type of consumer decision making, used when buying an unfamiliar, expensive product or an infrequently bought item; requires use of several criteria for evaluating options and much time for seeking information.

EXHIBIT 6.2

Continuum of Consumer Buying Decisions

	Routine	Limited	Extensive
Involvement	low	low to moderate	high
Time	short	short to moderate	long
Cost	low	low to moderate	high
Information Search	internal only	mostly internal	internal and external
Number of Alternatives	one	few	many

limited or extensive decision making to switch to another brand. And people who first use extensive decision making may then use limited or routine decision making for future purchases. For example, when a family gets a new puppy, they will spend a lot of time and energy trying out different toys to determine which one the dog prefers. Once the new owners learn that the dog prefers a bone to a ball, however, the purchase no longer requires extensive evaluation and will become routine.

Factors Determining the Level of Consumer Involvement

The level of involvement in the purchase depends on the following five factors:

Luxury cars are a sign of higher social class status.

☛ *Previous experience:* When consumers have had previous experience with a good or service, the level of involvement typically decreases. After repeated product trials, consumers learn to make quick choices. Because consumers are familiar with the product and know whether it will satisfy their needs, they become less involved in the purchase. For example, a consumer purchasing cereal has many brands to choose from—just think of any grocery store cereal aisle. If the consumer always buys the same brand because it satisfies his hunger, then he has a low level of involvement. When a consumer purchases cereal for the first time, however, it likely will be a much more involved purchase.

☛ *Interest:* Involvement is directly related to consumer interests, as in cars, music, movies, bicycling, or electronics. Naturally, these areas of interest vary from one individual to another. A person highly involved in bike racing will be very interested in the type of bike she owns and will spend quite a bit of time evaluating different bikes. If a person wants a bike only for recreation, however, he may be fairly uninvolved in the purchase and just look for a bike from the most convenient location.

☛ *Perceived risk of negative consequences:* As the perceived risk in purchasing a product increases, so does a consumer's level of involvement. The types of risks that concern consumers include financial risk, social risk, and psychological risk. First, financial risk is exposure to loss of wealth or purchasing power. Because high risk is associated with high-priced purchases, consumers tend to become extremely involved. Therefore, price and involvement are usually directly related: As price increases, so does the level of involvement. For example, someone who is purchasing a new car for the first time (higher perceived risk) will spend a lot of time and effort making this purchase. Second, consumers take social risks when they buy products that can affect people's social opinions of them (for example, driving an old, beat-up car or wearing unstylish clothes). Third, buyers undergo psychological risk if they feel that making the wrong decision might cause some concern or anxiety. For example, some consumers feel guilty about eating foods that are not healthy, such as regular ice cream rather than fat-free frozen yogurt.

☛ *Situation:* The circumstances of a purchase may temporarily transform a low-involvement decision into a high-involvement one. High involvement comes into play when the consumer perceives risk in a specific situation. For example, an individual might routinely buy low-priced brands of liquor and wine. When the boss visits, however, the consumer might make a high-involvement decision and buy more prestigious brands.

☛ *Social visibility:* Involvement also increases as the social visibility of a product increases. Products often on social display include clothing (especially designer labels), jewelry, cars, and furniture. All these items make a statement about the purchaser and, therefore, carry a social risk.

Marketing Implications of Involvement

Marketing strategy varies according to the level of involvement associated with the product. For high-involvement product purchases, marketing managers have several responsibilities. First, promotion to the target market should be extensive and informative. A good ad gives consumers the information they need for making the purchase decision, as well as specifying the benefits and unique advantages of owning the product. For example, a recent two-page ad for Toyota's Camry Hybrid provides extensive information on the personal and planet-wide benefits of choosing their vehicle. Photos of a wide-eyed young girl and a globe are meant to appeal to the customer's care for the future, while captions on interior photos of the car and its engine note the vehicle's unique technology that "drives just like a regular car," benefits that might appeal to the consumer's need for performance.[8] Another ad featured in earlier pages of the same magazine shows the Camry Hybrid being driven along a country road, surrounded by green pastures and grazing horses. The ad is meant to appeal to the consumer who cares that the vehicle is built in the United States and that Toyota is committed to America, its air, its communities, and its future.

For low-involvement product purchases, consumers may not recognize their wants until they are in the store. Therefore, in-store promotion is an important tool when promoting low-involvement products. Marketing managers focus on package design so the product will be eye-catching and easily recognized on the shelf. Examples of products that take this approach are Campbell's soups, Tide detergent, Velveeta cheese, and Heinz ketchup. In-store displays also stimulate sales of low-involvement products. A good display can explain the product's purpose and prompt recognition of a want. Displays of health and beauty aid items in supermarkets have been known to increase sales many times above normal. Coupons, cents-off deals, and two-for-one offers also effectively promote low-involvement items.

Linking a product to a higher-involvement issue is another tactic that marketing managers can use to increase the sales or positive publicity of a low-involvement product. For example, in response to government and consumer concerns about childhood obesity, food manufacturers that advertise to children, such as Kellogg's, Hershey, McDonald's, and General Mills, have pledged to devote at least half of their marketing to the promotion of healthy dietary choices and lifestyles. In Kellogg's case, nearly $206 million in advertising dollars is at stake.[9]

REVIEW LEARNING OUTCOME

LO 4 Identify the types of consumer buying decisions and discuss the significance of consumer involvement

Previous experience
Interest
Perceived risk of negative consequences
Situation
Social visibility

Extensive

Limited

Routine

FACTORS INFLUENCING CONSUMER BUYING DECISIONS

The consumer decision-making process does not occur in a vacuum. On the contrary, underlying cultural, social, individual, and psychological factors strongly influence the decision process. These factors have an effect from the time a consumer perceives a stimulus through postpurchase behavior. Cultural factors, which include culture and values, subculture, and social class, exert a broad influence over consumer decision making. Social factors sum up the social interactions between a consumer and influential groups of people, such as reference groups, opinion leaders, and family members.

EXHIBIT 6.3

Factors That Affect the Consumer Decision-Making Process

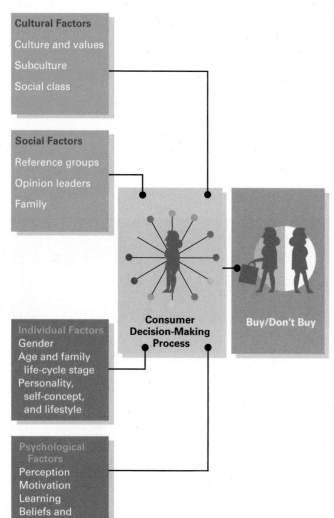

Cultural Factors
Culture and values
Subculture
Social class

Social Factors
Reference groups
Opinion leaders
Family

Individual Factors
Gender
Age and family life-cycle stage
Personality, self-concept, and lifestyle

Psychological Factors
Perception
Motivation
Learning
Beliefs and attitudes

Consumer Decision-Making Process

Buy/Don't Buy

Individual factors, which include gender, age, family life-cycle stage, personality, self-concept, and lifestyle, are unique to each individual and play a major role in the type of products and services consumers want. Psychological factors determine how consumers perceive and interact with their environments and influence the ultimate decisions consumers make. They include perception, motivation, learning, beliefs, and attitudes. Exhibit 6.3 summarizes these influences.

CULTURAL INFLUENCES ON CONSUMER BUYING DECISIONS

Of all the factors that affect consumer decision making, cultural factors exert the broadest and deepest influence. Marketers must understand the way people's culture and its accompanying values, as well as their subculture and social class, influence their buying behavior.

Culture and Values

Culture is the essential character of a society that distinguishes it from other societal groups. The underlying elements of every culture are the values, language, myths, customs, rituals, and laws that shape the behavior of the people, as well as the material artifacts, or products, of that behavior as they are transmitted from one generation to the next. Exhibit 6.4 lists some defining components of American culture.

Culture is pervasive. Cultural values and influences are the ocean in which individuals swim, and yet most are completely unaware that it is there. What people eat, how they dress, what they think and feel, and what language they speak are all dimensions of culture. It encompasses all the things consumers do without conscious choice because their culture's values, customs, and rituals are ingrained in their daily habits.

Culture is functional. Human interaction creates values and prescribes acceptable behavior for each culture. By

EXHIBIT 6.4

Components of American Culture

COMPONENT	EXAMPLES
Values	Success through hard work; Emphasis on personal freedom
Language	English as the dominant language
Myths	George Washington never told a lie. Abraham Lincoln walked a mile to return a penny.
Customs	Bathing daily; Shaking hands when greeting new people; Standard gratuity of 15 to 20 percent at restaurants
Rituals	Thanksgiving Day dinner; Singing the "Star Spangled Banner" before baseball games; Going to religious services on the appropriate day
Laws	Child labor laws; Sherman Anti-Trust Act guarantees competition
Material artifacts	Diamond engagement rings; Cell phones

Source: Adapted from *Consumer Behavior* by William D. Wells and David Prensky. Copyright © 1996 by John Wiley & Sons, Inc. Reprinted by permission of John Wiley & Sons, Inc. All Rights Reserved.

establishing common expectations, culture gives order to society. Sometimes these expectations are enacted into laws. For example, drivers in our culture must stop at a red light. Other times these expectations are taken for granted. For example, grocery stores and hospitals are open 24 hours, whereas banks are open only during bankers' hours.

Culture is learned. Consumers are not born knowing the values and norms of their society. Instead, they must learn what is acceptable from family and friends. Children learn the values that will govern their behavior from parents, teachers, and peers. As members of our society, they learn to shake hands when they greet someone, to drive on the right-hand side of the road, and to eat pizza and drink Coca-Cola.

Culture is dynamic. It adapts to changing needs and an evolving environment. The rapid growth of technology in today's world has accelerated the rate of cultural change. Television has changed entertainment patterns and family communication and has heightened public awareness of political and other news events. Automation has increased the amount of leisure time we have and, in some ways, has changed the traditional work ethic. Cultural norms will continue to evolve because of our need for social patterns that solve problems.

In the United States, rapidly increasing diversity is causing major shifts in culture. For example, the growth of the Hispanic community is influencing American food, music, clothing, and entertainment. Additionally, African American culture has been embraced by the mainstream. Indeed, African American women make up one of the fastest-growing segments of the American population. The projected growth rate of this segment is 8 percent, compared to 4 percent for the total U.S. population. Additionally, one in two married black women is the primary decision maker in buying a house, versus one in four married white women. Traditionally, marketers have not taken advantage of the opportunity to market to African American women. Now, however, many companies are taking note of this rapidly growing segment of the population. For example, Kraft's Honey Bunches of Oats cereal developed an advertising campaign that focused on black women. Research showed that African American women do not like to eat cereal when others are around, so the print ad shows a black woman eating a bowl of cereal alone with the caption "Take a breather. This moment is yours. Just you and your bowl of Honey Bunches of Oats."[10]

The most defining element of a culture is its values—the enduring beliefs shared by a society that a specific mode of conduct is personally or socially preferable to another mode of conduct. People's value systems have a great effect on their consumer behavior. Consumers with similar value systems tend to react alike to prices and other marketing-related inducements. Values also correspond to consumption patterns. For example, Americans place a high value on convenience. This value has created lucrative markets for products such as breakfast bars, energy bars, and nutrition bars that allow consumers to eat on the go. Values can also influence consumers' TV viewing habits or the magazines they read. For instance, people who strongly object to violence avoid crime shows, and those who oppose pornography do not buy *Hustler*. Core American values—those considered central to the American way of life—are presented in Exhibit 6.5.

Values represent what is most important in people's lives. Therefore, marketers watch carefully for shifts in consumers' values over time. For example, millions of Americans have an interest in spirituality, as evidenced by the soaring sales of books with religious or spiritual themes and the popularity of television shows with similar themes. Similarly, after the September 11 terrorist attacks, when many people were fearful and concerned about self-protection, gun sales soared as did the sale of drugs to cure anthrax.

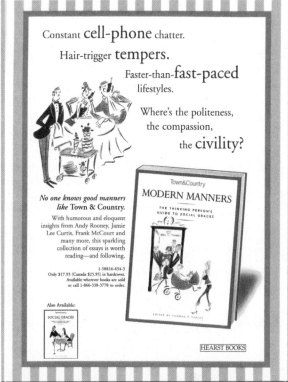

Modern Manners explores the ways in which new technologies, such as cell phones, have changed American culture.

culture
The set of values, norms, attitudes, and other meaningful symbols that shape human behavior, and the artifacts, or products, of that behavior as they are transmitted from one generation to the next.

value
The enduring belief that a specific mode of conduct is personally or socially preferable to another mode of conduct.

EXHIBIT 6.5

Core American Values

Success	Americans admire hard work, entrepreneurship, achievement, and success. Those achieving success in American society are rewarded with money, status, and prestige. For example, Bill Gates, once a nerdy computer buff, built Microsoft Corporation into an internationally known giant. Gates is now one of the richest people in the world.
Materialism	Americans value owning tangible goods. American society encourages consumption, ownership, and possession. Americans judge others based on their material possessions; for example, the type of car they own, where they live, and what type of clothes they wear.
Freedom	The American culture was founded on the principle of religious and political freedom. The U.S. Constitution and the Bill of Rights assure American citizens the right to life, liberty, and the pursuit of happiness. These freedoms are fundamental to the legal system and the moral fiber of American culture. The Internet, for example, is built on the principle of the right to free speech. Lawmakers who have attempted to limit the material available on the Internet have met with tough opposition from proponents of free speech. Spam has become such a major problem in recent years, however, that individuals are becoming more receptive to laws restricting spam even if they limit spammers' free speech.
Progress	Technological advances, as well as advances in medicine, science, health, and the quality of products and services, are important to Americans. Each year, for example, more than 20,000 new or improved consumer products are introduced on America's supermarket shelves.*
Youth	Americans are obsessed with youth and spend a good deal of time on products and procedures that make them feel and look younger. Americans spend millions each year on health and beauty aids, health clubs, and healthy foods. Media and advertising encourage the quest for youth by using young, attractive, slim models, such as those in ads from fashion designer Calvin Klein.
Capitalism	Americans believe in a free enterprise system characterized by competition and the chance for monetary success. Capitalism creates choices, quality, and value for Americans. Laws prohibit monopolistic control of a market and regulate free trade. Americans encourage small business success, such as that found by Apple Computer, Wal-Mart, and McDonald's, all of which started as small enterprises with a better idea that toppled the competition.

*Data obtained from the Food Marketing Institute Web site at **http://www.fmi.org,** 2004.
Source: *Consumer Behavior* by William D. Wells and David Prensky. Copyright © 1996 John Wiley & Sons, Inc. Reprinted by permission of John Wiley & Sons, Inc. All Rights Reserved.

subculture
A homogeneous group of people who share elements of the overall culture as well as unique elements of their own group.

James Stengel, global marketing director for Procter & Gamble, had this to say about the changes he's seen in today's consumers, "The biggest thing going on with U.S. consumers is that they want to trust something. They want to be understood, they want to be respected, [and] they want to be listened to. They don't want to be talked to. It's trust in the largest sense of the word. People really do care what's behind the brand, what's behind the business. They care about the values of a brand and the values of a company. We can never forget that. We can never be complacent about that."[11]

Understanding Cultural Differences

As more companies expand their operations globally, the need to understand the cultures of foreign countries becomes more important. A firm has little chance of selling products in a culture it does not understand. Like people, products have cultural values and rules that influence their perception and use. Culture, therefore, must be understood before the behavior of individuals within the cultural context can be understood. Colors, for example, may have different meanings in global markets than they do at home. In China, white is the color of mourning, and brides wear red. In the United States, black is for mourning, and brides wear white.

Language is another important aspect of culture that global marketers must deal with. When translating product names, slogans, and promotional messages into foreign languages, they must be careful not to convey the wrong message. General Motors discovered too late that Nova (the name of an economical car) literally means "doesn't go" in Spanish; Coors encouraged its English-speaking customers to "Turn it loose," but the phrase in Spanish means "Suffer from diarrhea."

Though marketers expanding into global markets generally adapt their products and business formats to the local culture, some fear that increasing globalization, as well as the proliferation of the Internet, will result in a homogeneous world culture in the future. U.S. companies in particular, they fear, are Americanizing the world by exporting bastions of American culture, such as McDonald's fast-food restaurants, Starbucks coffeehouses, Microsoft software, and American movies and entertainment.

One of the world's fastest growing countries is China. Perhaps the most important aspect of a multinational firm's success in selling in any country is understanding the culture. The Global Perspectives box illustrates one firm's attempt at modifying its products based upon culture.

Subculture

A culture can be divided into subcultures on the basis of demographic characteristics, geographic regions, national and ethnic background, political beliefs, and religious beliefs. A subculture is a homogeneous group of people who share elements of the overall culture as well as cultural elements unique to their own group. Within subcultures, people's attitudes, values, and purchase decisions are even more similar than they are within the broader culture. Subcultural differences may result in considerable variation within a culture in what, how, when, and where people buy goods and services.

In the United States alone, countless subcultures can be identified. Many are concentrated geographically. People belonging to the Mormon religion, for example, are clustered mainly in Utah; Cajuns are located in the bayou regions of southern Louisiana. Many Hispanics live in states bordering Mexico, whereas the majority of Chinese, Japanese, and Korean Americans are found on the West Coast. Other subcultures are geographically dispersed. Computer hackers, people who are hearing or visually impaired, Harley-Davidson bikers, military families, university

PepsiCo vies with Coca-Cola Co. in the world's fastest-growing soft-drinks arena—China. China's expanding market is the biggest after the United States and Mexico for the competing drinks giants. Which marketing elements do you think will give Pepsi an advantage over Coca-Cola or vice versa?

GLOBAL Perspectives

Fisher-Price's Global Game Plan is Based upon Understanding Local Cultures

Between 2006 and 2008, the average gross domestic product per capita in China has passed $2,000, and now is close to $2,500. That core of perhaps 250 million Chinese consumers—especially in coastal cities—actually earns closer to $10,000 a year on average. Given modest living expenses, they are left with considerable disposable income. They are eager to spend this income.

Fisher-Price wants to capture a piece of that disposable income. In developing a line of talking toys aimed at children in China, engineers at Fisher-Price had to struggle to perfect the Mandarin "Sh" sound, which involves a soft hiss that was difficult to encode on sound-data chips embedded in the toys. Developers finally solved the problem of recording the phrase "It's learning time!" in Mandarin, but new challenges are ahead. The company

will soon be examining the LCD screens on learning toys to determine whether Chinese characters can be displayed clearly.

Fisher-Price is pursuing other developing markets as well, including Brazil, Russia, and Poland. Each presents its own cultural challenges. For example, the company ran into trouble with a reading toy called "Storybook Rhymes" that featured a traditional Turkish poem paired with an illustration of a pig. "We realized this wasn't appropriate for a Muslim country," says Kelly Chapman, who heads product design, referring to cultural restrictions on pork. In development, the company replaced the pig with pictures of cats.[12]

Why is culture so important to multinational firms? Can you think of a product or service sold in the global marketplace where culture doesn't matter?

professors, and gays may be found throughout the country. Yet they have identifiable attitudes, values, and needs that distinguish them from the larger culture.

Once marketers identify subcultures, they can design special marketing programs to serve their needs. According to the U.S. Census Bureau, the Hispanic population is the largest and fastest-growing subculture, increasing four times as fast as the general population. To tap into this large and growing segment, marketers have been forming partnerships with broadcasters that have an established Latino audience. The Univision Radio network covers approximately 73 percent of the U.S. Hispanic population and has over 10 million listeners weekly. State Farm has partnered with Julie Stav, the leading financial expert to the Latino community, to sponsor evening broadcasts of her hugely successful Spanish-language radio show. When Sweden-based furniture manufacturer IKEA found that it wasn't capturing the large Latino demographic in U.S. cities, it started advertising in Spanish. It also launched a series of commercials featuring Latina soap opera stars on Telemundo—the second-largest U.S. Spanish-language broadcaster. IKEA saw immediate results with more Latinos in their stores.[13]

Social Class

The United States, like other societies, has a social class system. A social class is a group of people who are considered nearly equal in status or community esteem, who regularly socialize among themselves both formally and informally, and who share behavioral norms.

A number of techniques have been used to measure social class, and a number of criteria have been used to define it. One view of contemporary U.S. status structure is shown in Exhibit 6.6.

As you can see from Exhibit 6.6, the upper and upper-middle classes comprise the small segment of affluent and wealthy Americans. In terms of consumer buying patterns, the affluent are more likely to own their own home and purchase new cars and trucks and are less likely to smoke. The very rich flex their financial muscles by spending more on vacation homes, vacations and cruises, and housekeeping and gardening services. The most affluent consumers are more likely to attend art auctions and galleries, dance performances, operas, the theater, museums, concerts, and sporting events. Marketers often pay attention to the superwealthy. For example, the Mercedes-Benz Maybach 62, touted as the "world's most luxurious car," is aimed at this group. Priced at $375,000, the car features electronic doors, reclining seats with footrests, a workstation with media capability, a champagne cooler, and lots more. Similarly, New York-based designer Calvin Stewart sells A.P.O. jeans featuring fully customized denim embellished with diamond, gold, and platinum details—starting at $1,000 a pair.

The majority of Americans today define themselves as middle class, regardless of their actual income or educational attainment. This phenomenon most likely occurs because working-class Americans tend to aspire to the middle-class lifestyle while some of those who do achieve affluence may downwardly aspire to respectable middle-class status as a matter of

An ad such as this one for Avon featuring an admired celebrity like Salma Hayek, entices consumers who aspire to a certain lifestyle (or think they deserve it) to use the product being used by the celebrity.

IMAGE COURTESY OF THE ADVERTISING ARCHIVES

EXHIBIT 6.6

U.S. Social Classes

Upper Classes		
Capitalist class	1 percent	People whose investment decisions shape the national economy; income mostly from assets, earned or inherited; university connections
Upper-middle class	14 percent	Upper-level managers, professionals, owners of medium-sized businesses; well-to-do, stay-at-home homemakers who decline occupational work by choice; college educated; family income well above national average
Middle Classes		
Middle class	33 percent	Middle-level white-collar, top-level blue-collar; education past high school typical; income somewhat above national average; loss of manufacturing jobs has reduced the population of this class
Working class	32 percent	Middle-level blue-collar, lower-level white-collar; income below national average; largely working in skilled or semiskilled service jobs
Lower Classes		
Working poor	11–12 percent	Low-paid service workers and operatives; some high school education; below mainstream in living standard; crime and hunger are daily threats
Underclass	8–9 percent	People who are not regularly employed and who depend primarily on the welfare system for sustenance; little schooling; living standard below poverty line

Source: Adapted from Richard P. Coleman, "The Continuing Significance of Social Class to Marketing," *Journal of Consumer Research*, December 1983, 267; Dennis Gilbert and Joseph A. Kahl, *The American Class Structure: A Synthesis* (Homewood, IL: Dorsey Press, 1982), ch. 11, accessed online at **http://en.wikipedia.org/wiki/social_structure_of_the_united_states**, May 2008.

principle. Attaining goals and achieving status and prestige are important to middle-class consumers. People falling into the middle class live in the gap between the haves and the have-nots. They aspire to the lifestyle of the more affluent, but are constrained by the economic realities and cautious attitudes they share with the working class.

A recent poll asked whether the United States is split into "haves" and "have-nots"; 48 percent said it is and 48 percent said it isn't. (The rest declined to choose.) The researchers also asked people to say which class they belong to, if they had to pick. While a large percentage said they're "haves" (45 percent), that's down from the 52 percent who did so in 2001 and down even more from the 59 percent saying so in 1988. The rest said they fit in neither group or refused to pick. More women than men situated themselves among the have-nots (37 percent vs. 30 percent). Even 32 percent of middle-income consumers said that they were have-nots, meaning that they perceived their standard of living as inadequate for their purchasing power.[14]

The working class is a distinct subset of the middle class. Interest in organized labor is one of the most common attributes among the working class. This group often rates job security as the most important reason for taking a job. The working-class person depends heavily on relatives and the community for economic and emotional support. The emphasis on family ties is one sign of the group's intensely local view of the world. They like the local news far more than do middle-class audiences who favor national and world coverage. They are also more likely to vacation closer to home.

Lifestyle distinctions between the social classes are greater than the distinctions within a given class. The most significant difference between the classes occurs between the middle and lower classes, where there is a major shift in lifestyles. Members of the lower class typically have incomes at or below the poverty level. This social class has the highest unemployment rate, and many individuals or families are subsidized through the welfare system. Many are illiterate, with little formal education. Compared to more affluent consumers, lower-class consumers have poorer diets and typically purchase very different types of foods when they shop.

EXHIBIT 6.7

Social Class and Education

Educational Profile	Median Household Income
Those with less than a 9th grade education	$ 17,261
Those with a 9th–12th grade education (no diploma)	$ 21,737
High school graduates	$ 35,744
College graduates, BA	$ 64,406
College graduates, MA	$ 74,476
Professional degree holders	$ 100,000

Source: U.S. Census, available at http://www.pbs.org/peoplelikeus/resources/stats.html, May 2005.

Social class is typically measured as a combination of occupation, income, education, wealth, and other variables. For instance, affluent upper-class consumers are more likely to be salaried executives or self-employed professionals with at least an undergraduate degree. Working-class or middle-class consumers are more likely to be hourly service workers or blue-collar employees with only a high school education. Educational attainment, however, seems to be the most reliable indicator of a person's social and economic status (see Exhibit 6.7). Those with college degrees or graduate degrees are more likely to fall into the upper classes, while those people with some college experience fall closest to traditional concepts of the middle class.

Marketers are interested in social class for two main reasons. First, social class often indicates which medium to use for advertising. Suppose an insurance company seeks to sell its policies to middle-class families. It might advertise during the local evening news because middle-class families tend to watch more television than other classes do. If the company wants to sell more policies to upscale individuals, it might place a print ad in a business publication like *The Wall Street Journal*. The Internet, long the domain of more educated and affluent families, is becoming an increasingly important advertising outlet for advertisers hoping to reach blue-collar workers and homemakers. As the middle class rapidly adopts the medium, marketers have to do more research to find out which Web sites will reach their audience.

Second, knowing what products appeal to which social classes can help marketers determine where to best distribute their products. Affluent Americans, a fifth of the U.S. population, were responsible for nearly half of all new car and truck sales and over half of hotel stays and vacation homes. This same group spent nearly twice as much as less-affluent Americans on restaurant fare, alcohol, sporting events, plays, and club memberships.[15]

For the first time in a long while, however, industry analysts are seeing shares of discount chains faring better than their full-priced and upscale counterparts. These days, analysts say, the big-box and discount retailers' greatest challenge has been courting consumers who fall in the middle-income level. The result is a fiercely competitive retail environment where discount retailers have focused less on their core, low-income consumers, who are most impacted by rising housing and gas costs. Overall, however, shares of discount chains are faring better during this particular penny-pinching economy than their full-priced and upscale counterparts, because discount retailers have focused on getting current customers to purchase a wider array of products in the store, rather than trying to attract new shoppers.[16]

REVIEW LEARNING OUTCOME

LO 5 Identify and understand the cultural factors that affect consumer buying decisions

SOCIAL INFLUENCES ON CONSUMER BUYING DECISIONS

Many consumers seek out the opinions of others to reduce their search and evaluation effort or uncertainty, especially as the perceived risk of the decision increases. Consumers may also seek out others' opinions for guidance on new products or services, products with image-related attributes, or products where attribute information is lacking or uninformative. Specifically, consumers interact socially with reference groups, opinion leaders, and family members to obtain product information and decision approval.

Reference Groups

All the formal and informal groups that influence the buying behavior of an individual are that person's reference groups. Consumers may use products or brands to identify with or become a member of a group. They learn from observing how members of their reference groups consume, and they use the same criteria to make their own consumer decisions.

Reference groups can be categorized very broadly as either direct or indirect (see Exhibit 6.8). Direct reference groups are face-to-face membership groups that touch people's lives directly. They can be either primary or secondary. Primary membership groups include all groups with which people interact regularly in an informal, face-to-face manner, such as family, friends, and coworkers. In contrast, people associate with secondary membership groups less consistently and more formally. These groups might include clubs, professional groups, and religious groups.

Consumers also are influenced by many indirect, nonmembership reference groups they do not belong to. Aspirational reference groups are those a person would like to join. To join an aspirational group, a person must at least conform to the norms of that group. (Norms are the values and attitudes deemed acceptable by the group.) Thus, a person who wants to be elected to public office may begin to dress more conservatively, as other politicians do. He or she may go to many of the restaurants and social engagements that city and business leaders attend and try to play a role that is acceptable to voters and other influential people. Similarly, teenagers today may dye their hair and

reference group
A group in society that influences an individual's purchasing behavior.

primary membership group
A reference group with which people interact regularly in an informal, face-to-face manner, such as family, friends, or fellow employees.

secondary membership group
A reference group with which people associate less consistently and more formally than a primary membership group, such as a club, professional group, or religious group.

aspirational reference group
A group that someone would like to join.

norm
A value or attitude deemed acceptable by a group.

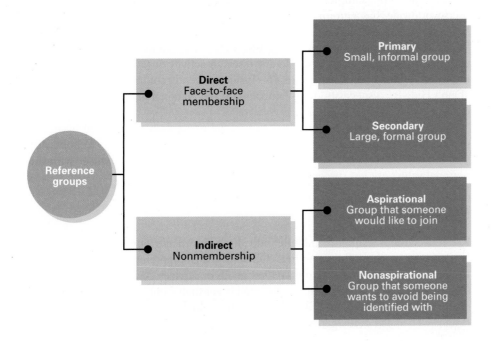

Reference groups

Direct
Face-to-face membership

Indirect
Nonmembership

Primary
Small, informal group

Secondary
Large, formal group

Aspirational
Group that someone would like to join

Nonaspirational
Group that someone wants to avoid being identified with

EXHIBIT 6.8
Types of Reference Groups

experiment with body piercing and tattoos. Athletes are an aspirational group for several market segments. To appeal to the younger market, Coca-Cola signed basketball star LeBron James to be the spokesperson for its Sprite and POWERade brands, and Nike signed a sneaker deal with him reportedly worth $90 million. Coca-Cola and Nike assumed James would encourage consumers to drink Coke brands and buy Nike shoes because they would like to identify with James.

Nonaspirational reference groups, or dissociative groups, influence our behavior when we try to maintain distance from them. A consumer may avoid buying some types of clothing or car, going to certain restaurants or stores, or even buying a home in a certain neighborhood in order to avoid being associated with a particular group.

The activities, values, and goals of reference groups directly influence consumer behavior. For marketers, reference groups have three important implications: (1) they serve as information sources and influence perceptions, (2) they affect an individual's aspiration levels, and (3) their norms either constrain or stimulate consumer behavior. For example, research firms devoted to uncovering what's cool in the teen market have identified a couple of influential groups among today's teens based on their interests in clothes, music, and activities. Tracking these groups reveals how products become cool and how groups influence the adoption of cool products by other groups. A trend or fad often starts with teens who have the most innovative tastes. These teens are on the cutting edge of fashion and music, and they wear their attitude all over their bodies in the form of tattoos, body piercing, studded jewelry, or colored tresses. Certain fads embraced by these "Edgers" will spark an interest in the small group of teens researchers call "Influencers," who project the look other teens covet. Influencers also create their own trends in music and clothing choices. Once a fad is embraced and adopted by Influencers, the look becomes cool and desirable. The remaining groups that compose the majority of the teen population will not embrace a fad until it gets its seal of approval from the Influencers.

Understanding the effect of reference groups on a product is important for marketers as they track the life cycle of their products. Retailer Abercrombie & Fitch noticed it was beginning to lose its target audience of college students when its stores began attracting large numbers of high school students trying to be more like college students. To solve the problem, A&F created its Hollister store chain specifically for high school students. The retailer also opened a chain called Abercrombie for a target market of boys and girls, ages seven to fourteen. Another A&F chain, Ruehl, offers Greenwich Village–inspired clothing for the post-college-age market.

Marketers and researchers can now gauge teen opinions, test new product ideas, and even get help creating marketing buzz by tapping into the ever-expanding online teen communities. For example, Piczo, an online community with 28 million registered users worldwide, has a group of influential "insiders" who will advise brands on how to best leverage the site. "Piczo Insiders" exchange opinions and offer feedback on marketing campaigns that are running on the Piczo site. These teens will collaborate online with marketers and are responsive to any research activity or project that they think will improve the Piczo user experience. The Insiders recently contributed real-life stories to "Don't Hide It," a successful new campaign for the National Society for the Prevention of Cruelty to Children (NSPCC).

Research has shown that reference groups are particularly powerful in influencing purchases of fragrances, wine, snack food, candy, clothing, and sodas.[17] People with well-formed networks of somewhat overlapping reference groups and those with strong personal values are less susceptible to reference group influences.[18]

Opinion Leaders

Reference groups frequently include individuals known as group leaders, or opinion leaders—those who influence others. Obviously, it is important for marketing managers to persuade such people to purchase their goods or services. Many products and services that are integral parts of Americans' lives today got their initial boost from opinion leaders. For example, DVDs and SUVs (sport-utility vehicles) were purchased by opinion leaders well ahead of the general public.

Opinion leaders are often the first to try new products and services out of pure curiosity. They are typically self-indulgent and status-seeking, making them more likely to explore unproven but intriguing products and services.[19] Technology companies have found that teenagers, because of their willingness to experiment, are key opinion leaders for the success of new technologies.

Opinion leadership is a casual, face-to-face phenomenon and is usually inconspicuous, so locating opinion leaders can be a challenge. Thus, marketers often try to create opinion leaders. They may use high school cheerleaders to model new fall fashions or civic leaders to promote insurance, new cars, and other merchandise. On a national level, companies sometimes use movie stars, sports figures, and other celebrities to promote products, hoping they are appropriate opinion leaders. The effectiveness of celebrity endorsements varies, though, depending largely on how credible and attractive the spokesperson is and how familiar people are with him or her. Endorsements are most likely to succeed if a reasonable association between the spokesperson and the product can be established.

Celebrities and sports figures aren't the only people marketers consider opinion leaders, however. Managers at BMW are rethinking who the U.S. opinion leaders are for their brand. Historically, the automaker targeted car enthusiasts. Today, the company is looking at the "idea class," a group composed of roughly 1.5 million architects, professionals, innovators, and entrepreneurs who are more interested in design, authenticity, and independent thinking. Over a five-year period, BMW has increased U.S. sales by 62 percent, but still has less than a 2 percent share of the U.S. market.[20]

Respected organizations such as the American Heart Association and the American Cancer Society may also serve as opinion leaders. Marketers may seek endorsements from them as well as from schools, churches, cities, the military, and fraternal organizations as a form of group opinion leadership. Salespeople often ask to use opinion leaders' names as a means of achieving greater personal influence in a sales presentation.

Yes. She checks herself out in the mirror.

1 in 5 Americans will develop skin cancer in their lifetime. That's why Jennifer Garner made a promise to herself to examine her skin every month and see her dermatologist for a screening every year.

The Neutrogena Partnership for Skin Health, working with the American Academy of Dermatology (AAD), invites you to join them in their mission to stop skin cancer before it strikes. Empower their cause by wearing broad-spectrum sun protection, covering up and seeking shade between 10:00 am and 4:00 pm. Perform self-examinations regularly and report any changes in existing moles or birthmarks to your doctor. Because with early detection, skin cancer is 99% curable. And that's a statistic we love to share.

Protect yourself starting today.
The AAD and the Neutrogena Partnership for Skin Health encourage you to get a free skin cancer screening in May, June or July. Find one in your area by visiting aad.org or neutrogenaskinhealth.com. Mark the date of your screening on this slip as a healthy reminder.

© 2008 Neutrogena Corp.

Neutrogena® PARTNERSHIP FOR SKIN HEALTH

The activities, values, and goals of reference groups directly influence consumer behavior. Consumers may use the Neutrogena brand—and participate in skin cancer prevention behavior as she does—because they aspire to be like actress Jennifer Garner.

How Blogs Are Defining Today's Opinion Leaders Increasingly, marketers are looking to Web logs, or blogs, as they're commonly called, to find opinion leaders. A new blog is created every second of every day according to Technorati, a blog-monitoring site, so it's getting harder to separate the true opinion leaders from intermediate Web users who are just looking to share random thoughts or vacation photos with family and friends. As of this printing, Technorati monitors 35.3 million blogs, Feedster monitors 80 million, and Nielsen BuzzMetrics boasts coverage of more than 25 million blogs.[21] The fashion industry used to dismiss bloggers as irrelevant and small-time, effectively limiting their access to hot events during semi-annual fashion week shows. Now, however, fashion bloggers have the attention of the fashion establishment because many are claiming bigger followings than traditional media. Still, not all fashion blogs are equal. Bloggers from FashionTribes.com and Bagtrends.com received tickets to some fall 2006 shows, but shopology.com and Coutorture.com were denied access because their audiences were too small.[22]

EXHIBIT 6.9

Tweens and Teens Weigh in on Advertising Tactics

Ad Tactic	Like		Dislike	
	8–12 yrs	13–18 yrs	8–12 yrs	13–18 yrs
Famous person uses product	39%	21%	12%	22%
Person in a movie uses product	33%	20%	12%	19%
Cartoon or TV show about product	31%	13%	25%	34%
Popular kids given free product	24%	12%	43%	44%
Product advertised on cell phones	5%	4%	41%	55%
Product mentioned in online chats	5%	4%	37%	45%
Product written about on a blog site	14%	10%	24%	32%

Source: Adapted from "Today's Youth Look to Advertising as Much as Their Friends When Making Purchase Decisions", *PR Newswire*, August 21, 2006.

socialization process
How cultural values and norms are passed down to children.

One way marketers are identifying true opinion leaders is by looking to teen blogs to identify the social trends that are shaping consumer behavior. During the research phase of development for its teen-targeted RED Blogs service, AOL discovered that over 50 percent of teens do not mind sharing their feelings in public forums. This is especially evident at social networking sites like MySpace, Facebook, and Xanga, where teens and twentysomethings post extensive personal profiles, photo collections, links to user groups they belong to, and detailed descriptions of their social events.

Raised with MTV, 500-channel cable services, a rapidly maturing Internet, and ever-expanding cell phone capabilities, teens have unprecedented access to the world around them. Furthermore, they are no longer passive observers of the culture their parents have created. They can follow their favorite bands, actors, or athletes via their Web sites and blogs and expect to interact with them instead of just admiring them from afar. With their unprecedented ability to network and communicate with each other, young people rely on each others' opinions more than marketing messages when making purchase decisions. And blogs are becoming a key way that teens communicate their opinions (see Exhibit 6.9). Consequently, today's marketers are reading teen blogs, developing products that meet the very specific needs that teens express there, and learning unique and creative ways to put key influencers in charge of marketing their brands for them.

Family

The family is the most important social institution for many consumers, strongly influencing values, attitudes, self-concept—and buying behavior. For example, a family that strongly values good health will have a grocery list distinctly different from that of a family that views every dinner as a gourmet event. Moreover, the family is responsible for the socialization process, the passing down of cultural values and norms to children. Children learn by observing their parents' consumption patterns, and so they will tend to shop in a similar pattern.

Decision-making roles among family members tend to vary significantly, depending on the type of item purchased. Family members assume a variety of roles in the purchase process. *Initiators* suggest, initiate, or plant the seed for the purchase process. The initiator can be any member of the family. For example, Sister might initiate the product search by asking for a new bicycle as a birthday present. *Influencers* are those members of the family whose opinions are valued. In our example, Mom might function as a price-range watchdog, an influencer whose main role is to veto or approve price ranges. Brother may give his opinion on certain makes of bicycles. The *decision maker* is the family member who actually makes the decision to buy or not to buy. For example, Dad or Mom is likely to choose the final brand and model of bicycle to buy after seeking further information from Sister about cosmetic features such as color, and then imposing additional criteria of his or her own, such as durability and safety. The *purchaser* (probably Dad or Mom) is the one who actually exchanges money for the product. Finally, the *consumer* is the actual user—Sister, in the case of the bicycle.

Marketers should consider family purchase situations along with the distribution of consumer and decision-maker roles among family members. Ordinary marketing views the individual as both decision maker and consumer. Family marketing adds several other possibilities: Sometimes more than one family member or all family members are involved in the decision; sometimes only children are involved in the decision; sometimes more than one consumer is involved; sometimes the decision maker and the consumer are different people. Exhibit 6.10 represents the patterns of family purchasing relationships that are possible.

In most households when parental joint decisions are being made, spouses consider their partner's needs and perceptions to maintain decision fairness and harmony.[23] This tends to minimize family conflict. Research also shows that in harmonious households the spouse that has "won" a previous decision is less likely to use strong influence in a subsequent decision.[24] This balancing factor is key in maintaining long-term family harmony.

Children can have great influence over the purchase decisions of their parents. In many families, with both parents working and short on time, children are encouraged to participate. In addition, children in single-parent households become more involved in family decisions at an earlier age. Children are especially influential in decisions about food and eating out. Exactly how much of an influence kids have varies depending on factors such as age, race, socioeconomic status, and region. For example, *Restaurants & Institutions'* New American Diner study shows that children age 5 or younger frequently influence restaurant visits, while children ages 6 to 18 have only occasional influence. Females, Generation Xers, Asian American diners, and Midwesterners are most likely to say children influence which restaurants they visit.[25] Children influence purchase decisions for many more products and services than food. Even though they are usually not the actual purchasers of such items, children often participate in decisions about toys, clothes, vacations, recreation, automobiles, and many other products. And if those children happen to be teenagers? American teens have a total income of $80 billion of their own, and parents spend an additional $110 billion each year on them. Recent data shows that while teens make up only 7 percent of the U.S. population, they actually contribute to 11 percent of U.S. spending. [26]

Traditionally, children learn about consumption from their parents. In today's technologically overloaded world, that trend is reversing. Teenagers and adult children often contribute information and influence the purchase of parents' technology products.[27] Often they even help with installation and show the parents how to use the product!

EXHIBIT 6.10

Relationships among Purchasers and Consumers in the Family

		Purchase Decision Maker		
		Parent(s) Only	Child/Children Only	Some or All Family Members
Consumer	Parent(s)	golf clubs cosmetics wine	Mother's Day card	Christmas gifts minivan
	Child/ Children	diapers breakfast cereal	candy small toys	bicycle
	Some Family Members	videos long-distance phone service	children's movies	computers sports events
	All Family Members	clothing life insurance	fast-food restaurant	swim club membership vacations

Source: Reprinted with permission from "Pulling the Family's Strings" by Robert Boutillier in *American Demographics*.

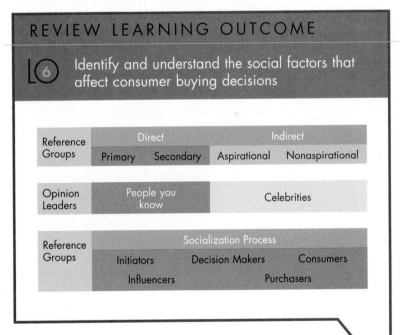

REVIEW LEARNING OUTCOME

LO6 Identify and understand the social factors that affect consumer buying decisions

Reference Groups	Direct		Indirect	
	Primary	Secondary	Aspirational	Nonaspirational

Opinion Leaders	People you know	Celebrities

Reference Groups	Socialization Process		
	Initiators	Decision Makers	Consumers
	Influencers		Purchasers

INDIVIDUAL INFLUENCES ON CONSUMER BUYING DECISIONS

A person's buying decisions are also influenced by personal characteristics that are unique to each individual, such as gender; age and life-cycle stage; and personality, self-concept, and lifestyle. Individual characteristics are generally stable over the course of one's life. For instance, most people do not change their gender, and the act of changing personality or lifestyle requires a complete reorientation of one's life. In the case of age and life-cycle stage, these changes occur gradually over time.

Gender

Physiological differences between men and women result in different needs, such as health and beauty products. Just as important are the distinct cultural, social, and economic roles played by men and women and the effects that these have on their decision-making processes. For example, many networks have programming targeted to women, while Spike TV calls itself the "first network for men." Two magazines are geared to men who like to shop: *Details* is an upscale fashion magazine for affluent men in their 20s and 30s; *Complex* is a magazine for younger men whose fashions range from hip-hop and skateboarding to mainstream style.

Trends in gender marketing are influenced by the changing roles of men and women in society. For example, men used to rely on the women in their lives to shop for them. Today, however, more men are shopping for themselves. The number of men shopping online was up to 57 percent in 2007 from 38 percent in 2006. Census Bureau figures show that in March 2003, the latest year for which Census statistics are available, there were 299,000 married-family households in which the husband was at home with at least one child under six. This figure was up 29 percent from 1993.[28] Men who have begun staying at home with their young children have noticed how few baby items, such as diaper bags, are made with a man's use in mind. One man went so far as to create his own product line, at **dadgear.com.** The first year the products hit the market, revenue was slightly higher than $40,000; projected revenue for 2006 was $800,000 to $1 million.[29] Whether because of the advent of online shopping or retailers wising up to the way men like to shop, today more men are comfortable shopping for themselves. A study commissioned by *GQ* found that 84 percent of men said they purchase their own clothes, compared with 65 percent four years ago.[30]

Men's roles aren't the only ones that are changing. Women around the world are working and earning more, and many industries are attracting new customers by marketing to women. For example, nearly 40 percent, or 50 million, of American Airlines' customers are women. If AA raises that number by 2 percent, it will make another $94 million in revenue each year. Acknowledging that, American has launched an online community resource especially for women travelers at **www.aa.com/women.** Wyndham Hotels and Resorts developed a program called Women On Their Way to enhance the experience of their female guests. American and Wyndham believe that by listening and responding to their female customers' insights, the travel experience for all of their customers will improve. These special programs are also designed to foster women travelers' belief that their business is valued.

The changing roles of women are also forcing companies that have traditionally targeted women to develop new strategies. One reason is because women's decision making tends to be multi-minded and integrative, meaning that they consider and move back and forth among many criteria, as opposed to being single-minded and focused. They tend to view shopping as a learning process, educating themselves on the available options and typically adding criteria as they learn more. It is not unusual for a woman to shift back to an earlier stage of the decision process as she learns something that may cause her even to change categories. For example, a woman may have decided to buy an SUV because her friends all love theirs and she likes the looks of the new models. Once on the showroom floor, however, she may see a new minivan that offers great storage and fuel mileage. Suddenly, she's including minivans in her consideration set and has added two new criteria to the qualifying list.

Age and Family Life-Cycle Stage

The age and family life-cycle stage of a consumer can have a significant impact on consumer behavior. How old a consumer is generally indicates what products he or she may be interested in purchasing. Consumer tastes in food, clothing, cars, furniture, and recreation are often age related. The table in Exhibit 6.11 uses data compiled by the Bureau of Labor Statistics to show the differences in spending on certain items by Americans by age.

EXHIBIT 6.11

Average Annual Expenditures by Age

Item	Age					
	<25	25–34	35–44	45–54	55–64	>65
Food at home	$2,265	$3,210	$4,125	$4,003	$3,457	$2,905
Food away from home	1,876	2,790	3,268	3,178	2,784	1,610
Household furnishings and equipment	925	2,034	2,198	1,933	1,944	1,235
Apparel and services	1,477	2,106	2,335	2,191	1,888	1,040
Vehicle purchases	2,273	3,930	4,183	3,223	3,348	1,977
Entertainment	1,448	2,462	3,551	3,163	2,730	1,966
Personal care products and services	337	512	662	686	632	528

Source: Bureau of Labor Statistics, 2005, by the U.S. Census Bureau.

Related to a person's age is his or her place in the family life cycle. As Chapter 8 explains in more detail, the *family life cycle* is an orderly series of stages through which consumers' attitudes and behavioral tendencies evolve through maturity, experience, and changing income and status. Marketers often define their target markets in terms of family life cycle, such as "young singles," "young married with children," and "middle-aged married without children." For instance, young singles spend more than average on alcoholic beverages, education, and entertainment. New parents typically increase their spending on health care, clothing, housing, and food and decrease their spending on alcohol, education, and transportation. Households with older children spend more on food, entertainment, personal care products, and education, as well as cars and gasoline. After their children leave home, spending by older couples on vehicles, women's clothing, health care, and long-distance calls typically increases. For instance, the presence of children in the home is the most significant determinant of the type of vehicle that's driven off the new-car lot. Parents are the ultimate need-driven car consumers, requiring larger cars and trucks to haul their children and all their belongings. It comes as no surprise then that for all households with children, SUVs rank either first or second among new-vehicle purchases, followed by minivans.

Marketers should also be aware of the many nontraditional life-cycle paths that are common today and provide insights into the needs and wants of such consumers as divorced parents, lifelong singles, and childless couples. Three decades ago, married couples with children under the age of 18 accounted for about half of U.S. households. Today, such families make up only 23 percent of all households, while people living alone or with nonfamily members represent more than 30 percent. Furthermore, according to the U.S. Census Bureau, the number of single-mother households grew by 25 percent over the last decade. The shift toward more single-parent households is part of a broader societal change that has put more women on the career track. Although many marketers continue to be wary of targeting nontraditional families, Charles Schwab targeted single mothers in an advertising campaign featuring Sarah Ferguson, the Duchess of York and a divorced mom. The idea was to appeal to single mothers' heightened awareness of the need for financial self-sufficiency.

Life Events Another way to look at the life cycle is to look at major events in one's life over time. Life-changing events can occur at any time. A few examples are: death of a spouse, moving to a different place, birth or adoption of a child, retirement, getting fired, divorce, and marriage. Typically, such events are quite stressful and consumers often take steps to minimize that stress. Many times such life-changing events will mean new consumption patterns.[31] A recently divorced person may try to improve his or her appearance by joining a health club and dieting. A person moving to a different

personality
A way of organizing and grouping the consistencies of an individual's reactions to situations.

self-concept
How consumers perceive themselves in terms of attitudes, perceptions, beliefs, and self-evaluations.

ideal self-image
The way an individual would like to be.

real self-image
The way an individual actually perceives himself or herself.

lifestyle
A mode of living as identified by a person's activities, interests, and opinions.

city will need a new dentist, grocery store, auto service center, and doctor, to name a few shops and service providers. Marketers realize that life-events often mean a chance to gain a new customer. The Welcome Wagon offers a number of free gifts and services for area newcomers. Lowe's sends out a discount coupon to those moving to a new community. And when you put your home on the market, very quickly you start getting flyers from moving companies promising a great price on moving your household goods.

Personality, Self-Concept, and Lifestyle

Each consumer has a unique personality. Personality is a broad concept that can be thought of as a way of organizing and grouping how an individual typically reacts to situations. Thus, personality combines psychological makeup and environmental forces. It includes people's underlying dispositions, especially their most dominant characteristics. Although personality is one of the least useful concepts in the study of consumer behavior, some marketers believe that personality influences the types and brands of products purchased. For instance, the type of car, clothes, or jewelry a consumer buys may reflect one or more personality traits.

Self-concept, or self-perception, is how consumers perceive themselves. Self-concept includes attitudes, perceptions, beliefs, and self-evaluations. Although self-concept may change, the change is often gradual. Through self-concept, people define their identity, which in turn provides for consistent and coherent behavior.

Self-concept combines the ideal self-image (the way an individual would like to be) and the real self-image (how an individual actually perceives himself or herself). Generally, we try to raise our real self-image toward our ideal (or at least narrow the gap). Consumers seldom buy products that jeopardize their self-image. For example, someone who sees herself as a trendsetter wouldn't buy clothing that doesn't project a contemporary image.

Human behavior depends largely on self-concept. Because consumers want to protect their identity as individuals, the products they buy, the stores they patronize, and the credit cards they carry support their self-image. No other product quite reflects a person's self-image as much as the car he or she drives. For example, many young consumers do not like family sedans like the Honda Accord or Toyota Camry and say they would buy one for their mom, but not for themselves. Likewise, younger parents may avoid purchasing minivans because they do not want to sacrifice the youthful image they have of themselves just because they have new responsibilities. To combat decreasing sales, marketers of the Nissan Quest minivan decided to reposition it as something other than a "mom mobile" or "soccer mom car." They chose the ad copy "Passion built it. Passion will fill it up," followed by "What if we made a minivan that changed the way people think of minivans?"

By influencing the degree to which consumers perceive a good or service to be self-relevant, marketers can affect consumers' motivation to learn about, shop for, and buy a certain brand. Marketers also consider self-concept important because it helps explain the relationship between individuals' perceptions of themselves and their consumer behavior.

Personality and self-concept are reflected in lifestyle. A lifestyle is a mode of living, as identified by a person's activities, interests, and opinions. Psychographics is the analytical technique used to examine consumer lifestyles and to categorize consumers. Unlike personality characteristics, which are hard to describe and measure, lifestyle characteristics are useful in segmenting and targeting consumers. Lifestyle and psychographic analysis explicitly addresses the way consumers outwardly express their inner selves in their social and cultural environment.

Many companies now use psychographics to better understand their market segments. For many years, marketers selling products to mothers conveniently assumed that all moms were fairly homogeneous and concerned about the same things—the health and well-being of their children—and that they could all be reached with a similar message. But recent lifestyle research has shown that there are traditional, blended, and nontraditional moms, and companies like Procter & Gamble and Pillsbury are using strategies to reach these different types of mothers. Psychographics is also effective with other market segments.

An example of a lifestyle segment are those people who are snackers. Snacking can be part of a healthy diet or it can be loaded with junk food. Thus, there are healthy and unhealthy snackers. Today, 21 percent of all meals are snacks.[32] A few findings on snacks and snackers are:

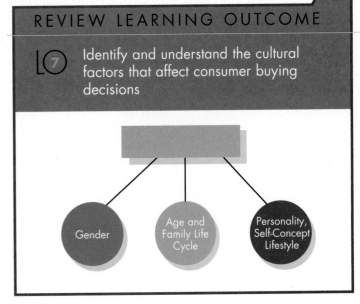

- ☞ While late-night refrigerator trips are still the most common (38.3 percent), morning snacks are rapidly growing (28.4 percent). Snack foods replaced breakfast more than any other meal. At-home afternoon snacking came in at 29.3 percent, followed by carried snacks (3.8 percent).

- ☞ Fruit is the top food eaten between meals at home and consumption is up from five years ago. Cookies, candy/gum, ice cream, and chips round out the top five most popular snack foods, respectively.

- ☞ Snack-oriented foods are not only eaten between meals; sometimes they serve as side dishes or replace a meal entirely.

- ☞ Most snack foods are purchased more than a day ahead. One in 10 snacks is bought within 30 minutes of consumption.

- ☞ Snack consumption is currently most popular among kids ages 6 to 12, but declining among children 2 to 5, adults ages 18 to 34, and those over 55.[33]

Psychographics and lifestyle segmentation are discussed in more detail in Chapter 8.

LO8 PSYCHOLOGICAL INFLUENCES ON CONSUMER BUYING DECISIONS

An individual's buying decisions are further influenced by psychological factors: perception, motivation, learning, and beliefs and attitudes. These factors are what consumers use to interact with their world. They are the tools consumers use to recognize their feelings, gather and analyze information, formulate thoughts and opinions, and take action. Unlike the other three influences on consumer behavior, psychological influences can be affected by a person's environment because they are applied on specific occasions. For example, you will perceive different stimuli and process these stimuli in different ways depending on whether you are sitting in class concentrating on the instructor, sitting outside of class talking to friends, or sitting in your dorm room watching television.

Perception

The world is full of stimuli. A stimulus is any unit of input affecting one or more of the five senses: sight, smell, taste, touch, and hearing. The process by which we select, organize, and interpret these stimuli into a meaningful and coherent picture is called perception. In essence, perception is how we see the world around us and how we recognize that we need some help in making a purchasing decision.

People cannot perceive every stimulus in their environment. Therefore, they use selective exposure to decide which stimuli to notice and which to ignore. A typical

perception
The process by which people select, organize, and interpret stimuli into a meaningful and coherent picture.

selective exposure
The process whereby a consumer notices certain stimuli and ignores others.

selective distortion
A process whereby a consumer changes or distorts information that conflicts with his or her feelings or beliefs.

selective retention
A process whereby a consumer remembers only that information that supports his or her personal beliefs.

consumer is exposed to more than 2,500 advertising messages a day, but notices only between 11 and 20.

The familiarity of an object, contrast, movement, intensity (such as increased volume), and smell are cues that influence perception. Consumers use these cues to identify and define products and brands. The shape of a product's packaging, such as Coca-Cola's signature contour bottle, for instance, can influence perception. Color is another cue, and it plays a key role in consumers' perceptions. Packaged foods manufacturers use color to trigger unconscious associations for grocery shoppers who typically make their shopping decisions in the blink of an eye. When Pepsi departed from its usual blue can for a red can in a marketing campaign for the 2008 Olympics in China, they risked brand confusion with Coke products. One Pepsi drinker in China said, "This is so weird. I usually just go for the blue can; it's easy to spot. . . the red can just doesn't look right." Pepsi officials say they coordinated the can with the color of China's flag to highlight their sponsorship of Team China. Pepsi had used national colors on promotional packages before, such as yellow and green cans to sponsor Brazilian teams.[34]

Ampacet, a world leader in color additives for plastics, reported in 2007 that nature-inspired colors and organic values were becoming more popular as the economy and global focus shifted from the tech-boom to bio- or eco-boom. Ecological consequences and concerns have resulted in marketing initiatives such as "going green." Packaging colors like natural greens, earthy browns, and strong yellows are in, as well as metallics such as steely silver, carbon black, gold, and copper. Color researchers speculate that technological overload has led to resurgence in the appreciation of simplistic luxury. Color names for fabrics and makeup reflect that trend with names such as Grounded, Champagne Chic, and Serene Blue.[35]

What is perceived by consumers may also depend on the stimuli's vividness or shock value. Graphic warnings of the hazards associated with a product's use are perceived more readily and remembered more accurately than less vivid warnings or warnings that are written in text. "Sexier" ads excel at attracting the attention of younger consumers. Companies like Calvin Klein and Guess use sensuous ads intended to create a fantasy or mood to capture the attention of the target audience. Fragrance advertisements often make promises of the "outcome" of wearing their product, often the promise of a role transformation on the part of the wearer. David Rubin, brand development director for Axe deodorant, says Axe's theme from the very start has been "giving guys an edge in the mating game."[36]

Two other concepts closely related to selective exposure are selective distortion and selective retention. Selective distortion occurs when consumers change or distort information that conflicts with their feelings or beliefs. For example, suppose a college student buys a SonicBlue Rio MP3 player. After the purchase, if the student gets new information about an alternative brand, such as an Apple iPod, he or she may distort the information to make it more consistent with the prior view that the SonicBlue Rio is just as good as the iPod, if not better. Business travelers who fly often may distort or discount information about airline crashes because they must use air travel constantly in their jobs.

Selective retention is remembering only information that supports personal feelings or beliefs. The consumer forgets all information that may be inconsistent. After reading a pamphlet that contradicts one's political beliefs, for instance, a person may forget many of the points outlined in it. Similarly, consumers may see a news report on suspected illegal practices by their favorite retail store, but soon forget the reason the store was featured on the news.

Which stimuli will be perceived often depends on the individual. People can be exposed to the same stimuli under identical conditions but perceive them very differently. For example, two people viewing a TV commercial may have different interpretations of the advertising message. One person may be thoroughly engrossed by the message and become highly motivated to buy the product. Thirty seconds after the ad ends, the second person may not be able to recall the content of the message or even the product advertised.

Marketing Implications of Perception Marketers must recognize the importance of cues, or signals, in consumers' perception of products. Marketing managers first identify the important attributes, such as price or quality, that the targeted consumers want in a product and then design signals to communicate these attributes. For example, consumers will pay more for candy in expensive-looking foil packages. But shiny labels on wine bottles signify less expensive wines; dull labels indicate more expensive wines. Marketers also often use price as a signal to consumers that the product is of higher quality than competing products. Gibson Guitar Corporation briefly cut prices on many of its guitars to compete with Japanese rivals Yamaha and Ibanez, but found that it sold more guitars when it charged more for them. Consumers perceived that the higher price indicated a better quality instrument.[37]

Of course, brand names send signals to consumers. The brand names of Close-Up toothpaste, DieHard batteries, and Caress moisturizing soap, for example, identify important product qualities. Names chosen for search engines and sites on the Internet, such as Yahoo!, Amazon.com, and Excite, are intended to convey excitement, intensity, and vastness. Companies may even change their names to send a message to consumers. As today's utility companies increasingly enter unregulated markets, many are shaking their stodgy "Power & Light & Electric" names in favor of those that let consumers know they are not just about electricity anymore, such as Reliant Resources, Entergy, and Cinergy.

Consumers also associate quality and reliability with certain brand names. Companies watch their brand identity closely, in large part because a strong link has been established between perceived brand value and customer loyalty. Brand names that consistently enjoy high perceived value from consumers include Kodak, Disney, National Geographic, Mercedes-Benz, and Fisher-Price. Naming a product after a place can also add perceived value by association. Brand names using the words Santa Fe, Dakota, or Texas convey a sense of openness, freedom, and youth, but products named after other locations might conjure up images of pollution and crime.

Marketing managers are also interested in the *threshold level of perception*: the minimum difference in a stimulus that the consumer will notice. This concept is sometimes referred to as the "just-noticeable difference." For example, how much would Apple have to drop the price of its iPod Shuffle before consumers recognized it as a bargain—$25? $50? or more? One study found that the just-noticeable difference in a stimulus is about a 20 percent change. For example, consumers will likely notice a 20 percent price decrease more quickly than a 15 percent decrease. This marketing principle can be applied to other marketing variables as well, such as package size or loudness of a broadcast advertisement.[38]

© LEIGH PRATHER/SHUTTERSTOCK.COM

" *Consumers will likely notice a 20 percent price decrease more quickly than a 15 percent decrease.* "

Besides changing such stimuli as price, package size, and volume, marketers can change the product or attempt to reposition its image. But marketers must be careful when adding features. How many new services will discounter Target Stores need to add before consumers perceive it as a full-service department store? How many sporty features will General Motors have to add to a basic two-door sedan before consumers start perceiving it as a sports car?

Marketing managers who intend to do business in global markets should be aware of how foreign consumers perceive their products. For instance, in Japan, product labels are often written in English or French, even though they may not translate into anything meaningful. Many Japanese associate foreign words on product labels with the exotic, the expensive, and high quality.

Marketers have often been suspected of sending advertising messages subconsciously to consumers in what is known as *subliminal perception*. The controversy began when a researcher claimed to have increased popcorn and Coca-Cola sales at a movie theater after flashing "Eat popcorn" and "Drink Coca-Cola" on the screen every five seconds for 1/300th of a second, although the audience did not consciously recognize the messages. Almost immediately consumer protection groups became concerned that advertisers were brainwashing consumers, and this practice was pronounced illegal in California and Canada. Although the researcher later admitted to making up the data and scientists have been unable to replicate the study since, consumers are still wary of hidden messages that advertisers may be sending.

Motivation

By studying motivation, marketers can analyze the major forces influencing consumers to buy or not buy products. When you buy a product, you usually do so to fulfill some kind of need. These needs become motives when aroused sufficiently. For instance, suppose this morning you were so hungry before class that you needed to eat something. In response to that need, you stopped at McDonald's for an Egg McMuffin. In other words, you were motivated by hunger to stop at McDonald's. Motives are the driving forces that cause a person to take action to satisfy specific needs.

Why are people driven by particular needs at particular times? One popular theory is Maslow's hierarchy of needs, shown in Exhibit 6.12, which arranges needs in ascending order of importance: physiological, safety, social, esteem, and self-actualization. As a person fulfills one need, a higher-level need becomes more important.

The most basic human needs are *physiological*—that is, the needs for food, water, and shelter. Because they are essential to survival, these needs must be satisfied first. Ads showing a juicy hamburger or a runner gulping down Gatorade after a marathon are examples of appeals to satisfy the physiological needs of hunger and thirst.

Safety needs include security and freedom from pain and discomfort. Marketers sometimes appeal to consumers' fears and anxieties about safety to sell their products. For example, aware of the aging population's health fears, the retail medical imaging centers Heart Check America and HealthScreen America advertise that they offer consumers a full body scan for early detection of health problems such as coronary disease and cancer. On the other hand, some companies or industries advertise to allay consumer fears. For example, in the wake of the September 11 terrorist attacks, the airline industry found itself having to conduct an image campaign to reassure consumers about the safety of air travel.

After physiological and safety needs have been fulfilled, *social needs*—especially love and a sense of belonging—become the focus. Love includes acceptance by one's peers, as well as sex and romantic love. Marketing managers probably appeal more to this need than to any other. Ads for clothes, cosmetics, and vacation packages suggest that buying the product can bring love. The need to belong is also a favorite of marketers, especially those marketing products to teens.

Teens consider the iPod to be not only their favorite brand but also as defining their generation. Other such brands include American Eagle Outfitters, Axe, Baby Phat, Facebook, Google, Hollister, MTV, MySpace, Vans, and YouTube. The VP of Research at MTV says marketers need to understand a new dynamic in the "millennial generation" consumer. The relationship this generation has with their parents is completely different from previous generations'. Parents can be a best friend. Brands that become too focused on "influential" teens can miss that parents can be the biggest influencer on this age group, especially when it comes to big-ticket items.[39]

Love is acceptance without regard to one's contribution. Esteem is

EXHIBIT 6.12

Maslow's Hierarchy of Needs

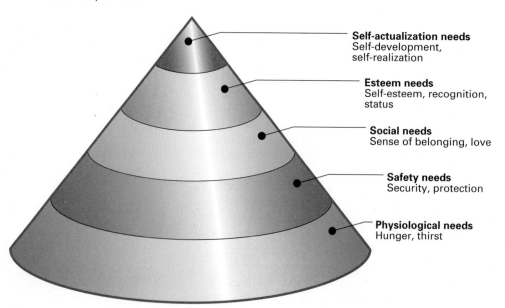

Self-actualization needs
Self-development, self-realization

Esteem needs
Self-esteem, recognition, status

Social needs
Sense of belonging, love

Safety needs
Security, protection

Physiological needs
Hunger, thirst

acceptance based on one's contribution to the group. *Self-esteem needs* include self-respect and a sense of accomplishment. Esteem needs also include prestige, fame, and recognition of one's accomplishments. Montblanc pens, Mercedes-Benz automobiles, and Neiman Marcus stores all appeal to esteem needs. Most high-end spas and health clubs appeal to consumers' self-esteem needs. Like exclusive country clubs, clubs such as Chicago's East Bank Club are designed to make members feel proud of their commitment to fitness while also giving them a sense of social accomplishment. In fact, the clubs can be so effective that even during an economic recession, patrons will not give up their membership because to do so would be a public admission of financial problems.

Asian consumers, in particular, are strongly motivated by status and appearance. Asians tend to be conscious of their place in a group, institution, or society as a whole. The importance of gaining social recognition turns Asians into some of the most image-conscious consumers in the world. Status-conscious Asians will not hesitate to spend freely on premium brands, such as BMW, Mercedes-Benz, and the best Scotch whiskey and French cognac. Indeed, marketers of luxury products such as Gucci, Louis Vuitton, and Prada find that demand for their products is so strong among image-conscious consumers that their sales are generally unaffected by economic downturns. In some cases, companies have been able to make up for sluggish European and U.S. sales by raising prices and volume in Asia.

The highest human need is *self-actualization*. It refers to finding self-fulfillment and self-expression, reaching the point in life at which "people are what they feel they should be." Maslow felt that very few people ever attain this level. Even so, advertisements may focus on this type of need. For example, American Express ads convey the message that acquiring its card is one of the highest attainments in life. Microsoft appealed to consumers' needs for self-actualization when it chose "Your Potential. Our Passion" as the Windows XP slogan; similarly, the U.S. Army changed its slogan from "Be all that you can be" to "Army of One," and the U.S. Navy adopted a slogan urging young people to "Accelerate Your Life."

Learning

Almost all consumer behavior results from learning, which is the process that creates changes in behavior through experience and practice. It is not possible to observe learning directly, but we can infer when it has occurred by a person's actions. For example, suppose you see an advertisement for a new and improved cold medicine. If you go to the store that day and buy that remedy, we infer that you have learned something about the cold medicine.

There are two types of learning: experiential and conceptual. *Experiential learning* occurs when an experience changes your behavior. For example, if the new cold medicine does not relieve your symptoms, you may not buy that brand again. *Conceptual learning*, which is not acquired through direct experience, is the second type of learning. Assume, for example, that you are standing at a soft drink machine and notice a new diet flavor with an artificial sweetener. Because someone has told you that diet beverages leave an aftertaste, you choose a different drink. You have learned that you would not like this new diet drink without ever trying it.

Reinforcement and repetition boost learning. Reinforcement can be positive or negative. If you see a vendor selling frozen yogurt (stimulus), buy it (response), and find the yogurt to be quite refreshing (reward), your behavior has been positively reinforced. On the other hand, if you buy a new flavor of yogurt and it does not taste good (negative reinforcement), you will not buy that flavor of yogurt again (response). Without positive or negative reinforcement, a person will not be motivated to repeat the behavior pattern or to avoid it. Thus, if a new brand evokes neutral feelings, some marketing activity, such as a price change or an increase in promotion, may be required to induce further consumption. Learning theory is helpful in reminding marketers that concrete and timely actions are what reinforce desired consumer behavior.

Repetition is a key strategy in promotional campaigns because it can lead to increased learning. Most marketers use repetitive advertising so that consumers will learn what their

learning
A process that creates changes in behavior, immediate or expected, through experience and practice.

unique advantage is over the competition. Generally, to heighten learning, advertising messages should be spread out over time rather than clustered together.

A related learning concept useful to marketing managers is stimulus generalization. In theory, stimulus generalization occurs when one response is extended to a second stimulus similar to the first. Marketers often use a successful, well-known brand name for a family of products because it gives consumers familiarity with and knowledge about each product in the family. Such brand-name families spur the introduction of new products and facilitate the sale of existing items. Jell-O frozen pudding pops rely on the familiarity of Jell-O gelatin; Clorox bathroom cleaner relies on familiarity with Clorox bleach; and Dove shampoo relies on familiarity with Dove soap. Microsoft entered the video game industry, hoping that the Microsoft brand would guarantee sales for the Xbox. Initial response to the Xbox was strong based on Microsoft's reputation. Since then, Microsoft has worked hard to be successful in an industry dominated by other brand giants Sony and Nintendo. The latest generation Xbox 360 Elite has jaw-dropping high-definition graphics, unmatched online play, and compelling digital entertainment; it plays music and movies stored in an array of devices, including MP3 players, and displays photos from digital cameras. Branding is examined in more detail in Chapter 10.

Another form of stimulus generalization occurs when retailers or wholesalers design their packages to resemble well-known manufacturers' brands. Such imitation often confuses consumers, who buy the imitation thinking it's the original. U.S. manufacturers in foreign markets have sometimes found little, if any, brand protection. BMW and Daimler-Chrysler recently sued Chinese car manufacturers for creating near-exact replicas of their cars. Cosmetics giant L'Oreal, maker of Gucci and other luxury brands, is threatening legal action against eBay unless the auction site cracks down on sales of counterfeit L'Oreal products on its site. DVD piracy is rampant in China; so much so that special DVD-counterfeit-sniffing dogs have become a common sight in international airports. After the terrorist attacks of September 11 and subsequent stepped-up security regulations, authentication technologies have been used successfully in identifying fake passports, currency, and credit cards. Those same technologies—and others, such as embedded microchips, holographic symbols, and tamperproof packaging—are now being used in everyday products such as clothing, footwear, computers, cell phones, video games, jewelry, software, pharmaceuticals, and medical devices, making it easier for importers and retailers to spot fakes.[40]

The opposite of stimulus generalization is stimulus discrimination, which means learning to differentiate among similar products. Consumers may perceive one product as more rewarding or stimulating. For example, some consumers prefer Coca-Cola and others prefer Pepsi. Many insist they can taste a difference between the two brands.

With some types of products—such as aspirin, gasoline, bleach, and paper towels—marketers rely on promotion to point out brand differences that consumers would otherwise not recognize. This process, called *product differentiation*, is discussed in more detail in Chapter 8. Usually, product differentiation is based on superficial differences. For example, Bayer tells consumers that it's the aspirin "doctors recommend most."

Beliefs and Attitudes

Beliefs and attitudes are closely linked to values. A belief is an organized pattern of knowledge that an individual holds as true about his or her world. A consumer may believe that Sony's camcorder makes the best home videos, tolerates hard use, and is reasonably priced. These beliefs may be based on knowledge, faith, or hearsay. Consumers tend to develop a set of beliefs about a product's attributes and then, through these beliefs, form a *brand image*—a set of beliefs about a particular brand. In turn, the brand image shapes consumers' attitudes toward the product.

An attitude is a learned tendency to respond consistently toward a given object, such as a brand. Attitudes rest on an individual's value system, which represents personal standards of good and bad, right and wrong, and so forth; therefore, attitudes tend to be more enduring and complex than beliefs.

For an example of the nature of attitudes, consider the differing attitudes of consumers around the world toward the practice of purchasing on credit. Americans have long been enthusiastic about charging goods and services and are willing to pay high interest rates for the privilege of postponing payment. To many European consumers, doing what amounts to taking out a loan—even a small one—to pay for anything seems absurd. Germans especially are reluctant to buy on credit. Italy has a sophisticated credit and banking system well suited to handling credit cards, but Italians prefer to carry cash, often huge wads of it. Although most Japanese consumers have credit cards, card purchases amount to less than 1 percent of all consumer transactions. The Japanese have long looked down on credit purchases, but acquire cards to use while traveling abroad.

If a good or service is meeting its profit goals, positive attitudes toward the product merely need to be reinforced. If the brand is not succeeding, however, the marketing manager must strive to change target consumers' attitudes toward it. Changes in attitude tend to grow out of an individual's attempt to reconcile long-held values with a constant stream of new information. This change can be accomplished in three ways: changing beliefs about the brand's attributes, changing the relative importance of these beliefs, and adding new beliefs.

Changing Beliefs about Attributes The first technique is to turn neutral, negative, or incorrect beliefs about product attributes into positive ones. Assume that 24 Hour Fitness does a survey among persons considering joining a health club. They find that most respondents believe that 24 Hour Fitness offers fewer classes and less variety than Shapes, Curves for Women, or Lifestyle Family Fitness. In fact, 24 Hour Fitness offers greater variety and more classes than any other health and fitness center. Thus, target consumers have incorrect beliefs and the service's attributes (number of classes and variety). So 24 Hour Fitness must advertise and do other forms of promotion, such as an open house, to correct the misimpressions.

Changing beliefs about a service can be more difficult because service attributes are usually intangible. Convincing consumers to switch hairstylists or lawyers or go to a mall dental clinic can be much more difficult than getting them to change brands of razor blades. Image, which is also largely intangible, significantly determines service patronage.

Usually changing beliefs about a product attribute is easier. For example, GE has created a new light bulb, a compact fluorescent lamp (CFL), that uses 1/3 the energy of a traditional bulb, lasts nearly 10 times longer, and can save up to $30 in energy costs over its lifetime. GE's new campaign urges the use of its new bulb by appealing to Americans' burgeoning ecological awareness, while exhibiting its own "care" for the world's resources. How could the consumer possibly resist when GE has made it so easy to participate? If every American swapped one standard bulb for a CFL, it would collectively prevent burning 30 billion pounds of coal and remove two million cars' worth of greenhouse gas emissions from the atmosphere.[41]

Changing the Importance of Beliefs The second approach to modifying attitudes is to change the relative importance of beliefs about an attribute. Cole Haan, originally a men's shoe outfitter, used boats and cars in its ads for years to associate the brand with active lifestyles, an important attribute for men. Now that it is selling women's products, such as handbags and shoes, some of its ads use models and emphasize how the products look, an important attribute for women. The company hopes the ads will change customers' perceptions and beliefs that it only sells men's products.[42]

Marketers can also emphasize the importance of some beliefs over others. For example, when consumers think of full-sized SUVs, good gas mileage doesn't often come to mind. Now, Cadillac wants to raise the importance of fuel efficiency to buyers of full-size SUVs.

LO 8   Identify and understand the psychological factors that affect consumer buying decisions

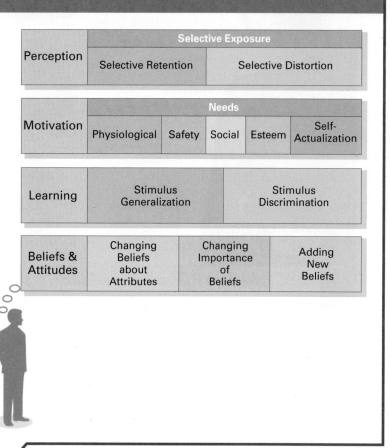

Perception	Selective Exposure	
	Selective Retention	Selective Distortion

Motivation	Needs				
	Physiological	Safety	Social	Esteem	Self-Actualization

Learning	Stimulus Generalization	Stimulus Discrimination

Beliefs & Attitudes	Changing Beliefs about Attributes	Changing Importance of Beliefs	Adding New Beliefs

The promotion for the 2009 Escalade Hybrid says, "Finally, a full-size luxury SUV confident enough to talk about fuel efficiency."[43]

Adding New Beliefs The third approach to transforming attitudes is to add new beliefs. Although changes in consumption patterns often come slowly, cereal marketers are betting that consumers will eventually warm up to the idea of cereal as a snack. A print ad for General Mills Cookie-Crisp cereal features a boy popping the sugary nuggets into his mouth while he does his homework. Koch Industries, the manufacturer of Dixie paper products, is also attempting to add new beliefs about the uses of its paper plates and cups with an advertising campaign aimed at positioning its product as a "home cleanup replacement." Commercials pitch Dixie paper plates as an alternative to washing dishes after everyday meals and not just for picnics.

U.S. companies attempting to market their goods overseas may need to help consumers add new beliefs about a product in general. Coca-Cola and PepsiCo have both found it challenging to sell their diet cola brands to consumers in India partly because diet foods of any kind are a new concept in that country where malnutrition was widespread not too many years ago. Indians also have deep-rooted attitudes that anything labeled "diet" is meant for a sick person, such as a diabetic. As a general rule, most Indians are not diet-conscious, preferring food prepared in the traditional manner that tastes good. Indians are also suspicious of the artificial sweeteners used in diet colas. India's Health Ministry has required warning labels on cans and bottles of Diet Coke and Diet Pepsi saying "Not Recommended for Children."[44]

5 ◄ number of factors determining the 3 types of consumer buying decisions

Kellogg's cereal advertising budget ► **$206 million**

4% ◄ projected growth rate for the U.S. population

projected growth rate for the population of African American women ► **8%**

73 ◄ Pecentage American Hispanics reached by Univision Radio

reported worth of Nike's endorsement deal with LeBron James ▼ **$90 million**

28 million ◄ number of registered users of the online community Piczo

number of blogs monitored by Technorati ▼ **35.3 million**

ANATOMY OF a Buying Decision: Car

For a high-involvement purchase, such as buying a car, a consumer typically practices extensive decision making. Several factors ultimately affect her buying decision.

SOCIAL FACTORS

Before deciding to buy a car, this woman may seek out others' opinions or observe what others purchase.

ADVICE FROM HER REFERENCE GROUP

EXAMPLE OF OPINION LEADER

© iStockphoto.com/ digitalskillet

© iStockphoto.com/ Palto

INDIVIDUAL FACTORS:

LIFESTYLE

SELF-CONCEPT

Her buying decision will be influenced by her personality, self-concept, and lifestyle.

© iStockphoto.com/ Richard Hobson

© iStockphoto.com/Brad Killer

PSYCHOLOGICAL FACTORS:

The consumer's perception, motivation, learning, values, beliefs, and attitudes will influence her decision on which car to buy, too.

ATTITUDE

"Should I try a new brand, or stick with the familiar one?"

?

© iStockphoto.com/Justin Horrocks

Stockphoto.com/ Niko Guido

REVIEW AND APPLICATIONS

LO ① Explain why marketing managers should understand consumer behavior. Consumer behavior describes how consumers make purchase decisions and how they use and dispose of the products they buy. An understanding of consumer behavior reduces marketing managers' uncertainty when they are defining a target market and designing a marketing mix.

1.1 The type of decision making a consumer uses for a product does not necessarily remain constant. Why? Support your answer with an example from your own experience.

LO ② Analyze the components of the consumer decision-making process. The consumer decision-making process begins with need recognition, when stimuli trigger awareness of an unfulfilled want. If additional information is required to make a purchase decision, the consumer may engage in an internal or external information search. The consumer then evaluates the additional information and establishes purchase guidelines. Finally, a purchase decision is made.

2.1 Visit Carpoint's Web site at **http://autos.msn.com/.** How does the site assist consumers in the evaluation stage of choosing a new car? Develop your own hypothetical evoked set of three or four car models and present your comparisons. Which vehicle attributes would be most important in your purchase decision?

LO ③ Explain the consumer's postpurchase evaluation process. Consumer postpurchase evaluation is influenced by prepurchase expectations, the prepurchase information search, and the consumer's general level of self-confidence. Cognitive dissonance is the inner tension that a consumer experiences after recognizing a purchased product's disadvantages. When a purchase creates cognitive dissonance, consumers tend to react by seeking positive reinforcement for the purchase decision, avoiding negative information about the purchase decision, or revoking the purchase decision by returning the product.

3.1 Recall an occasion when you experienced cognitive dissonance about a purchase. In a letter to a friend, describe the event and explain what you did about it.

LO ④ Identify the types of consumer buying decisions and discuss the significance of consumer involvement. Consumer decision making falls into three broad categories. First, consumers exhibit routine response behavior for frequently purchased, low-cost items that require very little decision effort; routine response behavior is typically characterized by brand loyalty. Second, consumers engage in limited decision making for occasional purchases or for unfamiliar brands in familiar product categories. Third, consumers practice extensive decision making when making unfamiliar, expensive, or infrequent purchases. High-involvement decisions usually include an extensive information search and a thorough evaluation of alternatives. In contrast, low-involvement decisions are characterized by brand loyalty and a lack of personal identification with the product. The main factors affecting the level of consumer involvement are previous experience, interest, perceived risk of negative consequences (financial, social, and psychological), situation, and social visibility.

4.1 Describe the three categories of consumer decision-making behavior. Name typical products for which each type of consumer behavior is used.

4.2 Describe the level of involvement and the involvement factors likely to be associated with buying a new computer. Do you think Apple's Web site at

www.apple.com simplifies or complicates the process for the average consumer? Explain.

Identify and understand the cultural factors that affect consumer buying decisions. Cultural influences on consumer buying decisions include culture and values, subculture, and social class. Culture is the essential character of a society that distinguishes it from other cultural groups. The underlying elements of every culture are the values, language, myths, customs, rituals, laws, and artifacts, or products, which are transmitted from one generation to the next. The most defining element of a culture is its values—the enduring beliefs shared by a society that a specific mode of conduct is personally or socially preferable to another mode of conduct. A culture can be divided into subcultures on the basis of demographic characteristics, geographic regions, national and ethnic background, political beliefs, and religious beliefs. Subcultures share elements of the overall culture as well as cultural elements unique to their own group. A social class is a group of people who are considered nearly equal in status or community esteem, who regularly socialize among themselves both formally and informally, and who share behavioral norms.

5.1   You are a new marketing manager for a firm that produces a line of athletic shoes to be targeted to the college student subculture. In a memo to your boss, list some product attributes that might appeal to this subculture and the steps in your customers' purchase processes, and recommend some marketing strategies that can influence their decision.

Identify and understand the social factors that affect consumer buying decisions. Social factors include such external influences as reference groups, opinion leaders, and family. Consumers seek out others' opinions for guidance on new products or services and products with image-related attributes or because attribute information is lacking or uninformative. Consumers may use products or brands to identify with or become a member of a reference group. Opinion leaders are members of reference groups who influence others' purchase decisions. Family members also influence purchase decisions; children tend to shop in similar patterns as their parents.

6.1   Family members play many different roles in the buying process: initiator, influencer, decision maker, purchaser, and consumer. Identify the person in your family who might play each of these roles in the purchase of a dinner at Pizza Hut, a summer vacation, Froot Loops breakfast cereal, an Abercrombie & Fitch sweater, golf clubs, an Internet service provider, and a new car.

Identify and understand the individual factors that affect consumer buying decisions. Individual factors that affect consumer buying decisions include gender; age and family life-cycle stage; and personality, self-concept, and lifestyle. Beyond obvious physiological differences, men and women differ in their social and economic roles, and that affects consumer buying decisions. How old a consumer is generally indicates what products he or she may be interested in purchasing. Marketers often define their target markets in terms of consumers' life-cycle stage, following changes in consumers' attitudes and behavioral tendencies as they mature. Finally, certain products and brands reflect consumers' personality, self-concept, and lifestyle.

7.1   Assume you are involved in the following consumer decision situations: (a) renting a DVD to watch with your roommates, (b) choosing a fast-food restaurant to go to with a new friend, (c) buying a popular music compact disc, (d) buying jeans to wear to class. List the individual factors that would influence your decision in each situation and explain your responses.

Identify and understand the psychological factors that affect consumer buying decisions. Psychological factors include perception, motivation, learning, values, beliefs, and attitudes. These factors allow consumers to interact with the world around them, recognize their feelings, gather and analyze information, formulate thoughts and opinions, and take action. Perception allows consumers to recognize their consumption problems. Motivation is what drives consumers to take action to satisfy specific consumption needs. Almost all consumer behavior results from learning, which is the process that creates changes in behavior through experience. Consumers with similar beliefs and attitudes tend to react alike to marketing-related inducements.

8.1 How do beliefs and attitudes influence consumer behavior? How can negative attitudes toward a product be changed? How can marketers alter beliefs about a product? Give some examples of how marketers have changed negative attitudes about a product or added or altered beliefs about a product.

KEY TERMS

aspirational reference group	207	lifestyle	214	real self-image	214
attitude	220	limited decision making	197	reference group	207
belief	220	marketing-controlled		routine response behavior	197
brand extensions	194	information source	192	secondary membership group	207
cognitive dissonance	195	Maslow's hierarchy of needs	218	selective distortion	216
consumer behavior	189	motive	218	selective exposure	215
consumer decision-making		need recognition	190	selective retention	216
process	189	nonaspirational reference		self-concept	214
culture	200	group	208	social class	204
evoked set (consideration set)	193	nonmarketing-controlled		socialization process	210
extensive decision making	197	information source	191	stimulus	190
external information search	191	norm	207	stimulus discrimination	220
ideal self-image	214	opinion leader	208	stimulus generalization	220
internal information search	191	perception	215	subculture	203
involvement	197	personality	214	value	201
learning	219	primary membership group	207	want	190

EXERCISES

APPLICATION EXERCISE

Principles of consumer behavior are evident in many areas of marketing. Perhaps the easiest place to see this critical foundation of marketing activity is in print ads.

Activities

1. Review the main concepts in this chapter and create a checklist that itemizes them. Then, comb through your favorite magazines and newspapers for advertisements that illustrate each concept. To get a wide variety of ads, you will need to look through several magazines. If you don't have many magazines at your disposal, go to the campus library periodical room. Photocopy the ads you select to support this chapter.

2. Because pictures can help reinforce understanding, consider doing this exercise for each chapter in the book. At the end of the semester, you will have a portfolio of ads that illustrate the concepts in the entire book, which

can help you study. Simply look through your portfolio and try to recall the concepts at work in each advertisement. This exercise can be a prelude to a longer study session for comprehensive exams.

ETHICS EXERCISE

EyeOnU operates a Web filter service for public schools and libraries to protect students from inappropriate material on the Internet. Like the industry as a whole, the company's market share has been stagnant for the past two years. Looking for new sources of revenue, the company is considering selling the data it has collected about student surfing habits to marketers trying to learn more about students' behavior on the Web. The data are anonymous, but privacy advocates are concerned about the precedent of selling information about children to marketers.

Questions

1. What should EyeOnU do? Should it protect the student's data, or should it take the opportunity to create new revenues?

2. Visit the COPPA site dedicated to distributing information about the Children's Online Privacy Protection Act at **www.coppa.org/comply.htm.** Then write a brief paragraph on the responsibilities a Web site operator has to protect children's privacy and safety online and how that relates to EyeOnU's dilemma.

MARKETING PLAN EXERCISE

The next step in preparing a marketing plan for the company you chose in Part 1 is to get a thorough understanding of the marketing opportunities in terms of marketing to customers. Once you've completed the marketing plan exercise for each chapter in Part 2 of this textbook, you can complete the Part 2 Marketing Planning Worksheet on your companion Web site at **www.cengage.com/marketing/lamb.** Complete the following exercises:

1. Describe the decision-making process that customers go through when purchasing your company's product or service. What are the critical factors that influence this purchase-behavior process? How will this decision-making affect your e-marketing focus and your market offering? If you have a brick-and-mortar presence, will you encourage any existing customers to shop online? Why or why not?

2. Nonmarketing periodicals can help you understand consumer behavior and apply what you've learned to your marketing plan. Research articles from such publications as the *Journal of Psychology*, *Journal of American Ethnic History*, *Psychology Today*, *Race and Class*, *Working Woman*, *Society*, and others. Select and read three articles that explore different topics (i.e., do not select three articles on psychology). Then, make a list of factors you think could affect consumer purchasing behavior. Include with each factor a way marketers could use this information to their benefit.

CASE STUDY: ETHEL'S CHOCOLATE LOUNGES

BACK TO THE FUTURE? CHOCOLATE LOUNGES TASTE SWEET SUCCESS

The chocolate house dates back to 17th-century London, when members of society's elite would gather in luxurious surroundings to relax and sip hot chocolate. Later, Europeans expanded on that idea and developed solid chocolate treats that sold in upscale boutiques. Lacking the resources and economy of established continentals, bootstrapping American settlers pioneered the development of cheaper chocolate bars for the masses.

Centuries have passed, however, and the American palate has tired of the taste of mass-produced chocolate. The U.S. chocolate industry has experienced growth of less than 3 percent since the turn of the millennium, and the lack of industry innovation has left a bad taste in chocolate purveyors' mouths, too. Enter Ethel's Chocolate Lounges, named in honor of the matriarch of the Mars family, who founded the candy company with her husband Frank in 1911.

Now Ethel Mars's name adorns the signs at the company's latest attempt to breathe fresh life into chocolate. Aware that chocolate sales at upscale retail outlets, like Godiva and Starbucks grew by nearly 20 percent from 2002 to 2004, Mars opened Ethel's Chocolate Lounge in the Lincoln Park neighborhood of Chicago in April 2005. More Ethel's Lounges have opened since then, and the chic chocolate houses are Mars's bet that well-heeled and sweet-toothed consumers will take to premium chocolate the same way that well-to-do coffee lovers flock to Starbucks for high-priced java. Ethel's Lounges are designed to coddle patrons in the lap of luxury, but Mars president John Haugh maintains that what makes Ethel's special is that it offers "approachable gourmet chocolate." In other words, you don't have to be a millionaire to enjoy the sweet taste of the good life.

Prices are not for everyone's wallet, however. Truffles and Tea for Two, which features all 11 of Ethel's truffles served on a silver platter, sells for $15. Chocolates and Cocoa for Two includes two cocoas and 10 pieces of chocolate for $18, and a box of 48 chocolates is $42. Five "Collections" offer over 50 individual chocolates that sell for between $.90 and $1.50.

Supporting Haugh's claim of approachability, though, the menus at Ethel's feature icons and descriptions of the chocolates' contents so that customers won't experience an unwanted surprise. A multitude of hot and cold beverages give visitors more reasons to extend their stays.

But it's not just the chocolate that makes Ethel's such a desirable destination. Advertising describes Ethel's as "a place for chocolate and chitchat." Generously stuffed pink couches with brown accents combine upscale modern and traditional looks to give the stores a hip and classy feel. For those who don't immediately get it, a sign behind the counter reads, "Chocolate is the new black." The stores' appeal is their relaxing ambience and neighborhood vibe—like a modern American coffeehouse, these shops encourage socializing and extended lounging. The effect is carefully planned. Mars's research revealed that even calorie-conscious consumers will splurge for the good stuff as long as a broader social experience comes with it.

Parallels to the Starbucks-led American coffee revival are obvious and inescapable. Confectionary industry insiders note that chocolate cafés are taking hold, and research confirms their belief. Datamonitor, a research firm specializing in trend identification, described chocolate as "the new coffee" on its list of the top ten trends to watch in 2006. The popularity of the Chocolate Bar in New York, billed as a "candy store for grown-ups," and South Bend Chocolate's ten chocolate cafés shows that the trend is for real. Even some Hershey's stores now offer seating for patrons.

Joan Steuer, president of Chocolate Marketing, claims that, for women, enjoying chocolate in a luxurious lounge is like taking a candle-lit bubble bath. She notes, too, that much of the appeal is that the experience is testimony to the person's upward mobility. It's a perfect way to cater to the American desire to have the best that money can buy.[45]

Source: Amy Chozick and Timothy Martin, "A Place for Cocoa Nuts?", *Wall Street Journal*, 7/15/2005, B1, B3; "Ethel's Launches First-Ever Approachable, Everyday Gourmet Chocolate and Chocolate Lounges, Opens First Two Stores in Chicago, Expected to Expand to Six by End of Summer", *PR Newswire*, 6/6/2005; Karen Hawkins, 'Chocolate Lounges' Present Themselves as "Sweet Alternative to Coffee Shops, Bars", *AP*, 2/13/2006; Melinda Murphy, "Trend Report: Chocolate Is Hot", *CBS News Online*, 02/07/2006.

Questions

1. What type of consumer buying decision best describes the choice to indulge at Ethel's?

2. List the factors that might influence a consumer to spend money and time at Ethel's. Which factor do you think will motivate a consumer the most? Why?

3. Review the core American values in Exhibit 6.5. Which value does the Ethel's experience appeal to most? Explain.

COMPANY CLIPS

READYMADE—DO-IT-YOURSELF

In 2001 when Grace Hawthorne, CEO, and Shoshana Berger, Editor-in-Chief, came up with their idea for *ReadyMade*, there were no other publications with their unique do-it-yourself (DIY) theme. *ReadyMade* was to be a magazine about fun and creative projects for the home. Since its development, the bimonthly magazine has enjoyed a loyal subscriber base and continues to gain readership across the country. All issues include numerous DIY projects, each rated by their level of difficulty, as well as several feature articles exploring the latest in innovation and design. In this video, pay attention to *ReadyMade*'s methods as they launched their magazine. Note also how *ReadyMade* uses its knowledge of its consumer base to tailor the product.

Questions

1. While the *ReadyMade* magazine was still in the design stages, very little research was done to determine whether an interested market existed. Did this adversely affect the magazine as it moved forward to publication? Explain.

2. How does the cover of *ReadyMade* magazine reflect the principles of packaging design as influenced by the known behaviors of its consumers?

3. To what extent does *ReadyMade* rely on opinion leaders to promote the magazine? Is this a successful tactic?

Marketing & You Results

High scores suggest that you tend to shop for value, whereas lower scores indicate compulsive buying, or excessive shopping relative to your disposable income. Lower scores also suggest that you may use excessive shopping to deal with undesirable moods or negative feelings. Even though your mood might improve afterward, beware: The change is temporary, compulsive shopping behavior is very difficult to stop, and you can experience harmful consequences as a result.

Segmenting and Targeting Markets

LEARNING OUTCOMES

1. Describe the characteristics of markets and market segments

2. Explain the importance of market segmentation

3. Discuss criteria for successful market segmentation

4. Describe the bases commonly used to segment consumer markets

5. Describe the bases for segmenting business markets

6. List the steps involved in segmenting markets

7. Discuss alternative strategies for selecting target markets

8. Explain one-to-one marketing

9. Explain how and why firms implement positioning strategies and how product differentiation plays a role

MARKET SEGMENTATION

The term *market* means different things to different people. We are all familiar with the supermarket, stock market, labor market, fish market, and flea market. All these types of markets share several characteristics. First, they are composed of people (consumer markets) or organizations (business markets). Second, these people or organizations have wants and needs that can be satisfied by particular product categories. Third, they have the ability to buy the products they seek. Fourth, they are willing to exchange their resources, usually money or credit, for desired products. In sum, a market is (1) people or organizations with (2) needs or wants and with (3) the ability and (4) the willingness to buy. A group of people or an organization that lacks any one of these characteristics is not a market.

Within a market, a market segment is a subgroup of people or organizations sharing one or more characteristics that cause them to have similar product needs. At one extreme, we can define every person and every organization in the world as a market segment because each is unique. At the other extreme, we can define the entire consumer market as one large market segment and the business market as another large segment. All people have some similar characteristics and needs, as do all organizations.

From a marketing perspective, market segments can be described as somewhere between the two extremes. The process of dividing a market into meaningful, relatively similar, and identifiable segments or groups is called market segmentation. The purpose of market segmentation is to enable the marketer to tailor marketing mixes to meet the needs of one or more specific segments.

Exhibit 8.1 illustrates the concept of market segmentation. Each box represents a market consisting of seven persons. This market might vary as follows: one homogeneous market of seven people, a market consisting of seven individual segments, a market composed of two segments based on gender, a market composed of three age segments; or a market composed of five age and gender market segments. Age and gender and many other bases for segmenting markets are examined later in this chapter.

market
People or organizations with needs or wants and the ability and willingness to buy.

market segment
A subgroup of people or organizations sharing one or more characteristics that cause them to have similar product needs.

market segmentation
The process of dividing a market into meaningful, relatively similar, and identifiable segments or groups.

Marketing & You

Please note your opinion on each of the following questions.

Using the following scale, enter your opinion.

1 2 3 4 5 6
Strongly agree   Strongly disagree

___ I frequently have problems making ends meet.

___ My budgeting is always tight.

___ I often have to spend more money than I have available.

___ I do not consider myself financially well off.

___ I am generally on a tight budget.

___ Meeting an unexpected expense of $1,000 would be a financial hardship.

Total your score. Now, read the chapter and find out what your score means at the end.

Source: From Scale #646, *Marketing Scales Handbook*, G. Bruner, K. James, H. Hensel, eds., Vol. III. © by American Marketing Association.

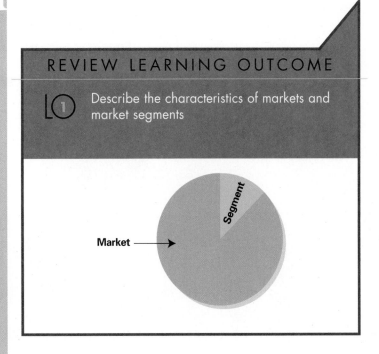

REVIEW LEARNING OUTCOME

Describe the characteristics of markets and market segments

EXHIBIT 8.1

Concept of Market
Segmentation

No market segmentation

Fully segmented market

Market segmentation
by gender: M, F

Market segmentation
by age group: 1, 2, 3

Market segmentation
by gender and age group

LO ②
THE IMPORTANCE OF MARKET SEGMENTATION

Until the 1960s, few firms practiced market segmentation. When they did, it was more likely a haphazard effort than a formal marketing strategy. Before 1960, for example, the Coca-Cola Company produced only one beverage and aimed it at the entire soft drink market. Today, Coca-Cola offers over a dozen different products to market segments based on diverse consumer preferences for flavors and calorie and caffeine content. Coca-Cola offers traditional soft drinks, energy drinks (such as POWERade), flavored teas, fruit drinks (Fruitopia), and water (Dasani).

Market segmentation plays a key role in the marketing strategy of almost all successful organizations and is a powerful marketing tool for several reasons. Most importantly, nearly all markets include groups of people or organizations with different product needs and preferences. Market segmentation helps marketers define customer needs and wants more precisely. Because market segments differ in size and potential, segmentation helps decision makers to more accurately define marketing objectives and better allocate resources. In turn, performance can be better evaluated when objectives are more precise.

How many ways can you slice the market for beverages? Coca-Cola has over a dozen beverages on the market with loyal fans for each one.

Chico's, a successful women's fashion retailer, thrives by marketing to women aged 35 to 55 who like to wear comfortable, yet stylish, clothing. It sells private-label clothing that comes in just a few nonjudgmental sizes: zero (regular sizes 4–6), one (8–10), two (10–12), and three (14–16). Another example is Best Buy, which identifies the needs of customers depending on their geographic location. For example, the store in Baytown, Texas, caters to Eastern European workers from cargo ships or oil tankers that are temporarily docked at the city's busy port. These workers don't have a lot of time to shop, so the Baytown Best Buy moved the iPods from the back corner of the store to the front, paired them with overseas power converters, and made the signage simpler.[1]

REVIEW LEARNING OUTCOME

 Explain the importance of market segmentation

Market segmentation → More precise definition of consumer needs and wants → More accurate marketing objectives → Improved resource allocation → Better marketing results

LO3

CRITERIA FOR SUCCESSFUL SEGMENTATION

Marketers segment markets for three important reasons. First, segmentation enables marketers to identify groups of customers with similar needs and to analyze the characteristics and buying behavior of these groups. Second, segmentation provides marketers with information to help them design marketing mixes specifically matched with the characteristics and desires of one or more segments. Third, segmentation is consistent with the marketing concept of satisfying customer wants and needs while meeting the organization's objectives.

To be useful, a segmentation scheme must produce segments that meet four basic criteria:

- *Substantiality:* A segment must be large enough to warrant developing and maintaining a special marketing mix. This criterion does not necessarily mean that a segment must have many potential customers. Marketers of custom-designed homes and business buildings, commercial airplanes, and large computer systems typically develop marketing programs tailored to each potential customer's needs. In most cases, however, a market segment needs many potential customers to make commercial sense. In the 1980s, home banking failed because not enough people owned personal computers. Today, a larger number of people own computers, and home banking is a thriving industry.

- *Identifiability and measurability:* Segments must be identifiable and their size measurable. Data about the population within geographic boundaries, the number of people in various age categories, and other social and demographic characteristics are often easy to get, and they provide fairly concrete measures of segment

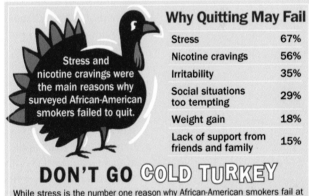

Why Quitting May Fail

Stress	67%
Nicotine cravings	56%
Irritability	35%
Social situations too tempting	29%
Weight gain	18%
Lack of support from friends and family	15%

Stress and nicotine cravings were the main reasons why surveyed African-American smokers failed to quit.

DON'T GO COLD TURKEY

While stress is the number one reason why African-American smokers fail at their quit attempt, going cold turkey may also be a significant factor. Quitting cold turkey does not address the nicotine cravings that effect smokers during their quit attempt, yet for 83 percent of African-American smokers surveyed, this is their quitting method of choice. Nicotine replacement therapies such as Nicorette® gum, NicoDerm® CQ® patch and the Commit® lozenge help address these cravings. To make quitting easier, the oral quit aids are available in flavors such as mint, fruit and cherry, and there is a more flexible patch.

Source: GlaxoSmithKline Consumer Healthcare, 2006 African-American Smoking Trend Survey conducted by Kelton Research

A successful segmentation scheme must identify and measure its target customer base. GlaxoSmithKline surveyed the African American smoking population and found that, for the majority, quitting cold turkey wasn't working for them. These data justify a campaign to promote GlaxoSmithKline's product for gradually quitting smoking to that population.

Useful
segment?

✓ Substantial

✓ Identifiable and measurable

✓ Accessible

✓ Responsive

Then, yes: Use segmentation

size. Suppose that a social service agency wants to identify segments by their readiness to participate in a drug and alcohol program or in prenatal care. Unless the agency can measure how many people are willing, indifferent, or unwilling to participate, it will have trouble gauging whether there are enough people to justify setting up the service.

☛ *Accessibility:* The firm must be able to reach members of targeted segments with customized marketing mixes. Some market segments are hard to reach—for example, senior citizens (especially those with reading or hearing disabilities), individuals who don't speak English, and the illiterate.

☛ *Responsiveness:* As Exhibit 8.1 illustrates, markets can be segmented using any criteria that seem logical. Unless one market segment responds to a marketing mix differently from other segments, however, that segment need not be treated separately. For instance, if all customers are equally price-conscious about a product, there is no need to offer high-, medium-, and low-priced versions to different segments.

segmentation bases (variables)
Characteristics of individuals, groups, or organizations.

geographic segmentation
Segmenting markets by region of a country or the world, market size, market density, or climate.

L◯ ④
BASES FOR SEGMENTING CONSUMER MARKETS

Marketers use segmentation bases, or variables, which are characteristics of individuals, groups, or organizations, to divide a total market into segments. The choice of segmentation bases is crucial because an inappropriate segmentation strategy may lead to lost sales and missed profit opportunities. The key is to identify bases that will produce substantial, measurable, and accessible segments that exhibit different response patterns to marketing mixes.

Markets can be segmented using a single variable, such as age group, or several variables, such as age group, gender, and education. Although it is less precise, single-variable segmentation has the advantage of being simpler and easier to use than multiple-variable segmentation. The disadvantages of multiple-variable segmentation are that it is often harder to use than single-variable segmentation; usable secondary data are less likely to be available; and as the number of segmentation bases increases, the size of individual segments decreases. Nevertheless, the current trend is toward using more rather than fewer variables to segment most markets. Multiple-variable segmentation is clearly more precise than single-variable segmentation.

Consumer goods marketers commonly use one or more of the following characteristics to segment markets: geography, demographics, psychographics, benefits sought, and usage rate.

Geographic Segmentation

Geographic segmentation refers to segmenting markets by region of a country or the world, market size, market density, or climate. Market density means the number of people within a unit of land, such as a census tract. Climate is commonly used for geographic segmentation because of its dramatic impact on residents'

ETHICS in Marketing

Behavioral Targeting and Consumer Privacy[4]

Behavioral targeting segments consumers based on observed and measured online data, including pages or sites that users visit, content examined, search inquiries entered, and ads clicked. This data is then combined with the time, length, and frequency of site visits. Behavioral targeting offers many potential benefits. For marketers, effective behavioral targeting can lead to ad campaigns that are more likely to persuade their audience. The CEO of online media network Specific Media claims that compared to targeting by customer category (e.g., "sports fans"), or by only looking at click-through data, behavioral targeting has doubled marketing's efficiency. For the public, it could mean that Internet ads become more relevant to their needs. While currently behavioral targeting represents a relatively small proportion of overall Internet ad spending, eMarketer projects that spending on this technique will reach $4.4 billion by the end of 2012.

However, companies that use behavioral targeting must face the ongoing challenge of balancing online ad targeting and consumer privacy. In a recent survey, 45 percent of consumers said that they were not comfortable with policies that allow behavioral targeting. Companies have access to both customer identity (IP address) and customer personality (online behavior). Behavioral targeting relies on "cookies," small pieces of data used to track and maintain the online actions of a user, such as sites visited and items stored in an electronic shopping cart.

The U.S. Senate Commerce, Science, and Transportation Committee has held hearings on privacy issues raised by online advertising. Critics are questioning whether behavioral targeting practices violate wiretap laws, which prevent carriers from monitoring customer communications. Based on consumer privacy concerns, CenturyTel, Inc. and Charter Communications have stopped plans to use behavioral targeting. Denver-based Wide Open West has also canceled its use of behavioral targeting software.

Do you think that behavioral targeting is an ethical issue for marketers? Why or why not? What could companies using behavioral targeting do to ease consumers' privacy concerns?

needs and purchasing behavior. Snowblowers, water and snow skis, clothing, and air-conditioning and heating systems are products with varying appeal, depending on climate.

Consumer goods companies take a regional approach to marketing for four reasons. First, many firms need to find new ways to generate sales because of sluggish and intensely competitive markets. Second, computerized checkout stations with scanners give retailers an accurate assessment of which brands sell best in their region. Third, many packaged-goods manufacturers are introducing new regional brands intended to appeal to local preferences. Fourth, a more regional approach allows consumer goods companies to react more quickly to competition. For example, research showed Saks Fifth Avenue's customers differ significantly at stores around the country. At the New York store, Saks' core shopper is a mid-40s woman with a classic style. By contrast, core shoppers at its Birmingham, Alabama, store are more brand-savvy, fashion-loving, and slightly younger.[2] Macy's is another retailer that uses geographic segmentation. The company has changed the merchandise mix so that 15 percent of the merchandise in stores reflect local preferences of its customers.[3]

Demographic Segmentation

Marketers often segment markets on the basis of demographic information because it is widely available and often related to consumers' buying and consuming behavior. Some common bases of demographic segmentation are age, gender, income, ethnic background, and family life cycle.

> **demographic segmentation**
> Segmenting markets by age, gender, income, ethnic background, and family life cycle.

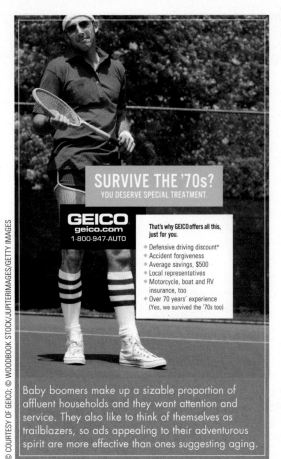

Baby boomers make up a sizable proportion of affluent households and they want attention and service. They also like to think of themselves as trailblazers, so ads appealing to their adventurous spirit are more effective than ones suggesting aging.

Age Segmentation Marketers use a variety of terms to refer to different age groups. Examples include newborns, infants, young children, tweens, teens and young adults (Generation Y), adults (Generation X), baby boomers, and seniors. Age segmentation can be an important tool, as a brief exploration of the market potential of several age segments illustrates.

Through allowances, earnings, and gifts, children account for, and influence, a great deal of consumption. For example, tweens (roughly 9–14 years old) in the United States spend billions of their own dollars each year on purchases for themselves, and also have a considerable influence over major family purchase decisions. They are technology savvy and very social consumers.[5] Tweens desire to be kids, but also want some of the fun of being a teenager. Many retailers, such as Abercrombie Kids, serve this market with clothing that is similar in style to that worn by teenagers and young adults. The Generation Y market, or the Millennial Generation, spans the age groups of 14 through 29. This group also has formidable purchasing power. They like to try whatever is new and trendy, tend to change their minds quickly about things, and covet status brands.[6] The teens in this group spend most of their money on clothing, entertainment, and food. They are aware of brands and also of marketing strategies. Therefore, obvious marketing techniques won't work. Teens consider brands such as iPod, American Eagle Outfitters, Facebook, and MTV to be not only their favorites, but also as defining their generation.[7] They are environmentally conscious, and say they would shop at an environmentally friendly retailer more, and spend more money if services, products, and brands were environmentally friendly.[8] When Procter & Gamble acquired Herbal Essences, the brand was struggling to compete with other shampoos. So its marketers choose to target Gen Y and millennial women by redesigning the packaging and adding cute style names like "drama clean." The changes were successful and Herbal Essences sales began growing again.[9]

Generation X is the group that was born after the baby boomers. Members of Generation X, or Xers, tend to be disloyal to brands and skeptical of big business. Many of them are becoming parents, and they make purchasing decisions with thought for and input from their families. Xers desire an experience, not just a product. For example, Starbucks developed a market for expensive coffee by encompassing it in the coffee-drinking experience that appeals to this consumer segment.[10]

People born between 1946 and 1964 are often called "baby boomers." Boomers spend $2.1 trillion a year, and represent half of all spending in the United States. For the next 18 years, one baby boomer will turn 60 every seven seconds. They make up 49 percent of affluent households, and they want attention and service when they shop.[11] This group spends big money on products such as travel, electronics, and automobiles. Baby boomers are not particularly brand loyal, and they are a very diverse group. Some may be the parents of a baby, while others are empty nesters. The Hallmark Channel, owned and operated by Crown Media (owned by Hallmark Cards), targets those of the baby boom generation because of their wealth, and the fact that they are more engaged in TV than are members of other groups.[12] The challenges facing marketers who target boomers are great. Unlike yesterday's generation of 50-plus-year-olds, today's boomers refuse to believe they're aging, so marketers who want to appeal to this segment cannot use any kind of messaging that refers to aging. Rather, they must appeal to boomers' interests, lifestyles, and values—anything but age. Companies as diverse as Whirlpool, Gap, Moen, Fila, and OXO are doing this with great success. The president of OXO, the company that makes Good Grips cooking utensils with the thick black handles, says, "The last thing they want is the kind of patronizing, help-me-do-something kind of tools. We have almost a cult-like following among older consumers. At the same time, we have just as strong a following from people in the 20-to-40 age range because the products look cool."[13]

Consumers in their early 60s and older represent people who are part of the War Generation (ages 61 to 66), the Depression Generation (ages 67 to 76), and the G.I. Generation (age 77 and up). Collectively, they are sometimes called the "Golden Generation" (a term coined by Focalyst, a research and consultancy firm focused on older consumers). Many in this group view retirement not as a passive time, but as an active time they use to explore new knowledge, travel, volunteer, and spend time with family and friends. They are living longer and are healthier than older consumers 20 years ago. However, marketers need to be aware that physical changes in hearing, eyesight, and mobility still occur in this segment. The Hartford Financial Services Group provides auto and homeowner insurance to AARP members. The company's voice self-service system has a low-pitched male voice that is easier for their older members to hear. The Hartford trains its employees to deal with conditions such as hearing impairment and other conditions of aging, and has nine gerontologists on staff to advise on issues relating to those in their golden years.[14]

Gender Segmentation In the United States, women handle 75 percent of family finances and make or influence 80 percent of consumer purchases. They buy 51 percent of the new electronics sold, 75 percent of over-the-counter drugs, and 65 percent of new cars. That means that women are making decisions when it comes to the purchase of a huge variety of goods and services, not just the packaged goods that have traditionally been marketed to them.[15]

Women are buying and playing video games in rapidly increasing numbers. Forty percent of gamers are women, and they outnumber under-17 males by nearly two to one in the gaming world. The video game industry has been forced to respond by developing more games with female protagonists and changing its advertising strategy. A recent commercial for EA Sports featured real video gamers—some of them women—instead of actors, and presented video game playing as an interactive social activity.[16] Other marketers that traditionally focused most of their attention on males are also recognizing the potential of the female market segment. For example, the number of women shopping at hardware stores such as Home Depot and Lowe's Home Improvement Warehouse has been rising in recent years. Home Depot is testing a new store concept that is designed to attract more women shoppers. These stores will focus more on upscale home décor and organization, using showrooms that are more extravagant and carry more products.[17]

Similarly, other brands that have been targeted to men, such as Gillette razors and Rogaine baldness remedy, are increasing their efforts to attract women. For example, athletic apparel manufacturers such as Nike and Reebok have typically targeted men, and when they did target women, just copied the hard-edged, sports-marketing strategies that made them so popular with men. But these companies are now taking women's unique needs regarding athletics into consideration when they design clothing and shoes for them. The Fairmont Princess Resort in Scottsdale, Arizona, hired a cultural anthropologist when it wanted to target men in addition to its female clientele. Intrinsic differences in the way men and women approached a spa were uncovered. Research led the resort to

Many companies have profited from redesigning traditionally feminine products and marketing them towards men. Here, Lancôme advertises an anti-wrinkle cream that has been packaged to appeal to men.

- ☛ Use darker woods and colors to create a club-like ambiance so men wouldn't feel they were entering female territory.

- ☛ Install televisions in locker rooms (to reduce awkwardness felt by males in spa wear).

- ☛ Develop customized packages, including "Keep Your Shorts On" and "Golf Performance Treatment."

- ☛ Reposition the "European Facial," as translated for men into "Barber Facial."[18]

Marketers of products such as clothing, cosmetics, personal-care items, magazines, jewelry, and gifts still commonly segment markets by gender. For instance, one Internet retailer, **CoolStuffForDads.com,** targets shoppers with a wide variety of gifts that men would enjoy.[19] Grocers market differently to men shopping alone, who make up about 18 percent of grocery shoppers. A recent study found that compared to women, men place a higher priority on location and convenience, don't like loyalty cards, and often vary from their lists, creating opportunities for grocers to encourage impulse buys.[20]

Income Segmentation Income is a popular demographic variable for segmenting markets because income level influences consumers' wants and determines their buying power. Many markets are segmented by income, including the markets for housing, clothing, automobiles, and food. Wholesale club stores such as Costco and Sam's Club appeal to many income segments. According to a Nielsen study, affluent households (those that earn more than $100,000 annually) are twice as likely to shop warehouse stores compared to households that earn $20,000 or less a year, and the affluent shopper spends an average $46 more than the lower-income shopper per trip.[21] High-income customers looking for luxury want outstanding customer service. For example, fashion companies use computer technology to customize upscale products that are designed specifically for their wealthy customers' needs.[22] Other companies try to appeal to low income customers. Casual Male has launched a big-and-tall brand of men's apparel aimed at the lower-income market. Procter & Gamble has introduced Bounty Basic paper towels and Charmin Basic bath tissue to attract more price-sensitive consumers.[23]

Ethnic Segmentation In the past, ethnic groups in the United States were expected to conform to a homogenized, Anglo-centric ideal. This was evident both in the marketing of mass-marketed products and in the selective way that films, television, advertisements, and popular music portrayed America's diverse population. Until the 1970s, ethnic foods were rarely sold except in specialty stores. The racial barrier in entertainment lasted nearly as long, except for supporting movie and TV roles—often based on stereotypes dating back to the nineteenth century.[24] Increasing numbers of ethnic minorities in the United States, along with increased buying power, have changed this. Hispanic Americans, African Americans, and Asian Americans are the three largest ethnic groups in the United States. In 2006, these three groups accounted for 88 million people and, by 2010, are expected to represent about a third of the total U.S. population.[25] Today, companies such as Procter & Gamble, Allstate Insurance, Bank of America, and Reebok have developed multicultural marketing initiatives designed to better understand and serve the wants and preferences of U.S. minority groups. Many consumer goods companies spend 5 to 10 percent of their marketing budgets specifically targeting multicultural consumers; this proportion will likely increase in the future as ethnic groups represent larger and larger percentages of the U.S. population.

The U.S. Census Bureau estimates that the number of Hispanic Americans was 44.3 million in 2006, growing to 47.8 million by 2011. Within this segment exists a variety of nationalities (people come from nearly 24 countries), languages, degrees of acculturation, income, and education levels. The Hispanic segment also is younger than is the total U.S. population.[26] Food retailers should understand not only that Hispanic shoppers like full-flavored products, but also that Mexico has different regional variations in preferences and that menus and tastes also vary among people from Central and South

America.[27] Research shows that one-fourth of Hispanic Americans must be served in Spanish if retailers want their business. After their Spanish-speaking customers told Home Depot they prefer shopping in Spanish even if they are bilingual, the company developed a Spanish-language version of its Web site. It is one of only a few retailers offering the online option in Spanish.[28] Similarly, Amazon introduced the Software en Español Store that offers Spanish-language and bilingual software products.[29] The African American segment now makes up more than 13 percent of the U.S. population, and will continue to grow. Some characteristics of this group: (1) they are twice as likely to trust black media as they are to trust mainstream media; (2) eight in ten households watch black television at least once a week; and (3) overall, 68 percent of African Americans are online, while over 90 percent of African American teens are online.[30]

Companies that have been successful in appealing to groups within this segment include Nissan, Merrill Lynch, and AARP. Nissan found that a sense of inclusion among other ethnic groups was preferable to being singled out, so its ad campaign for the Nissan Altima incorporated people of various ethnic backgrounds. Merrill Lynch & Company sponsors community-based events such as the Lasting Foundations: The Art of Architecture in Africa in New York. A membership benefits campaign for AARP recognized that African Americans are not typically close to retirement at age 50. Thus, the organization focused on immediate benefits, such as volunteer opportunities, grandparenting programs, and discounts on travel and health care.[31] Asians in America represent a segment that has higher than average household incomes and education levels than the general population.[32] This group also makes more online purchases a year than African American and Caucasian consumers. More packaged-goods companies such as Kraft Foods and Procter & Gamble are showing interest in Asian Americans due to the growth of Asian supermarket chains. At the same time, the number of Asian media is growing rapidly. Sovereign Bank in Boston has a branch that is staffed by all Chinese Americans. Their customers are so loyal they come from around the Northeast to do business there. It's not only that the employees speak Cantonese, but also that they have the cultural sensitivity to know, for example, not to insult their customers by talking to them about saving for a vacation when they take care of their parents before they do anything else.[33]

Family Life-Cycle Segmentation The demographic factors of gender, age, and income often do not sufficiently explain why consumer buying behavior varies. Frequently, consumption patterns among people of the same age and gender differ because they are in different stages of the family life cycle. The family life cycle (FLC) is a series of stages determined by a combination of age, marital status, and the presence or absence of children.

The life-cycle stage consisting of the married-couple household used to be considered the traditional family in the United States. Today, however, married couples make up just about half of households, down from nearly 80 percent in the 1950s. This means that the 86 million single adults in the United States could soon define the new majority. Already, unmarried Americans make up 42 percent of the workforce, 40 percent of home buyers, and one of the most potent consumer groups on record. Exhibit 8.2 illustrates numerous FLC patterns and shows how families' needs, incomes, resources, and expenditures differ at each stage. The horizontal flow shows the traditional family life cycle. The lower part of the exhibit gives some of the characteristics and purchase patterns of families in each stage of the traditional life cycle. The exhibit also acknowledges that many first marriages end in divorce. When young marrieds move into the young divorced stage, their consumption patterns often revert to those of the young single stage of the cycle. Divorced persons frequently remarry by middle age and reenter the traditional life cycle, as indicated by the "recycled flow" in the exhibit.

Consumers are especially receptive to marketing efforts at certain points in the life cycle. Dating and engaged couples are big spenders. In the two and half years before marriage, many spend over $40,000 on vacations, jewelry, dining, and wedding expenses.[34] NBC Universal and Wal-Mart Stores have struck an advertising sales deal to target the

family life cycle (FLC)
A series of stages determined by a combination of age, marital status, and the presence or absence of children.

EXHIBIT 8.2

Family Life Cycle

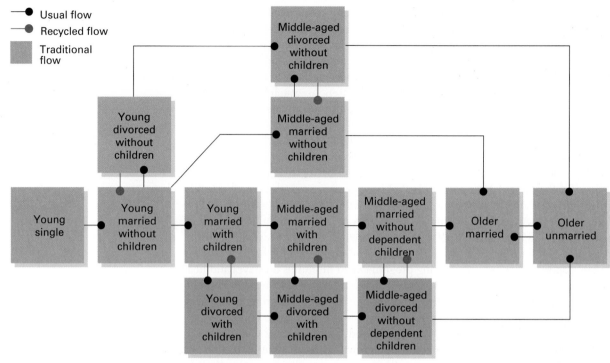

Young single	Young married or divorced without children	Young married or divorced with children	Middle-aged married or divorced with or without children	Middle-aged married or divorced without children	Older married	Older unmarried
Few financial burdens	Better off financially than they will be in near future	Home purchasing at peak	Financial position still better	Home ownership at peak	Drastic cut in income	Drastic cut in income
Fashion opinion leaders	Highest purchase rate and highest average purchase of durables	Liquid assets low	More wives work	Most satisfied with financial position and money saved	Keep home	Special need for attention, affection, and security
Recreation-oriented	Buy: cars, refrigerators, stoves, sensible and durable furniture, vacations	Dissatisfied with financial position and amount of money saved	Some children get jobs	Interested in travel, recreation, self-education	Buy: medical appliances, medical care, products that aid health, sleep, and digestion	Buy: same medical and product needs as other retired group
Buy: basic kitchen equipment, basic furniture, cars, equipment for mating game, vacations		Interested in new products	Hard to influence with advertising	Make gifts and contributions		
		Like advertised products	High average purchase of durables	Not interested in new products		
		Buy: washers, dryers, televisions, baby food, chest rubs, cough medicine, vitamins, dolls, wagons, sleds, skates	Buy: new and more tasteful furniture, auto travel, unnecessary appliances, boats, dental services, magazines	Buy: vacations, luxuries, home improvements		

"momtourage"—a group of people who help mothers to be better parents, including babysitters, neighbors, teachers, and neighbors. Wal-Mart is sponsoring momtourage material that appears on two NBC outlets: the iVillage Web site and the *"Today"* show. The information featured will focus on subjects like child care and fixing family meals.[35]

Research has found that the overriding factor in describing baby boomer subsegments is the presence of children in the house. The Nielsen study discovered eight specific segments: four segments with children under 18 represented about 40 percent of the boomers, and four segments without children represented 60 percent.[36]

Psychographic Segmentation

Age, gender, income, ethnicity, family life-cycle stage, and other demographic variables are usually helpful in developing segmentation strategies, but often they don't paint the entire picture. Demographics provide the skeleton, but psychographics add meat to the bones. **Psychographic segmentation** is market segmentation on the basis of the following variables:

☛ *Personality:* Personality reflects a person's traits, attitudes, and habits. According to a national survey by Roper, almost half of Americans believe their cars match their personalities. For example, SUVs deliver the heady feeling of being independent and above it all. Convertibles epitomize wind-in-the-hair freedom, and off-roaders convey outdoor adventure. About 25 percent of people surveyed say that their cars make them feel powerful.[37]

☛ *Motives:* Marketers of baby products and life insurance appeal to consumers' emotional motives—namely, to care for their loved ones. Using appeals to economy, reliability, and dependability, carmakers like Subaru and Suzuki target customers with rational motives. Carmakers like Mercedes-Benz, Jaguar, and Cadillac appeal to customers with status-related motives.

☛ *Lifestyles:* Lifestyle segmentation divides people into groups according to the way they spend their time, the importance of the things around them, their beliefs, and socioeconomic characteristics such as income and education. For example, the companies behind the sport Nordic walking are targeting couch potatoes and other nonathletic types. They hope to make the activity appealing to those for whom regular exercise has been a challenge.[38] Pepsi-Cola is promoting its low-calorie, vitamin-enhanced water, Aquafina Alive, to consumers who are health conscious.[39]

☛ *Geodemographics:* Geodemographic segmentation clusters potential customers into neighborhood lifestyle categories. It combines geographic, demographic, and lifestyle segmentations. Geodemographic segmentation helps marketers develop marketing programs tailored to prospective buyers who live in small geographic regions, such as neighborhoods, or who have very specific lifestyle and demographic characteristics. H-E-B Grocery Company, a 304-store, Texas-based supermarket chain, specializes in developing its own branded products designed to meet the needs and tastes of specific communities. In the Rio Grande Valley, where summers are hot and many residents don't have air-conditioning, H-E-B markets its own brand of rubbing oil that helps cool the skin while adding moisturizers. Along the southern border, the grocer stocks *discos*, large metal disks that Mexican Americans use to cook brisket. In Detroit, Home Depot has stores in some neighborhoods that have charcoal barbecue grills, while others offer gas grills.[40]

Psychographic variables can be used individually to segment markets or be combined with other variables to provide more detailed descriptions of market segments. One combination approach is the Claritas PRIZM Lifestyle software program that divides Americans into 66 "clusters," or consumer types, all with catchy names. The clusters combine basic demographic data such as age, ethnicity, and income with lifestyle information, such as magazine and sports preferences, taken from consumer surveys. For example,

psychographic segmentation
Market segmentation on the basis of personality, motives, lifestyles, and geodemographics.

geodemographic segmentation
Segmenting potential customers into neighborhood lifestyle categories.

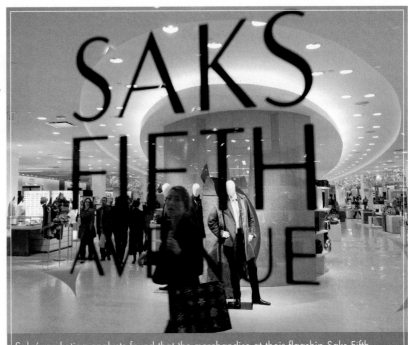

Saks' marketing analysts found that the merchandise at their flagship Saks Fifth Avenue store in New York City doesn't necessarily appeal to Saks customers nationwide. To bolster sales, Saks' marketing analysts use geodemographic research to determine what merchandise will appeal to customers in each of their 54 retail stores, from Birmingham, Alabama, to Bellevue, Washington.

© AP IMAGES/CHITOSE SUZUKI

benefit segmentation
The process of grouping customers
into market segments according
to the benefits they seek from the
product.

the "Kids and Cul-de-Sacs" group consists of upscale, married couples with children who live in recently built subdivisions. These families have a median household income of $70,233, tend to own a Honda Odyssey, and are likely to spend large sums of money for child-centered products and services such as video games and Chuck E. Cheese. The "Bohemian Mix" cluster is made up of urbanites under age 35. These young singles, couples, students, and professionals have a median income of $51,100, are early adopters in many product categories, tend to shop at Banana Republic, and are likely to read *Vanity Fair* magazine.[41] The program also predicts to which neighborhoods across the country these clusters are likely to gravitate.

Benefit Segmentation

Benefit segmentation is the process of grouping customers into market segments according to the benefits they seek from the product. Most types of market segmentation are based on the assumption that this variable and customers' needs are related. Benefit segmentation is different because it groups potential customers on the basis of their needs or wants rather than some other characteristic, such as age or gender. The snack-food market, for example, can be divided into six benefit segments, as shown in Exhibit 8.3.

Customer profiles can be developed by examining demographic information associated with people seeking certain benefits. This information can be used to match marketing strategies with selected target markets. The many different types of performance energy bars with various combinations of nutrients are aimed at consumers looking for different benefits. For example, PowerBar is designed for athletes looking for long-lasting fuel, while PowerBar Protein Plus is aimed at those who want extra protein for replenishing muscles after strength training. Carb Solutions High Protein Bars are for those on low-carb diets; Luna Bars are targeted to women who want a bar with fewer calories, soy protein, and calcium; and Clif Bars are for people who want a natural bar with ingredients like rolled oats, soybeans, and organic soy flour. Dannon introduced its Activia probiotic yogurt as a daily health booster by highlighting its benefits for the digestive tract and immune system.

EXHIBIT 8.3

Lifestyle Segmentation of the Snack-Food Market

	Nutritional Snackers	Weight Watchers	Guilty Snackers	Party Snackers	Indiscriminate Snackers	Economical Snackers
% of Snackers	22 %	14 %	9 %	15 %	15 %	18 %
Lifestyle Characteristics	Self-assured, controlled	Outdoorsy, influential, adventuresome	Highly anxious, isolated	Sociable	Hedonistic	Self-assured, price-oriented
Benefits Sought	Nutritious, without artificial ingredients, natural	Low in calories, quick energy	Low in calories, good tasting	Good to serve guests, goes well with beverages	Good tasting, satisfies hunger	Low in price, best value
Consumption Level of Snacks	Light	Light	Heavy	Average	Heavy	Average
Type of Snacks Usually Eaten	Fruits, vegetables, cheese	Yogurt, vegetables	Yogurt, cookies, crackers, candy	Nuts, potato chips, crackers, pretzels	Candy, ice cream, cookies, potato chips, pretzels, popcorn	No specific products
Demographics	Better educated, have young children	Young, single	Younger or older, female, lower socio-economic status	Middle-aged, no urban	Teenager	Have large family, better educated

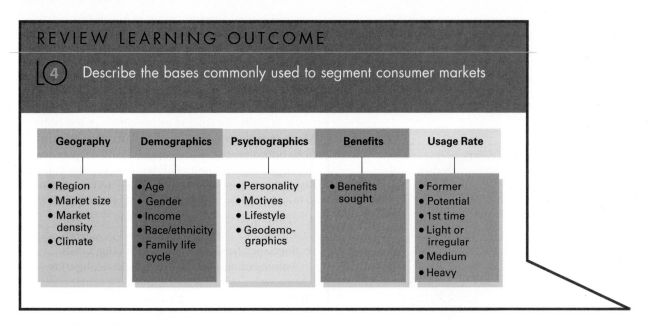

LO 4 Describe the bases commonly used to segment consumer markets

Geography	Demographics	Psychographics	Benefits	Usage Rate
• Region • Market size • Market density • Climate	• Age • Gender • Income • Race/ethnicity • Family life cycle	• Personality • Motives • Lifestyle • Geodemographics	• Benefits sought	• Former • Potential • 1st time • Light or irregular • Medium • Heavy

Usage-Rate Segmentation

Usage-rate segmentation divides a market by the amount of product bought or consumed. Categories vary with the product, but they are likely to include some combination of the following: former users, potential users, first-time users, light or irregular users, medium users, and heavy users. Segmenting by usage rate enables marketers to focus their efforts on heavy users or to develop multiple marketing mixes aimed at different segments. Because heavy users often account for a sizable portion of all product sales, some marketers focus on the heavy-user segment.

The 80/20 principle holds that 20 percent of all customers generate 80 percent of the demand. Although the percentages usually are not exact, the general idea often holds true. For example, in the fast-food industry, the heavy user accounts for only one of five fast-food patrons, but makes about 60 percent of all visits to fast-food restaurants. The needs of heavy users differ from the needs of other usage-rate groups. They have intense needs for product and service selection and a variety of types of information, as well as an emotional attachment to the product category. Individuals in this group spend four to fourteen times as much in their favored product category than do light users.[42]

Developing customers into heavy users is the goal behind many frequency/loyalty programs like the airlines' frequent flyer programs. Many supermarkets and other retailers have also designed loyalty programs that reward the heavy-user segment with deals available only to them, such as in-store coupon dispensing systems, loyalty card programs, and special price deals on selected merchandise.

LO 5

BASES FOR SEGMENTING BUSINESS MARKETS

The business market consists of four broad segments: producers, resellers, government, and institutions. (For a detailed discussion of the characteristics of these segments, see Chapter 7.) Whether marketers focus on only one or on all four of these segments, they are likely to find diversity among potential customers. Thus, further market segmentation offers just as many benefits to business marketers as it does to consumer-product marketers.

Company Characteristics

Company characteristics, such as geographic location, type of company, company size, and product use, can be important segmentation variables. Some markets tend to be regional because buyers prefer to purchase from local suppliers, and distant suppliers

usage-rate segmentation
Dividing a market by the amount of product bought or consumed.

80/20 principle
A principle holding that 20 percent of all customers generate 80 percent of the demand.

LO 5 Describe the bases for segmenting business markets

Company Characteristics

Producers	Resellers
Governments	Institutions

Buying Process

may have difficulty competing in terms of price and service. Therefore, firms that sell to geographically concentrated industries benefit by locating close to their markets.

Segmenting by customer type allows business marketers to tailor their marketing mixes to the unique needs of particular types of organizations or industries. Many companies are finding this form of segmentation to be quite effective. For example, Home Depot, one of the largest do-it-yourself retail businesses in the United States, has targeted professional repair and remodeling contractors in addition to consumers. Procter & Gamble is beginning to target business customers by focusing on janitors, fast-food workers, maids, and launderers with products specific to each group's cleaning needs.[43]

Volume of purchase (heavy, moderate, light) is a commonly used basis for business segmentation. Another is the buying organization's size, which may affect its purchasing procedures, the types and quantities of products it needs, and its responses to different marketing mixes. Banks frequently offer different services, lines of credit, and overall attention to commercial customers based on their size.

Many products, especially raw materials like steel, wood, and petroleum, have diverse applications. How customers use a product may influence the amount they buy, their buying criteria, and their selection of vendors. For example, a producer of springs may have customers that use the product in applications as diverse as making machine tools, bicycles, surgical devices, office equipment, telephones, and missile systems.

Buying Processes

Many business marketers find it helpful to segment customers and prospective customers on the basis of how they buy. For example, companies can segment some business markets by ranking key purchasing criteria, such as price, quality, technical support, and service. Atlas Corporation has developed a commanding position in the industrial door market by providing customized products in just 4 weeks, which is much faster than the industry average of 12 to 15 weeks. Atlas's primary market is companies with an immediate need for customized doors.

The purchasing strategies of buyers may provide useful segments. Two purchasing profiles that have been identified are satisficers and optimizers. Satisficers contact familiar suppliers and place the order with the first one to satisfy product and delivery requirements. Optimizers consider numerous suppliers (both familiar and unfamiliar), solicit bids, and study all proposals carefully before selecting one.

The personal characteristics of the buyers themselves (their demographic characteristics, decision style, tolerance for risk, confidence level, job responsibilities, etc.) influence their buying behavior and thus offer a viable basis for segmenting some business markets. IBM computer buyers, for example, are sometimes characterized as being more risk averse than buyers of less expensive computers that perform essentially the same functions. In advertising, therefore, IBM stressed its reputation for high quality and reliability.

satisficers
Business customers who place an order with the first familiar supplier to satisfy product and delivery requirements.

optimizers
Business customers who consider numerous suppliers, both familiar and unfamiliar, solicit bids, and study all proposals carefully before selecting one.

LO 6

STEPS IN SEGMENTING A MARKET

The purpose of market segmentation, in both consumer and business markets, is to identify marketing opportunities.

1. *Select a market or product category for study:* Define the overall market or product category to be studied. It may be a market in which the firm already competes, a new but related market or product category, or a totally new one. For instance, Anheuser-Busch closely examined the beer market before introducing Michelob Light and Bud Light. Anheuser-Busch also carefully studied the market for salty snacks before introducing the Eagle brand.

2. *Choose a basis or bases for segmenting the market:* This step requires managerial insight, creativity, and market knowledge. There are no scientific procedures for selecting segmentation variables. However, a successful segmentation scheme must produce segments that meet the four basic criteria discussed earlier in this chapter.

3. *Select segmentation descriptors:* After choosing one or more bases, the marketer must select the segmentation descriptors. Descriptors identify the specific segmentation variables to use. For example, if a company selects demographics as a basis of segmentation, it may use age, occupation, and income as descriptors. A company that selects usage segmentation needs to decide whether to go after heavy users, nonusers, or light users.

4. *Profile and analyze segments:* The profile should include the segments' size, expected growth, purchase frequency, current brand usage, brand loyalty, and long-term sales and profit potential. This information can then be used to rank potential market segments by profit opportunity, risk, consistency with organizational mission and objectives, and other factors important to the firm.

5. *Select target markets:* Selecting target markets is not a part of but a natural outcome of the segmentation process. It is a major decision that influences and often directly determines the firm's marketing mix. This topic is examined in greater detail later in this chapter.

6. *Design, implement, and maintain appropriate marketing mixes:* The marketing mix has been described as product, place (distribution), promotion, and pricing strategies intended to bring about mutually satisfying exchange relationships with target markets. Chapter 10 explores these topics in detail.

Markets are dynamic, so it is important that companies proactively monitor their segmentation strategies over time. Often, once customers or prospects have been assigned to a segment, marketers think their task is done. Once customers are assigned to an age segment, for example, they stay there until they reach the next age bracket or category, which could be ten years in the future. Thus, the segmentation classifications are static, but the customers and prospects are changing. Dynamic segmentation approaches adjust to fit the changes that occur in customers' lives. Abercrombie and Fitch, an apparel store that targets teenagers, has opened a new store called Ruehl No. 925 that

REVIEW LEARNING OUTCOME

LO6 List the steps involved in segmenting markets

1	2	3	4	5	6
Select a market or product category for study.	Choose a basis or bases for segmenting the market.	Select segmentation descriptors.	Profile and analyze segments.	Select target markets.	Design, implement, and maintain appropriate marketing mixes.

Note that steps 5 and 6 are actually marketing activities that follow market segmentation (steps 1 through 4).

target market
A group of people or organizations for which an organization designs, implements, and maintains a marketing mix intended to meet the needs of that group, resulting in mutually satisfying exchanges.

undifferentiated targeting strategy
A marketing approach that views the market as one big market with no individual segments and thus uses a single marketing mix.

caters to 20- to 35-year-olds, and Aeropostale owns Jimmy'Z, which stocks clothing for 18- to 25-year-olds that is higher priced than at its flagship stores for teens.

STRATEGIES FOR SELECTING TARGET MARKETS

So far this chapter has focused on the market segmentation process, which is only the first step in deciding whom to approach about buying a product. The next task is to choose one or more target markets. A target market is a group of people or organizations for which an organization designs, implements, and maintains a marketing mix intended to meet the needs of that group, resulting in mutually satisfying exchanges. Because most markets will include customers with different characteristics, lifestyles, backgrounds, and income levels, it is unlikely that a single marketing mix will attract all segments of the market. Thus, if a marketer wishes to appeal to more than one segment of the market, it must develop different marketing mixes. For example, Buick targets people in their 60s with the Lucerne sedan, a luxury car with a V8 engine and extras like OnStar service. The company also targets younger, Generation Y customers with the Enclave, a crossover SUV. The three general strategies for selecting target markets— undifferentiated, concentrated, and multisegment targeting—are illustrated in Exhibit 8.4. Exhibit 8.5 illustrates the advantages and disadvantages of each targeting strategy.

Undifferentiated Targeting

A firm using an undifferentiated targeting strategy essentially adopts a mass-market philosophy, viewing the market as one big market with no individual segments. The firm uses one marketing mix for the entire market. A firm that adopts an undifferentiated targeting strategy assumes that individual customers have similar needs that can be met with a common marketing mix.

The first firm in an industry sometimes uses an undifferentiated targeting strategy. With no competition, the firm may not need to tailor marketing mixes to the preferences of market segments. Henry Ford's famous comment about the Model T is a classic example of an undifferentiated targeting strategy: "They can have their car in any color they want, as long as it's black." At one time, Coca-Cola used this strategy with a single product and a single size of its familiar green bottle. Marketers of commodity products, such as flour and sugar, are also likely to use an undifferentiated targeting strategy.

EXHIBIT 8.4

Three Strategies for Selecting Target Markets

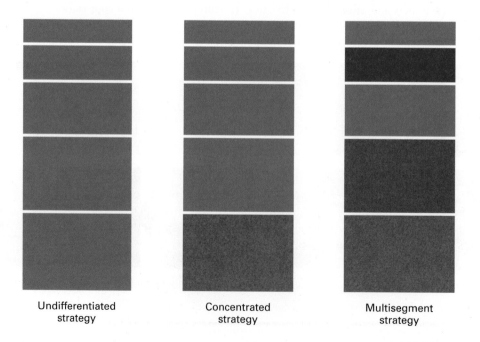

Undifferentiated strategy

Concentrated strategy

Multisegment strategy

Targeting Strategy	Advantages	Disadvantages
Undifferentiated Targeting	• Potential savings on production/ marketing costs	• Unimaginative product offerings
	• Company more susceptible to competition	
Concentrated Targeting	• Concentration of resources	• Segments too small, or changing
	• Can better meet the needs of a narrowly defined segment	• Large competitors may more effectively market to niche segment
	• Allows some small firms to better compete with larger firms	
	• Strong positioning	
Multisegment Targeting	• Greater financial success	• High costs
	• Economies of scale in producing/marketing	• Cannibalization

One advantage of undifferentiated marketing is the potential for saving on production and marketing. Because only one item is produced, the firm should be able to achieve economies of mass production. Also, marketing costs may be lower when there is only one product to promote and a single channel of distribution. Too often, however, an undifferentiated strategy emerges by default rather than by design, reflecting a failure to consider the advantages of a segmented approach. The result is often sterile, unimaginative product offerings that have little appeal to anyone.

Another problem associated with undifferentiated targeting is that it makes the company more susceptible to competitive inroads. Hershey lost a big share of the candy market to Mars and other candy companies before it changed to a multisegment targeting strategy. Coca-Cola forfeited its position as the leading seller of cola drinks in supermarkets to Pepsi-Cola in the late 1950s when Pepsi began offering several sizes of containers.

You might think a firm producing a standard product like toilet tissue would adopt an undifferentiated strategy. However, this market has industrial segments and consumer segments. Industrial buyers want an economical, single-ply product sold in boxes of a hundred rolls. The consumer market demands a more versatile product in smaller quantities. Within the consumer market, the product is differentiated with designer print or no print, cushioned or noncushioned, and economy priced or luxury priced. Fort Howard Corporation, the market share leader in industrial toilet paper, does not even sell to the consumer market.

Undifferentiated marketing can succeed in certain situations, though. A small grocery store in a small, isolated town may define all of the people that live in the town as its target market. It may offer one marketing mix and generally satisfy everyone in town. This strategy is not likely to be as effective if there are three or four grocery stores in the town.

Concentrated Targeting

With a concentrated targeting strategy, a firm selects a market niche (one segment of a market) for targeting its marketing efforts. Because the firm is appealing to a single segment, it can concentrate on understanding the needs, motives, and satisfactions of that segment's members and on developing and maintaining a highly specialized marketing mix. Some firms find that concentrating resources and meeting the needs of a narrowly defined market segment is more profitable than spreading resources over several different segments.

For example, Starbucks became successful by focusing on consumers who want gourmet coffee products. America Online (AOL) became one of the world's leading Internet providers by targeting Internet newcomers. By making the Internet interface easy to use, AOL was able to attract millions of people who otherwise might not have subscribed to an online service. Watchmakers Patek Philippe, Rolex, and Breguet, which sell watches priced at $200,000 or more, are definitely pursuing a concentrated targeting strategy. AARP pursues a concentrated strategy if you consider people over 50 years old to be a single market segment of the overall population.

concentrated targeting strategy
A strategy used to select one segment of a market for targeting marketing efforts.

niche
One segment of a market.

Small firms often adopt a concentrated targeting strategy to compete effectively with much larger firms. For example, Enterprise Rent-A-Car rose to number one in the car rental industry by catering to people with cars in the shop. It has now expanded into the airport rental market. Celebrity pots and pans are a growing niche market. They now represent 10 percent of the $2 billion U.S. cookware market—an increase of 7 percent in the past decade.[44] Charming Shoppes Inc. competes with other clothing sellers by appealing to plus-size teens; it sells designer labels in sizes 14 through 32.[45] Some firms, on the other hand, use a concentrated strategy to establish a strong position in a desirable market segment. Porsche, for instance, targets an upscale automobile market through "class appeal, not mass appeal."

Concentrated targeting violates the adage, "Don't put all your eggs in one basket." If the chosen segment is too small or if it shrinks because of environmental changes, the firm may suffer negative consequences. For instance, OshKosh B'Gosh, Inc., was highly successful selling children's wear in the 1980s. It was so successful, however, that the children's line came to define OshKosh's image to the extent that the company could not sell clothes to anyone else. Attempts at marketing older children's clothing, women's casual clothes, and maternity wear were all abandoned. Recognizing it was in the children's wear business, the company expanded into products such as kids' shoes, children's eyewear, and plush toys.

A concentrated strategy can also be disastrous for a firm that is not successful in its narrowly defined target market. Before Procter & Gamble introduced Head and Shoulders shampoo, several small firms were already selling antidandruff shampoos. Head and Shoulders was introduced with a large promotional campaign, and the new brand captured over half the market immediately. Within a year, several of the firms

CUSTOMER Experience

Trader Joe's Adventure[46]

In the 1960s, Trader Joe's was a small convenience store chain called "Pronto Markets" in the Los Angeles area trying to compete with 7-Eleven. It succeeded by offering customers a unique food and beverage buying experience. The stores are decked out with cedar plank walls and nautical décor. The Captain (store manager), the First Mate (assistant store manager) and the Crew Members (employees) wear colorful Hawaiian shirts. The name Trader Joe's was chosen by the original owner because the name belonged to a trader/adventurer he had read about.

Using a niche targeting strategy, the company offers wine and stocks a limited assortment of inexpensive (mostly private label) gourmet food products in smaller stores. A trip to Trader Joe's is an adventure, and the retailer is a brand with a cultlike following. Today, Trader Joe's uses this same strategy to compete with industry giants like Wal-Mart. The company now has 250 stores in 20 states, and is still growing.

Trader Joe's mission is to bring its customers the best food and beverage values and the information to make informed purchase decisions. It carries more than 2,000 unique grocery items (compared to the approximately 30,000 items a typical supermarket carries) under its house label, and offer its products at everyday low prices. The retailer has a tasting panel that tries every product before it buys the product, and if customers don't like something, they can return it for a no-hassle refund.

Another quality aspect of the Trader Joe's experience is its superior customer service. Its Crew Members are friendly, knowledgeable, and happy to see customers. Its stores regularly cook new and interesting products for their customers to try. If a customer asks an employee about a product, he or she will find the product and join the customer in a taste test. A popular radio ad for the company features its CEO making fun of other supermarkets that have put in flat-screen TVs for customers to watch at checkout counters. At Trader Joe's, he says, customers can entertain themselves by actually talking to employees.

Would you enjoy the Trader Joe's experience? Explain your answer. Can you think of other retail formats that could use a similar niche targeting strategy to develop a unique shopping experience compared to competitors?

that had been concentrating on this market segment went out of business.

Multisegment Targeting

A firm that chooses to serve two or more well-defined market segments and develops a distinct marketing mix for each has a multisegment targeting strategy. Many universities offer full-time (day) MBA programs, professional (evening) programs, and executive (weekend) programs, each targeted at a distinctly different market segment. Many programs are targeting mothers returning to the workplace. Cosmetics companies seek to increase sales and market share by targeting multiple age and ethnic groups. Maybelline and CoverGirl, for example, market different lines to teenage women, young adult women, older women, and African American women. CitiCard offers its Upromise Card to those who want to earn money to save for college, its Platinum Select Card to those who want no annual fee and a competitive interest rate, its Diamond Preferred Rewards Card to customers who want to earn free rewards like travel and brand-name merchandise, and its Citi AAdvantage Card to those who want to earn American Airlines Advantage frequent-flyer miles to redeem for travel. Many credit-card companies even have programs specifically designed for tweens, teens, and college students. Wal-Mart has historically followed a concentrated strategy that targeted lower income segments. Recently, however, the company has segmented its customers into three core groups based on the type of value they seek at the stores. "Brand Aspirationals" are low income customers who like to buy brand names like KitchenAid, "Price-Sensitive Affluents" are wealthier shoppers who love deals, and "Value-Price Shoppers" who like low prices and can't afford much more.[47]

Sometimes organizations use different promotional appeals, rather than completely different marketing mixes, as the basis for a multisegment strategy. Beer marketers such as Adolph Coors and Anheuser-Busch advertise and promote special events targeted toward African American, Hispanic American, and Asian American market segments. The beverages and containers, however, do not differ by ethnic market segment.

Gap, Inc., takes a different approach. It uses family and individual branding for its alternative format outlets that target different market segments. Stores operating under the family brand include Gap, Gapkids, babyGap, GapBody, and Gap Outlet. Individual brands other than Gap include Banana Republic and Old Navy. Multisegment targeting offers many potential benefits to firms, including greater sales volume, higher profits, larger market share, and economies of scale in manufacturing and marketing. Yet it may also involve greater product design, production, promotion, inventory, marketing research, and management costs. Before deciding to use this strategy, firms should compare the benefits and costs of multisegment targeting to those of undifferentiated and concentrated targeting.

Another potential cost of multisegment targeting is cannibalization, which occurs when sales of a new product cut into sales of a firm's existing products.

REVIEW LEARNING OUTCOME

LO 7 Discuss alternative strategies for selecting target markets

Undifferentiated   Multisegment   Concentrated

Brands with a multisegment targeting approach develop marketing mixes for more than one distinct market segment. In this advertisement, Ralph Lauren displays the versatility of its brand by pointing out that it makes clothing for children as well as for teenagers and young adults.

RALPH LAUREN

143 New Bond Street London

IMAGE COURTESY OF THE ADVERTISING ARCHIVES

cannibalization
A situation that occurs when sales of a new product cut into sales of a firm's existing products.

> *The difference between one-to-one marketing and the traditional mass-marketing approach can be compared to shooting a rifle and a shotgun.*

In many cases, however, companies prefer to steal sales from their own brands rather than lose sales to a competitor. Also, in today's fast-paced world of Internet business, some companies are willing to cannibalize existing business to build new business.

L8 ONE-TO-ONE MARKETING

one-to-one marketing
An individualized marketing method that utilizes customer information to build long-term, personalized, and profitable relationships with each customer.

Most businesses today use a mass-marketing approach designed to increase *market share* by selling their products to the greatest number of people. For many businesses, however, it is more efficient and profitable to use one-to-one marketing to increase *share of customer*—in other words, to sell more products to each customer. One-to-one marketing is an individualized marketing method that utilizes customer information to build long-term, personalized, and profitable relationships with each customer. The goal is to reduce costs through customer retention and increase revenue through customer loyalty. For example, Tesco, the British supermarket chain, sends out a mailing each quarter to 11 million households—but it produces 4 million different versions, tailored to the interests of its diverse customer base.

The difference between one-to-one marketing and the traditional mass-marketing approach can be compared to shooting a rifle and a shotgun. If you have good aim, a rifle is the more efficient weapon to use. A shotgun, on the other hand, increases your odds of hitting the target when it is more difficult to focus. Instead of scattering messages far and wide across the spectrum of mass media (the shotgun approach), one-to-one marketers look for opportunities to communicate with each individual customer (the rifle approach).

Teen retailer Karmaloop developed a system on their Web site that allows customers to preselect by brand or clothing category what types of merchandise they wanted to get e-mails about.[48] Lands' End also engages in one-to-one marketing by custom designing clothing. On Lands' End's Web site, customers provide information by answering a series of questions that takes about 20 minutes. Customer sizing information is saved, and reordering is simple. Customers who customize have been found to be more loyal.

Several factors suggest that personalized communications and product customization will continue to expand as more companies understand why and how

Carl's Jr. and Hardee's Web sites feature a 3-D bachelor-pad living room, a live-action video roommate, and a loyalty program which rewards their customers for purchasing food and for interacting with the Web site.

© AP IMAGES/PRNEWSFOTO/CKE RESTAURANTS, INC.

their customers make and execute purchase decisions. At least four trends will lead to the continuing growth of one-to-one marketing.

First, the one-size-fits-all marketing is no longer relevant. Consumers want to be treated as the individuals they are, with their own unique sets of needs and wants. By its personalized nature, one-to-one marketing can fulfill this desire.

Second, direct and personal marketing efforts will continue to grow to meet the needs of consumers who no longer have the time to spend shopping and making purchase decisions. With the personal and targeted nature of one-to-one marketing, consumers can spend less time making purchase decisions and more time doing the things that are important.

Third, consumers will be loyal only to those companies and brands that have earned their loyalty and reinforced it at every purchase occasion. One-to-one marketing techniques focus on finding a firm's best customers, rewarding them for their loyalty, and thanking them for their business.

Fourth, mass-media approaches will decline in importance as advances in market research and database technology allow marketers to collect detailed information on their customers. New technology offers one-to-one marketers a more cost-effective way to reach customers and enables businesses to personalize their messages. For example, **MyYahoo.com** greets each user by name and offers information in which the user has expressed interest. Similarly, **RedEnvelope.com** helps customers keep track of special occasions and offers personalized gift recommendations. With the help of database technology, one-to-one marketers can track their customers as individuals, even if they number in the millions.

One-to-one marketing is a huge commitment and often requires a 180-degree turn-around for marketers who spent the last half of the twentieth century developing and implementing mass-marketing efforts. Although mass marketing will probably continue to be used, especially to create brand awareness or to remind consumers of a product, the advantages of one-to-one marketing cannot be ignored.

REVIEW LEARNING OUTCOME

LO 8 Explain one-to-one marketing

Traditional Marketing

One-to-One Marketing

Increase market share

Increase share of customer

Market

ABC Company   ABC   ABC   ABC

POSITIONING

The development of any marketing mix depends on positioning, a process that influences potential customers' overall perception of a brand, product line, or organization in general. Position is the place a product, brand, or group of products occupies in consumers' minds relative to competing offerings. Consumer goods marketers are particularly concerned with positioning. Procter & Gamble, for example, markets 11 different laundry detergents, each with a unique position, as illustrated in Exhibit 8.6.

Positioning assumes that consumers compare products on the basis of important features. Marketing efforts that emphasize irrelevant features are therefore likely to misfire. For example, Crystal Pepsi and a clear version of Coca-Cola's Tab failed because consumers perceived the "clear" positioning as more of a marketing gimmick than a benefit.

Effective positioning requires assessing the positions occupied by competing products, determining the important dimensions underlying these positions, and choosing a position in the market where the organization's marketing efforts will have the greatest

positioning
Developing a specific marketing mix to influence potential customers' overall perception of a brand, product line, or organization in general.

position
The place a product, brand, or group of products occupies in consumers' minds relative to competing offerings.

EXHIBIT 8.6

Positioning of Procter & Gamble Detergents

Brand	Positioning	Market Share
Tide	Tough, powerful cleaning	31.1 percent
Cheer	Tough cleaning and color protection	8.2 percent
Bold	Detergent plus fabric softener	2.9 percent
Gain	Sunshine scent and odor-removing formula	2.6 percent
Era	Stain treatment and stain removal	2.2 percent
Dash	Value brand	1.8 percent
Oxide	Bleach-boosted formula, whitening	1.4 percent
Solo	Detergent and fabric softener in liquid form	1.2 percent
Dreft	Outstanding cleaning for baby clothes, safe for tender skin	1.0 percent
Ivory Snow	Fabric and skin safety on baby clothes and fine washables	0.7 percent
Ariel	Tough cleaner, aimed at Hispanic market	0.1 percent

product differentiation
A positioning strategy that some firms use to distinguish their products from those of competitors.

repositioning
Changing consumers' perceptions of a brand in relation to competing brands.

EXHIBIT 8.7

Perceptual Map and Positioning Strategy for Saks Department Stores

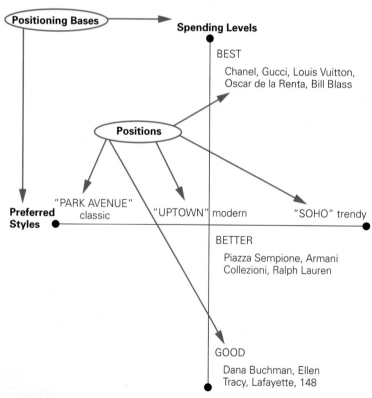

Source: Based on Vanessa O'Connell, "Park Avenue Classic or Soho Trendy?" *The Wall Street Journal*, April 20, 2007, B1.

impact. For example, AT&T's wireless company has positioned itself as mobility-centric, offering seamless mobility for customers whose lifestyles are not tied to one place.[49] Callaway Golf positions its new line of clubs and balls as innovative and technologically superior, using the tagline "A better game by design."[50] As the previous examples illustrate, product differentiation is a positioning strategy that many firms use to distinguish their products from those of competitors. The distinctions can be either real or perceived. Tandem Computers designed machines with two central processing units and two memories for computer systems that can never afford to be down or lose their databases (for example, an airline reservation system). In this case, Tandem used product differentiation to create a product with very real advantages for the target market. However, many everyday products, such as bleaches, aspirin, unleaded regular gasoline, and some soaps, are differentiated by such trivial means as brand names, packaging, color, smell, or "secret" additives. The marketer attempts to convince consumers that a particular brand is distinctive and that they should demand it over competing brands.

Some firms, instead of using product differentiation, position their products as being similar to competing products or brands. Two examples of this positioning include artificial sweeteners advertised as tasting like sugar or margarine tasting like butter.

Perceptual Mapping

Perceptual mapping is a means of displaying or graphing, in two or more dimensions, the location of products, brands, or groups of products in customers' minds. For example, Saks Inc., the tony department store chain, stumbled in sales when it tried to attract a younger core customer. To recover, Saks invested in research to determine its core customers in its 54 stores across the country. The perceptual map in Exhibit 8.7 shows how Saks Inc. uses customer demographics, such as a matrix that charts the best mix of clothes and accessories to stock in each store.

Positioning Bases

Firms use a variety of bases for positioning, including the following:

☛ *Attribute:* A product is associated with an attribute, product feature, or customer benefit. Kleenex has designed a tissue that contains substances to kill germs in an effort to differentiate its product from competing tissues.[51]

- *Price and quality*: This positioning base may stress high price as a signal of quality or emphasize low price as an indication of value. Neiman Marcus uses the high-price strategy; Wal-Mart has successfully followed the low-price and value strategies. The mass merchandiser Target has developed an interesting position based on price and quality. It is an "upscale discounter," sticking to low prices but offering higher quality and design than most discount chains.

- *Use or application*: Stressing uses or applications can be an effective means of positioning a product with buyers. Kahlúa liqueur used advertising to point out 228 ways to consume the product. Snapple introduced a new drink called "Snapple a Day" that is intended for use as a meal replacement.

- *Product user*: This positioning base focuses on a personality or type of user. Zale Corporation has several jewelry store concepts, each positioned to a different user. The Zales stores cater to middle-of-the-road consumers with traditional styles. Its Gordon's stores appeal to a slightly older clientele with a contemporary look. Guild is positioned for the more affluent 50-plus consumer.

- *Product class*: The objective here is to position the product as being associated with a particular category of products; for example, positioning a margarine brand with butter. Alternatively, products can be disassociated with a category. Del Monte introduced Fruit Chillers, a shelf-stable sorbet that consumers freeze themselves when they're ready to eat it. Fruit Chillers are sold next to single-serve fruit cups, positioned as fruit rather than as a frozen dessert.[52]

- *Competitor*: Positioning against competitors is part of any positioning strategy. The original Hertz rental car positioning as number two compared to Enterprise exemplifies positioning against specific competitors.

- *Emotion*: Positioning using emotion focuses on how the product makes customers feel. A number of companies use this approach. For example, Nike's "Just Do It" campaign didn't tell consumers what "it" was, but most got the emotional message of achievement and courage. Budweiser's advertising featuring talking frogs and lizards emphasized fun. Sears is drawing on the nostalgia of its brand name by remodeling a store outside Atlanta to resemble its stores of the past. The focus is on tapping into Sears' heritage and its legacy as America's store.[53]

Repositioning

Sometimes products or companies are repositioned in order to sustain growth in slow markets or to correct positioning mistakes. Repositioning is changing consumers' perceptions of a brand in relation to competing brands. For example, Procter & Gamble increased its baby-care business in the early 2000s when they changed Pampers' position from being about dryness to being about helping Mom with her baby's development. P&G also repositioned Olay from being a pink liquid that moisturizes to helping women look better and feel better as they age.[54] An entire industry of firms that need to think about repositioning is the supermarket industry. For over a decade, Wal-Mart has been expanding in both rural and metro areas. The result has generally been devastating to competitors, especially independent grocers. Consulting firm Retail Forward predicts that two supermarkets will go out of business for every Wal-Mart Supercenter that opens in the United States. The Strategic Resource Group adds that 27 leading national and regional supermarket operators have either gone bankrupt or have liquidated since Wal-Mart went national with Supercenters.[55] So what are competitors to do? Wal-Mart owns the low price position. Successful competitors will have to establish viable alternative positions.

H-E-B stores in Hispanic areas in Texas are tailoring their product mix to appeal to this market segment. H-E-B has also opened Asian wet markets in some stores. Its Central Market format is definitely upscale with unique products and very high-quality perishables. Research shows that over half of all families with incomes between $50,000 and $100,000 are willing to pay more for high-quality items in a more pleasant shopping environment.[56] Safeway is trying to avoid Wal-Mart by repositioning itself as upscale with about half its stores converted to "Lifestyle" markets with wood floors, on-site bakeries, and high-end private label brands.[57]

perceptual mapping
A means of displaying or graphing, in two or more dimensions, the location of products, brands, or groups of products in customers' minds.

It is too early to tell which, if any, of these repositioning strategies will be successful. Clearly, though, competing head-on with Wal-Mart is not a good idea.

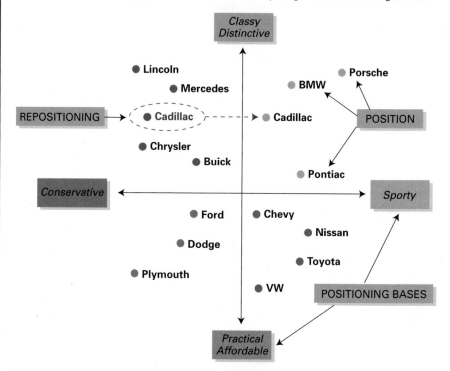

REVIEW AND APPLICATIONS

Describe the characteristics of markets and market segments. A market is composed of individuals or organizations with the ability and willingness to make purchases to fulfill their needs or wants. A market segment is a group of individuals or organizations with similar product needs as a result of one or more common characteristics.

1.1 Mercedes-Benz is thinking about advertising its cars to college students. Do you think that college students are a viable potential market for Mercedes? Why or why not?

1.2 Go to the Web site **www.careermag.com.** How are visitors to the site segmented when seeking relevant job openings? Report your results.

Explain the importance of market segmentation. Before the 1960s, few businesses targeted specific market segments. Today, segmentation is a crucial marketing strategy for nearly all successful organizations. Market segmentation enables marketers to tailor marketing mixes to meet the needs of particular population segments. Segmentation helps marketers identify consumer needs and preferences, areas of declining demand, and new marketing opportunities.

2.1 Describe market segmentation in terms of the historical evolution of marketing.

Discuss criteria for successful market segmentation. Successful market segmentation depends on four basic criteria: (1) a market segment must be substantial and have enough potential customers to be viable, (2) a market segment must be identifiable and measurable, (3) members of a market segment must be accessible to marketing efforts, and (4) a market segment must respond to particular marketing efforts in a way that distinguishes it from other segments.

3.1 As a marketing consultant for a chain of hair salons, you have been asked to evaluate the kids' market as a potential segment for the chain to target. Write a memo to your client discussing your evaluation of the kids' segment in terms of the four criteria for successful market segmentation.

Describe the bases commonly used to segment consumer markets. Five bases are commonly used for segmenting consumer markets. Geographic segmentation is based on region, size, density, and climate characteristics. Demographic segmentation is based on age, gender, income level, ethnicity, and family life-cycle characteristics. Psychographic segmentation includes personality, motives, and lifestyle characteristics. Benefits sought is a type of segmentation that identifies customers according to the benefits they seek in a product. Finally, usage segmentation divides a market by the amount of product purchased or consumed.

4.1 Choose magazine ads for five different consumer products. For each ad, write a description of what you think the demographic characteristics of the targeted market are.

4.2 Investigate how Delta Air Lines (**www.delta.com**) uses its Web site to cater to its market segments.

4.3 Is it possible to identify a single market for two distinctly different products? For example, how substantial is the market composed of consumers who use Apple *and* who drive Volkswagens? Can you think of other product combinations that would interest a single market? (Do not use products that are complementary, like a bike and a bike helmet. Think of products, like the iPod and the car, that are very different.) Complete the following sentences and describe the market for each set of products you pair together.

Consumers of:

Propel fitness water could also be a target market for _____.

Proactiv Solution skin care products could also be a target market for _____.

Alienware computers could also be a target market for _____.

Specialty luggage tags could also be a target market for _____.

LO 5 Describe the bases for segmenting business markets. Business markets can be segmented on two general bases: First, businesses segment markets based on company characteristics, such as customers' geographic location, type of company, company size, and product use. Second, companies may segment customers based on the buying processes those customers use.

5.1 Choose five ads from business publications such as *The Wall Street Journal*, *Fortune*, and *BusinessWeek*. For each ad, write a description of how you think the company has segmented its business market.

LO 6 List the steps involved in segmenting markets. Six steps are involved when segmenting markets: (1) selecting a market or product category for study; (2) choosing a basis or bases for segmenting the market; (3) selecting segmentation descriptors; (4) profiling and evaluating segments; (5) selecting target markets; and (6) designing, implementing, and maintaining appropriate marketing mixes.

6.1 Write a letter to the president of your bank suggesting ideas for increasing profits and enhancing customer service by improving segmentation and targeting strategies.

LO 7 Discuss alternative strategies for selecting target markets. Marketers select target markets using three different strategies: undifferentiated targeting, concentrated targeting, and multisegment targeting. An undifferentiated targeting strategy assumes that all members of a market have similar needs that can be met with a single marketing mix. A concentrated targeting strategy focuses all marketing efforts on a single market segment. Multisegment targeting is a strategy that uses two or more marketing mixes to target two or more market segments.

7.1 Form a team with two or three other students. Create an idea for a new product. Describe the segment (or segments) you are going to target with the product and explain why you chose the targeting strategy you did.

7.2 Go to the Web sites of JCPenney, **www.jcpenney.com,** and Target, **www. target.com.** Compare the presentation of women's fashions at the Web sites. What are the major differences? Which site is more designer focused, and which is more brand focused? Which company's approach do you think will appeal more to the "Holy Grail" target market of 25- to 35-year-old women?

LO 8 Explain one-to-one marketing. One-to-one marketing is an individualized marketing method that utilizes customer information to build long-term, personalized, and profitable relationships with each customer. Successful one-to-one marketing comes from understanding customers and collaborating with them rather than using them as targets for generic messages. Database technology makes it possible for companies to interact with customers on a personal, one-to-one basis.

8.1 You are the marketing manager for a specialty retailer that sells customized handbags. Write a memo to your boss describing how the company could benefit from one-to-one marketing.

LO 9 Explain how and why firms implement positioning strategies and how product differentiation plays a role. Positioning is used to influence consumer perceptions of a particular brand, product line, or organization in relation to competitors. The term *position* refers to the place that the offering occupies in consumers' minds. To establish a unique position, many firms use product differentiation, emphasizing the real or perceived differences between competing offerings. Products may be differentiated on the basis of attribute, price and quality, use or application, product user, product class, or competitor.

9.1 Choose a product category (e.g., pickup trucks), and identify at least three different brands and their respective positioning strategies. How is each position communicated to the target audience?

KEY TERMS

80/20 principle	271	market segment	259	psychographic	
benefit segmentation	270	market segmentation	259	segmentation	269
cannibalization	277	multisegment targeting		repositioning	281
concentrated targeting		strategy	276	satisficers	272
strategy	275	niche	275	segmentation bases	
demographic segmentation	263	one-to-one marketing	278	(variables)	262
family life cycle (FLC)	267	optimizers	272	target market	274
geodemographic		perceptual mapping	281	undifferentiated targeting	
segmentation	269	position	279	strategy	274
geographic segmentation	262	positioning	279	usage-rate segmentation	271
market	259	product differentiation	280		

EXERCISES

APPLICATION EXERCISE

How tightly do you fit into a particular market segment? Do you think you can be neatly classified? If you think your purchasing habits make you an enigma to marketers, you may need to think again.[58]

Activities

1. Go to the Claritas Web site (**www.claritas.com/MyBestSegments/Default. jsp?ID=20**) and follow its "You Are Where You Live" link to find out what your ZIP code says about you. The database will generate many cluster descriptions based on your ZIP code. Depending on the functionality of the Web site at the time you access the database, you may need to reenter your ZIP code multiple times if you want to read all the cluster descriptions.

2. Now pick a product category, like automobiles, athletic shoes, beverages, or health and beauty products. Then think about which products in that category would appeal to each of the clusters generated by your ZIP code search. For example, a car that appeals to a cluster titled "Young Bohemians" may not be the car of choice for the cluster "Pools and Patios." If your search generated only one cluster type, you may wish to enter other ZIP codes for your area of town or for your region.

3. Create a perceptual map for the product you chose. Write a short statement that describes the overall position of each product with an explanation of why you located it where you did on the perceptual map.

ETHICS EXERCISE

Tobacco companies are frequently criticized for targeting potential customers below the legal age to purchase and use their products. Critics cite Joe Camel and the Marlboro Man as images meant to make smoking appealing to young people. If tobacco companies are actually following this particular demographic targeting strategy, most would agree that it is unethical if not illegal.

Questions

1. Is marketing tobacco products to younger consumers unethical?

2. Many are beginning to argue that fast-food companies, such as McDonald's and Burger King, are knowingly marketing unhealthy food to consumers. Is it unethical for fast-food companies to market kids' meals to children?

3. What does the AMA Statement of Ethics have to say about marketing unhealthy or harmful products to consumers, particularly children and young adults? Go to the AMA Web site at **www.marketingpower.com** to review the statement of ethics (**www.marketingpower.com/AboutAMA/Pages/Statement of Ethics.aspx**). Write a brief paragraph summarizing where the AMA stands on this important issue.

MARKETING PLAN EXERCISE

Once you've completed the marketing plan exercise for each chapter in Part 2 of this textbook, you can complete the Part 2 Marketing Planning Worksheet on your companion Web site at **www.cengage.com/marketing/lamb.** Complete the following exercises to continue the marketing plan you began in Chapter 2:

1. To whom does your company market (consumer, industrial, government, not-for-profit, or a combination of targets)? Within each market, are there specific segments or niches that your company can concentrate on? If so, which one(s) would you focus on and why? What are the factors used to create these segments? What are the Internet capabilities in those markets? If you try to encourage those segments to access your product or service via the Internet, will that change which segments are most important to your business? How? What are the factors used to create these segments? Which segments should your company focus on and why?

2. Describe your company's target market segment(s). Use demographics, psychographics, geographics, economic factors, size, growth rates, trends, NAICS codes, and any other appropriate descriptors. What role does the Internet play in your target market's life? How is the target market for your Internet business different from that of a traditional business in your market?

3. Using the list of key competitive advantages you described in Part 1 of your marketing plan, create a series of positioning grids, using two factors each as dimensions. (See grids in LO9 in your textbook, for an example.) Then plot the list of key competitors you identified earlier onto these positioning grids. Is your company too close to a key competitor? Are there spaces where the consumer needs and wants are unsatisfied? Consider how the Internet changes what factors are important to your success in your market space. Is technology the most important factor for your firm, or are there other ways for you to differentiate from and beat your competition?

CASE STUDY: COKE ZERO

DO REAL MEN DRINK DIET COKE?

When a couple of marketing managers for Coca-Cola told attorney Elizabeth Finn Johnson that they wanted to sue their Coke Zero colleagues for "taste infringement,"

© VICKI BEAVER

she was baffled. She tried to talk them out of it, but they were determined. They argued that Coca-Cola Classic should be protected from the age discrimination it would suffer with the introduction of a newer, younger soft drink that tasted exactly the same as the original. Frustrated, Finn Johnson held up the Coke can and shouted, "It's not a person! Title VII doesn't cover these things!"

What she didn't know was that the marketing managers were actors. Hidden cameras had been planted around the meeting room to capture the reactions of several unsuspecting attorneys who had been asked to consider the case, including an immigration lawyer who was asked if he could get the Coke Zero marketing head deported back to Canada. The short videos were strategically placed on Web sites such as **www.youtube.com** to promote Coke Zero as the hip, new alternative to Diet Coke for men.

The Coca-Cola Company knows it has to be creative if it's going to sell more soda after sales dropped two years in a row in 2005 and 2006. Morgan Stanley analyst Bill Pecoriello explains, "Consumers are becoming ever more health-conscious, and the image of regular carbonated soft drinks is deteriorating rapidly." In an attempt to appeal to consumers concerned with nutrition, Coke introduced Diet Coke Plus in 2007, a sweeter version of Diet Coke fortified with vitamins and minerals. But what they really needed was a way to reach young male consumers, and Diet Coke Plus, marketed with tagline like "Your Best Friend Just Got Friendlier!" wasn't going to do it.

A few new products appealed to certain male demographics, such as Coca-Cola Blak, a cola with coffee essence created for older, more sophisticated consumers who are willing to pay more, and Full Throttle Blue Demon, an energy drink with an agave azule flavor (think margaritas) designed to appeal to Hispanic men. However, research showed that there was still a big demographic hole to fill as young men between the ages of 18 and 34 were abandoning the Coca-Cola brand altogether. They didn't want all the calories of regular Coke, but they weren't willing to make the move to Diet Coke, either, which has traditionally been marketed to women who want to lose weight.

Katie Bayne, chief marketing officer for Coca-Cola North America, says that the men who weren't put off by the "feminine stigma" of Diet Coke often rejected it anyway because of its aspartame-sweetened aftertaste. "What we were seeing before Zero launched was that more and more younger people were interested in no-calorie beverages but weren't going to sacrifice taste," Bayne said. "So when they got interested in no-calorie, they were like, 'Forget it, I'm not going to Diet Coke.'"

Testing showed that the name "Coke Zero" would be an effective way to sell a low-calorie cola to men without using the word "*diet*." And advances in artificial sweeteners made it possible for Coke to finally create a product that tasted more like the Real Thing. So expectations were high when Coke Zero was introduced in 2005 with a big marketing push, including a commercial that remade the famous 1971 "Hilltop/I'd Like to Teach the World to Sing" ad—this time with rapper G. Love on a rooftop singing that he'd like to teach the world to "chill." Unfortunately, the commercial didn't catch on, and neither did the product it was selling.

Despite disappointing sales in the United States, however, Coke Zero was an immediate hit in Australia, selling more than three times the number of cases expected during its first year on the market. In the United States, the packaging was white and silver, making it difficult for consumers to see the difference between Coke Zero and Diet Coke. In Australia, the bottles and cans were black, making the product stand out on the shelves and look more like the "bloke's Coke" it was intended to be.

The U.S. marketing team took notice and reintroduced Coke Zero with a black and silver label in 2007. Coca-Cola is now investing more money in Coke Zero than any other brand its size, hoping it will someday be a megabrand for the company alongside Coca-Cola Classic and Diet Coke. Chief marketing officer Bayne is enthusiastic about the impact it may have on the company. "We do see this as potentially a bit of a white knight. There's huge opportunity to grow here."[59]

Questions

1. Describe the specific type of consumer that the Coca-Cola Company is targeting with each of the following products: Diet Coke, Coke Zero, Diet Coke Plus, Coca-Cola Blak, and Full Throttle Blue Demon. What types of demographic segmentation is each product's marketing most likely to include?

2. Some industry analysts think soft-drink companies should develop products that will bring new customers into the market rather than just creating variants on the old. They warn that products like Coke Zero will cannibalize lost market share from other soft drink categories instead of increasing the number of consumers overall. Which Coca-Cola products are most likely to lose customers to Coke Zero?

3. Why do you think that the hidden-camera videos used to promote Coke Zero were an effective way to reach its target market? Do you think a similar strategy with a viral marketing campaign on the Internet would appeal to the target market for Diet Coke Plus?

4. Do you think Diet Coke could have been repositioned to change consumers' perceptions of it enough to be considered a drink equally appealing to men? Why or why not?

COMPANY CLIPS

© NKP MEDIA, INC./CENGAGE

READYMADE—FOCUS AND SEGMENTATION

ReadyMade markets itself as a magazine catering to GenNest, the group of consumers ages 25 to 35 who are just settling down after college.

The young couples that make up this group are buying their first houses and taking on domestic and decorating roles for the first time. They are interested in being stylish, while at the same time maintaining their own unique personalities. But *ReadyMade* appeals to a wider variety of readers than just GenNest. The magazine has subscribers in all age groups, from teens looking to spruce up their rooms to retirees looking for projects to enliven their homes. This diversity offers a unique challenge to *ReadyMade* as it tries to promote itself to advertisers who need to know what sort of people will be reached through advertisements appearing in the publication.

Questions

1. How does *ReadyMade* communicate the demographics of its reader base to advertisers who want to see specific statistics that do not easily represent *ReadyMade*'s target market?

2. What sort of segmentation does *ReadyMade* use when it markets to businesses and investors?

3. What ideas do you have that would help *ReadyMade* reach out to new subscribers without alienating its loyal base?

Marketing & You Results

A high score indicates that you operate within budget constraints. Living on a budget doesn't necessarily mean that you change your shopping behavior or your price comparison behavior, however. Low scores relate to financial health and a tendency to be brand loyal. After reading Chapter 8, you can see why income and financial situation can be an important segmentation variable!

Essentials of Marketing

7e

Lamb ▪ Hair ▪ McDaniel

Decision Support Systems and Marketing Research

LEARNING OUTCOMES

LO 1 Explain the concept and purpose of a marketing decision support system

LO 2 Define marketing research and explain its importance to marketing decision making

LO 3 Describe the steps involved in conducting a marketing research project

LO 4 Discuss the profound impact of the Internet on marketing research

LO 5 Discuss the growing importance of scanner-based research

LO 6 Explain the concept of competitive intelligence

MARKETING DECISION SUPPORT SYSTEMS

Accurate and timely information is the lifeblood of marketing decision making. Good information can help an organization maximize sales and efficiently use scarce company resources. To prepare and adjust marketing plans, managers need a system for gathering everyday information about developments in the marketing environment—that is, for gathering marketing information. The system most commonly used these days for gathering marketing information is called a *marketing decision support system*.

A marketing decision support system (DSS) is an interactive, flexible computerized information system that enables managers to obtain and manipulate information as they are making decisions. A DSS bypasses the information-processing specialist and gives managers access to useful data from their own desks.

These are the characteristics of a true DSS:

☛ *Interactive:* Managers give simple instructions and see immediate results. The process is under their direct control; no computer programmer is needed. Managers don't have to wait for scheduled reports.

☛ *Flexible:* A DSS can sort, regroup, total, average, and manipulate the data in various ways. It will shift gears as the user changes topics, matching information to the problem at hand. For example, the CEO can see highly aggregated figures, and the marketing analyst can view very detailed breakouts.

☛ *Discovery-oriented:* Managers can probe for trends, isolate problems, and ask "what if" questions.

☛ *Accessible:* Managers who aren't skilled with computers can easily learn how to use a DSS. Novice users should be able to choose a standard, or default, method of using the system. They can bypass optional features so they can work with the basic system right away while gradually learning to apply its advanced features.

Marketing & You

Please note your opinion on each of the following questions.

Using the following scale, enter your opinion.

1	2	3	4	5	6	7
Strongly disagree						Strongly agree

During a marketing project, a marketing manager should have formal or informal processes for continuously:

___ collecting information from customers.

___ collecting information about competitors' activities.

___ collecting information about relevant publics other than customers and competitors.

___ reexamining the value of information collected in previous studies.

___ collecting information from external experts, such as consultants.

Total your score. Now, read the chapter and find out what your score means at the end.

Source: From Scale #66, *Marketing Scales Handbook,* G. Bruner, James, H. Hensel, eds. Vol.III. © by American Marketing Association.

As a hypothetical example of how a DSS can be used, consider Renee Smith, vice president and manager of new products for Central Corporation. To evaluate sales of a recently introduced product, Renee can "call up" sales by the week, then by the month, breaking them out at her option by, say, customer segments. As she works at her desktop computer, her inquiries can go in several directions, depending on the decision at hand. If her train of thought raises questions about monthly sales last quarter compared to forecasts, she can use her DSS to analyze problems immediately. Renee might see that her new product's sales were significantly below forecasts. Were her forecasts too optimistic? She compares other products' sales to her forecasts and finds that the targets were very accurate. Was something wrong with the product? Is her sales department getting insufficient leads, or is it

marketing information
Everyday information about developments in the marketing environment that managers use to prepare and adjust marketing plans.

decision support system (DSS)
An interactive, flexible computerized information system that enables managers to obtain and manipulate information as they are making decisions.

> ❝ *Huge databases can raise a number of concerns about the safety and use of personal data.* ❞

database marketing
The creation of a large computerized file of customers' and potential customers' profiles and purchase patterns.

marketing research
The process of planning, collecting, and analyzing data relevant to a marketing decision.

not putting leads to good use? Thinking a minute about how to examine that question, she checks ratios of leads converted to sales, product by product. The results disturb her. Only 5 percent of the new product's leads generated orders, compared to the company's 12 percent all-product average. Why? Renee guesses that the salesforce is not supporting the new product vigorously enough. Quantitative information from the DSS could perhaps provide more evidence to back that suspicion. But already having enough quantitative knowledge to satisfy herself, the VP acts on her intuition and experience and decides to have a chat with her sales manager.

Perhaps the fastest-growing use of DSSs is for database marketing, which is the creation of a large computerized file of customers' and potential customers' profiles and purchase patterns. It is usually the key tool for successful one-to-one marketing, which relies on very specific information about a market. Huge databases can raise a number of concerns about the safety and use of personal data.

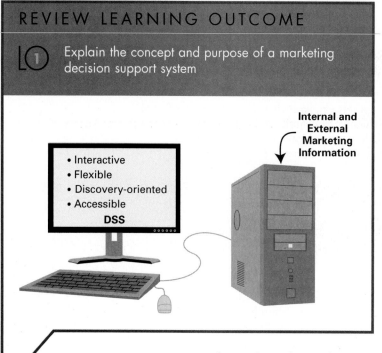

REVIEW LEARNING OUTCOME

LO 1 Explain the concept and purpose of a marketing decision support system

- Interactive
- Flexible
- Discovery-oriented
- Accessible
DSS

Internal and External Marketing Information

LO 2
THE ROLE OF MARKETING RESEARCH

Marketing research is the process of planning, collecting, and analyzing data relevant to a marketing decision. The results of this analysis are then communicated to management. Thus, marketing research is the function that links the consumer, customer, and public to the marketer through information. Marketing research plays a key role in the marketing system. It provides decision makers with data on the effectiveness of the current marketing mix and also with insights for necessary changes. Furthermore, marketing research is a main data source for both management information systems and DSS. In other words, the findings of a marketing research project become data in a DSS.

Each year over $7 billion is spent on marketing research in the United States. That money is used to study products, advertising, prices, packages, names, logos, services, buying habits, taglines, colors, uses, awareness, familiarity, new concepts, traffic patterns, wants, needs, and politics.

Marketing research has three roles: descriptive, diagnostic, and predictive. Its *descriptive* role includes gathering and presenting factual statements. For example, what is the historic sales trend in the industry? What are consumers' attitudes toward a product and its advertising? Its *diagnostic* role includes explaining data. For instance, what was the impact on sales of a change in the design of the package? Its *predictive* function is to address "what if" questions. For example, how can the researcher use the descriptive and diagnostic research to predict the results of a planned marketing decision?

Management Uses of Marketing Research

Marketing research can help managers in several ways. It improves the quality of decision making and helps managers trace problems. Most important, sound marketing research helps managers focus on the paramount importance of keeping existing customers, aids them in better understanding the marketplace, and alerts them to marketplace trends.

Marketing research also helps managers gauge the perceived value of their goods and services as well as the level of customer satisfaction. For example, research revealed which brands of plumbing fixtures were traditional to New York City. This helped the Brooklyn Home Depot's store manager Rich Kantor to arrange his small pilot store so that it was designed to meet the needs of urban communities.

Improving the Quality of Decision Making Managers can sharpen their decision making by using marketing research to explore the desirability of various marketing alternatives. For example, on the heels of the successful launch of its Young & Tender line of bagged spinach, NewStar, a Salinas, California-based produce firm, was wondering what to do for an encore. A line of salad kits featuring spinach in combination with a dressing and/or other ingredients seemed like a natural idea. But rather than introducing a me-too product to the already-crowded salad kit market, the company wanted to add a gourmet twist.

The process began with an idea generation phase, says Christie Hoyer, vice president of product development and evaluation at the National Food Laboratory (NFL). Sessions were conducted with NFL chefs, food technologists, and other culinary arts workers. "We did a number of brainstorming sessions, game-playing, and other, more coordinated exercises. From that we came up with numerous flavor concepts for the salads and the sauté mixes."

Next came the first round of consumer testing. At this stage, Hoyer says, NFL wanted to validate the product concepts and also gauge reactions to them. A four-phase process was conducted with male and female consumers ages 21 to 64 who were their family's primary grocery shopper and were positive toward spinach salad and cooked fresh spinach.

The first phase gathered reactions to the concept of a line of gourmet salad and sauté kits and determined purchase intent for each flavor (based on descriptions of the flavors, not actual tasting). Next, the respondents tried the product prototypes, which were rotated so that half of the group tried the sautés first and half tried the salads first.

The third phase was a test of packaging. Respondents were taken to a separate area featuring a mock store display of three packaging concepts and were asked to rank their preferences for the different graphics. In the fourth phase, the consumers viewed a large copy of the nutritional information for a salad kit and a sauté kit. "Without specifically asking about it, we were interested in their reaction to things such as fat content," Hoyer says.

Since the salad and sauté mixes were introduced, they have been a hit with retailers and with consumers. Marketing research paved the way![1]

Because kids eat over 5 billion ounces of ketchup each year, Heinz decided that the heavy users (kids) should have a lot to say (via marketing research) about how to make ketchup fun. Heinz listened and watched children using ketchup, which resulted in a new bottle design, name selection, and color. The true ketchup connoisseurs helped create Heinz EZ Squirt green ketchup.

Opening a pack of bacon is a messy job. Bacon lovers have to reach into the package and if they only pull out a few slices, there's no easy way to store the remainder. Oscar Mayer marketing researchers hear plenty from consumers about what they disliked about its former bacon packaging. So marketers figured the best solution would be a packaging innovation that eliminated the chore of placing the opened packed in a resealable plastic bag or wrapping it in plastic or foil. This unwanted task was done so the last piece of bacon would be as fresh as the first.

Recently, Oscar Mayer Center Cut Bacon was introduced in a new "Stay-Fresh Reclosable Tray." The flip-top lid allows easy access

Managers can sharpen their decision making by using marketing research to explore various marketing alternatives. Heinz used the results of its marketing research—that is, listening to and watching children using ketchup—to create a new bottle design, name selection, and color for its EZ Squirt ketchup.

© SUSAN VAN ETTEN

to the bacon inside. The top snaps closed, making it readily resealable. The flat tray makes for simplified storage in the refrigerator.[2]

Tracing Problems When Something Goes Wrong Another way managers use marketing research is to find out why a plan backfired. Was the initial decision incorrect? Did an unforeseen change in the external environment cause the plan to fail? How can the same mistake be avoided in the future?

Keebler introduced Sweet Spots, a shortbread cookie with a huge chocolate drop on it. It has had acceptable sales and is still on the market, but only after the company used marketing research to overcome several problems. Soon after the cookie's introduction, Keebler increased the box size from 10 ounces at $2.29 to 15 ounces at $3.19. Demand immediately fell. Market research showed that Sweet Spots were now considered more of a luxury than an everyday item. Keebler lowered the price and went back to the 10-ounce box. Even though Sweet Spots originally was aimed at upscale adult females, the company also tried to appeal to kids. In subsequent research, Keebler found that the package graphics appealed to mothers but not to children.

Focusing on the Paramount Importance of Keeping Existing Customers An inextricable link exists between customer satisfaction and customer loyalty. Long-term relationships don't just happen but are grounded in the delivery of service and value by the firm. Customer retention pays big dividends for organizations. Powered by repeat sales and referrals, revenues and market share grow. Costs fall because firms spend less money and energy attempting to replace defectors. Steady customers are easy to serve because they understand the modus operandi and make fewer demands on employees' time. Increased customer retention also drives job satisfaction and pride, which lead to higher employee retention. In turn, the knowledge employees acquire as they stay longer increases productivity. A Bain & Co. study estimated that a 5 percent decrease in the customer defection rate can boost profits by 25 to 95 percent.[3] Another study found that the customer retention rate has a major impact on the value of the firm.[4]

Recently, Dunkin' Donuts paid dozens of faithful customers in Phoenix, Chicago, and Charlotte, N.C., $100 a week to buy coffee at Starbucks instead. At the same time, the no-frills coffee chain paid Starbucks customers to make the opposite switch.

© AP IMAGES/PRNEWSFOTO/PROCTER & GAMBLE

When it later debriefed the two groups, Dunkin' says it found them so polarized that company researchers dubbed them "tribes"—each of whom loathed the very things that made the other tribe loyal to their coffee shop. Dunkin' fans viewed Starbucks as pretentious and trendy, while Starbucks loyalists saw Dunkin' as austere and unoriginal.

Bridging some of the divide between Starbucks and Dunkin' Donuts customers—but not too much—is key to Dunkin' Donuts' ambitious plan to expand its largely Eastern coffee chain into a national powerhouse that's as synonymous with coffee as Starbucks.

Dunkin' researchers concluded that it wasn't income that set the two tribes apart, as much as an ideal: Dunkin' tribe members wanted to be part of a crowd, while members of the Starbucks tribe had a desire to stand out as individuals. Dunkin' executives made dozens of decisions, big and small, ranging from where to put the espresso machines to how much of its signature pink and orange color scheme to retain to where to display its fresh-baked goods.

Out went the square laminate tables, to be replaced by round imitation-granite tabletops and sleek chairs. Dunkin' covered store walls in espresso brown and dialed down the pink and orange tones. Executives considered but held off on installing wireless Internet access because customers "just don't feel it's Dunkin' Donuts," says Joe Scafido, chief creative and innovation officer.[5]

One company that always goes the extra mile to provide quality service and to deliver customer satisfaction is the Ritz-Carlton hotel chain. Their training program is described in the Customer Experience box below.

CUSTOMER Experience

Ritz-Carlton Always Goes the Extra Mile

Ritz-Carlton is the only service company to have won the prestigious Malcolm Baldrige National Quality Award twice. The chain placed first in guest satisfaction among luxury hotels in the most recent J.D. Power & Associates hotel survey. Ritz-Carlton spends about $5,000 to train each new hire. First is a two-day introduction to company values (it's all about the service) and the 20 Ritz-Carlton "basics." (Basic 13 is "Never lose a guest.") Next comes a 21-day course focused on job responsibilities, such as a bellman's 28 steps to greeting a guest. Each employee carries a plastic card imprinted with the credo and the basics, as well as the "employee promise" and the three steps of service. Step 1: "A warm and sincere greeting. Use the guests' name, if and when possible."

Porters and doormen wear headsets, so when they spot your name on luggage tags, they can radio the information to the front desk. In addition, an in-house database called the Customer Loyalty Anticipation Satisfaction System stores guest preferences, such as whether an individual likes Seagram's ginger ale or Canada Dry. The software also alerts front-desk clerks when a guest who's stayed at other Ritz-Carltons has a habit of inquiring about the best sushi in town.[6]

Where does marketing research come into play at Ritz-Carlton? Is it really necessary for the Ritz-Carlton to provide such a high level of service to keep its customers?

UNDERSTANDING THE EVER-CHANGING MARKETPLACE

Marketing research also helps managers understand what is going on in the marketplace and take advantage of opportunities. Historically, marketing research has been practiced for as long as marketing has existed. The early Phoenicians carried out market demand studies as they traded in the various ports of the Mediterranean Sea. Marco Polo's diary indicates he was performing marketing research as he traveled to China. There is even evidence that the Spanish systematically conducted "market surveys" as they explored the New World, and there are examples of marketing research conducted during the Renaissance.

As the price of gasoline hit $4.00 plus per gallon, more and more manufacturers began looking at the hybrid car market. However, before committing hundreds of millions of dollars to producing hybrids, they need a better understanding of the market. Thus, the marketers turn to marketing research. When consumers were asked whether they would consider a hybrid version of their new vehicle had it been available, roughly 7 in 10 indicated they would have. In addition to their high likelihood to consider hybrid vehicles, when asked what type of alternative fuel they found most appealing, vehicle buyers most often indicate hybrid vehicles are their preferred alternative fuel type.

Also, there has been an increased interest in pure electric vehicles. The uptick likely reflects new developments in electric engines and public relations activities surrounding them. When considering purchasing a new vehicle, those who choose hybrids are motivated by a desire to obtain an environmentally friendly vehicle, but even more importantly, to achieve the greatest level of fuel economy. Those who chose hybrids are more likely than owners in general to consider issues such as style, comfort, roominess and even price to be significantly less important.

However, despite obtaining higher miles per gallon (MPG) and greater satisfaction with it, hybrid owners report their MPG falls far short of their expectations. In fact, hybrid owners are significantly more likely than vehicle purchasers in general to obtain lower-than-expected MPG.[7]

Why marketing research?

☑ Improve quality of decision making

☑ Trace problems

☑ Focus on keeping existing customers

☑ Understand changes in marketplace

Although the material above is just a tiny piece of a nationwide study of over 100,000 vehicle owners, you can see how the insights from such a study can be extremely valuable to car manufacturers.

L◯3

STEPS IN A MARKETING RESEARCH PROJECT

Virtually all firms that have adopted the marketing concept engage in some marketing research because it offers decision makers many benefits. Some companies spend millions on marketing research; others, particularly smaller firms, conduct informal, limited-scale research studies. For example, when Eurasia restaurant, serving Eurasian cuisine, first opened along Chicago's ritzy Michigan Avenue, it drew novelty seekers. But it turned off the important business lunch crowd, and sales began to decline. The owner surveyed several hundred businesspeople working within a mile of the restaurant. He found that they were confused by Eurasia's concept and wanted more traditional Asian fare at lower prices. In response, the restaurant altered its concept; it hired a Thai chef, revamped the menu, and cut prices. The dining room was soon full again.

Whether a research project costs $200 or $2 million, the same general process should be followed. The marketing research process is a scientific approach to decision making that maximizes the chance of getting accurate and meaningful results. Exhibit 9.1 traces the steps: (1) identifying and formulating the problem/opportunity, (2) planning the research design and gathering primary data, (3) specifying the sampling procedures, (4) collecting the data, (5) analyzing the data, (6) preparing and presenting the report, and (7) following up.

The research process begins with the recognition of a marketing problem or opportunity. As changes occur in the firm's external environment, marketing managers are faced with the questions, "Should we change the existing marketing mix?" and, if so, "How?" Marketing research may be used to evaluate product, promotion, distribution, or pricing alternatives.

Using marketing research helped the WD-40 Company successfully reposition its X-14 cleaning products in the marketplace. The research also identified opportunities to extend the X-14 brand.

Though famous for its well-known line of household lubricants, San Diego-based WD-40 Co. has repositioned one of its product lines as essential bathroom cleaners—the result of a research process.

Sales of the company's six household product brands (of which X-14 is one) make up a sizable percentage—more than 31 percent—of the overall portfolio. However, rival brands were more popular. Which elements in the company's marketing mix could be adjusted to gain more share of the cleaning products market?

The repositioning of WD-40's X-14 line helped the $287 million company find the brand's niche. "We previously had products that focused on the bathroom, but there wasn't a unified line in its positioning. We had a line of cleaning products that were not meeting their potential in the marketplace," says Heidi Noorany, director of marketing. The marketing research indicated that there was a need for a "bathroom expert" line of products. "We knew we had the positioning and the quality of products within the current line, but we had to communicate it," Noorany adds. That would be translated through the line's more cohesive packaging design characterized by a variety of pinks, oranges, and blues as well as several bottle designs.

Consumer research was also used to measure product effectiveness versus competitors' products, and found that the X-14 Foaming Bathroom Cleaner scored 4.5 on a scale of 1 to 5 and that its Trigger Bathroom Cleaner scored a 91 percent approval rating, placing it higher than four other competing brands. The research also found that consumers engage in two types of cleaning—weekly deep cleanings and quick daily cleanings. "We saw an opportunity for a bathroom expert line of products," says Noorany. Not only did WD-40 learn how to best reposition the X-14 line, but it also garnered enough insight from the research process that it could use the data in future product development.[8]

The WD-40 story illustrates an important point about problem/opportunity definition. The marketing research problem is information oriented. It involves determining what information is needed and how that information can be obtained efficiently and effectively. The marketing research objective, then, is to provide insightful decision-making information. This requires specific pieces of information needed to answer the marketing research problem. Managers must combine this information with their own experience and other information to make a proper decision. WD-40's marketing research problem was to gather information on how consumers clean and how they shop for cleaning products. The marketing research objective was several-fold: identify a better positioning strategy for X-14 and identify opportunities to add new items to the X-14 brand.

Whereas the marketing research problem is information-oriented, the management decision problem is action-oriented. Management problems tend to be much broader in scope and far more general than marketing research problems, which must be narrowly defined and specific if the research effort is to be successful. Sometimes several research studies must be conducted to solve a broad management problem. The management decision problem was: "How do we grow sales of X-14 family brand?" Management then decided to reposition X-14 as The Bathroom Expert—the centerpiece around which its new product line reenters the market. Completely redesigned, the line provides a family look for the set of products rather than a disjointed set of similar products. Yet it also includes two additions: Foaming Bathroom Cleaner and Bathroom Cleaner, which combines oxy and citrus (hydrogen peroxide with citric acid) for general bathroom cleaning. Additionally, several future products are expected to be released soon.[9]

Secondary Data

A valuable tool throughout the research process, but particularly in the problem/ opportunity identification stage is secondary data—data previously collected for any purpose other than the one at hand. Secondary information originating within the company includes documents such as annual reports, reports to stockholders, product testing results perhaps made available to the news media, and house periodicals composed by the company's personnel for communication to employees, customers, or others. Often this information is incorporated into a company's internal database.

Innumerable outside sources of secondary information also exist, principally coming from government departments and agencies (federal, state, and local) that compile and publish summaries of business data. Trade and industry associations also publish secondary data. Still more data are available in business periodicals and other news media that regularly publish studies and articles on the economy, specific industries, and even individual companies. The unpublished summarized secondary information from these sources corresponds to internal reports, memos, or special-purpose analyses with limited circulation. Economic considerations or priorities in the organization may preclude publication of these summaries. Most of the sources listed above can be found on the Internet.

Secondary data save time and money if they help solve the researcher's problem. Even if the problem is not solved, secondary data have other advantages. They can aid in formulating the problem statement and suggest research methods and other types of data needed for solving the problem. In addition, secondary data can pinpoint the kinds of people to approach and their locations and serve as a basis of comparison for other data.

EXHIBIT 9.1

The Marketing Research Process

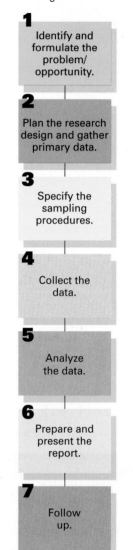

1 Identify and formulate the problem/ opportunity.

2 Plan the research design and gather primary data.

3 Specify the sampling procedures.

4 Collect the data.

5 Analyze the data.

6 Prepare and present the report.

7 Follow up.

marketing research problem
Determining what information is needed and how that information can be obtained efficiently and effectively.

marketing research objective
The specific information needed to solve a marketing research problem; the objective should be to provide insightful decision-making information.

management decision problem
A broad-based problem that uses marketing research in order for managers to take proper actions.

secondary data
Data previously collected for any purpose other than the one at hand.

The disadvantages of secondary data stem mainly from a mismatch between the researcher's unique problem and the purpose for which the secondary data were originally gathered, which are typically different. For example, a major consumer-products manufacturer wanted to determine the market potential for a fireplace log made of coal rather than compressed wood by-products. The researcher found plenty of secondary data about total wood consumed as fuel, quantities consumed in each state, and types of wood burned. Secondary data were also available about consumer attitudes and purchase patterns of wood by-product fireplace logs. The wealth of secondary data provided the researcher with many insights into the artificial log market. Yet, nowhere was there any information that would tell the firm whether consumers would buy artificial logs made of coal.

The quality of secondary data may also pose a problem. Often, secondary data sources do not give detailed information that would enable a researcher to assess their quality or relevance. Whenever possible, a researcher needs to address these important questions: Who gathered the data? Why were the data obtained? What methodology was used? How were classifications (such as heavy users versus light users) developed and defined? When was the information gathered?

The New Age of Secondary Information: The Internet

Gathering secondary data, though necessary in almost any research project, has traditionally been a tedious and boring job. The researcher often had to write to government agencies, trade associations, or other secondary data providers and then wait days or weeks for a reply that might never come. Often, one or more trips to the library were required, and the researcher might find that needed reports were checked out or missing. Now, however, the rapid development of the Internet has eliminated much of the drudgery associated with the collection of secondary data. A few popular sites used by marketing researchers are shown in Exhibit 9.2.

EXHIBIT 9.2

Popular Secondary Data Sites Used by Marketing Researchers

Organization	URL	Description
American Marketing Association	www.marketingpower.com	Enables users to search all of the AMA's publications by using keywords.
BLS Consumer Expenditure Surveys	http://www.bls.gov/cex/	Provides information on the buying habits of consumers, including data on their expenditures, income, and credit ratings.
U.S. Census Bureau	www.census.gov	Is a very useful source of virtually all census data.
U.S. Government	www.fedstats.gov	Source for statistics and reports for more than 100 government agencies. Also links to other sources of relevant information. Highly recommended site but you may have to dig a little.
WorldOpinion	www.worldopinion.com	Offers thousands of marketing research reports. This is perhaps the premier site for the marketing research industry.
Nielsen/NetRatings	www.nielsen-netratings.com	Is a source of Internet audience information. Researchers can find data on Internet growth and user patterns.
USADATA	www.usadata.com	Provides access to consumer lifestyle data on a local, regional, and national level.
FIND/SVP	www.findsvp.com	Offers consulting and research services. The site claims to offer access to the largest private information center for global data in the United States.

MARKETING RESEARCH AGGREGATORS

The **marketing research aggregator** industry is a $120 million business that is growing by about 6 percent a year. Companies in this field acquire, catalog, reformat, segment, and resell reports already published by large and small marketing research firms. Even Amazon.com has added a marketing research aggregation area to its high-profile e-commerce site.

The role of aggregator firms is growing because their databases of research reports are getting bigger and more comprehensive—and more useful—as marketing research firms get more comfortable using resellers as a sales channel. Meanwhile, advances in Web technology are making the databases easier to search and deliveries speedier. Research aggregators are also indirectly tapping new markets for traditional research firms. By slicing and repackaging research reports into narrower, more specialized sections for resale to small and medium-sized clients that often cannot afford to commission their own studies or buy full reports, the aggregators are nurturing a new target market for the information.

Prior to the emergence of research aggregators, a lot of marketing research was available only as premium-priced subscription services. For example, a 17-chapter $2,800 report from Wintergreen Research (based in Lexington, Massachusetts) was recently broken up and sold for $350 per chapter, significantly boosting the overall revenue generated by the report. Other major aggregators are **Mindbranch.com**, **Aarkstore.com**, and **USADATA.com**.

Planning the Research Design and Gathering Primary Data

Good secondary data can help researchers conduct a thorough situation analysis. With that information, researchers can list their unanswered questions and rank them. Researchers must then decide the exact information required to answer the questions. The research design specifies which research questions must be answered, how and when the data will be gathered, and how the data will be analyzed. Typically, the project budget is finalized after the research design has been approved.

Sometimes research questions can be answered by gathering more secondary data; otherwise, primary data may be needed. Primary data, or information collected for the first time, is used for solving the particular problem under investigation. The main advantage of primary data is that they will answer a specific research question that secondary data cannot answer. For example, suppose Pillsbury has two new recipes for refrigerated dough for sugar cookies. Which one will consumers like better? Secondary data will not help answer this question. Instead, targeted consumers must try each recipe and evaluate the taste, texture, and appearance of each cookie. Moreover, primary data are current, and researchers know the source. Sometimes researchers gather the data themselves rather than assign projects to outside companies. Researchers also specify the methodology of the research. Secrecy can be maintained because the information is proprietary. In contrast, much secondary data is available to all interested parties for relatively small fees or for free.

Gathering primary data is expensive; costs can range from a few thousand dollars for a limited survey to several million for a nationwide study. For instance, a nationwide, 15-minute telephone interview with 1,000 adult males can cost $50,000 for everything,

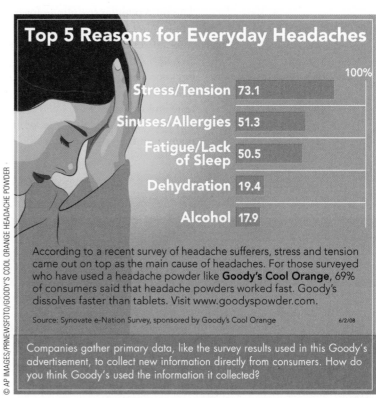

Top 5 Reasons for Everyday Headaches

	100%
Stress/Tension	73.1
Sinuses/Allergies	51.3
Fatigue/Lack of Sleep	50.5
Dehydration	19.4
Alcohol	17.9

According to a recent survey of headache sufferers, stress and tension came out on top as the main cause of headaches. For those surveyed who have used a headache powder like **Goody's Cool Orange**, 69% of consumers said that headache powders worked fast. Goody's dissolves faster than tablets. Visit www.goodyspowder.com.

Source: Synovate e-Nation Survey, sponsored by Goody's Cool Orange   6/2/08

Companies gather primary data, like the survey results used in this Goody's advertisement, to collect new information directly from consumers. How do you think Goody's used the information it collected?

© AP IMAGES/PRNEWSFOTO/GOODY'S COOL ORANGE HEADACHE POWDER

marketing research aggregator
A company that acquires, catalogs, reformats, segments, and resells reports already published by marketing research firms.

research design
Specifies which research questions must be answered, how and when the data will be gathered, and how the data will be analyzed.

primary data
Information that is collected for the first time; used for solving the particular problem under investigation.

including a data analysis and report. Because primary data gathering in person is so expensive, many firms now use an Internet study instead. Larger companies that conduct many research projects use another cost-saving technique. They *piggyback studies*, or gather data on two different projects using one questionnaire. The drawback is that answering questions about, say, dog food and gourmet coffee may be confusing to respondents. Piggybacking also requires a longer interview (sometimes a half hour or longer), which tires respondents. The quality of the answers typically declines, with people giving curt replies and thinking, "When will this end!" A lengthy interview also makes people less likely to participate in other research surveys.

Nevertheless, the disadvantages of primary data gathering are usually offset by the advantages. It is often the only way of solving a research problem. And with a variety of techniques available for research—including surveys, observations, and experiments—primary research can address almost any marketing question.

Survey Research

The most popular technique for gathering primary data is survey research, in which a researcher interacts with people to obtain facts, opinions, and attitudes. Exhibit 9.3 summarizes the characteristics of traditional forms of survey research.

In-Home Personal Interviews Although in-home personal interviews often provide high-quality information, they tend to be very expensive because of the interviewers' travel time and mileage costs. Therefore, they are rapidly disappearing from the American and European marketing researcher's survey toolbox. They are, however, still popular in many countries around the globe.

EXHIBIT 9.3

Characteristics of Traditional Forms of Survey Research

Characteristic	In-Home Personal Interviews	Mall Intercept Interviews	Central Location Telephone Interviews	Self-Administered and One-Time Mail Surveys	Mail Panel Surveys	Executive Interviews	Focus Groups
Cost	High	Moderate	Moderate	Low	Moderate	High	Low
Time span	Moderate	Moderate	Fast	Slow	Relatively slow	Moderate	Fast
Use of interviewer	Yes	Yes	Yes	No	No	Yes	Yes
Ability to show concepts to respondent	Yes (also taste tests)	Yes (also taste tests)	No	Yes	Yes	Yes	Yes
Management control over interviewer	Low	Moderate	High	N/A	N/A	Moderate	High
General data quality	High	Moderate	High to moderate	Moderate to low	Moderate to low	High	Moderate
Ability to collect large amounts of data	High	Moderate	Moderate to low	Low to moderate	Moderate	Moderate	Moderate
Ability to handle complex questionnaires	High	Moderate	High, if computer-aided	Low	Low	High	N/A

Mall Intercept Interviews The mall intercept interview is conducted in the common area of a shopping mall or in a market research office within the mall. It is the economy version of the door-to-door interview with personal contact between interviewer and respondent, because the interviewer saves on travel time and mileage costs. To conduct this type of interview, the research firm rents office space in the mall or pays a significant daily fee. One drawback is that it is hard to get a representative sample of the population this way.

However, an interviewer can also probe when necessary—a technique used to clarify a person's response. For example, an interviewer might ask, "What did you like best about the salad dressing you just tried?" The respondent might reply, "Taste." This answer doesn't provide a lot of information, so the interviewer could probe by saying, "Can you tell me a little bit more about taste?" The respondent then elaborates: "Yes, it's not too sweet, it has the right amount of pepper, and I love that hint of garlic."

Mall intercept interviews must be brief. Only the shortest ones are conducted while respondents are standing. Usually, researchers invite respondents to their office for interviews, which are still generally less than 15 minutes long. The researchers often show respondents concepts for new products or a test commercial or have them taste a new food product. The overall quality of mall intercept interviews is about the same as telephone interviews.

Marketing researchers are applying computer technology in mall interviewing. The first technique is computer-assisted personal interviewing. The researcher conducts in-person interviews, reads questions to the respondent off a computer screen, and directly keys the respondent's answers into the computer. A second approach is computer-assisted self-interviewing. A mall interviewer intercepts and directs willing respondents to nearby computers. Each respondent reads questions off a computer screen and directly keys his or her answers into a computer. The third use of technology is fully automated self-interviewing. Respondents are guided by interviewers or independently approach a centrally located computer station or kiosk, read questions off a screen, and directly key their answers into the station's computer.

Telephone Interviews Compared to the personal interview, the telephone interview costs less, but cost is rapidly increasing due to respondent refusals to participate. Most telephone interviewing is conducted from a specially designed phone room called a central-location telephone (CLT) facility. A phone room has many phone lines, individual interviewing stations, sometimes monitoring equipment, and headsets. The research firm typically will interview people nationwide from a single location. The federal "Do Not Call" law does not apply to survey research.

Most CLT facilities offer computer-assisted interviewing. The interviewer reads the questions from a computer screen and enters the respondent's data directly into the computer. The researcher can stop the survey at any point and immediately print out the survey results. Thus, a researcher can get a sense of the project as it unfolds and fine-tune the research design as necessary. An online interviewing system can also save time and money because data entry occurs as the response is recorded rather than as a separate process after the interview. Hallmark Cards found that an interviewer administered a printed questionnaire for its Shoebox greeting cards in 28 minutes. The same questionnaire administered with computer assistance took only 18 minutes.

Mail Surveys Mail surveys have several benefits: relatively low cost, elimination of interviewers and field supervisors, centralized control, and actual or promised anonymity for respondents (which may draw more candid responses). Some researchers feel that mail questionnaires give the respondent a chance to reply more thoughtfully and to check records, talk to family members, and so forth. A disadvantage is that mail questionnaires usually produce low response rates.

Low response rates pose a problem because certain elements of the population tend to respond more than others. The resulting sample may therefore not represent the surveyed population. For example, the sample may have too many retired people and too few working people. In this instance, answers to a question about attitudes toward government

mall intercept interview
A survey research method that involves interviewing people in the common areas of shopping malls.

computer-assisted personal interviewing
An interviewing method in which the interviewer reads the questions from a computer screen and enters the respondent's data directly into the computer.

computer-assisted self-interviewing
An interviewing method in which a mall interviewer intercepts and directs willing respondents to nearby computers where the respondent reads questions off a computer screen and directly keys his or her answers into a computer.

central-location telephone (CLT) facility
A specially designed phone room used to conduct telephone interviewing.

executive interviews
A type of survey that involves interviewing businesspeople at their offices concerning industrial products or services.

focus group
Seven to ten people who participate in a group discussion led by a moderator.

group dynamics
Group interaction essential to the success of focus-group research.

programs to aid senior citizens might indicate a much more favorable overall view of the system than is actually the case. Another serious problem with mail surveys is that no one probes respondents to clarify or elaborate on their answers.

Mail panels like those operated by Synovate, IPSOS, and NPD Research offer an alternative to the one-shot mail survey. A mail panel consists of a sample of households recruited to participate by mail for a given period. Panel members often receive gifts in return for their participation. Essentially, the panel is a sample used several times. In contrast to onetime mail surveys, the response rates from mail panels are high. Rates of 70 percent (of those who agree to participate) are not uncommon.

Executive Interviews Marketing researchers use executive interviews to conduct the industrial equivalent of door-to-door interviewing. This type of survey involves interviewing businesspeople, at their offices, concerning industrial products or services. For example, if Dell wanted information regarding user preferences for different features that might be offered in a new line of computer printers, it would need to interview prospective user-purchasers of the printers. It is appropriate to locate and interview these people at their offices.

This type of interviewing is very expensive. First, individuals involved in the purchase decision for the product in question must be identified and located. Sometimes lists can be obtained from various sources, but more frequently screening must be conducted over the telephone. A particular company is likely to have individuals of the type being sought, but locating those people within a large organization can be expensive and time-consuming. Once a qualified person is located, the next step is to get that person to agree to be interviewed and to set a time for the interview. This is not as hard as it might seem because most professionals seem to enjoy talking about topics related to their work.

Finally, an interviewer must go to the particular place at the appointed time. Long waits are frequently encountered, and cancellations are not uncommon. This type of survey requires the very best interviewers because they are frequently interviewing on topics that they know very little about. Executive interviewing has essentially the same advantages and disadvantages as in-home interviewing.

Focus Groups A focus group is a type of personal interviewing. Often recruited by random telephone screening, seven to ten people with certain desired characteristics form a focus group. These qualified consumers are usually offered an incentive (typically $50 to $75) to participate in a group discussion. The meeting place (sometimes resembling a living room, sometimes featuring a conference table) has audiotaping and perhaps videotaping equipment. It also likely has a viewing room with a one-way mirror so that clients (manufacturers or retailers) may watch the session. During the session, a moderator, hired by the research company, leads the group discussion.

Focus groups are much more than question-and-answer interviews. Market researchers draw a distinction between "group dynamics" and "group interviewing." The interaction provided in group dynamics

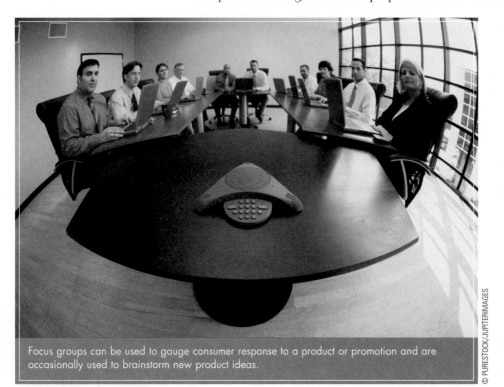

Focus groups can be used to gauge consumer response to a product or promotion and are occasionally used to brainstorm new product ideas.

© PURESTOCK/JUPITERIMAGES

is essential to the success of focus-group research; this interaction is the reason for conducting group rather than individual research. One of the essential postulates of group-session usage is the idea that a response from one person may become a stimulus for another, thereby generating an interplay of responses that may yield more information than if the same number of people had contributed independently.

Lewis Stone, former manager of Colgate-Palmolive's research and development division, says the following about focus groups: "If it weren't for focus groups, Colgate-Palmolive Co. might never know that some women squeeze their bottles of dishwashing soap, others squeeeeeze them, and still others squeeeeeeeeeze out the desired amount. Then there are the ones who use the soap 'neat.' That is, they put the product directly on a sponge or washcloth and wash the dishes under running water until the suds run out. Then they apply more detergent."

Stone was explaining how body language, exhibited during focus groups, provides insights into a product that are not apparent from reading questionnaires on habits and practices. Focus groups represent a most efficient way of learning how one's products are actually used in the home. By drawing out the panelists to describe in detail how they do certain tasks, you can learn a great deal about possible need-gaps that could be filled by new or improved products, and also how a new product might be received. It is estimated that over 600,000 focus groups are conducted around the world each year.[10]

A system created by FocusVision allows client companies and advertising agencies to view live focus groups in over 350 cities worldwide. For example, the private satellite network lets a Taco Bell researcher observing a San Diego focus group control two cameras in the viewing room. The researcher can get a full-group view or a close-up, zoom, or pan the participants. The researcher can also communicate directly with the moderator using an ear receiver. Ogilvy & Mather (a large New York advertising agency whose clients include StarKist Seafood, Seagram's, MasterCard, and Burger King) has installed the system.

Increasingly, focus groups are being conducted online. Online focus groups are examined in detail later in the chapter.

Questionnaire Design

All forms of survey research require a questionnaire. Questionnaires ensure that all respondents will be asked the same series of questions. Questionnaires include three basic types of questions: open-ended, closed-ended, and scaled-response (see Exhibit 9.4). An open-ended question encourages an answer phrased in the respondent's own words. Researchers get a rich array of information based on the respondent's frame of reference. In contrast, a closed-ended question asks the respondent to make a selection from a limited list of responses. Traditionally, marketing researchers separate the two-choice question (called *dichotomous*) from the many-item type (often called *multiple choice*). A scaled-response question is a closed-ended question designed to measure the intensity of a respondent's answer.

open-ended question
An interview question that encourages an answer phrased in the respondent's own words.

closed-ended question
An interview question that asks the respondent to make a selection from a limited list of responses.

scaled-response question
A closed-ended question designed to measure the intensity of a respondent's answer.

Closed-ended and scaled-response questions are easier to tabulate than open-ended questions because response choices are fixed. On the other hand, unless the researcher designs the closed-ended question very carefully, an important choice may be omitted.

For example, suppose a food study asked this question: "Besides meat, which of the following items do you normally add to a taco that you prepare at home?"

Avocado	1	Olives (black/green)	6
Cheese (Monterey Jack/cheddar)	2	Onions (red/white)	7
Guacamole	3	Peppers (red/green)	8
Lettuce	4	Pimento	9
Mexican hot sauce	5	Sour cream	0

© ISTOCKPHOTO.COM/C CATHLEEN CLAPPER

The list seems complete, doesn't it? However, consider the following responses: "I usually add a green, avocado-tasting hot sauce"; "I cut up a mixture of lettuce and spinach"; "I'm a vegetarian—I don't use meat at all"; or "My taco

EXHIBIT 9.4

Types of Questions Found on Questionnaires for National Market Research

Open-Ended Questions	Closed-Ended Questions	Scaled-Response Question
1. What advantages, if any, do you think ordering from a mail-order catalog offers compared to shopping at a local retail outlet? (*Probe:* What else?)	**Dichotomous** 1. Did you heat the Danish product before serving it? Yes . . . . 1 No 2	Now that you have used the rug cleaner, would you say that you . . . (*Circle one.*) Would definitely buy it . . . . 1 Would probably buy it . . . . 2 Might or might not buy it . . . . 3 Probably would not buy it . . . . 4 Definitely would not buy it 5
2. Why do you have one or more of your rugs or carpets professionally cleaned rather than cleaning them yourself or having someone else in the household clean them?	2. The federal government doesn't care what people like me think. Agree . . . . 1 Disagree. 2	
3. What is it about the color of the eye shadow that makes you like it the best?	**Multiple choice** 1. I'd like you to think back to the last footwear of any kind that you bought. I'll read you a list of descriptions and would like for you to tell me which category they fall into. (*Read list and circle proper category.*) Dress and/or formal. . . . . 1 Casual . . . . 2 Canvas/trainer/gym shoes . . . . . . 3 Specialized athletic shoes . . . . 4 Boots. . . . . 5 2. In the last three months, have you used Noxzema skin cream . . . (*Circle all that apply.*) As a facial wash . . . . 1 For moisturizing the skin . . . . 2 For treating blemishes . . . . 3 For cleansing the skin . . . . 4 For treating dry skin . . . . 5 For softening skin . . . . 6 For sunburn . . . . 7 For making the facial skin smooth . . . 8	

is filled only with guacamole." How would you code these replies? As you can see, the question needs an "other" category.

A good question must also be clear and concise, and ambiguous language must be avoided. Take, for example, the question "Do you live within ten minutes of here?" The answer depends on the mode of transportation (maybe the person walks), driving speed, perceived time, and other factors. Instead, respondents should see a map with certain areas highlighted and be asked whether they live in one of those areas.

Clarity also implies using reasonable terminology. A questionnaire is not a vocabulary test. Jargon should be avoided, and language should be geared to the target audience. A question such as "What is the level of efficacy of your preponderant dishwasher powder?" would probably be greeted by a lot of blank stares. It would be much simpler to say "Are you (1) very satisfied, (2) somewhat satisfied, or (3) not satisfied with your current brand of dishwasher powder?"

Stating the survey's purpose at the beginning of the interview also improves clarity. The respondents should understand the study's intentions and the interviewer's expectations.

Sometimes, of course, to get an unbiased response, the interviewer must disguise the true purpose of the study. If an interviewer says, "We're conducting an image study for American National Bank" and then proceeds to ask a series of questions about the bank, chances are the responses will be biased. Many times respondents will try to provide answers that they believe are "correct" or that the interviewer wants to hear.

Finally, to ensure clarity, the interviewer should avoid asking two questions in one; for example, "How did you like the taste and texture of the Pepperidge Farm coffee cake?" This should be divided into two questions, one concerning taste and the other texture.

A question should also be unbiased. A question such as "Have you purchased any quality Black & Decker tools in the past six months?" biases respondents to think of the topic in a certain way (in this case, to link quality and Black & Decker tools). Questions can also be leading: "Weren't you pleased with the good service you received last night at the Holiday Inn?" (The respondent is all but instructed to say yes.) These examples are quite obvious; unfortunately, bias is usually more subtle. Even an interviewer's clothing or gestures can create bias.

Observation Research

In contrast to survey research, observation research depends on watching what people do. Specifically, it can be defined as the systematic process of recording the behavioral patterns of people, objects, and occurrences without questioning them. A market researcher using the observation technique witnesses and records information as events occur or compiles evidence from records of past events. Carried a step further, observation may involve watching people or phenomena and may be conducted by human observers or machines. Examples of these various observational situations are shown in Exhibit 9.5.

© AP IMAGES/RICHARD DREW

Hundreds of children tested hundreds of toys at a recent Toys"R"Us opening to come up with a list of the season's favorites.

Two common forms of people-watching-people research are one-way mirror observations and mystery shoppers.

At the Fisher-Price Play Laboratory, children are invited to spend 12 sessions playing with toys. Toy designers watch through one-way mirrors to see how children react to Fisher-Price's and other makers' toys. A one-way mirror allows the researchers to see the participants but they cannot see the researchers. Fisher-Price, for example, had difficulty designing a toy lawn mower that children would play with. A designer, observing behind the mirror, noticed the children's fascination with soap bubbles. He then created a lawn mower that spewed soap bubbles. It sold over a million units in the first year.

Mystery shoppers are researchers posing as customers who gather observational data about a store (e.g., are the shelves neatly stocked?) and collect data about customer/employee interactions. In the latter case, of course, there is communication between the mystery shopper and the employee. The mystery shopper may ask, "How much is

observation research
A research method that relies on four types of observation: people watching people, people watching an activity, machines watching people, and machines watching an activity.

mystery shoppers
Researchers posing as customers who gather observational data about a store.

EXHIBIT 9.5

Observational Situations

Situation	Example
People watching people	Observers stationed in supermarkets watch consumers select frozen Mexican dinners; the purpose is to see how much comparison shopping people do at the point of purchase.
People watching phenomena	Observer stationed at an intersection counts traffic moving in various directions.
Machines watching people	Movie or videotape cameras record behavior as in the people-watching-people example above.
Machines watching phenomena	Traffic-counting machines monitor traffic flow.

ethnographic research
The study of human behavior in its
natural context; involves observation
of behavior and physical setting.

this item?"; "Do you have this in blue?"; or "Can you deliver this by Friday?" The inter-action is not an interview, and communication occurs only so that the mystery shopper can observe the actions and comments of the employee. Mystery shopping is, therefore, classified as an observational marketing research method even though communication is often involved.

Mystery shopping can provide a variety of benefits and insights, including:

☛ Enabling an organization to monitor compliance with product/service delivery stan-dards and specifications (Eddie Bauer requires its sales staff to make three attempts to sell "add-ons" to each customer—would you like a tie, belt, and sunglasses to go with that shirt).

☛ Enabling marketers to examine the gap between promises made through advertising/sales promotion and actual service delivery.

☛ Helping monitor the impact of training and performance improvement initiatives.

☛ Identifying differences in the customer experience across different times of day, locations, product/service types, and other potential sources of variation in product/service quality.[11]

Mystery shopping typically has three different levels:

Level 1—The mystery shopper either makes a phone call or shops online. The mys-tery shopper follows a fixed script or set of instructions and evaluates the level of service. The scenario would involve a live online conversation with a service representative. For example, the mystery shopper claims that she is having a problem with some software that she recently purchased from the firm.

Level 2—The mystery shopper visits an establishment and makes a quick purchase with very little, if any, customer-service employee interaction. For example, buying gasoline at a Shell service station or going to a movie at a Cinemark movie theater. The shopper evaluates the purchase and the image of the facility.

Level 3—The mystery shopper visits a business and has significant interaction with the personnel. Restaurant chains such as McDonald's, Starbucks, Chipotle, T.G.I. Friday's, Sonic, IHOP, and Olive Garden strive for consistent execution of service and quality across their many stores. Results of the mystery shopping research are tied to employee incentives such as bonuses and rewards. Typical items that are evaluated include: hostess attitude and skills, food quality and presentation, condition of the restaurant (such as clean floors and walls), cleanli-ness of the restrooms, parking lot condition, interaction with the server (such as the introduction and suggestion selling), and the visibility of and interaction with the management staff.

Not only does management use mystery shopping as a motivator for employees but also as a coaching tool when results are not meeting standards. Thus, mystery shopping is ultimately a monitor of quality assurance.

Ethnographic Research

Ethnographic research comes to marketing from the field of anthropology. The technique is becoming increasingly popular in commercial marketing research. Ethnographic research, or the study of human behavior in its natural context, involves observation of behavior and physical setting. Ethnographers directly observe the popula-tion they are studying. As "participant observers," ethnographers can use their intimacy with the people they are studying to gain richer, deeper insights into culture and behav-ior—in short, what makes people do what they do. Ethnographers often question those being observed to gain a fuller understanding of what they are seeing.

Ethnographers can record

☛ what is happening, including what objects are being created or manipulated.

☛ where it is happening.

- flow of what is happening.
- order of what is happening.
- time spent on what is happening.
- who is doing what.
- what is being communicated verbally and nonverbally.
- reactions of the various participants (which are critical).[12]

Marriott hired IDEO Inc., an ethnographic research firm, to rethink the hotel experience for an increasingly important customer: the young, tech-savvy road warrior. "This is all about looking freshly at business travel and how people behave and what they need," explains Michael E. Jannini, Marriott's executive vice-president for brand management.[13]

To better understand Marriott's customers, IDEO dispatched a team of seven consultants, including a designer, anthropologist, writer, and architect, on a six-week trip. Covering 12 cities, the group hung out in hotel lobbies, cafes, and bars, and asked guests to graph what they were doing hour by hour. What they learned: Hotels are generally good at serving large parties but not small groups of business travelers. Researchers noted that hotel lobbies tend to be dark and better suited to killing time than conducting casual business. Marriott lacked places where guests could comfortably combine work with pleasure outside their rooms. IDEO consultant and Marriott project manager Dana Cho recalls watching a female business traveler drink wine in the lobby while trying not to spill it on papers spread out on a desk. "There are very few hotel services that address [such] problems," says Cho.[14]

Having studied IDEO's findings, Marriott announced plans to reinvent the lobbies of its Marriott and Renaissance Hotels, creating for each a social zone, with small tables, brighter lights, and wireless Web access, that is better suited to meetings. Another area will allow solo travelers to work or unwind in larger, quiet, semiprivate spaces where they won't have to worry about spilling coffee on their laptops or papers.[15]

Observation Research and Virtual Shopping

Advances in computer technology have enabled researchers to simulate an actual retail store environment on a computer screen. Depending on the type of simulation, a shopper can "pick up" a package by touching its image on the monitor and rotate it to examine all sides. Like buying on most online retailers, the shopper touches the shopping cart to add an item to the basket. During the shopping process, the computer unobtrusively records the amount of time the consumer spends shopping in each product category, the time the consumer spends examining each side of a package, the quantity of product the consumer purchases, and the order in which items are purchased.

Computer-simulated environments like this one offer a number of advantages over older research methods. First, unlike focus groups, concept tests, and other laboratory approaches, the virtual store duplicates the distracting clutter of an actual market. Consumers can shop in an environment with a realistic level of complexity and variety. Second, researchers can set up and alter the tests very quickly. Once images of the product are scanned into the computer, the researcher can make changes in the assortment of brands, product packaging, pricing, promotions, and shelf space within minutes. Data collection is also fast and error-free because the information generated by the purchase is automatically tabulated and stored by the computer. Third, production costs are low because displays are created electronically. Once the hardware and software are in place, the cost of a test is largely a function of the number of respondents, who generally are given a small incentive to participate. Fourth, the simulation has a high degree of flexibility. It can be used to test entirely new marketing concepts or to fine-tune existing programs. The simulation also makes it possible to eliminate much of the noise that exists in field experiments.[16]

experiment
A method a researcher uses to gather primary data.

sample
A subset from a larger population.

Kimberly-Clark has refined the virtual shopping experience even more. Located in Appleton, Wisconsin, the firm's virtual testing lab has a woman standing in a room surrounded by three screens showing a store aisle, a retina-tracking device recording her every glance. Asked by a Kimberly-Clark researcher to find a "big box" of Huggies Natural Fit diapers in size three, she pushed forward on a handle like that of a shopping cart, and the video simulated her progress down the aisle. Spotting Huggies' red packages, she turned the handle to the right to face a dizzying array of diapers. After pushing a button to get a kneeling view of the shelves, she reached forward and tapped the screen to put the box she wanted in her virtual cart. Kimberly-Clark hopes these virtual shopping aisles will help it better understand consumer behavior and make the testing of new products faster, more convenient, and more precise.[17]

Kimberly-Clark's lab also features a U-shaped floor-to-ceiling screen that re-creates in vivid detail interiors of the big retailers that sell the company's products—a tool that the company will use in presentations to executives in bids to win shelf space. A separate area is reserved for real replicas of store interiors, which can be customized to match the flooring, light fixtures, and shelves of retailers such as Target Corp. and Wal-Mart Stores, Inc.[18]

Kimberly-Clark says its studio allows researchers and designers to get a fast read on new product designs and displays without having to stage real-life tests in the early stages of development. Doing the research in a windowless basement, rather than an actual test market, also avoids tipping off competitors early in the development process. "We're trying to test ideas faster, cheaper, and better," says Ramin Eivaz, a vice president at Kimberly-Clark focusing on strategy. Before, new product testing typically took eight months to two years. Now, that time is cut in half, he says. Projects that test well with the virtual-reality tools will be fast-tracked to real-store trials.[19]

Virtual shopping research is growing rapidly as companies such as Frito-Lay, Goodyear, Procter & Gamble, General Mills, and Coca-Cola realize the benefits from this type of observation research. About 40,000 new consumer package goods are introduced in the United States each year.[20] All are vying for very limited retail shelf space. Any process, such as virtual shopping, that can speed product development time and lower costs is always welcomed by manufacturers.

Experiments

An experiment is a method a researcher can use to gather primary data. The researcher alters one or more variables—price, package design, shelf space, advertising theme, advertising expenditures—while observing the effects of those alterations on another variable (usually sales). The best experiments are those in which all factors are held constant except the ones being manipulated. The researcher can then observe that changes in sales, for example, result from changes in the amount of money spent on advertising.

Holding all other factors constant in the external environment is a monumental and costly, if not impossible, task. Such factors as competitors' actions, weather, and economic conditions are beyond the researcher's control. Yet market researchers have ways to account for the ever-changing external environment. Mars, the candy company, was losing sales to other candy companies. Traditional surveys showed that the shrinking candy bar was not perceived as a good value. Mars wondered whether a bigger bar sold at the same price would increase sales enough to offset the higher ingredient costs. The company designed an experiment in which the marketing mix stayed the same in different markets but the size of the candy bar varied. The substantial increase in sales of the bigger bar quickly proved that the additional costs would be more than covered by the additional revenue. Mars increased the bar size—and its market share and profits.

Specifying the Sampling Procedures

Once the researchers decide how they will collect primary data, their next step is to select the sampling procedures they will use. A firm can seldom take a census of all possible users of a new product, nor can they all be interviewed. Therefore, a firm must select a sample of the group to be interviewed. A sample is a subset from a larger population.

EXHIBIT 9.6
Types of Samples

	Probability Samples
Simple Random Sample	Every member of the population has a known and equal chance of selection.
Stratified Sample	The population is divided into mutually exclusive groups (such as gender or age); then random samples are drawn from each group.
Cluster Sample	The population is divided into mutually exclusive groups (such as geographic areas); then a random sample of clusters is selected. The researcher then collects data from all the elements in the selected clusters or from a probability sample of elements within each selected cluster.
Systematic Sample	A list of the population is obtained—e.g., all persons with a checking account at XYZ Bank—and a *skip interval* is obtained by dividing the sample size by the population size. If the sample size is 100 and the bank has 1,000 customers, then the skip interval is 10. The beginning number is randomly chosen within the skip interval. If the beginning number is 8, then the skip pattern would be 8, 18, 28, ...
	Nonprobability Samples
Convenience Sample	The researcher selects the easiest population members from which to obtain information.
Judgment Sample	The researcher's selection criteria are based on personal judgment that the elements (persons) chosen will likely give accurate information.
Quota Sample	The researcher finds a prescribed number of people in several categories—e.g., owners of large dogs versus owners of small dogs. Respondents are not selected on probability sampling criteria.
Snowball Sample	Additional respondents are selected on the basis of referrals from the initial respondents. This method is used when a desired type of respondent is hard to find—e.g., persons who have taken round-the-world cruises in the last three years. This technique employs the old adage "Birds of a feather flock together."

Several questions must be answered before a sampling plan is chosen. First, the population, or universe, of interest must be defined. This is the group from which the sample will be drawn. It should include all the people whose opinions, behavior, preferences, attitudes, and so on are of interest to the marketer. For example, in a study whose purpose is to determine the market for a new canned dog food, the universe might be defined to include all current buyers of canned dog food.

After the universe has been defined, the next question is whether the sample must be representative of the population. If the answer is yes, a probability sample is needed. Otherwise, a nonprobability sample might be considered.

Probability Samples A probability sample is a sample in which every element in the population has a known statistical likelihood of being selected. Its most desirable feature is that scientific rules can be used to ensure that the sample represents the population.

One type of probability sample is a random sample—a sample arranged in such a way that every element of the population has an equal chance of being selected as part of the sample. For example, suppose a university is interested in getting a cross section of student opinions on a proposed sports complex to be built using student activity fees. If the university can acquire an up-to-date list of all the enrolled students, it can draw a random sample by using random numbers from a table (found in most statistics books) to select students from the list. Common forms of probability and nonprobability samples are shown in Exhibit 9.6.

Nonprobability Samples Any sample in which little or no attempt is made to get a representative cross section of the population can be considered a nonprobability sample. Therefore, the probability of selection of each sampling unit is not known. A common

universe
The population from which a sample will be drawn.

probability sample
A sample in which every element in the population has a known statistical likelihood of being selected.

random sample
A sample arranged in such a way that every element of the population has an equal chance of being selected as part of the sample.

nonprobability sample
Any sample in which little or no attempt is made to get a representative cross section of the population.

convenience sample
A form of nonprobability sample using respondents who are convenient or readily accessible to the researcher—for example, employees, friends, or relatives.

measurement error
An error that occurs when there is a difference between the information desired by the researcher and the information provided by the measurement process.

sampling error
An error that occurs when a sample somehow does not represent the target population.

frame error
An error that occurs when a sample drawn from a population differs from the target population.

random error
An error that occurs when the selected sample is an imperfect representation of the overall population.

field service firm
A firm that specializes in interviewing respondents on a subcontracted basis.

cross-tabulation
A method of analyzing data that lets the analyst look at the responses to one question in relation to the responses to one or more other questions.

form of a nonprobability sample is the convenience sample, which uses respondents who are convenient or readily accessible to the researcher—for instance, employees, friends, or relatives.

Nonprobability samples are acceptable as long as the researcher understands their nonrepresentative nature. Because of their lower cost, nonprobability samples are the basis of much marketing research.

Types of Errors Whenever a sample is used in marketing research, two major types of errors may occur: measurement error and sampling error. Measurement error occurs when there is a difference between the information desired by the researcher and the information provided by the measurement process. For example, people may tell an interviewer that they purchase Coors beer when they do not. Measurement error generally tends to be larger than sampling error.

Sampling error occurs when a sample somehow does not represent the target population. Sampling error can be one of several types. Nonresponse error occurs when the sample actually interviewed differs from the sample drawn. This error happens because the original people selected to be interviewed either refused to cooperate or were inaccessible. For example, people who feel embarrassed about their drinking habits may refuse to talk about them.

Frame error, another type of sampling error, arises if the sample drawn from a population differs from the target population. For instance, suppose a telephone survey is conducted to find out Chicago beer drinkers' attitudes toward Coors. If a Chicago telephone directory is used as the *frame* (the device or list from which the respondents are selected), the survey will contain a frame error. Not all Chicago beer drinkers have a phone, and many phone numbers are unlisted. An ideal sample (for example, a sample with no frame error) matches all important characteristics of the target population to be surveyed. Could you find a perfect frame for Chicago beer drinkers?

Random error occurs when the selected sample is an imperfect representation of the overall population. Random error represents how accurately the chosen sample's true average (mean) value reflects the population's true average (mean) value. For example, we might take a random sample of beer drinkers in Chicago and find that 16 percent regularly drink Coors beer. The next day we might repeat the same sampling procedure and discover that 14 percent regularly drink Coors beer. The difference is due to random error.

Error is common to all surveys, yet it is often not reported or is underreported. Typically, the only error mentioned in a written report is sampling error. When errors are ignored, misleading results can result in poor information and, perhaps, bad decisions.

Collecting the Data

Marketing research field service firms collect most primary data. A field service firm specializes in interviewing respondents on a subcontracted basis. Many have offices, often in malls, throughout the country. A typical marketing research study involves data collection in several cities, requiring the marketer to work with a comparable number of field service firms. Besides conducting interviews, field service firms provide focus-group facilities, mall intercept locations, test product storage, and kitchen facilities to prepare test food products.

Analyzing the Data

After collecting the data, the marketing researcher proceeds to the next step in the research process: data analysis. The purpose of this analysis is to interpret and draw conclusions from the mass of collected data. The marketing researcher tries to organize and analyze those data by using one or more techniques common to marketing research: one-way frequency counts, cross-tabulations, and more sophisticated statistical analysis. Of these three techniques, one-way frequency counts are the simplest. One-way frequency tables record the responses to a question. For example, the answers to the question "What brand of microwave popcorn do you buy most often?" would provide a one-way frequency distribution. One-way frequency tables are always done in data analysis, at least as a first step, because they provide the researcher with a general picture of the study's results.

A cross-tabulation, or "cross-tab," lets the analyst look at the responses to one question in relation to the responses to one or more other questions. For example, what is the association between gender and the brand of microwave popcorn bought most frequently? Hypothetical answers to this question are shown in Exhibit 9.7.

Although the Orville Reddenbacher brand was popular with both males and females, it was more popular with females. Compared with women, men strongly preferred Pop Rite, whereas women were more likely than men to buy Weight Watchers popcorn.

Researchers can use many other more powerful and sophisticated statistical techniques, such as hypothesis testing, measures of association, and regression analysis. A description of these techniques goes beyond the scope of this book, but can be found in any good marketing research textbook. The use of sophisticated statistical techniques depends on the researchers' objectives and the nature of the data gathered.

EXHIBIT 9.7

Hypothetical Cross-Tabulation between Gender and Brand of Microwave Popcorn Purchased Most Frequently

Brand	Purchase by Gender	
	Male	Female
Orville Reddenbacher	31%	48%
T.V. Time	12	6
Pop Rite	38	4
Act II	7	23
Weight Watchers	4	18
Other	8	0

GLOBAL Perspectives

GLOBAL

The Challenges of Global Marketing Research

Karl Feld, Research Manager at D3 Systems Incorporated, a Vienna, Virginia, marketing research firm, explains how global research can create unique problems not found in the United States. The story is told in his words.

Imagine you're driving a vehicle of unknown manufacture with dials you can't read down a muddy or dusty dirt track with no name to find a house with no number to make sure your contractor's employee interviewed the right respondent in a language you don't speak. You've been doing this for days, maybe even weeks. There's no running water, no electricity, no telephones, no mail service, and possibly no food other than what you've brought with you. Welcome to collecting research data from most of the world's people.

Questionnaire design in multicultural, multilingual research must use both the proper language and cultural context to elicit the desired responses. Context applies both to the language in the survey and the way it is administered, which is often more important than the questionnaire design itself. People in some cultures better relate to conversational interviewing styles than fixed questionnaire order. Some cultures require sensitive questions to be in a different order than others. In some places, people will only talk in particular settings. In research that I conducted in Bosnia-Herzegovina, for example, questionnaires had to be administered in a neutral location not affiliated with any local ethnic group.

Similarly, research in Arabic, Muslim countries which involve women generally must be conducted under the watchful eyes of the responsible male family leader, as social custom requires women not meet with outsiders without male presence. In Russia, it used to be extremely difficult to get face-to-face interviews inside people's homes. Public places were preferred. In Japan, it is only in private places like the home that face-to-face interviews will capture meaningful data.

In my experience in yesterday's Russia and Moldova, and in today's China, respondents asked questions of substance often will refuse to provide meaningful answers without approval from another authority. This is especially the case when interviewing professionals. Appropriate lag time, or preapproval, needs to be factored into timelines and interviewing environment to allow for this phenomenon.

I was also involved in a research study completed in South Africa. The study's sample frame was to draw from all adults in South Africa. Given that many South African villages lack building addresses, roads, and convenient grid layouts, sampling had to be designed using satellite maps to select dwelling units using an interval formula. A similar problem exists in Mexico, where streets are unidentified and houses unnumbered, compounded by walls and servants who keep strangers out. In Saudi Arabia, there is no officially recognized census of population and there are no elections and therefore no voter registration records or maps of population centers.[21]

Do you think that conducting research in developing countries is worth the effort? Do you think that doing marketing research in Western Europe is the same as the United States?

Describe the steps involved in conducting a marketing research project

1 Identify problem

Management decision ———▶ Action

Marketing research (research secondary data) ———▶ Information

2 Plan research design

3 Select sampling procedures

Probability (measure sampling error)

Nonprobability

4 Collect data

Primary data
- survey
- observation
- experiment
- ethnographic

Secondary data
- traditional
- Internet

5 Analyze data

Frequency counts
Cross-tabulation

Advanced statistical analysis

6 Prepare and present the report

7 Follow up

Preparing and Presenting the Report

After data analysis has been completed, the researcher must prepare the report and communicate the conclusions and recommendations to management. This is a key step in the process. If the marketing researcher wants managers to carry out the recommendations, he or she must convince them that the results are credible and justified by the data collected.

Researchers are usually required to present both written and oral reports on the project. Today, the written report is no more than a copy of the PowerPoint slides used in the oral presentation. Both reports should be tailored to the audience. They should begin with a clear, concise statement of the research objectives, followed by a complete, but brief and simple, explanation of the research design or methodology employed. A summary of major findings should come next. The conclusion of the report should also present recommendations to management.

Most people who enter marketing will become research users rather than research suppliers. Thus, they must know what to notice in a report. As with many other items we purchase, quality is not always readily apparent. Nor does a high price guarantee superior quality. The basis for measuring the quality of a marketing research report is the research proposal. Did the report meet the objectives established in the proposal? Was the methodology outlined in the proposal followed? Are the conclusions based on logical deductions from the data analysis? Do the recommendations seem prudent, given the conclusions?

Following Up

The final step in the marketing research process is to follow up. The researcher should determine why management did or did not carry out the recommendations in the report. Was sufficient decision-making information included? What could have been done to make the report more useful to management? A good rapport between the product manager, or whoever authorized the project, and the market researcher is essential. Often they must work together on many studies throughout the year.

Typically, the research process flows rather smoothly from one step to the next in the United States. However, conducting research in international markets can create a whole host of problems and challenges. These are discussed in the Global Perspectives box on page 311.

THE PROFOUND IMPACT OF THE INTERNET ON MARKETING RESEARCH

The world's Internet population will be about 1.3 billion users by the time you read this paragraph. That's right—about one-fifth of the world's population is online. In the United States, 70 percent of the population is online spanning every ethnic, socioeconomic, and educational divide. It is no wonder then that most managers accept that online research can, under appropriate conditions, accurately represent U.S. consumers as a whole.[22] Non-adopters of the Internet tend to be older, low-income consumers (aged 65+ and with household income less than $30,000).[23] These consumers are not the target market for many companies' goods and services.

The popularity of online research continues to grow with over 90 percent of America's marketing research companies conducting some form of online research.[24] Today online survey research has replaced computer-assisted telephone interviewing (CATI) as the most popular mode of data collection.[25] Internet data collection is also rated as having the greatest potential for further growth. Having said this, we must also report that there is no sign that other types of surveys are disappearing as two-thirds of the market research companies are still relying on them.[26]

There are several reasons for the success of Internet marketing research:

☛ It allows for better and faster decision making through much more rapid access to business intelligence.

☛ It improves the ability to respond quickly to customer needs and market shifts.

☛ It makes follow-up studies and tracking research much easier to conduct and more fruitful.

☛ It slashes labor- and time-intensive research activities (and associated costs), including mailing, telephone solicitation, data entry, data tabulation, and reporting.

Advantages of Internet Surveys

The huge growth in the popularity of Internet surveys is the result of the many advantages offered by the Internet. The specific advantages of Internet surveys are related to many factors:

☛ *Rapid development, real-time reporting:* Internet surveys can be broadcast to thousands of potential respondents simultaneously. Respondents complete surveys simultaneously; then results are tabulated and posted for corporate clients to view as the returns arrive. The result: Survey results can be in a client's hands in significantly less time than would be required for traditional surveys.

☛ *Dramatically reduced costs:* The Internet can cut costs by 25 to 40 percent and provide results in half the time it takes to do traditional telephone surveys. Data collection costs account for a large proportion of any traditional market research budget. Telephone surveys are labor-intensive efforts incurring training, telecommunications, and management costs. Electronic methods eliminate these completely. While costs for traditional survey techniques rise proportionally with the number of interviews desired, electronic solicitations can grow in volume with little increase in project costs.

☛ *Personalized questions and data:* Internet surveys can be highly personalized for greater relevance to each respondent's own situation, thus speeding the response process. Respondents enjoy a personalized survey because they are asked to answer only pertinent questions, can pause and resume the survey as needed, and can see previous responses and correct inconsistencies.

☛ *Improved respondent participation:* Busy respondents may be growing increasingly intolerant of "snail mail" or telephone-based surveys. Internet surveys take half as much time to complete as phone interviews, can be accomplished at the respondent's convenience (after work hours), and are much more stimulating and engaging. Graphics, interactivity, links to incentive sites and real-time summary reports make the interview enjoyable. The result? Much higher response rates.

☛ *Contact with the hard-to-reach:* Certain groups—doctors, high-income professionals, top management in Global 2000 firms—are among the most surveyed on the planet and the most difficult to reach. Many of these groups are well represented online. Internet surveys provide convenient anytime/anywhere access that makes it easy for busy professionals to participate.

Uses of the Internet by Marketing Researchers

Marketing researchers are using the Internet to administer surveys, conduct focus groups and observation research, and perform a variety of other types of marketing research.

Methods of Conducting Online Surveys

There are several basic methods for conducting online surveys: Web survey systems, survey design Web sites, and Web hosting. Each of these methods is briefly discussed.

Web Survey Systems Web survey systems are software systems specifically designed for Web questionnaire construction and delivery. They consist of an integrated questionnaire designer, Web server, database, and data delivery program, designed for use by nonprogrammers. In a typical use, the questionnaire is constructed with an easy-to-use edit feature, using a visual interface, and then automatically transmitted to the Web server system. The Web server distributes the questionnaire and files responses in a database. The user can query the server at any time via the Web for completion statistics, descriptive statistics on responses, and graphical displays of data. Several popular online survey research software packages are SPSS Quanquest, Inquisite, Sawtooth CiW, Web Survent, Infopoll, SurveyMonkey, and SurveyPro.

Survey Design and Web Hosting Sites Several Web sites allow the researcher to design a survey online without loading design software. The survey is then administered on the design site's server. Some offer tabulation and analysis packages as well. Two popular sites that offer Web hosting are WebSurveyor and Perseus. Several of the other firms mentioned in the previous paragraph also offer Web hosting.

Online Panel Providers

Designing a questionnaire is one step in the online survey process, another is procuring a sample to survey. Sometimes do-it-yourself researchers already have a sample or census of those they wish to survey, so sampling is not a problem. For example, members of a country club, persons who just purchased a new Toyota, students at a university, or customers at Best Buy. Often, however, researchers don't have a sample available, so they turn to online panel providers. The online panel providers such as Survey Sampling, Decision Analyst, Greenfield Online, Common Knowledge, and e-Rewards pre-recruit people who agree to opt-in to participate in online market research surveys.

Some online panels are created for specific industries such as construction, medical, or technology and may have a few thousand panel members, while the large commercial online panels have millions of people who have opted-in to participate in online surveys of varying topics. When people join most online panels, they answer an extensive profiling questionnaire which records demographic, lifestyle, and psychographic information, typically with hundreds of dimensions. This profiling information enables the panel provider to record detailed information on every panel member. Using this information, the panel provider can then target research efforts to panel members who meet specific criteria.

For example, a research study may require surveying avid golfers who play golf at least once a week, people who own an HDTV, or people who make decisions regarding information technology and work in companies with over 1,000 employees. Finding people who meet these criteria can be difficult, but online panel providers may be able to more easily identify these people based on their profiling information. By having millions of people pre-recruited and engaged in the research process, online panels help reduce recruitment cost and field time needed to complete a research project. For the really low-incidence groups, many of the larger panel providers, such as e-Rewards or Harris Interactive, are able to develop specialty panels for hard-to-reach audiences, such as small business owners, affluent consumers, and healthcare providers.

Online Focus Groups

A recent development in qualitative research is the online focus group. A number of organizations are currently offering this new means of conducting focus groups. The process is fairly simple.

- ☛ The research firm builds a database of respondents via a screening questionnaire on its Web site.
- ☛ When a client comes to a firm with a need for a particular focus group, the firm goes to its database and identifies individuals who appear to qualify. It sends an e-mail message to these individuals, asking them to log on to a particular site at a particular time scheduled for the group. The firm pays them an incentive for their participation.
- ☛ The firm develops a discussion guide similar to the one used for a conventional focus group.
- ☛ A moderator runs the group by typing in questions online for all to see. The group operates in an environment similar to that of a chat room so that all participants see all questions and all responses.
- ☛ The firm captures the complete text of the focus group and makes it available for review after the group has finished.

The Moderator's Role The basic way the moderator communicates with respondents in an online focus group is "freestyle" or "on the fly." That is, the moderator types in all questions, instructions, and probes into the text-entry area of the chat room in real-time (live, on-the-spot). In a variation on this method, the moderator copies and pastes questions from an electronic version of the guide into the text-entry area. Here, the moderator will toggle back and forth between the document and the chat room. An advantage of the freestyle method is that it forces the moderator to adapt to the group rather than use a series of canned questions. A disadvantage is that typing everything freestyle (or even copying and pasting from a separate document) takes time.

One way respondents can see stimuli (e.g., a concept statement, a mockup of a print ad, or a short product demonstration on video) is for the moderator to give the respondents a URL. Respondents then copy the URL from the chat stream, open another browser window, paste in the URL, and view it. An advantage of this approach is its simplicity. However, there are several disadvantages. First, if the respondents do not copy the URL correctly, they will not see it. Another disadvantage is that once respondents open another browser, they have "left the room" and the moderator has lost their attention; researchers must hope that respondents will return within the specified amount of time.

More advanced virtual focus group software reserves a frame (section) of the screen for stimuli to be shown. Here, the moderator has control over what is shown in the stimulus area. The advantage of this approach is that the respondent does not have to do any work to see the stimuli.

Types of Online Focus Groups Decision Analyst, one of America's most progressive firms in applying Internet technology to marketing research, offers two types of online focus groups:

1. *Real-time online focus groups:* These are live, interactive sessions with four to six participants and a moderator in a chat room format. The typical session does not last longer than 45 to 50 minutes. This technique is best for simple, straightforward issues that can be covered in limited time. The results tend to be superficial compared to in-person focus groups—but this is acceptable for certain types of projects. Typically, three to four groups are recommended as a minimum. Clients can view the chat room as the session unfolds and communicate with the moderator.

2. *Time-extended online focus groups:* These sessions follow a message board format and usually last five to ten days. The 15 to 20 participants must comment at least two or three times per day and spend 15 minutes a day logged in to the discussion. The moderator reviews respondents' comments several times per day (and night) and probes or redirects the discussion as needed. This technique provides three to four times as much content as the average in-person focus group. Time-extended online focus groups give participants time to reflect, talk to others, visit a store, or check the pantry. This extra time translates into richer content and deeper insights. Clients can view the online content as it is posted and may communicate with the moderator at any time.[27]

Using Channel M2 to Conduct Online Focus Groups Channel M2 provides market researchers with user-friendly virtual interview rooms, recruiting, and technical support for conducting virtual qualitative research, efficiently and effectively. By using Channel M2, the moderator and client can see and hear every respondent. You can see a demo at **www.channelM2.com.**

To recruit focus groups (from a global panel with access to over 15 million online consumers), Channel M2 uses a blend of e-mail and telephone verification and confirmation. Specifically, e-mails elicit involvement and direct participants to an online qualification questionnaire to ensure that each meets screening criteria. Telephone follow-up confirms that respondents qualify. Participants are sent a Web camera so that both verbal and nonverbal reactions can be recorded. Channel M2 tech support helps participants install the Webcam one to two days prior to the interview. Before participating, respondents must show a photo ID (their driver's license) to their Webcam so that their identity can be verified.

Participants are then provided instructions via e-mail, including a link to the Channel M2 interviewing room and a toll-free teleconference number to call. Upon clicking on the link, participants sign on and see the Channel M2 interview room, complete with live video of the other participants, text chat, screen or slide sharing, and whiteboard. (See Exhibit 9.8.)

Thus, in a Channel M2 focus group, all the participants can see and hear each other and communicate in a group setting. Once the focus group is under way, questions and answers occur in "real time" in a lively setting. Participants comment spontaneously, both verbally

EXHIBIT 9.8

An M2 Online Focus Group Under Way

Source: From http://www.ChannelM2.com, accessed January, 2009.

© 2005 CHANNEL M2, LLC

and via text messaging, yet the moderator can provide direction exactly as would be done in a traditional setting.[28]

Advantages of Online Focus Groups Many advantages are claimed for cyber groups. Cyber Dialogue, a marketing research company specializing in cyber groups, lists the following benefits of online focus groups on its Web site:

- *Speed:* Typically, focus groups can be recruited and conducted, with delivery of results, within five days of client approval.

- *Cost-effectiveness:* Off-line focus groups incur costs for facility rental, airfare, hotel, and food. None of these costs is incurred with online focus groups.

- *Broad geographic scope:* In a given focus group, you can speak to people in Boise, Idaho, and Miami, Florida, at the same time.

- *Accessibility:* Online focus groups give you access to individuals who otherwise might be difficult to recruit (e.g., business travelers, doctors, mothers with infants).

- *Honesty:* From behind their screen names, respondents are anonymous to other respondents and tend to talk more freely about issues that might create inhibitions in a face-to-face group.

Web Community Research

A Web community is a carefully selected group of consumers who agree to participate in an ongoing dialogue with a particular corporation.[29] All community interaction takes place on a custom-designed Web site. During the life of the community—which may last anywhere from six months to a year or more—community members respond to questions posed by the corporation on a regular basis. These discussions, which typically take the form of qualitative "dialogues," are augmented by the ability of community members to talk to one another about topics that are of interest to them as well.

The popularity and power of Web communities initially came from several key benefits. They

- engage customers in a space where they are most comfortable, allowing clients to interact with them on a deeper level;

- uncover "exciters" and "eureka moments," resulting in customer-derived innovations;

- establish brand advocates who are emotionally invested in a company's success;

- offer real-time results, enabling clients to explore ideas that normal time constraints prohibit; and

- create a forum where natural dialogue allows customers to initiate topics important to them.[30]

Additionally, Web communities help companies create a customer-focused organization by putting employees into direct contact with consumers from the comfort of their own desks. Since communities provide advantages in speed, flexibility, and 24/7 access to consumers, they let the organization be agile in its research decision-making and prudent in its spending.

By adding a research focus to the Web community, it becomes a way to

- map the thinking of consumer segments;

- brainstorm new ideas;

- create and test new products; and

- observe natural consumer behavior.[31]

Web community
A carefully selected group of consumers who agree to participate in an ongoing dialogue with a particular corporation.

The Role of Consumer Generated Media in Marketing Research

Consumer generated media (CGM) is that media which consumers generate themselves and share among themselves. Because it is consumer-based, it is trusted more than traditional forms of advertising and promotion.[32] CGM originates from

- Blogs
- Message boards and forums
- Public discussions (Usenet newsgroups)
- Discussions and forums on large e-mail portals (Yahoo!, AOL, MSN)
- Online opinion/review sites and services
- Online feedback/complaint sites
- Shared videos and photos
- Podcasts

It is estimated that 2 billion CGM comments are archived on the Web today, with 83 million content creators active in 2008. Those numbers grow by about 30 percent annually.[33]

CGM can be influenced but not controlled by marketers. To influence CGM, one must first understand what is being said or shown. Nielsen BuzzMetrics is the leading marketing research firm tracking CGM. The firm uses sophisticated data mining and other technologies to help marketers understand what is being said about their company and brands on the Web. BrandPulse is BuzzMetrics' most popular product. BrandPulse can tell a company about the spread and influence of CGM. How much "buzz" exists? Where is online discussion taking place, and by whom? What issues are most important? Is the tone of discussion negative or positive?

BrandPulse enables clients to listen in on unaided consumer conversations that take place on Internet forums, boards, Usenet newsgroups, and blogs, providing timely understanding of the opinions and trends affecting a company or brand.

A second product, BrandPulse Insight reports, focuses on specific issues and concerns such as

- What's the buzz about a certain issue, trend, product, or piece of news?
- Who's active online, and what are these online consumers saying?
- Are current trends building or waning?
- Can any emerging trends be detected early, before they catch fire (or fizzle out prematurely)?
- What key motivators influence and affect consumer behavior?
- What are consumer/customer moods and emotions on a particular topic, or about a specific brand?
- Which online consumers are likely candidates for influencer panels and relationship marketing programs?[34]

A marketer wanting to know about the latest diet trend, technological gadget, automotive perceptions, or health-related concerns can tap into BrandPulse Insights to understand what's being said.

Nielsen BuzzMetrics offers a free service titled BlogPulse, **www.blogpulse.com**, which is a blog search engine and a trend tracker. You can easily create your own graphs plotting blog buzz by entering a search term. Alternatively, you can check out popular blog trends, follow a story trail between two bloggers, or see profiles of popular bloggers.

Behavioral Targeting

Behavioral targeting (BT) is fairly new with "intelligent" behavioral targeting beginning in 2000 with an online ad company called DoubleClick. BT began as a simple process by placing cookies on users' browsers to track which Web sites they visited. Researchers could determine pages visited, time at each page, and the number and type of searches made. The objective is to match the Internet user with ads for products and services that they will most likely purchase. Today, the more sophisticated forms of BT combine a consumer's online activity with psychographic and demographic profiles inferred from databases. Thus, the BT firms claim that they use IP addresses and not an individual's actual name and address. Because of the potential effectiveness of BT advertising, its popularity is skyrocketing. Over 24 percent of all online advertisers used BT in 2008.[35] That is almost double from the previous year.

The most exciting growth area of BT is in the area of social networking where users share personal information with "friends." The information that a member of MySpace, Facebook, or Friendslator shares plus marrying the information with demographic and psychographic databases becomes a very powerful tool for ad placement. Critics have called this form of BT "conversational eavesdropping analysis." Tom Kendall, a Facebook executive, counters by saying that it is simply "user-declared information targeting."[36] This is because much of it is derived from what members provide in their profile such as gender, age, political views, hobbies, college, and occupation. This type of data is much more powerful for marketers than clickstream information. For example, if a member says that they have a strong interest in kayaking, this is much more useful than knowing that someone using the same computer went to the kayaking site, Kayakonline.com. It could have been a friend using the computer.

BT has raised a number of privacy issues, particularly the latest forms of the technology that is integrated with social networking sites. Yet, according to the latest research, only 7 percent of the respondents in a nationwide survey were concerned about their ISP tracking their activity; 54 percent were worried about viruses; and 52 percent about identity theft/fraud.[37] Also, 29 percent claimed that they would rather receive appropriately targeted ads rather than random ones.

Companies using behavioral targeting include Allstate, American Express, IBM, and TDAmeritrade to name a few. When Pepsi wanted to make a splash on the Web promoting its new low-calorie vitamin-enhanced water, Aquafina Alive, the company didn't run ads just anywhere on the Internet. It placed ads only on sites it knew would be visited by people interested in healthy lifestyles. Pepsi was using behavioral targeting.

Pepsi worked with Tacoda to identify health-conscious people by looking at traffic to sites about healthy lifestyles over a month-long period. Then Pepsi arranged to place Aquafina Alive ads on some of the 4,000 Web sites affiliated with Tacoda so the ads would pop up whenever these health-conscious consumers visited. The result? Pepsi recorded a threefold increase in the number of people clicking on its Aquafina Alive ads compared with previous campaigns.[38] Pepsi's success illustrates why behavioral targeting advertising was over $1 billion in 2008.[39]

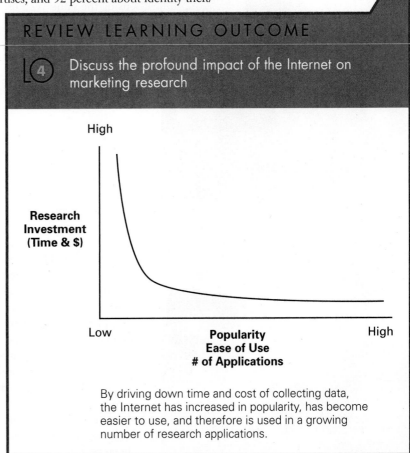

REVIEW LEARNING OUTCOME

LO**4** Discuss the profound impact of the Internet on marketing research

By driving down time and cost of collecting data, the Internet has increased in popularity, has become easier to use, and therefore is used in a growing number of research applications.

Other Uses of the Internet by Marketing Researchers

The Internet revolution in marketing research has had an impact on more than just the way surveys and focus groups are conducted. The management of the research process and the dissemination of information have also been greatly enhanced by the Internet. Several key areas have been affected by the Internet:

☛ *The distribution of requests for proposals (RFPs) and proposals:* Companies can now quickly and efficiently send RFPs to a select e-mail list of research suppliers. In turn, research suppliers can develop proposals and e-mail them back to clients. A process that used to take days using snail mail now occurs in a matter of hours.

☛ *Collaboration between the client and the research supplier in the management of a research project:* Now a researcher and client may both be looking at a proposal, RFP, report, or some type of statistical analysis at the same time on their respective computer screens while discussing it over the telephone. This is very powerful and efficient. Changes in the sample size, quotas, and other aspects of the research plan can be discussed and made immediately.

☛ *Data management and online analysis:* Clients can access their survey via the research supplier's secure Web site and monitor the data gathering in real time. The client can use sophisticated tools to actually do data analysis as the survey develops. This real-time analysis may result in changes in the questionnaire, sample size, or the types of respondents being interviewed. The research supplier and the client become partners in "just-in-time" marketing research.

☛ *Publication and distribution of reports:* Reports can be published to the Web directly from programs such as PowerPoint and all the latest versions of leading word-processing, spreadsheet, and presentation software packages. This means that results are available to appropriate managers worldwide on an almost instantaneous basis. Reports can be searched for the content of interest using the same Web browser used to view the report.

☛ *Viewing of oral presentations of marketing research surveys by widely scattered audiences:* By placing oral presentations on password-protected Web sites, managers throughout the world can see and hear the actual client presentation. This saves time and money by avoiding the need for the managers to travel to a central meeting site.[40]

LO 5

SCANNER-BASED RESEARCH

Scanner-based research is a system for gathering information from a single group of respondents by continuously monitoring the advertising, promotion, and pricing they are exposed to and the things they buy. The variables measured are advertising campaigns, coupons, displays, and product prices. The result is a huge database of marketing efforts and consumer behavior. Scanner-based research is bringing ever closer the Holy Grail of marketing research: an accurate, objective picture of the direct causal relationship between different kinds of marketing efforts and actual sales.

The two major scanner-based suppliers are Information Resources, Inc. (IRI), and the A. C. Nielsen Company. Each has about half the market. However, IRI is the founder of scanner-based research.

IRI's first product is called **BehaviorScan**. A household panel (a group of 3,000 long-term participants in the research project) has been recruited and maintained in each BehaviorScan town. Panel

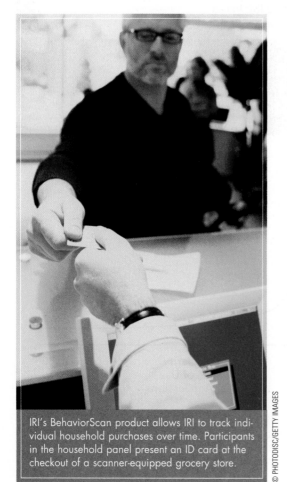

IRI's BehaviorScan product allows IRI to track individual household purchases over time. Participants in the household panel present an ID card at the checkout of a scanner-equipped grocery store.

© PHOTODISC/GETTY IMAGES

members shop with an ID card, which is presented at the checkout in scanner-equipped grocery stores and drugstores, allowing IRI to track electronically each household's purchases, item by item, over time. It uses microcomputers to measure TV viewing in each panel household and can send special commercials to panel member television sets. With such a measure of household purchasing, it is possible to manipulate marketing variables, such as TV advertising or consumer promotions, or to introduce a new product and analyze real changes in consumer buying behavior.

IRI's most successful product is InfoScan Reviews—a scanner-based sales-tracking service for the consumer packaged-goods industry. Retail sales, detailed consumer purchasing information (including measurement of store loyalty and total grocery basket expenditures), and promotional activity by manufacturers and retailers are monitored and evaluated for all bar-coded products. Data are collected weekly from more than 34,000 supermarkets, drugstores, and mass merchandisers.

When Should Marketing Research Be Conducted?

When managers have several possible solutions to a problem, they should not instinctively call for marketing research. In fact, the first decision to make is whether to conduct marketing research at all.

Some companies have been conducting research in certain markets for many years. Such firms understand the characteristics of target customers and their likes and dislikes about existing products. Under these circumstances, further research would be repetitive and waste money. Procter & Gamble, for example, has extensive knowledge of the coffee market. After it conducted initial taste tests with Folgers Instant Coffee, P&G went into national distribution without further research. Consolidated Foods Kitchen of Sara Lee followed the same strategy with its frozen croissants, as did Quaker Oats with Chewy Granola Bars. This tactic, however, does not always work. P&G marketers thought they understood the pain reliever market thoroughly, so they bypassed market research for Encaprin aspirin in capsules. Because it lacked a distinct competitive advantage over existing products, however, the product failed and was withdrawn from the market.

Managers rarely have such great trust in their judgment that they would refuse more information if it were available and free. But they might have enough confidence that they would be unwilling to pay very much for the information or to wait a long time to receive it. The willingness to acquire additional decision-making information depends on managers' perceptions of its quality, price, and timing. Of course, if perfect information were available—that is, the data conclusively showed which alternative to choose—decision makers would be willing to pay more for it than for information that still left uncertainty. In summary, research should be undertaken only when the expected value of the information is greater than the cost of obtaining it.

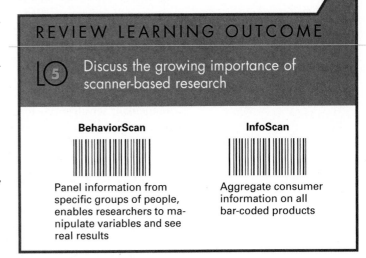

REVIEW LEARNING OUTCOME

LO 5 Discuss the growing importance of scanner-based research

BehaviorScan	InfoScan
Panel information from specific groups of people, enables researchers to manipulate variables and see real results	Aggregate consumer information on all bar-coded products

COMPETITIVE INTELLIGENCE

Derived from military intelligence, competitive intelligence is an important tool for helping a firm overcome a competitor's advantage. Specifically, competitive intelligence can help identify the advantage and play a major role in determining how it was achieved.

InfoScan
A scanner-based sales-tracking service for the consumer packaged-goods industry.

Competitive intelligence (CI) helps managers assess their competitors and their vendors in order to become a more efficient and effective competitor. Intelligence is analyzed information. It becomes decision-making intelligence when it has implications for the organization. For example, one of your firm's primary competitors may have plans to introduce a product with performance standards equal to your own but with a 15 percent cost advantage. The new product will reach the market in eight months. This intelligence has important decision-making and policy consequences for management. Competitive intelligence and environmental scanning (where management gathers data about the external environment—see Chapter 4) combine to create marketing intelligence. Marketing intelligence is then used as input into a marketing decision support system. Nine out of ten large companies have employees dedicated to the CI function. Many firms spend several million dollars a year on the function.

The top corporate CI officer at a multibillion-dollar global technology company claims that competitive intelligence helped his company recover after it began losing market share to a competitor. The rival, after competing directly with the company for years, had figured out its bidding strategy. Instead of competing on price with an off-the-shelf offering, the rival was beginning to offer prospects a customized solution—and it was winning. When the CI officer's company changed to a customized approach, it won hundreds of millions of dollars in new business the following year. At Pergo, Inc., a maker of laminate flooring, CI helped win a major contract. When Pergo told a national retailer what it had learned from a mutual supplier—that the rival would not be able to launch a new product when it said it would—the retailer signed with Pergo instead.

Conferences and professional courses led by rival executives are great places to gather information. A former competitive intelligence chief at telecom-software vendor Telcordia, says his firm hit the jackpot when one of its accountants attended a professional course taught by a competitor's CFO. The CFO used his company as the case for the class, revealing all kinds of tantalizing private financial information. Listening in on competitors' presentations to analysts at investment conferences and on conference calls is another good way to get financial data.

Executives, marketers and engineers tend to enjoy talking about what's new or what is coming in the future at their companies. Talking to these people at trade shows or even watching regulatory proceedings can yield fruitful CI. When drug maker Bristol-Myers Squibb (BMS) told Congress it needed to increase its harvest of environmentally sensitive yew trees, says a former intelligence executive at SmithKline Beecham, he knew there was a good chance that BMS would soon seek Food and Drug Administration approval for a drug using yew bark.

Sources of Competitive Intelligence

The Internet and its databases are a great source of CI. CI researchers can use Internet databases to answer these and other questions:

- What articles were written about this market?
- What companies are associated with this product group?
- What patents have been filed for this technology?
- What are the major magazines or texts in this industry?
- What are the chances that I will find something in print on the target company?
- How many companies are in the same industry as the target company?
- Who are the reporters studying this industry?
- How can I be updated on industry and company events without having to constantly request the information?

☞ How can I compile a list of the leading experts in the industry and the key institutions they are associated with?

Non-computer-based sources of CI can be found in a variety of areas:

☞ A company's salespeople, who can directly observe and ask questions about the competition.

☞ Experts with in-depth knowledge of a subject or activity.

☞ CI consultants, who can use their knowledge and experience to gather needed information quickly and efficiently.

☞ Government agencies, a valuable source of all types of data.

☞ Uniform Commercial Code (UCC) filings, a system that identifies goods that are leased or pledged as collateral. This is an excellent source for learning about a company's latest additions to plant assets.

☞ Suppliers, a group that may offer information on products shipped to a competitor.

☞ Periodicals, a good source for timely articles on successes, failures, opportunities, and threats.

☞ The Yellow Pages, which often provide data on a number of competitors, trading areas, and special offerings.

☞ Trade shows, official gatherings where competitors display their latest offerings.

This list is not exhaustive, but it does provide an idea of how CI can be gathered.

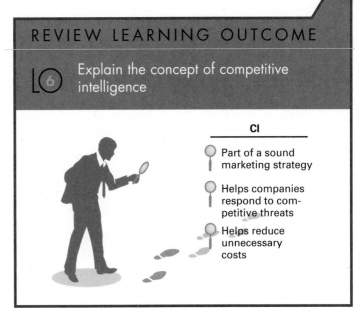

REVIEW LEARNING OUTCOME

LO 6 Explain the concept of competitive intelligence

CI

- Part of a sound marketing strategy
- Helps companies respond to competitive threats
- Helps reduce unnecessary costs

$7 billion ◀ amount that U.S. marketers spend on research each year

ounces of ketchup consumed by children each year ▶ **5 billion**

$2,800 ◀ cost of a 17-chapter report from Wintergreen Research aggregator

cost of a single chapter ▶ **$350**

$50,000 ◀ cost of a 15-minute telephone interview with 1,000 men

28 ◀ minutes required to complete a printed questionnaire for Hallmark's Shoebox Greeting Cards

18 ◀ minutes required to complete the same questionnaire with computer assistance

88 ◀ percentage of U.S. research firms conducting marketing research online

members on the Internet panel Survey Spot ▶ **5 million**

34,000 ◀ stores from which InfoScan tracks data

REVIEW AND APPLICATIONS

 Explain the concept and purpose of a marketing decision support system. A decision support system (DSS) makes data instantly available to marketing managers and allows them to manipulate the data themselves to make marketing decisions. Four characteristics make DSSs especially useful to marketing managers: They are interactive, flexible, discovery oriented, and accessible. That is, they give managers access to information immediately and without outside assistance, they allow users to manipulate data in a variety of ways and to answer "what if" questions, and they are accessible to novice computer users.

- *Interactive:* Managers give simple instructions and see immediate results. The process is under their direct control; no computer programmer is needed. Managers don't have to wait for scheduled reports.

- *Flexible:* A DSS can sort, regroup, total, average, and manipulate the data in various ways. It will shift gears as the user changes topics, matching information to the problem at hand. For example, the CEO can see highly aggregated figures, and the marketing analyst can view very detailed breakouts.

- *Discovery-oriented:* Managers can probe for trends, isolate problems, and ask "what if" questions.

- *Accessible:* Managers who aren't skilled with computers can easily learn how to use a DSS. Novice users should be able to choose a standard, or default, method of using the system. They can bypass optional features so they can work with the basic system right away while gradually learning to apply its advanced features.

1.1 In the absence of company problems, is there any reason to develop a marketing DSS?

1.2 Explain the difference between marketing research and a DSS.

 Define marketing research and explain its importance to marketing decision making. Marketing research is a process of collecting and analyzing data for the purpose of solving specific marketing problems. Marketers use marketing research to explore the profitability of marketing strategies. They can examine why particular strategies failed and analyze characteristics of specific market segments. Managers can use research findings to help keep current customers. Moreover, marketing research allows management to behave proactively, rather than reactively, by identifying newly emerging patterns in society and the economy.

2.1 The task of marketing is to create exchanges. What role might marketing research play in the facilitation of the exchange process?

2.2 Marketing research has traditionally been associated with manufacturers of consumer goods. Today, however, an increasing number of organizations, both profit and nonprofit, are using marketing research. Why do you think this trend exists? Give some examples of specific reasons why organizations might use marketing research.

 2.3 Write a reply to the following statement: "I own a restaurant in the downtown area. I see customers every day who I know on a first-name basis. I understand their likes and dislikes. If I put something on the menu and it doesn't sell, I know that they didn't like it. I also read the magazine *Modern Restaurants*, so I know what the trends are in the industry. This is all of the marketing research I need to do."

2.4 Give an example of (a) the descriptive role of marketing research, (b) the diagnostic role, and (c) the predictive function of marketing research.

 Describe the steps involved in conducting a marketing research project. The marketing research process involves several basic steps. First, the researcher and the decision maker must agree on a problem statement or set of research objectives. The researcher then creates an overall research design to specify how primary data will be gathered and analyzed. Before collecting data, the researcher decides whether the group to be interviewed will be a probability or nonprobability sample. Field service firms are often hired to carry out data collection. Once data have been collected, the researcher analyzes them using statistical analysis. The researcher then prepares and presents oral and written reports, with conclusions and recommendations, to management. As a final step, the researcher determines whether the recommendations were implemented and what could have been done to make the project more successful.

3.1 Critique the following methodologies and suggest more appropriate alternatives:

a. A supermarket was interested in determining its image. It dropped a short questionnaire into the grocery bag of each customer before putting in the groceries.

b. To assess the extent of its trade area, a shopping mall stationed interviewers in the parking lot every Monday and Friday evening. Interviewers walked up to people after they had parked their cars and asked them for their ZIP codes.

c. To assess the popularity of a new movie, a major studio invited people to call a 900 number and vote yes, they would see it again, or no, they would not. Each caller was billed a $2 charge.

3.2 You have been charged with determining how to attract more business majors to your school. Write an outline of the steps you would take, including the sampling procedures, to accomplish the task.

3.3 Why are secondary data sometimes preferable to primary data?

3.4 What is a marketing research aggregator? What role do these aggregators play in marketing research?

3.5 Discuss when focus groups should and should not be used.

3.6 Divide the class into teams of eight persons. Each group will conduct a focus group on the quality and number of services that your college is providing to its students. One person from each group should be chosen to act as moderator. Remember, it is the moderator's job to facilitate discussion, not to lead the discussion. These groups should last approximately 45 minutes. If possible, the groups should be videotaped or recorded. Upon completion, each group should write a brief report of its results. Consider offering to meet with the dean of students to share the results of your research.

3.7 Why do companies hire mystery shoppers?

3.8 Ethnographic research is a new (and expensive) trend in marketing research. Find an article on ethnographic research. Read and summarize the article. What is your opinion of ethnographic research? Do you think it will be the wave of the future? Explain your reasoning.

Discuss the profound impact of the Internet on marketing research. The Internet has vastly simplified the secondary data search process, placing more sources of information in front of researchers than ever before. Internet survey research is surging in popularity. Internet surveys can be created rapidly and reported in real time. They are also relatively inexpensive and can easily be personalized. Often researchers can use the Internet to contact respondents who are difficult to reach by other means. The Internet can also be used to conduct focus groups, analyze consumer-generated media, engage in behavioral targeting, distribute research proposals and reports, and to facilitate collaboration between the client and the research supplier. Clients can access real-time data and analyze the information as the collection process continues.

4.1 Go to **www.strategicbusinessinsights.com/vals/presurvey.shtml** and take the VALS Survey. Report on how marketing researchers are using this information.

4.2 Divide the class into teams. Each team should go to a different opt-in survey site on the Web and participate in an online survey. A spokesperson for each team should report the results to the class.

4.3 What are various ways to obtain respondents for online surveys?

4.4 Describe the advantages and disadvantages of online surveys.

 Discuss the growing importance of scanner-based research. A scanner-based research system enables marketers to monitor a market panel's exposure and reaction to such variables as advertising, coupons, store displays, packaging, and price. By analyzing these variables in relation to the panel's subsequent buying behavior, marketers gain useful insight into sales and marketing strategies.

5.1 Why has scanner-based research been seen as "the ultimate answer" for marketing researchers? Do you see any disadvantages of this methodology?

5.2 Detractors claim that scanner-based research is like "driving a car down the road looking only in the rearview mirror." What does this mean? Do you agree?

 Explain the concept of competitive intelligence. Competitive intelligence (CI) helps managers assess their competition and their vendors in order to become more efficient and effective competitors. Intelligence is analyzed information, and it becomes decision-making intelligence when it has implications for the organization.

By helping managers assess their competition and vendors, CI leads to fewer surprises. CI allows managers to predict changes in business relationships, guard against threats, forecast a competitor's strategy, and develop a successful marketing plan.

The Internet and databases accessed via the Internet offer excellent sources of CI. Company personnel, particularly sales and service representatives, are usually good sources of CI. Many companies require their salespersons to routinely fill out CI reports. Other external sources of CI include experts, CI consultants, government agencies, UCC filings, suppliers, newspapers and other publications, Yellow Pages, and trade shows.

6.1 Why do you think that CI is so hot in today's environment?

6.2 Prepare a memo to your boss at JetBlue Airlines and outline why the organization needs a CI unit.

6.3 Form a team with three other students. Each team must choose a firm in the PC manufacturing industry and then go to the Web site of the firm and acquire as much CI as possible. Each team will then prepare a five-minute oral presentation on its findings.

KEY TERMS

behavioral targeting (BT)	319	experiment	308	nonprobability sample	309
BehaviorScan	320	field service firm	310	observation research	305
central-location telephone (CLT) facility	301	focus group	302	open-ended question	303
		frame error	310	primary data	299
closed-ended question	303	group dynamics	302	probability sample	309
competitive intelligence (CI)	322	InfoScan	321	random error	310
computer-assisted personal interviewing	301	mall intercept interview	301	random sample	309
		management decision problem	297	research design	299
computer-assisted self-interviewing	301	marketing information	291	sample	308
				sampling error	310
consumer generated media	318	marketing research	292	scaled-response question	303
convenience sample	310	marketing research aggregator	299	scanner-based research	320
cross-tabulation	311	marketing research objective	297	secondary data	297
database marketing	292	marketing research problem	297	survey research	300
decision support system (DSS)	291	measurement error	310	universe	309
ethnographic research	306	mystery shoppers	305	Web community	317
executive interviews	302				

EXERCISES

APPLICATION EXERCISE

For its study, *Teens and Healthy Eating: Oxymoron or Trend?*, New York–based BuzzBack Market Research focused on snacking. Among its findings: Teens eat an average of three snacks per day; breakfast is the meal they skip most often. Though scads of snacks are stacked on store shelves, when it comes to healthier treats targeting adolescents, it's a bit of a teenage wasteland. BuzzBack asked 532 teen respondents to conjure up new foods they'd gobble up. The following are some of their ideas:

- "Travel fruit. Why can't fruit be in travel bags like chips or cookies? Canned fruit is too messy. Maybe have a dip or something sold with it, too."—Female, age 17.

- "A drink that contains five servings of fruits and vegetables."—Male, age 16, Caucasian.

- "I would invent all natural and fat-free, vitamin-enhanced cookies and chips that had great flavor."—Female, age 16.

- "I would make fruit-based cookies."—Male, age 16, Caucasian.

- "Low-carb trail mix, because trail mix is easy to eat but it has a lot of fat/carbs."—Female, age 15, Caucasian.

- "I would create some sort of microwavable spaghetti."—Male, age 16, Caucasian.

- "Something quick and easy to make that's also cheap. I'll be in college next year, and I'm trying to find things that are affordable, healthier than cafeteria food, and easy to make."—Female, age 17.

- "*Good* vegan mac 'n' cheese."—Female, age 18, Caucasian.

- "A smoothie where you could get all the nutrients you need, that tastes good, helps you stay in shape, and is good for you. Has vitamins A, B^3, B_{12}, C, ginkgo. Packaging would be bright."—Female, age 16, African American.

- "A breakfast shake for teens. Something easy that tastes good, not necessarily for dieters like Slim·Fast, etc. Something to balance you off in the morning."—Male, age 18.

Activities

1. You are a new-product development specialist at Kraft. What guidance can you get from the BuzzBack study?

2. Choose one of the suggestions from the above list of healthy snack concepts. Imagine that your company is interested in turning the idea into a new product but wants to conduct market research before investing in product development. Design a marketing research plan that will give company managers the information they need before engaging in new-product development of the idea. (Hint: Use steps 1–3 in Exhibit 9.1 as a guide.)

3. Once you have finished your plan, collect the data. Depending on the data-collection methods you have outlined in your plan, you may need to make adjustments so that you can collect actual data to analyze.

4. Analyze the data you collected, and create a report for your company either recommending that the company pursue the idea you chose or investigate another.

ETHICS EXERCISE

John Michael Smythe owns a small marketing research firm in Cleveland, Ohio, which employs 75 people. Most employees are the sole breadwinners in their families. John's firm has not fared well for the past two years and is on the verge of bankruptcy. The company recently surveyed over 2,500 people in Ohio about new-car purchase plans for the Ohio Department of Economic Development. Because the study identified many hot prospects for new cars, a car dealer has offered John $8,000 for the names and phone numbers of people saying they are "likely" or "very likely" to buy a new car within the next 12 months. John needs the money to avoid laying off a number of employees.

Questions

1. Should John Smythe sell the names?

2. Does the AMA Statement of Ethics address this issue? Go to **www. marketingpower.com/AboutAMA/Pages/Statement of Ethics.aspx.** Then write a brief paragraph on what the AMA Statement of Ethics contains that relates to John Smythe's dilemma.

MARKETING PLAN EXERCISE

For the marketing plan exercise in Chapter 6, you considered the consumer decision-making process as it applies to your marketing plan; in Chapter 7, you analyzed your potential business markets. In Chapter 8, you identified your company's target market and its various segments. Now complete the following exercises to find out more about your competitors and customers through marketing research—a key to any strategic marketing plan. Once completed, you can use your answers to complete the Marketing Plan Worksheet for Part 2, which you can find on your companion Web site at **www.cengage.com/marketing/lamb.**

1. Are there any critical issues that must be explored with primary marketing research before you can implement your marketing plan for your chosen company? These might include items such as customer demand, purchase intentions, customer perceptions of product quality, price perceptions, and reaction to critical promotion. List some critical research questions and decide which form of research you would use.

2. Design a brief Internet customer satisfaction survey that you could place on your company Web site. Use the "Survey Wiz" to help you with your questionnaire at **http://psych.fullerton.edu/mbirnbaum/programs/surveyWiz.HTM.**

3. What type of competitive intelligence will you need to gather in order to monitor your market space? How can analyzing the job offerings, mission or "about us" statement, products and services descriptions, or other general information on your competitors' Web sites help you figure our their strategic direction? What areas of a Web site could you scan to gather competitive information?

CASE STUDY: RED LOBSTER

MARKET RESEARCH REVEALS WHAT'S FRESH TODAY

Remember the Red Lobster commercials featuring lots of fried shrimp bouncing around and lobster claws dripping with butter? They've been replaced by scenes of steaming fresh fish, rice, and vegetables. The old slogan, "For the Seafood Lover in You" has also been canned. Now Red Lobster wants you to "Come See What's Fresh Today." The restaurants themselves will soon look different, too, with a more streamlined, contemporary décor that downplays the traditional nautical themes.

These changes and more are part of an effort to make over the seafood chain after marketing research revealed that the restaurant was considered outdated and unappealing to potential customers. Red Lobster president Kim Lodrup says that in the first stage of the makeover, the chain improved operations so that customers wouldn't have to wait so long for the food to reach their table. The second phase focused on improving the restaurant's image and shifting the focus from low prices to freshness. The third and final challenge will be to increase sales. Lodrup says, "We are positioning Red Lobster to be the best seafood restaurant on the planet."

Lodrup was originally hired as a marketing specialist to revive the sagging brand's image in 2003 when sales were falling and customer satisfaction was at an all-time low. He immediately put the kibosh on promotions like the All-You-Can-Eat Crab Legs Specials that had lost money for the company in the past and emphasized Red Lobster's seafood expertise instead. After sales increased in 2004, he was promoted to president, but he still relies on marketing research to keep his finger on the pulse of customer preferences.

"We find out what they want from idealized dining service and research how to deliver value to guests," Lodrup says. To do that, Red Lobster follows changing consumer habits and pays attention to which dishes patrons prefer. They use phone and Internet surveys to learn about guest attitudes toward the food they've tried and try to determine how well they might respond to new menu items or concept changes before instituting them. The guest-relations department "catalogs the nature of guest contact so we can see if there are changes in trends," Lodrup explains. "Emerging concerns or requests from consumers get captured weekly and recorded for our executives."

More in-depth research measures attitudes and trends that could affect the brand in the future. Before a promotion is launched, featured menu items are chosen through extensive consumer testing. Beginning with a large number of possible dishes, they narrow it down to the one that testers deem most appealing.

After studies indicated that freshness is the single biggest criterion consumers use to judge a seafood restaurant, the chain knew it was vital to get word out that fresh fish is delivered to Red Lobster restaurants six days a week. Interviews with former customers revealed that many still believed that Red Lobster's fish was frozen despite the company's extensive global connections and rapid seafood delivery system.

"It's really important to signal to people food is freshly prepared," says marketing V.P. Salli Setta, who created the Culinary Institute of Tuscany for Olive Garden before being hired by Red Lobster. The company is considering a similar seafood-related school in Maine to add authenticity to Red Lobster's menu. In the meantime, Setta hired a new team of executive chefs to create updated recipes with the herbs that customers said had fresher connotations than the traditional lemon and butter sauces.

They also introduced a separate Fresh Fish Menu that is updated twice a day at the restaurants. Even though fresh fin fish had been on the regular menu for years, it had never really been promoted. Research showed that this could make the restaurant more appealing to their lapsed customers, who tend to be affluent, educated, and over 50. Households with an annual income of more than $70,000 account for half of all food eaten in restaurants and have been shown to be most interested in seafood dining. Reeling these customers back in has become a top priority in the chain's turnaround.

So far the makeover is working. Red Lobster has been reporting same-store sales increases since 2004. Improvements in operations and other cost controls led to the highest operating margin in Red Lobster history and, Lodrup reports, "Every measure of guest satisfaction is at a record level." However, it continues to be a challenge for the chain to change old perceptions of itself. As one surveyed customer put it, "My wife swears by the fish. She just can't get her friends to try it."

Source: "Las Vegas Tourism Agency Announces 1.3 Percent Rise in Visitor Totals for 2003", *Las Vegas Review-Journal*, February 14, 2004; Jennifer Bjorhus, "Las Vegas Tourism Agency Executive Says Research, Marketing are Key to Success", *Las Vegas Review-Journal*, April 6, 2003; Chris Jones,

"Las Vegas Tourism Agency Executive Says Research Marketing Are Key to Success," Las Vegas Review-Journal, April 6, 2003; Chris Jones, "Las Vegas Tourism Chief Opposes Ads; Board Members Object to 'Sin City' Phrase"' Las Vegas Review-Journal, December 16, 2003; Chris Jones, "Las Vegas Tourism Officials Plan Marketing Blitz to Attract Canadian Tourist", Travel Weekly, March 3, 2003; Chris Jones, "New Las Vegas Tourism Ads Target Hispanics with Tradition-Focused Messages", Las Vegas Review-Journal, July 17, 2003.

Questions

1. Why do you think Red Lobster relies so much on Internet surveys to track customer opinions, preferences, and criticisms? What are the advantages of online questionnaires versus traditional surveys conducted over the phone or through the mail?

2. Go to **www.redlobster.com** and click around. How well do you think the site appeals to the educated, affluent, and over-50 crowd that the chain wants to reel in? What are the primary messages that it communicates about the restaurant, and how effective are they? How does the site attempt to capture information about its customers?

3. Red Lobster's closest competitor in the seafood-dining business is Joe's Crab Shack. Check out their Web site at **www.joescrabshack.com** and compare it to Red Lobster's. How does their marketing approach differ? Do you think it's appealing to the same types of customers? How does the Web site try to get information from its customers?

4. Suppose Red Lobster was wondering how well its new interior design was being received by customers at a redecorated restaurant in Columbus, Ohio, and hired you to create a questionnaire. Write one of each: an open-ended question, a closed-ended question (either dichotomous or multiple choice), and a scaled-response question.

COMPANY CLIPS

READYMADE—READY RESEARCH

Having been in business for five years, *ReadyMade* now has a lot of research on the various characteristics of its readers. Its knowledge of GenNesters has made the magazine a leader in identifying and describing that segment. As a new business, *ReadyMade* found that businesses had little interest in marketing to this group. Now that businesses have become more aware of GenNester influence, however, *ReadyMade* is able to fill the need for information. *ReadyMade* has statistics on the ages at which people are marrying and the interests of couples that have just married. Because the magazine is ahead of the curve on gathering information on this segment, *ReadyMade* can help other businesses figure out how to tailor their marketing efforts to fit the needs of GenNesters.

Questions

1. How has *ReadyMade* been able to help Toyota promote its new line of cars? What benefit has *ReadyMade* seen from the partnership?

2. How does *ReadyMade* use new technology to gain information about its consumers?

3. What sorts of long-term decisions is *ReadyMade* making that could be aided by research? What would you recommend?

Marketing & You Results

Higher scores indicate that you place greater importance on collecting primary and secondary information when developing marketing campaigns or projects. A lower score means you would be less aggressive in collecting information and might plow ahead regardless of how much information you do (or don't) have. After reading Chapter 9, you can see how involved gathering and analyzing market information can be, but also how critical it is to success.

Product and Distribution Decisions

PART 3

WHAT'S INSIDE

Product Concepts *332*

Developing and Managing Products *360*

Marketing Channels *388*

Retailing *432*

© FRANK CHMURA/ALAMY

10

Product Concepts

LEARNING OUTCOMES

LO1 Define the term *product*

LO2 Classify consumer products

LO3 Discuss the importance of services to the economy

LO4 Discuss the differences between services and goods

LO5 Define the terms *product item*, *product line*, and *product mix*

LO6 Describe marketing uses of branding

LO7 Describe marketing uses of packaging and labeling

LO8 Discuss global issues in branding and packaging

LO9 Describe how and why product warranties are important marketing tools

LO① WHAT IS A PRODUCT?

The product offering, the heart of an organization's marketing program, is usually the starting point in creating a marketing mix. A marketing manager cannot determine a price, design a promotion strategy, or create a distribution channel until the firm has a product to sell. Moreover, an excellent distribution channel, a persuasive promotion campaign, and a fair price have no value when the product offering is poor or inadequate.

A product may be defined as everything, both favorable and unfavorable, that a person receives in an exchange. A product may be a tangible good such as a pair of shoes, a service such as a haircut, an idea such as "don't litter," or any combination of these three. Packaging, style, color, options, and size are some typical product features. Just as important are intangibles such as service, the seller's image, the manufacturer's reputation, and the way consumers believe others will view the product.

To most people, the term *product* means a tangible good. However, services and ideas are also products. The marketing process identified in Chapter 1 is the same whether the product marketed is a good, a service, an idea, or some combination of these.

REVIEW LEARNING OUTCOME

LO① Define the term *product*

Product

- Good
- Service
- Idea

Marketing & You

Using the following scale, indicate your opinion on the line before each item.

1	2	3	4	5	6
Strongly disagree	Disagree	Neutral	Agree	Strongly agree	

__ I usually purchase brand-name products.

__ Store brands are of poor quality.*

__ All brands are about the same.*

__ The well-known national brands are best for me.

__ The more expensive brands are usually my choices.

__ The higher the price of a product, the better its quality.

__ Nice department and specialty stores offer me the best products.

Total your score, reversing your scores for the items followed by an asterisk. That is, if you answered 1, change it to 5 and vice versa. Read the chapter and find out what your score means at the end.

Source: From Scale #230, *Marketing Scales Handbook*, G. Bruner, K. James, H. Hesel, eds. Vol. IIII. © by American Marketing Association.

LO② TYPES OF CONSUMER PRODUCTS

Products can be classified as either business (industrial) or consumer products, depending on the buyer's intentions. The key distinction between the two types of products is their intended use. If the intended use is a business purpose, the product is classified as a business or industrial product. As explained in Chapter 7, a business product is used to manufacture other goods or services, to facilitate an organization's operations, or to resell to other customers. A consumer product is bought to satisfy an individual's personal wants. Sometimes the same item can be classified as either a business or a consumer product, depending on its intended use. Examples include lightbulbs, pencils and paper, and computers.

We need to know about product classifications because business and

product
Everything, both favorable and unfavorable, that a person receives in an exchange.

business product (industrial product)
A product used to manufacture other goods or services, to facilitate an organization's operations, or to resell to other customers.

consumer product
A product bought to satisfy an individual's personal wants.

convenience product
A relatively inexpensive item that merits little shopping effort.

shopping product
A product that requires comparison shopping because it is usually more expensive than a convenience product and is found in fewer stores.

specialty product
A particular item for which consumers search extensively and are very reluctant to accept substitutes.

unsought product
A product unknown to the potential buyer, or a known product that the buyer does not actively seek.

service
The result of applying human or mechanical efforts to people or objects.

consumer products are marketed differently. They are marketed to different target markets and tend to use different distribution, promotion, and pricing strategies.

Chapter 7 examined seven categories of business products: major equipment, accessory equipment, component parts, processed materials, raw materials, supplies, and services. The current chapter examines an effective way of categorizing consumer products. Although there are several ways to classify them, the most popular approach includes these four types: convenience products, shopping products, specialty products, and unsought products (see Exhibit 10.1). This approach classifies products according to how much effort is normally used to shop for them.

Convenience Products

A convenience product is a relatively inexpensive item that merits little shopping effort—that is, a consumer is unwilling to shop extensively for such an item. Candy, soft drinks, combs, aspirin, small hardware items, dry cleaning, and car washes fall into the convenience product category.

Consumers buy convenience products regularly, usually without much planning. Nevertheless, consumers do know the brand names of popular convenience products, such as Coca-Cola, Bayer aspirin, and Right Guard deodorant. Convenience products normally require wide distribution in order to sell sufficient quantities to meet profit goals. For example, the gum Dentyne Ice is available everywhere, including Wal-Mart, Walgreens, gas stations, newsstands, and vending machines.

Shopping Products

A shopping product is usually more expensive than a convenience product and is found in fewer stores. Consumers usually buy a shopping product only after comparing several brands or stores on style, practicality, price, and lifestyle compatibility. They are willing to invest some effort into this process to get the desired benefits.

EXHIBIT 10.1

Classification of Consumer Products

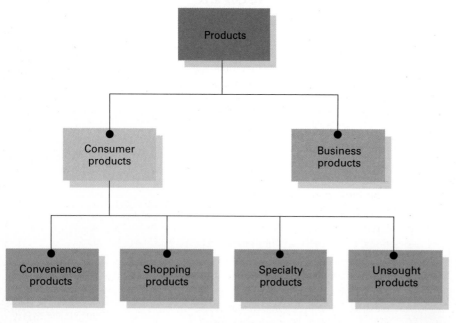

There are two types of shopping products: homogeneous and heterogeneous. Consumers perceive *homogeneous* shopping products as basically similar—for example, washers, dryers, refrigerators, and televisions. With homogeneous shopping products, consumers typically look for the lowest-priced brand that has the desired features. For example, they might compare Kenmore, Whirlpool, and General Electric refrigerators.

In contrast, consumers perceive *heterogeneous* shopping products as essentially different—for example, furniture, clothing, housing, and universities. Consumers often have trouble comparing heterogeneous shopping products because the prices, quality, and features vary so much. The benefit of comparing heterogeneous shopping products is "finding the best product or brand for me"; this decision is often highly individual. For example, it would be difficult to compare a small, private university with a large, public university.

Specialty Products

When consumers search extensively for a particular item and are very reluctant to accept substitutes, that item is a specialty product. Rolex watches, Rolls-Royce automobiles, Bose speakers, and highly specialized forms of medical care are generally considered specialty products.

Marketers of specialty products often use selective, status-conscious advertising to maintain their product's exclusive image. Distribution is often limited to one or a very few outlets in a geographic area. Brand names and quality of service are often very important.

Unsought Products

A product unknown to the potential buyer or a known product that the buyer does not actively seek is referred to as an unsought product. New products fall into this category until advertising and distribution increase consumer awareness of them.

Some goods are always marketed as unsought items, especially needed products we do not like to think about or care to spend money on. Insurance, burial plots, and similar items require aggressive personal selling and highly persuasive advertising. Salespeople actively seek leads to potential buyers. Because consumers usually do not seek out this type of product, the company must go directly to them through a salesperson, direct mail, or direct-response advertising.

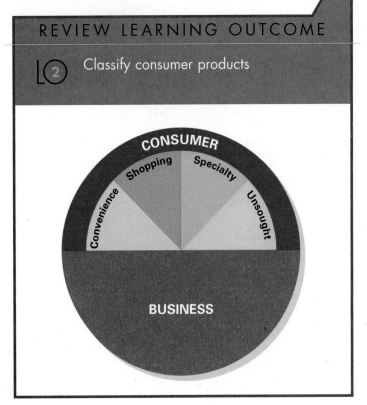

REVIEW LEARNING OUTCOME

LO 2 Classify consumer products

THE IMPORTANCE OF SERVICES

A service is the result of applying human or mechanical efforts to people or objects. Services involve a deed, a performance, or an effort that cannot be physically possessed.

Today, the service sector substantially influences the U.S. economy, accounting for 81 percent of both U.S. gross domestic product and U.S. employment.[1] The demand for services is expected to continue. According to the Bureau of Labor Statistics, service occupations will be responsible for nearly all net job growth through the year 2016.[2] Much of this demand results from demographics. An aging population will need nurses, home health care, physical therapists, and social workers. Two-earner families need child-care, housecleaning, and lawn-care services. Also increasing will be the demand for information managers, such as computer engineers and systems analysts. There is also a growing market for service companies worldwide.

The marketing process described in Chapter 1 is the same for all types of products, whether they are goods or services. Many ideas and strategies discussed throughout this book have been illustrated with service examples. In many ways, marketing is marketing, regardless of the product's characteristics. In addition, although a comparison of goods and services marketing can be beneficial,

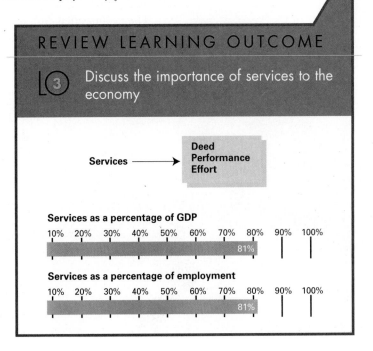

REVIEW LEARNING OUTCOME

LO 3 Discuss the importance of services to the economy

intangibility
The inability of services to be touched, seen, tasted, heard, or felt in the same manner that goods can be sensed.

search quality
A characteristic that can be easily assessed before purchase.

experience quality
A characteristic that can be assessed only after use.

credence quality
A characteristic that consumers may have difficulty assessing even after purchase because they do not have the necessary knowledge or experience.

inseparability
The inability of the production and consumption of a service to be separated. Consumers must be present during the production.

in reality it is hard to distinguish clearly between manufacturing and service firms. Indeed, many manufacturing firms can point to service as a major factor in their success. For example, maintenance and repair services offered by the manufacturer are important to buyers of copy machines. General Electric makes most of its revenues from finance operations rather than from products. Nevertheless, services have some unique characteristics that distinguish them from goods, and marketing strategies need to be adjusted for these characteristics.

HOW SERVICES DIFFER FROM GOODS

Services have four unique characteristics that distinguish them from goods. Services are intangible, inseparable, heterogeneous, and perishable.

Intangibility

The basic difference between services and goods is that services are intangible performances. Because of their intangibility, they cannot be touched, seen, tasted, heard, or felt in the same manner that goods can be sensed. Services cannot be stored and are often easy to duplicate.

Evaluating the quality of services before or even after making a purchase is harder than evaluating the quality of goods because, compared to goods, services tend to exhibit fewer search qualities. A search quality is a characteristic that can be easily assessed before purchase—for instance, the color of an appliance or automobile. At the same time, services tend to exhibit more experience and credence qualities. An experience quality is a characteristic that can be assessed only after use, such as the quality of a meal in a restaurant or the actual experience of a vacation. A credence quality is a characteristic that consumers may have difficulty assessing even after purchase because they do not have the necessary knowledge or experience. Medical and consulting services are examples of services that exhibit credence qualities.

These characteristics also make it harder for marketers to communicate the benefits of an intangible service than to communicate the benefits of tangible goods. Thus, marketers often rely on tangible cues to communicate a service's nature and quality. For example, Travelers Insurance Company's use of the umbrella symbol helped make tangible the benefit of protection that insurance provides.

The facilities that customers visit, or from which services are delivered, are a critical tangible part of the total service offering. Messages about the organization are communicated to customers through elements such as the décor, the clutter or neatness of service areas, and the staff's manners and dress. Reflecting this idea, the design and development team at Bass Pro Shops believes that in-store displays are not just fixtures, but marketing tools that will attract customers if designed to reflect local culture. So, for example, the Destin, Florida, store incorporates indigenous seagulls and swordfish in the chandeliers.[3]

The facilities that customers visit or from which services are delivered, such as those in a hair stylist's shop, are a critical tangible part of the total service offering.

© VICKI BEAVER

Inseparability

Goods are produced, sold, and then consumed. In contrast, services are often sold, produced, and consumed at the same time. In other words, their production and consumption are inseparable activities. This inseparability means that, because consumers must be present during the production of services like haircuts or surgery, they are actually involved in the production of the services they buy. That type of consumer involvement is rare in goods manufacturing. Inseparability also means that customers have an opportunity to provide input into their service experience and outcome. For example, individuals getting a haircut can provide feedback during the process so that their hair looks the way they want it to look.

Simultaneous production and consumption also means that services normally cannot be produced in a centralized location and consumed in decentralized locations, as goods typically are. Services are also inseparable from the perspective of the service provider. Thus, the quality of service that firms are able to deliver depends on the quality of their employees.

Heterogeneity

One great strength of McDonald's is consistency. Whether customers order a Big Mac and french fries in Fort Worth, Tokyo, or Moscow, they know exactly what they are going to get. This is not the case with many service providers. Because services have greater heterogeneity, or variability of inputs and outputs, they tend to be less standardized and uniform than goods. For example, physicians in a group practice or barbers in a barber shop differ from one another in their technical and interpersonal skills. A given physician's or barber's performance may even vary depending on time of day, physical health, or some other factor. Because services tend to be labor-intensive, and production and consumption are inseparable, consistency and quality control can be hard to achieve.

Standardization and training help increase consistency and reliability. Limited-menu restaurants like Pizza Hut and KFC offer customers high consistency from one visit to the next because of standardized preparation procedures. Another way to increase consistency is to mechanize the process. Banks have reduced the inconsistency of teller services by providing automated teller machines (ATMs). Automatic coin receptacles and electronic toll collection systems such as E-Z Pass have replaced human collectors on toll roads.

Perishability

The fourth characteristic of services is their perishability, which means that they cannot be stored, warehoused, or inventoried. An empty hotel room or airplane seat produces no revenue that day. The revenue is lost. Yet service organizations are often forced to turn away full-price customers during peak periods.

One of the most important challenges in many service industries is finding ways to synchronize supply and demand. The philosophy that some revenue is better than none has prompted many hotels to offer deep discounts on weekends and during the off-season and has prompted airlines to adopt similar pricing strategies during off-peak hours. Car rental agencies, movie theaters, and restaurants also use discounts to encourage demand during nonpeak periods.

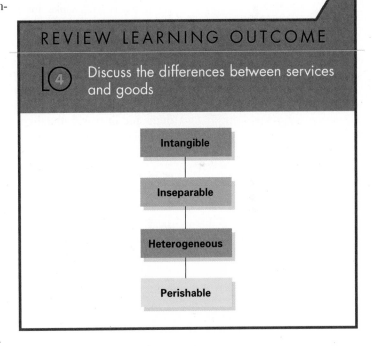

REVIEW LEARNING OUTCOME

LO 4 Discuss the differences between services and goods

- Intangible
- Inseparable
- Heterogeneous
- Perishable

LO 5
PRODUCT ITEMS, LINES, AND MIXES

Rarely does a company sell a single product. More often, it sells a variety of things. A product item is a specific version of a product that can be designated as a distinct offering among an organization's products. Campbell's Creamy Chicken soup is an example of a product item (see Exhibit 10.2).

heterogeneity
The variability of the inputs and outputs of services, which causes services to tend to be less standardized and less uniform than goods.

perishability
The inability of services to be stored, warehoused, or inventoried.

product item
A specific version of a product that can be designated as a distinct offering among an organization's products.

EXHIBIT 10.2

Campbell's Product Lines and Product Mix

Depth of the Product Lines	Width of the Product Mix				
	Canned Soups	Microwave Soups	Gravies	Meal Kits	Tomato Juice
	Chicken Noodle	Creamy Tomato	Beef	Chicken Pasta	Regular
	Tomato	Vegetable	Turkey	Stroganoff Pasta	Low Sodium
	Vegetable Beef	Chicken Noodle	Mushroom	Chicken With Rice	Organic
	French Onion	Creamy Chicken	Chicken	Pork Chops With Stuffing	Healthy Request
	More	More	More	More	

Source: Campbell's Web site: http://www.campbellsoup.com, June 10, 2008.

product line
A group of closely related product items.

product mix
All products that an organization sells.

product mix width
The number of product lines an organization offers.

product line depth
The number of product items in a product line.

A group of closely related product items is a product line. For example, the column in Exhibit 10.2 titled "Canned Soups" and "Microwave Soups" represents one of Campbell's product lines. Different container sizes and shapes also distinguish items in a product line. Diet Coke, for example, is available in cans and various plastic containers. Each size and each container are separate product items.

An organization's product mix includes all the products it sells. Together, all of Campbell's products—canned soups, microwave soups, gravies, meal kits, and tomato juice—constitute its product mix. Each product item in the product mix may require a separate marketing strategy. In some cases, however, product lines and even entire product mixes share some marketing strategy components. Nike promotes all of its product items and lines with the theme "Just Do It."

Organizations derive several benefits from organizing related items into product lines, including the following:

☛ *Advertising economies:* Product lines provide economies of scale in advertising. Several products can be advertised under the umbrella of the line. Campbell's can talk about its soup being "Mm! Mm! Good!" and promote the entire line.

☛ *Package uniformity:* A product line can benefit from package uniformity. All packages in the line may have a common look and still keep their individual identities. Again, Campbell's soup is a good example.

☛ *Standardized components:* Product lines allow firms to standardize components, thus reducing manufacturing and inventory costs. For example, many of the components Samsonite uses in its folding tables and chairs are also used in its patio furniture. General Motors uses the same parts on many automobile makes and models.

☛ *Efficient sales and distribution:* A product line enables sales personnel for companies like Procter & Gamble to provide a full range of choices to customers. Distributors and retailers are often more inclined to stock the company's products if it offers a full line. Transportation and warehousing costs are likely to be lower for a product line than for a collection of individual items.

☛ *Equivalent quality:* Purchasers usually expect and believe that all products in a line are about equal in quality. Consumers expect that all Campbell's soups and all Mary Kay cosmetics will be of similar quality.

Product mix width (or breadth) refers to the number of product lines an organization offers. In Exhibit 10.2, the width of Campbell's product mix is five product lines. Product line depth is the number of product items in a product line. As shown in Exhibit 10.2, the Tomato Juice product line consists of four product items; the Gravies product line includes more than four product items.

Firms increase the *width* of their product mix to diversify risk. To generate sales and boost profits, firms spread risk across many product lines rather than depend on only one or two. Firms also widen their product mix to capitalize on established reputations. The Oreo Cookie brand has been extended to include items such as breakfast cereal, ice cream, Jell-O pudding, and cake mix.

Firms increase the *depth* of their product lines to attract buyers with different preferences, to increase sales and profits by further segmenting the market, to capitalize on economies of scale in production and marketing, and to even out seasonal sales patterns. Coca-Cola and PepsiCo are introducing soft drinks in the United States using the natural, plant-based sweetener stevia. These companies are targeting consumers looking for healthier sweetener alternatives.[4] As another example, Oreo Cookies now come in a variety of flavors, including Double Delight Mint Creme, Chocolate Creme, Uh-Oh Oreos (vanilla cookie, chocolate filling), Double Delight Peanut Butter, and Chocolate Fudge Sundae Creme.

Adjustments to Product Items, Lines, and Mixes

Over time, firms change product items, lines, and mixes to take advantage of new technical or product developments or to respond to changes in the environment. They may adjust by modifying products, repositioning products, or extending or contracting product lines.

Product Modification Marketing managers must decide if and when to modify existing products. Product modification changes one or more of a product's characteristics:

☛ *Quality modification*: change in a product's dependability or durability. Reducing a product's quality may let the manufacturer lower the price and appeal to target markets unable to afford the original product. Conversely, increasing quality can help the firm compete with rival firms. Increasing quality can also result in increased brand loyalty, greater ability to raise prices, or new opportunities for market segmentation. Inexpensive ink-jet printers have improved in quality to the point that they produce photo-quality images. These printers are now competing with camera film. To appeal to a more upscale market, Robert Mondavi Winery introduced a high-end wine called Twin Oaks to prestigious restaurants and hotels. This wine is positioned as a higher-quality wine than the one Mondavi sells in supermarkets.

☛ *Functional modification*: change in a product's versatility, effectiveness, convenience, or safety. Tide with Downy combines the functions of cleaning power and fabric softening into one product. Lea & Perrins offers its steak sauce in a value-priced squeeze bottle with a "no mess, stay clean" cap.

☛ *Style modification*: aesthetic product change, rather than a quality or functional change. Procter & Gamble has added Febreze scents to its Tide liquid laundry detergent, Downy liquid fabric softener, and Bounce dryer sheets. These products all promise their usual function, with a touch of scent to improve the aesthetics of each brand.[5] Clothing and auto manufacturers also commonly use style modifications to motivate customers to replace products before they are worn out. Planned obsolescence is a term commonly used to describe the practice of modifying products so that those that have already been sold become obsolete before they actually need replacement. For example, products such as printers and cell phones become obsolete because technology changes so quickly. Some argue that planned obsolescence is wasteful; some claim it is unethical. Marketers respond that consumers favor style modifications because they like changes in the appearance of goods such as clothing and cars. Marketers also contend that consumers, not manufacturers and marketers, decide when styles are obsolete.

Repositioning Repositioning, as Chapter 8 explained, involves changing consumers' perceptions of a brand. Kool-Aid, the soft drink brand that has stood for fun and refreshment for many years, is adding better-for-you options by introducing new and

product modification
Changing one or more of a product's characteristics.

planned obsolescence
The practice of modifying products so those that have already been sold become obsolete before they actually need replacement.

© VICKI BEAVER

reformulated products. They are repositioning the brand as supporting a healthier family lifestyle.[6]

Changing demographics, declining sales, or changes in the social environment often motivate firms to reposition established brands. The clothing retailer Banana Republic started out selling safari-style clothing, but the concept soon became outdated. Gap acquired the chain and repositioned it as a more upscale retailer offering business casual clothing. Procter & Gamble is redesigning its Dawn liquid detergent line, including adding new products, sizes and graphics. For example, its Dawn Plus line will be positioned as a tough cleaning brand, reformulated with an added enzyme to fight stuck-on foods.[7]

Product Line Extensions A product line extension occurs when a company's management decides to add products to an existing product line in order to compete more broadly in the industry. Procter & Gamble extended its Febreze odor freshener line with Febreze to Go aimed at travelers.[8] Kraft extended a number of its popular Nabisco brands by adding small-portioned packages. Campbell's offers its soups in cans and in microwavable containers and its sells its Swanson Broth in "chef" size cartons for serious cooks and 16 ounce packages for simple side dishes.[9]

Product Line Contraction Does the world really need 31 varieties of Head and Shoulders shampoo? Or 52 versions of Crest? Or numerous brands of apparel? When Steve Jobs took over Apple, the company sold over 40 products. He immediately simplified by cutting the product line down to four computers—two desktop and two laptops that Apple could focus on perfecting. This move helped Apple double its market share.[10] Symptoms of product line overextension include the following:

☞ Some products in the line do not contribute to profits because of low sales or because they cannibalize sales of other items in the line.

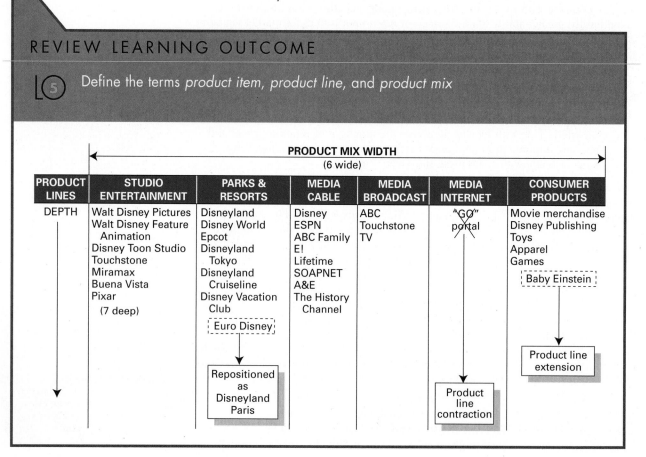

- Manufacturing or marketing resources are disproportionately allocated to slow-moving products.
- Some items in the line are obsolete because of new product entries in the line or new products offered by competitors.

Three major benefits are likely when a firm contracts its overextended product lines. First, resources become concentrated on the most important products. Second, managers no longer waste resources trying to improve the sales and profits of poorly performing products. Third, new product items have a greater chance of being successful because more financial and human resources are available to manage them.

BRANDING

The success of any business or consumer product depends in part on the target market's ability to distinguish one product from another. Branding is the main tool marketers use to distinguish their products from the competition's.

A brand is a name, term, symbol, design, or combination thereof that identifies a seller's products and differentiates them from competitors' products. A brand name is that part of a brand that can be spoken, including letters (GM, YMCA), words (Chevrolet), and numbers (WD-40, 7-Eleven). The elements of a brand that cannot be spoken are called the brand mark—for example, the well-known Mercedes-Benz and Delta Air Lines symbols.

> " *Brand identity is essential to developing brand loyalty.* "

Benefits of Branding

Branding has three main purposes: product identification, repeat sales, and new-product sales. The most important purpose is *product identification*. Branding allows marketers to distinguish their products from all others. Many brand names are familiar to consumers and indicate quality.

The term brand equity refers to the value of company and brand names. A brand that has high awareness, perceived quality, and brand loyalty among customers has high brand equity. Starbucks, Volvo, and Dell are companies with high brand equity. A brand with strong brand equity is a valuable asset.

The term global brand refers to a brand that obtains at least a third of its earnings from outside its home country, is recognizable outside its home base of customers, and has publicly available marketing and financial data.[11] Exhibit 10.3 lists the top ten global brands. Although it's not on the top of this year's list, Yum! Brands, which owns Pizza Hut, KFC, and Taco Bell, is a good example of a company that has developed strong global brands. Yum believes that it has to adapt its restaurants to local tastes and different cultural and political climates. In Japan, for instance, KFC sells tempura crispy strips. In northern England, KFC focuses on gravy and potatoes, and in Thailand it offers rice with soy or sweet chili sauce.

The best generator of *repeat sales* is satisfied customers. Branding helps consumers identify products they wish to buy again and avoid those they do not. Brand loyalty, a consistent preference for one brand over all others, is quite high in some product categories. Over half the users in product categories such as cigarettes, mayonnaise, toothpaste, coffee, headache remedies, photographic film, bath soap, and ketchup are loyal to one brand. Many students come to college and purchase the same brands they used at home, rather than being "price" buyers. Brand identity is essential to developing brand loyalty.

The third main purpose of branding is to *facilitate new-product sales*. Company and brand names like those listed in Exhibit 10.3 are extremely useful when introducing new products.

The Internet provides firms with a new alternative for generating brand awareness, promoting a desired brand image, stimulating new and repeat brand sales, enhancing

:-
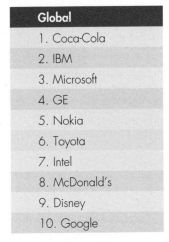

EXHIBIT 10.3

The Top Ten Global Brands

Global
1. Coca-Cola
2. IBM
3. Microsoft
4. GE
5. Nokia
6. Toyota
7. Intel
8. McDonald's
9. Disney
10. Google

Source: Reprinted from the September 29, 2008, issue of *Business Week* by special permission, copyright © 2007 by The McGraw-Hill Companies, Inc.

product line extension
Adding additional products to an existing product line in order to compete more broadly in the industry.

brand
A name, term, symbol, design, or combination thereof that identifies a seller's products and differentiates them from competitors' products.

brand name
That part of a brand that can be spoken, including letters, words, and numbers.

brand mark
The elements of a brand that cannot be spoken.

brand equity
The value of company and brand names.

global brand
A brand where at least one-third of the product is sold outside its home country or region.

brand loyalty
A consistent preference for one brand over all others.

EXHIBIT 10.4

Major Branding Decisions

© MEDIABLITZIMAGES (UK) LIMITED/ALAMY

manufacturer's brand
The brand name of a manufacturer.

private brand
A brand name owned by a wholesaler or a retailer.

captive brand
A brand that carries no evidence of a retailer's affiliation, is manufactured by a third party, and is sold exclusively at the retailer.

brand loyalty, and building brand equity. Nearly all packaged-goods firms have a presence online. Tide.com offers a useful feature called Stain Detective, a digital tip sheet on how to remove almost any substance from almost any fabric.

Branding Strategies

Firms face complex branding decisions. As Exhibit 10.4 illustrates, firms may choose to follow a policy of using manufacturers' brands, private (distributor) brands, or both. In either case, they must then decide among a policy of individual branding (different brands for different products), family branding (common names for different products), or a combination of individual branding and family branding.

Manufacturers' Brands versus Private Brands The brand name of a manufacturer—such as Kodak, La-Z-Boy, and Fruit of the Loom—is called a manufacturer's brand. Sometimes "national brand" is used as a synonym for "manufacturer's brand." This term is not always accurate, however, because many manufacturers serve only regional markets. Using "manufacturer's brand" more precisely defines the brand's owner.

A private brand, also known as a private label or store brand, is a brand name owned by a wholesaler or a retailer. Private brands include Wal-Mart's Ol' Roy dog food, which has surpassed Nestlé's Purina as the world's top-selling dog food, and the George line of apparel, which has knocked Liz Claiborne's clothing out of Wal-Mart. A survey conducted for the Private Manufacturers' Label Association found that 41 percent of shoppers identify themselves as frequent buyers of store brands, and 7 out of 10 feel the private-label products they buy are as good as, if not better than, their national brand counterparts.[12]

Retailers love consumers' greater acceptance of private brands. Because overhead is low and there are no marketing costs, private-label products bring 10 percent higher margins, on average, than manufacturers' brands. More than that, a trusted store brand can differentiate a chain from its competitors. For example, many shoppers will drive the extra mile to Costco, a wholesale club, to buy the store's Kirkland brands and will also buy other goods while they are there. Costco has recently introduced a Kirkland Signature brand of wines that compete at the premium and super premium price categories.[13] Exhibit 10.5 illustrates key issues that wholesalers and retailers should consider in deciding whether to sell manufacturers' brands or private brands. Many firms offer a combination of both. Instead of marketing private brands as cheaper, and inferior to manufacturer's brands, many retailers are creating and promoting their own captive brands. These brands carry no evidence of the store's affiliation, are manufactured by a third party and are sold exclusively at the chains. This strategy allows the retailer to ask a price similar to manufacturer's brands, and they are typically displayed alongside marketed mainstream products. For example, bioInfusion, a line of hair-care products

EXHIBIT 10.5

Comparing Manufacturers' and Private Brands from the Reseller's Perspective

Key Advantages of Carrying Manufacturers' Brands	Key Advantages of Carrying Private Brands
• Heavy advertising to the consumer by manufacturers like Procter & Gamble helps develop strong consumer loyalties.	• A wholesaler or retailer can usually earn higher profits on its own brand. In addition, because the private brand is exclusive, there is less pressure to mark the price down to meet competition.
• Well-known manufacturers' brands, such as Kodak and Fisher-Price, can attract new customers and enhance the dealer's (wholesaler's or retailer's) prestige.	• A manufacturer can decide to drop a brand or a reseller at any time or even to become a direct competitor to its dealers.
• Many manufacturers offer rapid delivery, enabling the dealer to carry less inventory.	• A private brand ties the customer to the wholesaler or retailer. A person who wants a DieHard battery must go to Sears.
• If a dealer happens to sell a manufacturer's brand of poor quality, the customer may simply switch brands and remain loyal to the dealer.	• Wholesalers and retailers have no control over the intensity of distribution of manufacturers' brands. Wal-Mart store managers don't have to worry about competing with other sellers of Sam's American Choice products or Ol' Roy dog food. They know that these brands are sold only in Wal-Mart and Sam's Wholesale Club stores.

available only at Walgreens, has grown to become one of the top brands in the entire hair care category.[14]

Individual Brands versus Family Brands Many companies use different brand names for different products, a practice referred to as individual branding. Companies use individual brands when their products vary greatly in use or performance. For instance, it would not make sense to use the same brand name for a pair of dress socks and a baseball bat. Procter & Gamble targets different segments of the laundry detergent market with Bold, Cheer, Dash, Dreft, Era, Gain, Ivory Snow, and Tide. Marriott International also targets different market segments with Courtyard by Marriott, Residence Inn, and Fairfield Inn.

In contrast, a company that markets several different products under the same brand name is using a family brand. Sony's family brand includes radios, television sets, stereos, and other electronic products. The Heinz brand name is attached to products such as ketchup, mustard, and pickles.

This image, featuring both Nike and Apple products, illustrates an example of cobranding. Cobranding is a useful strategy when a combination of brand names enhances the prestige or perceived value of a product.

© AP IMAGES/MARY ALTAFFER

Cobranding Cobranding entails placing two or more brand names on a product or its package. Three common types of cobranding are ingredient branding, cooperative branding, and complementary branding. *Ingredient branding* identifies the brand of a part that makes up the product. Examples of ingredient branding are Intel (a microprocessor) in a personal computer, such as Dell, or a satellite system (OnStar) in an automobile (Cadillac). Procter & Gamble has developed Mr. Clean Disinfecting Wipes with Febreze Freshness. Febreze is also cobranded with Tide, Bounce, and Downy.[15] *Cooperative branding* occurs when two brands receiving equal treatment (in the context of an advertisement) borrow from each other's brand equity. A promotional contest jointly sponsored by Ramada Inns, American Express, and Continental Airlines is an example of cooperative branding. Guests at Ramada who paid with an American Express card were automatically entered in the contest and were eligible to win more than a hundred getaways for two at any Ramada in the continental United States and round-trip airfare from Continental. Finally, with *complementary branding*, products are advertised or marketed together to suggest usage, such as a spirits brand (Seagram's) and a compatible mixer (7-Up). A partnership between Ann Taylor Loft women's clothing stores and Procter & Gamble will promote the use of Tide Total Care and Downy Total Care to clean clothing and cut down on dry cleaning bills. The store will give free samples and

individual branding
Using different brand names for different products.

family brand
Marketing several different products under the same brand name.

cobranding
Placing two or more brand names on a product or its package.

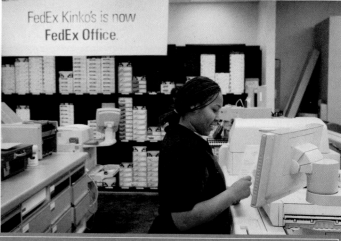

When FedEx purchased Kinko's in 2004, it merged the company's brand names to make one brand entity in the mind of the consumer. In late 2008, having successfully cobranded a shipping business and a copy/print/data center business, the company renamed the brand "FedEx Office."

coupons to customers who buy machine washable clothes, and posters and decals placed in the stores will call attention to the product's benefits.[16]

Cobranding is a useful strategy when a combination of brand names enhances the prestige or perceived value of a product, or when it benefits brand owners and users. When Intel launched its Centrino wireless processor, it established cobranding relationships with T-Mobile and hotel chains Marriott International and Westin Hotels & Resorts because there was mutual value in establishing these relationships.

CUSTOMER Experience

World of Coca-Cola Museum

The Coca-Cola Company has created a unique venue through which consumers can experience its brands. This venue is the World of Coca-Cola Museum in Atlanta, Georgia, opened in May 2007 on a 20-acre complex called Pemberton Place (named after John Pemberton, the inventor of Coca-Cola). The attraction has 92,000 square feet, with 60,000 feet of guest areas, and attracts 1.5 million visitors a year. More than 1,200 Coca-Cola artifacts from around the world are displayed along with a number of interactive exhibits such as a 4-D movie and a gallery dedicated to Coke and pop culture. Guests pay a fee to get in the museum, and average estimated visit time is 90 minutes.

The outside of the building features a bottle sculpture with lighted streams of red and white color. Guests entering "The Lobby" see large Coca-Cola bottles manufactured from materials obtained from around the world. They then go into "The Coca-Cola Loft," which has a collection of Coca-Cola advertising artifacts from as far back as 1905. Next is the "Happiness Factory Theatre," where guests view *Inside the Happiness Factory: A Documentary*, a mock documentary that shows characters of the Happiness Factory, a central focus of the brand's current advertising campaign, "The Coke Side of Life." After the video,

"The Hub" is revealed, from which guests can visit various attractions in whatever order they choose.

Attractions include posing for a picture with the Coca-Cola mascot, the Coca-Cola Polar Bear. They can listen to stories about the company's influence in the world. The "Milestones of Refreshment" attraction presents artifacts from Coca-Cola's branding efforts. For example, one item on display is a packing slip from 1888 that shows Coca-Cola U.S. sales figures. The "Bottle Works" gives visitors a tour of a fully functioning bottling line, which makes 8-ounce bottles of Coca-Cola Classic that can be received at the end of the tour. Coca-Cola's advertising campaigns are featured in three short films in the "Perfect Pauses Theater." A museum favorite is the tasting experience that provides visitors with an opportunity to sample nearly 60 different products from around the world. And the last stop is the Coca-Cola store, which offers thousands of Coca-Cola–themed products for sale. As trends and advertising campaigns change over time, the museum will update its attractions.[17]

Why do you think people visit (and pay a fee to get in) the World of Coca-Cola Museum? How does the museum support the Coca-Cola brand? Can you think of other brands that could benefit from a similar experiential attraction?

T-Mobile was able to set up global "hot spots" to reach Intel's target market of mobile professionals, while the hotel chains enabled Intel to target business professionals.

Cobranding may be used to increase a company's presence in markets where it has little or no market share. For example, Coach was able to build a presence in a whole new category when its leather upholstery with logo was used in Lexus automobiles. European firms have been slower to adopt cobranding than U.S. firms have. One reason is that European customers seem to be more skeptical than U.S. customers about trying new brands. European retailers also typically have less shelf space than their U.S. counterparts and are less willing to give new brands a try.

Trademarks

A trademark is the exclusive right to use a brand or part of a brand. Others are prohibited from using the brand without permission. A service mark performs the same function for services, such as H&R Block and Weight Watchers. Parts of a brand or other product identification may qualify for trademark protection. Some examples are

- ☞ Shapes, such as the Jeep front grille and the Coca-Cola bottle
- ☞ Ornamental color or design, such as the decoration on Nike tennis shoes, the black-and-copper color combination of a Duracell battery, Levi's tag on the left side of the rear pocket of its jeans, or the cutoff black cone on the top of Cross pens
- ☞ Catchy phrases, such as Prudential's "Own a piece of the rock," Mountain Dew's "Do the Dew," and Nike's "Just Do It"
- ☞ Abbreviations, such as Bud, Coke, or The Met
- ☞ Sounds, such as General Electric Broadcasting Company's ship's bell clock sound and the MGM lion's roar

It is important to understand that trademark rights come from use rather than registration. A company must have a genuine intention to use a trademark when it files an intent-to-use application with the U.S. Patent and Trademark Office and must actually use the mark within three years of the application being granted. Trademark protection lasts for as long as the mark is being used.

In November 1999, legislation went into effect that explicitly applies trademark law to the online world. This law includes financial penalties for those who violate trademarked products or register an otherwise trademarked term as a domain name.

Companies that fail to protect their trademarks face the possibility that their product names will become generic. A generic product name identifies a product by class or type and cannot be trademarked. Former brand names that were not sufficiently protected by their owners and were subsequently declared to be generic product names by U.S. courts include aspirin, cellophane, linoleum, thermos, kerosene, monopoly, cola, and shredded wheat.

Companies like Rolls-Royce, Cross, Xerox, Levi Strauss, Frigidaire, and McDonald's aggressively enforce their trademarks. Rolls-Royce, Coca-Cola, and Xerox even run newspaper and magazine ads stating that their names are trademarks and should not be used as descriptive or generic terms. Some ads threaten lawsuits against competitors that violate trademarks.

Despite severe penalties for trademark violations, trademark infringement lawsuits are not uncommon. One of the major battles is over brand names that closely resemble another brand name. The celebrity chef Wolfgang Puck filed a lawsuit against Wolfgang Zweiner when Zweiner opened Wolfgang's Steakhouse and confused fans began calling to make reservations at what they thought was the new Puck restaurant.[18]

Companies must also contend with fake or unauthorized brands, such as fake Levi's jeans, Microsoft software, Rolex watches, Reebok and Nike footwear, and Louis Vuitton handbags. Hasbro sued the makers of the online game Scrabulous, an obvious copy of Scrabble, including the rules, game pieces, and board colors, for copyright infringement on its Scrabble game.[19]

trademark
The exclusive right to use a brand or part of a brand.

service mark
A trademark for a service.

generic product name
Identifies a product by class or type and cannot be trademarked.

L◯6 Describe marketing uses of branding

Brand name: MGM

Brand mark:

©AP IMAGES PRNEWSFOTO/METRO-GOLDWYN-MAYER INC.

BRANDING

Benefits	Strategies
Brand equity (from product identfication)	Generic Brand Trademark — Manufacturer — Individual / Family / Combination — Private
Brand loyalty (from repeat sales)	
Brand recognition (to generate new product sales)	

In Europe, you can sue counterfeiters only if your brand, logo, or trademark is formally registered. Until recently, formal registration was required in each country in which a company sought protection. A company can now register its trademark in all European Union (EU) member countries with one application.

L◯7 PACKAGING

Packages have always served a practical function—that is, they hold contents together and protect goods as they move through the distribution channel. Today, however, packaging is also a container for promoting the product and making it easier and safer to use.

Packaging Functions

The three most important functions of packaging are to contain and protect products, promote products, and facilitate the storage, use, and convenience of products. A fourth function of packaging that is becoming increasingly important is to facilitate recycling and reduce environmental damage.

Containing and Protecting Products The most obvious function of packaging is to contain products that are liquid, granular, or otherwise divisible. Packaging also enables manufacturers, wholesalers, and retailers to market products in specific quantities, such as ounces.

Physical protection is another obvious function of packaging. Most products are handled several times between the time they are manufactured, harvested, or otherwise produced and the time they are consumed or used. Many products are shipped, stored, and inspected several times between production and consumption. Some, like milk, need to be refrigerated. Others, like beer, are sensitive to light. Still others, like medicines and bandages, need to be kept sterile. Packages protect products from breakage, evaporation, spillage, spoilage, light, heat, cold, infestation, and many other conditions.

Promoting Products Packaging does more than identify the brand, list the ingredients, specify features, and give directions. A package differentiates a product from competing products and may associate a new product with a family of other products from the same manufacturer. Welch's repackaged its line of grape juice–based jams, jellies, and juices to unify the line and get more impact on the shelf.

Packagers use designs, colors, shapes, and materials to try to influence consumers' perceptions and buying behavior. For example, marketing research shows that health-conscious consumers are likely

© AP IMAGES/ PRNEWSFOTO/AMERICAN DAIRY ASSOCIATION AND DAIRY COUNCIL, INC.

to think that any food is probably good for them as long as it comes in green packaging. Two top brands of low-fat foods—SnackWell's and Healthy Choice—use green packaging. Packaging can also influence consumers' perceptions of quality and/or prestige. Pennzoil redesigned its recognizable but dated package using a different color and engine part to convey a clean engine. Their focus group data told them that the only part that would be descriptive was the piston with a spot of white with shards of light coming from the part to portray cleanliness.[20] Packaging has a measurable effect on sales. Quaker Oats revised the package for Rice-A-Roni without making any other changes in marketing strategy and experienced a 44 percent increase in sales in one year.

Facilitating Storage, Use, and Convenience Wholesalers and retailers prefer packages that are easy to ship, store, and stock on shelves. They also like packages that protect products, prevent spoilage or breakage, and extend the product's shelf life.

Consumers' requirements for storage, use, and convenience cover many dimensions. Consumers are constantly seeking items that are easy to handle, open, and reclose, although some consumers want packages that are tamperproof or childproof. Research indicates that hard-to-open packages are among consumers' top complaints. Surveys conducted by *Sales & Marketing Management* magazine revealed that consumers dislike—and avoid buying—leaky ice cream boxes, overly heavy or fat vinegar bottles, immovable pry-up lids on glass bottles, key-opener sardine cans, and hard-to-pour cereal boxes. Such packaging innovations as zipper tear strips, hinged lids, tab slots, screw-on tops, and pour spouts were introduced to solve these and other problems. Nestlé improved all its packaging to make it easier for people to rip open its pouches, twist off its caps, and reseal its tubs. Easy openings are especially important for kids and aging baby boomers. The company's package designers spent nine months developing a plastic lid for ice cream that is easier to pull off when the ice cream is frozen and ribbed corners for ice cream cartons that are easier to grip when scooping.[21]

Some firms use packaging to segment markets. For example, a C&H sugar carton with an easy-to-pour, reclosable top is targeted to consumers who don't do a lot of baking and are willing to pay at least 20 cents more for the package. Different-size packages appeal to heavy, moderate, and light users. Salt is sold in package sizes ranging from single serving to picnic size to giant economy size. Campbell's soup is packaged in single-serving cans aimed at the elderly and singles market segments. Beer and soft drinks are similarly marketed in various package sizes and types. Packaging convenience can increase a product's utility and, therefore, its market share and profits. To appeal to women, Dutch Boy designed a square plastic paint container with a side handle and a spout to replace the traditional wire-handled round metal paint can. The Internet will soon give consumers more packaging options. Indeed, the Internet may significantly change the purpose and appearance of packaging. Packaging for products sold on the Internet will be more under the customer's control and will be customized by consumers to fit their needs. Some designers are already offering to personalize, for a fee, packages such as wine bottle labels.

Facilitating Recycling and Reducing Environmental Damage One of the most important packaging issues today is compatibility with the environment. In a recent study of consumers, a majority said they would give up the following conveniences if it would benefit the environment: packaging designed for easy stacking/storing, packaging that can be used for cooking, and packaging designed for easy transport.[22] Some firms use their packaging to target environmentally concerned market segments. The French winery, Boisset Family Estates, recently introduced TetraPak cartons of its French Rabbit chardonnay to offer consumers a playful and eco-friendly alternative to glass bottles. When the cartons sold well, other companies followed suit.[23] Dell has plans to cut by 10 percent the amount of materials used in its laptop and desktop packaging worldwide by 2012.[24] Groups like the Sustainable Packaging Coalition assist companies in creating perpetually recycled packaging so that materials don't ever end up in landfills, damaging the ecosystem.[25]

Greenwashing

There is a strong interest today in environmental awareness. More and more, consumers are supporting companies that provide environmentally friendly, or "green," products. Consequently, more companies are engaging in green marketing, claiming that their products are manufactured in a way that does not harm the environment. Some of this green marketing, critics claim, is actually greenwash.

Greenwash is a term used to describe the practice of companies stretching the truth when they promote their products as being environmentally friendly. Often, customers are misled into thinking an aspect of the product is good for the environment when in reality it is only a cost-cutting method for the company. For example, a company may insist that people use less toilet paper in order to save trees, when in reality the company does not want to buy as much toilet paper. The term is typically used when more time and money has been spent advertising being green (i.e., operating with consideration for the environment) than has been spending resources on environmentally sound practices.

Research conducted by TerraChoice Environmental Marketing surveyed six category-leading big box stores and that included over 1,000 consumer products having 1,753 environmental claims. Their results showed that 99 percent of green claims were either not true or misleading. For example, more than half of the eco-labels on today's products promote a small eco-friendly quality, such as recycled content, without mentioning more significant environmental drawbacks such as manufacturing intensity or travel costs. The study report identified the following "Six Sins of Greenwashing":

1. Sin of the Hidden Trade-off: for example, "energy efficient" electronics that contain hazardous materials.

2. Sin of No Proof: for example, shampoos claiming to be "certified organic," but without verifiable certification.

3. Sin of Vagueness: for example, products claiming to be 100% natural when many naturally occurring substances are hazardous (e.g., arsenic or formaldehyde).

4. Sin of Irrelevance: for example, products claiming to be CFC-free, even though CFCs were banned 20 years ago.

5. Sin of Fibbing: for example, products falsely claiming to be certified by an internationally recognized environmental standard, like Energy Star.

6. Sin of Lesser of Two Evils: For example, organic cigarettes or "environmentally friendly" pesticides.

EcoLogo is a government ecolabeling program that has been accredited by the Global Ecolabelling Network, an international association of ecolabeling programs, as meeting certain environmental marketing standards. The program provides a marketing incentive to manufacturers and suppliers of environmentally preferable products and services in more than 120 product categories. EcoLogo provides an insignia that helps consumers know that an independent, credible, and expert third party has verified a product's green qualifications.[27]

Do you think greenwashing is an unethical practice? Defend your answer.

Labeling

An integral part of any package is its label. Labeling generally takes one of two forms: persuasive or informational. Persuasive labeling focuses on a promotional theme or logo, and consumer information is secondary. Procter & Gamble put real photography on its new Downy fabric softener labels in order to make a more personal connection with consumers. Note that the standard promotional claims—such as "new," "improved," and "super"—are no longer very persuasive. Consumers have been saturated with "newness" and thus discount these claims.

Informational labeling, in contrast, is designed to help consumers make proper product selections and lower their cognitive dissonance after the purchase. Sears attaches a "label of confidence" to all its floor coverings. This label gives such product information as durability, color, features, cleanability, care instructions, and construction standards. Most major furniture manufacturers affix labels to their wares that explain the products' construction features, such as type of frame, number of coils, and fabric characteristics. The Nutritional Labeling and Education Act of 1990 mandated detailed nutritional information be placed on most food packages and standards for health claims on food packaging. An important outcome of this legislation has been guidelines from the Food and Drug Administration for using terms like *low fat, light, reduced cholesterol, low sodium, low calorie,* and *fresh.* Getting the right information is very important to consumers—so much so that almost 75 percent said they would be willing to pay extra, for example, to have products display country of origin information.[26]

Universal Product Codes

The universal product codes (UPCs) that appear on most items in supermarkets and other high-volume outlets were first introduced in 1974. Because the numerical codes appear as a series of thick and thin vertical lines, they are often called *bar codes.* The lines are read by computerized optical scanners that match codes with brand names, package sizes, and prices. They also print information on cash register tapes and help retailers rapidly and accurately prepare records of customer purchases, control inventories, and track sales. The UPC (bar code) system and scanners are also used in single-source research (see Chapter 9).

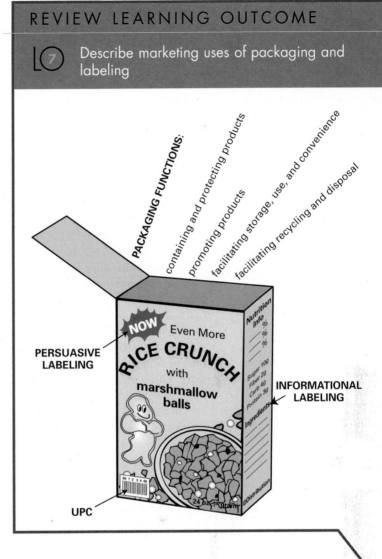

REVIEW LEARNING OUTCOME

LO 7 Describe marketing uses of packaging and labeling

PACKAGING FUNCTIONS:
- containing and protecting products
- promoting products
- facilitating storage, use, and convenience
- facilitating recycling and disposal

PERSUASIVE LABELING

INFORMATIONAL LABELING

UPC

LO 8
GLOBAL ISSUES IN BRANDING AND PACKAGING

International marketers must address several concerns regarding branding and packaging.

Branding

When planning to enter a foreign market with an existing product, a firm has three options for handling the brand name:

- *One brand name everywhere:* This strategy is useful when the company markets mainly one product and the brand name does not have negative connotations in any local market. The Coca-Cola Company uses a one-brand-name strategy in 195 countries around the world. The advantages of a one-brand-name strategy are greater identification of the product from market to market and ease of coordinating promotion from market to market.

- *Adaptations and modifications:* A one-brand-name strategy is not possible when the name cannot be pronounced in the local language, when the brand name is owned by someone else, or when the brand name has a negative or vulgar connotation in the local language. The Iranian detergent "Barf," for example, might encounter some problems in the U.S. market.

persuasive labeling
A type of package labeling that focuses on a promotional theme or logo with consumer information being secondary.

informational labeling
A type of package labeling designed to help consumers make proper product selections and lower their cognitive dissonance after the purchase.

universal product codes (UPCs)
A series of thick and thin vertical lines (bar codes), readable by computerized optical scanners, that represent numbers used to track products.

warranty
A confirmation of the quality or performance of a good or service.

express warranty
A written guarantee.

☛ *Different brand names in different markets:* Local brand names are often used when translation or pronunciation problems occur, when the marketer wants the brand to appear to be a local brand, or when regulations require localization. Gillette's Silkience hair conditioner is called Soyance in France and Sientel in Italy. Coca-Cola's Sprite brand had to be renamed Kin in South Korea to satisfy a government prohibition on the unnecessary use of foreign words. Because of the feminine connotations of the word *diet*, the European version of Diet Coke is Coca-Cola Light.

Packaging

Three aspects of packaging that are especially important in international marketing are labeling, aesthetics, and climate considerations. The major *labeling* concern is properly translating ingredient, promotional, and instructional information on labels. In Eastern Europe, packages of Ariel detergent are printed in 14 languages, from Latvian to Lithuanian. Care must also be employed in meeting all local labeling requirements. Several years ago, an Italian judge ordered that all bottles of Coca-Cola be removed from retail shelves because the ingredients were not properly labeled. Labeling is also harder in countries like Belgium and Finland, which require it to be bilingual.

Package *aesthetics* may also require some attention. The key is to stay attuned to cultural traits in host countries. For example, colors may have different connotations. Red is associated with witchcraft in some countries, green may be a sign of danger, and white may be symbolic of death. Aesthetics also influence package size. Soft drinks are not sold in six-packs in countries that lack refrigeration. In some countries, products such as detergent may be bought only in small quantities because of a lack of storage space. Other products, like cigarettes, may be bought in small quantities, and even single units, because of the low purchasing power of buyers.

On the other hand, simple visual elements of the brand, such as a symbol or logo, can be a standardizing element across products and countries. For example, in Mexico, Lay's potato chips are known as Sabritas, but the packaging carries the same brand mark and graphic elements as in the United States. Extreme *climates* and long-distance shipping necessitate sturdier and more durable packages for goods sold overseas. Spillage, spoilage, and breakage are all more important concerns when products are shipped long distances or frequently handled during shipping and storage. Packages may also have to ensure a longer product life if the time between production and consumption lengthens significantly.

REVIEW LEARNING OUTCOME

LO8 Discuss global issues in branding and packaging

	Branding choices:	Packaging considerations:
	One name	Labeling
	Modify or adapt one name	Aesthetics
	Different names in different markets	Climate

LO9
PRODUCT WARRANTIES

Just as a package is designed to protect the product, a warranty protects the buyer and gives essential information about the product. A warranty confirms the quality or performance of a good or service. An express warranty is a written guarantee. Express warranties range from simple statements—such as "100 percent cotton" (a guarantee of quality) and "complete satisfaction guaranteed" (a statement of performance)—to extensive documents written in technical language. In contrast, an implied warranty is an unwritten guarantee that the good or service is fit for the purpose for which it was sold. All sales have an implied warranty under the Uniform Commercial Code.

Congress passed the Magnuson-Moss Warranty–Federal Trade Commission Improvement Act in 1975 to help consumers understand warranties and get action from manufacturers and dealers. A manufacturer that promises a full warranty must meet certain minimum standards, including repair "within a reasonable time and without charge" of any defects and replacement of the merchandise or a full refund if the product does not work "after a reasonable number of attempts" at repair. Any warranty that does not live up to this tough prescription must be "conspicuously" promoted as a limited warranty.

REVIEW LEARNING OUTCOME

 LO9   Describe how and why product warranties are important marketing tools

Express warranty = written guarantee
Implied warranty = unwritten guarantee

implied warranty
An unwritten guarantee that the good or service is fit for the purpose for which it was sold.

3 years within which a company must use a trademark once it has been granted ▶

categories of consumer products ▶ **4**

41 ◀ percentage of shoppers who frequently buy store brands

Mattel updated Barbie's packaging to keep her fresh and familiar.

1 Familiar brand mark

2 Heat- and impact-tested packaging protects Barbie from damage.

3 Die cuts keep Barbie from shifting.

4 Plastic staples facilitate easy removal.

5 Persuasive labeling—"easy for me"—assures parents their kids can open it themselves.

COURTESY OF CHAPEL HOUSE PHOTOGRAPHY

REVIEW AND APPLICATIONS

Define the term product. A product is anything, desired or not, that a person or organization receives in an exchange. The basic goal of purchasing decisions is to receive the tangible and intangible benefits associated with a product. Tangible aspects include packaging, style, color, size, and features. Intangible qualities include service, the retailer's image, the manufacturer's reputation, and the social status associated with a product. An organization's product offering is the crucial element in any marketing mix.

1.1   Form a team of four or five members. Have the team determine what the tangible and intangible benefits are for a computer, a tube of toothpaste, a beauty salon, and a dentist.

Classify consumer products. Consumer products are classified into four categories: convenience products, shopping products, specialty products, and unsought products. Convenience products are relatively inexpensive and require limited shopping effort. Shopping products are of two types: homogeneous and heterogeneous. Because of the similarity of homogeneous products, they are differentiated mainly by price and features. In contrast, heterogeneous products appeal to consumers because of their distinct characteristics. Specialty products possess unique benefits that are highly desirable to certain customers. Finally, unsought products are either new products or products that require aggressive selling because they are generally avoided or overlooked by consumers.

2.1   Break into groups of four or five. Have the members of the group classify each of the following products into the category (convenience, shopping, specialty, unsought) that they think fits best from their perspective as consumers (i.e., if they were buying the product): Coca-Cola (brand), car stereo, winter coat, pair of shoes, life insurance, blue jeans, fast-food hamburgers, shampoo, canned vegetables, curtains.

2.2   Although major appliances, like washers and dryers, are usually considered homogeneous shopping products, the high-efficiency front-loaders that boast many more features than standard machines are gaining in popularity. Do you think high-efficiency technology is enough to make washers and dryers heterogeneous shopping products? Explain.

Discuss the importance of services to the economy. The service sector plays a crucial role in the U.S. economy, employing more than 80 percent of the workforce and accounting for a similar percentage of the gross domestic product.

3.1   To keep track of how service employment is affecting the U.S. economy, go to **www.bls.gov/bdm/.** Look at the right sidebar, which gives the latest numbers for Business Employment Dynamics. What trends to you see? Do the numbers support the information from the chapter?

Discuss the differences between services and goods. Services are distinguished by four characteristics. Services are intangible performances in that they lack clearly identifiable physical characteristics, making it difficult for marketers to communicate their specific benefits to potential customers. The production and consumption of services occur simultaneously. Services are heterogeneous because their quality depends on such elements as the service provider, individual consumer, location, and so on. Finally, services are perishable in the sense that they cannot be stored or saved. As a result, synchronizing supply with demand is particularly challenging in the service industry.

4.1   Assume that you are a manager of a bank branch. Write a list of the implications of intangibility for your firm.

4.2 Over 25 years ago, Tim and Nina Zagat began publishing leisure guides containing reviews of restaurants. Today, the renowned *Zagat* guides still contain reviews of restaurants, but they also rate hotels, entertainment, night-life, movies, shopping, and even music. Go to **www.zagat.com.**
In your opinion, are *Zagat* survey guides goods or services? Explain your reasoning.

Define the terms *product item, product line,* and *product mix.* A product item is a specific version of a product that can be designated as a distinct offering among an organization's products. A product line is a group of closely related products offered by an organization. An organization's product mix includes all the products it sells. Product mix width refers to the number of product lines an organization offers. Product line depth is the number of product items in a product line. Firms modify existing products by changing their quality, functional characteristics, or style. Product line extension occurs when a firm adds new products to existing product lines.

5.1 A local civic organization has asked you to give a luncheon presentation about planned obsolescence. Rather than pursuing a negative approach by talking about how businesses exploit customers through planned obsolescence, you have decided to talk about the benefits of producing products that do not last forever. Prepare a one-page outline of your presentation.

5.2 Go to Unilever's Web site at **www.unilever.com.** Can Unilever delete anything from its product lines? Visit the company's product category pages on its "Brands" Web page to see the number of existing products and new products planned. Write a proposal for contracting one of Unilever's product lines.

Describe marketing uses of branding. A brand is a name, term, or symbol that identifies and differentiates a firm's products. Established brands encourage customer loyalty and help new products succeed. Branding strategies require decisions about individual, family, manufacturers', and private brands.

6.1 A local supermarket would like to introduce its own brand of paper goods (e.g., paper towels, facial tissue, etc.) to sell alongside its current inventory. The company has hired you to generate a report outlining the advantages and disadvantages of doing so. Write the report.

6.2 How does Hormel use its Web site (**www.hormel.com**) to promote its store brands? Is the site designed more to promote the company or its brands? Check out the Spam Web site at **www.spam.com.** How do you think Hormel is able to successfully sustain this brand that is often the punch line to a joke?

Describe marketing uses of packaging and labeling. Packaging has four functions: containing and protecting products; promoting products; facilitating product storage, use, and convenience; and facilitating recycling and reducing environmental damage. As a tool for promotion, packaging identifies the brand and its features. It also serves the critical function of differentiating a product from competing products and linking it with related products from the same manufacturer. The label is an integral part of the package, with persuasive and informational functions. In essence, the package is the marketer's last chance to influence buyers before they make a purchase decision.

7.1 Find a product at home that has a distinctive package. Write a paragraph evaluating that package based on the four functions of packaging discussed in the chapter.

Discuss global issues in branding and packaging. In addition to brand piracy, international marketers must address a variety of concerns regarding branding and packaging, including choosing a brand-name policy, translating labels and meeting host-country labeling requirements, making packages aesthetically compatible with host-country cultures, and offering the sizes of packages preferred in host countries.

8.1 List the countries to which Levi Strauss & Co. markets through the Web site **www.levi.com.** How do the product offerings differ between the U.S. and European selections?

Describe how and why product warranties are important marketing tools. Product warranties are important tools because they offer consumers protection and help them gauge product quality.

9.1 Lands' End and L.L. Bean are renowned for their product guarantees. Find and read the exact wording of their guarantees on their Web sites (**www.landsend.com** and **www.llbean.com**). Do you think a company could successfully compete against either without offering the same guarantee?

KEY TERMS

brand	341	global brand	341	product line extension	340
brand equity	341	heterogeneity	337	product mix	338
brand loyalty	341	implied warranty	351	product mix width	338
brand mark	341	individual branding	343	product modification	339
brand name	341	informational labeling	348	search quality	336
business product (industrial		inseparability	336	service	335
product)	333	intangibility	336	service mark	345
captive brand	342	manufacturer's brand	342	shopping product	334
cobranding	343	perishability	337	specialty product	335
consumer product	333	persuasive labeling	348	trademark	345
convenience product	334	planned obsolescence	339	universal product code	
credence quality	336	private brand	342	(UPC; bar code)	349
experience quality	336	product	333	unsought product	335
express warranty	350	product item	337	warranty	350
family brand	343	product line	338		
generic product name	345	product line depth	338		

EXERCISES

APPLICATION EXERCISE

What is your favorite brand of sandwich cookie? If you're like most Americans, chances are it is Oreo. In fact, Oreos are so popular that many people think Oreo was the original sandwich cookie. But they're wrong. Sunshine first marketed its Hydrox sandwich cookie in 1908. Hydrox thrived until 1912, when Nabisco (now part of Kraft) launched Oreo. With Nabisco's superior distribution and advertising, Hydrox was soon outmatched. By 1998, Hydrox sales totaled $16 million, while Oreo's revenues were at $374 million. Hydrox has been purchased by Keebler, whose elves are trying to give the cookie a major facelift. You are part of the Keebler team deciding what to do with the Hydrox brand.

Activities

1. Can you re-create Hydrox through a name change? What kind of brand name could go head-to-head with Oreo? (Most people unfamiliar with Hydrox think it is a cleaning product.) Make a list of three to five possibilities.

2. How can you package your renewed sandwich cookie to make it more attractive on the shelf than Oreo? What about package size? Draft a brief packaging plan for the new Hydrox (or whatever name you chose).

3. Can you modify the original formula to make something new and more competitive? Will a brand extension work here? Why or why not?

ETHICS EXERCISE

A product that a potential buyer knows about but is not actively seeking is called an unsought product. Is the marketing of unsought products unethical? Discuss your answer in terms of the AMA Statement of Ethics, found at **www .marketingpower.com.**

MARKETING PLAN EXERCISE

In the first part of your strategic marketing plan, you stated your business mission and objectives, and performed a detailed SWOT analysis. In the second part of the plan, you identified and described target market segments and described their buying behaviors and decision-making processes. In addition, you identified sources of competitive intelligence and the need for any further marketing research before the marketing plan could be implemented. The next stages of the strategic planning process involve defining the elements of the marketing mix: (Part 3) product and place, (Part 4) promotion and pricing strategies.

After reading Chapter 10, you can use the following exercises to guide you through the third part of your strategic marketing plan:

1. How would you classify the offering to your customers? Is it a consumer product? A business-to-business product? A good or a service? How does this classification change the focus of your e-marketing plan? Is your product unique enough to be patented? Check with the U.S. Patent and Trademark Office at **www.uspto.gov.**

2. Place your company's offerings into a product portfolio. Consider the broader impact of marketing a product item within a line or mix. Factors to consider are those such as price, image, complementary products, distribution relationship, and so on. Are there any special product features that selling on the Internet would allow you to add or force you to take away?

3. Does your chosen company have a brand name and brand mark? If not, design both. If so, evaluate the ability of the brand name and mark to communicate effectively to the target market. Is strong branding more or less important in an Internet environment? Why? What makes branding so important?

4. What will your company Internet address be? To check and see what URLs are available, go to **www.companyname.com** and try some out. Should your URL be the same as your company name? Why or why not? What happens if a customer mistypes your name? Should you register under alternative spellings?

5. Is the product packaged and labeled? How should it be packaged and why? Does the package and label design match other communications tools? How is this an opportunity to communicate with your customers?

6. Evaluate warranties or guarantees offered by your firm, including product return policies. How will customers return products they purchased from the Web site? Design the parameters for warranties and return policies. Should your return policy be stricter online than off-line? Why or why not?

CASE STUDY: TERRACYCLE

© AP IMAGES/MEL EVANS

TURNING WORM POOP INTO A PRODUCT

Environmentally friendly products have never been as hot as they are now, and the number of brands touting their "green" credentials has never been higher, but TerraCycle Plant Food may be the ultimate organic product to hit the market. A college student named Tom Szaky founded TerraCycle in 2003 after buddies from Canada, "where they have more liberal rules about growing certain plants," he says, taught him how to use worm droppings as cheap and eco-friendly fertilizer.

Szaky based his business model on recycling, starting with the trash that TerraCycle turns into compost and feeds to millions of red worms. The worm castings are then liquefied and put into previously used plastic water and soda bottles. Even the company's shipping cartons come from recycled materials.

TerraCycle's organic plant food hit the shelves in 2004 with labels boasting that it "Contains Liquefied Worm Poop!" It didn't take long for the products to take off. By 2006, the company had been named "The Coolest Little Start-Up in America" by *Inc.* magazine and had passed the $1 million mark in sales, growing as much as 300 percent from the previous year. They snagged shelf space in retail giants such as Target, Wal-Mart, and Home Depot.

Founder and president Tom Szaky liked to refer to his company as "the anti-Miracle-Gro." But the industry giant disagreed. It turns out that Scotts Miracle-Gro thought that, if anything, TerraCycle was encroaching too closely on its territory. In March of 2007, Scotts sued Szaky's fledgling company for trademark infringement and for making "false claims" that its organic products are superior to synthetic versions.

Small companies can easily fold under the weight of such a lawsuit. Even if they win, the legal costs can cripple them. So TerraCycle took their case to the Internet with the blog **www.suedbyscotts.com,** hoping to stir public support and raise contributions for its legal fees.

"I knew there was no way I could out-lawyer Scotts," Tom Szaky says. "So as I thought about it, I wondered what core competency our company had that we could exploit. Guerrilla marketing seemed to be the obvious answer." He adds that they hoped to get so much public support for their cause that Scotts would drop their suit.

The blog offered a comparison chart titled "David vs. Goliath" that illustrated the differences between the two companies. A photo of TerraCycle's modest headquarters behind a chain-link fence in New Jersey was in stark contrast to Scotts's grand, pillared entryway in Ohio. The blog listed TerraCycle's CEO's "major perquisite" as "unlimited free worm poop," whereas Scotts's CEO enjoys "personal use of company-owned aircraft."

The blog also countered Scotts's claims that consumers might be confused by its "overly similar yellow and green packaging" by posting photographs of

TerraCycle's wacky and unusual bottles in their variety of shapes and sizes beside Miracle-Gro's uniform and professional looking ones. Scotts continued to insist that they change their labels, but TerraCycle's general counsel, Richard Ober Jr., says that changing packaging now would hurt their sales momentum. "There's the loss of customer recognition."

Su Lok, a Scotts spokesperson, argued that the blog was just one of TerraCycle's PR "tactics" and insisted that none of their arguments had merit. "We've spent a lot of time building up brands that consumers trust," she says, "and we are going to protect those brands."

Ira J. Levy, an intellectual property lawyer, warned that Scotts may have more to lose by pursuing TerraCycle than it's worth. "By pursuing a trade dress case," Levy says, "they can allow a small player to promote itself on the national stage. When word gets out that the mega-conglomerate is suing the little guy, you risk having bloggers launching boycotts, and the plaintiff ends up injuring his own business."

Which is precisely what Tom Szaky hoped would happen. The lawsuit wasn't something he would have wanted to fight, he said, but it was a chance to generate buzz. "It's like *The Art of War*," he explained. "You need to have a villain to be up against, and for us, that's Scotts."

Although the fight is over now (in September 2007 TerraCycle reached a settlement with Scotts and has agreed to change its packaging and its advertising claims), in its time, **www.suedbyscotts.com** gained massive media attention, leading major newspapers and magazines to cover the story, and hundreds of bloggers to defend TerraCycle's cause. Online donations actually totaled less than $1,000; however, overall company sales surged 122 percent within weeks of the blog's launch. And TerraCycle's main Web site, which averaged about 1,000 visitors a day, spiked to as high as 13,000.[28]

Questions

1. What type of consumer product is TerraCycle's plant food: convenience, shopping, specialty, or unsought? Why?

2. Go to **www.terracycle.net** and look at the types of products the company sells. Describe their product mix. How wide is it? Which basic product lines does it sell? How long are they?

3. Do you think that product line extension or product line contraction would make more sense for TerraCycle at this stage of the company's growth? Why?

4. How well do TerraCycle's bottles perform the four packaging functions discussed in this chapter? Compare TerraCycle's products to Miracle-Gro's (**www.scotts.com**). Do you think TerraCycle's package design distinguishes their products well enough from those of the industry giant, or are they similar enough to cause customer confusion?

COMPANY CLIPS

KODAK—REINVENTING THE BRAND

Unquestionably, Kodak is one of the most recognized brands in the United States and the world. For over a century, Kodak was known as the company that brought the technology of photography into the everyday, aptly summed up in the tagline, "Celebrate the Moments of Your Life." Grocery stores, convenience stores, and camera stores contained aisles full of little yellow boxes of Kodak film in every possible speed. But after Kodak invented the digital camera, the company was faced with the challenge of leveraging the equity of its brand in a new competitive market—one that didn't include film.

Questions

1. Using Exhibit 10.1 as a guide, create a diagram that organizes the Kodak products mentioned in the video. How are changes in the company's product mix necessitating changes to the way managers market Kodak's offerings?

2. List the attributes of the Kodak brand. What benefits of branding has the company experienced over time? Have there been pitfalls to having a brand with such strong associations?

3. Describe the functions of packaging of a disposable camera.

Marketing &You Results

A higher score on this scale indicates that you are very brand conscious when you shop. You prefer to buy brands that are nationally known rather than private brands or generic brands. Conversely, a lower score suggests that you are not so brand conscious and tend to choose lower-priced, lesser-known brands.

12

Marketing Channels and Supply Chain Management

LEARNING OUTCOMES

1. Explain what a marketing channel is and why intermediaries are needed
2. Define the types of channel intermediaries and describe their functions and activities
3. Describe the channel structures for consumer and business products and discuss alternative channel arrangements
4. Define the terms *supply chain* and *supply chain management*, and discuss the benefits of supply chain management
5. Discuss the issues that influence channel strategy
6. Describe the different channel relationship types and their unique costs and benefits
7. Describe the logistical components of the supply chain
8. Discuss new technology and emerging trends in supply chain management
9. Explain channel leadership, conflict, and partnering
10. Discuss channels and distribution decisions in global markets
11. Identify the special problems and opportunities associated with distribution in service organizations

MARKETING CHANNELS

The term *channel* is derived from the Latin word *canalis*, which means canal. A marketing channel can be viewed as a large canal or pipeline through which products, their ownership, communication, financing and payment, and accompanying risk flow to the consumer. Formally, a marketing channel (also called a channel of distribution) is a business structure of interdependent organizations that are involved in the process of making a product or service available for use or consumption by end customers or business users. Marketing channels facilitate the physical movement of goods from location to location, thus representing "place" or "distribution" in the marketing mix (product, price, promotion, and place) and encompassing the processes involved in getting the right product to the right place at the right time.

Many different types of organizations participate in marketing channels. Channel members (wholesalers, distributors, and retailers, also sometimes referred to as *intermediaries*, *resellers*, and *middlemen*) negotiate with one another, buy and sell products, and facilitate the change of ownership between buyer and seller in the course of moving the product from the manufacturer into the hands of the final consumer. As products move through channels, channel members facilitate the distribution process by providing specialization and division of labor, overcoming discrepancies, and providing contact efficiency.

Providing Specialization and Division of Labor

According to the concept of *specialization and division of labor*, breaking down a complex task into smaller, simpler ones and allocating them to specialists will create greater efficiency and lower average production costs. Manufacturers achieve economies of scale through the use of efficient equipment capable of producing large quantities of a single product.

Marketing channels can also attain economies of scale through specialization and division of labor by aiding producers who lack the motivation, financing, or expertise to market directly to end users or consumers. In some cases, as with most consumer convenience goods, such as soft drinks, the cost of marketing directly to millions of consumers—taking and shipping individual orders—is prohibitive. For this reason,

marketing channel (channel of distribution)
A set of interdependent organizations that ease the transfer of ownership as products move from producer to business user or consumer.

channel members
All parties in the marketing channel that negotiate with one another, buy and sell products, and facilitate the change of ownership between buyer and seller in the course of moving the product from the manufacturer into the hands of the final consumer.

Marketing & You

Using the following scale, indicate your opinions on the lines before the items.

1   2   3   4   5

Strongly disagree   Strongly agree

__ I would prefer to be a leader.

__ I see myself as a good leader.

__ I will be a success.

__ People always seem to recognize my authority.

__ I have a natural talent for influencing people.

__ I am assertive.

__ I like to have authority over other people.

__ I am a born leader.

Now, total your score. Read the chapter and find out what your score means at the end.

Source: Scale #119, *Marketing Scales Handbook*, G. Bruner, K. James, H. Hensel, eds., Vol. III. © by American Marketing Association. Used with permission of the American Marketing Association.

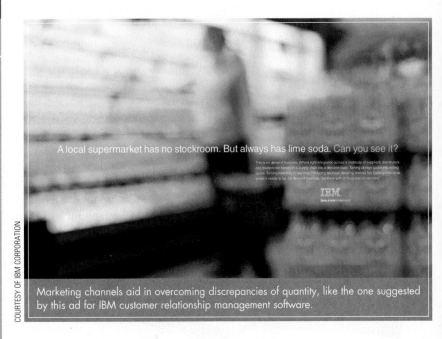

COURTESY OF IBM CORPORATION

A local supermarket has no stockroom. But always has lime soda. Can you see it?

IBM

Marketing channels aid in overcoming discrepancies of quantity, like the one suggested by this ad for IBM customer relationship management software.

Capturing a Bigger Slice of the Pie

The pizza delivery business is very competitive, with both local businesses and national chains competing for a $28.5 billion U.S. consumer market annually. Many of the delivery pizzas ordered in the United States each year are purchased by young adults and teenagers. Papa John's, a 2,700-unit national pizza restaurant chain, believed it could capture more market share if it could find a way to make ordering and delivery easier and more appealing to the technologically savvy members of the younger segment. And if it could do so, it could compete more effectively with larger national companies such as Pizza Hut and Domino's.

In early 2008, Papa John's introduced a new marketing and ordering channel designed to attract younger consumers, rolling out a new service so customers could order pizza from a cell phone or PDA via text message. Once a customer first established an online account, they could at any time simply tap in their preference for one of several favorite pizzas using an abbreviated code. The meal order would be delivered to any of several preprogrammed delivery addresses, and paid for with credit or debit card information already on file in a database, and delivered within a half hour from the closest retail location.

Key additional benefits of customers' willingness to opt into this unique channel arrangement are better overall marketing and customer awareness. By keeping a database of customer purchase behavior, customized promotions flow through the channel to pizza lovers, with great deals offered on favorite crusts, meats, and other toppings according to customer's past preferences. The electronic channel can also be engaged in other ways, such as sending customers digital coupons, providing updates on new menu items, and engaging customers with reminder advertising.

The results of employing this exciting new marketing and delivery channel have been impressive, with Papa John's share rising to 6.9 percent of the marketplace despite having far fewer locations than their major competitors. The company has also recently introduced Web site ordering to great success, with 65 million unique visitors in the first year of operations. The company is optimistic that these new channels will allow it to continue to compete strongly with the "big boys" in the world of pizza delivery.[1]

© FOODPIX/JUPITER IMAGES

producers hire channel members, such as wholesalers and retailers, to do what the producers are not equipped to do or what channel members are better prepared to do. Channel members can do some things more efficiently than producers because they have built good relationships with their customers. Therefore, their specialized expertise enhances the overall performance of the channel.

Overcoming Discrepancies

Marketing channels also aid in overcoming discrepancies of quantity, assortment, time, and space created by economies of scale in production. For example, assume that Pillsbury can efficiently produce its Hungry Jack instant pancake mix only at a rate of 5,000 units in a typical day. Not even the most ardent pancake fan could consume that amount in a year, much less in a day. The quantity produced to achieve low unit costs has created a discrepancy of quantity, which is the difference between the amount of product produced and the amount an end user wants to buy. By storing the product and distributing it in the appropriate amounts, marketing channels overcome quantity discrepancies by making products available in the quantities consumers desire.

Mass production creates not only discrepancies of quantity but also discrepancies of assortment. A discrepancy of assortment occurs when a consumer does not have all of the items needed to receive full satisfaction from a product. For pancakes to provide maximum satisfaction, several other products are required to complete the assortment. At the very least, most people want a knife, fork, plate, butter, and syrup. Others might add orange juice, coffee, cream, sugar, eggs, and bacon or sausage. Even though Pillsbury is a large consumer-products company, it does not come close to providing the optimal assortment to go with its Hungry Jack pancakes. To overcome discrepancies of assortment, marketing channels assemble in one place many of the products necessary to complete a consumer's needed assortment.

A temporal discrepancy is created when a product is produced, but a consumer is not ready to buy it. Marketing channels overcome temporal discrepancies by maintaining inventories in anticipation of demand. For example, manufacturers of seasonal merchandise, such as Christmas or Halloween decorations, are in operation all year even though consumer demand is concentrated during certain months of the year.

Furthermore, because mass production requires many potential buyers, markets are usually scattered over large geographic regions, creating a spatial discrepancy. Often global, or at least nationwide, markets are needed to absorb the outputs of mass producers. Marketing channels overcome spatial discrepancies by making products available in locations convenient to consumers. For example, if all the Hungry Jack pancake mix is produced in Boise, Idaho, then Pillsbury must use an intermediary to distribute the product to other regions of the United States. Consumers elsewhere would be unwilling to drive to Boise to purchase pancake mix.

Providing Contact Efficiency

The third need fulfilled by marketing channels is they provide contact efficiency. Marketing channels provide contact efficiencies by reducing the number of stores customers must shop in to complete their purchases. Think about how much time you would spend shopping if supermarkets, department stores, and shopping malls did not exist. For example, suppose you had to buy your milk at a dairy and your meat at a stockyard. Imagine buying your eggs and chicken at a hatchery and your fruits and vegetables at various farms. You would spend a great deal of time, money, and energy just shopping for a few groceries. Channels simplify distribution by cutting the number of transactions required to get products from manufacturers to consumers and making an assortment of goods available in one location. In addition, many consumers in recent years have begun shopping using a multichannel approach whereby they view products online, in catalogues, and in the brick-and-mortar retail outlet. Savvy retailers are capitalizing on these additional customer contacts by segmenting customers according to buying versus simply shopping channels and providing consistent messages to customers regardless of channel choice.

Consider the example illustrated in Exhibit 12.1. Four consumers each want to buy a television set. Without a retail intermediary like Best Buy, television manufacturers JVC, Zenith, RCA, Sony, and Toshiba would each have to make four contacts to reach the four buyers who are in the target market, for a total of 20 transactions. However, when Best Buy acts as an intermediary between the producer and consumers, each producer has to make only one contact, reducing the number of transactions to 9. Each producer sells to one retailer rather than to four consumers. In turn, consumers buy from one retailer instead of from five producers.

Contact efficiency is being enhanced even more by information technology. Better information on product availability and pricing increasingly is reducing the need for consumers to actually shop for bargains or view ads in a traditional manner. By making information on products and services easily accessible over the Internet, Google, Yahoo! and similar information assemblers are becoming the starting points for finding and buying products and services. As they cull and organize huge digital warehouses of news, images, traffic and weather reports, and information on automobiles, real estate, and other consumer products, inefficiencies will be reduced, as will prices. These developments are revolutionizing marketing channels and benefiting consumers because

discrepancy of quantity
The difference between the amount of product produced and the amount an end user wants to buy.

discrepancy of assortment
The lack of all the items a customer needs to receive full satisfaction from a product or products.

temporal discrepancy
A situation that occurs when a product is produced but a customer is not ready to buy it.

spatial discrepancy
The difference between the location of a producer and the location of widely scattered markets.

Without an intermediary: 5 producers × 4 consumers = 20 transactions

With an intermediary: 5 producers + 4 consumers = 9 transactions

shoppers can find out where the best bargains are without having to search for them.

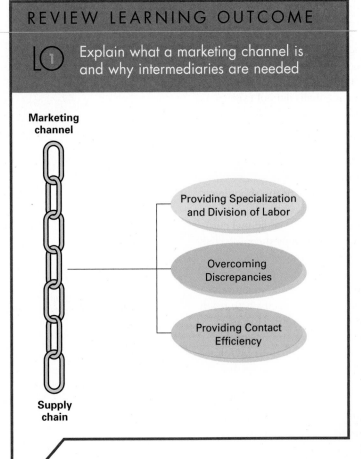

REVIEW LEARNING OUTCOME

LO 1 Explain what a marketing channel is and why intermediaries are needed

Marketing channel

- Providing Specialization and Division of Labor
- Overcoming Discrepancies
- Providing Contact Efficiency

Supply chain

LO 2

CHANNEL INTERMEDIARIES AND THEIR FUNCTIONS

Intermediaries in a channel negotiate with one another, facilitate the change of ownership between buyers and sellers, and physically move products from the manufacturer to the final consumer. The most prominent difference separating intermediaries is whether they take title to the product. *Taking title* means they own the merchandise and control the terms of the sale—for example, price and delivery date. Retailers and merchant wholesalers are examples of intermediaries that take title to products in the marketing channel and resell them. Retailers are firms that sell mainly to consumers. Retailers will be discussed in more detail in Chapter 13.

Merchant wholesalers are organizations that facilitate the movement of products and services from the manufacturer to producers, resellers, governments, institutions, and retailers. All merchant wholesalers take title to the goods they sell, and most of them operate one or more warehouses where they receive goods, store them, and later reship them. Customers are mostly small or medium-sized retailers, but merchant wholesalers also market to manufacturers and institutional clients.

Other intermediaries do not take title to goods and services they market but do facilitate the exchange of ownership between sellers and buyers. Agents and brokers simply facilitate the sale of a product from producer to end user by representing retailers, wholesalers, or manufacturers. Title reflects ownership, and ownership usually implies control.

Unlike wholesalers, agents or brokers only facilitate sales and generally have little input into the terms of the sale. They do, however, get a fee or commission based on sales volume. For example, when selling a home, the owner usually hires a real estate agent who then brings potential buyers to see the house. The agent facilitates the sale by bringing the buyer and owner together, but never actually takes ownership of the home.

Variations in channel structures are due in large part to variations in the numbers and types of wholesaling intermediaries. Generally, product characteristics, buyer considerations, and market conditions determine the type of intermediary the manufacturer should use.

> *Taking title means they own the merchandise and control the terms of the sale.*

- *Product characteristics* that may require a certain type of wholesaling intermediary include whether the product is standardized or customized, the complexity of the product, and the gross margin of the product. For example, a customized product such as insurance is sold through an insurance agent or broker who may represent one or multiple companies. In contrast, a standardized product such as gum is sold through a merchant wholesaler that takes possession of the gum and reships it to the appropriate retailers.

- *Buyer considerations* affecting the wholesaler choice include how often the product is purchased and how long the buyer is willing to wait to receive the product. For example, at the beginning of the school term, a student may be willing to wait a few days for a textbook to get a lower price by ordering online. Thus, this type of product can be distributed directly. But, if the student waits to buy the book until the night before an exam and needs the book immediately, it will have to be purchased at the school bookstore.

- *Market characteristics* determining the wholesaler type include how many buyers are in the market and whether they are concentrated in a general location or are widely dispersed. Gum and textbooks, for example, are produced in one location and consumed in many other locations. Therefore, a merchant wholesaler is needed to distribute the products. In contrast, in a home sale, the buyer and seller are localized in one area, which facilitates the use of an agent/broker relationship.

Channel Functions Performed by Intermediaries

Retailing and wholesaling intermediaries in marketing channels perform several essential functions that make the flow of goods between producer and buyer possible. The three basic functions that intermediaries perform are summarized in Exhibit 12.2.

retailer
A channel intermediary that sells mainly to consumers.

merchant wholesaler
An institution that buys goods from manufacturers and resells them to businesses, government agencies, and other wholesalers or retailers and that receives and takes title to goods, stores them in its own warehouses, and later ships them.

agents and brokers
Wholesaling intermediaries who do not take title to a product but facilitate its sale from producer to end user by representing retailers, wholesalers, or manufacturers.

EXHIBIT 12.2

Marketing Channel Functions Performed by Intermediaries

Type of Function	Description
Transactional functions	**Contacting and promoting:** Contacting potential customers, promoting products, and soliciting orders
	Negotiating: Determining how many goods or services to buy and sell, type of transportation to use, when to deliver, and method and timing of payment
	Risk taking: Assuming the risk of owning inventory
Logistical Functions	**Physically distributing:** Transporting and sorting goods to overcome temporal and spatial discrepancies
	Storing: Maintaining inventories and protecting goods
	Sorting: Overcoming discrepancies of quantity and assortment by
	Sorting out: Breaking down a heterogeneous supply into separate homogeneous stocks
	Accumulating: Combining similar stocks into a larger homogeneous supply
	Allocating: Breaking a homogeneous supply into smaller and smaller lots ("breaking bulk")
	Assorting: Combining products into collections or assortments that buyers want available at one place
Facilitating Functions	**Researching:** Gathering information about other channel members and consumers
	Financing: Extending credit and other financial services to facilitate the flow of goods through the channel to the final consumer

Transactional functions involve contacting and communicating with prospective buyers to make them aware of existing products and explain their features, advantages, and benefits. Intermediaries in the channel also provide *logistical* functions. Logistics is the efficient and cost-effective forward and reverse flow and storage of goods, services, and related information, into, through, and out of channel member companies. Logistics functions typically include transportation and storage of assets, as well as their sorting, accumulation, consolidation, and/or allocation for the purpose of conforming to customer requirements. For example, grading agricultural products typifies the sorting-out process, while consolidation of many lots of grade A eggs from different sources into one lot illustrates the accumulation process. Supermarkets or other retailers perform the sorting function by assembling thousands of different items that match their customers' desires. Similarly, while large companies typically have direct channels, many small companies depend on wholesalers to promote and distribute their products. For example, small beverage manufacturers like Jones Soda, Honest Tea, and Energy Brands depend on wholesalers to distribute their products in a marketplace dominated by large competitors like Coca-Cola and Pepsi. The management of logistics is a key component of supply chain management, which is discussed in greater detail in Learning Outcomes 4, 7, and 8.

The third basic channel function, *facilitating*, includes research and financing. Research provides information about channel members and consumers by getting answers to key questions: Who are the buyers? Where are they located? Why do they buy? Financing ensures that channel members have the money to keep products moving through the channel to the ultimate consumer.

A single company may provide one, two, or all three functions. Consider Kramer Beverage Company, a Coors beer distributor. As a beer distributor, Kramer provides transactional, logistical, and facilitating channel functions. Sales representatives contact local bars and restaurants to negotiate the terms of the sale, possibly giving the customer a discount for large purchases, and arrange for delivery of the beer. At the same time, Kramer also provides a facilitating function by extending credit to the customer. Kramer merchandising representatives, meanwhile, assist in promoting the beer on a local level by hanging Coors beer signs and posters. Kramer also provides logistical functions by accumulating the many types of Coors beer from the Coors manufacturing plant in Golden, Colorado, and storing them in its refrigerated warehouse. When an order needs to be filled, Kramer then sorts the beer into heterogeneous collections for each particular customer. For example, the local Chili's Grill & Bar may need two kegs of Coors, three kegs of Coors Light, and two cases of Killian's Red in bottles. The beer will then be loaded onto a refrigerated truck and transported to the restaurant. Upon arrival, the Kramer delivery person will transport the kegs and cases of beer into the restaurant's refrigerator and may also restock the coolers behind the bar.

Although individual members can be added to or deleted from a channel, someone must still perform these essential functions. They can be performed by producers, end users or consumers, channel intermediaries such as wholesalers and retailers, and sometimes nonmember channel participants. For example, if a manufacturer decides to eliminate its private fleet of trucks, it must still have a way to move the goods to the wholesaler. This task may be accomplished by the wholesaler, which may have its own fleet of trucks, or by a nonmember channel participant, such as an independent trucking firm. Nonmembers also provide many other essential functions that may at one time have been provided by a channel member. For example, research firms may perform the research function; advertising agencies may provide the promotion function; transportation and storage firms, the physical distribution function; and banks, the financing function.

REVIEW LEARNING OUTCOME

LO 2 Define the types of channel intermediaries and describe their functions and activities

CHANNEL INTERMEDIARIES		CHANNEL FUNCTIONS
Retailers Wholesalers Agents and Brokers	*Perform* →	Transactional Logistical Facilitating

CHANNEL STRUCTURES

A product can take many routes to reach its final consumer. Marketers search for the most efficient channel from the many alternatives available. Marketing a consumer convenience good like gum or candy differs from marketing a specialty good like a Mercedes-Benz. The two products require very different distribution channels. Likewise, the appropriate channel for a major equipment supplier like Boeing Company would be unsuitable for an accessory equipment producer like Black & Decker. The next sections discuss the structures of typical marketing channels for consumer and business-to-business products. Alternative channel structures are also discussed.

Channels for Consumer Products

Exhibit 12.3 illustrates the four ways manufacturers can route products to consumers. Producers use the direct channel to sell directly to consumers. Direct marketing activities—including telemarketing, mail-order and catalog shopping, and forms of electronic retailing like online shopping and shop-at-home television networks—are a good example of this type of channel structure. For example, home computer users can purchase Dell computers directly over the telephone or from Dell's Web site. There are no intermediaries. Producer-owned stores and factory outlet stores—like Sherwin-Williams, Polo Ralph Lauren, Oneida, and West Point Pepperell—are other examples of direct channels. Farmers' markets are also direct channels. Direct marketing and factory outlets are discussed in more detail in Chapter 13.

At the other end of the spectrum, an *agent/broker channel* involves a fairly complicated process. Agent/broker channels are typically used in markets with many small manufacturers and many retailers that lack the resources to find each other. Agents or brokers bring manufacturers and wholesalers together for negotiations, but they do not take title to merchandise. Ownership passes directly to one or more

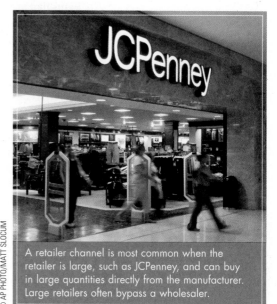

A retailer channel is most common when the retailer is large, such as JCPenney, and can buy in large quantities directly from the manufacturer. Large retailers often bypass a wholesaler.

direct channel
A distribution channel in which producers sell directly to consumers.

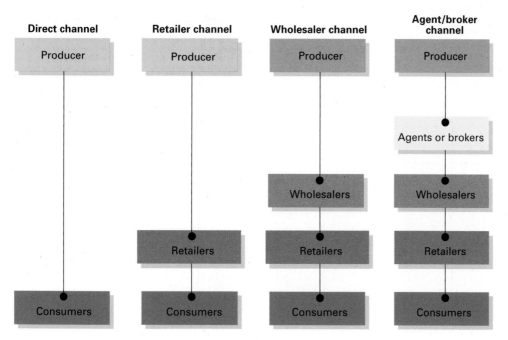

EXHIBIT 12.3

Marketing Channels for Consumer Products

wholesalers and then to retailers. Finally, retailers sell to the ultimate consumer of the product. For example, a food broker represents buyers and sellers of grocery products. The broker acts on behalf of many different producers and negotiates the sale of their products to wholesalers that specialize in foodstuffs. These wholesalers in turn sell to grocers and convenience stores.

Most consumer products are sold through distribution channels similar to the other two alternatives: the retailer channel and the wholesaler channel. A *retailer channel* is most common when the retailer is large and can buy in large quantities directly from the manufacturer. Wal-Mart, Target, JCPenney, and car dealers are examples of retailers that often bypass a wholesaler. A *wholesaler channel* is commonly used for low-cost items that are frequently purchased, such as candy, cigarettes, and magazines. For example, M&M/Mars sells candies and chocolates to wholesalers in large quantities. The wholesalers then break these quantities into smaller quantities to satisfy individual retailer orders.

Channels for Business and Industrial Products

As Exhibit 12.4 illustrates, five channel structures are common in business and industrial markets. First, direct channels are typical in business and industrial markets. For example, manufacturers buy large quantities of raw materials, major equipment, processed materials, and supplies directly from other manufacturers. Manufacturers that require suppliers to meet detailed technical specifications often prefer direct channels. The direct communication required between Ford Motor Company and its suppliers, for example, along with the tremendous size of the orders, makes anything but a direct channel impractical. The channel from producer to government buyers is also a direct channel. Because much government buying is done through bidding, a direct channel is attractive. Dell, for example, the top seller of desktop computers to federal, state, and local government agencies in the United States, sells the computers through direct channels.

Companies selling standardized items of moderate or low value often rely on *industrial distributors*. In many ways, an industrial distributor is like a supermarket for organizations. Industrial distributors are wholesalers and channel members that buy and take title to products. Moreover, they usually keep inventories of their products and sell

EXHIBIT 12.4

Channels for Business and Industrial Products

and service them. Often small manufacturers cannot afford to employ their own sales force. Instead, they rely on manufacturers' representatives or selling agents to sell to either industrial distributors or users.

Today, though, the traditional industrial distributor is facing many challenges. Manufacturers are getting bigger due to growth, mergers, and consolidation. Through technology, manufacturers and customers have access to information that in the past only the distributor had. Consequently, many manufacturers and customers are bypassing distributors and going direct, often via the Internet. The Internet has enabled virtual distributors to emerge and forced traditional industrial distributors to expand their business model. An example of how the Internet has revolutionized industrial distribution is **www.pumpbiz.com**, which sells pumps for chemicals, wastewater, sumps, water, coolants, and all other industrial process fluids. Pump types available include centrifugal, diaphragm, vertical, magnetic drive, and metering pumps. The site offers 24-7 purchasing and provides access to information on major manufacturers of pumps, including side-by-side comparisons and reviews; copies of manuals, diagrams, and other installation and repair documentation; warranted installers in the customer's local area; and instant access to past purchasing and related information on a customer's account.[2]

The Internet has also led to the emergence of three other new forms of industrial distribution. Some companies serve as agents that link buyers and sellers and charge a fee. For example, Expedia.com links business travelers to airlines, hotels, and car rental companies. A second form of marketplace has been developed by existing companies looking for a way to drop the intermediary from the channel. For example, the Worldwide Retail Exchange is a marketplace created by 17 major retailers including Target, JCPenney, and Walgreens. Retailers use the exchange to make purchases that in the past would have required telephone, fax, or face-to-face sales calls. Retailers using the exchange estimate they have saved approximately 15 percent in their purchasing costs. Finally, a third type of Internet marketplace is a "private exchange." Private exchanges allow companies to automate their channels while sharing information only with select suppliers. Ace Hardware and Hewlett-Packard, for example, use private exchanges to manage their inventory supplies. Another example is iTextiles.com which enables companies in the textile business to communicate over a secure online platform to place orders, update information, and standardize transactions.[3]

Alternative Channel Arrangements

Rarely does a producer use just one type of channel to move its product. It usually employs several different or alternative channels, which include multiple channels, nontraditional channels, and strategic channel alliances.

Multiple Channels When a producer selects two (or more) channels to distribute the same product to target markets, this arrangement is called dual distribution (or multiple distribution). As more people have access to the Internet and embrace online shopping, an increasing number of retailers are using multiple channels of distribution. For example, companies such as Limited Brands, which includes The Limited, Express, Victoria's Secret, and Bath and Body Works, sell in-store, online, and through catalogs. Other examples are Sears and Avon. Since Sears purchased Lands' End, a traditional direct business-to-consumer clothing manufacturer, Lands' End products are available in Sears's stores, and Sears credit cards are accepted on the Lands' End Web site. Avon, a direct supplier of health and beauty products for women, offers consumers four alternatives for purchasing products. They can contact a representative in person (the original business model), purchase on the Web, order direct from the company, or pick up products at an Avon Salon & Spa. The Limited, Sears/Lands' End, and Avon are each distributing identical products to existing markets using more than one channel of distribution.

Nontraditional Channels Often nontraditional channel arrangements help differentiate a firm's product from the competition. For example, manufacturers may decide to use nontraditional channels such as the Internet, mail-order channels, or infomercials to sell

dual distribution (multiple distribution)
The use of two (or more) channels to distribute the same product to target markets.

An increasing number of retailers use multiple channels of distribution. For example, Sears purchased Lands' End, a traditional direct business-to-consumer clothing manufacturer. Now Lands' End products are available in Sears's stores, and Sears credit cards are accepted on the Lands' End Web site.

© AP IMAGES/PRNEWSFOTO/LANDS' END

strategic channel alliance
A cooperative agreement between business firms to use the other's already established distribution channel.

products instead of going through traditional retailer channels. Although nontraditional channels may limit a brand's coverage, they can give a producer serving a niche market a way to gain market access and customer attention without having to establish channel intermediaries. Nontraditional channels can also provide another avenue of sales for larger firms. For example, a London publisher sells short stories through vending machines in the London Underground. Instead of the traditional book format, the stories are printed like folded maps, making them an easy-to-read alternative for commuters.

Kiosks, long a popular method for ordering and registering for wedding gifts, dispersing cash through ATMs, and facilitating airline check-in, are finding new uses. Ethan Allen furniture stores use kiosks as a product locator tool for consumers and salespeople. Kiosks on the campuses of Cheyney University allow students to register for classes, see their class schedule and grades, check account balances, and even print transcripts. The general public, when it has access to the kiosks, can use them to gather information about the university.[4]

Strategic Channel Alliances Companies often form strategic channel alliances. Such an alliance enables a company to use another manufacturer's already established channel. Alliances are used most often when the creation of marketing channel relationships may be too expensive and time-consuming. Starbucks, the world's premier coffee marketer, uses strategic alliances both domestically and around the world. When Starbucks wanted to develop ready-to-drink (RTD) coffee beverages for supermarkets and other outlets, it decided not to develop a new channel from scratch. Rather, Starbucks signed an agreement with Pepsi to develop and bottle a Starbucks brand of RTD coffee, a category that had been extremely difficult to develop. The resulting Frappuccino and DoubleShot were so successful when they were launched that they were constantly sold out. Pepsi is still the sole distributor for Starbucks RTD beverages like Frappuccino and DoubleShot, and Starbucks has continued access to the thousands of outlets where Pepsi is sold.[5] Similarly, Accenture and Cisco Systems have formed an alliance to work together in the joint development, marketing, and deployment of global network solutions. The combination of Accenture's network consulting services and Cisco's advanced technology will result in cost savings in asset acquisition and service delivery for their customers.[6] Strategic channel alliances are proving to be more successful for growing businesses than mergers and acquisitions. This is especially true in global markets where cultural differences, distance, and other barriers can prove challenging. For example, Heinz has a strategic alliance with Kagome, one of Japan's largest food companies. The companies are working together to find ways to reduce operating costs while expanding both brands' market presence globally.

REVIEW LEARNING OUTCOME

LO 3 Describe the channel structures for consumer and business products and discuss alternative channel arrangements

CONSUMER CHANNELS	BUSINESS CHANNELS	ALTERNATIVE CHANNELS
• Direct	• Direct	• Multiple
• Retail	• Industrial	• Nontraditional
• Wholesaler	• Agent/broker	• Strategic alliances
• Agent/broker	• Agent/broker–industrial	

SUPPLY CHAINS AND SUPPLY CHAIN MANAGEMENT

In today's sophisticated marketplace, many companies are focusing on their supply chain and turning to supply chain management for competitive advantages. A company's supply chain includes all of the companies involved in all of the upstream and downstream flows of products, services, finances, and information, from initial suppliers (the point of origin) to the ultimate customer (the point of consumption). The goal of supply chain management is to coordinate and integrate the activities performed by supply chain members into a collection of seamless end-to-end processes, ultimately giving supply chain managers "total visibility" of the supply chain both inside and outside the firm. The philosophy behind supply chain management is that by visualizing the entire supply chain, managers can maximize strengths and efficiencies at each level of the process to create a highly competitive, customer-driven supply system that is able to respond immediately to changes in supply and demand. Companies that have a supply chain orientation are those that recognize and embrace this philosophy, and therefore see the implications of managing the flows of products, services, and so on across their direct and indirect suppliers and customers.

An important element of supply chain management is that it is completely customer driven. During the era of mass production (c. 1865–1980), manufacturers produced standardized products that were "pushed" down through the supply channel to the consumer. In contrast, products in today's marketplace are being driven by customers, who expect to receive product configurations and services matched to their unique needs. For example, Dell builds computers only according to its customers' precise specifications, such as the amount of RAM memory; type of monitor, modem, or optical drive; and amount of hard disk space. Similarly, car companies offer customers the option to customize even economy-priced cars. For about $20,000, customers can order a Ford Mustang with a V-6 engine, a six-disc CD changer, MP3 player, and eight speakers. The focus is on pulling products into the marketplace and partnering with members of the supply chain to enhance customer value. Customizing an automobile is now possible because of new supply chain relationships between the automobile manufacturers and the after-market auto-parts industry.

This reversal of the flow of demand from a "push" to a "pull" system has resulted in a radical reformulation of market expectations as well as traditional marketing, production, and distribution functions. Through the coordinated partnership of suppliers, manufacturers, wholesalers, and retailers working together along the entire supply chain, supply chain management allows companies to respond with the unique product configuration and mix of services demanded by the customer. Today, supply chain management plays a dual role: first, as a *communicator* of customer demand that extends from the point of sale all the way back to the supplier and, second, as a *physical flow process* that engineers the timely and cost-effective movement of goods through the entire source-to-consumer supply pipeline. Boeing realized the importance of these supply chain processes when it struggled to get enough titanium fasteners to assemble the new 787 Dreamliner from its supplier, Alcoa, in time to launch its widely publicized new luxury airliner.[7] Better communication with Alcoa and its titanium ore suppliers, combined with better process flow synchronization, could have reduced the stress Boeing executives felt as they scrambled to find enough fasteners to meet the publicized launch date.

Supply chain managers are responsible for making strategic decisions, such as coordinating the sourcing and procurement of raw materials, scheduling production, processing orders, managing inventory, transporting and storing supplies and finished goods, dealing with returns, and coordinating customer service activities. Supply chain managers are also responsible for the management of information that flows

supply chain
The connected chain of all of the business entities, both internal and external to the company, that perform or support the logistics function.

supply chain management
A management system that coordinates and integrates all of the activities performed by supply chain members into a seamless process, from the source to the point of consumption, resulting in enhanced customer and economic value.

through the supply chain. Coordinating the relationships between the company and its external partners, such as vendors, carriers, and third-party companies, is also a critical function of supply chain management. Because supply chain managers play such a major role in both cost control and customer satisfaction, they are more valuable than ever. In fact, demand for supply chain managers has increased substantially in recent years. According to the Council of Supply Chain Management Professionals, the supply chain career field accounts for over 9.5 percent of the U.S. gross domestic product, with thousands of new, high-paying positions becoming available yearly.

In summary, supply chain managers are responsible for directing raw materials and parts to the production department and the finished or semifinished product through warehouses and eventually to the intermediary or end user. Above all, supply chain management begins and ends with the customer. Instead of forcing a product into the market that may or may not sell quickly, supply chain managers react to actual customer demand. By doing so, they minimize the flow of raw materials, finished product, and packaging materials at every point in the supply chain, resulting in lower costs and increased customer value. Exhibit 12.5 depicts a typical supply chain model that managers attempt to optimize for firm and customer benefit.

EXHIBIT 12.5

A Typical Supply Chain Management Process

Benefits of Supply Chain Management

Supply chain management is a key means of differentiation for a firm and a critical component in marketing and corporate strategy. Supply chain–oriented companies commonly report lower inventory, transportation, warehousing, and packaging costs; greater supply chain flexibility; improved customer service; and higher revenues. Research has shown a clear relationship between supply chain performance and profitability. Specific benefits from effective implementation of supply chain procedures include an almost 20 percent increase in cash flow, a more than 50 percent increase in flexibility of supply chain activities, and a reduction of 5 to 10 percent in supply chain costs, among other potential benefits.[8]

MAKING CHANNEL STRATEGY DECISIONS

Devising a marketing channel strategy requires several critical decisions. Managers must decide what role distribution will play in the overall marketing strategy. In addition, they must be sure that the channel strategy chosen is consistent with product, promotion, and pricing strategies. In making these decisions, marketing managers must determine what factors will influence the choice of channel and what level of distribution intensity will be appropriate.

REVIEW LEARNING OUTCOME

Define the terms *supply chain* and *supply chain management,* and discuss the benefits of supply chain management

Well-managed supply chains . . .

lead to . . .

✓ reduced costs
✓ increased flexibility
✓ improved customer service
✓ greater revenue

Factors Affecting Channel Choice

Managers must answer many questions before choosing a marketing channel. The final choice depends on the analysis of several factors, which often interact. These factors can be grouped as market factors, product factors, and producer factors.

Market Factors Among the most important market factors affecting the choice of distribution channel are target customer considerations. Specifically, managers should answer the following questions: Who are the potential customers? What do they buy? Where do they buy? When do they buy? How do they buy? Additionally, the choice of channel depends on whether the producer is selling to consumers or to industrial customers. Industrial customers' buying habits are very different from those of consumers. Industrial customers tend to buy in larger quantities and require more customer service. For example, Toyota Industrial Equipment manufactures the leading lift truck used to move materials in and out of warehouses and other industrial facilities. Its business customers buy large numbers of trucks at one time and require additional services such as data tracking on how the lift truck is used. In contrast, consumers usually buy in very small quantities and sometimes do not mind if they get little or no service, such as in a discount store like Wal-Mart or Target.

The geographic location and size of the market are also important to channel selection. As a rule, if the target market is concentrated in one or more specific areas, then direct selling through a sales force is appropriate. When markets are more widely dispersed, intermediaries would be less expensive. The size of the market also influences channel choice. Generally, larger markets require more intermediaries. For instance, Procter & Gamble has to reach millions of consumers with its many brands of household goods. It needs many intermediaries, including wholesalers and retailers.

Product Factors Products that are more complex, customized, and expensive tend to benefit from shorter and more direct marketing channels. These types of products sell better through a direct sales force. Examples include pharmaceuticals, scientific instruments, airplanes, and mainframe computer systems. On the other hand, the more standardized a product is, the longer its distribution channel can be and the greater the number of intermediaries that can be involved. For example, with the exception of flavor and shape, the formula for chewing gum is about the same from producer to producer. Chewing gum is also very inexpensive. As a result, the distribution channel for gum tends to involve many wholesalers and retailers.

The product's life cycle is also an important factor in choosing a marketing channel. In fact, the choice of channel may change over the life of the product. For example, when photocopiers were first available, they were typically sold by a direct sales force. Now, however, photocopiers can be found in several places, including warehouse clubs, electronics superstores, and mail-order catalogs. As products become more common and less intimidating to potential users, producers tend to look for alternative channels. Gatorade was originally sold to sports teams, gyms, and fitness clubs. As the drink became more popular, mainstream supermarket channels were added, followed by convenience stores and drugstores. Now Gatorade can be found in vending machines and even in some fast-food restaurants.

Another factor is the delicacy of the product. Perishable products like vegetables and milk have a relatively short life span. Fragile products like china and crystal require a minimum amount of handling. Therefore, both require fairly short marketing channels. Online retailers such as eBay facilitate the sale of unusual or difficult-to-find products that benefit from a direct channel.

Producer Factors Several factors pertaining to the producer itself are important to the selection of a marketing channel. In general, producers with large financial, managerial, and marketing resources are better able to use more direct channels. These producers have the ability to hire and train their own sales force, warehouse their own goods, and extend credit to their customers. For example, variety store Dollar Tree distributes products through retail locations at low prices. To increase cost-efficiency, Dollar Tree has a coast-to-coast logistics network of nine distribution centers to service its almost 3,000 stores.[9] Smaller or weaker firms, on the other hand, must rely on intermediaries to provide these services for them. Compared to producers with only one or two product lines, producers that sell several products in a related area are able to choose channels that are more direct. Sales expenses then can be spread over more products.

A producer's desire to control pricing, positioning, brand image, and customer support also tends to influence channel selection. For instance, firms that sell products with exclusive brand images, such as designer perfumes and clothing, usually avoid channels in which discount retailers are present. Manufacturers of upscale products, such as Gucci (handbags) and Godiva (chocolates), may sell their wares only in expensive stores in order to maintain an image of exclusivity. Many producers have opted to risk their image, however, and test sales in discount channels. Levi Strauss expanded its distribution to include JCPenney, Sears, and Wal-Mart.

Intensive distribution is susceptible to errors when intermediaries are expected to handle products in a prespecified manner detailed in buyer–seller agreements. For example, Scholastic executives were alarmed when copies of the final book in the Harry Potter series were mistakenly released a day earlier than the widely publicized release date.

© AP IMAGES/MARK BAKER

Levels of Distribution Intensity

Organizations have three options for intensity of distribution: intensive distribution, selective distribution, or exclusive distribution (see Exhibit 12.6).

EXHIBIT 12.6

Intensity of Distribution Levels

Intensity Level	Distribution Intensity Objective	Number of Intermediaries in Each Market	Examples
Intensive	Achieve mass-market selling; popular with health and beauty aids and convenience goods that must be available everywhere	Many	Pepsi-Cola, Frito-Lay potato chips, Huggies diapers, Alpo dog food, Crayola crayons
Selective	Work closely with selected intermediaries who meet certain criteria; typically used for shopping goods and some specialty goods	Several	Donna Karan clothing, Hewlett-Packard printers, Burton snowboards, Aveda aromatherapy products
Exclusive	Work with a single intermediary for products that require special resources or positioning; typically used for specialty goods and major industrial equipment	One	BMW cars, Rolex watches

Intensive Distribution Intensive distribution is a form of distribution aimed at maximum market coverage. The manufacturer tries to have the product available in every outlet where potential customers might want to buy it. If buyers are unwilling to search for a product (as is true of convenience goods and operating supplies), the product must be very accessible to buyers. A low-value product that is purchased frequently may require a lengthy channel. For example, candy, chips, and other snack foods are found in almost every type of retail store imaginable. These foods typically are sold to retailers in small quantities by food or candy wholesalers. The Wrigley Company could not afford to sell its gum directly to every service station, drugstore, supermarket, and discount store. The cost would be too high. Sysco delivers food and related products to restaurants and other food service companies that prepare meals for customers dining out. It is not economically feasible for restaurants to go to individual vendors for each product. Therefore, Sysco serves as an intermediary by delivering all products necessary to fulfill restaurants' needs.[10]

Most manufacturers pursuing an intensive distribution strategy sell to a large percentage of the wholesalers willing to stock their products. Retailers' willingness (or unwillingness) to handle items tends to control the manufacturer's ability to achieve intensive distribution. For example, a retailer already carrying ten brands of gum may show little enthusiasm for one more brand. Intensive distribution is also susceptible to errors when intermediaries who are shipped products are expected to handle them in a prespecified manner detailed in buyer–seller agreements. For example, executives at Scholastic Books were quite alarmed when some 1,200 of the 12 million copies of the final book in the Harry Potter series, *Harry Potter and the Deathly Hallows*, were mistakenly released through an Internet retailing Web site a day earlier than the widely publicized release date.[11]

Selective Distribution Selective distribution is achieved by screening dealers and retailers to eliminate all but a few in any single area. Because only a few are chosen, the consumer must seek out the product. For example, when Heeling Sports Ltd. launched Heelys, thick-soled sneakers with a wheel embedded in each heel, the company hired a group of 40 teens to perform Heelys exhibitions in targeted malls, skate parks, and college campuses across the country to create demand. Then the company made the decision to avoid large stores like Target and to distribute the shoes only through selected mall retailers and skate and surf shops in order to position the product as "cool and kind of irreverent." Selective distribution strategies often hinge on a manufacturer's desire to maintain a superior product image so as to be able to charge a premium price. DKNY clothing, for instance, is sold only in select retail outlets, mainly full-price department

intensive distribution
A form of distribution aimed at having a product available in every outlet where target customers might want to buy it.

selective distribution
A form of distribution achieved by screening dealers to eliminate all but a few in any single area.

stores. Likewise, premium pet food brands such as Hill's Pet Nutrition and Nestlé Purina's Pro Plan are distributed chiefly through specialty pet food stores and veterinarians, rather than mass retailers like Wal-Mart, so that a premium price can be charged. Manufacturers sometimes expand selective distribution strategies, believing that doing so will enhance revenues without diminishing their product's image. For example, when Procter & Gamble purchased premium pet food brand Iams, it expanded the brand's selective distribution strategy and began selling Iams food in mass retailer Target. Even though the new strategy created channel conflict with breeders and veterinarians who had supported the product, sales increased.[12] Similarly, Playboy Energy, a new energy drink manufactured and bottled by the media enterprise of the same name, uses selective distribution to position itself as a higher-end option versus more intensively distributed competitor Red Bull.[13] The drink has been introduced in luxurious nightclubs and upscale bars only in Boston, Miami, Las Vegas, and Los Angeles in order to draw the attention of "elite" customers prior to its broader release in grocery and convenience stores in the future.

Recently, a high-tech form of selective distribution has emerged whereby products are pushed through to the membership of exclusive virtual social networks. Scion Speak was developed as a social network Internet portal where Toyota Scion owners could design and share their own unique graffiti-type artwork which then could be airbrushed onto the body of their cars. Members of the network, which is managed by a quirky marketing firm called StrawberryFrog, have the exclusive rights to the car customization services, as well as to some available custom designs made by a professional artist contracted by the company. This type of service is among the first to leverage the power of social network Web sites as a product distribution medium.[14]

Exclusive Distribution The most restrictive form of market coverage is exclusive distribution, which entails only one or a few dealers within a given area. Because buyers may have to search or travel extensively to buy the product, exclusive distribution is usually confined to consumer specialty goods, a few shopping goods, and major industrial equipment. Products such as Rolls-Royce automobiles, Chris-Craft powerboats, and Pettibone tower cranes are distributed under exclusive arrangements. Sometimes exclusive territories are granted by new companies (such as franchisors) to obtain market coverage in a particular area. Limited distribution may also serve to project an exclusive image for the product.

Retailers and wholesalers may be unwilling to commit the time and money necessary to promote and service a product unless the manufacturer guarantees them an exclusive territory. This arrangement shields the dealer from direct competition and enables it to be the main beneficiary of the manufacturer's promotion efforts in that geographic area. With exclusive distribution, channels of communication are usually well established because the manufacturer works with a limited number of dealers rather than many accounts.

Exclusive distribution also takes place within a retailer's store rather than a geographic area—for example, when a retailer agrees not to sell a manufacturer's competing brands. Mossimo, traditionally an apparel wholesaler, developed an agreement with Target to design clothing and related items sold exclusively at Target stores. Other exclusive distributors involved in this successful model include Thomas O'Brien domestics, Sonia Kashuk makeup, Isaac Mizrahi domestics and apparel, and Todd Oldham home furnishings for college students.

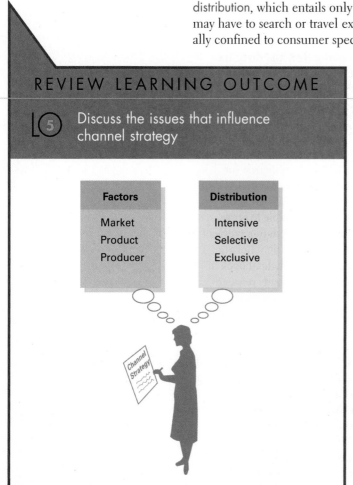

REVIEW LEARNING OUTCOME

LO 5   Discuss the issues that influence channel strategy

Factors	Distribution
Market	Intensive
Product	Selective
Producer	Exclusive

Channel Strategy

TYPES OF CHANNEL RELATIONSHIPS

A marketing channel is more than a set of institutions linked by economic ties. Social relationships play an important role in building unity among channel members. A critical aspect of channel management, therefore, is managing the social relationships among channel members to achieve synergy. Marketing managers should carefully consider the types of relationships they choose to foster between their company and other companies, and in doing so, pay close attention to the benefits and hazards associated with each relationship type.

Channel Relationship Types

Channel members must create and manage multiple relationships with other members in order to create an efficient environment for exchange. Relationships among channel members range from "loose" to "tight," taking the form of a continuum stretching from single transactions to complex interdependent relationships such as partnerships or alliances. The choice of relationship type is important for channel management because each relationship type carries with it different levels of time, financial, and resource investment. Three basic types of relationships, organized by degree of closeness, are commonly considered: Arm's-Length, integrated relationships, and cooperative.

Arm's-Length Relationships At one end of the relationship continuum are relationships considered by channel members to be temporary or one-time-only. These relationships are often referred to as "Arm's-Length" relationships due to the companies' unwillingness or lack of ability to develop a closer type of relationship. In Arm's-Length relationships, both parties retain their independence and pursue only their own interests while attempting to benefit from the goods or services provided by the other. This type of relationship is often used when a company has a sudden and/or unique need for a product or service and does not anticipate this need will arise again in the near future. For example, what might happen if Chevrolet were suddenly faced with an unusual situation where Bridgestone, its usual tire producer for the Chevy Tahoe, were unable to provide shipment of tires in reasonable time for a planned production run? One solution might be to engage in a temporary, Arm's-Length relationship with an alternate provider such as Michelin, who might be able to supply substitute tires on a temporary basis and thus save Chevrolet the costs associated with delaying the production run.

This sort of channel arrangement, however, involves a number of downsides. Because Chevrolet needs the tires on short notice, Michelin might decide to charge a somewhat higher price then usual, and furthermore, because the order placed was a onetime-only order and contained a fixed number of units, it is unlikely that Chevrolet would be able to take advantage of discounts available for customers buying in large quantities. In addition, because the relationship between Chevrolet and Michelin is new, there is no history or friendship to draw on in cases where disagreements or conflicts arise related to the terms of the agreement. In closer relationships, channel members might easily resolve their differences through communication, future promises, or bargaining. But in Arm's-Length relationships it is sometimes necessary to resolve Arm's-Length disputes through more formal and costly means such as arbitration or lawsuits. For all of these reasons, companies often find it appealing to develop more concrete, long-term relationships with other channel members.

Integrated Relationships At the opposite end of the relationship continuum from Arm's-Length relationships is a situation where one company (vertical integration) or several companies acting as one (a supply chain), perform all channel functions. These closely bonded types of relationships are collectively referred to as integrated relationships. Integrated relationships are characterized by formal arrangements that explicitly define the relationships to the involved channel members. For example, with vertical integration,

 ... (placed above)

> **Arm's-Length relationships**
> A relationship between companies that is loose, characterized by low relational investment and trust, and usually taking the form of a series of discrete transactions with no/low expectation of future interaction or service.
>
> **integrated relationships**
> A relationship between companies that is tightly connected, with linked processes across and between firm boundaries, and high levels of trust and interfirm commitment.

cooperative relationships
A relationship between companies that takes the form of informal partnership with moderate levels of trust and information sharing as needed to further each company's goals.

all of the related channel members are collectively owned by a single legal entity (which may be one of the channel members, or may be a third party), with ownership established through formal legal titles and/or agreements. This sort of relational arrangement has often been employed by McDonald's Corporation, whose subsidiary companies have owned dairy and potato farms and processing plants that grow and process components of the products served by the chain's fast-food restaurants. A supply chain consists of several companies acting together in a highly organized and efficient manner, while employing the same or similar techniques as a single vertically integrated company.

Based on these descriptions, it seems that integrated relationships would be the preferred relationship type in almost all company-to-company channel settings. However, highly integrated relationships also come with some significant costs and/or hazards. For example, the single-owner model is somewhat risky because a large amount of capital assets must be purchased or leased (requiring a potentially huge initial cash outlay), and the failure of any portion of the business may result in not only the economic loss of that portion, but may also reduce the value of the other business units (or render them totally worthless). Because these trade-offs are sometimes hard to justify, companies often look for a sort of "happy medium" between Arm's-Length and integrated relationships that enables them to maximize the advantages of both relationship types while limiting their potential risks.

REVIEW LEARNING OUTCOME

LO₆ Discuss the different channel relationship types and their unique costs and benefits

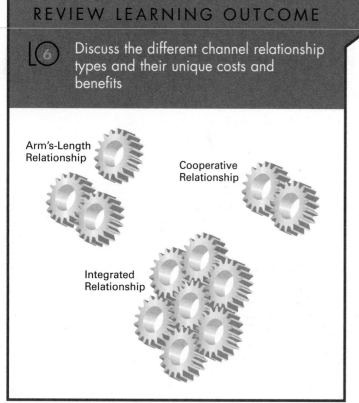

Arm's-Length Relationship

Cooperative Relationship

Integrated Relationship

Cooperative Relationships Cooperative relationships, which exist between Arm's-Length and integrated relationships in terms of their connectedness, take many different forms. Cooperative relationships include non-equity agreements such as franchising and licensing, as well as equity-based joint ventures and strategic alliances (see Chapter 5 for a review). In general, cooperative relationships are administered using some sort of formal contract. This is in contrast to Arm's-Length relationships, which are enforced through legal action (or the implied threat thereof), and integrated relationships that rely on informal social enforcement to secure the agreement based on trust, commitment, and loyalty. Cooperative relationships thus tend to be more flexible than integrated relationships, but are also structured with greater detail and depth than Arm's-Length relationships. They tend to be used when a company wants less ambiguity in the channel relationship than the Arm's-Length relationship can provide, but without the long-term and/or capital investment required to achieve full integration.

LO₇

THE LOGISTICS FUNCTION IN THE SUPPLY CHAIN

Now that you are familiar with the structure and strategy of supply chain management, it is important to also understand the physical means through which products move through the supply chain. As mentioned earlier, supply chain management coordinates and integrates all of the activities performed by supply chain members into a seamless process. The logistics function of the supply chain is responsible for the movement and delivery of goods and services into, through, and out of each firm in the supply chain network. The logistics function consists of several interrelated and integrated logistical components: (1) sourcing and procurement of raw materials and supplies,

(2) production scheduling, (3) order processing, (4) inventory management and control, (5) warehousing and materials-handling, and (6) transportation.

A logistics information system provides the technological link connecting all of the logistics components of the supply chain. The components of the system include, for example, software for materials acquisition and handling, warehouse-management and enterprise-wide solutions, data storage and integration in data warehouses, mobile communications, electronic data interchange, RFID chips, and the Internet. Working together, the components of the logistics information system are the fundamental enablers of successful supply chain management.

The supply chain team, leveraging the capabilities of the logistics information system, orchestrates the movement of goods, services, and information from the source to the consumer. Supply chain teams typically cut across organizational boundaries, embracing all parties who participate in moving the product to market. The best supply chain teams also move beyond the organization to include the external participants in the chain, such as suppliers, transportation carriers, and third-party logistics suppliers. Members of the supply chain communicate, coordinate, and cooperate extensively to make the logistics function as efficient and effective as possible.

Today's corporate supply chain logisticians have become so efficient that the U.S. Marine Corps is now consulting with companies like Wal-Mart, UPS, and Unilever to improve its own supply chain efficiency. The Marine Corps's goal is to reduce the time it takes to deliver supplies to the front lines from one week to 24 hours and lower costs by cutting inventories in half.

Sourcing and Procurement

One of the most important links in the supply chain is the one between the manufacturer and the supplier. Purchasing professionals are on the front lines of supply chain management. Purchasing departments plan purchasing strategies, develop specifications, select suppliers, and negotiate price and service levels. Often, goods are procured for use in local manufacturing processes from suppliers halfway around the world. This is especially true for the United States, which is the world's top importer with nearly $2 trillion worth of purchased merchandise entering the nation annually through its international ports.[15]

The goal of most sourcing and procurement activities is to reduce the costs of raw materials and supplies. Purchasing professionals have traditionally relied on tough negotiations to get the lowest price possible from suppliers of raw materials, supplies, and components. Perhaps the biggest contribution purchasing can make to supply chain management, however, is in the area of vendor relations. Companies can use the purchasing function to strategically manage suppliers in order to reduce the total cost of materials and services. Through enhanced vendor relations, buyers and sellers can develop cooperative relationships that reduce costs and improve efficiency with the aim of lowering prices and enriching profits. By integrating suppliers into their companies' businesses, purchasing managers have become better able to streamline purchasing processes, manage inventory levels, and reduce overall costs of the sourcing and procurement operations.

Order Processing

The order is often the catalyst that sets the supply chain in motion, especially in the build-to-order environments of leading computer manufacturers such as Dell. The order processing system processes the requirements of the customer and sends the information into the supply chain via the logistics information system. The order goes to the manufacturer's warehouse. If the product is in stock, the order is filled and arrangements are made to ship it. If the product is not in stock, it triggers a replenishment request that finds its way to the factory floor.

The role of proper order processing in providing good service cannot be overemphasized. As an order enters the system, management must monitor two flows: the flow of goods and the flow of information. Often marketers' best-laid plans get entangled in the order processing system. Obviously, good communication among sales representatives, office personnel, and warehouse and shipping personnel is essential to correct order

logistics information system
The link that connects all of the logistics components of the supply chain.

supply chain team
An entire group of individuals who orchestrate the movement of goods, services, and information from the source to the consumer.

order processing system
A system whereby orders are entered into the supply chain and filled.

electronic data interchange (EDI)
Information technology that replaces the paper documents that usually accompany business transactions, such as purchase orders and invoices, with electronic transmission of the needed information to reduce inventory levels, improve cash flow, streamline operations, and increase the speed and accuracy of information transmission.

inventory control system
A method of developing and maintaining an adequate assortment of materials or products to meet a manufacturer's or a customer's demand.

materials requirement planning (MRP) (materials management)
An inventory control system that manages the replenishment of raw materials, supplies, and components from the supplier to the manufacturer.

distribution resource planning (DRP)
An inventory control system that manages the replenishment of goods from the manufacturer to the final consumer.

processing. Shipping incorrect merchandise or partially filled orders can create just as much dissatisfaction as stockouts or slow deliveries. The flow of goods and information must be continually monitored so that mistakes can be corrected before an invoice is prepared and the merchandise shipped.

Order processing is becoming more automated through the use of computer technology known as electronic data interchange (EDI). The basic idea of EDI is to replace the paper documents that usually accompany business transactions, such as purchase orders and invoices, with electronic transmission of the needed information. A typical EDI message includes all the information that would traditionally be included on a paper invoice such as product code, quantity, and transportation details. The information is usually sent via private networks, which are more secure and reliable than the networks used for standard e-mail messages. Most importantly, the information can be read and processed by computers, significantly reducing costs and increasing efficiency. Companies that use EDI can reduce inventory levels, improve cash flow, streamline operations, and increase the speed and accuracy of information transmission. EDI also creates a closer relationship between buyers and sellers.

It should not be surprising that retailers have become major users of EDI. For Wal-Mart, Target, and the like, logistics speed and accuracy are crucial competitive tools in an overcrowded retail environment. Many big retailers are helping their suppliers acquire EDI technology so that they can be linked into the system. EDI works hand in hand with retailers' *efficient consumer response* programs, which are designed to have the right products on the shelf, in the right styles and colors, at the right time, through improved inventory, ordering, and distribution techniques.

Inventory Management and Control

Closely interrelated with the procurement, manufacturing, and ordering processes is the inventory control system—a method that develops and maintains an adequate assortment of materials or products to meet a manufacturer's or a customer's demands.

Inventory decisions, for both raw materials and finished goods, have a big impact on supply chain costs and the level of service provided. If too many products are kept in inventory, costs increase—as do risks of obsolescence, theft, and damage. If too few products are kept on hand, then the company risks product shortages and angry customers, and ultimately lost sales. For example, negative sales forecasts for the Christmas buying season in the past few years caused many retailers to cut back on orders because they were afraid of having to discount large end-of-the-year inventories. As a result, many companies, including Panasonic and Lands' End, lost sales due to inventory shortages on popular items. The goal of inventory management, therefore, is to keep inventory levels as low as possible while maintaining an adequate supply of goods to meet customer demand.

Managing inventory from the supplier to the manufacturer is called materials requirement planning (MRP), or materials management. This system also encompasses the sourcing and procurement operations, signaling purchasing when raw materials, supplies, or components will need to be replenished for the production of more goods. The system that manages the finished goods inventory from manufacturer to end user is commonly referred to as distribution resource planning (DRP). Both inventory systems use various inputs, such as sales forecasts, available inventory, outstanding orders, lead times, and

Most trading partners that adopt EDI do so for increased efficiencies and cost savings. Sometimes pressures from larger trading partners force smaller trading partners to use EDI. For instance, Wal-Mart will not do business with a supplier that doesn't agree to use its preferred EDI processes.

© AP IMAGES/JAE C. HONG

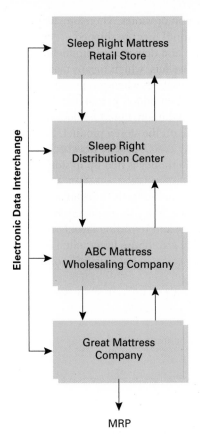

EXHIBIT 12.7

Inventory Replenishment Example

Sleep Right is planning a promotion on the Great Mattress Company's Gentle Rest mattress. Sales forecast is for 50 units to be sold. Sleep Right has 10 open Gentle Rest orders with its distribution center. New mattresses must be delivered in two weeks in time for the promotion.

Sleep Right's Distribution Center is electronically notified of the order of 50 new Gentle Rest mattresses. It currently has 20 Gentle Rest mattresses in inventory and begins putting together the transportation plans to deliver these to the Sleep Right Store. Delivery takes one day. It orders 40 new mattresses from its mattress wholesaler to make up the difference.

ABC Mattress Wholesaling Company is electronically notified of Sleep Right DC's order of 40 new Gentle Rest mattresses. It currently does not have any of these in stock but electronically orders 40 from the Great Mattress Company's factory. Once it receives the new mattresses, it can have them delivered to the Sleep Right DC in two days.

The Great Mattress Company electronically receives ABC's order and forwards it to the factory floor. Production of a new mattress takes 20 minutes. The total order of 40 mattresses can be ready to be shipped to ABC in two days. Delivery takes one day. Raw material supplies for this order are electronically requested from Great Mattress's supply partners, who deliver the needed materials just-in-time to its stitching machines.

mode of transportation to be used, to determine what actions must be taken to replenish goods at all points in the supply chain. Demand in the system is collected at each level in the supply chain, from the retailer back up the chain to the manufacturer. With the use of electronic data interchange, the information can be transmitted much faster to meet the quick-response needs of today's competitive marketplace. Exhibit 12.7 provides an example of inventory replenishment using DRP from the retailer to the manufacturer.

Other inventory management systems that have gained in popularity in recent years, however, use few or no forecasts at all during the scheduling of shipments. Known as automatic replenishment programs, these systems trigger shipments only once a good (usually something with a relatively predictable demand pattern) is sold to the customer. Using an EDI linkage connected with barcode scanners at the point of purchase, the supplier can view the inventory being held at the next tier of the supply chain in real time. When stock of a good at the customer location falls below preestablished safety levels, orders are automatically packed and shipped from the supplier location. Thus, in this type of system, the supplier takes responsibility for keeping inventory on the shelves or in the customer's warehouse; this usually results in reduced stockouts and lowers overall inventory levels.

Warehousing and Materials-Handling

Supply chain logisticians oversee the constant flow of raw materials from suppliers to manufacturer and finished goods from the manufacturer to the ultimate consumer. Although build-to-order manufacturing processes may eliminate the need to warehouse many raw materials, manufacturers may often keep some safety stock on hand in the event of an emergency, such as a strike at a supplier's plant or a catastrophic event that temporarily stops the flow of raw materials to the production line. Likewise, the final user may not need or want the goods at the same time the manufacturer produces and wants to sell them. Products like grain and corn are produced seasonally, but consumers demand them year-round. Other products, such as Christmas ornaments and turkeys, are produced

automatic replenishment program
An inventory management system that triggers shipments only once a good is sold to the customer; the program uses EDI linkage connected with barcode scanners at the point of purchase, so the supplier can view the inventory being held at the next tier of the supply chain in real time.

materials-handling system
A method of moving inventory into,
within, and out of the warehouse.

year-round, but consumers do not want them until autumn or winter. Therefore, management must have a storage system to hold these products until they are shipped.

Storage is what helps manufacturers manage supply and demand, or production and consumption. It provides time utility to buyers and sellers, which means that the seller stores the product until the buyer wants or needs it. Even when products are used regularly, not seasonally, many manufacturers store excess products in case the demand surpasses the amount produced at a given time. Storing additional product does have disadvantages, however, including the costs of insurance on the stored product, taxes, obsolescence or spoilage, theft, and warehouse operating costs. Another drawback is opportunity costs—that is, the opportunities lost because money is tied up in stored product instead of being used for something else.

Because businesses are focusing on cutting supply chain costs, the warehousing industry is also changing to better serve its customers. For example, many warehouses are putting greater emphasis on more efficient unloading and reloading layouts and customized services that move merchandise through the warehouse faster, often in the same day. They also are investing in services using sophisticated tracking technology such as materials-handling systems.

A materials-handling system moves inventory into, within, and out of the warehouse. Materials-handling includes these functions:

- Receiving goods into the warehouse or distribution center
- Identifying, sorting, and labeling the goods
- Dispatching the goods to a temporary storage area
- Recalling, selecting, or picking the goods for shipment (may include packaging the product in a protective container for shipping)

The goal of the materials-handling system is to move items quickly with minimal handling. With a manual, nonautomated materials-handling system, a product may be handled more than a dozen times. Each time it is handled, the cost and risk of damage increase; each lifting of a product stresses its package. Consequently, most manufacturers today have switched to automated systems. Scanners quickly identify goods entering and leaving a warehouse through bar-coded labels affixed to the packaging. Electronic storage and retrieval systems automatically store and pick goods in the warehouse or distribution center. Automated materials-handling systems decrease product handling, ensure accurate placement of product, and improve the accuracy of order picking and the rates of on-time shipment. In fact, many firms are relying on materials handling systems operated either partially, or in rare cases fully, by robots. For example, at office supply giant Staples, over 150 robots collect materials, process, and pack up to 8,000 orders daily.[16]

At Dell, the OptiPlex system runs the factory. The computer software receives orders, sends requests for parts to suppliers, orders components, organizes assembly of the product, and even arranges for it to be shipped. Thus, instead of hundreds of workers, often fewer than six are working at one time. An order for a few hundred computers can be filled in less than eight hours using the automated system. With the OptiPlex system, productivity has increased dramatically.

Transportation

Transportation typically accounts for 5 to 10 percent of the price of goods. Supply chain logisticians must decide which mode of transportation to use to move products from supplier to producer and from producer to buyer. These decisions are, of course, related to all other logistics decisions. The five major modes of transportation are railroads, motor carriers, pipelines, water transportation, and airways. Supply chain managers generally choose a mode of transportation on the basis of several criteria:

- *Cost:* The total amount a specific carrier charges to move the product from the point of origin to the destination

- *Transit time*: The total time a carrier has possession of goods, including the time required for pickup and delivery, handling, and movement between the point of origin and the destination

- *Reliability*: The consistency with which the carrier delivers goods on time and in acceptable condition

- *Capability*: The ability of the carrier to provide the appropriate equipment and conditions for moving specific kinds of goods, such as those that must be transported in a controlled environment (for example, under refrigeration)

- *Accessibility*: A carrier's ability to move goods over a specific route or network

- *Traceability*: The relative ease with which a shipment can be located and transferred

EXHIBIT 12.8

Criteria for Ranking Transportation Modes

	Highest				Lowest
Relative Cost	Air	Truck	Rail	Pipe	Water
Transit Time	Water	Rail	Pipe	Truck	Air
Reliability	Pipe	Truck	Rail	Air	Water
Capability	Water	Rail	Truck	Air	Pipe
Accessibility	Truck	Rail	Air	Water	Pipe
Traceability	Air	Truck	Rail	Water	Pipe

The mode of transportation used depends on the needs of the shipper, as they relate to these six criteria. Exhibit 12.8 compares the basic modes of transportation on these criteria.

The importance of transportation to modern companies is difficult to overstate. Many industry experts regard on-time delivery and shipment of products as the single most important supply chain management criteria leading to customer satisfaction. This perspective is reflected in companies' investment in transportation management systems—software applications designed to optimize transportation modes' routing, loading, unloading, and other functions. U.S. firms are expected to spend between $500 and $800 million annually on specialized transportation management software by 2011.[17]

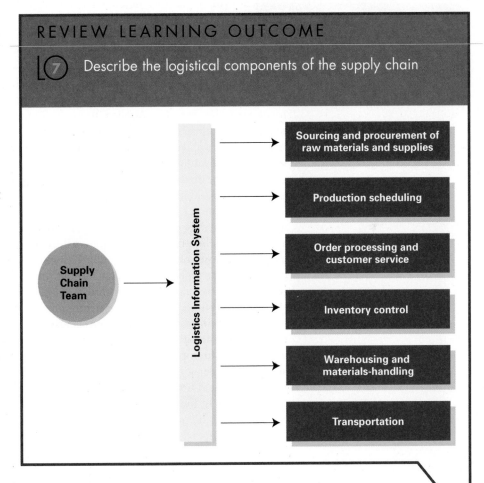

REVIEW LEARNING OUTCOME

LO7 Describe the logistical components of the supply chain

TRENDS IN SUPPLY CHAIN MANAGEMENT

Several technological advances and business trends are affecting the job of the supply chain manager today. Four of the most important trends are the globalization of supply chain management, advanced computer technology, outsourcing of logistics functions, and electronic distribution.

The multitude of global trade rules is why multinational companies like Eastman Kodak are so committed to working through the World Trade Organization to develop a global set of rules and to encourage countries to participate.

© VICKI BEAVER

Global Supply Chain Management

As global trade becomes a more decisive factor in success or failure for firms of all sizes, global supply chain management increases in importance. For example, one supply chain management consultant reported cost savings of 20 to 40 percent on finished goods imported from China versus their American counterparts.[18] In addition to savings, another supply chain research team estimated the output of the global economy will grow at a rate of 3 percent or more until the year 2030, with much of the growth occurring outside the United States, and thereby increasing the U.S. import base.[19] Thus, one of the most critical global supply chain issues for importers of any size is coping with the legalities of trade in other countries. Companies must be aware of the permits, licenses, and registrations they may need to acquire and, depending on the type of product they are importing, the tariffs, quotas, and other regulations that apply in each country. This multitude of different rules is why multinational companies like Eastman Kodak are so committed to working through the World Trade Organization to develop a global set of rules and to encourage countries to participate. Other goals for these companies include reducing trade barriers, such as tariffs. As these barriers fall, the flow of merchandise across borders is increasing due to more companies sourcing from multiple countries. For instance, a Kodak camera sold in France may have been assembled there, but the camera mechanism probably came from China and the film from the United States.

The presence of different rules hasn't slowed the spread of supply chain globalization, however. In spite of the added costs associated with importing and exporting goods, many companies are looking to other countries for their sourcing and procurement needs. For example, Applica, Inc., a U.S. maker of small appliances, is committed to using technology to improve its relationships with suppliers in Mexico. The company has linked its suppliers directly to sales data from Wal-Mart stores to help manage production and inventory costs. In another case, U.S. soap producers faced with increased prices for a key ingredient due to new government legislation were forced to look for substitutes in Indonesia and Malaysia in order to remain profitable.[20]

Transportation can also be a major issue for companies dealing with global supply chains. Uncertainty regarding shipping usually tops the list of reasons why companies, especially smaller ones, resist international markets. Even companies that have scored overseas successes often are vulnerable to logistical problems. Large companies have the capital to create global logistics systems, but smaller companies often must rely on the services of carriers and freight forwarders to get their products to overseas markets.

In some instances, poor infrastructure makes transportation dangerous and unreliable. And the process of moving goods across the borders of even the most industrialized nations can still be complicated by government regulations. For example, NAFTA was supposed to improve the flow of goods across the continent, but moving goods across the border still requires approvals from dozens of government agencies, broker intervention, and hours spent at border checks. Shipping companies like Ryder are working to make the process easier. Currently, Ryder operates a cross-border facility in San Antonio to help clients like General Motors and Xerox with customs and logistics costs. The company also is part of a pilot project to automate border crossings with technology similar to that of an E-Zpass. The new system sends and receives short-range radio signals containing information on the load to tollbooths, weigh stations, and border crossings. If the cargo meets requirements, the truck or train receives a green light to go ahead. Questionable cargo is set aside for further inspection. Transportation industry experts say the system can reduce delivery times by hours.

Advanced Computer Technology

Advanced computer technology has boosted the efficiency of logistics dramatically with tools such as automatic identification systems (auto ID) using bar coding and radio-frequency technology, communications technology, and supply chain software systems that help synchronize the flow of goods and information with customer demand. Amazon.com's state-of-the-art distribution centers, for instance, use sophisticated order picking systems that utilize computer terminals to guide workers through the picking and packing process. Radio-frequency technology, which uses radio signals that work with scanned bar codes to identify products, directs Amazon's workers to the exact locations in the warehouse where the product is stored. Warehouse management software examines pick rates, location, and picking and storage patterns, and builds combinations of customer orders for shipping. After installing these supply chain technology tools, Amazon saw a 70 percent improvement in operational efficiency.

Procter & Gamble and many other companies use RFID tags in shipments to Wal-Mart stores. RFID tags are chips attached to a pallet of goods that allow the goods to be tracked from the time they are packed at the manufacturing plant until the consumer purchases them. Benefits include increased revenue for Wal-Mart (because the shelves are always full) and reduced inventory management costs (because overstocking and time spent counting items is minimized). Best Buy is currently planning to use an RFID-enabled payment system to reduce and eventually eliminate checkout lines at the front of the store—customers with a personalized Best Buy RFID shopping card could simply load up their carts and walk out the front door, with their checking or credit card account debited for the price of their merchandise before they even unlock their car.[21] However, RFID has been slower than expected in penetrating the retail sector. While 44 percent of manufacturers have adopted RFID at some level, only about 10 percent of retailers have done so.[22] Though some experts attribute the slowness of retail adoption of RFID to its complexity of implementation, many others suggest that retailers are scared away because of difficulty in determining their return on RFID-related investment.

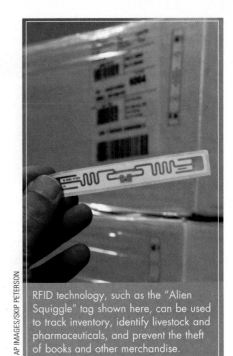

RFID technology, such as the "Alien Squiggle" tag shown here, can be used to track inventory, identify livestock and pharmaceuticals, and prevent the theft of books and other merchandise.

One of the other major goals of technology is to bring up-to-date information to the supply chain manager's desk. The transportation system has long been referred to as an informational "black hole," where products and materials fall out of sight until they reappear some time later in a plant, store, or warehouse. Now carriers have systems that track freight, monitor the speed and location of carriers, and make routing decisions on the spur of the moment. Roadway Express, named one of the "Top 100 U.S. Motor Carriers" by Inbound Logistics, handles more than 70,000 shipments a day, many for large retailers like Wal-Mart, Target, and Home Depot. Information technology systems enable each package to be tracked from the minute it is received at one of Roadway's terminals until it is delivered. Customers can check on the progress of their shipment anytime by logging on to Roadway's Web site and entering the tracking number. Companies needing trucking services can go to the Inbound Logistics Web site and use their Trucking Decision Support Tool to identify motor carriers that can meet their service needs.[23] Swedish-based communications giant Ericsson, whose operations span the globe, uses specialized supply chain software to gain visibility over the 50,000 outbound shipments it makes a year. As products leave its manufacturing facilities, transportation providers transmit status information at specified intervals to Ericsson's information system, which is accessible to management using a standard Web browser. The company has benefited greatly from the increased visibility of shipments the system has provided. Ericsson's management is now in a position to identify bottlenecks and respond before a crisis occurs, as well as measure the performance of its supply chain at different checkpoints.

Outsourcing Logistics Functions

External partners are becoming increasingly important in the efficient deployment of supply chain management. Outsourcing, or contract logistics, is a rapidly growing segment of the distribution industry in which a manufacturer or supplier turns over an entire function of the logistics system, such as buying and managing transportation or warehousing, to an independent third party. Many manufacturers are turning to outside

outsourcing (contract logistics) A manufacturer's or supplier's use of an independent third party to manage an entire function of the logistics system, such as transportation, warehousing, or order processing.

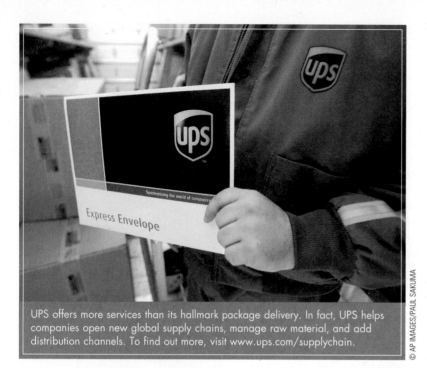

UPS offers more services than its hallmark package delivery. In fact, UPS helps companies open new global supply chains, manage raw material, and add distribution channels. To find out more, visit www.ups.com/supplychain.

© AP IMAGES/PAUL SAKUMA

electronic distribution
A distribution technique that includes any kind of product or service that can be distributed electronically, whether over traditional forms such as fiber-optic cable or through satellite transmission of electronic signals.

partners for their logistics expertise in an effort to focus on the core competencies that they do best. Partners create and manage entire solutions for getting products where they need to be, when they need to be there. Logistics partners offer staff, an infrastructure, and services that reach consumers virtually anywhere in the world. Because a logistics provider is focused, clients receive service in a timely, efficient manner, thereby increasing customers' level of satisfaction and boosting their perception of added value to a company's offerings.

Third-party contract logistics allows companies to cut inventories, locate stock at fewer plants and distribution centers, and still provide the same or increased level of service. The companies then can refocus investment on their core business. Ford Motor Company uses third-party logistics provider UPS Worldwide Logistics Group to manage the delivery of Ford and Lincoln cars and trucks in the United States, Canada, and Mexico. The alliance between Ford and UPS has substantially reduced the time it takes to move vehicles from Ford's assembly plants to dealers and customers. Moreover, the Web-based system enables Ford and its dealers to track an individual vehicle's location from production through delivery to the final destination. Similarly, in the hospitality industry, procurement services company Avendra enables Fairmont Hotels & Resorts, Hyatt Hotels, Intercontinental Hotels Group, Marriott International, and others to enjoy significant savings and value-added supply chain services.[24] Avendra negotiates with suppliers to obtain virtually everything a hotel might need, from food and beverages to golf course maintenance. By relying on Avendra to manage many aspects of the supply chain, the hotels are able to concentrate on their core function—providing hospitality.

Many firms are taking outsourcing one step further by allowing business partners to take over the final assembly of their product or its packaging in an effort to reduce inventory costs, speed up delivery, or better meet customer requirements. Ryder Truck Lines assembles and packages 22 different combinations of shrink-wrapped boxes that contain the ice trays, drawers, shelves, doors, and other accessories for the various refrigerator models Whirlpool sells. Similarly, outsourcing firm StarTek, Inc. packages and ships products for Microsoft, provides technical support to customers of America Online, and maintains AT&T communication systems.

Electronic Distribution

Electronic distribution is the most recent development in the logistics arena. Broadly defined, electronic distribution includes any kind of product or service that can be distributed electronically, whether over traditional forms such as fiber-optic cable or through satellite transmission of electronic signals. For instance, instead of buying and installing software from stores, computer users purchase and download software over the Internet or rent the same software from Internet services that have the program available for use on their servers. For example, Intuit, Inc., allows people to fill out their tax returns on its Web site for a fee rather than buying its TurboTax software. Consumers can purchase tickets to sporting events, concerts, and movies over the Internet and print the tickets at home. And music, television shows, and movies have long been delivered to consumers through electronic pipelines. Apple sells over 20 million songs and TV shows annually through iTunes.[25]

One of the most innovative electronic distribution ventures of late has come from ESPN. The sports broadcaster offers free access on the iPhone to the most comprehensive sports coverage available in a mobile format. Using an iPhone App, ESPN Mobile Web broadcasts a multimedia-rich sports information package unlike anything else, including breaking news and analysis, up-to-the-minute scores, ESPN Fantasy teams, ESPN columnists, the ESPN Podcenter, and more. There's also a special section where users can select to receive news and stats about their favorite players and teams.[26]

Supply Chain Security

Firms are expending more effort on securing their supply chains from external threats than at any time in recent memory. Natural disasters, widespread technology failures, political instability, terrorism, disease pandemics, and worker strikes are but a few of the major events that can cause a supply chain to shut down temporarily or for an extended amount of time. The supply chain must be guarded from end to end because it is only as strong as its weakest link.

Managing supply chain disruptions begins with identifying the risks potentially affecting each node and link in the supply chain network.[27] This is especially true when the supply chain is global, with nodes and links located in or across international boundaries. Global supply chains are particularly at risk because members in faraway places often fail to completely understand the political, legal, and technological culture of the local area. Once risks are identified and assessed, the firm should put controls in place to monitor dangerous or volatile situations, and buy insurance when it appears that things could go wrong in the supply chain. The very best supply chains with respect to security also build contingency plans that are able to address situations quickly in the event of an emergency and get the supply chain back online. In fact, some businesses have completely replicated their systems and facilities in different geographic locations and, in the event of a disaster, can activate these backups within 24 hours.

Green Supply Chain Management

In response to the need for firms to both gain cost savings and act as leaders in protecting the natural environment, many are adopting green supply chain management principles as a key part of their supply chain strategy. Green supply chain management involves the integration of environmentally conscious thinking into all phases of key supply chain management processes. Such activities include green materials sourcing, the design of products with consideration given to their environmental impact based on packaging, shipment and use, as well as end-of-life management for products including easy recycling and/or clean disposal. By enacting green supply chain management principles, firms hope to simultaneously generate cost savings and protect our natural resources from excess pollution, damage, and/or wastefulness.

A number of relatively simple changes to typical supply chain management processes can achieve significant positive environmental impacts.

REVIEW LEARNING OUTCOME

LO8 Discuss the new and emerging trends in supply chain management

Trends

Many companies are looking globally for their sourcing and procurement needs.

Computer technology increases efficiency.

Third-party logistics allow companies to focus on core business functions.

Electronic distribution of products and services collapses the supply chain.

channel power
The capacity of a particular marketing channel member to control or influence the behavior of other channel members.

channel control
A situation that occurs when one marketing channel member intentionally affects another member's behavior.

channel leader (channel captain)
A member of a marketing channel that exercises authority and power over the activities of other channel members.

channel conflict
A clash of goals and methods between distribution channel members.

Trucks can switch to alternative fuels on long routes; drivers can be retrained and routes revised to limit the amount of time trucks sit idling; excess materials from manufacturing and staff processes can be recycled, composted, or avoided altogether; and reusable shipping containers and pallets introduced into the supply chain.[28] Though these activities may seem costly at first, many firms are recognizing the long term benefits. Whereas the common assumption among supply chain managers used to be that greening the supply chain would increase costs, many companies are realizing that environmentally conscious supply chain management can increase profits. General Motors, for example, increased profitability by over $12 million annually by switching to reusable containers when receiving shipments from their suppliers.[29]

MANAGING CHANNEL RELATIONSHIPS

In addition to considering the multiple different types of channel relationships and their costs and benefits, managers must also be aware of the social dimensions that are constantly impacting their relationships. The basic social dimensions of channels are power, control, leadership, conflict, and partnering.

Channel Power, Control, and Leadership

Channel power is a channel member's ability to control or influence the behavior of other channel members. Channel control occurs when one channel member's power affects another member's behavior. To achieve control, a channel member assumes channel leadership and exercises authority and power. This member is termed the channel leader, or channel captain. In one marketing channel, a manufacturer may be the leader because it controls new-product designs and product availability. In another, a retailer may be the channel leader because it wields power and control over the retail price, inventory levels, and postsale service.

The exercise of channel power is a routine element of many business activities in which the outcome is often greater control over a company's brands. For example, the Sheraton Hotel chain operates hundreds of hotels across North America and worldwide, most of which are owned by franchisees. As with many franchises, it is in the best interest of the parent company to closely monitor and control operations to prevent the brand name from being devalued. However, when the chain asked its franchisees to invest nearly $4 billion of their own money to make improvements (such as redesigned lobbies and bathrooms) to keep the brand name from weakening, many owners balked and a power struggle ensued. Eventually, the parent company and ownership group came to an agreement detailing the hotel features Sheraton would control, such as lobby design, room layout, and even which coffee brand would be provided in the rooms, and which would be controlled by the owners (including the number of sheets provided on each bed).[30]

Channel Conflict

Inequitable channel relationships often lead to channel conflict, which is a clash of goals and methods among the members of a distribution channel. In a broad context, conflict may not be bad. Often it arises because staid, traditional channel members refuse to keep pace with the times. Removing an outdated intermediary may result in reduced costs for the entire channel. The Internet has forced many intermediaries to offer services such as merchandise tracking and inventory availability online.

© SUSAN VAN ETTEN

Conflicts among channel members can be due to many different situations and factors. Oftentimes, conflict arises because channel members have conflicting goals. For instance, athletic footwear retailers want to sell as many shoes as possible in order to maximize profits, regardless of whether the shoe is manufactured by Nike, Adidas, or Saucony, but the Nike manufacturer wants a certain sales volume and market share in each market.

Conflict can also arise when channel members fail to fulfill expectations of other channel members—for example, when a franchisee does not follow the rules set down by the franchisor or when communications channels break down between channel members. As another example, if a manufacturer shortens the period of warranty coverage and fails to inform dealers of this change, conflict may occur when dealers make repairs expecting that they will be reimbursed by the manufacturer. Further, ideological differences and different perceptions of reality can also cause conflict among channel members. For instance, retailers may believe "the customer is always right" and offer a very liberal return policy. Wholesalers and manufacturers may feel that people "try to get something for nothing" or don't follow product instructions carefully. Their differing views of allowable returns will undoubtedly conflict with those of retailers.

Conflict within a channel can be either horizontal or vertical. Horizontal conflict occurs among channel members on the same level, such as two or more different wholesalers or two or more different retailers that handle the same manufacturer's brands. This type of channel conflict is found most often when manufacturers practice dual or multiple distribution strategies. When Apple changed its distribution strategy and began opening its own stores, it angered Apple's traditional retail partners, some of whom ultimately filed lawsuits against the company. The primary allegation was that Apple stores were competing unfairly with them and that Apple favored its own stores when allocating desirable inventory (like iPods). Horizontal conflict can also occur when some channel members feel that other members on the same level are being treated differently by the manufacturer. For example, the American Booksellers Association, a group representing small independent booksellers, filed a lawsuit against bookstore giants Barnes & Noble and Borders, claiming they had violated antitrust laws by using their buying power to demand "illegal and secret" discounts from publishers. These deals, the association contended, put independent booksellers at a serious competitive disadvantage.

Many marketers and customers regard horizontal conflict as healthy competition. Much more serious is vertical conflict, which occurs between different levels in a marketing channel, most typically between the manufacturer and wholesaler or the manufacturer and retailer. Producer-versus-wholesaler conflict occurs when the producer chooses to bypass the wholesaler and deal directly with the consumer or retailer.

Dual distribution strategies can also cause vertical conflict in the channel. For example, high-end fashion designers traditionally sold their products through luxury retailers such as Neiman Marcus and Saks Fifth Avenue. Interested in increasing sales and gaining additional control over presentation, many designers such as Giorgio Armani, Donna Karan, and Louis Vuitton opened their own boutiques in the same shopping centers anchored by the luxury retailers. As a result, the retailers lost substantial revenues on the designers' items. Similarly, manufacturers experimenting with selling to customers directly over the Internet create conflict with their traditional retailing intermediaries. For example, Walgreens sells about 2 billion photo prints a year, all of which once were printed on Kodak paper using Kodak chemicals. When Kodak launched **KodakGallery.com**, a site where customers could upload digital prints to the Internet, view them, and order prints directly from Kodak, Walgreens took exception. It installed 2,300 traditional and digital photo kiosks made by Fuji, Kodak's main competitor.[31] The channel conflict cost Kodak an estimated $500 million a year in sales. In another case, Hollywood Studios petitioned federal regulators to allow them to release first-run movies over special cable and satellite channels in order to reduce the negative effects of movie piracy. Though the government has not yet ruled whether Hollywood's strategy will be allowed, the measure is being strongly opposed by DVD rental companies currently holding agreements with Hollywood, who would likely

horizontal conflict
A channel conflict that occurs among channel members on the same level.

vertical conflict
A channel conflict that occurs between different levels in a marketing channel, most typically between the manufacturer and wholesaler or between the manufacturer and retailer.

channel partnering
(channel cooperation)
The joint effort of all channel
members to create a channel that
serves customers and creates a
competitive advantage.

experience major sales losses if such first-run movies could be broadcast directly into homes rather than rented from their retail outlets.[32]

Producers and retailers may also disagree over the terms of the sale or other aspects of the business relationship. When Procter & Gamble introduced "everyday low pricing" to its retail channel members, a strategy designed to standardize wholesale prices and eliminate most trade promotions, many retailers retaliated. Some cut the variety of P&G sizes they carried or eliminated marginal brands. Others moved P&G brands from prime shelf space to less visible shelves.

Channel Partnering

Regardless of the locus of power, channel members rely heavily on one another. Even the most powerful manufacturers depend on dealers to sell their products; even the most powerful retailers require the products provided by suppliers. In sharp contrast to the adversarial relationships of the past between buyers and sellers, contemporary management thought emphasizes the development of close working partnerships among channel members. Channel partnering, or channel cooperation, is the joint effort of all channel members to create a channel that serves customers and creates a competitive advantage. Channel partnering is vital if each member is to gain something from other members. By cooperating, retailers, wholesalers, manufacturers, and suppliers can speed up inventory replenishment, improve customer service, and reduce the total costs of the marketing channel.

ETHICS in Marketing

ETHICS

Willbros Petroleum's Bribery Problem in Nigeria

As national economies become increasingly globalized, Western businesspeople are struggling with how to deal with local business corruption. Bribes, kickbacks, and under-the-table payments to both local channel partners and government officials are considered to be just "part of the cost of doing business" in many emerging nations. Though American law clearly makes such practices illegal, U.S. firms wanting to do business in places such as China, Russia, and Eastern Europe are increasingly finding they must develop tactics to address corrupt practices if they expect to succeed when developing these marketplaces.

Though many different types of corrupt activities are taking place, bribery is particularly problematic for American businesses doing business in foreign markets. For example, though Houston-based company Willbros had been working in Nigeria for nearly a half century, it was recently caught up in a bribery scandal that resulted in government allegations the firm had violated the Foreign Corrupt Practices Act (FCPA). The FCPA is a U.S. law that prohibits engaging in illicit business dealings both at home and abroad. In order to win more business, Willbros officials paid over $6 million to members of a government-run supplier consortium, with the result being their selection to build a $387 million natural gas pipeline, using those suppliers as partners throughout the project. The Willbros top management team was later blackmailed for an additional $1.5 million in payments in order to maintain the contract.

Willbros acknowledged as part of a plea for reduced punishment that members of its leadership team owned portions of some of Willbros' Nigerian customers and suppliers, and may have received illegal payments related to deals made with these companies and government officials. The results were predictable: The company was prosecuted by the U.S. Securities and Exchange Commission, and its leaders scrambled to cooperate with investigators in an attempt to avoid jail time. Yet, while Willbros was made an example of what can happen to U.S. businesses that participate in shady deals overseas, the problem of bribery remains one that continues to vex American companies wanting to expand their operations to new markets.

When attempting to increase business by entering emerging markets, how should U.S. companies handle local corruption by suppliers or governments? Should they "do as the Romans do" and risk prosecution at home, or attempt to impose Western values on foreign business cultures, and risk failure in entering the new marketplace? Payments to suppliers, bribes, money laundering, and kickback schemes are commonplace in many nations; how should a U.S. firm cope?[33]

Channel alliances and partnerships help managers create the parallel flow of materials and information required to leverage the channel's intellectual, material, and marketing resources. The rapid growth in channel partnering is due to new enabling technology and the need to lower costs. A comparison between companies that approach the marketplace unilaterally and those that engage in channel cooperation and form partnerships is detailed in Exhibit 12.9.

Collaborating channel partners meet the needs of consumers more effectively by ensuring that the right products are available at the right time and for a lower cost, thus boosting sales and profits. Forced to become more efficient, many companies are turning formerly adversarial relationships into partnerships. For example, Kraft is the largest coffee purchaser in the world. Rather than clash with coffee bean growers, Kraft partners with them to help build customer demand and develop "sustainable" coffee production (growing coffee in a way that reduces the impact on the environment, provides higher-quality ingredients for manufacturers to meet consumer needs, and is more valuable to the farmer).

EXHIBIT 12.9

Transaction-Based versus Partnership-Based Firms

Intensity Level	Transaction-Based	Partnership-Based
Relationships between Manufacturer and Supplier	• Short-term • Adversarial • Independent • Price more important	• Long-term • Cooperative • Dependent • Value-added services more important
Number of Suppliers	Many	Few
Level of Information Sharing	Minimal	High
Investment Required	Minimal	High

Source: David Frederick Ross, *Competing Through Supply Chain Management: Creating Market-Winning Strategies through Supply Chain Partnerships* (New York: Chapman & Hall, 1998), 61. Reprinted with kind permission from Springer Science and Business Media.

CHANNELS AND DISTRIBUTION DECISIONS FOR GLOBAL MARKETS

With the spread of free-trade agreements and treaties in recent decades, such as the European Union and the North American Free Trade Agreement (NAFTA), global marketing channels and management of the channels have become increasingly important to U.S. companies that export their products or manufacture abroad.

Developing Global Marketing Channels

Executives should recognize the unique cultural, economic, institutional, and legal aspects of each market before trying to design marketing channels in foreign countries. Manufacturers introducing products in global markets face a tough decision: what type of channel structure to use. Specifically, should the product be marketed directly, mostly by company salespeople, or through independent foreign intermediaries, such as agents and distributors? Using company salespeople generally provides more control and is less risky than using foreign intermediaries. However, setting up a sales force in a foreign country also entails a greater commitment, both financially and organizationally.

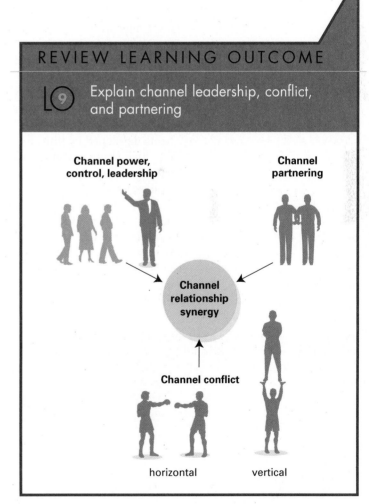

REVIEW LEARNING OUTCOME

LO9 Explain channel leadership, conflict, and partnering

Channel power, control, leadership

Channel partnering

Channel relationship synergy

Channel conflict

horizontal   vertical

© AP IMAGES/NG HAN GUAN

Marketers should be aware that channel structures and types abroad may differ from those in the United States. For instance, the more highly developed a nation is economically, the more specialized its channel types. Therefore, a marketer wishing to sell in Germany or Japan will have several channel types to choose from. Conversely, developing countries such as India, Ethiopia, and Venezuela have limited channel types available—there are typically few mail-order channels, vending machines, or specialized retailers and wholesalers. Some countries also regulate channel choices. Until 2004, Chinese regulations required foreign retailers to have a local partner. So when IKEA, the Swedish home furnishings retailer, opened its first two stores in China, it used joint ventures. When the regulations were lifted, however, IKEA opened its first wholly owned store in Guangzhou and then a Beijing store that is almost as big as eight football fields, second in size only to the company's flagship store in Stockholm.[34]

Developing effective marketing channels in emerging nations is further complicated due to different retail format preferences and differences in the ways locals shop. In many emerging nations, consumers shun large-scale formats popularized in the United States and Western Europe such as supercenter and other big-box retailers, in favor of tiny, independently owned street-side retailers that may be no larger than a closet. These small retailers (known at Procter & Gamble as "high frequency shops") provide small packages of goods that are intended to fulfill customer needs only for a day or two. Procter & Gamble estimates that over 620,000 such stores exist in Mexico alone, and that 80 percent of emerging nation citizens shop high-frequency stores multiple times per week. New channel strategies are currently being developed by firms like P&G in order to maximize sales and penetration into high-frequency shops, including reliance on local sales agents who are paid to ensure that popular products are placed as close as possible to the street and/or cash register.[35]

Marketers must also be aware that many countries have "gray" marketing channels in which products are distributed through unauthorized channel intermediaries. It is estimated that sales of counterfeit luxury items like Prada handbags and Big Bertha golf clubs have reached almost $2 billion a year. The new fakes are harder to detect and hit the market almost instantly. For instance, a fake Christian Dior saddlebag was available just weeks after the original arrived on retailers' shelves. Similarly, Chinese companies are producing so many knockoffs of Yamaha, Honda, and Suzuki motorcycles that the Japanese companies are seeing a drop in sales. What's more, many companies are getting so good at design piracy that they are beginning to launch their own new products.

The Internet has also proved to be a way for pirates to circumvent authorized distribution channels, especially in the case of popular prescription drugs. In recent years, the U.S. Customs Service has seized millions of dollars worth of prescription drugs, most of which were purchased from foreign Internet sites. Some were seized because they had not been approved for use in the United States, others because they did not comply with U.S. labeling laws. Most sites offer just a handful of the most popular drugs, such as Viagra. Consumers can get the drugs after obtaining the approval of a doctor, affiliated with the site, who never sees the patient.

REVIEW LEARNING OUTCOME

LO 10 Discuss channels and distribution decisions in global markets

- Distribute directly or through foreign partners
- Different channel structures than in domestic markets
- Illegitimate "gray" marketing channels
- Legal and infrastructure differences

CHANNELS AND DISTRIBUTION DECISIONS FOR SERVICES

The fastest-growing part of our economy is the service sector. Although distribution in the service sector is difficult to visualize, the same skills, techniques, and strategies used to manage inventory can also be used to manage service inventory—for instance, hospital beds, bank accounts, or airline seats. The quality of the planning and execution of distribution can have a major impact on costs and customer satisfaction.

One thing that sets service distribution apart from traditional manufacturing distribution is that, in a service environment, production and consumption are simultaneous. In manufacturing, a production setback can often be remedied by using safety stock or a faster mode of transportation. Such substitution is not possible with a service. The benefits of a service are also relatively intangible—that is, a consumer normally can't see the benefits of a service, such as a doctor's physical exam, but normally can see the benefits provided by a product—for example, cold medicine relieving a stuffy nose.

Because service industries are so customer-oriented, customer service is a priority. To manage customer relationships, many service providers, such as insurance carriers, physicians, hair salons, and financial services, use technology to schedule appointments, manage accounts, and disburse information. Service distribution focuses on three main areas:

☞ *Minimizing wait times*: Minimizing the amount of time customers wait in line to deposit a check, wait for their food at a restaurant, or wait in a doctor's office for an appointment is a key factor in maintaining the quality of service. People tend to overestimate the amount of time they spend waiting in line, researchers report, and unexplained waiting seems longer than explained waits. To reduce anxiety among waiting customers, some restaurants give patrons pagers that allow them to roam around or go to the bar. Banks sometimes install electronic boards displaying stock quotes or sports scores. Car rental companies reward repeat customers by eliminating their waits altogether. Airports have designed comfortable sitting areas with televisions and children's play areas for those waiting to board planes. Some service companies are using sophisticated technology to further ease their customers' waiting time. For example, many hotels and airlines are using electronic check-in kiosks. Travelers can insert their credit cards to check in upon arrival, receive their room key, get directions, print maps to area restaurants and attractions, and print out their hotel bills.

☞ *Managing service capacity*: For product manufacturers, inventory acts as a buffer, enabling them to provide the product during periods of peak demand without extraordinary efforts. Service firms don't have this luxury. If they don't have the capacity to meet demand, they must either turn down some prospective customers, let service levels slip, or expand capacity. For instance, at tax time a tax preparation firm may have so many customers desiring its services that it has to either turn business away or add temporary offices or preparers. Popular restaurants risk losing business when seating is unavailable or the wait is too long. To manage their capacity, travel Web sites allow users to find last-minute deals to fill up empty airline seats and hotel rooms.

☞ *Improving service delivery*: Like manufacturers, service firms are now experimenting with different distribution channels for their services. Choosing the right distribution channel can increase the times that services are available (such as using the Internet to disseminate information and services 24-7) or add to customer

© JEFF GREENBERG/ALAMY

GEICO's early business model—a first in the insurance industry—involved direct marketing to targeted customers without the use of agents. In its early years, GEICO contacted its customers by mail and telephone, but now it offers online service 24 hours a day, seven days a week.

Identify the special problems and opportunities associated with distribution in service organizations

Minimizing wait times is a key factor in maintaining service quality.

Managing service capability is critical to successful service distribution.

Improving service delivery makes it easier and more convenient for consumers to use the service.

convenience (like pizza delivery, walk-in medical clinics, or a dry cleaner located in a supermarket). The airline industry has found that using the Internet for ticket sales both reduces distribution costs and raises the level of customer service by making it easier for customers to plan their own travel. Cruise lines, on the other hand, have found that travel agents add value by helping customers sort through the abundance of information and complicated options available when booking a cruise. In the real estate industry, realtors are placing kiosks in local malls that enable consumers to directly access listings.

The Internet is quickly becoming an alternative channel for delivering services. Consumers can now purchase plane tickets, reserve a hotel room, pay bills, purchase mutual funds, and receive electronic newspapers in cyberspace. Insurance giant Allstate, for instance, now sells auto and home insurance directly to consumers in some states through the Internet in addition to its traditional network of agents. The effort reduces costs so that Allstate can stay competitive with rival insurance companies Progressive and GEICO that already target customers directly. Similarly, several real estate Web sites are making it easier for customers to shop for a new home on the Web. Traditionally, the only way for customers to gain access to realtors' listings was to work through a real estate agent, who would search the listings and then show customers' homes that met their requirements. The new companies offer direct access to the listings, enabling customers to review properties for sale on their own and choose which ones they would like to visit.

17 ◄ major retailers in the Worldwide Retail Exchange

percentage of purchasing costs saved by using the exchange ► **15**

3,000 ◄ Dollar Tree Stores

Dollar Tree distribution centers ► **9**

copies of *Harry Potter and the Deathly Hallows* mistakenly released early ► **1,200**

2 billion ◄ photo prints sold by Walgreens each year

yearly profits Kodak lost to channel conflict with Walgreens ► **$500 million**

small "high frequency" **620,000** stores in Mexico ►

percentages of emerging nation citizens who shop in such stores multiple times each week ► **80**

Channel members facilitate the distribution process by providing specialization and division of labor, overcoming discrepancies, and providing contact efficiency.

Producer

© iStockphoto.com/Andreas Reh

Au	Sn	Li
GOLD	TIN	LITHIUM

Materials used to make the components of electronic devices come from around the globe, for example, South America provides tin (solder), lithium (batteries), and gold (a/v cables).

Distributor

COURTESY CHAPEL HOUSE PHOTOGRAPHY

Customers have the option of buying their computer supplies online through a direct channel with the manufacturer.

Dual distribution: Consumers can buy directly from producers or through a retailer.

Wholesaler

© iStockphoto.com/tomczybartek

Wholesalers may transport and distribute products.

Electronics retailers (such as Best Buy) bridge the gap between companies and consumers.

Retailer

© COURTESY CHAPEL HOUSE PHOTOGRAPHY

Customer

© Image Source

REVIEW AND APPLICATIONS

Explain what a marketing channel is and why intermediaries are needed. A marketing channel is a business structure of interdependent organizations that reach from the point of product origin to the consumer with the purpose of physically moving products to their final consumption destination, representing "place" or "distribution" in the marketing mix, and encompassing the processes involved in getting the right product to the right place at the right time. Members of a marketing channel create a continuous and seamless system that performs or supports the marketing channel functions. Channel members provide economies to the distribution process in the form of specialization and division of labor; overcoming discrepancies in quantity, assortment, time, and space; and providing contact efficiency.

1.1 Your family runs a specialty ice cream parlor called Scoops. It manufactures its own ice cream in small batches and sells it only in pint-sized containers. After someone not affiliated with the company sent six pints of its ice cream to a popular talk-show host, she proclaimed on her national TV show that it was the best ice cream she had ever eaten. Immediately after the broadcast, orders came flooding in, overwhelming your small-batch production schedule and your limited distribution system. The company's shipping manager thinks she can handle it, but you disagree. List the reasons why you need to restructure your channel of distribution.

Define the types of channel intermediaries and describe their functions and activities. The most prominent difference separating intermediaries is whether they take title to the product. Retailers and merchant wholesalers take title, but agents and brokers do not. Retailers are firms that sell mainly to consumers. Merchant wholesalers are organizations that facilitate the movement of products and services from the manufacturer to producers, resellers, governments, institutions, and retailers. Agents and brokers do not take title to the goods and services they market, but they do facilitate the exchange of ownership between sellers and buyers. Channel intermediaries perform three basic types of functions. Transactional functions include contacting and promoting, negotiating, and risk taking. Logistical functions performed by channel members include physical distribution, storing, and sorting functions. Finally, channel members may perform facilitating functions, such as researching and financing.

2.1 What kind of marketing channel functions can be performed over the Internet? Why do you think so?

Describe the channel structures for consumer and business products and discuss alternative channel arrangements. Marketing channels for consumer and business products vary in degree of complexity. The simplest consumer-product channel involves direct selling from producers to consumers. Businesses may sell directly to business or government buyers. Marketing channels grow more complex as intermediaries become involved. Consumer-product channel intermediaries include agents, brokers, wholesalers, and retailers. Business-product channel intermediaries include agents, brokers, and industrial distributors. Marketers often use alternative channel arrangements to move their products to the consumer. With dual distribution or multiple distribution, they choose two or more different channels to distribute the same product. Nontraditional channels help differentiate a firm's product from the competitor's or provide a manufacturer with another avenue for sales. Finally, strategic channel alliances are arrangements that use another manufacturer's already established channel.

3.1 Describe the most likely marketing channel structure for each of these consumer products: candy bars, Tupperware products, nonfiction books, new automobiles, farmers' market produce, and stereo equipment. Now, construct alternative channels for these same products.

3.2 You have been hired to design an alternative marketing channel for a firm specializing in the manufacturing and marketing of novelties for college student organizations. In a memo to the president of the firm, describe how the channel operates.

3.3 Building on question 1.1 determine a new channel structure for Scoops. Write a proposal to present to your key managers.

Define the terms *supply chain* and *supply chain management*, and discuss the benefits of supply chain management. Supply chain management coordinates and integrates all of the activities performed by supply chain members into a seamless process from the source to the point of consumption. The responsibilities of a supply chain manager include developing channel design strategies, managing the relationships of supply chain members, sourcing and procurement of raw materials, scheduling production, processing orders, managing inventory and storing product, and selecting transportation modes. The supply chain manager is also responsible for managing customer service and the information that flows through the supply chain. The benefits of supply chain management include reduced costs in inventory management, transportation, warehousing, and packaging; improved service through techniques like time-based delivery and make-to-order; and enhanced revenues, which result from such supply chain-related achievements as higher product availability and more customized products.

4.1 Discuss the benefits of supply chain management. How does the implementation of supply chain management result in enhanced customer value?

Discuss the issues that influence channel strategy. When determining marketing channel strategy, the channel manager must determine what market, product, and producer factors will influence the choice of channel. The manager must also determine the appropriate level of distribution intensity. Intensive distribution is distribution aimed at maximum market coverage. Selective distribution is achieved by screening dealers to eliminate all but a few in any single area. The most restrictive form of market coverage is exclusive distribution, which entails only one or a few dealers within a given area.

5.1 Decide which distribution intensity level—intensive, selective, or exclusive—is used for each of the following products, and explain why: Piaget watches, Land Rover sport-utility vehicles, M&Ms, special edition Barbie dolls, Crest toothpaste.

5.2 Now that you have a basic channel structure for Scoops (from question 3.3), form a team of three to four students and list the market, product, and producer factors that will affect your final channel structure.

Describe the different channel relationship types and their unique costs and benefits. Channel relationships can be plotted on a continuum ranging from Arm's-Length to integrated, with cooperative relationships somewhere in between. Arm's-Length relationships generally consist of unique transactions that are intended to occur once or very infrequently, and are pursued when closer relationships are undesirable or impractical. Although Arm's-Length relationships are low risk, they also provide few benefits in terms of favorable conditions for the agreement, and disputes are often resolved in court. Integrated relationships, on the opposite end of the spectrum, are very close relationships that are backed by formal agreements and can result in great efficiency and effectiveness. However, given that integrated relationships tend either to involve high levels of expense (in the case of vertical integration) or require enormous amounts of trust in the partner company (as in the case of supply chains), many companies prefer cooperative relationships in some settings. Cooperative relationships are a hybrid form of relationship that is governed by formal contract, are temporary, and are enforced by the agreement itself.

6.1 Working with another student in the class, decide when it would be most advantageous for large companies like Procter & Gamble, IBM, and/or Ford Motor Company to develop integrated relationships with smaller suppliers. Would the same rules for integrated relationship development also apply to customers? Why or why not?

Describe the logistical components of the supply chain. The logistics supply chain consists of several interrelated and integrated logistical components: (1) sourcing and procurement of raw materials and supplies, (2) production scheduling, (3) order processing, (4) inventory control, (5) warehousing and materials-handling, and (6) transportation. The logistics information system is the link connecting all of the logistics components of the supply chain. Information technology connects the various components and partners of the supply chain into an integrated whole. The supply chain team, in concert with the logistics information system, orchestrates the movement of goods, services, and information from the source to the consumer. Supply chain teams typically cut across organizational boundaries, embracing all parties who participate in moving product to market. Procurement deals with the purchase of raw materials, supplies, and components according to production scheduling. Order processing monitors the flow of goods and information (order entry and order handling). Inventory control systems regulate when and how much to buy (order timing and order quantity). Warehousing provides storage of goods until needed by the customer while the materials-handling system moves inventory into, within, and out of the warehouse. Finally, the major modes of transportation are railroads, motor carriers, pipelines, waterways, and airways.

7.1 Assume that you are the supply chain manager for a producer of expensive, high-tech computer components. Identify the most suitable method(s) of transporting your product in terms of cost, transit time, reliability, capability, accessibility, and traceability. Now, assume you are the supply chain manager for a producer of milk. How does this change your choice of transportation?

Discuss new technology and emerging trends in supply chain management. Several emerging trends are changing the job of today's supply chain manager. Technology and automation are bringing up-to-date distribution information to the decision maker's desk. Technology is also linking suppliers, buyers, and carriers for joint decision making, and it has created a new electronic distribution channel. Many companies are saving money and time by outsourcing third-party carriers to handle some or all aspects of the distribution process. Firms are taking major steps toward the goal of securing their supply chains from external threats.

8.1 Visit the Web site of Menlo Logistics at **www.menlolog.com.** What logistics functions can this third-party logistics supplier provide? How does its mission fit in with the supply chain management philosophy?

Explain channel leadership, conflict, power, and partnering. Power, control, leadership, conflict, and partnering are the main social dimensions of marketing channel relationships. Channel power refers to the capacity of one channel member to control or influence other channel members. Channel control occurs when one channel member intentionally affects another member's behavior. Channel leadership is the exercise of authority and power. Channel conflict occurs when there is a clash of goals and methods among the members of a distribution channel. Channel conflict can be either horizontal, between channel members at the same level, or vertical, between channel members at different levels of the channel. Channel partnering is the joint effort of all channel members to create an integrated system that serves customers and creates a competitive advantage. Collaborating channel partners meet the needs of consumers more effectively by ensuring that the right products reach shelves at the right time and at a lower cost, boosting sales and profits.

9.1 Procter & Gamble and Wal-Mart are key partners in a shared channel. P&G is one of Wal-Mart's biggest suppliers, and Wal-Mart provides extremely detailed scanner data about customer purchases of P&G products. Wal-Mart has begun selling its own brand of Sam's Choice laundry detergent in bright orange bottles alongside P&G's Tide, but for a greatly reduced price. What do you think will be the impact of this new product on what has been a stable channel relationship?

Discuss channels and distribution decisions in global markets. Global marketing channels are becoming more important to U.S. companies seeking growth abroad. Manufacturers introducing products in foreign countries must decide what type of channel structure to use—in particular, whether the product should be marketed through direct channels or through foreign intermediaries. Marketers should be aware that channel structures in foreign markets may be very different from those they are accustomed to in the United States. Global distribution expertise is also emerging as an important skill for channel managers as many countries are removing trade barriers.

10.1 Go to the World Trade Organization's Web site at **www.wto.org.** What can you learn at the site about how globalization affects channel management and other aspects of business?

Identify the special problems and opportunities associated with distribution in service organizations. Managers in service industries use the same skills, techniques, and strategies to manage logistics functions as managers in goods-producing industries. The distribution of services focuses on three main areas: minimizing wait times, managing service capacity, and improving service delivery.

11.1 Assume that you are the marketing manager of a hospital. Write a report indicating the distribution functions that concern you. Discuss the similarities and dissimilarities of distribution for services and for goods.

KEY TERMS

agents and brokers	392	channel partnering (channel cooperation)	418	dual distribution (multiple distribution)	397
Arm's-Length relationships	405	channel power	416	electronic data interchange (EDI)	408
automatic replenishment program	409	cooperative relationships	406	electronic distribution	414
channel conflict	416	direct channel	395	exclusive distribution	404
channel control	416	discrepancy of assortment	391	horizontal conflict	417
channel leader (channel captain)	416	discrepancy of quantity	390	integrated relationships	405
channel members	389	distribution resource planning (DRP)	408	intensive distribution	403

inventory control system	408	merchant wholesaler	392	supply chain	399
logistics	394	order processing system	407	supply chain	
logistics information system	407	outsourcing (contract		management	399
marketing channel		logistics)	413	supply chain team	407
(channel of distribution)	389	retailer	392	temporal discrepancy	391
materials-handling system	410	selective distribution	403	vertical conflict	417
materials requirement		spatial discrepancy	391		
planning (MRP) (materials		strategic channel			
management)	408	alliance	398		

EXERCISES

APPLICATION EXERCISE

It may be easy to understand how distribution channels work just from reading, but you may still not appreciate their broad scope. This exercise will help you see for yourself how complex a single distribution channel is. Then, when you think of the number of products and services available on the market at any one time, you will understand how tremendous the national (and international) distribution network actually is.[36]

Activities

1. Create a list of approximately 20 products that you often purchase for personal use and/or that are present in your home.

2. For each of the products you listed, speculate whether the product was routed through the marketing channel using (a) exclusive, (b) selective, or (c) intensive distribution.

3. Now, for each product/distribution strategy combination, speculate as to the product, market, or producer factors that lead to this distribution strategy.

4. Finally, identify any potential alternative distribution channel options through which you might have purchased this product. Would the alternative channel choice have changed the way (location, timing, price) you purchased this good? Why or why not?

ETHICS EXERCISE

Wholesome Snacks, Inc., the maker of a variety of cookies and crackers, has just created a new vitamin-packed cookie. The new cookie has the potential to combat many of the health problems caused by malnutrition in children throughout poverty-stricken areas of the world. To date, however, many of the larger developing markets have resisted opening distribution channels to Wholesome's products. Wholesome realizes that its new cookie could also help open the door for the company to sell its less nutritious products in these markets. Therefore, the company is offering the new cookie at a low cost to government relief programs in exchange for the long-sought distribution channels. The company feels the deal is good for business, but the countries feel it is corporate bullying.

Questions

1. What do you think about Wholesome's idea for opening a new distribution channel?

2. Does the AMA Statement of Ethics address this issue? Go to **www.marketingpower.com** and review the code. Then, write a brief paragraph stating what the AMA Statement of Ethics contains that relates to distribution channels in developing nations.

MARKETING PLAN EXERCISE

In Part 1 of your strategic marketing plan, you stated your business mission and objectives and performed a detailed SWOT analysis. In Part 2 of the plan, you identified and described target market segments, identified sources of competitive intelligence and the need for further marketing research. In Part 3, you began the process of defining the marketing mix, starting with the first component: product. The next stage of the strategic planning process continues defining the elements of the marketing mix, and this section focuses on place, or distribution. Use the following exercises to guide you through the distribution part of your strategic marketing plan.

1. Discuss the implications of dual/multiple distribution. If your chosen company sells through a major department store and its own catalog and then decides to have an online site or open its own store in a factory outlet, what will happen to channel relationships? To the final price offered to consumers? To promotional vehicles? Most e-marketers assume that a direct distribution channel, with no intermediaries, is the most efficient and least costly method for getting product offerings to customers. However, if you decide on a different distribution channel, you will also have to identify warehouses, fulfillment services, transportation firms, packing companies, and many other facilitating agencies. Does your company have the capabilities to handle this, or should your company invest in channel members to take over these tasks and functions?

2. Decide what channel(s) your company should be using. Describe the intermediaries involved and their likely behavior. What are the implications of these channels? Describe the conflict that might arise from having both an e-marketing offering as well as a brick-and-mortar offering. If distribution costs are different, will your company set the same or different prices for end customers?

3. Which distribution intensity level would be best for your company's product? Justify your decision.

CASE STUDY: TIME WARNER/VIACOM

COUNTDOWN TO A BLACKOUT

Why is Dora crying? That was the question readers were faced with when they opened the *New York Times* and *LA Times* on December 31, 2008. Viacom, owner of the Nickelodeon television channel where Dora the Explorer shares the stage with SpongeBob SquarePants and many other favorite children's television stars, purchased full-page advertisements of the cartoon adventurer with a tear streaming down her cheek clutching her frightened-looking sidekick, Boots the Monkey. The image was accompanied by this alarming message: Time Warner Cable is taking Dora off the air tonight along with 19 of your favorite channels. Throughout the day, viewers of Viacom channels saw a ticker running across the bottom of their television screens alerting them to the impending blackout, and in the face of Viacom's aggressive media campaign, Time Warner found its call centers swamped by angry customers, many the parents of distraught children, demanding that Time Warner keep the Viacom channels on the air, or else they might look for another cable provider.

Time Warner is the second-largest cable provider in the United States with approximately 13.3 million subscribers. Viacom is one of the largest providers of cable TV channel programming, including MTV, VH-1, BET, Spike TV, Nickelodeon, and Comedy Central. Viacom's media campaign came at the climax of a growing dispute between the two companies as the agreement under which Viacom granted Time Warner the rights to broadcast its channels would come to an end at 12:01 on January 1st. If Time Warner did not come to terms

© AP IMAGES/PRNEWSFOTO/NICKELODEON

with the programmer, Viacom threatened to pull its channels. To renew the contract, Viacom asked Time Warner to pay an additional $37 million per year for its programming on top of the $300 million it was already paying—roughly a 12 percent rate increase. At the time, Viacom's programming constituted about 7.9 percent of Time Warner's programming costs.

Viacom argued that given the estimated 25 percent of cable viewers who tuned in to Viacom channels over the course of a given day, the amount that Time Warner was paying left Viacom's programming well underpriced in comparison to other channels. Costs for the Disney Channel amount to about 85 cents per subscriber per month, and ESPN costs about $4. In contrast, Viacom's MTV would cost 32 cents and Nickelodeon would cost 45 cents per month. Viacom's rate increase would amount to a monthly cost of about 23 cents per subscriber, a sum they claim is modest in comparison to the likes of ESPN's subscriber costs, especially considering it would cover Viacom's entire package.

Time Warner responded that in the current economic environment, such a rate increase could not be justified. As the company said in response to Viacom's media campaign, the majority of any rate increase would likely have to be absorbed by customers. Furthermore, Time Warner pointed out that in many cases, Viacom was offering the same programming that it was threatening to pull from Time Warner on the Internet for free. Time Warner argued that a rate increase would have Time Warner customers subsidizing Viacom's Internet programming, even going so far during negotiations as to threaten to provide customers a way to connect their laptops to their cable boxes and to stream programs from the Internet onto their TVs.

Fortunately for customers (or perhaps unfortunately, depending on how much of the cost they end up having to shoulder), in the midst of negotiations, Viacom agreed to suspend its decision to pull its programming, and the two companies were able to come to terms shortly after midnight when their previous contract expired. Traditionally, network programmers hold the upper hand in disputes over programming costs, but in this instance neither Viacom nor Time Warner could afford the fallout of a protracted channel blackout. Viacom's bid for increased subscription fees is not unique; as advertising revenues decreased over the course of the year, many network programmers looked to cable providers for higher fees to fund increasing programming costs. Any sort of blackout, however, would have greatly hurt whatever ad revenue Viacom was already generating. For Time Warner, while increased fees would be unpleasant, a blackout could send increasingly wary cable customers to competitors. In the end, no blackout occurred, and Dora was able to stay on the air.[37]

Questions

1. What is the channel arrangement described between Viacom, Time Warner, and consumers? Who are the intermediaries?

2. What is the channel conflict between Viacom and Time Warner?

3. Obviously the conflict between Viacom and Time Warner has strained their relationship. If you were in charge of one of these companies, what steps would you take to improve their channel relationships?

COMPANY CLIPS

©NKP MEDIA, INC./CENGAGE

SEPHORA—BUSINESS IS BEAUTIFUL

The beauty-retail store Sephora was founded in 1969 in France, and since then has become a leader in sales of heath and beauty-aid products. It opened its first store in the United States in 1998 on Fifth Avenue in New York City and prides itself on being ahead of the market in skin care trends. Its luxurious environment is the selling point for over 250 brands. On its shelves, Sephora maintains a balance of big brand names with lesser-known, up-and-coming brands. Sephora also carries its own private brand that it promotes independently in the store. Each sales representative in a Sephora store is trained to best help customers find the products that best fit their skin types and lifestyles. Watch the video to learn what techniques Sephora uses to keep its shelves stocked and customers happy.

Questions

1. Why is important to customers that Sephora keep detailed information about their inventory? What does Sephora do to insure their numbers are accurate?

2. How does Sephora manage its marketing channel? What information goes into deciding which suppliers become incorporated?

Marketing & You Results

A higher score indicates that you like to be a leader and use authority. Studies have linked authority to vanity, so a high score also suggests a high level of vanity. In particular, you have "achievement view vanity," which is strongly linked to authority. That means that you have very high opinions of your accomplishments and think that others consider you successful as well.

Promotion and Pricing Decisions

WHAT'S INSIDE

Marketing Communications
and Advertising *470*

Public Relations, Sales
Promotion, and Personal
Selling *524*

Pricing Concepts *558*

Cartier
Opening Soon
即将开幕

Marketing Communications and Advertising

LEARNING OUTCOMES

1. Discuss the role of promotion in the marketing mix
2. Describe the communication process
3. Explain the goals of promotion
4. Discuss the elements of the promotional mix
5. Discuss the AIDA concept and its relationship to the promotional mix
6. Discuss the concept of integrated marketing communications
7. Describe the factors that affect the promotional mix
8. Discuss the effects of advertising on market shares and consumers
9. Identify the major types of advertising
10. Discuss the creative decisions in developing an advertising campaign
11. Describe media evaluation and selection techniques

LO ① THE ROLE OF PROMOTION IN THE MARKETING MIX

Few goods or services, no matter how well developed, priced, or distributed, can survive in the marketplace without effective promotion—communication by marketers that informs, persuades, and reminds potential buyers of a product in order to influence their opinion or elicit a response.

Promotional strategy is a plan for the optimal use of the promotional mix elements: advertising, public relations, personal selling, and sales promotion. As Exhibit 14.1 shows, the marketing manager determines the goals of the company's promotional strategy in light of the firm's overall goals for the marketing mix—product, place (distribution), promotion, and price.

REVIEW LEARNING OUTCOME

LO ① Discuss the role of promotion in the marketing mix

Promotional Strategy

Promotional mix
Advertising
Public Relations
Sales Promotion
Personal Selling

Competitive advantage

Marketer

Consumer

EXHIBIT 14.1

Role of Promotion in the Marketing Mix

Overall marketing objectives

Marketing mix
• Product
• Place (distribution)
• Promotion
• Price

Promotional mix
• Advertising
• Public relations
• Sales promotion
• Personal selling

Target market

promotion
Communication by marketers that informs, persuades, and reminds potential buyers of a product in order to influence an opinion or elicit a response.

promotional strategy
A plan for the optimal use of the elements of promotion: advertising, public relations, personal selling, and sales promotion.

competitive advantage
One or more unique aspects of an organization that cause target consumers to patronize that firm rather than competitors.

communication
The process by which we exchange or share meanings through a common set of symbols.

Using these overall goals, marketers combine the elements of the promotional mix into a coordinated plan. This promotional plan defines the promotional strategy, which then becomes an integral part of the overall marketing strategy for reaching the target market.

The main function of a marketer's promotional strategy is to convince target customers that the goods and services offered provide a competitive advantage over the competition. A competitive advantage is the set of unique features of a company and its products that are perceived by the target market as significant and superior to the competition. Such features can include high product quality, rapid delivery, low prices, excellent service, or a feature not offered by the competition. For example, fast-food restaurant Subway promises fresh sandwiches that are better for you than a hamburger or pizza. Subway effectively communicates its competitive advantage through advertising featuring longtime "spokes-eater" Jared Fogle, who lost weight by eating at Subway every day.[1] Thus, promotion is a vital part of the marketing mix, informing consumers of a product's benefits and thereby positioning the product in the marketplace.

LO2
MARKETING COMMUNICATION

Promotional strategy is closely related to the process of communication. As humans, we assign meaning to feelings, ideas, facts, attitudes, and emotions. Communication is the process by which we exchange or share meanings through a common set of symbols. When a company develops a new product, changes an old one, or simply tries to increase sales

CUSTOMER Experience

Obama for President: The Ultimate IMC Campaign

Start with a young, relatively unknown black man with a Muslim-sounding name. His first opponent was the best-known woman in America married to one of the most successful politicians in history. His second competitor was a well-known and respected war hero with 40 years as a senator. But President Barack Obama had a better marketing strategy than either one of them: Change.

Obama's presidential campaign, launched in February 2007, began with the message of "change" and did not deviate from it. Ever. The message resonated with American voters and would-be voters. He kept the message simple and consistent through endless repetition. Obama also effectively defined the message so that all of the other candidates were also forced to talk about change. This follows classic marketing positioning principles.

But Team Obama went further. They used behavioral targeting to segment their voter audience so that each message was tailored specifically to the individual voter. Traditional media were used in untraditional ways—specifically by purchasing viewing time on big events, such as the Summer Olympics, and by airing a 30-minute infomercial on seven networks just days before the election. Team Obama raised the use of digital media to a completely new level and created content for online distribution.

They used text messaging and e-mail effectively by using the list sparingly through most of the campaign and then sending a flurry of e-mails during the last few weeks of the campaign urging supporters to make calls and visits, host parties, and volunteer. Obama had more than double John McCain's online traffic. The campaign even created their own social network of 2 million users, MyBarackObama.com, and leveraged other social networks such as Facebook and MySpace as well as specialized networks such as Eon and BlackPlanet. Search engine optimization was used to dispel negative information and Internet rumors. The campaign demonstrated not only knowledge of basic marketing principles, but also an understanding of ground-level tactics on everything from segmentation and database management to analytics, social networking, and online communities.

And consider the results. First there was the obvious landslide victory—even in states that Democrats have not captured in years. Second, the campaign set fund-raising records of more than half a billion dollars, specifically from everyday voters who donated less than an average of $100. Third, they have a database of more than 13 million engaged voters and 5 million supporters on social networks. With all of this momentum, the real question is how Obama will use his marketing skills to run the country.[2]

of an existing good or service, it must communicate its selling message to potential customers. Marketers communicate information about the firm and its products to the target market and various publics through its promotion programs. When Sara Lee Corp. decided to reinvigorate its legacy brand, Kiwi shoe polish, it began with communication: It asked people about their shoe care needs. After interviewing 3,500 people across eight countries, it found out that people cared more about fresh, comfortable shoes than whether those shoes were polished. Sara Lee's new CEO welcomes innovation. She found out which innovations would be welcome by communicating with Kiwi's consumers, marketers, and retailers; then she pushed the employees to "think outside the box—or inside the shoe." And it paid off. Kiwi's new products—including thin insoles with built-in fresheners and single-use polishes—pushed Kiwi's sales up by 4.4 percent (for the first time in a long time). Now Sara Lee is using that same innovation-driven-by-communication model and holding focus groups with its employees and customers to find out which new products will revive Sara Lee's other brands (**www.kiwicare.com**).[3]

Communication can be divided into two major categories: interpersonal communication and mass communication. Interpersonal communication is direct, face-to-face communication between two or more people. When communicating face-to-face, people see the other person's reaction and can respond almost immediately. A salesperson speaking directly with a client is an example of an interpersonal marketing communication. Mass communication involves communicating a concept or message to large audiences. A great deal of marketing communication is directed to consumers as a whole, usually through a mass medium such as television, newspapers, or the Internet. When a company advertises, it generally does not personally know the people with whom it is trying to communicate. Furthermore, the company is unable to respond immediately to consumers' reactions to its message. Instead, the marketing manager must wait to see whether people are reacting positively or negatively to the mass-communicated promotion. Any clutter from competitors' messages or other distractions in the environment can reduce the effectiveness of the mass-communication effort.

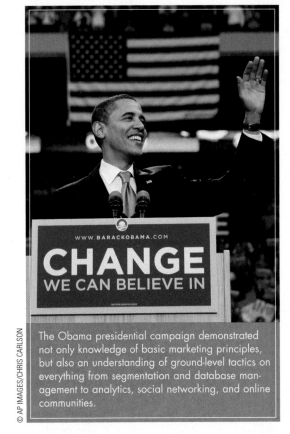

© AP IMAGES/CHRIS CARLSON

The Obama presidential campaign demonstrated not only knowledge of basic marketing principles, but also an understanding of ground-level tactics on everything from segmentation and database management to analytics, social networking, and online communities.

The Communication Process

Marketers are both senders, and receivers of messages. As *senders*, marketers attempt to inform, persuade, and remind the target market to adopt courses of action compatible with the need to promote the purchase of goods and services. As *receivers*, marketers attune themselves to the target market in order to develop the appropriate messages, adapt existing messages, and spot new communication opportunities. In this way, marketing communication is a two-way, rather than one-way, process. The two-way nature of the communication process is shown in Exhibit 14.2.

The Sender and Encoding The sender is the originator of the message in the communication process. In an interpersonal conversation, the sender may be a parent, a friend, or a salesperson. For an advertisement or press release, the sender is the company or organization itself. For example, the Swedish brand Absolut Vodka launched a marketing campaign using the theme "In an Absolut World." At the outset, the objective of the campaign was to increase Absolut's market share in the crowded and increasingly competitive U.S. vodka market. To appeal to this market, Absolut had to differentiate its message from the "rational benefits" (such as best taste or smooth feel) being claimed by so many of the upstarts in the vodka category. Absolut changed its near-legendary super-premium brand strategy—a print campaign pairing the iconic shape of its bottle with equally iconic art figures—to a campaign that would appeal to the "emotional benefits" of the brand.[4] Thus, Absolut launched a new campaign using

interpersonal communication
Direct, face-to-face communication between two or more people.

mass communication
The communication of a concept or message to large audiences.

sender
The originator of the message in the communication process.

EXHIBIT 14.2

Communication Process

Noise
• Other advertisements
• News articles
• Other store displays

Sender	Encoding the message	Message channel	Decoding the message	Receiver

Sender
• Marketing manager
• Advertising manager
• Advertising agency

Encoding the message
• Advertisement
• Sales presentation
• Store display
• Coupon
• Press release

Message channel
• Media
• Salesperson
• Retail store
• Local news show

Decoding the message
• Receiver interpretation of message

Receiver
• Customers
• Viewers/ listeners
• News media
• Clients

Feedback channel
• Market research
• Sales results
• Change in market share

encoding
The conversion of a sender's ideas and thoughts into a message, usually in the form of words or signs.

channel
A medium of communication—such as a voice, radio, or newspaper—for transmitting a message.

noise
Anything that interferes with, distorts, or slows down the transmission of information.

the phrase "Absolut World" to promote the message that its vodka was the brand to choose if the customer was intelligent, savvy, and wanted to challenge the status quo by taking on bold and optimistic new world views. The new ads assert that Absolut vodka is in a class by itself—indeed, in a world of its own, an "Absolut World." The ad campaign also invites Absolut's consumers to visualize a world that appeals to them— even a world that may be idealized or "fantastic."[5]

Encoding is the conversion of the sender's ideas and thoughts into a message, usually in the form of words or signs. A basic principle of encoding is that what matters is not what the source says but what the receiver hears. One way of conveying a message that the receiver will hear properly is to use concrete words and pictures. For example, Absolut's marketers encoded the message by a creating a series of life-size outdoor ads, wrapped buildings, and other media that imagined an "Absolut World" where factories emit harmless bubbles instead of smoke, ATMs dispense "free" money, politicians' noses grow if they lie, and people in bars wear buttons labeling their dating status and mind-set.[6]

Message Transmission Transmission of a message requires a channel—a voice, radio, newspaper, computer, or other communication medium. A facial expression or gesture can also serve as a channel.

Reception occurs when the message is detected by the receiver and enters his or her frame of reference. In a two-way conversation such as a sales pitch given by a sales representative to a potential client, reception is normally high. In contrast, the desired receivers may or may not detect the message when it is mass communicated because most media are cluttered by noise—anything that interferes with, distorts, or slows down the transmission of information. In some media overcrowded with advertisers, such as newspapers and television, the noise level is high and the reception level is low. For example, competing network advertisements, other entertainment option advertisements, or other programming on the network itself might hamper reception of the "Absolut World" advertising campaign message. Transmission can also be hindered by situational factors: physical surroundings such as light, sound, location, and weather; the presence of other people; or the temporary moods consumers might bring to the situation. Mass communication may not even reach all the right consumers. Some members of the target audience were likely watching television when Absolut's commercials were shown, but others probably were not.

The Receiver and Decoding Marketers communicate their message through a channel to customers, or receivers, who will decode the message. Decoding is the interpretation of the language and symbols sent by the source through a channel. Common understanding between two communicators, or a common frame of reference, is required for effective communication. Therefore, marketing managers must ensure a proper match between the message to be conveyed and the target market's attitudes and ideas.

Even though a message has been received, it will not necessarily be properly decoded—or even seen, viewed, or heard—because of selective exposure, distortion, and retention (see Chapter 6). Even when people receive a message, they tend to manipulate, alter, and modify it to reflect their own biases, needs, knowledge, and culture. Differences in age, social class, education, culture, and ethnicity can lead to miscommunication, for example. Further, because people don't always listen or read carefully, they can easily misinterpret what is said or written. In fact, researchers have found that consumers misunderstand a large proportion of both printed and televised communications. Bright colors and bold graphics have been shown to increase consumers' comprehension of marketing communication. Even these techniques are not foolproof, however. A classic example of miscommunication occurred when Lever Brothers mailed out samples of its then new dishwashing liquid, Sunlight, which contains real lemon juice. The package clearly stated that Sunlight was a household cleaning product. Nevertheless, many people saw the word *sunlight,* the large picture of lemons, and the phrase "with real lemon juice" and thought the product was lemon juice.

Marketers targeting consumers in foreign countries must also worry about the translation and possible miscommunication of their promotional messages by other cultures. An important issue for global marketers is whether to standardize or customize the message for each global market in which they sell. While Absolut's marketers used the "World" message globally, they tailored the ads to reflect how people in various regions might envision an "Absolut World." For example, a bus shelter on Second Avenue in New York City was wrapped to look like a subway entrance—a dream of many New York commuters.[7] In Germany, consumers were given a firsthand experience of the "Absolut World." For one week, a fleet of Porsche taxis chauffeured passengers quickly—and for free—around Hamburg, Munich, and Berlin. By the end of that week, the taxis had generated over 15 million media contacts through TV, print, and online news coverage.[8]

Feedback In interpersonal communication, the receiver's response to a message is direct feedback to the source. Feedback may be verbal, as in saying "I agree," or nonverbal, as in nodding, smiling, frowning, or gesturing.

Because mass communicators like Absolut's are often cut off from direct feedback, they must rely on market research or analysis of viewer responses from indirect feedback. Absolut might use such measurements as the percentage of television viewers who recognized, recalled, or stated they were exposed to Absolut's messages. Indirect feedback enables mass communicators to decide whether to continue, modify, or drop a message. Web sites also facilitate feedback. For example, Absolut could capture consumer feedback in e-mails, discussion boards, blogs, and other tools from its Web site.

The Impact of Web 2.0 on Marketing Communication

The Internet and related technologies are having a profound impact on marketing communication. When companies initially developed Web sites the primary formats

receiver
The person who decodes a message.

decoding
Interpretation of the language and symbols sent by the source through a channel.

feedback
The receiver's response to a message.

corporate blogs
Blogs that are sponsored by a
company or one of its brands and
maintained by one or more of the
company's employees.

noncorporate blogs
Independent blogs that are not
associated with the marketing
efforts of any particular company
or brand.

were either online brochures, where essentially the corporate brochure or catalog was put online, or e-commerce sites, where the companies could facilitate online sales of products. The next generation of the Internet, Web 2.0, facilitated consumer empowerment. For the first time, consumers were able to directly speak to other consumers, the company, and Web communities.

Web 2.0 tools include blogs (online journals), podcasting (online radio shows), vodcasts (online videos and newscasts), and social networks such as MySpace and Facebook. In the beginning, these tools were primarily used by individuals to express themselves. For example, a lawyer may develop a blog to talk about politics because that is a hobby. Or a college freshman may develop a profile on Facebook to stay in touch with high school friends. But soon, businesses began to see that these tools can be used to engage with consumers as well. The rise of blogging, for example, has created a completely new way for marketers to manage their image, connect with consumers, and generate interest in and desire for their companies' products.

Despite what could be considered a national obsession with blogs, measuring blogging activity remains challenging. According to Technorati, the first blog search engine, there were more than 28 million blogs online in 2006. But by early 2008, there were so many blogs that there was not a consistent number. While research companies agree that there are millions of blogs, comScore Media Metrix says that as of August 2008, there were 189 million blogs (counting Facebook) and Universal McCann reports there were 184 million blogs.[9] As part of its annual *State of the Blogosphere*, Technorati says the real trend is with the active blogosphere that tends to influence the mainstream media. Brands also permeate the blogosphere. Four of five bloggers post brand or product reviews, so even if a company does not have a formal social media strategy, chances are the brand is still out in the blogosphere thanks to the millions of bloggers. As such, companies are now reaching out to the most influential bloggers. Indeed, more than one-third of those with a blog have been approached to be a brand advocate.

The question then is whether blogging is a passing fad, representing at best an unreliable means of communicating, or an emerging trend. If it is a fad, why are marketers so interested in blogging as a promotional tool? The answer in part is that blogging alters the marketing communication process for the promotional elements that rely on mass communication—advertising, public relations, and sales promotion—by moving them away from impersonal, indirect communication toward a personalized, direct communication model.

Blogs can be divided into broad categories: corporate blogs and professional blogs versus noncorporate blogs (such as personal blogs). Corporate blogs are sponsored by a company or one of its brands and maintained by one or more of the company's employees. Corporate blogs disseminate marketing-controlled information. (Recall from Chapter 6 that marketing-controlled information is a source of product information that originates with marketers promoting the product.) Because blogs are designed to change daily, corporate blogs are dynamic and highly flexible, giving marketers the opportunity to adapt their messages more frequently than with any other communication channel. Initially, blogs were maintained by only the most technology-savvy companies. But today companies as diverse as Coca-Cola, Starwood Hotels, Honda, Nokia, Benetton, Ducati, Guinness, and HSBC have all launched corporate blogs. Undoubtedly, many more will appear in the near future.

In contrast, noncorporate blogs are independent and not associated with the marketing efforts of any particular company or brand. As such, noncorporate blogs function much like nonmarketing-controlled information: They provide a source of information and opinion perceived to be independent and more authentic than a corporate blog.[10] Michael Marx loves Barq's root beer. He wears Barq's T-shirts, brings the beverage to parties, and calls it his "beer." He established a blog dedicated to Barq's, **www.thebarqsman.com**, where he posted news about the brand, Barq's commercials he likes, and musings on why Barq's is superior to other root beers. Thebarqsman.com is not affiliated with Coca-Cola, the owner of the Barq's brand, which had no idea of the blog's existence until a *New York Times* reporter writing a story on brand blogs mentioned it. Even though thebarqsman.com is dedicated to a single brand, Marx's blog is an example of a noncorporate blog.[11]

Both corporate and noncorporate blogs have had an impact on the communication model depicted in Exhibit 14.2. That model shows the feedback channel as primarily impersonal and numbers-driven. In the traditional communication process, marketers can see the results of consumer behavior (e.g., a drop in sales), but are only able to explain them using their judgment. Even the information generated by market research is not as natural as that gleaned from bloggers. Corporate blogs allow marketers to personalize the feedback channel by opening the door for direct conversation with consumers. However, because there is no control over noncorporate blogs, there is a chance that comments and postings will be negative. Thus, many companies have a crisis communication strategy to deal with negative information in the blogosphere.

When marketers launch a corporate blog, they create an unfiltered feedback channel. For example, Enrico Minoli, CEO of Ducati, the Italian motorcycle brand, launched **blog.ducati.com.** He vowed to write "openly about what's going on at Ducati." Within three days, his postings had generated 99 responses, from motorcycle enthusiasts from Greece to Daytona Beach who all seemed most pleased that the CEO himself was a motorbike enthusiast. They began peppering him with questions about when new models would hit production and chatted with each other about their own bikes and biking experiences. Minoli's blog put a face on the impersonal nature of a large corporation.[12]

Noncorporate blogs have also personalized the feedback channel. But while corporate blogs create a *direct*, personalized feedback channel for masses of consumers, noncorporate blogs represent an *indirect*, personalized feedback channel. Because noncorporate blogs are independent, they are often perceived as more authentic. Blogging experts offer marketers some solid advice for giving their blogs the honest quality many bloggers associate with noncorporate blogs: open the feedback channel. Todd Copilevitz, a consultant specializing in digital marketing, says, "Blogs are not an environment where you just hold forth opinion and don't accept feedback. You have to have your wits about you to understand it's not the same old PR machine."[13]

REVIEW LEARNING OUTCOME

LO2 Describe the communication process

L③
THE GOALS OF PROMOTION

People communicate with one another for many reasons. They seek amusement, ask for help, give assistance or instructions, provide information, and express ideas and thoughts. Promotion, on the other hand, seeks to modify behavior and thoughts in some way. For example, promoters may try to persuade consumers to drink Pepsi rather than Coke, or to eat at Burger King instead of McDonald's. Promotion also strives to reinforce existing behavior—for instance, getting consumers to continue dining at Burger King once they have switched. The source (the seller) hopes to project a favorable image or to motivate purchase of the company's goods and services.

Effective promotion will achieve one or more of three goals: It will *inform* the target audience, *persuade* the target audience, or *remind* the target audience. Often a marketer will try to achieve two or more of these goals at the same time.

Informing

Informative promotion seeks to convert an existing need into a want or to stimulate interest in a new product. It is generally more prevalent during the early stages of the product life cycle. People typically will not buy a product or service or support a nonprofit organization until they know its purpose and its benefits to them. Informative messages are important for promoting complex and technical products such as automobiles, computers, and investment services. For example, Philips's original advertisement for the Magnavox flat-screen television showed young, urban consumers trying the flat-screen TV all over the house, including the ceiling. The ad focused on "how to" use the flat-screen TV rather than the Philips Magnavox brand or the technological capabilities.[14] Informative promotion is also important for a "new" brand being introduced into an "old" product class—for example, a new brand of frozen pizza (such as Kashi Frozen Pizza) entering the frozen pizza industry, which is dominated by well-known brands like Kraft's DiGiorno and Schwan's Grocery Products' Red Baron. Kashi Frozen Pizza cannot establish itself against more mature products unless potential buyers are aware of it, value its benefits, and understand its positioning in the marketplace.

© VICKI BEAVER

Persuading

Persuasive promotion is designed to stimulate a purchase or an action—for example, to eat more Doritos or use Verizon wireless mobile phone service. Persuasion normally becomes the main promotion goal when the product enters the growth stage of its life cycle. By this time, the target market should have general product awareness and some knowledge of how the product can fulfill their wants. Therefore, the promotional goal switches from informing consumers about the product category to persuading them to buy the company's brand rather than the competitor's. At this time, the promotional message emphasizes the product's real and perceived competitive advantages, often appealing to emotional needs such as love, belonging, self-esteem, and ego satisfaction. For example, the latest advertisement for the Philips Magnavox flat-screen television still features young, urban consumers. But the ad focuses on the product's benefits such as lifestyle enhancements, technological features like HDTV and Dolby digital surround sound, and the superiority of the brand.[15]

Persuasion can also be an important goal for very competitive mature product categories such as many household items, soft drinks, beer, and banking services. In a marketplace characterized by many competitors, the promotional message often encourages brand switching and aims to convert some buyers into loyal users. For example, to persuade new customers to switch their checking accounts, a bank's marketing manager may offer a year's worth of free checks with no fees.

Critics believe some promotional messages and techniques can be too persuasive, causing consumers to buy products and services they really don't need.

Reminding

Reminder promotion is used to keep the product and brand name in the public's mind. This type of promotion prevails during the maturity stage of the life cycle. It assumes that the target market has already been persuaded of the good's or service's merits. Its purpose is simply to trigger a memory. Crest toothpaste, Tide laundry detergent, Miller beer, and many other consumer products often use reminder promotion. Similarly, Philips Magnavox could advertise just the brand rather than the benefits of the product.

THE PROMOTIONAL MIX

As you read earlier, most promotional strategies use several elements or tools—which may include advertising, public relations, sales promotion, and personal selling—to reach a target market. That combination is called the promotional mix. The proper promotional mix is the one that management believes will meet the needs of the target market and fulfill the organization's overall goals. The more funds allocated to each promotional element and the more managerial emphasis placed on each technique, the more important that element is thought to be in the overall mix.

REVIEW LEARNING OUTCOME

LO 3 Explain the goals of promotion

- **Informative promotion**
  Increasing the awareness of a new brand, product class, or product attribute
  Explaining how the product works
  Suggesting new uses for a product
  Building a company image

- **Persuasive promotion**
  Encouraging brand switching
  Changing customers' perceptions of product attributes
  Influencing customers to buy now
  Persuading customers to call

- **Reminder promotion**
  Reminding consumers that the product may be needed in the near future
  Reminding consumers where to buy the product
  Maintaining consumer awareness

Advertising

Almost all companies selling a good or a service use some advertising, whether in the form of a multimillion-dollar campaign or a simple classified ad in a newspaper. *Advertising* is any form of impersonal (one-way) paid communication in which the sponsor or company is identified. One of the primary benefits of advertising is its ability to communicate to a large number of people at one time. Traditional media—such as television, radio, newspapers, magazines, books, direct mail, billboards, and transit cards (advertisements on buses and taxis and at bus stops)—are most commonly used to transmit advertisements to consumers. With the increasing fragmentation of traditional media choices, marketers are using other methods to send their advertisements to consumers, such as Web sites, e-mail, and interactive video kiosks located in department stores and supermarkets. However, as the Internet becomes a more vital component of many companies' promotion and marketing mix, consumers and lawmakers are increasingly concerned about possible violations of consumers' privacy. Read more about this issue in the Ethics in Marketing box about how social networking sites are using all the information that is freely collected.

DON'T YOU JUST HATE IT WHEN POPCORN GETS **STUCK** IN YOUR TEETH?

DenTek

DenTek

Flossing Made Easy!

ETHICS in Marketing

Who's Peeping at your Facebook? Privacy Concerns and Social Networks

Millions of people have embraced social networking sites such as Facebook (70 million U.S. users) and MySpace (110 million users) and increasingly specialized sites such as LinkedIn. While social networks are easy ways to keep in touch with friends and family, there are privacy concerns. A study at Carnegie Mellon found that a large portion of the Facebook users the researchers studied generously supplied plenty of personal data and limited privacy settings. Does this mean the users were oblivious to several privacy concerns? A simple viewing of personal information can make it easier for stalking and identify theft. More insidiously, Facebook and MySpace allow outside developers to create widgets or apps for the sites. Since 2007, 24,000 applications have been created by more than 400,000 developers and more than 95 percent of Facebook users have downloaded at least one application.

No big deal, right? Well, all of those developers are allowed to see your personal information to develop their applications. That's right. Twenty guys you don't know could be looking at your personal information and that of your friends. When a user installs an app, the developer can see everything but contact information. The data is available for only 24 hours, but once that data gets onto a third-party server, there is little Facebook or MySpace can do. Facebook states that developers are not allowed to share data with advertisers, but they can use the information to tailor features to users—in essence, they can use it during new product development. Developers interviewed for this case have not ruled out the prospect of using the data for targeted advertising; some think that leveraging this data does make sense for some marketing applications.

There are several things you can do to protect your privacy, such as not using friend lists; removing yourself from Facebook results; removing yourself from Google; avoiding photo tags; and others. Currently, there is no policy addressing concerns about privacy and social networks. Consumer advocates and the Center for Digital Democracy are urging the Federal Trade Commission to develop a policy surrounding third-party applications.[16] Do you think this gold mine of information should be leveraged as marketing research or should there be limits? And if limits are necessary, what should they be?

Public Relations

Concerned about how they are perceived by their target markets, organizations often spend large sums to build a positive public image. *Public relations* is the marketing function that evaluates public attitudes, identifies areas within the organization the public may be interested in, and executes a program of action to earn public understanding and acceptance. Public relations helps an organization communicate with its customers, suppliers, stockholders, government officials, employees, and the community in which it operates. Marketers use public relations not only to maintain a positive image but also to educate the public about the company's goals and objectives, introduce new products, and help support the sales effort. Public relations will be covered in more depth in Chapter 15.

Personal Selling

Personal selling is a purchase situation involving a personal, paid-for communication between two people in an attempt to influence each other. Traditional methods of personal selling include a planned presentation to one or more prospective buyers for the purpose of making a sale. More current notions on personal selling emphasize the relationship that develops between a salesperson and a buyer. Recently, both business-to-business and business-to-consumer selling focus on building long-term relationships rather than on making a onetime sale.

Personal selling, like other promotional mix elements, increasingly depends on the Internet. Most companies use their Web sites to attract potential buyers seeking information on products and services. While some companies sell products direct to consumers online, many do not. Instead, they rely on the Web site to drive customers to their physical locations where personal selling can close the sale. Whether it takes place face-to-face, over the phone, or online, personal selling attempts to persuade the buyer to accept a point of view or take some action. Personal selling is discussed further in Chapter 15.

Sales Promotion

Sales promotion consists of all marketing activities—other than personal selling, advertising, and public relations—that stimulate consumer purchasing and dealer effectiveness. Sales promotion is generally a short-run tool used to stimulate immediate increases in demand. In fact, marketers often use sales promotion to improve the effectiveness of other ingredients in the promotional mix, especially advertising and personal selling. Research shows that sales promotion complements advertising by yielding faster sales responses. Sales promotion can be aimed at end consumers, trade customers, or a company's employees. Sales promotions include free samples, contests, premiums, trade shows, giveaways, and coupons. A major promotional campaign might use several of these sales promotion tools. Sales promotion is discussed in more detail in Chapter 15.

> " *Sales promotion is generally a short-run tool used to stimulate immediate increases in demand.* "

The Communication Process and the Promotional Mix

The four elements of the promotional mix differ in their ability to affect the target audience. For instance, promotional mix elements may communicate with the consumer directly or indirectly. The message may flow one way or two ways. Feedback may be fast or slow, a little or a lot. Likewise, the communicator may have varying degrees of control over message delivery, content, and flexibility. Exhibit 14.3 outlines differences among the promotional mix elements with respect to mode of communication, marketer's control over the communication process, amount and speed of feedback, direction of message flow, marketer's control over the message, identification of the sender, speed in reaching large audiences, and message flexibility.

EXHIBIT 14.3

Characteristics of the Elements in the Promotional Mix

	Advertising	Public Relations	Sales Promotion	Personal Selling
Mode of Communication	Indirect and impersonal	Usually indirect and impersonal	Usually indirect and impersonal	Direct and face-to-face
Communicator Control over Situation	Low	Moderate to low	Moderate to low	High
Amount of Feedback	Little	Little	Little to moderate	Much
Speed of Feedback	Delayed	Delayed	Varies	Immediate
Direction of Message Flow	One-way	One-way	Mostly one-way	Two-way
Control over Message Content	Yes	No	Yes	Yes
Identification of Sponsor	Yes	No	Yes	Yes
Speed in Reaching Large Audience	Fast	Usually fast	Fast	Slow
Message Flexibility	Same message to all audiences	Usually no direct control over message	Same message to varied target audiences	Tailored to prospective buyer

Maintain image and educate consumers

Reach the masses

Stimulate purchase

Advertising

Public Relations

Sales Promotion

Personal Selling

Build relationships

Exhibit 14.3 illustrates that most elements of the promotional mix are indirect and impersonal when used to communicate with a target market, providing only one direction of message flow. For example, advertising, public relations, and sales promotion are generally impersonal, one-way means of mass communication. Because they provide little opportunity for direct feedback, it can be more difficult to adapt these promotional elements to changing consumer preferences, individual differences, and personal goals. One exception is how a company uses its Web site, which can provide a forum for some types of feedback.

Personal selling, on the other hand, is personal, two-way communication. The salesperson receives immediate feedback from the consumer and can adjust the message in response. Personal selling, however, is very slow in dispersing the marketer's message to large audiences. Because a salesperson can communicate to only one person or a small group of persons at one time, it is a poor choice if the marketer wants to send a message to many potential buyers.

LO ⑤
PROMOTIONAL GOALS AND THE AIDA CONCEPT

The ultimate goal of any promotion is to get someone to buy a good or service or, in the case of nonprofit organizations, to take some action (for instance, donate money or volunteer time). A classic model for reaching promotional goals is called the AIDA concept.[17] The acronym stands for *attention, interest, desire,* and *action*—the stages of consumer involvement with a promotional message.

This model proposes that consumers respond to marketing messages in a cognitive (thinking), affective (feeling), and conative (doing) sequence. First, a promotion manager may focus on attracting a person's *attention* by training a salesperson to use a friendly greeting and approach, or by using loud volume, unusual color contrasts, bold headlines, movement, bright colors, and the like in an advertisement. Next, a good sales presentation, demonstration, or advertisement creates *interest* in the product and then, by illustrating how the product's features will satisfy the consumer's needs, arouses *desire*. Finally, a special offer or a strong closing sales pitch may be used to obtain purchase *action*.

The AIDA concept assumes that promotion propels consumers along the following four steps in the purchase-decision process:

1. *Attention:* The advertiser must first gain the attention of the target market. A firm cannot sell something if the market does not know that the good or service exists. When Apple introduced the iPod, it was a new product for the company. To create awareness and gain attention for the new product, Apple had to advertise and promote it extensively through ads on TV, in magazines, and on the Internet. Because the iPod was a brand extension of the Apple computer, it required less effort than if it had been an entirely new brand. At the same time, because the iPod was an innovative new product line, the promotion had to get customers' attention and create awareness of a new idea from an established company.

2. *Interest:* Simple awareness of a brand seldom leads to a sale. The next step is to create interest in the product. A print ad or TV commercial cannot tell potential customers all the features and benefits of the iPod. Thus, Apple had to arrange iPod demonstrations and target messages to innovators and early adopters to create interest in the new portable music players.

3. *Desire:* Potential customers for the Apple iPod may like the concept of a portable music player, but they may not feel it is necessarily better than a Sony Walkman portable radio or a portable music player with fewer features. Therefore, Apple had to create brand preference with its iTunes Music Store, extended-life battery, clock and alarm, calendar and to-do list, photo storage, and other features. Specifically, Apple had to convince potential customers that the iPod was the best solution to meet their desire for a portable digital music player.

4. *Action:* Some potential target market customers may have been convinced to buy an iPod but had not yet made the actual purchase. To motivate them to take action, Apple continued advertising to more effectively communicate the features and benefits and also used promotions and price discounts.

Following the initial success of the iPod, to continue its market dominance of the portable digital music player market, Apple introduced new models such as the Nano and Shuffle that were smaller and lighter and yet had longer battery life and more storage. Then podcasting and video were added with access to thousands of network and cable shows and interfaces with auto, boat, and home equipment—and the iPod became a "portable media player."

With each product innovation, the cycle of attention, interest, desire, and action began again. But with the familiarity and success of earlier models, the time frame became shorter. In fact, during one Christmas season, Apple was selling more than 100 iPods per minute; by early 2009 it had sold over 150 million iPods. Moreover, Apple's iTunes Store now sells more music than any other retailer in the United States except for Wal-Mart—more than 4 billion songs to over 50 million customers.[18]

> **AIDA concept**
> A model that outlines the process for achieving promotional goals in terms of stages of consumer involvement with the message; the acronym stands for attention, interest, desire, and action.

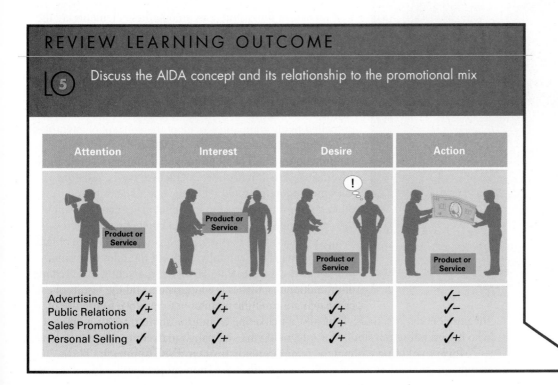

REVIEW LEARNING OUTCOME

LO 5 Discuss the AIDA concept and its relationship to the promotional mix

	Attention	Interest	Desire	Action
Advertising	✓+	✓+	✓	✓−
Public Relations	✓+	✓+	✓+	✓−
Sales Promotion	✓	✓	✓+	✓
Personal Selling	✓	✓+	✓+	✓+

Most buyers involved in high-involvement purchase situations pass through the four stages of the AIDA model on the way to making a purchase. The promoter's task is to determine where on the purchase ladder most of the target consumers are located and design a promotion plan to meet their needs. For instance, if Apple learned from its market research that many potential customers were in the desire stage but had not bought an iPod for some reason, then Apple could place advertising on Yahoo! or Google, and in video games as well, to target younger individuals who are the primary target market with specific messages to motivate them to take immediate action and buy an iPod.

The AIDA concept does not explain how all promotions influence purchase decisions. The model suggests that promotional effectiveness can be measured in terms of consumers progressing from one stage to the next. However, the order of stages in the model, as well as whether consumers go through all steps, has been much debated. For example, a purchase can occur without interest or desire, perhaps when a low-involvement product is bought on impulse. Regardless of the order of the stages or consumers' progression through these stages, the AIDA concept helps marketers by suggesting which promotional strategy—that is, which plan for using the promotional mix—will be most effective.[19]

L◯⑥ INTEGRATED MARKETING COMMUNICATIONS

Ideally, marketing communications from each promotional mix element (personal selling, advertising, sales promotion, and public relations) should be integrated—the message reaching the consumer should be the same regardless of whether it is from an advertisement, a salesperson in the field, a magazine article, or a coupon in a newspaper insert.

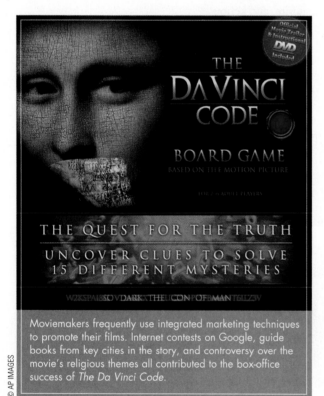

Moviemakers frequently use integrated marketing techniques to promote their films. Internet contests on Google, guide books from key cities in the story, and controversy over the movie's religious themes all contributed to the box-office success of *The Da Vinci Code.*

From the consumer's standpoint, a company's communications are already integrated. Consumers do not think in terms of the four elements of promotion: advertising, sales promotion, public relations, and personal selling. Instead, everything is an "ad." In general, the only people who recognize the distinctions among these elements are the marketers themselves. Unfortunately, many marketers neglect this fact when planning promotional messages and fail to integrate their communication efforts from one element to the next. The most common rift typically occurs between personal selling and the other elements of the promotional mix.

This unintegrated, disjointed approach to promotion has propelled many companies to adopt the concept of integrated marketing communications (IMC). IMC is the careful coordination of all promotional messages—traditional advertising, direct marketing, interactive, public relations, sales promotion, personal selling, event marketing, and other communications—for a product or service to ensure the consistency of messages at every contact point where a company meets the consumer. Following the concept of IMC, marketing managers carefully work out the roles that various promotional elements will play in the marketing mix. Timing of promotional activities is coordinated, and the results of each campaign are carefully monitored to improve future use of the promotional mix tools. Typically, a marketing communications director is appointed who has overall responsibility for integrating the company's marketing communications.

Movie marketing campaigns benefit greatly from an IMC approach. Those campaigns that are most integrated generally have more impact and make a deeper impression on potential moviegoers, leading to higher box-office sales. An integrated marketing approach was used to introduce *The Da Vinci Code*. Excitement about the release of the film gathered momentum months in advance as the trailer was shown on the Internet and television. Along with the release of the trailer, the movie was supported by numerous merchandising efforts. Bookstores and gift shops stocked hardback, paperback, and special illustrated editions, as well as *Da Vinci Code* walking tours of key cities in the story, playing cards, calligraphy sets, music CDs, video games, podcasts, and more. Google and Sony launched a game called "The Sony Ericsson Da Vinci Code Trail" in 22 languages. Players competed against each other online and then in a real-life challenge in Paris. The winner was awarded a two-week trip to Rome, Paris, London, and New York. The game did more than promote the movie, however. "Da Vinci Code Trail" familiarized people with Google's services beyond search and drove traffic to Sony's Web site, which rose 30 percent as a result of the promotion. Finally, before the movie's release, there were over 500,000 English language posts on blogs like Technorati, Google, IceRocket, and BlogPulse. The integrated marketing campaign (plus the religious controversy surrounding the story) helped the film generate over $77 million at the box office on opening weekend.[20]

The IMC concept has been growing in popularity for several reasons. First, the proliferation of thousands of media choices beyond traditional television has made promotion a more complicated task. Instead of promoting a product just through mass-media options, like television and magazines, promotional messages today can appear in many varied sources. Furthermore, the mass market has also fragmented—more selectively segmented markets and an increase in niche marketing have replaced the traditional broad market groups that marketers promoted to in years past. For instance, many popular magazines now have Spanish-language editions targeted toward America's growing Hispanic population. Finally, marketers have slashed their advertising spending in favor of promotional techniques that generate immediate sales responses and those whose effects are more easily measured, such as direct marketing. Thus, the interest in IMC is largely a reaction to the scrutiny that marketing communications has come under and, particularly, to suggestions that uncoordinated promotional activity leads to a strategy that is wasteful and inefficient.

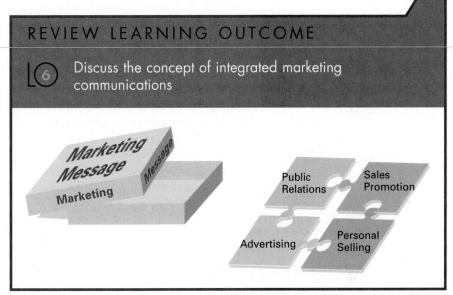

REVIEW LEARNING OUTCOME

LO 6 Discuss the concept of integrated marketing communications

Marketing Message

Marketing

Message

Public Relations   Sales Promotion

Advertising   Personal Selling

LO 7
FACTORS AFFECTING THE PROMOTIONAL MIX

Promotional mixes vary a great deal from one product and one industry to the next. Normally, advertising and personal selling are used to promote goods and services, and are supported and supplemented by sales promotion. Public relations helps develop a positive image for the organization and the product line. However, a firm may choose not to use all four promotional elements in its promotional mix, or it may choose to use them in varying degrees. The particular promotional mix chosen by a firm for a product or service depends on several factors: the nature of

Buying specialty products such as jewelry and clothing often involves a social risk. Many consumers depend on sales personnel for guidance and advice in making the "proper" choice.

the product, the stage in the product life cycle, target market characteristics, the type of buying decision, funds available for promotion, and whether a push or a pull strategy will be used.

Nature of the Product

Characteristics of the product itself can influence the promotional mix. For instance, a product can be classified as either a business product or a consumer product (refer to Chapters 7 and 10). As business products are often custom-tailored to the buyer's exact specifications, they are often not well suited to mass promotion. Therefore, producers of most business goods, such as computer systems or industrial machinery, rely more heavily on personal selling than on advertising. Informative personal selling is common for industrial installations, accessories, and component parts and materials. Advertising, however, still serves a purpose in promoting business goods. Advertisements in trade media may be used to create general buyer awareness and interest. Moreover, advertising can help locate potential customers for the sales force. For example, print media advertising often includes coupons soliciting the potential customer to "fill this out for more detailed information."

In contrast, because consumer products generally are not custom-made, they do not require the selling efforts of a company representative who can tailor them to the user's needs. Thus, consumer goods are promoted mainly through advertising to create brand familiarity. Television and radio advertising, consumer-oriented magazines, and the Internet and other highly targeted media are used extensively to promote consumer goods, especially nondurables. Sales promotion, the brand name, and the product's packaging are about twice as important for consumer goods as for business products. Persuasive personal selling is important at the retail level for shopping goods such as automobiles and appliances.

The costs and risks associated with a product also influence the promotional mix. As a general rule, when the costs or risks of using a product increase, personal selling becomes more important. Items that are a small part of a firm's budget (supply items) or of a consumer's budget (convenience products) do not require a salesperson to close the sale. In fact, inexpensive items cannot support the cost of a salesperson's time and effort unless the potential volume is high. On the other hand, expensive and complex machinery, new buildings, cars, and new homes represent a considerable investment. A salesperson must assure buyers that they are spending their money wisely and not taking an undue financial risk.

Social risk is an issue as well. Many consumer goods are not products of great social importance because they do not reflect social position. People do not experience much social risk in buying a loaf of bread or a candy bar. However, buying some shopping products and many specialty products such as jewelry and clothing does involve a social risk. Many consumers depend on sales personnel for guidance and advice in making the "proper" choice.

Stages in the Product Life Cycle

The product's stage in its life cycle is a big factor in designing a promotional mix. (See Exhibit 14.4.) During the *introduction stage*, the basic goal of promotion is to inform the target audience that the product is available. Initially, the emphasis is on the general product class—for example, mobile phones. The emphasis gradually changes to gaining attention for a particular brand, such as Nokia, Samsung, Sony Ericsson, or Motorola. Typically, both extensive advertising and public relations inform the target audience of the product class or brand and heighten awareness

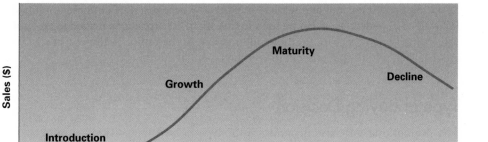

| Preintroduction publicity; small amounts of advertising near introduction | Heavy advertising and public relations to build awareness; sales promotion to induce trial; personal selling to obtain distribution | Heavy advertising and public relations to build brand loyalty; decreasing use of sales promotion; personal selling to maintain distribution | Advertising slightly decreased — more persuasive and reminder in nature; increased use of sales promotion to build market share; personal selling to maintain distribution | Advertising and public relations drastically decreased; sales promotion and personal selling maintained at low levels |

levels. Sales promotion encourages early trial of the product, and personal selling gets retailers to carry the product.

When the product reaches the *growth stage* of the life cycle, the promotion blend may shift. Often a change is necessary because different types of potential buyers are targeted. Although advertising and public relations continue to be major elements of the promotional mix, sales promotion can be reduced because consumers need fewer incentives to purchase. The promotional strategy is to emphasize the product's differential advantage over the competition. Persuasive promotion is used to build and maintain brand loyalty to support the product during the growth stage. By this stage, personal selling has usually succeeded in getting adequate distribution for the product.

As the product reaches the *maturity stage* of its life cycle, competition becomes much stronger, and thus persuasive and reminder advertising are more strongly emphasized. Sales promotion comes back into focus as product sellers try to increase their market share.

All promotion, especially advertising, is reduced as the product enters the *decline stage*. Nevertheless, personal selling and sales promotion efforts may be maintained, particularly at the retail level.

Target Market Characteristics

A target market characterized by widely scattered potential customers, highly informed buyers, and brand-loyal repeat purchasers generally requires a promotional mix with more advertising and sales promotion and less personal selling. Sometimes, however, personal selling is required even when buyers are well informed and geographically dispersed. Although industrial installations and component parts may be sold to extremely competent people with extensive education and work experience, salespeople must still be present to explain the product and work out the details of the purchase agreement.

Often firms sell goods and services in markets where potential customers are hard to locate. Print advertising can be used to find them. The reader is invited to go online, call, or mail in a reply card for more information. As the online inquiries, calls, or cards are received, salespeople are sent to visit the potential customers.

Type of Buying Decision

The promotional mix also depends on the type of buying decision (routine or complex). For example, the most effective promotion for routine consumer decisions, like buying toothpaste or soft drinks, calls attention to the brand or reminds the consumer about the brand. Advertising and, especially, sales promotion are the most productive promotion tools to use for routine decisions.

If the decision is neither routine nor complex, advertising and public relations help establish awareness for the good or service. Suppose a man is looking for a bottle of wine to serve to his dinner guests. As a beer drinker, he is not familiar with wines, yet he has seen advertising for Robert Mondavi wine and has also read an article in a popular magazine about the Robert Mondavi winery. He may be more likely to buy this brand because he is already aware of it. Indeed, online reviews can be important tools in this type of buying decision.

In contrast, consumers making complex buying decisions are more extensively involved. They rely on large amounts of information to help them reach a purchase decision. Personal selling is most effective in helping these consumers decide. For example, consumers thinking about buying a car typically research the car online using corporate and third party Web sites. However, few people buy a car without visiting the dealership. They depend on a salesperson to provide the information they need to reach a decision. In addition to online resources, print advertising and brochures may also be used for high-involvement purchase decisions because they can often provide a large amount of information to the consumer.

Available Funds

Money, or the lack of it, may easily be the most important factor in determining the promotional mix. A small, undercapitalized manufacturer may rely heavily on free publicity if its product is unique. If the situation warrants a sales force, a financially strained firm may turn to manufacturers' agents, who work on a commission basis with no advances or expense accounts. Even well-capitalized organizations may not be able to afford the advertising rates of publications like *Time Magazine, Reader's Digest,* and *The Wall Street Journal,* or the cost of running television commercials on *Desperate Housewives, American Idol,* or the Super Bowl. The price of a high-profile advertisement in these media could support several salespeople for an entire year.

When funds are available to permit a mix of promotional elements, a firm will generally try to optimize its return on promotion dollars while minimizing the *cost per contact,* or the cost of reaching one member of the target market. In general, the cost per contact is very high for personal selling, public relations, and sales promotions like sampling and demonstrations. On the other hand, given the number of people national advertising reaches, it has a very low cost per contact.

Usually, there is a trade-off among the funds available, the number of people in the target market, the quality of communication needed, and the relative costs of the promotional elements. A company may have to forgo a full-page, color advertisement in *People* magazine in order to pay for a personal selling effort. Although the magazine ad will reach more people than personal selling, the high cost of the magazine space is a problem. There are plenty of low cost options available to companies without a huge budget. Many of these include online strategies and public relations efforts, where the company relies on free publicity.

Push strategy

EXHIBIT 14.5

Push Strategy versus Pull Strategy

Pull strategy

Push and Pull Strategies

The last factor that affects the promotional mix is whether to use a push or a pull promotional strategy. Manufacturers may use aggressive personal selling and trade advertising to convince a wholesaler or a retailer to carry and sell their merchandise. This approach is known as a push strategy. (See Exhibit 14.5.) The wholesaler, in turn, must often push the merchandise forward by persuading the retailer to handle the goods. The retailer then uses advertising, displays, and other forms of promotion to convince the consumer to buy the "pushed" products. This concept also applies to services. For example, the Jamaican Tourism Board targets promotions to travel agencies, which, in turn, tell their customers about the benefits of vacationing in Jamaica.

At the other extreme is a pull strategy, which stimulates consumer demand to obtain product distribution. Rather than trying to sell to the wholesaler, the manufacturer using a pull strategy focuses its promotional efforts on end consumers or opinion leaders. For example, Procter & Gamble recently spent $100 million on an advertising campaign to promote its new toothpaste. P&G's new Crest Pro-Health claims to deliver everything a consumer could want in one tube—it supposedly protects against gingivitis, plaque, cavities, sensitivity, and stains, and it freshens breath. The theme of the campaign, targeted to the information-seeking customer, is "Healthy, beautiful smiles for life."[21] Consumers responded positively to the campaign and began demanding the product from their retailer. The retailer ordered the merchandise from the wholesaler. The wholesaler, confronted with rising demand, then placed an order for the "pulled" merchandise from the manufacturer. Consumer demand pulled the product through the channel of distribution. (See Exhibit 14.5.) Heavy sampling, introductory consumer advertising,

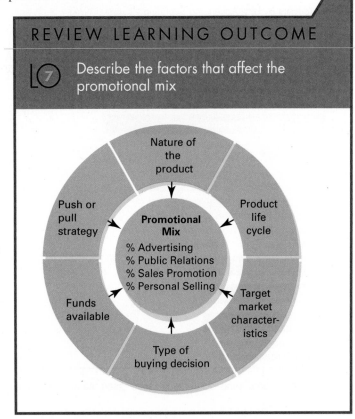

REVIEW LEARNING OUTCOME

LO7 Describe the factors that affect the promotional mix

cents-off campaigns, and couponing are part of a pull strategy. P&G flooded dental offices with product samples and informational materials in hopes of generating favorable testimonials from users. Similarly, Splenda No Calorie Sweetener offered free samples, recipes, and a coupon to potential consumers who tried Splenda.[22]

Rarely does a company use a pull or a push strategy exclusively. Instead, the mix will emphasize one of these strategies. For example, pharmaceutical companies generally use a push strategy, through personal selling and trade advertising, to promote their drugs and therapies to physicians. Sales presentations and advertisements in medical journals give physicians the detailed information they need to prescribe medication to their patients. Most pharmaceutical companies supplement their push promotional strategy with a pull strategy targeted directly to potential patients through advertisements in consumer magazines and on television.

LO ⑧
THE EFFECTS OF ADVERTISING

Advertising is defined as any form of impersonal, paid communication in which the sponsor or company is identified. It is a popular form of promotion, especially for consumer packaged goods and services. Advertising expenditures typically increase annually but were expected to decline in 2009, due to economic conditions. In recent years 30 companies spent over $1 billion each, with the top 100 global marketers spending more than $108 billion overall on measured media. Among the top brands advertised by these companies were Procter & Gamble ($9.4 billion), Unilever ($5.3 billion), L'Oreal ($3.4 billion), and General Motors Company ($3.3 billion).[23]

Advertising and marketing services agencies and other firms that provide marketing and communications services to marketers employ an estimated 750,000 people. About another 850,000 people work in media advertising, such as newspapers, broadcast and cable TV, radio, magazines, and Internet media companies.[24] This represents a decrease in both areas primarily due to economic conditions and much lower newspaper employment.

The money budgeted for advertising by some firms is staggering. (See Exhibit 14.6.) Procter & Gamble, Verizon, AT&T, General Motors, and Johnson & Johnson each spend anywhere from $2.5 billion to nearly $5 billion annually in the United States on national advertising alone. That's about $10 million a day on national advertising. If local advertising, sales promotion, and public relations are included, this figure rises much higher. Over 100 companies spend more than $300 million each on advertising every year.[25]

Spending on advertising varies by industry. For example, book publishers have one of the highest ratios of advertising dollars to sales. They spend roughly 27 cents on advertising for every dollar of book revenue. Similarly, for every dollar of merchandise sold in

EXHIBIT 14.6

Top Ten Leaders by U.S. Advertising Spending

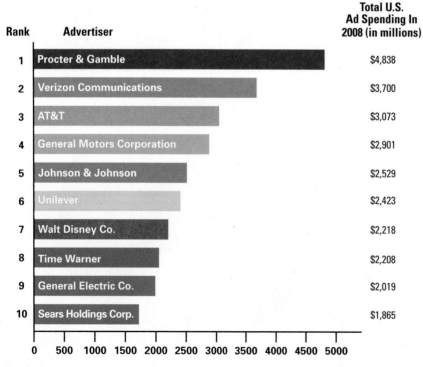

Rank	Advertiser	Total U.S. Ad Spending In 2008 (in millions)
1	Procter & Gamble	$4,838
2	Verizon Communications	$3,700
3	AT&T	$3,073
4	General Motors Corporation	$2,901
5	Johnson & Johnson	$2,529
6	Unilever	$2,423
7	Walt Disney Co.	$2,218
8	Time Warner	$2,208
9	General Electric Co.	$2,019
10	Sears Holdings Corp.	$1,865

Source: Reprinted with permission from the June 23, 2009, issue of *Advertising Age.* Copyright © Crain Communications, Inc.

the game and toy industry, about 12 to 15 cents is spent on advertising these products to consumers. Other consumer goods manufacturers that spend heavily on advertising in relation to total sales include sugar and confectionery products manufacturers, leather manufacturers, watchmakers, perfume and cosmetic manufacturers, detergent makers, and wine and liquor companies.[26]

Advertising and Market Share

Today's most successful brands of consumer goods, like Ivory soap and Coca-Cola, were built by heavy advertising and marketing investments long ago. Today's advertising dollars for successful consumer brands are spent on maintaining brand awareness and market share.

New brands with a small market share tend to spend proportionately more for advertising and sales promotion than those with a large market share, typically for two reasons. First, beyond a certain level of spending for advertising and sales promotion, diminishing returns set in. That is, sales or market share begins to decrease no matter how much is spent on advertising and sales promotion. This phenomenon is called the advertising response function. Understanding the advertising response function helps marketers use budgets wisely. A market leader like Johnson & Johnson's Neutrogena typically spends proportionately less on advertising than a newcomer like Jergens Natural Glow Daily Moisturizer brand. Jergens spends more on its brand to gain attention and increase market share. Neutrogena, on the other hand, spends only as much as is needed to maintain market share—anything more would produce diminishing benefits. Neutrogena has already captured the attention of the majority of its target market. It needs only to remind customers of its product.

The second reason new brands tend to require higher spending for advertising and sales promotion is that a certain minimum level of exposure is needed to measurably affect purchase habits. If Jergens advertised Natural Glow Daily Moisturizer in only one or two publications and bought only one or two television spots, it certainly would not achieve the exposure needed to penetrate consumers' perceptual defenses, gain attention, and ultimately affect purchase intentions. Instead, Natural Glow Daily Moisturizer was advertised in many different media for a sustained time.

The Effects of Advertising on Consumers

Advertising affects consumers' daily lives, informing them about products and services and influencing their attitudes, beliefs, and ultimately their purchases. The average U.S. citizen is exposed to hundreds of advertisements a day from all types of advertising media. In the television medium alone, researchers estimate that the average viewer watches at least six hours of commercial television messages a week. In addition, that person is exposed to countless print ads and promotional messages seen in other places. Advertising affects the TV programs people watch, the content of the newspapers they read, the politicians they elect, the medicines they take, and the toys their children play with. Consequently, the influence of advertising on the U.S. socioeconomic system has been the subject of extensive debate among economists, marketers, sociologists, psychologists, politicians, consumerists, and many others.

Though advertising cannot change consumers' deeply rooted values and attitudes, it may succeed in transforming a person's negative attitude toward a product into a positive one. For instance, serious or dramatic advertisements are more effective at changing consumers' negative attitudes. Humorous ads, on the other hand, have been shown to be more effective at shaping attitudes when consumers already have a positive image of the advertised brand.[27] However, as much as humor in advertising tends to improve brand recognition, it does not necessarily improve product recall, message credibility, or buying intentions. Consumers who find the ad funny may have good feelings about the product, but their purchasing decisions will not be affected unless they can actually recall the brand. The best results with humorous ads are achieved by making the message relevant

advertising response function
A phenomenon in which spending for advertising and sales promotion increases sales or market share up to a certain level but then produces diminishing returns.

to the product. For example, Taco Bell saw a substantial rise in sales after promoting a tiny talking Chihuahua who was crazy about their product, constantly demanding to be fed by saying, "Yo quiero Taco Bell." The phrase caught on and got people repeating—and remembering—the company's name across the country. The actual content of the commercial reinforced the company's message in a relevant manner.[28]

Advertising can also affect the way consumers rank a brand's attributes, such as color, taste, smell, and texture. For example, in years past, car ads emphasized brand attributes such as roominess, speed, and low maintenance. Today, however, car marketers have added safety, versatility, and customization to the list. Safety features such as antilock brakes, power door locks, and front and side air bags are now a standard part of the message in many carmakers' ads. Toyota Scion appeals to consumers' sense of individuality by allowing purchasers to custom-design their cars by selecting features such as the steering wheel color, multi-shade illuminated cup holders, and "sport" pedals.[29]

CUSTOMER Experience

CUSTOMER

Pepsi's New Look

PEPSI-COLA NORTH AMERICA BEVERAGES

How much does a brand logo makeover cost these days? Well more than one million dollars and five months if you are Pepsi-Cola. Pepsi recently revealed its new logo—only the 11th change since 1898, five changes coming in the last 21 years. According to Pepsi's top executives, part of the strategy was to move the brand from the traditional mass marketing and mass distribution era into the current culture of personalization. "By making the logo more dynamic and more alive . . . it is absolutely a huge step in the right direction," said Pepsi VP portfolio brands, Frank Cooper. While the $1 million dollars spent on design could be considered hefty, the real costs come in the other changes—from the trucks, vending machines, stadium signage, point of sale materials, and more. This could easily reach into the hundreds of millions of dollars.

So just what does the new logo signify? According to Pepsi, the new logo has a white band in the middle of the Pepsi circle that represents a series of smiles . . . a smile for Pepsi, a grin for Diet Pepsi, and a laugh for Pepsi Max. Branding experts are mixed: Some think the new look will make the logo less durable and classic while others feel that it is more adventurous and youthful. Indeed, Pepsi has succeeded in the past by targeting the "new generation."

There are also mixed consumer reviews. Some think the new logo looks like the old Diet Pepsi logo with the identical sans-serif typeface and the red and blue Pepsi wave in a diagonal slope. Others feel the new logo looks similar to the campaign for President Barack Obama. Regardless, there is a minimalist feel that has captured the attention of the iPod generation—that idea of simple elegance.

Interestingly, Pepsi's new advertising campaign also comes with a dose of optimism "every generation refreshes the world." However, arch rival Coca-Cola is also dosing out the optimism with its new advertising tagline "Open happiness."[30] While both companies have embraced this message at various times, never has this happened simultaneously. So the question is whether this helps or hurts the differentiation of each brand.

Return on advertising expense (in sales or market share)

Building sales/share

Maintaining sales/share

Advertising response function

Money spent

Advertising can
- ✓ change negative attitude to positive
- ✓ reinforce positive attitude
- ✓ affect how consumers rank brand attributes

LO⑨
MAJOR TYPES OF ADVERTISING

The firm's promotional objectives determine the type of advertising it uses. If the goal of the promotion plan is to build up the image of the company or the industry, institutional advertising may be used. In contrast, if the advertiser wants to enhance the sales of a specific good or service, product advertising is used.

Institutional Advertising

Historically, advertising in the United States has been product oriented. Today, however, companies market multiple products and need a different type of advertising. Institutional advertising, or corporate advertising, promotes the corporation as a whole and is designed to establish, change, or maintain the corporation's identity. It usually does not ask the audience to do anything but maintain a favorable attitude toward the advertiser and its goods and services. For example, when Time Warner dropped AOL from the company's corporate brand name, it hired a branding agency to develop institutional advertising to reposition the brand without the Internet unit and refocus the image on Time Warner as a media giant. In designing the "rebranding," executives did not want a radical change. Rather, they wanted to "freshen" the previous image and maintain its favorable status. The logo itself changed in texture, color, and typeface. In addition to changing the logo on buildings, business cards, and stationery, the company changed its stock ticker symbol to reflect the new image.[31]

A form of institutional advertising called advocacy advertising is typically used to safeguard against negative consumer attitudes and to enhance the company's credibility

institutional advertising
A form of advertising designed to enhance a company's image rather than promote a particular product.

product advertising
A form of advertising that touts the benefits of a specific good or service.

advocacy advertising
A form of advertising in which an organization expresses its views on controversial issues or responds to media attacks.

ENERGY FOR THE 21ST CENTURY

COAL

Today's technologies can convert U.S. coal into:

Clean Electricity to power growing cities.

Transportation Fuels to keep our economy moving.

Natural Gas to warm homes and families in winter.

Hydrogen to energize fuel cells of tomorrow.

Yeah... coal can do that.

Today, coal fuels more than 50% of U.S. electricity. America has the largest coal reserves in the world... and greater use of this clean and affordable fuel can reduce our reliance on foreign oil and liquefied natural gas.

Peabody Energy (NYSE: BTU) is the world's largest provider of coal to fuel 21st Century energy solutions.

CoalCanDoThat.com

Peabody

Institutional advertising is designed to promote, establish, change, or maintain a corporation's positive identity. Usually the audience isn't asked to do anything except maintain a favorable attitude toward the institution.

pioneering advertising
A form of advertising designed to stimulate primary demand for a new product or product category.

competitive advertising
A form of advertising designed to influence demand for a specific brand.

among consumers who already favor its position. Often corporations use advocacy advertising to express their views on controversial issues. At other times, firms' advocacy campaigns react to criticism or blame, some in direct response to criticism by the media. For example, oil and gas companies typically get blamed for high gas prices and high profits. One of the largest in the world, Chevron Texaco, recently launched a campaign called "The Power of Human Energy" to highlight the different areas of energy the company is investing in aside from oil exploration. BP, another global energy company, rebranded itself BP—Beyond Petroleum to highlight its investments in alternative energy sources.[32] Other advocacy campaigns may try to ward off increased regulation, damaging legislation, or an unfavorable outcome in a lawsuit. The tobacco companies have utilized "good citizen campaigns" in the United States and around the world in an effort to create a positive public image for themselves after losing several class-action suits and being accused of targeting children with their marketing campaigns. In an effort to improve its corporate image, Philip Morris has been spending more than $120 million a year promoting its environmental and community development programs, such as building homes for Habitat for Humanity, making donations to food banks, and supporting meal programs for seniors and shelters for battered women.[33]

Product Advertising

Unlike institutional advertising, product advertising promotes the benefits of a specific good or service. The product's stage in its life cycle often determines which type of product advertising is used: pioneering advertising, competitive advertising, or comparative advertising.

Pioneering Advertising Pioneering advertising is intended to stimulate primary demand for a new product or product category. Heavily used during the introductory stage of the product life cycle, pioneering advertising offers consumers in-depth information about the benefits of the product class. Pioneering advertising also seeks to create interest. Pharmaceutical companies are the latest big players in pioneering advertising. For instance, one pharma giant, Pfizer, has steadily ramped up consumer advertising of a new drug, Lyrica—first approved by the FDA to treat pain caused by diabetic nerve damage. Then Pfizer found a broader market for Lyrica when it was approved for treatment of the disputed pain condition fibromyalgia. In just six months Pfizer spent $46 million on a new ad campaign for Lyrica as a treatment for fibromyalgia, compared with $33 million the previous year, in spite of the protest by many doctors who do not believe fibromyalgia is a real medical condition. There are no biological tests to diagnose fibromyalgia, and the condition has not been linked to any environmental or biological causes. But worldwide sales of Lyrica reached $1.8 billion in 2007. Analysts predicted sales would rise an additional 30 percent in 2008, helped by consumer advertising and the interest from other drug companies who see the potential for a major new market in aggressively pursuing fibromyalgia treatments.[34]

Competitive Advertising Firms use competitive or brand advertising when a product enters the growth phase of the product life cycle and other companies begin to enter the marketplace. Instead of building demand for the product category, the goal of competitive advertising is to influence demand for a specific brand. Often promotion becomes less informative and appeals more to emotions during this phase. Advertisements may emphasize subtle differences between brands, focusing on building recall of a brand name and creating a favorable brand attitude. Automobile advertising has long used very competitive messages, drawing distinctions based on factors such as quality, performance, and image. Similarly, in an effort to obtain market share from competitors and to build brand awareness in the wireless industry, Nextel Communications signed a ten-year title sponsorship agreement with NASCAR. NASCAR executives, interested in building a younger fan base, consider the telecom industry one of the best ways to reach younger consumers because they always have a cell phone "stuck" to their ear.[35]

Comparative Advertising Comparative advertising directly or indirectly compares two or more competing brands on one or more specific attributes. Some advertisers even use comparative advertising against their own brands. Products experiencing slow growth or entering the marketplace against strong competitors are more likely to employ comparative claims in their advertising. For instance, the Mac versus PC ads for Apple have been masterful. The ads create an image of a stodgy PC battling with a hip, cool Mac. The campaign's success has escalated the battle between the two computer icons with each creating new ads aimed at the other. Other recent campaigns include Hoover versus Dyson vacuum cleaners, Miller Lite versus Bud Light, and Pampers versus Huggies. In addition to comparative advertising, some companies have brought back the "taste test." These include Progresso soups versus Campbell's Select Harvest soups and Dunkin' Donuts versus Starbucks (which is even supported by a microsite **www.dunkin-beatstarbucks.com**).[36]

Before the 1970s, comparative advertising was allowed only if the competing brand was veiled and unidentified. In 1971, however, the Federal Trade Commission (FTC) fostered the growth of comparative advertising by saying that it provided information to the customer and that advertisers were more skillful than the government in communicating this information. Federal rulings prohibit advertisers from falsely describing competitors' products and allow competitors to sue if ads show their products or mention their brand names in an incorrect or false manner.

FTC rules also apply to advertisers making false claims about their own products. For example, the FTC recently filed a false-advertising suit against a company that

The Mac vs. PC ads for Apple use comparative advertising by portraying the PC (and everything and everyone associated with it) as "stodgy" and constantly losing to a hip, cool Mac.

© A. MILLER/WENN/NEWSCOM

REVIEW LEARNING OUTCOME

LO 9 Identify the major types of advertising

	Introduction	Growth	Maturity	Decline

Institutional advertising (promote company rather than product)

PLC

Product Advertising

Comparative

Pioneering — Competitive

Stimulate demand / Influence demand for specific brand / Influence demand by highlighting weakness of the competition

comparative advertising
A form of advertising that compares two or more specifically named or shown competing brands on one or more specific attributes.

marketed a weight-loss product, claiming that its users could lose substantial amounts of weight rapidly, including as much as 18 pounds per week and as much as 50 percent of all excess weight in just 14 days, without dieting or exercise. The company also included (false) assurances that clinical studies prove those claims.[37]

Companies must be careful with comparative advertising approaches in other countries as well. Germany, Italy, Belgium, and France, for example, do not permit advertisers to claim that their products are the best or better than competitors' products, both of which are common claims in the United States. In the Netherlands, car manufacturers cannot make claims in their advertising about the fuel consumption or environmental aspects of the car. Similarly, Lands' End ran afoul of a German law prohibiting lifetime guarantee claims, which happen to be one of Lands' End's guiding principles. The law has made it difficult for the direct retailer to sell its products and advertise its lifetime guarantee through the Internet and direct mail in Germany.

In other countries, hard-hitting comparative advertising will not be effective because it offends cultural values. For example, Arabic culture generally encourages people not to compete with one another, and the sharing of wealth is common practice. Therefore, comparative advertising is not consistent with social values in Arabic countries. Japanese advertisers have also been reluctant to use comparative advertising because it is considered confrontational and doesn't promote the respectful treatment of consumers or portray a company in a respectful light. Nevertheless, although the Japanese have traditionally favored soft-sell advertising approaches, consumers are witnessing a trend toward comparative ads.

LO CREATIVE DECISIONS IN ADVERTISING

Advertising strategies typically are organized around an advertising campaign. An advertising campaign is a series of related advertisements focusing on a common theme, slogan, and set of advertising appeals. It is a specific advertising effort for a particular product that extends for a defined period of time. For example, Hewlett-Packard's celebrity-drenched global ad campaign, "The computer is personal again," helped HP gain the lead in worldwide market share for personal computers, and also imbued a once-faded brand with some cool. The glossy campaign, featuring print, video, and television ads, showcased achievers such as "CEO of Hip-Hop" Jay-Z, "Master of Snowboards" Shaun White, designer Vera Wang, and Brazilian author Paulo Coelho. Each celebrity was shown manipulating images that seemingly revolved around their laptop to show what's on their computer, what they do in their spare time, and why the PC is personal to them. A concurrent online campaign included a virtual motorcycle tour with the Orange County Choppers team, who were also the celebrity stars of HP's Super Bowl ad. That campaign was designed to create demand among 18- to 34-year-olds for the HP Pavilion entertainment notebook and specially designed Orange County Choppers "skins," or computer covers.[38]

Before any creative work can begin on an advertising campaign, it is important to determine what goals or objectives the advertising should achieve. An advertising objective identifies the specific communication task that a campaign should accomplish for a specified target audience during a specified period. The objectives of a specific advertising campaign often depend on the overall corporate objectives and the product being advertised. For example, McIlhenny Company's Tabasco Hot Sauce launched a print advertising campaign with the objective of educating consumers about how to use the product and the variety of flavors offered. The ads featured product information embedded in the label, which was blown up to cover the entire page. The ad copy for the Garlic Pepper Sauce read: "The only one potent enough to ward off both hypothermia and vampires at once." The original Tabasco Pepper Sauce ad copy read: "It's like love, you always want more no matter how badly you got burned last time." The ad campaign increased sales by over 11 percent in the first four weeks. The print medium was also supported by participation in special events, such as the National Collegiate Tailgate Tour.[39]

The DAGMAR approach (Defining Advertising Goals for Measured Advertising Results) is one method of setting objectives. According to this method, all advertising objectives should precisely define the target audience, the desired percentage change in some specified measure of effectiveness, and the time frame in which that change is to occur. For example, the objectives for an advertising campaign for Coca-Cola's revamped POWERade brand might be to achieve a 15 percent increase in its share of the sports-drink market within eight months.

Once objectives are defined, creative work can begin on the advertising campaign. Advertising campaigns often follow the AIDA model, which was discussed in Chapter 14. Depending on where consumers are in the AIDA process, the creative development of an advertising campaign might focus on creating attention, arousing interest, stimulating desire, or ultimately leading to the action of buying the product. Specifically, creative decisions include identifying product benefits, developing and evaluating advertising appeals, executing the message, and evaluating the effectiveness of the campaign.

Identifying Product Benefits

A well-known rule of thumb in the advertising industry is "Sell the sizzle, not the steak"—that is, in advertising the goal is to sell the benefits of the product, not its attributes. An attribute is simply a feature of the product such as its easy-open package or special formulation. A benefit is what consumers will receive or achieve by using the product. A benefit should answer the consumer's question, "What's in it for me?" Benefits might be such things as convenience, pleasure, savings, or relief. A quick test to determine whether you are offering attributes or benefits in your advertising is to ask, "So?" Consider this example:

- ☞ *Attribute:* "SoBe Life Water has reformulated five delicious, low-calorie flavors— Blackberry Grape, Pomegranate Cherry, Orange Tangerine, Strawberry Kiwi and Passionfruit Citrus—each infused with a unique mix of antioxidant vitamins C & E, essential B vitamins and healthy herbal ingredients . . ." "So . . . ?"

- ☞ *Benefit:* "So . . . SoBe Life Water is not only an enhanced water; it is a lifestyle unto itself . . . providing consumers the healthiest, most fun and refreshing products, delivering the incredibly positive benefits of hydration and unmatched brand experiences."[40]

Marketing research and intuition are usually used to unearth the perceived benefits of a product and to rank consumers' preferences for these benefits. Coke's rival, PepsiCo, has its own sports drink, Gatorade. Already positioned as *the* thirst-quencher, Gatorade's advertising touts its refueling benefits to serious athletes of mainstream sports. Similarly, Kellogg's ad campaign for its latest cereal, Frosted Flakes Gold, has partnered with ESPN to promote the new frosted flake as a product that provides longer-lasting energy because it's a whole grain cereal. The ads underscore the message of increased, longer-lasting energy by featuring adolescent athletes being cheered on by Tony the Tiger.[41]

Developing and Evaluating Advertising Appeals

An advertising appeal identifies a reason for a person to buy a product. Developing advertising appeals, a challenging task, is typically the responsibility of the creative people in the advertising agency. Advertising appeals typically play off of consumers' emotions, such as fear or love, or address some need or want the consumer has, such as a need for convenience or the desire to save money.

Advertising campaigns can focus on one or more advertising appeals. Often the appeals are quite general, thus allowing the firm to develop a number of subthemes or

advertising appeal
A reason for a person to buy a product.

© AP IMAGES/PR NEWSFOTO/PEPSI CO.

EXHIBIT 14.7

Common Advertising Appeals

Profit	Lets consumers know whether the product will save them money, make them money, or keep them from losing money
Health	Appeals to those who are body-conscious or who want to be healthy
Love or Romance	Is used often in selling cosmetics and perfumes
Fear	Can center around social embarrassment, growing old, or losing one's health; because of its power, requires advertiser to exercise care in execution
Admiration	Is the reason that celebrity spokespeople are used so often in advertising
Convenience	Is often used for fast-food restaurants and microwave foods
Fun and Pleasure	Are the key to advertising vacations, beer, amusement parks, and more
Vanity and Egotism	Are used most often for expensive or conspicuous items such as cars and clothing
Environmental Consciousness	Centers around protecting the environment and being considerate of others in the community

unique selling proposition
A desirable, exclusive, and believable advertising appeal selected as the theme for a campaign.

minicampaigns using both advertising and sales promotion. Several possible advertising appeals are listed in Exhibit 14.7.

Choosing the best appeal from those developed normally requires market research. Criteria for evaluation include desirability, exclusiveness, and believability. The appeal first must make a positive impression on and be desirable to the target market. It must also be exclusive or unique; consumers must be able to distinguish the advertiser's message from competitors' messages. Most importantly, the appeal should be believable. An appeal that makes extravagant claims not only wastes promotional dollars but also creates ill will for the advertiser.

The advertising appeal selected for the campaign becomes what advertisers call its unique selling proposition. The unique selling proposition usually becomes the campaign's slogan. For example, Red Bull's "Red Bull has wings" touts its benefits including improved concentration and reaction time, improved performance, and increased endurance (**www.redbullusa .com**). Similarly, POWERade's advertising campaign aimed at the sports enthusiast carries the slogan "Sport Is What You Make It." This is POWERade's unique selling proposition, implying that you can push yourself to the limit if you are motivated and use POWERade.[42]

Effective slogans often become so ingrained that consumers hearing the slogan immediately conjure up images of the product. For example, many consumers can easily name the companies and products behind these memorable slogans or even hum the jingle that goes along with them: "Have it your way," "Tastes great, less filling," "Ring around the collar," and "Tum te Tum Tum." Advertisers often revive old slogans or jingles in the hope that the nostalgia will create good feelings with consumers. Burger King brought back the King in its advertising. Maytag refreshed its campaign featuring its appliance pitchman by changing the actor who plays him and giving him a helper—the third change since the ads originated in 1967. And Hershey's Kit Kat bar's jingle "Gimme a Break" is so etched in consumers' minds that recently the agency hired a film crew to ask people on the street to sing the jingle for use on the Internet, in future ad campaigns, and in its Kit Kat "Gimme a Break" Café.[43]

Executing the Message

Message execution is the way an advertisement portrays its information. In general, the AIDA plan (see Chapter 14) is a good blueprint for executing an advertising message. Any ad should immediately draw the reader's, viewer's, or listener's attention. The advertiser must then use the message to hold interest, create desire for the good or service, and ultimately motivate action—a purchase.

The style in which the message is executed is one of the most creative elements of an advertisement. Exhibit 14.8 lists some examples of executional styles used by advertisers. Executional styles often dictate what type of media is to be employed to convey the message. Scientific executional styles lend themselves well to print advertising where more information can be conveyed. On the other hand, demonstration and musical styles are more likely found in broadcast advertising.

Testimonials by athletes are one of the more popular executional styles. Tiger Woods and Shaquille O'Neal are two of the most successful athlete spokespersons.

Read Shaq's own words about the power of marketing and advertising in Exhibit 14.9.

Injecting humor into an advertisement is a popular and effective executional style. Selection of a humorous approach is based on the communications goal. Humorous executional styles are more often used in radio and television advertising than in print or magazine advertising where humor is less easily communicated. Regardless of the advertising medium, however, humor can be tricky to use because not all people find the same things funny and marketers have to be sure the humor won't be misconstrued. For instance, a print and e-mail ad campaign for Timbuk2's limited-edition messenger bags caused an uproar even while the ad's creators protested it was supposed to be funny. The ad featured a photo of a crying girl in a prom dress next to a

This "talk-of-the-world, spectacular" outdoor ad welcoming visitors to the 2006 FIFA World Cup soccer match is an example of an aesthetically imaginative executional style.

EXHIBIT 14.8

Ten Common Executional Styles for Advertising

Slice-of-Life	Depicts people in normal settings, such as at the dinner table or in their car. McDonald's often uses slice-of-life styles showing youngsters munching french fries and Happy Meals on family outings.
Lifestyle	Shows how well the product will fit in with the consumer's lifestyle. As their Volkswagen Jetta moves through the streets of the French Quarter, the Gen X drivers plug in a techno music CD and marvel at how the rhythms of the world mimic the ambient vibe inside their vehicle.
Spokesperson/ Testimonial	Can feature a celebrity, company official, or typical consumer making a testimonial or endorsing a product. Sarah Michelle Gellar, star of *Buffy the Vampire Slayer*, endorses Maybelline cosmetics while country singer Shania Twain introduced Revlon's ColorStay Liquid Lip. Dell, Inc. founder Michael Dell touts his vision of the customer experience via Dell in television ads.
Fantasy	Creates a fantasy for the viewer built around use of the product. Carmakers often use this style to let viewers fantasize about how they would feel speeding around tight corners or down long country roads in their cars.
Humorous	Advertisers often use humor in their ads, such as Snickers' "Not Going Anywhere for a While" campaign featuring hundreds of souls waiting, sometimes impatiently, to get into heaven.
Real/Animated Product Symbols	Creates a character that represents the product in advertisements, such as the Energizer bunny, Starkist's Charlie the Tuna, or General Mills' longtime icon, Betty Crocker, redesigned for the new millennium.
Mood or Image	Builds a mood or image around the product, such as peace, love, or beauty. De Beers ads depicting shadowy silhouettes wearing diamond engagement rings and diamond necklaces portrayed passion and intimacy while extolling that a "diamond is forever."
Demonstration	Shows consumers the expected benefit. Many consumer products use this technique. Laundry-detergent spots are famous for demonstrating how their product will clean clothes whiter and brighter. Fort James Corporation demonstrated in television commercials how its Dixie Rinse & ReUse disposable stoneware product line can stand up to the heat of a blowtorch and survive a cycle in a clothes washer.
Musical	Conveys the message of the advertisement through song. For example, Nike's ads depicting a marathoner's tortured feet, skier Picabo Street's surgery-scarred knee, and a surfer's thigh scarred by a shark attack while strains of Joe Cocker's "You Are So Beautiful" are heard in the background.
Scientific	Uses research or scientific evidence to give a brand superiority over competitors. Pain relievers like Advil, Bayer, and Excedrin use scientific evidence in their ads.

While on the outside looking in, I did not realize that marketing was so complicated. I never knew that a person, such as an athlete, could have such a powerful effect on people's thought processes and purchasing behavior. The use of a well-known athlete in marketing a product or service can have a great impact on the sales of that product or service. Look at Michael Jordan. Almost overnight most every kid either was wearing or wanted to wear Air Jordan shoes.

Why does this happen? Is it the appeal of a great athlete or is it great marketing? The answer is "none of the above." It's both. In my years as a professional basketball player, I have seen firsthand the dramatic appeal that athletes have for the fans and public in general. Top-name athletes are like E. F. Hutton—when they talk, people listen. But why do they listen? I believe they listen to us, the athletes, because we have credibility. The effectiveness of celebrity endorsements depends largely on how credible and attractive the spokesperson is and how familiar people are with him or her. Companies sometimes use sports figures and other celebrities to promote products hoping they are appropriate opinion leaders.

Because of an athlete's fame and fortune, or attraction, the athlete can often have the right credibility to be a successful spokesperson. The best definition of credibility that I could find was by James Gordon in his book, *Rhetoric of Western Thought*. He said that attraction "can come from a person's observable talents, achievements, occupational position or status, personality and appearance, and style."* That may be why a famous athlete's personality and position can help him or her communicate more effectively than a not-so-famous athlete.

Credibility is a positive force in the persuasive promotion used predominantly by cola marketers like Pepsi because of what I like to call "dreamful attraction." For example, when I was young, I dreamed that I was like Dr. J., the famous basketball player for the Philadelphia 76ers. I would take his head off a poster and put my head on it. I wanted to be Dr. J. That is dreamful attraction. The youth of today are no different. Just the other day a kid stopped me and told me that he wanted to be like me. He had a dreamful attraction. This dreamful attraction can help sell products. In my case, Pepsi, Spalding, Kenner, and Reebok are hoping that they are able to package properly and market whatever dreamful attraction I might have for their target audience—kids.

There are many ways to communicate to my target audience. I find that the most effective way for me is through television commercials. This avenue gives me a chance to express myself and show my real feelings about a message we are trying to communicate—either visually or vocally. I feel that I have what Clint Eastwood has—"Sudden Impaq." My impact is revealed through my sense of humor and my nonverbal communication.

Why does Shaq sell? Communication. Although the verbal communication in many of my commercials is slim, the impact is still there. This makes me believe even more in the quote that who you are can almost be as important as what you say. But if you can blend the two together—who you are and what you have to say—then imagine how much more successful the communication message can be in the marketing process. Andre Agassi's favorite quote from his Canon commercial is "Image is everything." If it is not everything, it is almost everything. If you have the right image, match it with the right product, and market it properly, then success should follow.

I have been involved in commercials and the marketing of products for only a short time, but I have learned a great deal. If there is one formula for success in selling products, it would be this: Marketing plus credibility and image plus effective communications equals increase in sales—hopefully.

Now, you can call me Dr. Shaq, M.E. (Marketing Expert).

*James Gordon, *Rhetoric of Western Thought* (Dubuque, Iowa: Kendall-Hunt Publishing Co., 1976), 207.

photo of a tough-looking guy across whom was written: "Here today. Gone tomorrow. Just like that jerk who stole your virginity, these bags are only around for a short time." Timbuk2 finally pulled the ad in response to a storm of negative blog postings and e-mail protests against the ad saying that trying to be funny using a reference to date-rape was offensive.[44] Used appropriately, humor can be effective in attracting and holding audience attention. For example, Altoids used humor to create and reinforce its quirky yet strong persona. With a significantly lower budget than key competitors, the Altoids campaign helped the product grow from a sleepy brand to the number one mint in America based on flavor.[45]

Executional styles for foreign advertising are often quite different from those we are accustomed to in the United States. Sometimes they are sexually oriented or aesthetically imaginative. For example, Adidas commissioned a German ad company to come up with a "talk-of-the-world, spectacular" outdoor ad to welcome visitors to the FIFA World Cup soccer match. They designed a 65-meter, front-and-back billboard of soccer star Oliver Kahn diving to catch a soccer ball, which stretched across a four-lane highway near the airport in Munich, Germany. Four million cars drove under the installation, and it became the visual that accompanied almost every foreign news coverage of the World Cup event.[46] European advertising avoids the direct-sell approaches common in U.S. ads and instead is more indirect, more symbolic, and, above all, more visual. Nike, known in the United States for "in-your-face" advertising and irreverent slogans such as "Just Do It," discovered that its brash advertising did not appeal to Europeans.

Sometimes a company will modify its executional styles to make its advertising more effective. For decades, Procter & Gamble has advertised shampoo in China using a demonstrational executional style. Television ads demonstrated how the science of shampoo worked and then showed a woman with nice, shiny hair. Because today's urban Chinese customers are more financially secure, they no longer make solely utilitarian purchases. To reflect that shift, Procter & Gamble has begun incorporating more of an emotional appeal into its advertisements. A new set of TV ads shows a woman emerging from an animated cocoon as a sophisticated butterfly. A voice-over says, "Head & Shoulders metamorphosis—new life for hair."[47]

Post-Campaign Evaluation

Evaluating an advertising campaign can be the most demanding task facing advertisers. How do advertisers know whether the campaign led to an increase in sales or market share or elevated awareness of the product? Most advertising campaigns aim to create an image for the good or service instead of asking for action, so their real effect is unknown. So many variables shape the effectiveness of an ad that, in many cases, advertisers must guess whether their money has been well spent. Despite this gray area, marketers spend a considerable amount of time studying advertising effectiveness and its probable impact on sales, market share, or awareness.

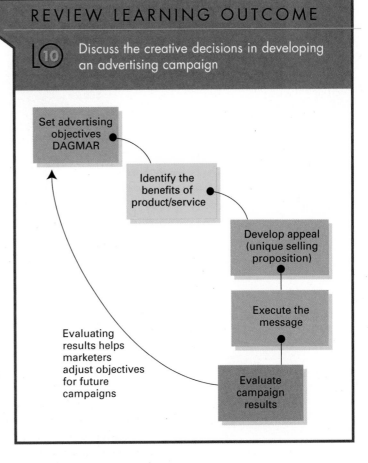

REVIEW LEARNING OUTCOME

LO 10 Discuss the creative decisions in developing an advertising campaign

- Set advertising objectives DAGMAR
- Identify the benefits of product/service
- Develop appeal (unique selling proposition)
- Execute the message
- Evaluate campaign results

Evaluating results helps marketers adjust objectives for future campaigns

Testing ad effectiveness can be done either before or after the campaign. Before a campaign is released, marketing managers use pretests to determine the best advertising appeal, layout, and media vehicle. After advertisers implement a campaign, they often conduct tests to measure its effectiveness. Several monitoring techniques can be used to determine whether the campaign has met its original goals. Even if a campaign has been highly successful, advertisers still typically do a post-campaign analysis. They assess how the campaign might have been more efficient and what factors contributed to its success. For example, Hallmark's market researchers wanted to capitalize on aging baby boomers. Research indicated that baby boomers do not want to age, but since that is inevitable, boomers want to see the positive side of aging. Therefore, Hallmark created the "Time of Your Life" series that flattered their egos. The cards were not successful, however, because they were placed in the "over 50" section of the store and baby boomers do not want to shop in that section.[48]

LO 11
MEDIA DECISIONS IN ADVERTISING

A major decision for advertisers is the choice of medium—the channel used to convey a message to a target market. Media planning, therefore, is the series of decisions advertisers make regarding the selection and use of media, allowing the marketer to optimally and cost-effectively communicate the message to the target audience. Specifically, advertisers must determine which types of media will best communicate the benefits of their product or service to the target audience and when and for how long the advertisement will run.

Promotional objectives and the appeal and executional style of the advertising strongly affect the selection of media. It is important to understand that both creative and media decisions are made at the same time. Creative work cannot be completed without knowing which medium will be used to convey the message to the target

medium
The channel used to convey a message to a target market.

media planning
The series of decisions advertisers make regarding the selection and use of media, allowing the marketer to optimally and cost-effectively communicate the message to the target audience.

EXHIBIT 14.10

Domestic Advertising Spending by
Media Type, in billions

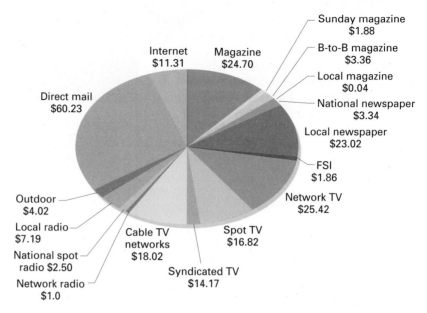

Internet $11.31

Magazine $24.70

Sunday magazine $1.88

B-to-B magazine $3.36

Local magazine $0.04

National newspaper $3.34

Local newspaper $23.02

FSI $1.86

Network TV $25.42

Direct mail $60.23

Outdoor $4.02

Local radio $7.19

National spot radio $2.50

Network radio $1.0

Cable TV networks $18.02

Syndicated TV $14.17

Spot TV $16.82

Source: Adapted from "Total U.S. Advertising Spending by Medium," *Advertising Age*, June 23, 2008.

cooperative advertising
An arrangement in which the manufacturer and the retailer split the costs of advertising the manufacturer's brand.

market. For instance, creative planning will likely differ for an ad to be displayed on a Web site versus one placed in a print medium, such as a newspaper or magazine. In many cases, the advertising objectives dictate the medium and the creative approach to be used. For example, if the objective is to demonstrate how fast a product operates, a TV commercial that shows this action may be the best choice.

U.S. advertisers spend about $300 billion on media advertising annually. Almost half of that is spent on media monitored by national reporting services—newspapers, magazines, Internet, radio, television, and outdoor media. The remainder is spent on unmonitored media, such as direct mail, trade exhibits, cooperative advertising, brochures, coupons, catalogs, and special events. Exhibit 14.10 shows advertising spending by media type. About 44 percent of every media dollar goes toward TV ads, 20 percent toward direct mail, and about 18 percent for newspaper ads.[49] But these traditional mass-market media are declining in usage and more targeted media are growing.[50]

Media Types

Advertising media are channels that advertisers use in mass communication. The six major advertising media are newspapers, magazines, radio, television, outdoor media, and the Internet. Exhibit 14.11 summarizes the advantages and disadvantages of these major channels. In recent years, however, alternative media vehicles have emerged that give advertisers innovative ways to reach their target audience and avoid advertising clutter.

Newspapers The advantages of newspaper advertising include geographic flexibility and timeliness. Because copywriters can usually prepare newspaper ads quickly and at a reasonable cost, local merchants can reach their target market almost daily. Because newspapers are generally a mass-market medium, however, they may not be the best vehicle for marketers trying to reach a very narrow market. For example, local newspapers are not the best media vehicles for reaching purchasers of specialty steel products or even tropical fish. These target consumers make up very small, specialized markets. Newspaper advertising also encounters a lot of distractions from competing ads and news stories; thus, one company's ad may not be particularly visible.

The main sources of newspaper ad revenue are local retailers, classified ads, and cooperative advertising. In cooperative advertising, the manufacturer and the retailer

EXHIBIT 14.11

Advantages and Disadvantages of Major Advertising Media

Medium	Advantages	Disadvantages
Newspapers	Geographic selectivity and flexibility; short-term advertiser commitments; news value and immediacy; year-round readership; high individual market coverage; co-op and local tie-in availability; short lead time	Little demographic selectivity; limited color capabilities; low pass-along rate; may be expensive
Magazines	Good reproduction, especially for color; demographic selectivity; regional selectivity; local market selectivity; relatively long advertising life; high pass-along rate	Long-term advertiser commitments; slow audience buildup; limited demonstration capabilities; lack of urgency; long lead time
Radio	Low cost; immediacy of message; can be scheduled on short notice; relatively no seasonal change in audience; highly portable; short-term advertiser commitments; entertainment carryover	No visual treatment; short advertising life of message; high frequency required to generate comprehension and retention; distractions from background sound; commercial clutter
Television	Ability to reach a wide, diverse audience; low cost per thousand; creative opportunities for demonstration; immediacy of messages; entertainment carryover; demographic selectivity with cable stations	Short life of message; some consumer skepticism about claims; high campaign cost; little demographic selectivity with network stations; long-term advertiser commitments; long lead times required for production; commercial clutter
Outdoor Media	Repetition; moderate cost; flexibility; geographic selectivity	Short message; lack of demographic selectivity; high "noise" level distracting audience
Internet	Fastest-growing medium; ability to reach a narrow target audience; relatively short lead time required for creating Web-based advertising; moderate cost	Difficult to measure ad effectiveness and return on investment; ad exposure relies on "click-through" from banner ads; not all consumers have access to the Internet

split the costs of advertising the manufacturer's brand. One reason that manufacturers use cooperative advertising is the impracticality of listing all their dealers in national advertising. Also, co-op advertising encourages retailers to devote more effort to the manufacturer's lines.

Magazines Compared to the cost of other media, the cost per contact in magazine advertising is usually high. The cost per potential customer may be much lower, however, because magazines are often targeted to specialized audiences and thus reach more potential customers. The types of products most frequently advertised in magazines include automobiles, apparel, computers, and cigarettes.

One of the main advantages of magazine advertising is its market selectivity. Magazines are published for virtually every market segment. For instance, *Lucky* "The Magazine about Shopping and Style" is a leading fashion magazine; *ESPN the Magazine* is a successful sports magazine; *Essence* is targeted toward African American women; *Marketing News* is a trade magazine for the marketing professional; and *The Source* is a niche publication geared to young urbanites with a passion for hip-hop music.

Philips Electronics used an innovative magazine advertising campaign by sponsoring the magazines' contents page. Issues of four Time Warner magazines (*Time, Fortune, People,* and *Business* 2.0) featured the table of contents on the first page rather than several pages later. The inside front cover featured a Philips ad with the following copy: "Philips Electronics is bringing the table of contents to the front of selected Time, Inc. magazines to make things easier for readers." In general, the placement of the contents page varies from magazine to magazine, but it is not uncommon for the contents to appear after numerous advertisements; as many as 24 pages of ads can appear before a magazine's contents page. Philips paid Time, Inc., $5 million to sponsor the contents pages in the four magazines for only one issue each.[51]

Radio Radio has several strengths as an advertising medium: selectivity and audience segmentation, a large out-of-home audience, low unit and production costs, timeliness, and geographic flexibility. Local advertisers are the most frequent users of radio advertising, contributing over three-quarters of all radio ad revenues. Like newspapers, radio also lends itself well to cooperative advertising.

Radio advertising is enjoying a resurgence in popularity. As Americans become more mobile and pressed for time, media such as network television and newspapers have lost viewers and readers, particularly in the youth market. Radio listening, however, has grown in step with population increases mainly because its immediate, portable nature meshes so well with a fast-paced lifestyle. The ability to target specific demographic groups is a major selling point for radio stations, attracting advertisers pursuing narrowly defined audiences that are more likely to respond to certain kinds of ads and products. Radio listeners also tend to listen habitually and at predictable times, especially during "drive time," when commuters form a vast captive audience. Finally, satellite radio has attracted new audiences that are exposed to ads when allowed on that format.

The ad-skipping functionality offered by TiVo and other digital video recorders has been the most significant recent trend to affect TV advertising.

infomercial
A 30-minute or longer advertisement that looks more like a TV talk show than a sales pitch.

Television Because television is an audiovisual medium, it provides advertisers with many creative opportunities. Television broadcasters include network television, independent stations, cable television, and a relative newcomer, direct broadcast satellite television. ABC, CBS, NBC, and the Fox Network dominate network television, which reaches a wide and diverse market. Conversely, cable television and direct broadcast satellite systems, such as DirecTV and Dish Network, offer consumers a multitude of channels devoted exclusively to particular audiences—for example, women, children, African Americans, nature lovers, senior citizens, Christians, Hispanics, sports fans, and fitness enthusiasts. Recent niche market entries include CSTV Network (college sports) and the NFL Network—focused exclusively on the sports enthusiast—and the casino and gambling channel. Because of its targeted channels, cable television is often characterized as "narrowcasting" by media buyers.

Advertising time on television can be very expensive, especially for network and popular cable channels. The top-ranked TV programs in recent years are aired on networks ABC, CBS, and Fox. The biggest draws are Fox's *American Idol* and *House*; ABC's *Dancing with the Stars, Lost*, and *Grey's Anatomy*; NBC's *Sunday Night Football* and *The Office*; and CBS's crime series *CSI*.[52] First-run prime-time shows and special events command the highest rates for a typical 30-second spot, with the least expensive ads costing about $300,000 and the more expensive costing $500,000. Super Bowl spots are the most expensive—a 30-second spot during the 2009 Super Bowl telecast cost advertisers an average of $3 million.[53] The two dozen or so marketers paying such a premium price include typical big ad spenders such as Procter & Gamble, Anheuser-Busch, Pepsi, and E-Trade. Most marketers consider the Super Bowl the "last bastion" of mass marketing available, with about 100 million viewers tuning in.[54]

One of the more successful recent television formats to emerge is the infomercial, a 30-minute or longer advertisement. Infomercials are an attractive advertising vehicle for many marketers because of the relatively inexpensive airtime and the lower production costs. Advertisers say the infomercial is an ideal way to present complicated information to potential customers, which other advertising vehicles typically don't allow time to do. Now a $200 billion-dollar industry, infomercials are increasingly being used by some mainstream marketers. Once relegated to late-night TV, infomercials are showing up in early evening time slots, such as Fox's *The O'Reilly Factor*, CBS's *60 Minutes*, CNBC's *Mad Money*. Consumers who might have been skeptical of an ad's veracity on shopping networks, are less likely to suspect an ad shown during prime-time television programs. A shorter direct-retail infomercial is more common in daytime programming, running an average of 120 seconds.[55]

Probably the most significant trend to affect television advertising is the rise in popularity of digital video recorders (DVRs) such as TiVo. For every hour of television programming, an average of 15 minutes is dedicated to nonprogram material (ads, public service announcements, and network promotions), so it's hardly surprising that viewers weary of ad breaks have embraced ad-skipping DVR technology as the solution to interruptions during their favorite shows. Marketers of the products featured in those advertisements are not the only ones trying to figure out ways to keep consumers from avoiding them; networks are also concerned about ad skipping. If consumers are not watching advertisements, then marketers will spend a greater proportion of their advertising budgets on alternative media, and a critical revenue stream for networks will disappear. While NBC ran a test to measure the effectiveness of running shorter blocks of advertising, the company also said that it has no intention of changing its business model relative to advertising sales. TiVo then began offering interactive banner ads to advertisers, making those sponsors' names visible as their ads are being fast-forwarded. The full impact of DVR technology on television as an advertising medium has yet to be determined, but research companies such as Nielsen have started to measure the number of people who time shift—that is, record a show and watch at their convenience.[56]

Outdoor Media Outdoor or out-of-home advertising is a flexible, low-cost medium that may take a variety of forms. Examples include billboards, skywriting, giant inflatables, mini-billboards in malls and on bus stop shelters, signs in sports arenas, lighted moving signs in bus terminals and airports, and ads painted on cars, trucks, buses, water towers, manhole covers, drinking glass coasters, and even people, called "living advertising." Students in London "rented" their foreheads for temporary tattoos of brands and then walked around specified areas of the city.[57] The plywood scaffolding that rings downtown construction sites can also carry ads. Manhattan's Times Square, with an estimated 1.5 million daily pedestrians, has been a popular area for outdoor advertising using scaffolding.

Outdoor advertising reaches a broad and diverse market and is, therefore, ideal for promoting convenience products and services as well as directing consumers to local businesses. One of outdoor's main advantages over other media is that its exposure frequency is very high, yet the amount of clutter from competing ads is very low. Outdoor advertising also has the ability to be customized to local marketing needs. For these reasons, local business establishments, such as local services and amusements, retailers, public transportation, and hotels and restaurants, are the leading outdoor advertisers. Outdoor advertising categories on the rise include telecommunications with a heavy emphasis on wireless services, financial services, and packaged goods.

Outdoor advertising is becoming more innovative. New technology is enabling outdoor ads to become interactive and to be more like online ads. For example, Nike commissioned a 23-story interactive, digital billboard on New York's Times Square. People passing the display on the sidewalk could use their cell phones to temporarily control

New technology is enabling outdoor ads to become more interactive. For example, Virgin Atlantic Airways projected ads onto skyscrapers inviting passersby to send a text message. That drove traffic to its Web site, which was accessible by Web-enabled mobile devices.

the billboard and design their own shoes.[58] Virgin Atlantic Airways projected ads onto New York's and Chicago's skyscrapers, inviting passersby to access the airline's "Love From Above" campaign rewards.[59]

Unusual outdoor advertising campaigns are not limited to the United States. Adidas Japan created a "living billboard" in the form of a vertical soccer field on the side of a skyscraper. The billboard featured live players and a ball attached by ropes to the side of the building.[60] Virgin Atlantic painted an ad on the grass next to the runway at South Africa's Johannesburg International Airport to greet arriving and departing passengers. A world's first, the ad required 1,000 liters of paint and nine separate permits from different regulatory authorities due to the sensitive nature of the site.[61]

The Internet and Alternative Media Marketing The Internet has dramatically changed the advertising industry. With ad revenues exceeding $26 billion annually, the Internet has become a solid advertising medium. Online advertising continues to grow at double-digit rates—well ahead of other advertising media.[62] In fact, online ad spending is expected to exceed $60 billion annually by 2012 and account for 18 percent of all marketing expenditures.[63] Internet advertising provides an interactive and versatile platform that offers rich data on consumer usage, enabling advertisers to improve their ad targetability and achieve measurable results.[64]

Popular Internet sites and search engines, such as Google and Yahoo!, as well as online service providers such as America Online, generally sell advertising space to marketers to promote their goods and services. Internet surfers click on these ads to be linked to more information about the advertised product or service. Established brands such as General Motors, Anheuser-Busch, Procter & Gamble, and Verizon have been adjusting their budgets to include Internet advertising, and other firms are not far behind. For example, Vonage, Circuit City, Ameritrade Brokerage, Amazon.com, Overstock.com, Netflix.com, and Monster.com have been among the top 50 advertisers on the Internet in recent years.

> *Marketers' primary objective in using search engine ads is to enhance brand awareness.*

The effectiveness of Internet advertising has been hotly debated, however. Early research on banner ads found response rates as high as 30 percent, but more recent studies indicate much lower response rates. With high-speed broadband spreading rapidly in the United States, advertisers increasingly are switching to other online approaches. For example, marketers are using ads that float, sing, or dance; video commercials similar to traditional TV spots; and ads that pop up in another window, use larger, hard-to-miss shapes, and include both online and offline cross-promotions. These new formats are often large enough for marketers to include their entire message so that users don't have to click through to another site.

Search Engine Ads One of the most popular approaches for Internet advertising is search engine ads. More than 120 billion searches are conducted annually in the United States with Google getting the lion's share—nearly 65 billion.[65] In second place is Yahoo! with more than two billion searches, followed by Microsoft's MSN with 940 million.[66] Google's market share of Internet search grew from 43 percent in 2005 to over 56 percent in 2008.[67] Marketers' primary objective in using search engine ads is to enhance brand awareness. Search engine optimization (SEO) accounted for the largest portion of online advertising expenditure with 41 percent of online marketing dollars going to SEO.

Advergaming Another popular Internet advertising format is advergaming. In advergaming, companies put ad messages in Web-based or video games to advertise or promote a product, service, organization, or issue. Sometimes

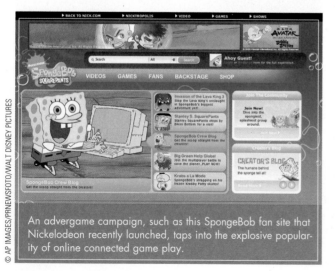

An advergame campaign, such as this SpongeBob fan site that Nickelodeon recently launched, taps into the explosive popularity of online connected game play.

the entire game amounts to a virtual commercial, other times advertisers sponsor games or buy ad space for product placement in them. Organizations using advergaming include Disney, Viacom's Nickelodeon, and even the U.S. Army.[68] The format encourages users to register for sweepstakes and other promotions and play the game. For example, a company with a heritage of aligning their products with gamers, Pepsi developed a multiplayer online game in which players get a chance to choose the next flavor of Mt. Dew. The site, dewmocracy.com, drew 700,000 unique visitors and 200,000 registered users who spent an average of 28 minutes per gaming session. Pepsi's "dewmocracy" advergame campaign taps into the explosive popularity of online connected game play, such as "World of Warcraft" with more than 10 million paying subscribers.[69]

An increasingly popular Internet advertising medium is social media marketing. Social media marketing is the collaboration and sharing of online content between the sender and the receiver—the brand and the consumer. The social media network, as one media pundit put it, "is where word-of-mouth meets word-of-mouse . . . where authentic brands are rewarded and fake brands (and their empty promises) are punished."[70] Social media is sometimes referred to as user-generated content, or consumer-generated media, and includes blogs, podcasts, forums, interactive video tours, social networks, and virtual worlds.[71] This new way of using the Internet is possible in part because of Internet-driven technology such as RSS (Really Simple Syndication)—a data exchange format that provides Internet users with quick access to frequently updated online content such as blogs and news headlines.[72]

Blogging Initially, blogs had no advertising. But the popularity of some blogs has made them an attractive medium for marketing messages. Budget Rent-A-Car recently bought ads on 177 blogs, Audi of America paid for advertising on 286 blogs, and MSNBC bought ads on more than 800 blogs.[73] Seed Media, which produces science publications in print and online, sells advertising on its network of more than 15 blogs just as it does in its magazine *Seed*. Seed Media contends that by advertising on its blog network, marketers will gain access to a group of bright, curious consumers who buy all kinds of products.[74]

Podcasts Podcasts are audio or video shows on computers, portable MP3 players, or other Web-connected devices. All that is needed to produce a podcast is a microphone connected to a computer and audio software. Most consumer-users promote their "show" on a Web site or a blog and submit their podcast to podcast directories. Many major broadcasters now participate in podcasting. Apple's iTunes directory, for instance, offers NPR, ABC News, CNN, Comedy Central, MTV, *The New York Times*, and PBS podcasts.[75]

Advertainment To cut through the clutter of traditional advertising media, advertisers are creating even more new media vehicles to advertise their products, some ordinary and others quite innovative. Alternative media vehicles can include shopping carts in grocery stores, computer screen savers, DVDs, interactive kiosks in department stores, advertisements run before movies at the cinema, and "advertainments"—"mini movies" that promote a product and are shown via the Internet.[76] For example, BMW shows films by recognized directors that run six to eight minutes and feature the cars in extreme situations.[77] Likewise, Coca-Cola sponsored a 25-minute advertainment program called "Sound Check" that was available only on TiVo. The program featured exclusive interviews, music videos, live shows, behind-the-scenes filming, and recordings by artists such as Ashanti, Sting, and Mary J. Blige.[78]

Indeed, almost anything can become a vehicle for displaying advertising. For instance, supermarkets have begun using "Flooranimation"—ads that are animated with graphics and sounds and installed on supermarket floors. Unanimated floor ads have been in use for some time, and research shows they increase sales 15 to 30 percent. Marketers are hoping that with animation and sound, sales will increase even more.[79] Billboards now include motion graphics, and sound, and as an additional advertising media, are an excellent way to communicate with consumers in the evenings in metro markets such as New York City, Chicago, Los Angeles, and San Francisco.[80] Marketers are also looking for more innovative ways to reach captive and often bored commuters. For instance, subway systems now show ads via lighted boxes installed along tunnel walls. As a train passes through the tunnel, the passengers view the illuminated boxes,

media mix
The combination of media to be
used for a promotional campaign.

cost per contact
The cost of reaching one member of
the target market.

reach
The number of target consumers
exposed to a commercial at least
once during a specific period,
usually four weeks.

which create the same kind of illusion as a child's flip book, in which the images appear to move as the pages are flipped rapidly.

Video Game Advertising When trying to reach males aged 18 to 34, video game advertising is emerging as an excellent medium, second only to prime-time *Monday Night Football.* The medium first attracted attention when Massive, Inc., (**http://www.massiveincorporated.com**) started a videogame advertising network and later established a partnership with Nielsen Entertainment, Inc., to provide ad ratings. Massive provides the capability to have ads with full motion and sound inserted into games played on Internet-connected computers. This is a big improvement over previous ads, which had to be inserted when the games were made and therefore quickly became obsolete. In 2006, Microsoft acquired Massive, a move that the company says will help it "deliver dynamic, relevant ads" across its online services including Xbox Live and MSN Games.[81]

Cell phones Cell phones are among the newest advertising media and are particularly useful for reaching the youth market. Mobile advertising has substantial upside potential when you consider there are more than four billion cell phone users in the world. In 2008, cell phone advertising sales was almost $1.6 billion in the United States and nearly $4.4 billion worldwide.[82] Mobile ad spending is expected to grow dramatically in the next few years. Today's data- and video-oriented phones can deliver advertisements and also have GPS capability, so they can receive "location-based" advertising; for example, a nearby restaurant can alert potential customers about specials. McDonald's enjoyed success doing this at locations in California where it gave away free McFlurry desserts. Marketers also are using text and video messages to notify customers of special deals, such as ring tone downloads. Cell phone advertising is less popular in the United States than in Europe and Asia, where cell phone owners use text messaging much more heavily. Although there is concern that cell phone spam will become as much of a problem as Internet spam, cell phone advertisers are targeting their ads to users who agree to receive the ads in exchange for premium services or who sign up on opt-in lists to learn about items that interest them, such as a particular band's next album or concert.[83]

Stealth Marketing The term "stealth" might conjure images of undercover operations, possibly even sneakiness. In marketing, however, stealth has come to mean a campaign of outsmarting the competition, rather than outspending them. Stealth marketing, also known as guerrilla marketing, or buzz, is usually just any unconventional way of performing marketing promotions on a low budget. Stealth marketing is often designed to leave the target audience unaware they have been marketed to, but that they have simply participated in something fun, or sometimes shocking. For instance, in a recent guerilla campaign to promote the film *The Water Horse: Legend of the Deep,* a 50-foot dragon (think Loch Ness monster) was created by way of hologram projection on the water surface of Tokyo Bay, in Japan. Conjuring a huge monster practically out of thin air created marketing "buzz" online, on the street, and in the media.[84]

Media Selection Considerations

An important element in any advertising campaign is the media mix, the combination of media to be used. Media mix decisions are typically based on several factors: cost per contact, reach, frequency, target audience considerations, flexibility of the medium, noise level, and the life span of the medium.

Cost per contact is the cost of reaching one member of the target market. Naturally, as the size of the audience increases, so does the total cost. Cost per contact enables an advertiser to compare media vehicles, such as television versus radio or magazine versus newspaper, or even the same media, such as *Newsweek* versus *Time.* An advertiser debating whether to spend local advertising dollars for TV spots or radio spots could consider the cost per contact of each. The advertiser might then pick the vehicle with the lowest cost per contact to maximize advertising punch for the money spent.

Reach is the number of different target consumers exposed to a commercial at least once during a specific period, usually four weeks. Media plans for product introductions and attempts at increasing brand awareness usually emphasize reach. For example, an advertiser might try to reach 70 percent of the target audience during the first three months of the campaign. Reach is related to a medium's ratings, generally referred to in the industry as *gross ratings points*, or GRP. A television program with a higher GRP means that more people are tuning in to the show and the reach is higher. Accordingly, as GRP increases for a particular medium, so does cost per contact.

Because the typical ad is short-lived and because often only a small portion of an ad may be perceived at one time, advertisers repeat their ads so that consumers will remember the message. Frequency is the number of times an individual is exposed to a message during a specific period. Advertisers use average frequency to measure the intensity of a specific medium's coverage. For example, Coca-Cola might want an average exposure frequency of five for its POWERade television ads. That means each of the television viewers who saw the ad saw it an average of five times.

Media selection is also a matter of matching the advertising medium with the product's target market. If marketers are trying to reach teenage females, they might select *Seventeen* magazine. If they are trying to reach consumers over 50 years old, they may choose *Modern Maturity* magazine. A medium's ability to reach a precisely defined market is its audience selectivity. Some media vehicles, like general newspapers and network television, appeal to a wide cross section of the population. Others—such as *Brides, Popular Mechanics, Architectural Digest, Lucky*, MTV, ESPN, and Christian radio stations—appeal to very specific groups.

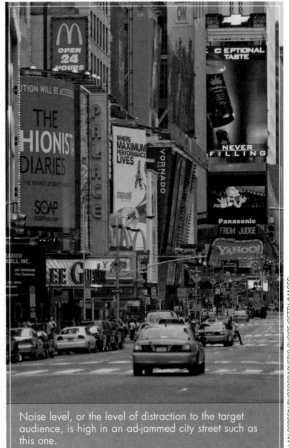

Noise level, or the level of distraction to the target audience, is high in an ad-jammed city street such as this one.

© ALAN COPSON/PHOTOGRAPHER'S CHOICE/GETTY IMAGES

The *flexibility* of a medium can be extremely important to an advertiser. In the past, because of printing timetables, production requirements, and so on, some magazines required final ad copy several months before publication. Therefore, magazine advertising traditionally could not adapt as rapidly to changing market conditions. While this is changing quickly due to computer technology that creates electronic ad images and layouts, the lead time for magazine advertising is still considerably longer. Radio and Internet advertising, on the other hand, provide maximum flexibility. Usually, the advertiser can change a radio ad on the day it is aired, if necessary. Similarly, advertisements on the Internet can be changed in minutes with the click of a few buttons.

Noise level is the level of distraction associated with a medium. For example, to understand a televised promotional message, viewers must watch and listen carefully. But they often watch television with others, who may well provide distractions. Noise can also be created by competing ads, as when a street is lined with billboards or when a television program is cluttered with competing ads. About two-thirds of a newspaper's pages are now filled with advertising. A recent Sunday issue of the *Los Angeles Times* contained over one thousand ads, not counting the small classifieds. Even more space is dedicated to ads in magazines. For example, 85 percent of the space in *Brides* magazine is typically devoted to advertisements. In contrast, direct mail is a private medium with a low noise level. Typically, no other advertising media or news stories compete for direct-mail readers' attention.

Media have either a short or a long life span. *Life span* means that messages can either quickly fade or persist as tangible copy to be carefully studied. For example, a radio commercial may last less than a minute. Listeners can't replay the commercial unless they have recorded the program. One way advertisers overcome this problem is by repeating radio ads often. In contrast, a magazine has a relatively long life span. A person may read several articles, put the magazine down, and pick it up a week later to

frequency
The number of times an individual is exposed to a given message during a specific period.

audience selectivity
The ability of an advertising medium to reach a precisely defined market.

media schedule
Designation of the media, the specific publications or programs, and the insertion dates of advertising.

continuous media schedule
A media scheduling strategy in which advertising is run steadily throughout the advertising period; used for products in the latter stages of the product life cycle.

continue reading. In addition, magazines often have a high pass-along rate. That is, one person will read the publication and then give it to someone else to read.

Media planners have traditionally relied on the above factors in selecting an effective media mix, with reach, frequency, and cost often the overriding criteria. But some experts question the reliance media planners have traditionally placed on reach and frequency. For instance, well-established brands with familiar messages probably need fewer exposures to be effective, while newer brands or brands with unfamiliar messages likely need more exposures to become familiar.

Additionally, media planners have hundreds more media options today than they had when network television reigned. For instance, there are over 1,600 television stations across the country. Similarly, in the Los Angeles market alone there are more than 80 radio stations, with 7 offering an "adult contemporary" format. The number of unique magazine titles has more than doubled over the last decade, with publications now targeting every possible market segment. Satellite television brings hundreds of channels into viewers' homes. The Internet provides media planners with even more targeted choices in which to send their messages. And alternative media choices are popping up in some very unlikely places. *Media fragmentation* is forcing media planners to pay as much attention to where they place their advertising, as to how often the advertisement is repeated. Indeed, experts recommend evaluating reach along with frequency in assessing the effectiveness of advertising. That is, in certain situations it may be important to reach potential consumers through as many media vehicles as possible. When this approach is considered, however, the budget must be large enough to achieve sufficient levels of frequency to have an impact. In evaluating reach versus frequency, therefore, the media planner ultimately must select an approach that is most likely to result in the ad being understood and remembered when a purchase decision is being made.

Advertisers also evaluate the qualitative factors involved in media selection. These qualitative factors include such things as attention to the commercial and the program, involvement, lack of distractions, how well the viewer likes the program, and other audience behaviors that affect the likelihood a commercial message is being seen and, hopefully, absorbed. While advertisers can advertise their product in as many media as possible and repeat the ad as many times as they like, the ad still may not be effective if the audience is not paying attention. Research on audience attentiveness for television, for example, shows that the longer viewers stay tuned to a particular program, the more memorable they find the commercials. Holding power, therefore, can be more important than ratings (the number of people tuning in to any part of the program) when selecting media vehicles, challenging the long-held assumption that the higher the rating of a program, the more effective the advertising run during the program, even though it is more costly. For instance, *ER*, once one of the top-rated shows among 25- to 54-year-olds, cost about $400,000 for a 30-second spot but ranked relatively low for holding power. In contrast, the low-rated *Candid Camera*, which ranked high in holding power, used to cost only about $55,000 for a 30-second spot.[85]

See the Global Perspectives box and consider what kind of media campaign would be most effective in promoting Bollywood movies.

Media Scheduling

After choosing the media for the advertising campaign, advertisers must schedule the ads. A media schedule designates the medium or media to be used (such as magazines, television, or radio), the specific vehicles (such as *People* magazine, the TV show *CSI*, or the American Top 40 national radio program), and the insertion dates of the advertising.

There are three basic types of media schedules:

- Products in the latter stages of the product life cycle, which are advertised on a reminder basis, use a continuous media schedule. A continuous schedule allows

GLOBAL Perspectives

Welcome to Bollywood

With the smashing success of the low budget film *Slumdog Millionaire* (which grossed more than $69 million in the United States and won countless awards around the globe), Hollywood is starting to take notice of Bollywood. Bollywood, shorthand for the Indian movie industry in Mumbai, pumps out more movies than Hollywood (1,200 in 2007 compared to 600 in the United States.). The budgets are much smaller as well—a big budget film runs about $15 million compared to Hollywood's $100 million blockbuster films. With the success of *Slumdog Millionaire*, as well as the size of the Indian market, Hollywood is starting to investigate partnerships with Indian film companies.

While the Indian movie industry has been around for almost 100 years, its appeal has been limited. The traditional Indian movie can be considered kitschy, with song and dance scenes and melodramatic plots. While that may not go over well in the United States, the partnership is more of a collaboration between India and the West. Many of the new movies blend Indian themes and storylines with American cinematic styles. Collaborations abound between movie companies, producers, directors, screenwriters, and actors. Some of the top actors in both countries are considering projects. This new blend of entertainment could have huge marketing and advertising implications in the United States.

This is especially true for the Desis. The Desis are Americans of Indian, Pakistani, Bangladeshi, Sri Lankan, Bhutanese, and Nepalese descent. They make up 2.5 million people in the United States—small by the standards represented by other groups such as Hispanics—and most of them are Indian. But unlike their other minority counterparts, Desis come to the United States with knowledge of English and an appreciation of the culture, even if it is primarily British influenced. Their median income is 50 percent higher than the U.S. national average and they represent $76 billion of disposable income. And they are educated; 64 percent hold a bachelor's degree compared to 24 percent of the U.S. population.

With the increasing influence of Indian culture in the United States, it will be interesting to see what happens with marketing and advertising campaigns. Already some companies have targeted the Desi subculture mostly by focusing on the community as opposed to traditional advertising. Community is an important characteristic in this large immigrant group. It will also be interesting to see what influence the United States has on Bollywood. Already some of the most popular actors are attractive and light skinned, as opposed to the dark skinned actors of earlier films.[86] The question remains how much will each culture influence the other? What kind of campaign would you use to promote Bollywood movies? How successful do you think Bollywood movies will be in the United States?

---

the advertising to run steadily throughout the advertising period. Examples include Ivory soap, Tide detergent, Bounty paper towels, and Charmin toilet tissue, which may have an ad in the newspaper every Sunday and a TV commercial on NBC every Wednesday at 7:30 P.M. over a three-month period.

☛ With a flighted media schedule, the advertiser may schedule the ads heavily every other month or every two weeks to achieve a greater impact with an increased frequency and reach at those times. Movie studios might schedule television advertising on Wednesday and Thursday nights, when moviegoers are deciding which films to see that weekend. A variation is the pulsing media schedule, which combines continuous scheduling with flighting. Continuous advertising is simply heavier during the best sale periods. A retail department store may advertise on a year-round basis but place more advertising during certain sale periods such as Thanksgiving, Christmas, and back-to-school.

☛ Certain times of the year call for a seasonal media schedule. Products like Contac cold tablets and Coppertone sunscreen lotion, which are used more during certain times of the year, tend to follow a seasonal strategy. Advertising for

flighted media schedule
A media scheduling strategy in which ads are run heavily every other month or every two weeks, to achieve a greater impact with an increased frequency and reach at those times.

pulsing media schedule
A media scheduling strategy that uses continuous scheduling throughout the year coupled with a flighted schedule during the best sales periods.

seasonal media schedule
A media scheduling strategy that runs advertising only during times of the year when the product is most likely to be used.

Describe media evaluation and selection techniques

Media Choices

Type:

Magazine
Radio
Television
Newspaper
Outdoor
Alternative
Internet

Considerations:

Mix	**(How much of each?)**
Cost per contact	**(How much per person?)**
Reach	**(How many people?)**
Frequency	**(How often?)**
Audience selectivity	**(How targeted is audience?)**

flexibility
noise
life span
fragmentation

Scheduling:

continuous →

flighted →

pulsing →

seasonal (e.g., back-to-school) →

Winter   Spring   Summer   Fall

champagne is concentrated during the weeks of Christmas and New Year's, whereas health clubs concentrate their advertising in January to take advantage of New Year's resolutions.

New research comparing continuous media schedules and flighted ones finds that continuous schedules for television advertisements are more effective than flighting in driving sales. The research suggests that it may be more important to get exposure as close as possible to the time when someone is going to make a purchase. For example, if a consumer shops on a weekly basis, the best time to reach that person is right before he or she shops. Therefore, the advertiser should maintain a continuous schedule over as long a time as possible. Often called *recency planning,* this theory of scheduling is now commonly used for scheduling television advertising for frequently purchased products, such as Coca-Cola or Tide detergent. Recency planning's main premise is that advertising works by influencing the brand choice of people who are ready to buy.

3,500 ◄ people interviewed by Sara Lee Corp. before it innovated Kiwi shoe polish

media ► **15 million** contacts generated by Absolut's Porsche taxis in Germany

112.8 ◄**million** blogs tracked by Technorati

10 ◄ percentage of blogs updated weekly

70 ◄ percentage of e-mail messages that are spam

100 ◄ iPods sold per minute during the 2005 Christmas season

$100 million ◄ cost of Procter & Gamble's recent advertising campaign for Crest Pro-Health

22 ◄ languages in which Google and Sony offered "The Sony Ericsson Da Vinci Code Trail"

30 ◄ percentage of increased traffic at Sony's Web site during the promotion

$77 million ◄ ticket sales for *The DaVinci Code*'s opening weekend

Lucasfilm Ltd. used integrated marketing communications to ensure that *Indiana Jones and the Kingdom of the Crystal Skull* was widely and consistently promoted before its release.

NASCAR cars increase publicity.

Hallmark greeting cards and Scholastic books hold kids' interest even after the movie leaves theaters.

Legos and Kellogg's cereal attract kids.

Burger King's "Indy Double Whopper" and Mar's M&M's tie the movie to summer fun.

INDIANA JONES
and the
KINGDOM OF
THE CRYSTAL SKULL

MAY 22

REVIEW AND APPLICATIONS

 Discuss the role of promotion in the marketing mix. Promotion is communication by marketers that informs, persuades, and reminds potential buyers of a product in order to influence an opinion or elicit a response. Promotional strategy is the plan for using the elements of promotion—advertising, public relations, sales promotion, and personal selling—to meet the firm's overall objectives and marketing goals. Based on these objectives, the elements of the promotional strategy become a coordinated promotion plan. The promotion plan then becomes an integral part of the total marketing strategy for reaching the target market along with product, distribution, and price.

1.1 What is a promotional strategy? Explain the concept of a competitive advantage in relation to promotional strategy.

 Describe the communication process. The communication process has several steps. When an individual or organization has a message it wishes to convey to a target audience, it encodes that message using language and symbols familiar to the intended receiver and sends the message through a channel of communication. Noise in the transmission channel distorts the source's intended message. Reception occurs if the message falls within the receiver's frame of reference. The receiver decodes the message and usually provides feedback to the source. Normally, feedback is direct for interpersonal communication and indirect for mass communication.

2.1 Why is understanding the target market a crucial aspect of the communication process?

 Explain the goals of promotion. The fundamental goals of promotion are to induce, modify, or reinforce behavior by informing, persuading, and reminding. Informative promotion explains a good's or service's purpose and benefits. Promotion that informs the consumer is typically used to increase demand for a general product category or to introduce a new good or service. Persuasive promotion is designed to stimulate a purchase or an action. Promotion that persuades the consumer to buy is essential during the growth stage of the product life cycle, when competition becomes fierce. Reminder promotion is used to keep the product and brand name in the public's mind. Promotions that remind are generally used during the maturity stage of the product life cycle.

3.1 Why might a marketing manager choose to promote his or her product using persuasion? Give some current examples of persuasive promotion.

 3.2 Choose a partner from class and go together to interview the owners or managers of several small businesses in your city. Ask them what their promotional objectives are and why. Are they trying to inform, persuade, or remind customers to do business with them? Also determine whether they believe they have an awareness problem or whether they need to persuade customers to come to them instead of to competitors. Ask them to list the characteristics of their primary market, the strengths and weaknesses of their direct competitors, and how they are positioning their store to compete. Prepare a report to present in class summarizing your findings.

 Discuss the elements of the promotional mix. The elements of the promotional mix include advertising, public relations, sales promotion, and personal selling.

Advertising is a form of impersonal, one-way mass communication paid for by the source. Public relations is the function of promotion concerned with a firm's public image. Sales promotion is typically used to back up other components of the promotional mix by stimulating immediate demand. Finally, personal selling typically involves direct communication, in person or by telephone; the seller tries to initiate a purchase by informing and persuading one or more potential buyers.

4.1 As the promotional manager for a new line of cosmetics targeted to preteen girls, you have been assigned the task of deciding which promotional mix elements—advertising, public relations, sales promotion, and personal selling—should be used in promoting it. Your budget for promoting the preteen cosmetics line is limited. Write a promotional plan explaining your choice of promotional mix elements given the nature of the product, the stage in the product life cycle, the target market characteristics, the type of buying decision, available funds, and the use of a pull or push strategy.

Discuss the AIDA concept and its relationship to the promotional mix. The AIDA model outlines the four basic stages in the purchase decision-making process, which are initiated and propelled by promotional activities: (1) attention, (2) interest, (3) desire, and (4) action. The components of the promotional mix have varying levels of influence at each stage of the AIDA model. Advertising is a good tool for increasing awareness and knowledge of a good or service. Sales promotion is effective when consumers are at the purchase stage of the decision-making process. Personal selling is most effective in developing customer interest and desire.

5.1 Discuss the AIDA concept. How do these different stages of consumer involvement affect the promotional mix?

5.2 How does a Web site's ease of use affect its ability to create attention, interest, desire, and action? Visit the kitchen and bath pages of Kohler's Web site (**www.kohler.com**), and determine how successful the company is at moving consumers through the AIDA process.

Discuss the concept of integrated marketing communications. Integrated marketing communications is the careful coordination of all promotional messages for a product or service to ensure the consistency of messages at every contact point where a company meets the consumer—advertising, sales promotion, personal selling, public relations, as well as direct marketing, packaging, and other forms of communication. Marketing managers carefully coordinate all promotional activities to ensure that consumers see and hear one message. Integrated marketing communications has received more attention in recent years due to the proliferation of media choices, the fragmentation of mass markets into more segmented niches, and the decrease in advertising spending in favor of promotional techniques that generate an immediate sales response.

6.1 Discuss the importance of integrated marketing communications. Give some current examples of companies that are and are not practicing IMC.

6.2 What do you think is the role of Hallmark's Web site (**www.hallmark .com**) in the company's integrated marketing communications plan? What seems to be the marketing function of the site? Do you think the site is effective?

Describe the factors that affect the promotional mix. Promotion managers consider many factors when creating promotional mixes. These factors include the nature of the product, product life-cycle stage, target market characteristics, the type of buying decision involved, availability of funds, and feasibility of push or pull strategies. Because most business products tend to be custom-tailored to the buyer's exact specifications, the marketing manager may choose a promotional mix that relies more heavily on personal selling. On the other hand, consumer products are generally mass produced and lend themselves more to mass promotional efforts such as advertising and sales promotion. As products move through different stages of the product life cycle, marketers will choose to use different promotional elements. For example, advertising is emphasized more in the introductory stage of the product life cycle than in the decline stage. Characteristics of the target market, such as geographic location of potential buyers and brand loyalty, influence the promotional mix as does whether the buying decision is complex or routine. The amount of funds a firm has to allocate to promotion may also help determine the promotional mix. Small firms with limited funds may rely more heavily on public relations, whereas larger firms may be able to afford broadcast or print advertising. Last, if a firm uses a push strategy to promote the product or service, the marketing manager may choose to use aggressive advertising and personal selling to wholesalers and retailers. If a pull strategy is chosen, then the manager often relies on aggressive mass promotion, such as advertising and sales promotion, to stimulate consumer demand.

7.1 Explain the difference between a "pull" and a "push" promotional strategy. Under what conditions should each strategy be used?

 7.2 Use Radioguide (**www.radioguide.fm**) to find a listing of radio Web sites in your area. View several of the stations' sites and compare the promotions featured. What conclusions can you draw about the target market of each station based on the types of promotions they are currently running? Would any of the promotions entice you to tune to a station that you normally don't listen to?

 7.3 Visit **www.teenresearch.com**. What research can this company offer about the size and growth of the teen market, the buying power of teenagers, and their buying habits? Why might these statistics be important to a company targeting teenagers in terms of marketing communications and promotion strategy?

 Discuss the effects of advertising on market share and consumers. Advertising helps marketers increase or maintain brand awareness as well as market share. Typically, more is spent to advertise new brands with a small market share than to advertise older brands. Brands with a large market share use advertising mainly to maintain their share of the market. Advertising affects consumers' daily lives as well as their purchases. Although advertising can seldom change strongly held consumer attitudes and values, it may transform a consumer's negative attitude toward a product into a positive one. Additionally, when consumers are highly loyal to a brand, they may buy more of that brand when advertising is increased. Lastly, advertising can also change the importance of a brand's attributes to consumers. By emphasizing different brand attributes, advertisers can change their appeal in response to consumers' changing needs or try to achieve an advantage over competing brands.

8.1 Discuss the reasons why new brands with a smaller market share spend proportionately more on advertising than brands with a larger market share.

8.2 Form a three-person team. Divide the responsibility for getting newspaper advertisements and menus for several local restaurants. While you are at the restaurants to obtain copies of their menus, observe the atmosphere and interview the manager to determine what he or she believes are the primary reasons people choose to dine there. Pool your information and develop a table comparing the restaurants in terms of convenience of location, value for the money, food variety and quality, atmosphere, and so on. Rank the restaurants in terms of their appeal to college students. Explain the basis of your rankings. What other market segment would be attracted to the restaurants and why? Do the newspaper advertisements emphasize the most effective appeal for a particular restaurant? Explain.

Identify the major types of advertising. Advertising is any form of impersonal, paid communication in which the sponsor or company is identified. The two major types of advertising are institutional advertising and product advertising. Institutional advertising is not product oriented; rather, its purpose is to foster a positive company image among the general public, investment community, customers, and employees. Product advertising is designed mainly to promote goods and services, and it is classified into three main categories: pioneering, competitive, and comparative. A product's place in the product life cycle is a major determinant of the type of advertising used to promote it.

9.1 At what stage in a product's life cycle are pioneering, competitive, and comparative advertising most likely to occur? Give a current example of each type of advertising.

Discuss the creative decisions in developing an advertising campaign. Before any creative work can begin on an advertising campaign, it is important to determine what goals or objectives the advertising should achieve. The objectives of a specific advertising campaign often depend on the overall corporate objectives and the product being advertised. Once objectives have been defined, creative work can begin on the advertising campaign. Creative decisions include identifying the product's benefits, developing possible advertising appeals, evaluating and selecting the advertising appeals, executing the advertising message, and evaluating the effectiveness of the campaign.

10.1 What is an advertising appeal? Give some examples of advertising appeals you have observed recently in the media.

10.2 Design a full-page magazine advertisement for a new brand of soft drink. The name of the new drink and its package design are at your discretion. On a separate sheet, specify the benefits stressed or appeals made in the advertisement.

Describe media evaluation and selection techniques. Media evaluation and selection make up a crucial step in the advertising campaign process. Major types of advertising media include newspapers, magazines, radio, television, outdoor advertising such as billboards and bus panels, and the Internet. Recent trends in advertising media include video shopping carts, computer screen savers, cinema and DVD advertising, cell phones, and videogames. Promotion managers choose the advertising campaign's media mix on the basis of the following variables: cost per contact, reach, frequency, characteristics of the target audience, flexibility of the medium, noise level, and the life span of the medium. After choosing the media mix, a media schedule designates when the advertisement will appear and the specific vehicles it will appear in.

11.1 What are the advantages of radio advertising? Why is radio expanding as an advertising medium?

11.2 You are the advertising manager of a sailing magazine, and one of your biggest potential advertisers has questioned your rates. Write the firm a letter explaining why you believe your audience selectivity is worth the extra expense for advertisers.

11.3 Identify an appropriate media mix for the following products:

 a. Chewing tobacco

 b. *People* magazine

 c. Weed-Eaters

 d. Foot odor killers

 e. "Drink responsibly" campaigns by beer brewers

11.4 How easy is it to find out about advertising options on the Internet? Go to LookSmart's and Yahoo!'s advertiser pages (**www.looksmart.com/aboutus/media** and **www.yahoo.com/info/advertising**). What kind of information do they require from you? Send an e-mail requesting information and compare what you receive.

KEY TERMS

advergaming	506
advertising	490
advertising appeal	497
advertising campaign	496
advertising objective	496
advertising response function	491
advocacy advertising	493
audience selectivity	509
AIDA concept	482
channel	474
communication	472
comparative advertising	495
competitive advantage	472
competitive advertising	494
continuous media schedule	510
cooperative advertising	502

corporate blogs	476
cost per contact	508
decoding	475
encoding	474
feedback	475
flighted media schedule	511
frequency	509
infomercial	504
institutional advertising	493
integrated marketing communications (IMC)	484
interpersonal communication	473
mass communication	473
media mix	508
media planning	501
media schedule	510

medium	501
noise	474
noncorporate blogs	476
pioneer advertising	494
product advertising	493
promotion	471
promotional mix	479
promotional strategy	471
pull strategy	489
pulsing media schedule	511
push strategy	489
reach	508
receiver	475
seasonal media schedule	511
sender	473
unique selling proposition	498

EXERCISES

APPLICATION EXERCISE 1

Many people are not aware of the rationale behind certain advertising messages. "Why do Infiniti ads show rocks and trees instead of automobiles?" "If car safety is so important, why do automobile ads often show cars skidding on wet, shiny surfaces?" "Target's ads are funky, with all the bright colors and product packaging, but what's the message?"

One way to understand the vagaries of the encoding process is to think of the popular board game *Taboo* by Hasbro. In this game, each team tries to get its members to guess a word without using obvious word clues. For example, to get the team to guess "apple," you may not say such words as *red, fruit, pie, cider,* or *core*. Sometimes advertising is like *Taboo* in that advertisers are not allowed to use certain words or descriptions. For example, pharmaceutical companies are not permitted to make certain claims or to say what a drug treats unless the ad also mentions the potential side effects. Language choices are also limited in advertising. To appreciate this, you can apply the *Taboo* game rules in an advertising format.[87]

Activities

1. Select a product from the list below, and then create a print advertisement or a television storyboard for that product. As part of the exercise, give your product a brand name. Taboo words, visuals, and concepts are given for each product type. *Taboo* items cannot be present in your work.

Product	Taboo Words, Visuals, and Concepts
Deodorant	Odor, underarm, perspiration, smell, sweat
Pain reliever	Pain, aches, fever, child-proof cap, gel
Soft drinks	Sugar-free, refreshing, thirst, swimwear, any celebrity

2. Now create a second ad or storyboard for your product. This time, however, you must use all the words, visuals, and concepts that are listed in the right column.

Product	Must-Use Words, Visuals, and Concepts
Deodorant	A romantic couple, monster trucks
Pain reliever	A mother and child, oatmeal, homework
Soft drinks	A cup of coffee, cookies, birthday cake, wine

APPLICATION EXERCISE 2

An important concept in promotion is semiotics, or the study of meaning and meaning-producing events. An understanding of semiotics can help you not only to identify objects (denotation) but also to grasp the utility of images and associations (connotation). By manipulating connotations of objects in advertising, you can create, change, or reinforce images for products. Thus, semiotics is a powerful tool for brand management and promotion.[86]

Activities

1. Make a list of ten images and associations that come to mind for each of the following items: baseball, vinyl record album, spoon, rubber band.

2. Look through magazines and see if you can find print advertisements that include each of the items (baseball, vinyl record album, spoon, rubber band) in a supporting role. What seems to be the message of each ad? How does the item help create or reinforce an image for the product being sold in the ad?

3. Think of an everyday object of your own. What are its likely connotations? For example, a dog in a car might signal a family vehicle, but a dog also connotes loyalty, "man's best friend," and dependability. What images and associations are likely with your item? Make a list of as many as you can.

4. Now use your object and list of associations to create an image for another product. Think of the likely connotations your object will have for a certain target market and how such connotations can support a brand image. For example, if your everyday object is a candle, you might choose lingerie for your product, based on a candle's romantic connotations.

ETHICS EXERCISE

Integrated Marketing Solutions is a consumer-products marketing services firm. Currently, the firm is handling the launch of a new book for one of its publishing clients. The campaign includes advance review copies for key book reviewers, "Coming Soon" posters for booksellers, an author book-signing tour, and several television interviews. Everything has been produced and scheduled for release next week. Today, Jane Kershaw, the account executive, has learned that although the book received numerous favorable reviews, the review quoted on all of the promotional materials is fabricated.

Questions

1. What should Jane do? Why?

2. What does the AMA Code of Ethics say about accuracy in promotional materials? Go to **www.marketingpower.com** and review the code. Then, write a brief paragraph describing how the AMA Code of Ethics relates to this issue.

MARKETING PLAN EXERCISE

In Part 3, you began the process of defining the marketing mix, starting with the components of product and distribution. The next stage of the strategic planning process continues defining the elements of the marketing mix, and this section—Part 4—focuses on promotion and communication decisions for the promotion mix, including advertising, public relations, sales promotion, and personal selling. Use the following exercises to guide you through the promotions part of your strategic marketing plan:

1. Define your promotional objectives. What specific results do you hope to accomplish, and which promotional tools will be responsible? How will you use promotions to differentiate yourself from your competition? Remember that promotions cannot be directly tied with sales because there are too many other factors (competition, environment, price, distribution, product, customer service, company reputation, and so on) that affect sales. State specific objectives that can be tied directly to the result of promotional activities—for example, number of people redeeming a coupon, share of audience during a commercial, percent attitude change before and after a telemarketing campaign, or number of people calling a toll-free information hotline. Remember to have offline promotions drive online traffic.

2.   Design a promotional message or theme. Does this message inform, remind, persuade, or educate the target market? Make sure this message will work across both traditional and electronic media. How is your promotional message consistent with your branding? Is this message or slogan unique and important enough to be copyrighted? Check with the U.S. Copyright Office at **http://lcweb.loc.gov/copyright.**

3.   Will you be designing and producing all your promotion tools in-house, or do you need to find an agency? What are the advantages of designing promotional tools in-house? Disadvantages? Try **http://www.agencyfinder.com** to assist in your decision.

CASE STUDY: HBO'S BLOOD VIRUS

When prominent occult film bloggers and fans began receiving strange letters written in dead languages and mailed in wax-sealed black envelopes, a shockwave of curiosity and excitement rippled through the horror-film fandom. A legion of bloggers and message-board posters set to work translating the letters from languages like Babylonian and Ugaritic into English, discovering that the missives led them to a mysterious and macabre Web site featuring an image of a seductive lady vampire. The site advertised a beverage called TruBlood—a synthetic blood developed by the Japanese, which vampires could drink as an alternative to feeding on humans. As visitors explored the site, they discovered short webisodes for the then-upcoming HBO television series which incorporates the TruBlood beverage into its storyline.

The letters and Web site were developed as part of a viral marketing campaign by HBO and Campfire Media, an independent agency founded by two of the creators of the successful 1999 film *The Blair Witch Project*. Viral marketing is the propagation of brand or product awareness through preexisting social networks, using unconventional media, with the hope that the campaign spreads as a cultural phenomenon. In addition to the letters, Campfire established a fictional blog and MySpace pages written by characters from the show, launched a human-vampire dating service, advertised TruBlood on vending machines, and strategically leaked tidbits of information and multimedia about the show. Campfire employees closely monitored popular horror blogs and message boards in order to gauge and encourage public interest, as well as orchestrate the release of new materials.

The campaign was an incredible, if somewhat subversive success—not only did Campfire generate momentous interest in the show, but a number of individuals actually tried to locate a TruBlood distributor. "We didn't mean to dupe people," said Zach Enterlin, HBO's vice president of advertising and promotions. "We just wanted a campaign that breaks through and resonates a little bit. It's a testament to how true to form the ads are. Some people aren't paying close attention." Viral marketing campaigns are ideal for shows like *True Blood*, whose fans fervently share and discuss ideas within Internet communities. In addition, as it's based on the popular Sookie Stackhouse series of books by Charlaine Harris, *True Blood* came with an avid built-in fan base of those already familiar with the story.

Viral marketing has been a successful part of many advertising campaigns, such as those of 2008 films *Cloverfield* and *The Dark Knight*.

Cloverfield, a film in which gargantuan monsters rampage through New York City, is captured on handheld video cameras. It was introduced to viewers through an untitled, unexplained teaser trailer that played before 2007's *Transformers* movie. As speculation mounted, *Cloverfield* marketers unveiled a number of enigmatic Web sites, as well as a tie-in campaign for the fictional Slusho! beverage and a Japanese drilling company, both of which play a part in *Cloverfield*'s mythology.

In May of 2007, 42 Entertainment began a viral campaign for *The Dark Knight*, a sequel to 2005's *Batman Begins*. The campaign focused on the film's antagonists: a Web site titled "I believe in Harvey Dent" was created as an advertisement for district attorney candidate Harvey Dent (played by Aaron Eckhart), as was a site titled "I Believe in Harvey Dent Too," a defiled version of the former which slowly revealed the first image of The Joker (played by Heath Ledger) as visitors sent e-mails through the site. The Joker's catchphrase "Why so serious?" spread virally on the Internet, and was used as the URL of a Web site that sent visitors on a Joker-themed scavenger hunt.

As *True Blood*'s premier drew near, HBO and Campfire turned to less obtuse, if still unorthodox, methods of advertisement. A prequel comic book about an elder vampire and the development of *True Blood* was handed out for free at 2008's San Diego Comic-Con, the largest pop cultural convention in the world. The first episode of *True Blood* was distributed on DVD for free to thousands of moviegoers at the 2008 Toronto International Film Festival, and was made available for rental from Blockbuster Video several days before it aired on television.

True Blood premiered on HBO on September 7, 2008—six months after Campfire's subtle marketing campaign began. According to Nielsen Co., the first three-quarters of 2008 saw HBO's viewership drop by nearly 23 percent compared to the previous year. However, thanks to interest in new shows such as *True Blood*, HBO saw a 2.4 percent increase in fourth-quarter viewership compared to 2007. Without question, the success of *True Blood* is due in part to the novel marketing developed by Campfire Media.[89]

Questions

1. What is the communication process for viral marketing? Is it different from conventional marketing? How so?

2. What was the initial promotional mix of the *True Blood* campaign, and how might it suggest an observance of IMC?

3. Did *Cloverfield* use a push or pull promotional strategy? What about *The Dark Knight*? Explain.

4. Why did *True Blood* shift its promotional mix as its premier neared? Was this a good or a bad strategy? Explain.

COMPANY CLIPS

VANS—OFF THE WALL AND ON TARGET

You have undoubtedly heard of Vans. The company has sold footwear, apparel, and extreme sports equipment for over 40 years using the distinct tagline, "Off the Wall." The company's founder wanted to control his own retail channel, so he transformed his manufacturing company into a marketing company. Always carefully protecting its unique brand image, Vans has crafted successful marketing messages and promotions that resonate with the youth culture that represents the company's target market. This video examines the carefully planned strategy that Vans developed to create loyalty in a fickle niche market.

Questions

1. Does Vans use a push or pull strategy to market its apparel? How does Steve feel about the two strategies?

2. What does Steve mean when he refers to tours and events as "planting seeds?"

3. Describe Vans' pyramid strategy. How does it protect the brand?

4. How does Steve's hands-on approach to events and promotion benefit the company?

Marketing & You Results

Higher scores on this scale indicate that others perceive you to be responsive, warm, and a good listener. A high score also corresponds to a willingness to mentor others. If your score is low, it indicates that you don't actively encourage other people to share information about themselves with you. That doesn't mean you are a poor listener, however. Rather, you prefer not to take the initiative in the interaction.

15

Public Relations, Sales Promotion, and Personal Selling

LEARNING OUTCOMES

LO1 Discuss the role of public relations in the promotional mix

LO2 Define and state the objectives of sales promotion

LO3 Discuss the most common forms of consumer sales promotion

LO4 List the most common forms of trade sales promotion

LO5 Describe personal selling

LO6 Discuss the key differences between relationship selling and traditional selling

LO7 List the steps in the selling process

LO ① PUBLIC RELATIONS

Public relations is the element in the promotional mix that evaluates public attitudes, identifies issues that may elicit public concern, and executes programs to gain public understanding and acceptance. Like advertising and sales promotion, public relations is a vital link in a company's marketing communication mix. Marketing managers plan solid public relations campaigns that fit into overall marketing plans and focus on targeted audiences. These campaigns strive to maintain a positive image of the corporation in the eyes of the public. Before launching public relations programs, managers evaluate public attitudes and company actions. Then they create programs to capitalize on factors that enhance the firm's image and minimize the factors that could generate a negative image.

In recent years, fast-food companies like McDonald's and soft drink companies like Coca-Cola have been criticized for contributing to childhood obesity, particularly in the United States. In response, the companies have undertaken public relations campaigns to try to minimize the impact on their reputations and ultimately sales. For example, Coca-Cola created the Beverage Institute for Health and Wellness to support nutrition research, education, and outreach. The company also spent $4 million to develop the "Live It" children's fitness campaign in schools across the country. Coke's nutrition communication manager says the campaign will not address childhood obesity or encourage students to drink Coke and that the company's logo will not appear on "Live It" materials. In addition to promoting the campaign, Coke is paying for campaign posters, pedometers, and nutrition education materials and offering prizes to children who meet the program's exercise goal of walking 10,000 steps a day. Such efforts are designed to offset a push by the Center for Science in the Public Interest to persuade the Food and Drug Administration to require labels on sodas warning about obesity, tooth decay, and diabetes.[1]

A public relations program can generate favorable publicity—public information about a company, product, service, or issue appearing in the mass media as a new item. Organizations generally do not pay for the publicity and are not identified as the source of the information, but they can benefit tremendously from it. For example, the rapid growth of the satellite radio industry is partly due to publicity. Subscribers were expected to top 20 million in 2009. Satellite radio's profile received a huge boost from the storm of publicity surrounding the decision by the country's most notorious and popular radio host, "shock jock" Howard Stern, to quit CBS radio and join censor-free Sirius satellite radio. Stern's first satellite broadcast was a major event, with the national media breathlessly reporting on the number of times he swore and looking for acceptable ways to report the more graphic—usually sexual—content of the show. Satellite radio, now called Sirius XM after the merger, benefited from the publicity

Marketing & You

What do you think of coupons? Enter your answers on the lines provided.

1 2 3 4 5
Strongly disagree — Strongly agree

__ Coupons can save a person a lot of money.

__ The money I can save by using coupons does not amount to much.*

__ I believe that people can help their families financially by using coupons.

__ Overall, I like using coupons.

__ Personally for me, using coupons for supermarket products is or would be useless.*

__ Taking everything into account, using coupons for supermarket shopping is wise.

Now, total your score, reversing your answers for the items followed by an asterisk (for example, if you answered 4, change it to 2). Find out what your score means after you read the chapter.

Source: Scale #115, *Marketing Scales Handbook,* G. Bruner, K. James, H. Hensel, eds., Vol. III. © by American Marketing Association.

public relations
The marketing function that evaluates public attitudes, identifies areas within the organization the public may be interested in, and executes a program of action to earn public understanding and acceptance.

publicity
Public information about a company, product, service, or issue appearing in the mass media as a news item.

product placement
A public relations strategy that involves getting a product, service, or company name to appear in a movie, television show, radio program, magazine, newspaper, video game, video or audio clip, book, or commercial for another product; on the Internet; or at special events.

Stern generated for the whole satellite broadcast medium as well as by signing up both Oprah Winfrey and reclusive music legend Bob Dylan to host shows.[2]

Again, although organizations do not directly pay for publicity, it should not be viewed as free. Preparing news releases, staging special events, and persuading media personnel to broadcast or print publicity messages costs money. Public relations departments may perform any or all of the following functions:

- ☛ *Press relations:* Placing positive, newsworthy information in the news media to attract attention to a product, a service, or a person associated with the firm or institution

- ☛ *Product publicity:* Publicizing specific products or services

- ☛ *Corporate communication:* Creating internal and external messages to promote a positive image of the firm or institution

- ☛ *Public affairs:* Building and maintaining national or local community relations

- ☛ *Lobbying:* Influencing legislators and government officials to promote or defeat legislation and regulation

- ☛ *Employee and investor relations:* Maintaining positive relationships with employees, shareholders, and others in the financial community

- ☛ *Crisis management:* Responding to unfavorable publicity or a negative event

Major Public Relations Tools

Public relations professionals commonly use several tools, including new-product publicity, product placement, consumer education, sponsorship, and Web sites. Although many of these tools require an active role on the part of the public relations professional, such as writing press releases and engaging in proactive media relations, some techniques create their own publicity.

New-Product Publicity Publicity is instrumental in introducing new products and services. Publicity can help advertisers explain what's different about their new product by prompting free news stories or positive word of mouth about it. During the introductory period, an especially innovative new product often needs more exposure than conventional, paid advertising affords. Public relations professionals write press releases or develop videos in an effort to generate news about their new product. They also jockey for exposure of their product or service at major events, on popular television and news shows, or in the hands of influential people.

Product Placement Marketers are increasingly using product placement to reinforce brand awareness and create favorable attitudes. Product placement is a strategy that involves getting one's product, service, or name to appear in a movie, television show, radio program, magazine, newspaper, video game, video or audio clip, book, or commercial for another product; on the Internet; or at special events. Including an actual product such as a can of Pepsi adds a sense of realism to a movie, TV show, video game, book, or similar vehicle that a can simply marked "soda" cannot. Product placements are arranged through barter (trade of product for placement), through paid placements, or at no charge when the product is viewed as enhancing the vehicle where it is placed.

Product placement expenditures amount to about $5 billion annually. Though this amount is small relative to other marketing expenditures, it is growing about 30 percent annually due to increasing audience fragmentation and the spread of ad-skipping technology.[3] More than two-thirds of product placements are in movies and TV shows, but placements in alternative media are growing, particularly on the Internet and in video games. Most product placements are for transportation, clothing, food, beverages, home furnishings, travel, and leisure time activities. Companies like BMW, Lexus, Coca-Cola, Pepsi, Procter & Gamble, and Hershey have frequently used product placement as a public relations strategy. Indeed, Pepsi appeared in seven top-ranked films in one year. Digital technology now enables companies to "virtually" place their products in any audio or video production. Virtual placement not only reduces the cost of product placement for new productions, but also enables companies to place products in previously produced programs, such as reruns of television shows and movies.

Companies obtain valuable product exposure, brand reinforcement, and increased sales through product placement, often at a much lower cost than in mass media like television ads. For example, Burger King products were woven into *The Apprentice* when contestants wore Burger King uniforms and flipped burgers as part of a challenge; Ford sponsored the show *24*, with the main character, Jack Bauer, driving a Ford Expedition; and S.C. Johnson placed the ant killer RAID in an episode of the popular HBO series *The Sopranos*. When Red Stripe, a Jamaican-brewed beer, appeared in the movie *The Firm*, its U.S. sales increased more than 50 percent in the first month after the movie was released.[4]

Consumer Education Some major firms believe that educated consumers are better, more loyal customers. BMW of North America, for example, sponsored an instructional driving school for teenagers in major cities across the United States. Teens received a special four-hour training session that included driving techniques, accident avoidance skills, and traction aid tricks from a professional driver. Financial planning firms often sponsor free educational seminars on money management, retirement planning, and investing in the hope that the seminar participants will choose the sponsoring organization for their future financial needs. Likewise, computer hardware and software firms, realizing that many consumers are intimidated by new technology and recognizing the strong relationship between learning and purchasing patterns, sponsor computer seminars and free in-store demonstrations.

Sponsorships Sponsorships are increasing both in number and as a proportion of companies' marketing budgets, with spending reaching $17 billion annually in the United States and Canada. Overall, global spending on sponsorships including North America was expected to exceed $44 billion in 2008. Probably the biggest reason for the increasing use of sponsorships is the difficulty of reaching audiences and differentiating a product from competing brands through the mass media. With a sponsorship, a company spends money to support an issue, cause, or event that is consistent with corporate objectives, such as improving brand awareness or enhancing corporate image. The biggest category is sports, which accounts for almost 70 percent of spending in sponsorships. Nonsports categories include entertainment tours and attractions, causes, arts, festivals, fairs and annual events, and association and membership organizations.[5] Typical examples of sponsorships include Jose Cuervo Tequila's sponsorship of the Pro Beach Volleyball Tour, Domino's Pizza's sponsorship of Michael Waltrip for NASCAR, Hilton Hotels' sponsorship of the Hilton Family Skating & Gymnastics Spectacular on NBC, Levi Strauss & Co.'s partnership with the San Francisco Giants to sponsor the right field section of the park to be named "Levi's Landing," and Anheuser-Busch's Bud Bowl that featured hip-hop star Snoop Dogg and rock band 3 Doors Down.[6] In addition, multiple companies sponsored the 2008 summer Olympics in Beijing.

Although companies have recently been turning to specialized events such as tie-ins with schools, charities, and other community service organizations, the most popular sponsorship events are still those involving sports, music, or the arts. McDonald's expanded its "I'm lovin' it" campaign to include sponsorships of NASCAR, the Pro Beach Volleyball Tour, and the Big Mac Challenge—a 20-stop lifestyle-oriented car

sponsorship
A public relations strategy in which a company spends money to support an issue, cause, or event that is consistent with corporate objectives, such as improving brand awareness or enhancing corporate image.

show including DJs and other youth-focused activities. And, Yahoo! sponsored a video game tour to promote Yahoo! Music Unlimited, Napster forged a deal with the Dew Action Sports Tour, and MSN Music hosted Milwaukee's Summerfest and Manchester, Tennessee's Bonnaroo Music and Arts Festival.[7]

Marketers sometimes create their own events tied around their products. The state of Hawaii organized its own mall touring event, titled "Experience Aloha: Hawaii on Tour," to promote the islands as a tourist destination. The tour traveled to 22 U.S. cities for weekend mall visits that included hula dancers, chefs cooking Hawaiian cuisine, lei-making demonstrations, and a virtual reality film simulating a helicopter ride over Hawaii's islands. Many other states also sponsor events promoting tourism.

Corporations sponsor issues as well as events. Sponsorship issues are quite diverse, but the three most popular are education, health care, and social programs. Firms often donate a percentage of sales or profits to a worthy cause favored by their target market.

A special type of sponsorship, cause-related marketing, involves the association of a for-profit company with a nonprofit organization. Through the sponsorship, the company's product or service is promoted, and money is raised for the nonprofit. In a common type of cause-related sponsorship, a company agrees to donate a percentage of the purchase price of a particular item to a charity, but some arrangements are more complex. In the United Kingdom, for example, Blockbuster Entertainment Ltd. works with Starlight Children's Foundation to raise money, and Tesco supermarkets raise money for computers in schools. Similarly, in the United States Avon, Yoplait Yogurt, and BMW support the Susan G. Komen Breast Cancer Foundation, and J. P. Morgan Chase & Co. Bank works with St. Jude Children's Research Hospital.[8] Recently, companies are partnering with nonprofit organizations to create new "cause brands." For example, the American Heart Association and several corporations have developed the "Go Red for Women" campaign to increase the awareness of heart disease for women (**www.goredforwomen.org**).[9] Findings from several studies suggest that some consumers consider a company's reputation when making purchasing decisions and that a company's community involvement boosts employee morale and loyalty.[10]

Internet Web Sites Companies increasingly are using the Internet in their public relations strategies. Company Web sites are used to introduce new products, promote existing products, obtain consumer feedback, post news releases, communicate legislative and regulatory information, showcase upcoming events, provide links to related sites, release financial information, interact with customers and potential customers, and perform many more marketing activities. Online reviews from opinion leaders and other consumers help marketers sway purchasing decisions in their favor. On its Web site for PlayStation 3 (**www.playstation.com**), Sony has online support, events and promotions, game trailers, and new and updated product releases such as *Killzone 2, Street Fighter IV, F.E.A.R. 2: Project Origin*, and *MLB 09*. The site also includes message boards where the gaming community posts notes and chats, exchanges tips on games, votes on lifestyle issues like music and videos, and learns about promotional events.[11]

Web sites are also being incorporated into integrated marketing communications strategies. For example, CBS integrated broadcast advertising with product placement by placing a bonus scene from *CSI: Miami* on its Web site featuring a plot twist that was not revealed to television viewers until later in the season. The bonus scene page was sponsored by General Motors' Hummer brand, which also appeared in the bonus scene itself.[12]

More and more often, companies are also using blogs—both corporate and noncorporate—as a tool to manage their public images. Noncorporate blogs cannot be controlled, but marketers must monitor them to be aware of and respond to negative information and encourage positive content. Wal-Mart has been especially active in cultivating bloggers to get the company's message out. Mona Williams, Wal-Mart's spokeswoman, says, "We reach out to bloggers in the same way we reach out to reporters. A lot of people are looking to bloggers for their news source, and this is a good way to get our message out."[13] The company hired a public relations firm to combat negative publicity. The publicist assigned to the Wal-Mart account, Marshall Manson, contacts bloggers who write pro-Wal-Mart content and asks if he can send them materials to use in their commentaries. Those who agree become champions for the giant retailer.[14]

In addition to "getting the message out," companies are using blogs to create communities of consumers who feel positively about the brand. The hope is that the positive attitude toward the brand will build into strong word-of-mouth marketing. Companies must exercise caution when diving into corporate blogging, however. Coca-Cola launched a blog authored by a fictional character that did little except parrot the company line. Consumers immediately saw the blog for what it was (a transparent public relations platform) and lambasted Coca-Cola for its insincerity.[15]

Managing Unfavorable Publicity

Although marketers try to avoid unpleasant situations, crises do happen. In our free-press environment, publicity is not easily controlled, especially in a crisis. Crisis management is the coordinated effort to handle the effects of unfavorable publicity, ensuring fast and accurate communication in times of emergency.

A good public relations staff is as important in bad times as in good. Companies must have a communication policy firmly in hand before a disaster occurs, because timing is uncontrollable. For example, McDonald's was caught off-guard by the wave of negative publicity that followed the release of *Super Size Me*, a documentary film which chronicled the deterioration of filmmaker Morgan Spurlock's health while he experimented with an all-McDonald's diet. In anticipation of a similar response to the movie version of Eric Schlosser's best seller *Fast Food Nation*, McDonald's contemplated dispatching a "truth squad" and a team of "ambassadors of the brand" to remind consumers that the restaurant offers a healthy menu and provides good

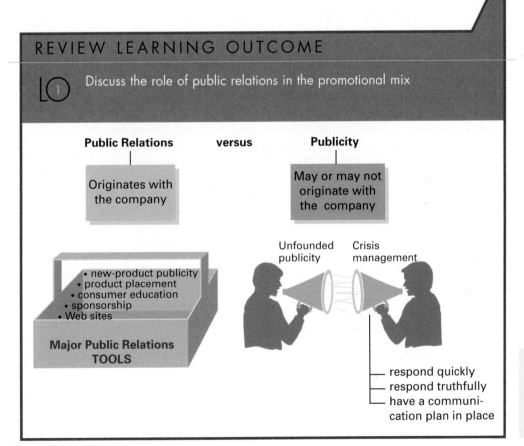

REVIEW LEARNING OUTCOME

LO 1 Discuss the role of public relations in the promotional mix

Public Relations versus Publicity

Originates with the company

May or may not originate with the company

• new-product publicity
• product placement
• consumer education
• sponsorship
• Web sites

Major Public Relations TOOLS

Unfounded publicity   Crisis management

— respond quickly
— respond truthfully
— have a communication plan in place

crisis management
A coordinated effort to handle all the effects of unfavorable publicity or of another unexpected unfavorable event.

sales promotion
Marketing activities—other than personal selling, advertising, and public relations—that stimulate consumer buying and dealer effectiveness.

consumer sales promotion
Sales promotion activities targeting the ultimate consumer.

trade sales promotion
Sales promotion activities targeting a channel member, such as a wholesaler or retailer.

jobs. The company also modified its menu to include more salads and apple dippers. McDonald's new marketing communication focused on the importance of a balanced lifestyle appears to have offset potential negative publicity resulting from the documentary.[16]

When Wal-Mart became the target of negative publicity regarding its low wages and sparse benefits, publicist Marshall Manson sent a special missive to his network of bloggers. It revealed that unions were hiring homeless and day laborers to protest at nonunion businesses, including Wal-Mart. The unions paid the picketers minimum wage and gave them no benefits. Manson's release was used by numerous bloggers and represented a counterattack in the publicity war over Wal-Mart's employment practices.[17]

LO 2
SALES PROMOTION

In addition to using advertising, public relations, and personal selling, marketing managers can use sales promotion to increase the effectiveness of their promotional efforts. Sales promotion is marketing communication activities, other than advertising, personal selling, and public relations, in which a short-term incentive motivates consumers or members of the distribution channel to purchase a good or service immediately, either by lowering the price or by adding value.

Advertising offers the consumer a reason to buy. Sales promotion offers an incentive to buy. Both are important, but sales promotion is usually cheaper than advertising and easier to measure. A major national TV advertising campaign often costs over $5 million or more to create, produce, and place. In contrast, promotional campaigns using the Internet or direct marketing methods can cost less than half that amount. It is also very difficult to determine how many people buy a product or service as a result of radio or TV ads. But with sales promotion, marketers know the precise number of coupons redeemed or the number of contest entries.

Sales promotion is usually targeted toward either of two distinctly different markets. Consumer sales promotion is targeted to the ultimate consumer market. Trade sales promotion is directed to members of the marketing channel, such as wholesalers and retailers. Sales promotion has become an important element in a marketer's integrated marketing communications program. Sales promotion expenditures have been steadily increasing over the last several years as a result of increased competition, the everexpanding array of available media choices, consumers and retailers demanding more deals from manufacturers, and the continued reliance on accountable and measurable marketing strategies. In addition, product and service marketers that have traditionally ignored sales promotion activities, such as power companies and restaurants, have discovered the marketing power of sales promotion. In fact, annual expenditures on promotion marketing in the United States now exceed $400 billion. Direct mail is the most widely used promotional medium, accounting for 50 percent of annual promotional expenditures.[18] The next two most widely used media are sampling and in-store promotions. Examples of these include point-of-purchase promotions (17 percent of expenditures), events and sponsorships (14 percent), and promotions via Internet and mobile devices (7 percent).[19]

The Objectives of Sales Promotion

Sales promotion usually has more effect on behavior than on attitudes. Immediate purchase is the goal of sales promotion, regardless of the form it takes. Therefore, it seems to make more sense when planning a sales promotion campaign to target customers according to their general behavior. For instance, is the consumer loyal to your product or to your competitor's? Does the consumer switch brands readily in favor of the best deal? Does the consumer buy only the least expensive product, no matter what? Does the consumer buy any products in your category at all?

The objectives of a promotion depend on the general behavior of target consumers. (See Exhibit 15.1.) For example, marketers targeting loyal users of their product do not want to change behavior. Instead, they need to reinforce existing behavior or increase product usage. An effective tool for strengthening brand loyalty is the *frequent buyer program* that rewards consumers for repeat purchases. Other types of promotions are more effective with customers prone to brand switching or with those who are loyal to a competitor's product. A cents-off coupon, free sample, or eye-catching display in a store will often entice shoppers to try a different brand. Consumers who do not use the product may be enticed to try it through the distribution of free samples.

Once marketers understand the dynamics occurring within their product category and have determined the particular consumers and consumer behaviors they want to influence, they can then go about selecting promotional tools to achieve these goals.

REVIEW LEARNING OUTCOME

LO2 Define and state the objectives of sales promotion

Sales Promotion → Consumer / Trade → $1.99

Goal = Drive immediate purchase

= Influence <u>Behavior</u> not ~~Attitude~~

EXHIBIT 15.1

Types of Consumers and Sales Promotion Goals

Type of Buyer	Desired Results	Sales Promotion Examples
Loyal customers People who buy your product most or all of the time	Reinforce behavior, increase consumption, change purchase timing	• Loyalty marketing programs, such as frequent buyer cards or frequent shopper clubs • Bonus packs that give loyal consumers an incentive to stock up or premiums offered in return for proofs of purchase
Competitor's customers People who buy a competitor's product most or all of the time	Break loyalty, persuade to switch to your brand	• Sampling to introduce your product's superior qualities compared to their brand • Sweepstakes, contests, or premiums that create interest in the product
Brand switchers People who buy a variety of products in the category	Persuade to buy your brand more often	• Any promotion that lowers the price of the product, such as coupons, price-off packages, and bonus packs • Trade deals that help make the product more readily available than competing products
Price buyers People who consistently buy the least expensive brand	Appeal with low prices or supply added value that makes price less important	• Coupons, price-off packages, refunds, or trade deals that reduce the price of the brand to match that of the brand that would have been purchased

Source: From *Sales Promotion Essentials*, 2nd ed., by Don E. Schultz, William A. Robinson, and Lisa A. Petrison. Reprinted by permission of NTC Publishing Group, 4255 Touhy Ave., Lincolnwood, IL 60048.

Has Starbucks Lost Its Mojo with Average Joes?

Once considered a master at branding and one of the most admired companies in the world, the company that taught America about coffee and provided a "third place" to enjoy it has lost its luster. At one point, Starbucks was opening a new store a day. It still has more than 15,000 stores in 44 countries and Starbucks represents more than half (2.9 billion servings) of total coffee consumption (4.6 billion servings) according to NPD Group/Crest. But sales of specialty coffee were down in 2008 (the first decline in 5 years), and many people have traded down to other new (and less expensive) competitors, such as Dunkin' Donuts and McDonald's. However, Starbucks' slide started long before the economy took a downturn.

The real reason behind Starbucks' trouble is that management began to ignore the customer. While trying to solve some customer complaints, Starbucks degraded the overall customer experience, becoming less passionate about customer relationships and their coffee experience. For example, when some customers complained about the length of the lines and the pace of the service, Starbucks elected to take out some of the sofas and comfortable chairs that made Starbucks unique. This made space for more people in line, but not much room for people to relax. And in order to speed up the service, Starbucks got rid of the coffee bean grinders, which took a lot of time. Hand-pulled shots also took up time and were shuttered. But once the couches and coffee bean smells were gone, so was much of the Starbucks experience. Soon customers began to realize the price they paid for their lattes was pretty expensive relative to the experience.

When Starbucks stock prices and sales began to tumble, management attempted to recover; founder Howard Schultz returned as CEO after 8 years away from the role. Starbucks planned to reignite the customer connection, slow store growth, shut down underperforming stores, increase global expansion, and improve the state of the U.S. business. New coffee blends, new products (particularly hot food), and even coupons were introduced. So far, Starbucks has not had much luck. In 2008, 600 stores were closed and more are expected to be shut down in light of the economic downturn.

Starbucks created and profited from the specialty coffee category, but customer preferences and loyalties changed. Indeed, in the 2006 Customer Loyalty Engagement Index Starbucks dominated its competitors; by the end of 2007 Starbucks had surrendered its dominance to Dunkin' Donuts. A Lightspeed Research study revealed that more than 60 percent of Americans scaled back on expensive coffee in the past six months. This is good news for "low rung" coffee companies like McDonald's; it has plans to open coffee bars in 14,000 U.S. restaurants.[20] So, how can Starbucks return to the "Starbucks Experience"?

TOOLS FOR CONSUMER SALES PROMOTION

Marketing managers must decide which consumer sales promotion devices to use in a specific campaign. The methods chosen must match the objectives to ensure success of the overall promotion plan. Popular tools for consumer sales promotion are coupons and rebates, premiums, loyalty marketing programs, contests and sweepstakes, sampling, and point-of-purchase promotion. Consumer sales promotion tools have also been easily transferred to online versions to entice Internet users to visit sites, purchase products, or use services on the Web.

Coupons and Rebates

A coupon is a certificate that entitles consumers to an immediate price reduction when they buy the product. Coupons are a particularly good way to encourage product trial and repurchase. They are also likely to increase the amount of a product bought.

Traditional types of coupon distribution, such as newspapers, direct mail, and magazines, had been declining but began increasing in recent years. For example, consumer packaged goods marketers issued over 300 billion coupons valued at almost $400 billion in 2008. To make coupons more attractive, the average value was increased, and the result was the first increase in redemption rates (from about 1.5 percent to 2.6 percent) in 25 years.[21] Online and in-store distribution of coupons also has been increasing. These trends are the result of intense competition in the consumer packaged goods category and the introduction of over 1,200 new products each year, as well as the economic downturn. Though coupons are often criticized for reaching customers who have no interest in the product or service, or for encouraging repeat purchase by regular users, studies indicate coupons promote new-product use and are likely to stimulate purchases. The use of colorful free-standing inserts (FSIs), mostly in Sunday newspapers, continues to grow despite declines in newspaper readership. FSIs are the most frequent way marketers distribute coupons (88.1 percent) followed by handouts (4.7 percent), direct mail (2.2 percent), magazines (2.1 percent), newspapers (1.2 percent), in/on pack (1.2 percent), and Internet (0.4 percent). But online coupon distribution sites such as **www.coolsavings.com** and **www.valpak.com** are emerging as major coupon distribution outlets. Unfortunately, redemption rates for coupons often are 2 percent or lower.[22]

To overcome the low redemption rates for coupons, marketers are using new strategies. For example, by shortening the time in which coupons can be redeemed or reducing the requirement for multiple purchases, some marketers have increased the redemption rate by creating a greater sense of urgency to redeem the coupon. Some marketers are de-emphasizing their use of coupons in favor of everyday low pricing, while others are distributing single, all-purpose coupons that can be redeemed for several brands.

In-store coupons have become popular because they are more likely to influence customers' buying decisions. Instant coupons on product packages, coupons distributed from on-shelf coupon-dispensing machines, and electronic coupons issued at the checkout counter are achieving much higher redemption rates. Indeed, instant coupons are redeemed more than 15 times more frequently than traditional newspaper coupons, indicating that consumers are making more in-store purchase decisions.

Starbucks has taken in-store coupons to a new level by installing interactive units on grocery store shelves. Each unit provides consumers with product information related to brewing, coffee education, and a taste matcher. In one test the units resulted in a 200 percent increase in sales. Internet coupons are also gaining in popularity. For example, Kroger has launched "Coupons that you click. Not clip." on Kroger.com. Registered Kroger Plus Shopper card members just log on to the Web site and click on the coupons they want. Coupons are automatically loaded on to the Kroger Plus card and redeemed at checkout when the shopper's Kroger Plus card is scanned.[23]

As marketing tactics grow more sophisticated, coupons are no longer viewed as a stand-alone tactic, but as an integral component of a larger promotional campaign. For example, Papa John's Pizza teamed up with Warner Bros. Home Entertainment and DC Comics to offer an instantly redeemable $3 coupon for online purchases as well as a limited edition "Dark Knight" gift card that could be redeemed for Papa John's products in store or online. Exclusive content and trailers from the movie are available on the restaurant's Web site. Subway restaurants in Buffalo, New York, developed a campaign that offers consumer alerts and discount coupons via customers' mobile phones. This was a major breakthrough in marketing to the 18- to 34-year-old customer. Other firms are experimenting with mobile phone coupons as well while working out the technical issues such as using the coupons at the cashier.[24] Rebates are similar to coupons in that they offer the purchaser a price reduction; however, because the purchaser must mail in a rebate form and usually some proof of purchase, the reward is not as immediate. Traditionally used by food and cigarette

coupon
A certificate that entitles consumers to an immediate price reduction when they buy the product.

rebate
A cash refund given for the purchase of a product during a specific period.

premium
An extra item offered to the consumer, usually in exchange for some proof of purchase of the promoted product.

loyalty marketing program
A promotional program designed to build long-term, mutually beneficial relationships between a company and its key customers.

frequent buyer program
A loyalty program in which loyal consumers are rewarded for making multiple purchases of a particular good or service.

manufacturers, rebates now appear on all types of products, from computers and software to film and cell phones. In the run-up to Super Bowl XL, Pepsi-Cola offered consumers a $10 dollar rebate as an incentive to stock up on the company's soda products and Frito-Lay brand chips in time for the big game.[25]

Manufacturers prefer rebates for several reasons. Rebates enable manufacturers to offer price cuts directly to consumers. Manufacturers have more control over rebate promotions because they can be rolled out and shut off quickly. Further, because buyers must fill out forms with their names, addresses, and other data, manufacturers use rebate programs to build customer databases. Perhaps the best reason of all to offer rebates is that although rebates are particularly good at enticing purchase, most consumers never bother to redeem them. Studies show only about one-half of customers eligible for rebates actually collect them.[26]

Premiums

A premium is an extra item offered to the consumer, usually in exchange for some proof that the promoted product has been purchased. Premiums reinforce the consumer's purchase decision, increase consumption, and persuade nonusers to switch brands. Premiums like telephones, tote bags, and umbrellas are given away when consumers buy cosmetics, magazines, bank services, rental cars, and so on. Probably the best example of the use of premiums is the McDonald's Happy Meal, which rewards children with a small toy. Many companies have been built around furnishing clients with customized premiums. Because of the widespread use of premiums, especially in trade relationships, it is getting harder to capture someone's attention with a premium. Kellogg's decided to use the animated character Shrek in a mix of premium-based promotions to get kids to eat healthy. Three games aimed at healthy lifestyles were created and appeared on 100 million cereal boxes. And for the first time, a bilingual promotional insert was included in Spanish using Puss 'n' Boots, Shrek's Latin sidekick. As a result, 125,000 cereal bowls, 85,000 boogie boards, 43,000 helmet covers, 37,000 talking key chains, and 16,000 soccer balls were redeemed. Kellogg's also saw major sales increases for Rice Krispies (21.5 percent), Froot Loops (16.7 percent), and Corn Pops (5.6 percent).[27]

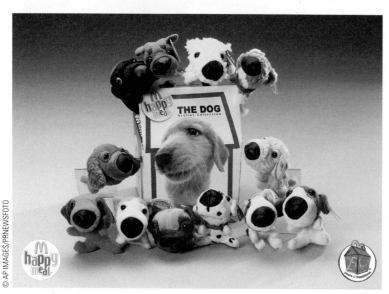

© AP IMAGES/PRNEWSFOTO

Premiums can also include more product for the regular price, such as two-for-the-price-of-one bonus packs or packages that include more of the product. Kellogg's, for instance, added two more pastries and waffles to its Pop-Tarts and Eggo packages without increasing the price in an effort to boost market share lost to private-label brands and new competitors. The promotion was so successful the company decided to keep the additional product in its regular packaging. Another possibility is to attach a premium to the product's package. For example, when research showed that consumers who drink tequila are often trendsetters who entertain at home, 1-800-Tequila launched a holiday promotion that included an instant camera and entertainment guide attached to the bottle.[28]

Loyalty Marketing Programs

Loyalty marketing programs and frequent buyer programs reward loyal consumers for making multiple purchases. Promotional spending related to loyalty programs has increased almost 4 percent to $2.1 billion. Popularized by the airline industry through frequent-flyer programs, loyalty marketing enables companies to strategically invest sales promotion dollars in activities designed to capture greater profits from customers already loyal to the product or company. This is critical, as studies show that consumer loyalty is on the decline. Forrester Research showed the percentage of consumers ranking price as more important than brand rose from 41 to 47 percent over 3 years. According to research conducted by Gartner, more than 75 percent of consumers have more than one loyalty card that rewards them with redeemable points. Furthermore, there are almost 1.5 billion loyalty program memberships in the United States, with the average household participating in 12 programs.[29]

The objective of loyalty marketing programs is to build long-term, mutually beneficial relationships between a company and its key customers. In the retail sector, programs such as My Coke Rewards and Nike Plus are enabling these brands to learn more about what customers buy and their choice of rewards. Frequent shopper card programs offered by many supermarkets and other retailers have exploded in popularity. Research from Forrester shows that 54 percent of primary grocery shoppers belong to two or more supermarket loyalty programs. Although this speaks to the popularity of loyalty cards, it also shows that customers are pledging "loyalty" to more than one store: 15 percent of primary grocery shoppers are cardholders in at least three programs, and 4 percent participate in four or five programs.[30] Combined with the statistics on the growing importance of price over brands, frequent shopper programs need to offer something more than just discounts to build customer loyalty. One of the more successful recent premium promotions is Starbucks' Duetto Card, which combines a Visa credit card with a reloadable Starbucks card. The card allows members to collect "Duetto Dollars" that can be redeemed for anything they want to purchase at a Starbucks location. Starbucks also sends members quarterly opportunities based on usage, such as product samples and previews. One study reported that over 60 percent of Duetto cardholders said they were more likely to purchase Starbucks products as a result of the program.[31]

Cobranded credit cards are an increasingly popular loyalty marketing tool. Annually over 6 billion direct marketing appeals for a cobranded credit card are sent to potential customers in the United States. Gap, Sony, and American Airlines are only a few examples of companies sponsoring cobranded Visa, MasterCard, or American Express cards. Target has a card (Take Charge of Education) that enables consumers to identify the school they would like to give money to (**www.target.com**). In addition, many nonprofit organizations participate in these cobranded affinity programs. American Express has a program with Space Adventures, a company that offers simulated space flight experiences.[32]

Through loyalty programs, shoppers receive discounts, alerts on new products, and other enticing offers. In exchange, retailers are able to build customer databases that help them better understand customer preferences. Verizon Wireless builds loyalty with its "New Every Two" program. Consumers who have been Verizon customers for 2 years are eligible for a $100 credit toward a new digital phone.[33]

Companies increasingly are using the Internet to build customer loyalty through e-mail and blogs. Over 80 percent of supermarket chains are using e-mail to register customers for their loyalty programs and to entice them with coupons, flyers, and promotional campaigns.[34] Blogs are becoming a critical component of some companies' loyalty marketing programs. Blogging technology enables marketers to create a community of consumers who feel positively about the company's brand and to build deeper relationships with them. Starwood Hotels launched a corporate blog called TheLobby .com. Although the blog is open to the public, the company is aiming the content specifically at members of the Starwood Preferred Guest loyalty program. Features include postings about special events at specific Starwood properties and how travelers can earn loyalty points through special promotions. The company's goal is to combine advertising with useful information to create a Web destination for its guests—and divert them away from other travel blogs that might contain negative postings about Starwood hotels.[35]

Companies like McDonald's and Cannondale are also using blogging technology to create communities around their brands. Robin Hopper, CEO of iUpload, the company that hosts the blogs for these two companies, says that companies publish blogs to build social networks around their brands. "It's a whole new way to market," he says. "People willingly provide all sorts of demographic information on blogs" that companies can use to target them more effectively.[36]

Contests and Sweepstakes

Contests and sweepstakes are generally designed to create interest in a good or service, often to encourage brand switching. *Contests* are promotions in which participants use some skill or ability to compete for prizes. A consumer contest usually requires entrants to answer questions, complete sentences, or write a paragraph about the product and submit proof of purchase. Winning a *sweepstakes*, on the other hand, depends on chance or luck, and participation is free. Sweepstakes usually draw about ten times more entries than contests do. Marketers were expected to spend almost $2 billion in 2009 building games, contests, and sweepstakes. Contests and sweepstakes calling for consumer-generated content remain the favorite. For example, Dole launched its Sweet Retreat contest using blogs and parfait parties. In order to enter, people have to submit photos of themselves enjoying Dole's parfaits and include a caption about their "indulgent moment." Consumers then vote on the winners who then receive a variety of prizes. Bloggers that focus on moms, health, and wellness were asked to talk about the Dole parfait parties. Last, specific groups like book clubs, scrapbooking groups, and others were identified in several cities to participate in the parfait parties.[37]

While contests and sweepstakes may draw considerable interest and publicity, generally they are not effective tools for generating long-term sales. To increase their effectiveness, sales promotion managers must make certain the award will appeal to the target market. For example, Home & Garden Television Network's annual "Dream Home Giveaway" sweepstakes awards a fully furnished, custom-built home to one lucky viewer. The promotion is cosponsored by General Motors, which fills the garage with a new sport-utility vehicle, and other home-related companies such as Sherwin-Williams paint, Lumber Liquidators flooring, California Closets, and Jeld-Wen windows and doors. The annual sweepstakes typically draws over four million entries.[38] Offering several smaller prizes to many winners instead of one huge prize to just one person often will increase the effectiveness of the promotion, but there's no denying the attractiveness of a jackpot-type prize.

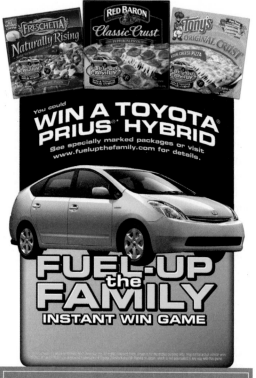

Red Baron, Freschetta, and Tony's pizzas' mega event "Fuel-Up The Family" gives consumers an opportunity to win a Toyota Prius. To participate, consumers enter the UPC code from specially marked packages and play an Instant Win game on an interactive Web site.

Sampling

Consumers generally perceive a certain amount of risk in trying new products. Many are afraid of trying something they will not like (such as a new food item) or spending too much money and getting little reward. Sampling enables customers to try a product risk-free. Sampling can increase retail sales by more than 40 percent. It is no surprise, therefore, that product sampling is the dominant in-store marketing method when it comes to influencing consumer purchase decisions.[39]

Spending on sampling increased by 5 percent in 2008, to $2.3 billion.[40] Sampling can be accomplished by directly mailing the sample to the customer, delivering the sample door-to-door, packaging the sample with another product, or demonstrating or sampling the product at a retail store or service outlet. Coca-Cola partnered with Domino's Pizza to sample its Coca-Cola Zero beverage. Every Domino's customer placing an order got a complimentary 20-ounce bottle of Coca-Cola Zero.[41] Kleenex launched its broadest sampling program ever for the new enhanced tissue with lotion product. The campaign put 60 million samples in places consumers would not typically find tissues, such as free-standing dispensers so consumers could try it. Kleenex supported the effort with magazine advertising and a sampling van tour. Similarly, when Masterfoods wanted to increase sales of its Dove "Promises" product line of dark and milk chocolates, it used both print media and sampling. To reach the upscale target market, samples were handed out at high-end hotels, spas, and gourmet cooking shows.[42]

Sampling at special events is a popular, effective, and high-profile distribution method that permits marketers to piggyback onto fun-based consumer activities—including sporting events, college fests, fairs and festivals, beach events, and chili cook-offs. General Mills used 500 "meal assembly kitchens" to provide samples of its Chocolate Turtle Chex Mix where busy moms could prepare ready-to-eat food. Companies like Tabasco, Juicy Juice, and Lipton Iced Tea are also sampling in these kitchens. Product sampling during tailgating at college and professional football stadiums enables marketers to reach from 10,000 to 100,000 consumers in a single afternoon. H.J. Heinz tests products such as new barbecue sauces and ketchups to get immediate feedback about what consumers like and dislike about the products.[43]

Distributing samples to specific location types where consumers regularly meet for a common objective or interest, such as health clubs, churches, or doctors' offices, is one of the most efficient methods of sampling. What better way to get consumers to try a product than to offer a sample exactly when it is needed most? If someone visits a health club regularly, chances are he or she is a good prospect for a health-food product or vitamin supplement. Health club instructors are also handing out body wash, deodorant, and face cloths to sweating participants at the end of class, and, more surprisingly, hot drinks! Dunkin' Donuts used a sampling program in more than 200 health clubs to promote its new Latte Lite drink, a zero percent fat product that gives health-conscious consumers a lighter alternative.[44] Meanwhile, makers of stain removers and hand cleansers are giving away samples in mall food courts and petting zoos. Likewise, pharmaceutical companies offer free samples of new and expensive drugs as a tactic to entice doctors and consumers to become loyal to a product. Online sampling is gaining momentum as Web communities bring people together with common interests in trying new products, often using blogs to spread the word. Nail polish company OPI used SheSpeaks.com to encourage trials of new lacquer nail polish pens. Consumers had to register and then order one of five color pens and coupons. Consumers also blogged about the new pens and passed along the coupons to friends.[45]

Point-of-Purchase Promotion

Point-of-purchase (P-O-P) promotion includes any promotional display set up at the retailer's location to build traffic, advertise the product, or induce impulse buying. Point-of-purchase promotions include shelf "talkers" (signs attached to store shelves), shelf extenders (attachments that extend shelves so products stand out), ads on grocery carts and bags, end-aisle and floor-stand displays, television monitors at supermarket checkout counters, in-store audio messages, and audiovisual displays. One big advantage of P-O-P promotion is that it offers manufacturers a captive audience in retail stores. Another advantage is between 70 and 80 percent of all retail purchase decisions are made in-store, so P-O-P promotions can be very effective. P-O-P promotions can increase sales by as much as 65 percent. Strategies to increase sales include adding header or riser cards, changing messages on base or case wraps, adding inflatable or mobile displays, and using signs that advertise the brand's sports, movie, or charity tie-in.[46] When Hershey launched its new Swoops, a "chip" version of popular candy bars such as Almond Joy, Reese's, and Hershey Bars, it successfully used in-store displays to stimulate in-store, impulse purchases of the new candy.[47]

point-of-purchase display (P-O-P)
A promotional display set up at the retailer's location to build traffic, advertise the product, or induce impulse buying.

Online Sales Promotion

Online sales promotions have expanded dramatically in recent years. Marketers are now spending billions of dollars annually on such promotions. Sales promotions

trade allowance
A price reduction offered by manufacturers to intermediaries, such as wholesalers and retailers.

push money
Money offered to channel intermediaries to encourage them to "push" products—that is, to encourage other members of the channel to sell the products.

online have proved effective and cost-efficient, generating response rates three to five times higher than off-line promotions. The most effective types of online sales promotions are free merchandise, sweepstakes, free shipping with purchases, and coupons.

Eager to boost traffic, Internet retailers are busy giving away free services or equipment, such as personal computers and travel, to lure consumers not only to their own Web sites, but to the Internet in general. Another goal is to add potential customers to their databases. For example, Heineken USA, Inc. launched the "Headline Hoax" online promotional campaign in which consumers (hoaxers) trick a friend (victim). The hoax is a fake headline with a photograph that looks as though it is on the front page of a major magazine's Web page such as *Maxim* or *The Sporting News*. The hoaxer can choose from a selection of pictures and headlines. One photo shows two football players attacking one another and the tackler has one hand inside the other's shirt and another hand pulling on his shorts; the headline reads "[Person's Name] is too touchy at touch football game." Once the victim opens this e-mail, other friends on the hoaxer's list are alerted to the joke. At the start of the campaign, Heineken had only 5,000 e-mail addresses in its database. Within six months, it had collected an additional 95,000 e-mail addresses. The program has been so successful that it has been updated and expanded to the "Heineken Holiday Headline Hoax" and similar programs.[48]

Marketers have discovered that online coupon distribution provides another vehicle for promoting their products. Online coupons often have a redemption rate of more than 20 percent, as much as 10 times higher than for traditional coupons.[49] In fact, nearly 50 percent of consumers who purchase something online use a coupon or discount promotional code. According to CMS, a coupon-management company, over 2.6 billion coupons are redeemed annually, representing $331 billion in potential consumer savings. Moreover, almost 142 million U.S. consumers use coupons each year, with substantial usage across ethnic and demographic lines.[50] In addition, e-coupons can help marketers lure new customers. Lucky Brand Jeans created a program in which users controlled a green-nosed reindeer that tried to "buck off" various holiday characters for discounts in store and online. The discounts could go up to 30 percent off. The Lucky Buck Off was also augmented with street teams in various cities. Similarly, Staples.com jumped from 23rd to 14th among retail Web sites with the most buyers through an e-coupon promotion that offered $25 off on purchases of $75 or more.[51]

Online versions of loyalty programs are also popping up, and although many types of companies have these programs, the most successful are those run by hotel and airline companies. But other programs such as the Starbucks "I'm In" program, that promoted volunteerism by getting consumers to go online and pledge five hours in return for a free coffee, have also been successful at engaging consumers (**www.starbucks.com**).

REVIEW LEARNING OUTCOME

LO3   Discuss the most common forms of consumer sales promotion

CONSUMER SALES PROMOTION

- Coupons and rebates
- Premiums
- Loyalty marketing program
- Contests and sweepstakes
- Sampling
- P-O-P
- Online

LO 4
TOOLS FOR TRADE SALES PROMOTION

Whereas consumer promotions *pull* a product through the channel by creating demand, trade promotions *push* a product through the distribution channel. (See Chapter 14.) When selling to members of the distribution channel, manufacturers use many of the same sales promotion tools used in consumer promotions—such as sales contests, premiums, and point-of-purchase displays. Several tools, however, are unique to manufacturers and intermediaries:

☛ *Trade allowances:* A trade allowance is a price reduction offered by manufacturers to intermediaries such as wholesalers and retailers. The price reduction or rebate is given in exchange for doing something specific, such as allocating space for a new product or buying something during special periods. For example, a local Best Buy outlet could receive a special discount for running its own promotion on Sony Surround Sound Systems.

☛ *Push money:* Intermediaries receive push money as a bonus for pushing the manufacturer's brand through the distribution channel. Often the push money is directed toward a retailer's salespeople. LinoColor, the leading high-end scanner company, produces a Picture Perfect Rewards catalog filled with merchandise retailers can purchase with points accrued for every LinoColor scanner they sell. The cover of the catalog features a wave runner that was brought to three industry trade shows and given away in a sweepstakes to one of the dealers who had visited all the product displays and passed a quiz. The program resulted in a 26 percent increase in LinoColor sales, and the manufacturer recruited 32 new dealers to carry the product line.[52]

☛ *Training:* Sometimes a manufacturer will train an intermediary's personnel if the product is rather complex—as frequently occurs in the computer and telecommunication industries. For example, representatives of a TV manufacturer like Toshiba may train salespeople in how to demonstrate the new features of the latest models of TVs to consumers. This is particularly helpful when salespeople must explain the features to older consumers who are less technology oriented.

☛ *Free merchandise:* Often a manufacturer offers retailers free merchandise in lieu of quantity discounts. For example, a breakfast cereal manufacturer may throw in one case of free cereal for every 20 cases ordered by the retailer. Occasionally, free merchandise is used as payment for trade allowances normally provided through other sales promotions. Instead of giving a retailer a price reduction for buying a certain quantity of merchandise, the manufacturer may throw in extra merchandise "free" (that is, at a cost that would equal the price reduction).

☛ *Store demonstrations:* Manufacturers can also arrange with retailers to perform an in-store demonstration. Food manufacturers often send representatives to grocery stores and supermarkets to let customers sample a product while shopping. Cosmetic companies also send their representatives to department stores to promote their beauty aids by performing facials and makeovers for customers.

☛ *Business meetings, conventions, and trade shows:* Trade association meetings, conferences, and conventions are an important aspect of sales promotion and a growing, multibillion-dollar market. At these shows, manufacturers, distributors, and other vendors have the chance to display their goods or describe their services to customers and potential customers. Moreover, the cost of closing leads generated at trade shows is often less than 50 percent of those developed in the field.[53] Trade shows have been uniquely effective in introducing new

In a multisensory sampling campaign, Stove Top stuffing workers handed out samples to commuters and shoppers in Chicago. The campaign also included heated bus shelters and bus shelter print ads.

© AP IMAGES/PRNEWSFOTO/KRAFT FOODS INC.; STOVE TOP, AYNSLEY FLOYD

List the most common forms of trade sales promotion

Training

Business Meetings

Conventions

Push Money

Trade Allowance

Store Demonstrations

Free Merchandise

Trade Shows

Trade Sales Promotion Tools

products; they can establish products in the marketplace more quickly than advertising, direct marketing, or sales calls can. Companies participate in trade shows to attract and identify new prospects, serve current customers, introduce new products, enhance corporate image, test the market response to new products, enhance corporate morale, and gather competitive product information.

Trade promotions are popular among manufacturers for many reasons. Trade sales promotion tools help manufacturers gain new distributors for their products, obtain wholesaler and retailer support for consumer sales promotions, build or reduce dealer inventories, and improve trade relations. Car manufacturers annually sponsor dozens of auto shows for consumers. Many of the displays feature interactive computer stations where consumers enter vehicle specifications and get a printout of prices and local dealer names. In return, the local car dealers get the names of good prospects. The shows attract millions of consumers, providing dealers with increased store traffic as well as good leads.

personal selling
A purchase situation involving a personal, paid-for communication between two people in an attempt to influence each other.

LO ⑤
PERSONAL SELLING

As mentioned in Chapter 14, personal selling is direct communication between a sales representative and one or more prospective buyers in an attempt to influence each other in a purchase situation.

In a sense, all businesspeople are sales people. An individual may become a plant manager, a chemist, an engineer, or a member of any profession and yet still have to sell. During a job search, applicants must "sell" themselves to prospective employers in an interview. To reach the top in most organizations, individuals need to sell ideas to peers, superiors, and subordinates. Most important, people must sell themselves and their ideas to just about everyone with whom they have a continuing relationship and to many other people they see only once or twice. Chances are that students majoring in business or marketing will start their professional careers in sales. Even students in non-business majors may pursue a sales career.

Personal selling offers several advantages over other forms of promotion:

- Personal selling provides a detailed explanation or demonstration of the product. This capability is especially needed for complex or new goods and services.

- The sales message can be varied according to the motivations and interests of each prospective customer. Moreover, when the prospect has questions or raises objections, the salesperson is there to provide explanations. In contrast, advertising and sales promotion can respond only to the objections the copywriter thinks are important to customers.

- Personal selling can be directed only to qualified prospects. Other forms of promotion include some unavoidable waste because many people in the audience are not prospective customers.

EXHIBIT 15.2

Comparison of Personal Selling and Advertising/Sales Promotion

Personal selling is more important if . . .	Advertising and sales promotion are more important if . . .
The product has a high value. It is a custom-made product. There are few customers. The product is technically complex. Customers are concentrated.	The product has a low value. It is a standardized product. There are many customers. The product is easy to understand. Customers are geographically dispersed.
Examples: insurance policies, custom windows, airplane engines	**Examples:** soap, magazine subscriptions, cotton T-shirts

☛ Personal selling costs can be controlled by adjusting the size of the sales force (and resulting expenses) in one-person increments. On the other hand, advertising and sales promotion must often be purchased in fairly large amounts.

☛ Perhaps the most important advantage is that personal selling is considerably more effective than other forms of promotion in obtaining a sale and gaining a satisfied customer.

Personal selling may work better than other forms of promotion given certain customer and product characteristics. Generally speaking, personal selling becomes more important as the number of potential customers decreases, as the complexity of the product increases, and as the value of the product grows. (See Exhibit 15.2.) When there are relatively few potential customers and the value of the good or service is relatively high, the time and travel costs of personally visiting each prospect are justifiable. For highly complex goods, such as business jets or private communication systems, a salesperson is needed to determine the prospective customer's needs, explain the product's basic advantages, and propose the exact features and accessories that will meet the client's needs.

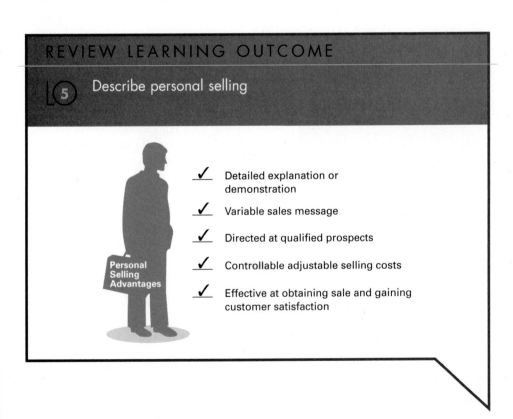

REVIEW LEARNING OUTCOME

LO 5   Describe personal selling

Personal Selling Advantages

✓ Detailed explanation or demonstration

✓ Variable sales message

✓ Directed at qualified prospects

✓ Controllable adjustable selling costs

✓ Effective at obtaining sale and gaining customer satisfaction

relationship selling (consultative selling) A sales practice that involves building, maintaining, and enhancing interactions with customers in order to develop long-term satisfaction through mutually beneficial partnerships.

LO ⑥
RELATIONSHIP SELLING

Until recently, marketing theory and practice concerning personal selling focused almost entirely on a planned presentation to prospective customers for the sole purpose of making the sale. In contrast, modern views of personal selling emphasize the relationship that develops between a salesperson and a buyer. Relationship selling, or consultative selling, is a multistage process that emphasizes personalization and empathy as key ingredients in identifying prospects and developing them as long-term, satisfied customers. The old way was to sell a product, but with relationship selling, the objective is to build long-term branded relationships with consumers/buyers. Thus, the focus is on building mutual trust between the buyer and seller through the delivery of anticipated, long-term, value-added benefits to the buyer.

Relationship or consultative salespeople, therefore, become consultants, partners, and problem solvers for their customers. They strive to build long-term relationships with key accounts by developing trust over time. The emphasis shifts from a one-time sale to a long-term relationship in which the salesperson works with the customer to develop solutions for enhancing the customer's bottom line. Moreover, research has shown that positive customer-salesperson relationships contribute to trust, increased customer loyalty, and the intent to continue the relationship with the salesperson.[54] Thus, relationship selling promotes a win–win situation for both buyer and seller.

The result of relationship selling tends to be loyal customers who purchase from the company time after time. A relationship selling strategy focused on retaining customers costs a company less than constantly prospecting and selling to new customers. Companies that focus on customer retention through high customer service gain 6 percent market share per year, while companies that offer low customer service lose 2 percent market share per year.[55] In fact, it typically costs businesses six times more to gain a new customer than to retain a current one.[56]

Relationship selling is more typical with selling situations for industrial-type goods, such as heavy machinery or computer systems, and services, such as airlines and insurance, than for consumer goods. For example, FedEx Kinko's has built a long-term business relationship with PeopleSoft. The software maker now gives many of its training and educational materials printing jobs to FedEx Kinko's—a deal worth close to $5 million in revenues. FedEx Kinko's forged such a close relationship with the company that their representatives were even invited to sit in on internal planning meetings in PeopleSoft's human resources department at the company's headquarters.

"Webinars" (online seminars lasting about an hour) are a popular way to support relationship selling tasks like lead generation, client support, sales training, and corporate meetings. For example, 3Com, a computer data networking system, held a webinar that was attended by 1,300 executives in 80 countries; the session generated 60 percent of 3Com's five-month lead generation goals. Similarly, SpectraLink, a provider of wireless phone and text messaging systems to Verizon and AT&T, uses webinars to give new-product demonstrations so that channel managers can focus on other tasks. DMReview, a Web-based

> ❝ *It typically costs businesses six times more to gain a new customer than to retain a current one.* ❞

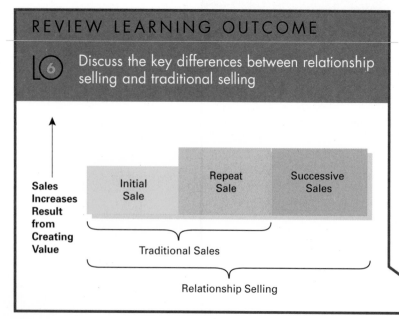

REVIEW LEARNING OUTCOME

LO ⑥ Discuss the key differences between relationship selling and traditional selling

Sales Increases Result from Creating Value

Initial Sale | Repeat Sale | Successive Sales

Traditional Sales

Relationship Selling

EXHIBIT 15.3

Key Differences between Traditional Selling and Relationship Selling

Traditional Personal Selling	Relationship or Consultative Selling
Sell products (goods and services)	Sell advice, assistance, and counsel
Focus on closing sales	Focus on improving the customer's bottom line
Limited sales planning	Consider sales planning as top priority
Spend most contact time telling customers about product	Spend most contact time attempting to build a problem-solving environment with the customer
Conduct "product-specific" needs assessment	Conduct discovery in the full scope of the customer's operations
"Lone wolf" approach to the account	Team approach to the account
Proposals and presentations based on pricing and product features	Proposals and presentations based on profit impact and strategic benefits to the customer
Sales follow-up is short term, focused on product delivery	Sales follow-up is long term, focused on long-term relationship enhancement

Source: Robert M. Peterson, Patrick L. Schul, and George H. Lucas, Jr., "Consultative Selling: Walking the Walk in the New Selling Environment," National Conference on Sales Management, *Proceedings*, March 1996.

portal on technology, has found webinars to be so successful that it offers them continuously "on demand" on business intelligence and data mining topics. The webinars are cosponsored by major firms in insurance, banking, health care, and related fields. To maximize the opportunities provided by webcasting, marketers are using technology that effectively delivers content to other audiences using devices such as mobile phones, TiVo-type digital video recorders, and game consoles.[57]

Exhibit 15.3 lists the key differences between traditional personal selling and relationship or consultative selling. These differences will become more apparent as we explore the personal selling process later in the chapter.

STEPS IN THE SELLING PROCESS

Although personal selling may sound like a relatively simple task, completing a sale actually requires several steps. The sales process, or sales cycle, is simply the set of steps a salesperson goes through to sell a particular product or service. The sales process or cycle can be unique for each product or service, depending on the features of the product or service, characteristics of customer segments, and internal processes in place within the firm, such as how leads are gathered.

Some sales take only a few minutes, but others may take much longer to complete. Sales of technical products, such as a Boeing or Airbus airplane, and customized goods and services typically take many months, perhaps even years, to complete. On the other end of the spectrum, sales of less technical products such as copy machines or office supplies are generally more routine and may take only a few days. Whether a salesperson spends a few minutes or a few years on a sale, these are the seven basic steps in the personal selling process:

1. Generating leads

2. Qualifying leads

3. Approaching the customer and probing needs

4. Developing and proposing solutions

sales process (sales cycle)
The set of steps a salesperson goes through in a particular organization to sell a particular product or service.

lead generation (prospecting)
Identification of those firms and
people most likely to buy the seller's
offerings.

5. Handling objections

6. Closing the sale

7. Following up

Like other forms of promotion, these steps of selling follow the AIDA concept discussed in Chapter 14. Once a salesperson has located a prospect with the authority to buy, he or she tries to get the prospect's attention. A thorough needs assessment turned into an effective sales proposal and presentation should generate interest. After developing the customer's initial desire (preferably during the presentation of the sales proposal), the salesperson seeks action in the close by trying to get an agreement to buy. Follow-up after the sale, the final step in the selling process, not only lowers cognitive dissonance (refer to Chapter 6) but also may open up opportunities to discuss future sales. Effective follow-up will also lead to repeat business in which the process may start all over again at the needs assessment step.

Traditional selling and relationship selling follow the same basic steps. They differ in the relative importance placed on key steps in the process. (See Exhibit 15.4.) Traditional selling efforts are transaction oriented, focusing on generating as many leads as possible, making as many presentations as possible, and closing as many sales as possible. Minimal effort is placed on asking questions to identify customer needs and wants or matching these needs and wants to the benefits of the product or service. In contrast, salespeople practicing relationship selling emphasize an up-front investment in the time and effort needed to uncover each customer's specific needs and wants and match the product or service offering to them as closely as possible. By doing their homework up front, relationship salespeople create the conditions necessary for a relatively straightforward close. Let's look at each step of the selling process individually.

Generating Leads

Initial groundwork must precede communication between the potential buyer and the salesperson. Lead generation, or prospecting, is the identification of the firms and people most likely to buy the seller's offerings. These firms or people become "sales leads" or "prospects."

Sales leads can be obtained in several different ways, most notably through advertising, trade shows and conventions, or direct-mail and telemarketing programs. One accounting firm used direct mail, telephone, sales visits, and seminars in a four-step process aimed at generating business-to-business leads. The initial step was a direct-mail piece, in the form of an introductory letter from a firm partner. The second piece, sent one month later, was a black-and-white direct-mail circular with company contact information. The third step was a follow-up call from a firm partner to arrange a meeting. In the last stage, partners contacted prospects who had initially declined appointments and invited them to attend a free tax seminar the following month. Of the 1,100 businesses targeted, 200 prospects set up meetings. Favorable publicity also helps to create leads. Company records of past client purchases are another excellent source of leads. Many sales professionals are also securing valuable leads from their firm's Internet Web site. For example, Chrysler's use of interactive media to create ongoing interaction with online consumers is paying off. The company recently sponsored 42 online video

EXHIBIT 15.4

Relative Amount of Time Spent in Key Steps of the Selling Process

Key Selling Steps	Traditional Selling	Relationship/ Consultative Selling
Generating leads	High	Low
Qualifying leads	Low	High
Approaching the customer and probing needs	Low	High
Developing and proposing solutions	Low	High
Handling objections	High	Low
Closing the sale	High	Low
Following up	Low	High

games featuring Chrysler, Jeep, and Dodge vehicles, generating more than 10,000 sales leads among the estimated 3.5 million consumers who downloaded the games. The company generates an estimated 40,000 sales leads monthly through its Web site and other online venues.[58]

Another way to gather a lead is through a referral— a recommendation from a customer or business associate. The advantages of referrals over other forms of prospecting include highly qualified leads, higher closing rates, larger initial transactions, and shorter sales cycles. Simply put, the salesperson and the company can earn more money in less time when prospecting using referrals. Referrals typically are as much as ten times more productive in generating sales than are cold calls. Unfortunately, although most clients are willing to give referrals, many salespeople do not ask for them. Effective sales training can help to overcome this reluctance to ask for referrals. To increase the number of referrals, some companies even pay or send small gifts to customers or suppliers that provide referrals.

Networking is using friends, business contacts, coworkers, acquaintances, and fellow members in professional and civic organizations to identify potential clients. Indeed, a number of national networking clubs have been started for the sole purpose of generating leads and providing valuable business advice. The networking clubs usually have between 15 and 30 members in noncompeting business categories. During weekly breakfast or lunch meetings, each member is allowed to talk about the company he or she represents for an allotted period of time. Then members exchange lead cards. Research suggests that, on average, chapter members see an increase in business volume of between 16 and 25 percent after they've been with their group for three to six months. Increasingly, sales professionals are also using online networking sites such as Ryze, LinkedIn, and The Ladders to connect with targeted leads and clients around the world 24 hours a day. Some of LinkedIn's estimated 4.8 million users have reported response rates between 50 and 60 percent, versus 3 percent from direct marketing efforts.[59]

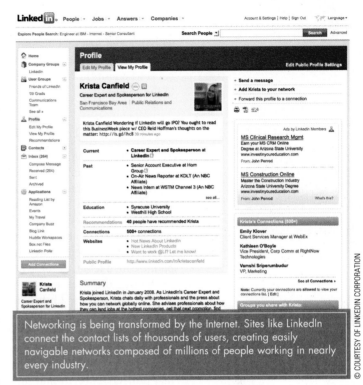

Networking is being transformed by the Internet. Sites like LinkedIn connect the contact lists of thousands of users, creating easily navigable networks composed of millions of people working in nearly every industry.

Qualifying Leads

When a prospect shows interest in learning more about a product, the salesperson has the opportunity to follow up, or qualify, the lead. Personally visiting unqualified prospects wastes valuable salesperson time and company resources. Often many leads go unanswered because salespeople are given no indication as to how qualified the leads are in terms of interest and ability to purchase. Unqualified prospects give vague or incomplete answers to a salesperson's specific questions, try to evade questions on budgets, and request changes in standard procedures like prices or terms of sale. In contrast, qualified leads are real prospects that answer questions, value your time, and are realistic about money and when they are prepared to buy. Salespersons given accurate information on qualified leads are more than twice as likely to follow up.[60]

Lead qualification involves determining whether the prospect has three things: a recognized need, willingness to see a salesperson, and buying power. Lead qualification is often handled by a telemarketing group or a sales support person who prequalifies the lead for the salesperson. But companies are increasingly using Web sites to qualify leads. When leads are qualified online, companies want visitors to register, indicate the products and services they are interested in, and provide information on their time frame and resources. Leads from the Internet can then be prioritized

referral
A recommendation to a salesperson from a customer or business associate.

networking
A process of finding out about potential clients from friends, business contacts, coworkers, acquaintances, and fellow members in professional and civic organizations.

lead qualification
Determination of a sales prospect's (1) recognized need, (2) buying power, and (3) receptivity and accessibility.

preapproach
A process that describes the "homework" that must be done by a salesperson before he or she contacts a prospect.

needs assessment
A determination of the customer's specific needs and wants, and the range of options the customer has for satisfying them.

sales proposal
A formal written document or professional presentation that outlines how the salesperson's product or service will meet or exceed the prospect's needs.

(those indicating a short time frame, for instance, given a higher priority) and then transferred to salespeople. Often Web site visitors can be enticed to answer questions with offers of free merchandise or information. Enticing visitors to register also enables companies to customize future electronic interactions—for example, by giving prospects who visit the Web site their choice from a menu of products tailored specifically to their needs.

Approaching the Customer and Probing Needs

Before approaching customers, the salesperson should learn as much as possible about the prospect's organization and its buyers. This process, called the preapproach, describes the "homework" that must be done by the salesperson before contacting the prospect. This may include visiting company Web sites, consulting standard reference sources such as Moody's, Standard & Poor's, or Dun & Bradstreet, or contacting acquaintances or others who may have information about the prospect. Another preapproach task is to determine whether the actual approach should be a personal visit, a phone call, a letter, or some other form of communication.

During the sales approach, the salesperson either talks to the prospect or secures an appointment for a future time in which to probe the prospect further as to his or her needs. Relationship selling theorists suggest that salespeople should begin developing mutual trust with their prospect during the approach. Salespeople should use the approach as a way of introducing themselves and their company and products. They must sell themselves before they can sell the product. Small talk that projects sincerity and some suggestion of friendship is encouraged because it builds rapport with the prospect, but remarks that could be construed as insincere should be avoided.

The salesperson's ultimate goal during the approach is to conduct a needs assessment to find out as much as possible about the prospect's situation. This involves interviewing the customer to determine his or her specific needs and wants and the range of options the customer has for satisfying them. The salesperson should be determining how to maximize the fit between what he or she can offer and what the prospective customer wants. In conducting a needs assessment, consultative salespeople must learn about the product or service, the customers and their needs, the competition, and the industry. Using this information, a customer profile is created.

Creating a *customer profile* during the approach helps salespeople optimize their time and resources. This profile is then used to help develop an intelligent analysis of the prospect's needs in preparation for the next step, developing and proposing solutions. Customer profile information is typically stored and manipulated using sales force automation software packages designed for use on laptop computers. Sales force automation software provides sales reps with a computerized and efficient method of collecting customer information for use during the entire sales process. Further, customer and sales data stored in a computer database can be easily shared among sales team members. The information can also be appended with industry statistics, sales or meeting notes, billing data, and other information that may be pertinent to the prospect or the prospect's company. The more salespeople know about their prospects, the better they can meet their prospects' needs.

Developing and Proposing Solutions

Once the salesperson has gathered the appropriate information about the client's needs and wants, the next step is to determine whether his or her company's products or services match the needs of the prospective customer. The salesperson then develops a solution, or possibly several solutions, in which the salesperson's product or service solves the client's problems or meets a specific need.

These solutions are typically offered to the client in the form of a sales proposal delivered during a sales presentation. A sales proposal is a written document or professional presentation that outlines how the company's product or service will meet or exceed the client's needs. The sales presentation is the formal meeting in which the salesperson has the opportunity to present the sales proposal. The presentation should be explicitly tied to the prospect's expressed needs. Further, the prospect should be involved in the presentation by being encouraged to participate in demonstrations or by exposure to computer exercises, slides, video or audio, flip charts, photographs, and the like.

Technology has become an important part of presenting solutions for many salespeople. Pen manufacturer BIC uses the Internet to connect with its wholesale and convenience store customers. Before launching BIClink.com, BIC received 80 percent of its order volume by fax. Processing these orders was time-consuming, and the orders often were filled with errors. BIClink.com has eliminated the potential for errors and made it easier and faster to validate purchase order numbers, ship dates, case quantities, and pricing. When customers sign on (through a secure, password-protected system), the welcome screen is personalized with their company's name and the name of their BIC rep. On placing an order, customers receive both a hard copy and e-mail confirmation statement with the salesperson's name and contact information including e-mail, voice mail, phone, and fax numbers. Virtually all of BIC's customers now order online.[61]

Because the salesperson often has only one opportunity to present solutions, the quality of both the sales proposal and presentation can make or break the sale. Salespeople must be able to present the proposal and handle any customer objections confidently and professionally. For a powerful presentation, salespeople must be well prepared, use direct eye contact, ask open-ended questions, be poised, use hand gestures and voice inflection, focus on the customer's needs, incorporate visual elements that impart valuable information, know how to operate the audio/visual or computer equipment being used for the presentation, make sure the equipment works, and practice, practice, practice.[62] Nothing dies faster than a boring presentation. If the salesperson doesn't have a convincing and confident manner, then the prospect will very often forget the information. Prospects take in body language, voice patterns, dress, and body type. Customers are more likely to remember how salespeople present themselves than what they say.

Handling Objections

Rarely does a prospect say "I'll buy it" right after a presentation. Instead, the prospect often raises objections or asks questions about the proposal and the product. The potential buyer may insist that the price is too high, that he or she does not have enough information to make a decision, or that the good or service will not satisfy the present need. The buyer may also lack confidence in the seller's organization or product.

One of the first lessons every salesperson learns is that objections to the product should not be taken personally as confrontations or insults. Rather, salespeople should view objections as requests for information. A good salesperson considers objections a legitimate part of the purchase decision. To handle objections effectively, the salesperson should anticipate specific objections, such as concerns about price, fully investigate the objection with the customer, be aware of what the competition is offering, and, above all, stay calm. When Dell introduced its direct selling model, salespeople anticipated that customers would worry that they would not receive the same level of service and dedication as they would get from a reseller. As a result, the salespeople included assurances about service and support following the sale in their sales presentations.

Zig Ziglar, a renowned sales trainer, created a popular method for handling objections: "When an objection occurs, always use the fundamentals of FEEL, FELT, FOUND. It gives you an extra cushion of time and allows the prospect to identify with others." For example: "I see how

sales presentation
A formal meeting in which the salesperson presents a sales proposal to a prospective buyer.

© PETER LILLJA/GETTY IMAGES

negotiation
The process during which both the salesperson and the prospect offer special concessions in an attempt to arrive at a sales agreement.

follow-up
The final step of the selling process, in which the salesperson ensures that delivery schedules are met, that the goods or services perform as promised, and that the buyers' employees are properly trained to use the products.

you FEEL! Others have FELT the same way too until they FOUND. . . ." Imagine a copy machine salesperson pitching his machine to a doctor. The doctor might say, "The copy machine seems to be very expensive." Using the Zig Ziglar method the salesperson would respond, "I see how you *feel*. Other doctors have *felt* the same way until they *found* out how much money they were saving after the first year."[63]

Often salespeople can use objections to close the sale. If the customer tries to pit suppliers against each other to drive down the price, the salesperson should be prepared to point out weaknesses in the competitor's offer and stand by the quality in his or her own proposal.

Closing the Sale

At the end of the presentation, the salesperson should ask the customer how he or she would like to proceed. If the customer exhibits signs that he or she is ready to purchase and all questions have been answered and objections have been met, then the salesperson can try to close the sale. Customers often give signals during or after the presentation that they are ready to buy or are not interested. Examples include changes in facial expressions, gestures, and questions asked. The salesperson should look for these signals and respond appropriately.

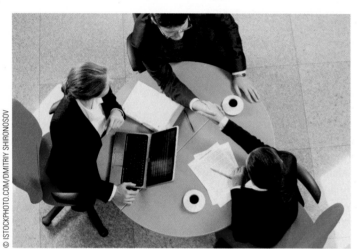

Closing requires courage and skill. Naturally, the salesperson wants to avoid rejection, and asking for a sale carries with it the risk of a negative answer. A salesperson should keep an open mind when asking for the sale and be prepared for either a yes or a no. Rarely is a sale closed on the first call. In fact, the typical salesperson makes several hundred sales calls a year, many of which are repeat calls to the same client in an attempt to make a sale. Some salespeople may negotiate with large accounts for several years before closing a sale. As you can see, building a good relationship with the customer is very important. Often, if the salesperson has developed a strong relationship with the customer, only minimal efforts are needed to close a sale.

Negotiation often plays a key role in the closing of the sale. Negotiation is the process during which both the salesperson and the prospect offer special concessions in an attempt to arrive at a sales agreement. For example, the salesperson may offer a price cut, free installation, free service, or a trial order. Effective negotiators, however, avoid using price as a negotiation tool because cutting price directly affects a company's profitability. Because companies spend millions on advertising and product development to create value, when salespeople give in to price negotiations too quickly, it decreases the value of the product. Instead, effective salespeople should emphasize value to the customer, rendering price a nonissue. Salespeople should also be prepared to ask for trade-offs and try to avoid giving unilateral concessions. If you're making only a 30 percent margin on a product, and you need at least a 40 percent margin, raise your prices or drop the product. Moreover, if the customer asks for a 5 percent discount, the salesperson should ask for something in return, such as higher volume or more flexibility in delivery schedules.

Following Up

Unfortunately, many salespeople have the attitude that making the sale is all that's important. Once the sale is made, they can forget about their customers. They are wrong. Salespeople's responsibilities do not end with making the sales and placing the orders. One of the most important aspects of their jobs is follow-up—the final step in the selling process, in which they must ensure that delivery schedules are met, that

© ISTOCKPHOTO.COM/DMITRIY SHIRONOSOV

PART 4   Promotion and Pricing Decisions

the goods or services perform as promised, and that the buyers' employees are properly trained to use the products.

In the traditional sales approach, follow-up with the customer is generally limited to successful product delivery and performance. A basic goal of relationship selling is to motivate customers to come back, again and again, by developing and nurturing long-term relationships. Most businesses depend on repeat sales, and repeat sales depend on thorough and continued follow-up by the salesperson. Finding a new customer is far more expensive than retaining an existing customer. When customers feel abandoned, cognitive dissonance arises and repeat sales decline. Today, this issue is more pertinent than ever because customers are far less loyal to brands and vendors. Buyers are more inclined to look for the best deal, especially in the case of poor after-the-sale follow-up. More and more buyers favor building a relationship with sellers. One Farmers Insurance agent suggests following up on insurance claims with a question to determine the customer's level of satisfaction. For example, he may ask, "Were you happy with the way your claim was handled?" Depending on the response, the agent can either get a referral from the customer or try to fix any problems so that the customer does not choose another agency in the future. This agent also makes telephone and personal follow-up visits after a marriage, death, birth, or birthday in the customer's family. These visits are used as sales opportunities to cross-sell products such as life insurance.[64]

Automated e-mail follow-up marketing—a combination of sales automation and Internet technology—is enhancing customer satisfaction as well as bringing in more business for some marketers. Here's how it works: After the initial contact with a prospect, a software program automatically sends a series of personalized e-mails over a period. CollegeRecruiter.com is one company taking advantage of this technology. The company posts ads for businesses recruiting recent college graduates on its Web site and has seen phenomenal results from auto-response marketing. Prospects start receiving a series of e-mails once they have visited the site and requested advertising rates. The first message goes out immediately. The next two go out in 4 to 11 days. From there, e-mails go out monthly. Using the automated follow-up e-mail system has helped CollegeRecruiter.com become the highest traffic career site used by job-hunting students and recent graduates. Its Web site regularly posts more than 100,000 job openings.[65]

REVIEW LEARNING OUTCOME

LO 7 List the steps in the selling process

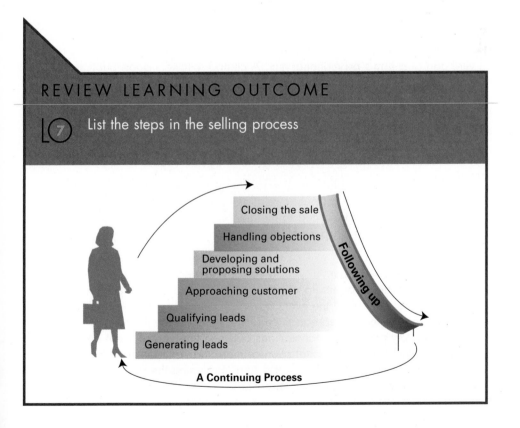

Closing the sale
Handling objections
Developing and proposing solutions
Approaching customer
Qualifying leads
Generating leads

Following up

A Continuing Process

$5 million
▲ cost of creating, producing, and placing a national TV advertising campaign

new products introduced ▶ **1,200**

2 ◀ percentage of coupons that are redeemed

20 ◀ percentage of online coupons that are redeemed

loyalty program memberships in the U.S.
1.5 billion ◀

health clubs in which Dunkin' Donuts distributed samples of its Latte Lite drink ▶ **200**

percentage of market share gained each by companies with high customer service ▶ **6**

percentage of market share lost by companies with low customer service ▶ **2**

online video games sponsored by Chrysler and featuring their vehicles ▶ **42**

job openings on CollegeRecruiter.com ▼
100,000

REVIEW AND APPLICATIONS

LO ① Discuss the role of public relations in the promotional mix. Public relations is a vital part of a firm's promotional mix. A company fosters good publicity to enhance its image and promote its products. Popular public relations tools include new-product publicity, product placements, consumer education, sponsorships, and Web sites. An equally important aspect of public relations is managing unfavorable publicity to minimize damage to a firm's image.

1.1 How can advertising and publicity work together? Give an example.

1.2 As the new public relations director for a sportswear company, you have been asked to set public relations objectives for a new line of athletic shoes to be introduced to the teen market. Draft a memo outlining the objectives you propose for the shoe's introduction and your reasons for them.

1.3 Review the newspapers in your area for one week. Try to review several and varied newspapers (local, campus, cultural, countercultural, etc.) During this period, cut out all the event advertisements that list sponsors. Once you have your collection, spread them out so you can see them all at once. Identify any patterns or connections between the type of event and its sponsors. Identify companies that sponsor more than one event. What do sponsors tell you about target markets? After analyzing the ads, write a brief paragraph summarizing your discoveries.

Define and state the objectives of sales promotion. Sales promotion consists of those marketing communication activities, other than advertising, personal selling, and public relations, in which a short-term incentive motivates consumers or members of the distribution channel to purchase a good or service immediately, either by lowering the price or by adding value. The main objectives of sales promotion are to increase trial purchases, consumer inventories, and repeat purchases. Sales promotion is also used to encourage brand switching and to build brand loyalty. Sales promotion supports advertising activities.

2.1 What is the primary factor that determines sales promotion objectives? Name some different types of sales promotion techniques, and explain the type of customer they are intended to influence.

2.2 You have recently been assigned the task of developing promotional techniques to introduce your company's new product, a Cajun chicken sandwich. Advertising spending is limited, so the introduction will include only some low-budget sales promotion techniques. Write a sales promotion plan that will increase awareness of your new sandwich and allow your customer base to try it risk-free.

Discuss the most common forms of consumer sales promotion. Consumer forms of sales promotion include coupons and rebates, premiums, loyalty marketing programs, contests and sweepstakes, sampling, and point-of-purchase displays. Coupons are certificates entitling consumers to an immediate price reduction when they purchase a product or service. Coupons are a particularly good way to encourage product trial and brand switching. Similar to coupons, rebates provide purchasers with a price reduction, although it is not immediate. To receive a rebate, consumers generally must mail in a rebate form with a proof of purchase. Premiums offer an extra item or incentive to the consumer for buying a product or service. Premiums reinforce the consumer's purchase decision, increase consumption, and persuade nonusers to switch brands. Rewarding loyal customers is the basis of loyalty marketing programs. Loyalty programs are extremely effective at building long-term, mutually beneficial relationships between a company and its key customers. Contests and sweepstakes are generally designed to create interest, often to encourage brand switching. Because consumers perceive risk in trying new products, sampling is an effective method for gaining new customers. Finally, point-of-purchase displays set up at the retailer's location build traffic, advertise the product, and induce impulse buying.

3.1 Discuss how different forms of sales promotion can erode or build brand loyalty. If a company's objective is to enhance customer loyalty to its products, what sales promotion techniques will be most appropriate?

3.2 What forms of consumer sales promotion might induce impulse purchases? What forms of sales promotion are more effective at persuading consumers to switch brands?

3.3 Consider the different consumer sales promotion tools. Give an example of how each type of tool has influenced you to purchase—or purchase more of—a product or service.

3.4 Not everyone thinks supermarket shopper cards are a bargain. Go to **www.nocards.org** and read several pages. Is the information on the site compelling? What do you think of shopper cards? You may want to use the Internet to research shopper cards in more detail before forming an opinion.

3.5 Contests and sweepstakes are very common in the entertainment industry. Radio stations have contests almost weekly (some daily); local television morning shows quiz viewers on trivia; even movies offer sweepstakes in conjunction with film previews and premiere nights. Think of a television or radio program unlikely to have contests or sweepstakes (things like *Cops, The View, Scooby Doo,* or your local classical music radio station, for example). Once you have chosen your program, design a contest or sweepstake to promote the show or the channel on which it airs. List the objectives, and describe the rationale behind each part of your promotion.

3.6 How can uPromote.com help you with your sales promotions efforts (visit **www.upromote.com**)? What kind of marketing budget would you need to take advantage of its services? What kind of company would be best served by uPromote.com?

List the most common forms of trade sales promotion. Manufacturers use many of the same sales promotion tools used in consumer promotions, such as sales contests, premiums, and point-of-purchase displays. In addition, manufacturers and channel intermediaries use several unique promotional strategies: trade allowances, push money, training programs, free merchandise, store demonstrations, and meetings, conventions, and trade shows.

4.1 How does trade sales promotion differ from consumer sales promotion? How is it the same?

4.2 What are the main forms of trade sales promotion? Which type might be most enticing to a grocery store manager? To a buyer for a major electronics chain?

4.3 Form a team of three to five students. As marketing managers, you are in charge of selling Dixie cups. Design a consumer sales promotion plan and trade sales promotion plan for your product. Incorporate at least three different promotion tools into each plan. Share your results with the other teams in the class.

Describe personal selling. Personal selling is direct communication between a sales representative and one or more prospective buyers in an attempt to influence each other in a purchase situation. Broadly speaking, all businesspeople use personal selling to promote themselves and their ideas. Personal selling offers several advantages over other forms of promotion. Personal selling allows salespeople to thoroughly explain and demonstrate a product. Salespeople have the flexibility to tailor a sales proposal to the needs and preferences of individual customers. Personal selling is more efficient than other forms of promotion because salespeople target qualified prospects and avoid wasting efforts on unlikely buyers. Personal selling affords greater managerial control over promotion costs. Finally, personal selling is the most effective method of closing a sale and producing satisfied customers.

5.1 Discuss the role of personal selling in promoting products. What advantages does personal selling offer over other forms of promotion?

5.2 What are the major advantages of personal selling to the company selling a product? What are the advantages to the person or company buying the product?

Discuss the key differences between relationship selling and traditional selling. Relationship selling is the practice of building, maintaining, and enhancing interactions with customers in order to develop long-term satisfaction through mutually beneficial partnerships. Traditional selling, on the other hand, is transaction focused. That is, the salesperson is most concerned with making onetime sales and moving on to the next prospect. Salespeople practicing relationship selling spend more time understanding a prospect's needs and developing solutions to meet those needs.

6.1 What are the key differences between relationship selling and traditional methods of selling? What types of products or services do you think would be conducive to relationship selling?

6.2 Based on the key differences between traditional and relationship selling, which type of sales approach would you use as a salesperson? Do the different approaches require different personal strengths or attributes?

List the steps in the selling process. The selling process is composed of seven basic steps: (1) generating leads, (2) qualifying leads, (3) approaching the customer and probing needs, (4) developing and proposing solutions, (5) handling objections, (6) closing the sale, and (7) following up.

7.1 You are a new salesperson for a well-known medical software company, and one of your clients is a large group of physicians. You have just arranged an initial meeting with the office manager. Develop a list of questions you might ask at this meeting to uncover the group's specific needs.

7.2 What does sales follow-up entail? Why is it an essential step in the selling process, particularly from the perspective of relationship selling? How does it relate to cognitive dissonance?

7.3 How many ways can zapdata (**www.zapdata.com**) benefit salespeople? Which of its services would be most useful to marketing managers? Other businesspeople?

7.4 Consider each step in the selling process. Which steps could be conducted through technology (Internet, webinars, etc.)? Which are most important to handle "face-to-face"?

KEY TERMS

cause-related marketing	528	negotiation	548	relationship selling	
consumer sales		networking	545	(consultative selling)	542
promotion	530	personal selling	540	sales presentation	547
coupon	532	point-of-purchase display		sales process (sales	
crisis management	529	(P-O-P)	537	cycle)	543
follow-up	548	preapproach	546	sales promotion	530
frequent buyer program	534	premium	534	sales proposal	546
lead generation		product placement	526	sampling	536
(prospecting)	544	public relations	525	sponsorship	527
lead qualification	545	publicity	525	trade allowance	539
loyalty marketing		push money	539	trade sales promotion	530
program	534	rebate	533		
needs assessment	546	referral	545		

EXERCISES

APPLICATION EXERCISE

Have you ever waited forever to get a fast-food hamburger? Have you even been left to languish in a dressing room by a salesperson who left for a coffee break? If so, you already know that sales and customer service are integral parts of marketing. While you are working on this chapter, keep a journal of your personal sales and/or customer service experiences with local merchants. Don't ignore the details. Even such things as how crowded a store or restaurant is when you visit may affect your perceptions of the service you received.[66]

Activities

1. Keep your journal for a week, recording all sales and service transactions, if possible, on the day they occur.

2. At the end of the week, examine your journal, and pick the most noteworthy entry. Provide the basic information about the transaction: company where it occurred, type of transaction (purchase, return, complaint, etc.), type of good or service involved, and so forth.

3. Once you have the outlined the situation, evaluate the experience. Use the information about selling in this chapter as support for your evaluation. For example, did the salesperson seem to treat the situation as an individual, discrete transaction, or did he or she seem interested in building a relationship?

4. Finally, make recommendations as to how the company can improve its sales and/or service. Suggestions should be logical and achievable (meaning you have to consider the cost of implementing your suggestion).

ETHICS EXERCISE

Sally Burke works for Hi-Tech Electronics. Her responsibilities include selecting items to advertise in her company's Sunday newspaper FSIs. One hot item is a 50-inch flat-panel plasma TV. The list price is $4,999, but her manager tells her to advertise it at $3,999, since customers can apply for a $1,000 mail-in rebate. The advertised price has attracted many people to buy the TV; however, Sally has heard several complaints from customers who found the rebate process unusually complex and were denied a rebate because the manufacturer claimed they hadn't provided the required information. She would prefer to advertise the "real" list price, knowing that customers are not guaranteed to receive a rebate.

Questions

1. Is it unethical to advertise products at their post-rebate price in order to increase sales? Why or why not? What is another sales promotion method Hi-Tech Electronics could use to persuade customers to buy their plasma TV at the store?

2. Rebate programs are commonly used by electronics manufacturers because the rebates arouse consumers' interest in buying products; yet only half of purchasers ultimately claim their rebates. Is a rebate program itself unethical if the manufacturer knows consumers are unlikely to receive their money?

3. Visit a local electronics store—or Web site—and find a product being sold with a mail-in rebate offer. Are the rebate instructions clear? Would you take the time to complete the process?

MARKETING PLAN EXERCISE

For the next stage of the strategic planning process you'll focus on your chosen company's sales promotion and personal selling decisions. Use the following exercises to guide you through the final elements of Part 4 of your strategic marketing plan:

1.   Evaluate or create printed materials for you chosen company (such as data sheets, brochures, stationery, or rate cards). Does the literature sufficiently answer questions? Provide enough information for further contact? Effectively promote product features and customer service? Note a differential or competitive advantage?

2.   Think about ways your promotions could turn a first-time customer or deal-hunter into a repeat, loyal customer. Which sales promotion tools should your company use? What trade shows could your firm attend? Search the Eventline database for trade shows appropriate to your firm. Order media kits and explore the feasibility and costs of attending those trade shows. For a listing of tradeshows, go to **www.exhibitornet.com** and look for the directory of shows, or the Trade Show News Network at **www.tsnn.com**.

3.   What other sales promotion tools could your firm use? What are the costs? What is the impact of using these methods on pricing?

4.   Will you need a sales force? Identify and justify the best type (internal or external) and structure (product, customer, geographic, etc.) for your firm's sales force. You may find that in e-marketing, a sales force is more of a customer service and customer relations management tool. True selling activities may be limited to selling and buying online media space and links. In many circumstances, forming strategic partnerships and distribution deals have replaced traditional sales in the Internet space. What types of alliances and partnerships will you pursue? Will you work with other online firms, offline firms, or both?

CASE STUDY: RON POPEIL

© ROSE ALCORN

RON POPEIL WHEELS, DEALS, HAS MASS APPEAL

At age 71, Ron "Ronco" Popeil is an avid inventor, tireless entrepreneur, clever marketer, and master salesman all in one. He just happens to be an American icon, too. The godfather of the infomercial, Popeil even has his famous Veg-O-Matic on display in the Smithsonian Institution as an American cultural artifact. His other famous products include the food dehydrator, the Ronco spray gun, and the Popeil Pocket Fisherman.

As a teenager, Popeil helped his father sell his kitchen gadgets at local Woolworth's and later, in the 1950s, on the Chicago fair circuit. That is probably why his famous shtick, which included such memorable catchphrases as "But wait, there's more," "Priced so low," and "Operators are standing by," always seemed like a blend between sincere eccentric inventor and excitable carnival barker. The combination suited him well and brought him enough financial success that he could afford to take his act to television. In the 1960s, he incorporated Ronco, and its name became synonymous with gadgets like the smokeless ashtray and Mr. Microphone.

Regardless of the product he is selling or the catchy pitch phrases he invents on the fly to sell them, Popeil is always sincere. "The easiest thing to do in the world is to sell a product I believe in," he has said. "If I spent two years creating a product, conceiving it, tinkering with it, I can get up and sell it. Who can sell it better than the guy who invented it?" Len Green, a professor in entrepreneurship at Babson College, says, "Ron is one of a kind. He is different from the rest because he not only invents, he sells. Most entrepreneurs come up with a concept and then give it to others to manufacture or sell. He's his own best salesman."

Though Popeil has suffered his fair share of flops, like spray-on hair and a brief bankruptcy in 1987, he has always managed to bounce back. Returning from bankruptcy, he relaunched the popular food dehydrator in 1990, and 8 years later he designed and sold his most successful product ever, the Showtime rotisserie BBQ. Having sold over seven million units for four installments of $39.95 each, the rotisserie alone has grossed over $1 billion in sales. During the taping of the infomercial for that product, the live studio audience was treated to yet another of Popeil's catchphrases that has become part of the fabric of American speech. "Just set it and forget it!" is now used to sell all kinds of non-Popeil products from VCRs and digital video recorders to ovens and coffeemaker.

Through the medium of television, Popeil was able to reach tens of millions of people. With an innate ability to invent or improve on everyday household products, his live product demonstrations captured the imaginations and dollars of generations of consumers. In 1976, he was even the subject of what was probably Dan Aykroyd's most famous bit on *Saturday Night Live*. Parodying Popeil, Aykroyd hawked "Rovco's Super Bass-O-Matic '76," which was capable of turning a bass or any other "small aquatic creature" into liquid without any "scaling, cutting or gutting."

Having recently sold Ronco to an investment group for over $55 million and accumulated a personal net worth of over $100 million, Popeil has had the last laugh. He will continue to serve as a product developer, pitchman, and consultant for the new company and already promises an even bigger hit than the Showtime rotisserie. Having identified a market of over 20 million Americans who fry turkeys every year, Popeil says he has a new fryer on the way that will make it possible to safely fry a 20-pound turkey in 70 minutes—indoors. Given that he has created over 150 products and invented personal selling via the mass marketing medium, there is little reason to doubt him.

As Barbara Gross, professor of marketing at California State University, Northridge, states, "His success speaks for itself; probably that has more to do with his personality. He's comfortable and sincere. He comes across like he really believes in it. When you hear him talk, you never feel like he's lying to you."[67]

Source: "Ron Popeil, He of the Pocket Fisherman and Spray-On Hair, Has Perfected His Formula for Success: Invent, Market, and Sell with a Passion," *Business Week Online*, October 3, 2005; Brent Hopkins, "How Ron Popeil Invented Himself", *Knight-Ridder/Tribune Business News*, August 31, 2005; Matt Myerhoff, "Informercial King Sells Company, Ronco Goes Public for Expansion", *Los Angeles Business Journal*, July 29, 2005, p. 1; http://snltranscripts.jt.org/75/75qbassamatic.phtml.

Questions

1. What does Ron Popeil bring to personal selling that makes him so effective?

2. What trade sales promotion tools does he use? Why does he use sales promotion tools when he is selling direct to consumers?

3. Explain how Popeil's selling tactics allow him to achieve the desired objectives of sales promotions.

4. Do you think it is likely that America will ever see someone like Ron Popeil in the future? Why or why not?

COMPANY CLIPS

VANS—OFF THE WALL PROMOTIONS

Steve Van Doren, son of Vans founder, is the self-proclaimed "ambassador of fun" at Vans. Because the company doesn't want to discount its products or lower its

CAFTA See *Central America Free Trade Agreement.*

cannibalization A situation that occurs when sales of a new product cut into sales of a firm's existing products.

capital-intensive Using more capital than labor in the production process.

captive brand A brand that carries no evidence of a retailer's affiliation, is manufactured by a third party, and is sold exclusively at the retailers.

cash cow In the portfolio matrix, a business unit that usually generates more cash than it needs to maintain its market share.

casuist ethical theory A theory that compares a current ethical dilemma with examples of similar ethical dilemmas and their outcomes.

category killers Specialty discount stores that heavily dominate their narrow merchandise segment.

cause-related marketing The cooperative marketing efforts between a "for-profit" firm and a "nonprofit organization."

Central America Free Trade Agreement (CAFTA) A trade agreement, instituted in 2005, that includes Costa Rica, the Dominican Republic, El Salvador, Guatemala, Honduras, Nicaragua, and the United States.

central-location telephone (CLT) facility A specially designed phone room used to conduct telephone interviewing.

CGM See *consumer generated media.*

chain stores Stores owned and operated as a group by a single organization.

channel A medium of communication—such as a voice, radio, or newspaper—for transmitting a message.

channel captain See *channel leader.*

channel conflict A clash of goals and methods between distribution channel members.

channel control A situation that occurs when one marketing channel member intentionally affects another member's behavior.

channel cooperation See *channel partnering.*

channel leader (channel captain) A member of a marketing channel that exercises authority and power over the activities of other channel members.

channel members All parties in the marketing channel that negotiate with one another, buy and sell products, and facilitate the change of ownership between buyer and seller in the course of moving the product from the manufacturer into the hands of the final consumer.

channel of distribution See *marketing channel.*

channel partnering (channel cooperation) The joint effort of all channel members to create a channel that serves customers and creates a competitive advantage.

channel power The capacity of a particular marketing channel member to control or influence the behavior of other channel members.

CI See *competitive intelligence.*

closed-ended question An interview question that asks the respondent to make a selection from a limited list of responses.

CLT See *central-location telephone facility.*

cobranding Placing two or more brand names on a product or its package.

code of ethics A guideline to help marketing managers and other employees make better decisions.

cognitive dissonance Inner tension that a consumer experiences after recognizing an inconsistency between behavior and values or opinions.

commercialization The decision to market a product.

communication The process by which we exchange or share meanings through a common set of symbols.

comparative advertising A form of advertising that compares two or more specifically named or shown competing brands on one or more specific attributes.

competitive advantage The set of unique features of a company and its products that are perceived by the target market as significant and superior to the competition.

competitive advertising A form of advertising designed to influence demand for a specific brand.

competitive intelligence (CI) An intelligence system that helps managers assess their competition and vendors in order to become more efficient and effective competitors.

component lifestyles The practice of choosing goods and services that meet one's diverse needs and interests rather than conforming to a single, traditional lifestyle.

component parts Either finished items ready for assembly or products that need very little processing before becoming part of some other product.

computer-assisted personal interviewing An interviewing method in which the interviewer reads the questions from a computer screen and enters the respondent's data directly into the computer.

computer-assisted self-interviewing An interviewing method in which a mall interviewer intercepts and directs willing respondents to nearby computers where the respondent reads questions off a computer screen and directly keys his or her answers into a computer.

concentrated targeting strategy A strategy used to select one segment of a market for targeting marketing efforts.

concept test A test to evaluate a new-product idea, usually before any prototype has been created.

consideration set See *evoked set.*

consultative selling See *relationship selling.*

consumer behavior Processes a consumer uses to make purchase decisions, as well as to use and dispose of purchased goods or services; also includes factors that influence purchase decisions and product use.

consumer decision-making process A five-step process used by consumers when buying goods or services.

consumer generated media (CGM) Media which is consumer generated and shared with other consumers.

consumer product A product bought to satisfy an individual's personal wants.

Consumer Product Safety Commission (CPSC) A federal agency established to protect the health and safety of consumers in and around their homes.

consumer sales promotion Sales promotion activities targeting the ultimate consumer.

continuous media schedule A media scheduling strategy in which advertising is run steadily throughout the advertising period; used for products in the latter stages of the product life cycle.

contract logistics See *outsourcing.*

contract manufacturing Private-label manufacturing by a foreign company.

control Provides the mechanisms for evaluating marketing results in light of the plan's objectives and for correcting actions that do not help the organization reach those objectives within budget guidelines.

convenience product A relatively inexpensive item that merits little shopping effort.

convenience sample A form of nonprobability sample using respondents who are convenient or readily accessible to the researcher—for example, employees, friends, or relatives.

convenience store A miniature supermarket, carrying only a limited line of high-turnover convenience goods.

cooperative advertising An arrangement in which the manufacturer and the retailer split the costs of advertising the manufacturer's brand.

cooperative relationship A relationship between companies that takes the form of informal partnership with moderate levels of trust and information sharing as needed to further each company's goals.

corporate blogs Blogs that are sponsored by a company or one of its brands and maintained by one or more of the company's employees.

corporate social responsibility Business's concern for society's welfare.

cost competitive advantage Being the low-cost competitor in an industry while maintaining satisfactory profit margins.

cost per contact The cost of reaching one member of the target market.

countertrade A form of trade in which all or part of the payment for goods or services is in the form of other goods or services.

coupon A certificate that entitles consumers to an immediate price reduction when they buy the product.

CPSC See *Consumer Product Safety Commission.*

credence quality A characteristic that consumers may have difficulty assessing even after purchase because they do not have the necessary knowledge or experience.

crisis management A coordinated effort to handle all the effects of unfavorable publicity or of another unexpected unfavorable event.

cross-tabulation A method of analyzing data that lets the analyst look at the responses to one question in relation to the responses to one or more other questions.

culture The set of values, norms, attitudes, and other meaningful symbols that shape human behavior, and the artifacts, or products, of that behavior as they are transmitted from one generation to the next.

customer satisfaction Customers' evaluation of a good or service in terms of whether it has met their needs and expectations.

customer value The relationship between benefits and the sacrifice necessary to obtain those benefits.

D

database marketing The creation of a large computerized file of customers' and potential customers' profiles and purchase patterns.

decision support system (DSS) An interactive, flexible computerized information system that enables managers to obtain and manipulate information as they are making decisions.

decline stage The fourth stage of the product life cycle, characterized by a long-run drop in sales.

decoding Interpretation of the language and symbols sent by the source through a channel.

demand The quantity of a product that will be sold in the market at various prices for a specified period.

demographic segmentation Segmenting markets by age, gender, income, ethnic background, and family life cycle.

demography The study of people's vital statistics, such as their age, race and ethnicity, and location.

deontological ethical theory A theory that states that people should adhere to their obligations and duties when analyzing an ethical dilemma.

department store A store housing several departments under one roof.

derived demand The demand for business products.

destination stores Stores that consumers purposefully plan to visit.

development The stage in the product development process in which a prototype is developed and a marketing strategy is outlined.

diffusion The process by which the adoption of an innovation spreads.

direct channel A distribution channel in which producers sell directly to consumers.

direct foreign investment Active ownership of a foreign company or of overseas manufacturing or marketing facilities.

direct marketing (direct-response marketing) Techniques used to get consumers to make a purchase from their home, office, or another nonretail setting.

direct retailing The selling of products by representatives who work door-to-door, office-to-office, or at-home parties.

direct-response marketing See *direct marketing.*

discount store A retailer that competes on the basis of low prices, high turnover, and high volume.

discrepancy of assortment The lack of all the items a customer needs to receive full satisfaction from a product or products.

discrepancy of quantity The difference between the amount of product produced and the amount an end user wants to buy.

disintermediation The elimination of intermediaries such as wholesalers or distributors from a marketing channel.

distribution resource planning (DRP) An inventory control system that manages the replenishment of goods from the manufacturer to the final consumer.

diversification A strategy of increasing sales by introducing new products into new markets.

dog In the portfolio matrix, a business unit that has low growth potential and a small market share.

DRP See *distribution resource planning.*

drugstore A retail store that stocks pharmacy-related products and services as its main draw.

DSS See *decision support system.*

dual distribution (multiple distribution) The use of two (or more) channels to distribute the same product to target markets.

dumping The sale of an exported product at a price lower than that charged for the same or a like product in the "home" market of the exporter.

E

EDI See *electronic data interchange.*

elastic demand A situation in which consumer demand is sensitive to changes in price.

elasticity of demand Consumers' responsiveness or sensitivity to changes in price.

electronic data interchange (EDI) Information technology that replaces the paper documents that usually accompany business transactions, such as purchase orders and invoices, with electronic transmission of the needed information to reduce inventory levels, improve cash flow, streamline operations, and increase the speed and accuracy of information transmission.

electronic distribution A distribution technique that includes any kind of product or service that can be distributed electronically, whether over traditional forms such as fiber-optic cable or through satellite transmission of electronic signals.

empowerment Delegation of authority to solve customers' problems quickly–usually by the first person that the customer notifies regarding a problem.

encoding The conversion of a sender's ideas and thoughts into a message, usually in the form of words or signs.

environmental management When a company implements strategies that attempt to shape the external environment within which it operates.

environmental scanning Collection and interpretation of information about forces, events, and relationships in the external environment that may affect the future of the organization or the implementation of the marketing plan.

ethics The moral principles or values that generally govern the conduct of an individual.

ethnographic research The study of human behavior in its natural context; involves observation of behavior and physical setting.

EU See *European Union.*

European Union (EU) A free trade zone encompassing 27 European countries.

evaluation Gauging the extent to which the marketing objectives have been achieved during the specified time.

evoked set (consideration set) A group of brands, resulting from an information search, from which a buyer can choose.

exchange People giving up something to receive something they would rather have.

exclusive distribution A form of distribution that establishes one or a few dealers within a given area.

executive interviews A type of survey that involves interviewing businesspeople at their offices concerning industrial products or services.

experience curves Curves that show costs declining at a predictable rate as experience with a product increases.

experience quality A characteristic that can be assessed only after use.

experiment A method a researcher uses to gather primary data.

export agent An intermediary who acts like a manufacturer's agent for the exporter. The export agent lives in the foreign market.

export broker An intermediary who plays the traditional broker's role by bringing buyer and seller together.

exporting Selling domestically produced products to buyers in another country.

express warranty A written guarantee.

extensive decision making The most complex type of consumer decision making, used when buying an unfamiliar, expensive product or an infrequently bought item; requires use of several criteria for evaluating options and much time for seeking information.

external information search The process of seeking information in the outside environment.

F

factory outlet An off-price retailer that is owned and operated by a manufacturer.

family brand Marketing several different products under the same brand name.

family life cycle (FLC) A series of stages determined by a combination of age, marital status, and the presence or absence of children.

FDA See *Food and Drug Administration*.

Federal Trade Commission (FTC) A federal agency empowered to prevent persons or corporations from using unfair methods of competition in commerce.

feedback The receiver's response to a message.

field service firm A firm that specializes in interviewing respondents on a subcontracted basis.

fixed cost A cost that does not change as output is increased or decreased.

FLC See *family life cycle*.

flighted media schedule A media scheduling strategy in which ads are run heavily every other month or every two weeks, to achieve a greater impact with an increased frequency and reach at those times.

floating exchange rates Prices of different currencies move up and down based on the demand for and the supply of each currency.

focus group Seven to ten people who participate in a group discussion led by a moderator.

follow-up The final step of the selling process, in which the salesperson ensures that delivery schedules are met, that the goods or services perform as promised, and that the buyers' employees are properly trained to use the products.

Food and Drug Administration (FDA) A federal agency charged with enforcing regulations against selling and distributing adulterated, misbranded, or hazardous food and drug products.

Foreign Corrupt Practices Act A law that prohibits U.S. corporations from making illegal payments to public officials of foreign governments to obtain business rights or to enhance their business dealings in those countries.

four Ps Product, place, promotion, and price, which together make up the marketing mix.

frame error An error that occurs when a sample drawn from a population differs from the target population.

franchise The right to operate a business or to sell a product.

franchisee An individual or business that is granted the right to sell another party's product.

franchisor The originator of a trade name, product, methods of operation, and so on that grants operating rights to another party to sell its product.

frequency The number of times an individual is exposed to a given message during a specific period.

frequent buyer program A loyalty program in which loyal consumers are rewarded for making multiple purchases of a particular good or service.

FTC See *Federal Trade Commission*.

full-line discount stores A retailer that offers consumers very limited service and carries a broad assortment of well-known, nationally branded "hard goods."

G

GATT See *General Agreement on Tariffs and Trade*.

General Agreement on Tariffs and Trade (GATT) A trade agreement that contained loopholes that enabled countries to avoid trade-barrier reduction agreements.

Generation X People born between 1965 and 1978.

Generation Y People born between 1979 and 1994.

generic product name Identifies a product by class or type and cannot be trademarked.

geodemographic segmentation Segmenting potential customers into neighborhood lifestyle categories.

geographic segmentation Segmenting markets by region of a country or the world, market size, market density, or climate.

global brand A brand where at least one-third of the product is sold outside its home country or region.

global marketing Marketing that targets markets throughout the world.

global marketing standardization Production of uniform products that can be sold the same way all over the world.

global vision Recognizing and reacting to international marketing opportunities, using effective global marketing strategies, and being aware of threats from foreign competitors in all markets.

gross margin The amount of money the retailer makes as a percentage of sales after the cost of goods sold is subtracted.

group dynamics Group interaction essential to the success of focus-group research.

growth stage The second stage of the product life cycle when sales typically grow at an increasing rate, many competitors enter the market, large companies may start acquiring small pioneering firms, and profits are healthy.

H

heterogeneity The variability of the inputs and outputs of services, which causes services to tend to be less standardized and less uniform than goods.

horizontal conflict A channel conflict that occurs among channel members on the same level.

I

ideal self-image The way an individual would like to be.

IMC See *integrated marketing communications*.

IMF See *International Monetary Fund*.

implementation The process that turns a marketing plan into action assignments and ensures that these assignments are executed in a way that accomplishes the plan's objectives.

implied warranty An unwritten guarantee that the good or service is fit for the purpose for which it was sold.

independent retailers Retailers owned by a single person or partnership and not operated as part of a larger retail institution.

individual branding Using different brand names for different products.

industrial product See *business product*.

inelastic demand A situation in which an increase or a decrease in price will not significantly affect demand for the product.

inflation A measure of the decrease in the value of money, expressed as the percentage reduction in value since the previous year.

infomercial A 30-minute or longer advertisement that looks more like a TV talk show than a sales pitch.

informational labeling A type of package labeling designed to help consumers make proper product selections and lower their cognitive dissonance after the purchase.

InfoScan A scanner-based sales-tracking service for the consumer packaged-goods industry.

innovation A product perceived as new by a potential adopter.

inseparability The inability of the production and consumption of a service to be separated. Consumers must be present during the production.

installations See *major equipment*.

institutional advertising A form of advertising designed to enhance a company's image rather than promote a particular product.

intangibility The inability of services to be touched, seen, tasted, heard, or felt in the same manner that goods can be sensed.

integrated marketing communications (IMC) The careful coordination of all promotional messages for a product or a service to assure the consistency of messages at every contact point where a company meets the consumer.

integrated relationship A relationship between companies that is tightly connected, with linked processes across and between firm boundaries, and high levels of trust and interfirm commitment.

intensive distribution A form of distribution aimed at having a product available in every outlet where target customers might want to buy it.

internal information search The process of recalling past information stored in the memory.

International Monetary Fund (IMF) An international organization that acts as a lender of last resort, providing loans to troubled nations, and works to promote trade through financial cooperation.

interpersonal communication Direct, face-to-face communication between two or more people.

introductory stage The first stage of the product life cycle in which the full-scale launch of a new product into the marketplace occurs.

inventory control system A method of developing and maintaining an adequate assortment of materials or products to meet a manufacturer's or a customer's demand.

involvement The amount of time and effort a buyer invests in the search, evaluation, and decision processes of consumer behavior.

J

joint demand The demand for two or more items used together in a final product.

joint venture When a domestic firm buys part of a foreign company or joins with a foreign company to create a new entity.

K

keiretsu A network of interlocking corporate affiliates.

keystoning The practice of marking up prices by 100 percent, or doubling the cost.

L

laboratory market testing See *simulated market testing*.

lead generation (prospecting) Identification of those firms and people most likely to buy the seller's offerings.

lead qualification Determination of a sales prospect's (1) recognized need, (2) buying power, and (3) receptivity and accessibility.

learning A process that creates changes in behavior, immediate or expected, through experience and practice.

licensing The legal process whereby a licensor agrees to let another firm use its manufacturing process, trademarks, patents, trade secrets, or other proprietary knowledge.

lifestyle A mode of living as identified by a person's activities, interests, and opinions.

limited decision making The type of decision making that requires a moderate amount of time for gathering information and deliberating about an unfamiliar brand in a familiar product category.

logistics The efficient and cost-effective forward and reverse flow as well as storage of goods, services, and related information, into, through, and out of channel member companies. Logistics functions typically include transportation and storage of assets, as well as their sorting, accumulation, consolidation, and/or allocation for the purpose of meeting customer requirements.

logistics information system The link that connects all of the logistics components of the supply chain.

loss-leader pricing See *leader pricing*.

loyalty marketing program A promotional program designed to build long-term, mutually beneficial relationships between a company and its key customers.

M

major equipment (installations) Capital goods such as large or expensive machines, mainframe computers, blast furnaces, generators, airplanes, and buildings.

mall intercept interview A survey research method that involves interviewing people in the common areas of shopping malls.

management decision problem A broad-based problem that uses marketing research in order for managers to take proper actions.

manufacturer's brand The brand name of a manufacturer.

marginal cost (MC) The change in total costs associated with a one-unit change in output.

marginal revenue (MR) The extra revenue associated with selling an extra unit of output or the change in total revenue with a one-unit change in output.

market People or organizations with needs or wants and the ability and willingness to buy.

market development A marketing strategy that entails attracting new customers to existing products.

market opportunity analysis (MOA) The description and estimation of the size and sales potential of market segments that are of interest to the firm and the assessment of key competitors in these market segments.

market orientation A philosophy that assumes that a sale does not depend on an aggressive sales force but rather on a customer's decision to purchase a product. It is synonymous with the marketing concept.

market penetration A marketing strategy that tries to increase market share among existing customers.

market segment A subgroup of people or organizations sharing one or more characteristics that cause them to have similar product needs.

market segmentation The process of dividing a market into meaningful, relatively similar, and identifiable segments or groups.

market share A company's product sales as a percentage of total sales for that industry.

marketing The activity, set of institutions, and processes for creating, communicating, delivering, and exchanging offerings that have value for customers, clients, partners, and society at large.

marketing audit A thorough, systematic, periodic evaluation of the objectives, strategies, structure, and performance of the marketing organization.

marketing channel (channel of distribution) A set of interdependent organizations that ease the transfer of ownership as products move from producer to business user or consumer.

marketing concept The idea that the social and economic justification for an organization's existence is the satisfaction of customer wants and needs while meeting organizational objectives.

marketing information Everyday information about developments in the marketing environment that managers use to prepare and adjust marketing plans.

marketing mix A unique blend of product, place, promotion, and pricing strategies designed to produce mutually satisfying exchanges with a target market.

marketing myopia Defining a business in terms of goods and services rather than in terms of the benefits that customers seek.

marketing objective A statement of what is to be accomplished through marketing activities.

marketing plan A written document that acts as a guidebook of marketing activities for the marketing manager.

marketing planning Designing activities relating to marketing objectives and the changing marketing environment.

marketing research The process of planning, collecting, and analyzing data relevant to a marketing decision.

marketing research aggregator A company that acquires, catalogs, reformats, segments, and resells reports already published by marketing research firms.

marketing research objective The specific information needed to solve a marketing research problem; the objective should be to provide insightful decision-making information.

marketing research problem Determining what information is needed and how that information can be obtained efficiently and effectively.

marketing strategy The activities of selecting and describing one or more target markets and of developing and maintaining a marketing mix that will produce mutually satisfying exchanges with target markets.

marketing-controlled information source A product information source that originates with marketers promoting the product.

markup pricing The cost of buying the product from the producer plus amounts for profit and for expenses not otherwise accounted for.

Maslow's hierarchy of needs A method of classifying human needs and motivations into five categories in ascending order of importance: physiological, safety, social, esteem, and self-actualization.

mass communication The communication of a concept or message to large audiences.

mass merchandising A retailing strategy using moderate to low prices on large quantities of merchandise and lower service to stimulate high turnover of products.

materials management See *materials requirement planning*.

materials requirement planning (MRP) (materials management) An inventory control system that manages the replenishment of raw materials, supplies, and components from the supplier to the manufacturer.

materials-handling system A method of moving inventory into, within, and out of the warehouse.

maturity stage The third stage of the product life cycle during which sales increase at a decreasing rate.

MC See *marginal cost*.

measurement error An error that occurs when there is a difference between the information desired by the researcher and the information provided by the measurement process.

media mix The combination of media to be used for a promotional campaign.

media planning The series of decisions advertisers make regarding the selection and use of media, allowing the marketer to optimally and cost-effectively communicate the message to the target audience.

media schedule Designation of the media, the specific publications or programs, and the insertion dates of advertising.

medium The channel used to convey a message to a target market.

merchant wholesaler An institution that buys goods from manufacturers and resells them to businesses, government agencies, and other wholesalers or retailers and that receives and takes title to goods, stores them in its own warehouses, and later ships them.

Mercosur The largest Latin American trade agreement; includes Argentina, Bolivia, Brazil, Chile, Colombia, Ecuador, Paraguay, Peru, Venezuela, and Uruguay.

mission statement A statement of the firm's business based on a careful analysis of benefits sought by present and potential customers and an analysis of existing and anticipated environmental conditions.

MOA See *market opportunity analysis*.

modified rebuy A situation where the purchaser wants some change in the original good or service.

moral relativists Persons who believe that ethical truths depend on the individuals and groups holding them.

morals The rules people develop as a result of cultural values and norms.

motive A driving force that causes a person to take action to satisfy specific needs.

MR See *marginal revenue*.

MRP See *materials requirement planning*.

multiculturalism When all major ethnic groups in an area—such as a city, county, or census tract—are roughly equally represented.

multinational corporation A company that is heavily engaged in international trade, beyond exporting and importing.

multiple distribution See *dual distribution*.

multiplier effect (accelerator principle) Phenomenon in which a small increase or decrease in consumer demand can produce a much larger change in demand for the facilities and equipment needed to make the consumer product.

multisegment targeting strategy A strategy that chooses two or more well-defined market segments and develops a distinct marketing mix for each.

mystery shoppers Researchers posing as customers who gather observational data about a store.

N

NAFTA See *North American Free Trade Agreement*.

NAICS See *North American Industry Classification System*.

need recognition Result of an imbalance between actual and desired states.

needs assessment A determination of the customer's specific needs and wants, and the range of options the customer has for satisfying them.

negotiation The process during which both the salesperson and the prospect offer special concessions in an attempt to arrive at a sales agreement.

networking A process of finding out about potential clients from friends, business contacts, coworkers, acquaintances, and fellow members in professional and civic organizations.

new buy A situation requiring the purchase of a product for the first time.

new product A product new to the world, the market, the producer, the seller, or some combination of these.

new-product strategy A plan that links the new-product development process with the objectives of the marketing department, the business unit, and the corporation.

niche One segment of a market.

niche competitive advantage The advantage achieved when a firm seeks to target and effectively serve a small segment of the market.

noise Anything that interferes with, distorts, or slows down the transmission of information.

nonaspirational reference group A group with which an individual does not want to associate.

noncorporate blogs Independent blogs that are not associated with the marketing efforts of any particular company or brand.

nonmarketing-controlled information source A product information source that is not associated with advertising or promotion.

nonprobability sample Any sample in which little or no attempt is made to get a representative cross section of the population.

nonstore retailing Selling to customers through other means than by visiting a store.

norm A value or attitude deemed acceptable by a group.

North American Free Trade Agreement (NAFTA) An agreement between Canada, the United States, and Mexico to reduce trade barriers between the countries.

North American Industry Classification System (NAICS) A detailed numbering system developed by the United States, Canada, and Mexico to classify North American business establishments by their main production processes.

O

observation research A research method that relies on four types of observation: people watching people, people watching an activity, machines watching people, and machines watching an activity.

OEMs See *original equipment manufacturers.*

off-price retailer A retailer that sells at prices 25 percent or more below traditional department store prices because it pays cash for its stock and usually doesn't ask for return privileges.

one-to-one marketing An individualized marketing method that utilizes customer information to build long-term, personalized, and profitable relationships with each customer.

online retailing A type of shopping available to consumers with access to the Internet.

open-ended question An interview question that encourages an answer phrased in the respondent's own words.

opinion leader An individual who influences the opinions of others.

optimizers Business customers who consider numerous suppliers, both familiar and unfamiliar, solicit bids, and study all proposals carefully before selecting one.

order processing system A system whereby orders are entered into the supply chain and filled.

original equipment manufacturers (OEMs) Individuals and organizations that buy business goods and incorporate them into the products that they produce for eventual sale to other producers or to consumers.

outsourcing (contract logistics) A manufacturer's or supplier's use of an independent third party to manage an entire function of the logistics system, such as transportation, warehousing, or order processing.

P

penetration pricing A pricing policy whereby a firm charges a relatively low price for a product initially as a way to reach the mass market.

perception The process by which people select, organize, and interpret stimuli into a meaningful and coherent picture.

perceptual mapping A means of displaying or graphing, in two or more dimensions, the location of products, brands, or groups of products in customers' minds.

perishability The inability of services to be stored, warehoused, or inventoried.

personal selling A purchase situation involving a personal, paid-for communication between two people in an attempt to influence each other.

personality A way of organizing and grouping the consistencies of an individual's reactions to situations.

persuasive labeling A type of package labeling that focuses on a promotional theme or logo with consumer information being secondary.

pioneer advertising A form of advertising designed to stimulate primary demand for a new product or product category.

planned obsolescence The practice of modifying products so those that have already been sold become obsolete before they actually need replacement.

planning The process of anticipating future events and determining strategies to achieve organizational objectives in the future.

PLC See *product life cycle.*

point-of-purchase display (POP) A promotional display set up at the retailer's location to build traffic, advertise the product, or induce impulse buying.

pop-up shops Temporary retail establishments that provide flexible locations without a long-term commitment.

portfolio matrix A tool for allocating resources among products or strategic business units on the basis of relative market share and market growth rate.

position The place a product, brand, or group of products occupies in consumers' minds relative to competing offerings.

positioning Developing a specific marketing mix to influence potential customers' overall perception of a brand, product line, or organization in general.

preapproach A process that describes the "homework" that must be done by a salesperson before he or she contacts a prospect.

predatory pricing The practice of charging a very low price for a product with the intent of driving competitors out of business or out of a market.

premium An extra item offered to the consumer, usually in exchange for some proof of purchase of the promoted product.

prestige pricing Charging a high price to help promote a high-quality image.

price That which is given up in an exchange to acquire a good or service.

price equilibrium The price at which demand and supply are equal.

price fixing An agreement between two or more firms on the price they will charge for a product.

price skimming A pricing policy whereby a firm charges a high introductory price, often coupled with heavy promotion.

price strategy A basic, long-term pricing framework, which establishes the initial price for a product and the intended direction for price movements over the product life cycle.

primary data Information that is collected for the first time; used for solving the particular problem under investigation.

primary membership group A reference group with which people interact regularly in an informal, face-to-face manner, such as family, friends, or fellow employees.

private brand A brand name owned by a wholesaler or a retailer.

probability sample A sample in which every element in the population has a known statistical likelihood of being selected.

problem child (question mark) In the portfolio matrix, a business unit that shows rapid growth but poor profit margins.

processed materials Products used directly in manufacturing other products.

product Everything, both favorable and unfavorable, that a person receives in an exchange.

product advertising A form of advertising that touts the benefits of a specific good or service.

product category All brands that satisfy a particular type of need.

product development A marketing strategy that entails the creation of new products for current customers.

product differentiation A positioning strategy that some firms use to distinguish their products from those of competitors.

product item A specific version of a product that can be designated as a distinct offering among an organization's products.

product life cycle (PLC) A biological metaphor that traces the stages of a product's acceptance, from its introduction (birth) to its decline (death).

product line A group of closely related product items.

product line depth The number of product items in a product line.

product line extension Adding additional products to an existing product line in order to compete more broadly in the industry.

product mix All products that an organization sells.

product mix width The number of product lines an organization offers.

product modification Changing one or more of a product's characteristics.

product offering The mix of products offered to the consumer by the retailer; also called the *product assortment* or *merchandise mix.*

product orientation A philosophy that focuses on the internal capabilities of the firm rather than on the desires and needs of the marketplace.

product placement A public relations strategy that involves getting a product, service, or company name to appear in a movie, television show, radio program, magazine, newspaper, video game, video or audio clip, book, or commercial for another product; on the Internet; or at special events.

product/service differentiation competitive advantage The provision of something that is unique and valuable to buyers beyond simply offering a lower price than the competition's.

production orientation A philosophy that focuses on the internal capabilities of the firm rather than on the desires and needs of the marketplace.

profit Revenue minus expenses.

profit maximization A method of setting prices that occurs when marginal revenue equals marginal cost.

promotion Communication by marketers that informs, persuades, and reminds potential buyers of a product in order to influence an opinion or elicit a response.

promotional mix The combination of promotional tools—including advertising, public relations, personal selling, and sales promotion—used to reach the target market and fulfill the organization's overall goals.

promotional strategy A plan for the optimal use of the elements of promotion: advertising, public relations, personal selling, and sales promotion.

prospecting See *lead generation*.

psychographic segmentation Market segmentation on the basis of personality, motives, lifestyles, and geodemographics.

public relations The marketing function that evaluates public attitudes, identifies areas within the organization the public may be interested in, and executes a program of action to earn public understanding and acceptance.

publicity Public information about a company, product, service, or issue appearing in the mass media as a news item.

pull strategy A marketing strategy that stimulates consumer demand to obtain product distribution.

pulsing media schedule A media scheduling strategy that uses continuous scheduling throughout the year coupled with a flighted schedule during the best sales periods.

purchasing power A comparison of income versus the relative cost of a set standard of goods and services in different geographic areas.

push money Money offered to channel intermediaries to encourage them to "push" products—that is, to encourage other members of the channel to sell the products.

push strategy A marketing strategy that uses aggressive personal selling and trade advertising to convince a wholesaler or a retailer to carry and sell particular merchandise.

pyramid of corporate social responsibility A model that suggests corporate social responsibility is composed of economic, legal, ethical, and philanthropic responsibilities and that the firm's economic performance supports the entire structure.

Q

question mark See *problem child*.

R

random error An error that occurs when the selected sample is an imperfect representation of the overall population.

random sample A sample arranged in such a way that every element of the population has an equal chance of being selected as part of the sample.

raw materials Unprocessed extractive or agricultural products, such as mineral ore, timber, wheat, corn, fruits, vegetables, and fish.

reach The number of target consumers exposed to a commercial at least once during a specific period, usually four weeks.

real self-image The way an individual actually perceives himself or herself.

rebate A cash refund given for the purchase of a product during a specific period.

receiver The person who decodes a message.

recession A period of economic activity characterized by negative growth, which reduces demand for goods and services.

reciprocity The practice of business purchasers choosing to buy from their own customers.

reference group A group in society that influences an individual's purchasing behavior.

referral A recommendation to a salesperson from a customer or business associate.

reintermediation The reintroduction of an intermediary between producers and users.

relationship commitment A firm's belief that an ongoing relationship with another firm is so important that the relationship warrants maximum efforts at maintaining it indefinitely.

relationship marketing A strategy that focuses on keeping and improving relationships with current customers.

relationship selling (consultative selling) A sales practice that involves building, maintaining, and enhancing interactions with customers in order to develop long-term satisfaction through mutually beneficial partnerships.

repositioning Changing consumers' perceptions of a brand in relation to competing brands.

resale price maintenance A manufacturer, and its distributors, agree that retailers will sell products at a certain price floor.

research design Specifies which research questions must be answered, how and when the data will be gathered, and how the data will be analyzed.

retailer A channel intermediary that sells mainly to consumers.

retailing All the activities directly related to the sale of goods and services to the ultimate consumer for personal, nonbusiness use.

retailing mix A combination of the six Ps—product, place, promotion, price, presentation, and personnel—to sell goods and services to the ultimate consumer.

return on investment (ROI) Net profit after taxes divided by total assets.

revenue The price charged to customers multiplied by the number of units sold.

routine response behavior The type of decision making exhibited by consumers buying frequently purchased, low-cost goods and services; requires little search and decision time.

S

sales cycle See *sales process*.

sales orientation The idea that people will buy more goods and services if aggressive sales techniques are used and that high sales result in high profits.

sales presentation A formal meeting in which the salesperson presents a sales proposal to a prospective buyer.

sales process (sales cycle) The set of steps a salesperson goes through in a particular organization to sell a particular product or service.

sales promotion Marketing activities—other than personal selling, advertising, and public relations—that stimulate consumer buying and dealer effectiveness.

sales proposal A formal written document or professional presentation that outlines how the salesperson's product or service will meet or exceed the prospect's needs.

sample A subset from a larger population.

sampling A promotional program that allows the consumer the opportunity to try a product or service for free.

sampling error An error that occurs when a sample somehow does not represent the target population.

satisficers Business customers who place an order with the first familiar supplier to satisfy product and delivery requirements.

SBU See *strategic business unit*.

scaled-response question A closed-ended question designed to measure the intensity of a respondent's answer.

scanner-based research A system for gathering information from a single group of respondents by continuously monitoring the advertising, promotion, and pricing they are exposed to and the things they buy.

scrambled merchandising The tendency to offer a wide variety of nontraditional goods and services under one roof.

screening The first filter in the product development process, which eliminates ideas that are inconsistent with the organization's new-product strategy or are obviously inappropriate for some other reason.

search quality A characteristic that can be easily assessed before purchase.

seasonal media schedule A media scheduling strategy that runs advertising only during times of the year when the product is most likely to be used.

secondary data Data previously collected for any purpose other than the one at hand.

secondary membership group A reference group with which people associate less consistently and more formally than a primary membership group, such as a club, professional group, or religious group.

segmentation bases (variables) Characteristics of individuals, groups, or organizations.

selective distortion A process whereby a consumer changes or distorts information that conflicts with his or her feelings or beliefs.

selective distribution A form of distribution achieved by screening dealers to eliminate all but a few in any single area.

selective exposure The process whereby a consumer notices certain stimuli and ignores others.

selective retention A process whereby a consumer remembers only that information that supports his or her personal beliefs.

self-concept How consumers perceive themselves in terms of attitudes, perceptions, beliefs, and self-evaluations.

selling against the brand Stocking well-known branded items at high prices in order to sell store brands at discounted prices.

sender The originator of the message in the communication process.

service The result of applying human or mechanical efforts to people or objects.

service mark A trademark for a service.

shopping product A product that requires comparison shopping because it is usually more expensive than a convenience product and is found in fewer stores.

simulated (laboratory) market testing The presentation of advertising and other promotion materials for several products, including a test product, to members of the product's target market.

simultaneous product development A team-oriented approach to new-product development.

site reach See *stickiness*.

social class A group of people in a society who are considered nearly equal in status or community esteem, who regularly socialize among themselves both formally and informally, and who share behavioral norms.

socialization process How cultural values and norms are passed down to children.

societal marketing orientation The idea that an organization exists not only to satisfy customer wants and needs and to meet organizational objectives, but also to preserve or enhance individuals' and society's long-term best interests.

spatial discrepancy The difference between the location of a producer and the location of widely scattered markets.

specialty discount store A retail store that offers a nearly complete selection of single-line merchandise and uses self-service, discount prices, high volume, and high turnover.

specialty product A particular item for which consumers search extensively and are very reluctant to accept substitutes.

specialty store A retail store specializing in a given type of merchandise.

sponsorship A public relations strategy in which a company spends money to support an issue, cause, or event that is consistent with corporate objectives, such as improving brand awareness or enhancing corporate image.

stakeholder theory A theory that holds that social responsibility is paying attention to the interest of every affected stakeholder in every aspect of a firm's operation.

star In the portfolio matrix, a business unit that is a fast-growing market leader.

status quo pricing A pricing objective that maintains existing prices or meets the competition's prices.

stickiness (site reach) A measure of a Web site's effectiveness; calculated by multiplying the frequency of visits times the duration of a visit times the number of pages viewed during each visit.

stimulus Any unit of input affecting one or more of the five senses: sight, smell, taste, touch, hearing.

stimulus discrimination A learned ability to differentiate among similar products.

stimulus generalization A form of learning that occurs when one response is extended to a second stimulus similar to the first.

straight rebuy A situation in which the purchaser reorders the same goods or services without looking for new information or investigating other suppliers.

strategic alliance (strategic partnership) A cooperative agreement between business firms.

strategic business unit (SBU) A subgroup of a single business or a collection of related businesses within the larger organization.

strategic channel alliance A cooperative agreement between business firms to use the other's already established distribution channel.

strategic partnership See *strategic alliance*.

strategic planning The managerial process of creating and maintaining a fit between the organization's objectives and resources and evolving market opportunities.

subculture A homogeneous group of people who share elements of the overall culture as well as unique elements of their own group.

supercenter A retail store that combines groceries and general merchandise goods with a wide range of services.

supermarket A large, departmentalized, self-service retailer that specializes in food and some nonfood items.

supplies Consumable items that do not become part of the final product.

supply The quantity of a product that will be offered to the market by suppliers at various prices for a specified period.

supply chain The connected chain of all of the business entities, both internal and external to the company, that perform or support the logistics function.

supply chain management A management system that coordinates and integrates all of the activities performed by supply chain members into a seamless process, from the source to the point of consumption, resulting in enhanced customer and economic value.

supply chain orientation The connected chain of all of the business entities, both internal and external to the company, that perform or support the logistics function.

supply chain team An entire group of individuals who orchestrate the movement of goods, services, and information from the source to the consumer.

survey research The most popular technique for gathering primary data, in which a researcher interacts with people to obtain facts, opinions, and attitudes.

sustainability The idea that socially responsible companies will outperform their peers by focusing on the world's social problems and viewing them as opportunities to build profits and help the world at the same time.

sustainable competitive advantage An advantage that cannot be copied by the competition.

SWOT analysis Identifying internal strengths (S) and weaknesses (W) and examining external opportunities (O) and threats (T).

T

target market A defined group most likely to buy a firm's product.

target market A group of people or organizations for which an organization designs, implements, and maintains a marketing mix intended to meet the needs of that group, resulting in mutually satisfying exchanges.

teamwork Collaborative efforts of people to accomplish common objectives.

telemarketing The use of the telephone to sell directly to consumers.

temporal discrepancy A situation that occurs when a product is produced but a customer is not ready to buy it.

test marketing The limited introduction of a product and a marketing program to determine the reactions of potential customers in a market situation.

trade allowance A price reduction offered by manufacturers to intermediaries, such as wholesalers and retailers. See *promotional allowance*.

trade discount See *functional discount*.

trade sales promotion Sales promotion activities targeting a channel member, such as a wholesaler or retailer.

trademark The exclusive right to use a brand or part of a brand.

trust The condition that exists when one party has confidence in an exchange partner's reliability and integrity.

U

undifferentiated targeting strategy A marketing approach that views the market as one big market with no individual segments and thus uses a single marketing mix.

unfair trade practice acts Laws that prohibit wholesalers and retailers from selling below cost.

unique selling proposition A desirable, exclusive, and believable advertising appeal selected as the theme for a campaign.

unitary elasticity A situation in which total revenue remains the same when prices change.

universal product codes (UPCs) A series of thick and thin vertical lines (bar codes), readable by computerized optical scanners, that represent numbers used to track products.

universe The population from which a sample will be drawn.

unsought product A product unknown to the potential buyer, or a known product that the buyer does not actively seek.

UPCs See *universal product codes*.

Uruguay Round An agreement to dramatically lower trade barriers worldwide; created the World Trade Organization.

usage-rate segmentation Dividing a market by the amount of product bought or consumed.

utilitarian ethical theory A theory that holds that the choice that yields the greatest benefit to the most people is the choice that is ethically correct.

V

value The enduring belief that a specific mode of conduct is personally or socially preferable to another mode of conduct.

variable cost A cost that varies with changes in the level of output.

variable pricing See *flexible pricing*.

variables See *segmentation bases*.

vertical conflict A channel conflict that occurs between different levels in a marketing channel, most typically between the manufacturer and wholesaler or between the manufacturer and retailer.

virtue A character trait valued as being good.

W

want The way a consumer goes about addressing a need.

warehouse membership clubs Limited-service merchant wholesalers that sell a limited selection of brand-name appliances, household items, and groceries on a cash-and-carry basis to members, usually small businesses and groups.

warranty A confirmation of the quality or performance of a good or service.

Web community A carefully selected group of consumers who agree to participate in an ongoing dialogue with a particular corporation.

World Bank An international bank that offers low-interest loans, advice, and information to developing nations.

World Trade Organization (WTO) A trade organization that replaced the old General Agreement on Tariffs and Trade (GATT).

WTO See *World Trade Organization*.

Y

yield management systems (YMS) A technique for adjusting prices that uses complex mathematical software to profitably fill unused capacity by discounting early purchases, limiting early sales at these discounted prices, and overbooking capacity.

YMS See *yield management systems*.

ENDNOTES

CHAPTER 1

1. Announcement to the AMA Academic Council from Patricia K. Goodrich, Senior Director, Professional Development, American Marketing Association, October 25, 2007.
2. George Anderson, "Satisfied Workers Generate Greater Returns," *Retailwire*, online, January 16, 2008.
3. Ann Zimmerman, "Home Depot Chief Renovates," *The Wall Street Journal*, June 5, 2008, B1, B2.
4. Robert Levering and Milton Moskowitz, "The 100 Best Companies to Work For," *Fortune*, January 25, 2005, 73.
5. Philip Kotler and Kevin Lane Keller, "*A Framework for Marketing Management*, 3rd ed. (Upper Saddle River, NJ: Prentice-Hall, 2007), 3.
6. Woody Driggs, "Serving Up Customer Delight," *Customer Relationship Management*, April 2008, 14.
7. Ibid.
8. George Anderson, "Customer Service Tops NRF Agenda," *Retailwire*, January 16, 2008, online; "The Bean Delivers," *Marketing News*, February 15, 2008, 5.
9. Jena McGregor, "Customer Service Champs," *BusinessWeek*, March 3, 2008, 37–42.
10. Anya Kamenetz, "Cleaning Solution," *Fast Company*, September 2008, 121–124.
11. Ibid.
12. Todd Wasserman, "P&G's Green Guru Tells Us Why There's No Green Tide," *Brandweek*, May 26, 2008, 15, 17.
13. Elena Malykhina, "Purex Detergent Joins the 'Green' Movement," **Brandweek.com**, online, July 15, 2008.
14. Becky Ebenkamp, "Study: 'Green' Products Leave Consumers Puzzled," **Brandweek.com**, online, July 15, 2008.
15. Marc Gunther, "Coca-Cola's Green Crusader," *Fortune*, April 28, 2008, 150.
16. Rachel Tobin Ramos, "UPS, Coke, Home Depot Push Green Strategies," **ajc.com**, online, April 23, 2008.
17. Ibid.; "Wal-Mart Says More Consumers Looking For 'Green' Products," **homeworld business.com**, online, April 22, 2008.
18. Todd Wasserman, "Mintel: 'Green' Products Top 5,933 in 2007," **Brandweek.com**, online, May 21, 2008.
19. Nora Isaccs, "Crash and Burn," **upsidetoday.com**, online.
20. A. G. Lafley and Rom Charan, "The Consumer is Boss," *Fortune*, March 17, 2008, 121–126.
21. Ibid., used by permission.
22. "The Importance of Great Customer Experiences and the Best Ways to Deliver Them," *Insight*, November 2007, 32.

23. Ibid.
24. Phred Dvorak, "Next in Line for Reinvention: The Art of Selling," *The Wall Street Journal*, January 28, 2008, B3.
25. Christopher Musico, "7 Essential Consumer Service Processes," **destinationcrm.com**, online, January 16, 2008.
26. Brian Hindo, "Satisfaction Not Guaranteed," *BusinessWeek*, June 19, 2006, 32–36.
27. Jena McGregor, "Customer Service Champs," *BusinessWeek*, March 5, 2007, 52–64.
28. "Many Companies Not Working to Earn Loyalty," *Quirk's Marketing Research Review*, October 2008, 80.
29. Jena McGregor, "Customer Service Champs."
30. Jeffrey M. O'Brien, "A Perfect Season," *Fortune*, February 4, 2008, 61–66.
31. Julie Barker, "Power to the People: Reducing Turnover With Empowerment," *Incentive*, online, February 8, 2008.
32. Samuel Fromartz, "Good Enough to Eat," *Fast Company*, September 2008, 29.
33. Lafley and Charan, "The Consumer is Boss," 122.
34. **http://en.wikipedia.org/wiki/ demographics_of_the_United_States**
35. The application exercises throughout the book are based on the winning entries in the "Best of the Great Ideas in Teaching Marketing" contest held in conjunction with the publication of the Eighth Edition of *Marketing*. Ideas came from marketing professors all across the country who teach many different sizes and types of marketing courses. Information on ways to implement these great ideas in the classroom can be found in the Instructor Manual that accompanies this text.
36. Sources: Don Steinberg, "Just Play," *Inc. Magazine*, October 2008, 124–134; Ethan Smith, Yutari Iwatani Kane, Sam Schechner, "Beatles Tunes Join Rock Band Game", *The Wall Street Journal*, October 30, 2008. Available at **http://online.wsj.com/article/ SB122531701276881747.html** (accessed January 5, 2009); Dan Gallagher, "Is 'Guitar Hero' Hitting Its Peak?" Market Watch, December 12, 2008. Available at **http://www.marketwatch.com/news/ story/guitar-hero-rock-band-games/story.aspx?g uid=%7B5CC35A95%2DB667%2D4E97%2DACB7 %2D3BA37BACA0FC%7D&dist=TQP_Mod_mktwN** (accessed January 5, 2009).

CHAPTER 2

1. Kate Maddox, "Marketer of the Year: Dan Henson, VP-CMO, General Electric, Co.," *BtoB's Best*, October 22, 2007.
2. Joseph Pereira, "Toys 'R' Us Unwraps Plans for Expansion," *The Wall Street Journal*, May 22, 2008, B1.

3. Melanie Warner, "McDonald's' Push a Boon for Produce," *The Star Telegram*, February 26, 2005, C1.
4. Ben & Jerry's, online, **www.benjerry.com**, (accessed December 1, 2008).
5. Mark Gongloff, "Golden Arches Offer Shelter in Storm," *The Wall Street Journal*, July 23, 2008, C1; Suzanne Vranica, "Marketers Find Ways to Exploit Gas Prices," *The Wall Street Journal*, July 7, 2008, B5.
6. Nike's site at **www.nike.com**, December 5, 2007.
7. Sarah Butrymowitz and Jayne O'Donnell, "Malls Get Creative to Draw More Shoppers in Tough Economy," **usatoday.com**, July 17, 2008; Store Review: Bass Pro Shops, **flyfishingabout.com**, December 1, 2008.
8. Julie Jargon, "New Leaf for Sara Lee, Kraft: Salads," *The Wall Street Journal*, March 26, 2007, A9.
9. John Brodie, "The Many Faces of Ralph Lauren," **money.cnn.com**, September 5, 2007.
10. Niraj Sherth, "India Liquor, Tobacco Firms Shift Tack," *The Wall Street Journal*, May 6, 2008, B8; Kounteya Sinha, "Surrogate Ads Luring Kids to Smoking: Study," **epaper.timesofindia .com**, December 1, 2008; "Surrogate Ads Will be Stopped, Assures I&B," **timesofindia.indiatimes .com**, December 1, 2008.
11. Richard Siklos, "Bob Iger Rocks Disney," *Fortune*, January 19, 2009. 80–86; Peter Sanders, "Disney Focuses on Boys," *The Wall Street Journal*, January 8, 2009. Available at **online.wsj.com/article/SB123137513996262627 .html** (accessed January 14, 2009).

MARKETING PLAN APPENDIX

The authors would like to thank e-motion software for allowing us to include its marketing plan in the Eleventh Edition of *Marketing*. We greatly appreciate Mr. Keohane's contribution of a real plan used by his growing company, which demonstrates to students the level of detail and the elements required to build an effective plan.

CHAPTER 3

1. "Report to the Principal, Big Shot," *BusinessWeek*, July 30, 2007, 9.
2. Partially adapted from: Edwin M. Epstein, "The Good Company: Rhetoric or Reality? Corporate Social Responsibility and Business Ethics Redux," *American Business Law Journal*, July 1, 2007, 207.
3. Neil Parmer, "Taking Care of Business," *SmartMoney*, October 2008, 77–82.
4. Ibid.
5. Marianne M. Jennings, *Business Ethics, 5th Ed.* (Mason, Ohio: Thomson Higher Education), 2006, 5–6.

6. These ethical theories are from: Catherine Rainbow, "Descriptions of Ethical Theories and Principles," **www.bio.davidson.edu/people/Kabernd/Indep/carainbow.htm** (June 22, 2005).

7. Jennings, 7.

8. Ibid.

9. Based on Edward Stevens, *Business Ethics* (New York: Paulist Press, 1979). Reprinted with permission. Used with permission of Paulist Press.

10. Anusorn Singhapakdi, Skott Vitell, and Kenneth Kraft, "Moral Intensity and Ethical Decision-making of Marketing Professionals," *Journal of Business Research 36*, March 1996, 245–255; Ishmael Akaah and Edward Riordan, "Judgments of Marketing Professionals about Ethical Issues in Marketing Research: A Replication and Extension," *Journal of Marketing Research*, February 1989, 112–120. See also Shelby Hunt, Lawrence Chonko, and James Wilcox, "Ethical Problems of Marketing Researchers," *Journal of Marketing Research*, August 1984, 309–324; Kenneth Andrews, "Ethics in Practice," *Harvard Business Review*, September/October 1989, 99–104; Thomas Dunfee, Craig Smith, and William T. Ross, Jr., "Social Contracts and Marketing Ethics," *Journal of Marketing*, July 1999, 14–32; Jan Handleman and Stephen Arnold, "The Role of Marketing Actions with a Social Dimension: Appeals to the Institutional Environment," *Journal of Marketing*, July 1999, 33–48; David Turnipseed, "Are Good Soldiers Good? Exploring the Link between Organizational Citizenship Behavior and Personal Ethics," *Journal of Business Research*, January 2002, 1–16; Tim Barnett and Sean Valentine, "Issue Contingencies and Marketers' Recognition of Ethical Issues, Ethical Judgments and Behavioral Intentions," *Journal of Business Research*, April 2004, 338–346.

11. "The Stat," *BusinessWeek*, September 12, 2005, 16.

12. Ibid.

13. "Actions Contributing Most to Ethical Behavior and Compliance Identified," *Workspan*, February 1, 2007, 1.

14. "Taser Settled 10 of 52 Cases It Said Were Dismissed," **Bloomberg.com**, August 28, 2007.

15. Ibid.

16. Erin White, "'What Would You Do?' Ethics Courses Get Context," *The Wall Street Journal*, June 12, 2006, B3.

17. Ibid.

18. Angelina MacKewn and K. W. VanVuren, "Business Training, Reasoning Skills, and Philosophical Orientation: Correlates of Ethical Decision-Making," *International Journal of Management and Marketing Research 1*, no. 1 (2008): 111–121; and Deloise Frisque and Judith Kolb, "The Effects of Ethics Training Programs On Attitude, Knowledge, and Transfer of Training of Office Professionals: A Treatment and Control Design," *Human Resource Development Quarterly*, March 2008, 35–53.

19. Kellye Whitney, "Ernst & Young Ethics Training: Part of the Company Fabric," **clomedia.com** (July 2007).

20. "Wal-Mart Raises Bar on Toy-Safety Standards," *The Wall Street Journal*, May 14, 2008, B1–B2.

21. "Wal-Mart Suppliers Face Energy, Other Mandates," *The Wall Street Journal*, October 22, 2008, B1, B4.

22. Remi Trudel and June Cotte, "Does Being Ethical Pay?" *The Wall Street Journal*, May 12, 2008, R4.

23. "Study Links Ethics and Profits," *Quality Progress*, March 2008, 26.

24. **www.cdc.gov/tobacco**, August 29, 2007.

25. This section is partially adapted from Jennings, *Business Ethics*, 72–75.

26. Milton Friedman, "The Social Responsibility of Business Is to Increase Its Profits," *The New York Times*, September 1962, 126.

27. "Valero To Pay Pollution Fines," *Oil Daily*, August 30, 2007.

28. John Carey, "Big Strides to Become the Jolly Green Giant," *BusinessWeek*, January 29, 57.

29. Xueming Luo and C. B. Bhattacharya, "Corporate Social Responsibility, Customer Satisfaction, and Market Value," *Journal of Marketing*, October 2006, 1–18.

30. "Globally, Companies are Giving Back," *HR Magazine*, June 1, 2007, 30.

31. "Americans Seek More Responsibility from Companies," *Daytona Beach News Journal*, May 26, 2007, 3B.

32. **www.unglobalcompact.org/participantsandstakeholders/index/htm** (October 27, 2008).

33. "Secretary-General Opens Global Compact Leaders Summit as Business, Government, Civil Society Leaders Rally for Corporate Citizenship," *UNESCAP Press Release*, July 5, 2007, Press Release No. L/38/2007.

34. The Heinz story is from "A Clear Mission," *PR Week*, July 16, 2007, 12.

35. Jennifer Alsever, "Chiquita Cleans Up Its Act," *Fortune*, November 27, 2007, 73.

36. Joe Nocera, "The Promise and Limits of Good Works," *International Herald Tribune*, August 9–10, 2008, 11–12.

37. Michael Liedtke, "AOL Enters Settlement Over Cancellation Process," *Marketing News*, August 15, 2007, 14.

38. **www.marketingpower.com** (accessed October 28, 2008).

39. "Marketing a Green Product," *BusinessWeek Online*, March 5, 2007, 13.

40. Ibid.

41. "It's Not Easy Being Green," **www.usbusinessreview.com** (July–August 2008), 14–15.

42. "Easy but Green, Rider," *Marketing Magazine*, July 14, 2008, 29.

43. **www.wm.com** (accessed October 21, 2008).

44. "Shopping Can Boost Donations to Charity," *Augusta Chronicle*, May 29, 2007, C7.

45. "Shoppers Without A Cause," *BusinessWeek*, July 9, 2007, 14.

46. Larry Chiagouris and Ipshita Ray, "Saving the World With Cause-Related Marketing," *Marketing Management*, July/August 2007, 48–51.

47. "Cause-tied Marketing Not Perfect," *The Toronto Star*, July 16, 2007, AA02.

48. "Op-Ed: Cause Efforts Go Deeper Than Dollars," *PR Week*, April 16, 2007, 8.

49. "Susan G. Komen Breast Cancer Foundation Creates Five Questions to Ask Before Participating in a Cause-Related Marketing Program," *PR Newswire*, September 28, 2005; also see Michael Barone, Andrew Norman, and Anthony Miyazakij, "Consumer Response to Retailer Use of Cause-Related Marketing: Is More Better?" *Journal of Retailing*, December 2007, 437–445.

50. Laura Heller, "Think Pink. Shop RED," *Retailing Today*, November 20, 2006; Betsy Spethmann, "The RED Brigade," *Prism Business Media*, January 1, 2007; Geoffrey Gray, "Achtung, Bono! Activists See Red: Alliance with Gap Upsets Anti-Sweatshop Types," *New York*, October 30, 2006; Soo Youn, "Owner of Gap Releases Details of Operations at Textile Factories Worldwide," *Daily News*, May 13, 2004; **www.joinred.com; www.theglobalfund.org; www.myspace.com/joinred**.

CHAPTER 4

1. "A Shift in Dining Scene: Nicks, a Once-Hot Chain," *The Wall Street Journal*, June 29, 2007, A1, A13.

2. "Get in the Loop," *Marketing News*, May 1, 2008, 5.

3. Kerry Capell, "Thinking Simple at Philips," *BusinessWeek*, December 11, 2006, 50.

4. Calvin P. Duncan, Constance O'Hare, and John M. Mathews, "Raising Your Market IQ," *The Wall Street Journal*, December 102, 2007, R4.

5. "TJX: Dressed to Kill for the Downturn," *BusinessWeek*, October 27, 2008, 60.

6. The material on personality and geography is adapted from: Stephanie Simon, "The United States of Mind," *The Wall Street Journal*, September 23, 2008, A26.

7. "Stats on Women in Business," **www.score.org** (September 4, 2007).

8. "Women Want Home Improvement Retailers to Boost Service; National Survey Reveals Gaps in Service, Product Knowledge," *PR Newswire*, February 27, 2006.

9. "Single Women in U.S. Buying More Homes," *New York Times*, May 25, 2007, G6.

10. "Young Women Earn More than Men in Big U.S. Cities," *Renters News*, August 3, 2007.

11. Author's projection based upon J. Walker Smith, "Make Time Worth It," *Marketing Management*, July/August 2005, 56.

12. "Another Casualty Emerges From the Crises: Family Time," *The Wall Street Journal*, October 15, 2008, B1.

13. Michael Mandel, "The Real Reasons You're Working So Hard," *BusinessWeek*, October 3, 2005, 60.

14. Smith, "Make Time Worth It."

15. Elisabeth A. Sullivan, "HOG—Harley-Davidson Shows Brand Strength As It Navigates Down New Roads—And Picks Up More Female Riders Along the Way," *Marketing News*, November 1, 2008, 8.

16. "Changing Consumer Lifestyles Create New American Neighborhood," *Marketing Matters Newsletter*, **www.marketingpower.com**; (accessed October 28, 2008).

17. "American Time Use Survey—2007 Results," (Washington: Bureau of Labor Statistics) June 25, 2008.

18. "Changing Consumer Lifestyles...."

19. June Kronholz, "The Coming Crunch," *The Wall Street Journal*, October 13, 2006, B1, B8; U.S. Census Press Release, **www.census.gov/Press-Release/www/releases/archives/population/012496.html**, August 14, 2008.

20. "Fewer Americans Are Relocating Within the U.S.," *The Wall Street Journal*, July 10, 2008, A3.

21. "Targeting Tweens," *Chain Store Age*, July 1, 2007.

22. "Filling a Niche for Tweens," *Houston Chronicle*, August 23, 2007, 5.

23. "Celling to Tweens," *New York Post*, June 10, 2007, 32.

24. "Coming of Age in Consumerdom," *American Demographics*, April 2004, 14.

25. "Literal Fitness for Kids," *Brandweek*, September 24, 2007, 16.

26. "Spas for the Pre-Tween Set: More Businesses Are Offering Pampered-Treatment Packages for Kids," *Vancouver Sun*, October 30, 2006, C3.

27. "Tween Trend Report Investigates the World of Generation Y," *Harrison Group/VNU* (2006).

28. "Teens Prefer Real Friends to Online Ones," *Quirk's Marketing Research Review*, August 2008, 6.

29. "Retailers Sell to Teens in Virtual Worlds," *The Wall Street Journal*, August 19, 2008, B8.

30. "Understanding Tweens and Teens," *Youth Markets Alert*, August 1, 2007, 7; and "EPM Offers Advice for Marketing to Tweens and Teens," *Research Alert*, June 1, 1007, 5.

31. Karen Akers, "Generation Y: Marketing to the Young and the Restless," *Successful Promotions*, January/February 2005, 33–38.

32. "Young, Rich, and Famous," *USA Today*, January 10, 2007, 6B, 7B.

33. "Gen Y's Fave: Whole Foods," *Brandweek*, July 28, 2008, 13.

34. "Gen X More Involved Than Boomers," *USA Today*, April 4, 2007, D5.

35. "Gen Xers and Their Concerns Are Reshaping the Retail Landscape: Be True to Your Word, When Marketing to Them, Researcher Advises," *Montreal Gazette*, June 13, 2007, B1

36. "Gen X Wants No-Debt," *American Demographics*, April 2004, 43.

37. "Gen X Slackers Get Serious," *Brandweek*, June 30, 2008, 8.

38. "The Changing Face of the U.S. Consumer," *Advertising Age*, July 7, 2008, 1–10.

39. Ibid.

40. Louise Lee, "Love Those Boomers," *BusinessWeek*, October 24, 2005, 94–101.

41. "Boomer Bust," *The Wall Street Journal*, October 21, 2008, A13.

42. "Baby Boomers Delay Retirement," *The Wall Street Journal*, September 22, 2008, A4.

43. Lee, "Love Those…."

44. Dick Chay, "New Segments of Boomers Reveal New Marketing Implications," *Marketing News*, March 14, 2005, 24.

45. "Marketers Rethink Retail; Boomers Get Fresh Look," *Brandweek*, May 21, 2007, 10.

46. "Personal Touch," *Marketing Management*, May/June 2007, 4.

47. Robert J. Morais, "It's Time to Connect With Baby Boomers," *Brandweek*, March 6, 2006, 20.

48. "Minority Population Tops 100 Million," *US Fed News*, May 17, 2007.

49. "Nonwhites to Be Majority in U.S. by 2042," *The Wall Street Journal*, August 14, 2008, A4.

50. Ibid.

51. Ibid.

52. "Minority Population…."

53. Projections by the authors.

54. "Pepsi, Vowing Diversity Isn't Just Image Polish, Seeks Inclusive Culture," *The Wall Street Journal*, April 19, 2005, B1.

55. "Give Me Your Tired, Your Poor, Your Beloved Products," *Business 2.0*, October 2005, 29–30.

56. "Wal-Mart's Hispanic Outreach," *The Wall Street Journal*, May 31, 2005, B9.

57. "Claim That Tune," *Adweek Media*, January 14, 2008, 1.

58. "Online Shopping By Minorities Up Sharply," *Quirk's Marketing Research Review*, June 2008, 80.

59. "To Woo Gen Y, Marketers Push Culture, Not Language," *Brandweek*, January 1, 2007, 5.

60. "Has This Group Been Left Behind?" *Brandweek*, March 14, 2005, 35.

61. "African-American TV Usage and Buying Power Highlighted," **www.marketingcharts.com**, accessed November 12, 2008.

62. "Affluent African Americans Making Impact on Consumer Economy," **www.marketingcharts .com**, accessed November 12, 2008.

63. Ibid.

64. "Coca Cola Kicks Off 2007 With New Advertising and 'American Idol' Integration in the U.S.," *PR Newswire*, January 17, 2007; also see Sonya Grier, Anne Brumbaugh, and Corliss Thornton, "Crossover Dreams: Consumer Responses to Ethnic-Oriented Products," *Journal of Marketing*, April 2006, 35–51.

65. "Affluent African Americans Wield $29.8 Billion in Spending Power," **www.market-ingcharts.com**, accessed November 12, 2008.

66. Ibid.

67. "The Asian-American Market," *delivermagazine*, September 2008, 8.

68. Ibid.

69. "The Asian-American Market Is a Diverse Group, and There Are Cultural Nuances Particular to Each," *National Jeweler*, September 1, 2006.

70. Jerry Goodbody, "Taking the Pulse of Asian Americans," *Adweek's Marketing Week*, August 12, 2001, 32.

71. "The Invisible Market," *Brandweek*, January 30, 2006, 22–26.

72. U.S. Census Bureau, data with projections by the authors.

73. **http://earnmydegree.com**, accessed November 9, 2008.

74. U.S. Income gap widens, richest share hits record," **www.reuters.com/article/domes-ticNews/idUSN1241503820071012**, accessed November 9, 2008.

75. Christopher Conkey, "Snapshot of America: Who's Richest, Poorest, Where the Single Men Are," *The Wall Street Journal*, August 30, 2006, D1, D3.

76. "At the Supermarket Checkout, Frugality Trumps Brand Loyalty," *The Wall Street Journal*, November 6, 2008, D1.

77. "The Recession Could Be Mild But Long," *BusinessWeek*, October 20, 2008, 12.

78. "At the Supermarket Checkout…."

79. "Why Some Brands Cheer a Sour Economy," *Brandweek*, October 13, 2008, 5.

80. "Looking for Cost Cuts in Lots of New Places," *The Wall Street Journal*, October 16, 2008, B5.

81. "Costco's Artful Discounts," *BusinessWeek*, October 20, 2008, 58–60.

82. "How Technology Delivers for UPS," *BusinessWeek*, March 5, 2007, 60.

83. Diane Brady, "Reaping the Wind," *BusinessWeek*, October 11, 2004, 201.

84. "Creativity Pays. Here's How Much," *BusinessWeek*, April 24, 2006, 45.

85. "Yes, Innovations Do Pay Off, Study Finds," *International Herald Tribune*, August 30–31, 2008, 15.

86. Cornelia Dean, "Maybe Science Can Save the Planet: But Should It?" *International Herald Tribune*, August 13, 2008, 2.

87. "More Paper Tiger Than Watchdog?" *BusinessWeek*, September 3, 2007, 45.

88. "Spamalot No More," *Marketing Management*, October 2008, 47–50.

89. "Editorial: Shop With Cash," *The Providence Journal*, February 9, 2007, B4.

90. "Identity Theft Protection Bill Clears Hurdle," *Associates Press Newswires*, May 4, 2007.

91. "K-C, P&G's Lotion Tissue War Is Nothing to Sneeze At," *Brandweek*, September 18, 2008, 12–13.

92. Ibid.

93. "Home Economics," *BusinessWeek*, March 14, 2005, 12.

94. "DHL Beats a Retreat from the U.S.," *The Wall Street Journal*, November 11, 2008, B1.

CHAPTER 5

1. William Wrigley Jr. Company, news release, July 2, 2007.

2. *Trade and American Jobs: The Impact of Trade on U.S. and State-Level Employment* (Washington: Business Roundtable), February 2007.

3. Ibid.

4. Ibid.

5. "Top U.S. Trade Partners," U.S. Department of Commerce, Census Bureau, Foreign Trade Division, International Trade Administration, October 2008.

6. David Wessel and Bod Davis, "Pain from Free Trade Spurs Second Thoughts," *The Wall Street Journal*, March 28, 2007, A1, A14. Reprinted with permission of *The Wall Street Journal*, © 2007 Dow Jones & Company, Inc. All Rights Reserved Worldwide.

7. Ibid.

8. Ibid.

9. "Can the U.S. Bring Jobs Back from China?" *BusinessWeek*, June 30, 2008, 39–43.

10. Ibid.

11. "Globalization's Gains Come with a Price," *The Wall Street Journal*, May 24, 2007, A1, A12.

12. "Multinationals: Are They Good for America?" *BusinessWeek*, March 10, 2008, 41–45.

13. Ibid.

14. Ibid.

15. "Foreign Investors Face New Hurdles Across the Globe," *The Wall Street Journal*, July 6, 2007, A1, A7.

16. Theodore Levitt, "The Globalization of Markets," *Harvard Business Review*, May/June 1983, 92–100.

17. "Levi's Marketers Hope One Size Fits All," *The Wall Street Journal*, July 18, 2008, B7.

18. Ibid.

19. The Italian cleaning products stories are from "Convenience Is a Dirty Word to These Italian Consumers," *Quirk's Marketing Research Review*, October 2006, 6.

20. "Slacker Nation? Young Japanese Shun Promotions," *The Wall Street Journal*, November 1–2, 2008, A1, A6.

21. "French Protestors Wage War on Billboards," *The Wall Street Journal*, September 26, 2008, B5.

22. Ibid.

23. "Indian Farmers Threaten to Renew Nano Protests," *International Herald Tribune*, September 12, 2008, 17.

24. **www.finfacts.com**, November 22, 2005.

25. "World's Most Expensive Cities," **CNNMoney.com**, June 18, 2007.

26. The China/India story is from Anil K. Gupta and Haiyan Wang, "How to Get China and India Right," *The Wall Street Journal*, April 28–29, 2007, R9. Reprinted with permission of *The Wall Street Journal* © 2007 Dow Jones & Company, Inc. All Rights Reserved Worldwide.

27. "China Pushes Foreign Companies to Unionize," *The Global Edition of the New York Times*, September 12, 2008, 14.

28. Ibid.

29. "Doing Business 2008," The World Bank.

30. Ibid.

31. "Global Ties Under Stress As Nations Grab Power," *The Wall Street Journal*, April 28, 2008, A1, A16.

32. Ibid.

33. "China Says It Is Free to Set High Tariffs," *The Wall Street Journal*, July 30, 2008, A9; and "China Sides With Developing Nations in Trade Talks," *The Wall Street Journal*, July 30, 2008, A10.

34. "The End of Free Trade?" *The Wall Street Journal*, July 31, 2008, A14.

35. "South Korea Looks to the West," *Fortune*, October 31, 2008, 52; and "Liberalizing Trans-Atlantic Trade," *The Wall Street Journal*, September 5, 2008, 5.

36. "The Trade Stimulus," *International Trade Administrator*, October 27, 2008, 1.

37. "Most Canadians, Americans Support NAFTA: Poll," *Xinhua News Agency*, October 1, 2007.

38. "5 Myths About NAFTA," *The Fort Worth Star Telegram*, April 14, 2008, 9B.

39. "Top U.S. Trading Partners," *Top U.S. Export Markets*, Washington: International Trade Association, Summer 2008, 4.

40. Jack Welch, "A Punching Bag Named NAFTA," *BusinessWeek*, April 28, 2008, 138.

41. "Refighting NAFTA," *BusinessWeek*, March 31, 2008, 56–59; also see: "Make the World Go Away," *Fortune*, February 4, 2008, 105–107.

42. "U.S. Central America-Dominican Republic Free Trade Agreement (CAFTA-DR) Analysis," (Washington: International Trade Association), Summer 2008, 12.

43. **www.eurunion.org**, accessed November 5, 2008.

44. Ibid.

45. Ibid.

46. "European Union's Kroes Says U.S. Criticism of Microsoft Ruling Is Unacceptable," *Associated Press Newswires*, September 19, 2007.

47. Jonathan Bensky, "World's Biggest Market: European Union Offers Great Opportunities for U.S. Companies, But There Are Also Plenty of Challenges," *Shipping Digest*, July 30, 2007.

48. Ibid.

49. "World Bank Group 2008 Global Poll: Overcoming Poverty Remains Biggest Challenge to Developing Countries," press release, The World Bank, October 31, 2008.

50. **www.sba.gov**, accessed November 4, 2008.

51. **www.exim.gov**, October 3, 2007.

52. "$187 Billion Global Licensing Industry Comes to Life," **www.reuters.com** (press release), June 6, 2008.

53. "Entertainment/Character Licenses Generated Largest Share of Worldwide Sales," *Licensing Letter*, June 6, 2005.

54. **www.franchise.org**, December 5, 2005.

55. "Foreign Flavors," *The Wall Street Journal*, September 25, 2006, R8.

56. Roger Parloff, "Not Exactly Counterfeit," *Fortune*, May 1, 2006, 109–116.

57. "Dangerous Fakes," *BusinessWeek*, October 13, 2008, 34–44.

58. Andrew R. Thomas, Timothy J. Wilkinson, and Jon M. Hawes, "Making It in China," *The Wall Street Journal*, May 12, 2008, R11.

59. "GM's China Partner Looms as a New Rival," *The Wall Street Journal*, April 20, 2007, A1, A8.

60. "Partners Fight over Wahaha in China," *The Wall Street Journal*, July 28, 2008, B1.

61. "Danone's China Strategy in Set Back," *The Wall Street Journal*, June 15, 2007, A10.

62. **www.walmartstores.com/FactsNews**, accessed November 8, 2008.

63. "Investment Will Favor International Markets," *The Toronto Star*, October 29, 2008, BO2.

64. "Toyota Eyes India Market, Builds School to Get Edge," *The Wall Street Journal*, November 3, 2008, B1–B2.

65. "Starbucks Expansion Plan in China Unchanged," *China Knowledge Press*, August 7, 2008.

66. Kenneth Hein, "Emerging Markets Still Like U.S. Brands," *BrandWeek*, April 16, 2007, 4. Used by permission of Aegis Group, plc.; also see "Best Global Brands," September 29, 2008, 52–57.

67. "Fad Marketing's Balancing Act," *BusinessWeek*, August 6, 2007, 42.

68. "Machines for the Masses," *The Wall Street Journal*, December 9, 2005, A4.

69. Peter Gumbel, "Big Mac's Local Flavor," *Fortune*, May 5, 2008, 115–121.

70. "Kraft Reformulates Oreo, Scores in China," *The Wall Street Journal*, May 1, 2008, B1, B7.

71. "If Only 'Krispy Kreme' Meant 'Makes You Smarter,'" *Business 2.0*, August 2005, 108.

72. Amy Chozick, "The Samurai Sell: Lexus Dealers Bow to Move Swank Cars," *The Wall Street Journal*, July 9, 2007, A1, A12.

73. Jane Lanhee Lee, "China Hurdle: Lack of Refrigeration," *The Wall Street Journal*, August 30, 2007, A7.

74. Eric Bellmann and Cecilie Rohwedder, "Western Grocer Modernizes Passage to India's Markets," *The Wall Street Journal*, November 28, 2007, B1.

75. "UPS Battles Traffic to Gain Ground in India," *The Wall Street Journal*, January 25, 2008, B1, B2.

76. Michael Arndt, "Knock, Knock, It's Your Big Mac," *BusinessWeek*, July 23, 2007, 36.

77. "Vietnam Denies Garment Dumping in U.S. Market," *Thai News Service*, October 1, 2007.

78. Lacey Rose, "The World's Best-Paid Male Athletes," *Forbes*, August 8, 2008; Tom Van Riper and Kurt Badenhausen, "Top-Earning Female Athletes," *Forbes*, July 22, 2008; Kurt Badenhausen, Michael Ozanian, Christina Settimi, "The Richest Game," *Forbes*, September 11, 2008; Len Pasquarelli, "NFL Europa Failed to Produce Players, Profits," ESPN, June 29, 2007; Mike Carlson, "Saints Put on a Show for 'Home' Crowd at Wembley," NFL.com, October 27, 2008; Lisa Altobelli, "Think Globally: NFL Visits England to Increase Awareness of Football," *Sports Illustrated*, October 24, 2008; Associated Press, "NFL Hoping Rules, Jargon Doesn't Prevent Chinese From Learning Game," ESPN, June 29, 2007; Matthew Futterman, "Football Tries a New Play to Score Overseas," *The Wall Street Journal*, October 9, 2008.

CHAPTER 6

1. **www.persil.com/persil_products/pfam_home/**, February 2006; **www.eu.pg.com/our-brands/ariel.html**, February 2006.

2. "Virtually Satisfied," *Marketing News*, October 15, 2008, 26.

3. Allen Weiss, Nicholas Lurie, and Deborah MacInnis, "Listening to Strangers: Whose Responses Are Valuable, How Valuable Are They, and Why?" *Journal of Marketing Research*, August 2008, 450–461.

4. Jonah Berger and Grainne Fitzsimons, "Dogs on the Street, Pumas on Your Feet: How Cues in the Environment Influence Product Evaluation and Choice," *Journal of Marketing Research*, February 2008, 1–14.

5. The section on categorization is adapted from: Roger Blackwell, Paul Miniard, and James Engel, *Consumer Behavior*, 10th Edition (Mason, Ohio: Cengage Learning), 2006, 132–133.

6. Jeffrey Inman and Russell Winer, "Impulse Buys," *The Wall Street Journal*, April 15, 1999, A1; and David Silvera, Anne Lavack, and Fredric Kropp, "Impulse Buying: The Role of Affect, Social Influence, and Subjective Well-Being," *Journal of Consumer Research*, 25, no. 1 (2008), 23–33.

7. Paula Andruss, "Delivering Wow Through Service," *Marketing News*, October 15, 2008, 10.

8. Toyota ad, *Wired*, March, 2007, 72–73.

9. Ira Teinowitz, "Kellogg Move Bodes Ill for Ads to Kids," *Advertising Age*, June 18, 2007.

10. Sandra Yin, "Color Bind," *American Demographics*, September 2003, 24, 26.

11. Geoff Colvin, "Selling P&G," *Fortune*, September 17, 2007, 156, 6, 163.

12. "Thank God for the Chinese Consumer," *The Wall Street Journal*, August 8, 2008, A15; and Nicholas Casey, "Fisher-Price Game Plan: Pursue Toy Sales in Developing Markets," *The Wall Street Journal*, May 29, 2008, B1, B2.

13. Lorenza Muñoz," Selling Spanish TV to Ad Buyers," *Los Angeles Times*, May 15, 2007.

14. "Rise of the Have-Nots," *Adweek*, October 1, 2007, 29.

15. Bradley Johnson, "Mo' Money, Mo' Buyin'," *Advertising Age*, January 15, 2007, 78, 3, 29.

16. "TJX: Dressed to Kill for the Downturn," *BusinessWeek*, October 27, 2008, 60.

17. Ulrich Orth and Lynn Kahle, "Intrapersonal Variation in Consumer Susceptibility to Normative Influence: Toward a Better Understanding of Brand Choice Decisions," *Journal of Social Psychology*, August 8, 2008, 423–448.

18. Ibid.

19. Ronald Clark, James Zboja, and Ronald Goldsmith, "Status Consumption and Role-Relaxed Consumption: A Tale of Two Retail

Consumers," *Journal of Retailing and Consumer Services*, January 2007, 45–59.

20. Neil E. Boudette and Gina Ghon, "Brawny BMW Seeks 'the Idea Class'," *The Wall Street Journal*, August 2, 2006, B1.

21. Katie Delahaye Paine, "How Do Blogs Measure Up? Forget Reach and Frequency. Success in Today's Marketplace is Measured Not by How Broad Your Reach is But by How Deep Your Network Is," *Communication World*, Sept–Oct 2007, 24, 5, 30.

22. Rachel Dodes, "Bloggers Get Under the Tent," *The Wall Street Journal, September* 12, 2006, B1, B2.

23. Chenting See, Kevin Zheng Zhou, Nan Zhou, and Julie Juan Li, "Harmonizing Conflict in Husband-Wife Purchase Decision-Making: Perceived Fairness and Spousal Influence Dynamics," *Journal of the Academy of Marketing Science* (Fall 2008), 378–394; also see: Michel Laroche, Zhiyong Yang, Kim Chankon, and Marie-Odile Richard, "How Culture Matters in Children's Purchase Influence: A Multi-level Investigation," *Journal of the Academy of Marketing Science* (Spring 2007), 113–116.

24. Ibid.

25. Derek Gale, "Who's the Boss?" *Restaurants & Institutions*, February 1, 2007, 117, 2, 50.

26. Jeanine Poggi, "Teen Queens; The Age Group's Spending Is on the Rise, Making It a Coveted—Albeit Fickle—Market," *WWD*, June 28, 2007, 85.

27. Karin Ekstrom, "Parental Consumer Learning or 'Keeping Up With Their Children'," *Journal of Consumer Behavior* (July/August 2007), 203–217.

28. Bureau of Labor Statistics, Consumer Expenditures Annual Reports: 2005, Census Bureau, **www.bls.gov/ces/**.

29. Stephanie Rosenbloom, "My Dad, American Inventor," *The New York Times*, August 16, 2007.

30. Nanette Byrnes, "Secrets Of the Male Shopper," *BusinessWeek*, online, **www.businessweek.com/magazine/content/06_36/b3999001.htm**, accessed August 17, 2007; also see: Xin He, Jeffrey Inman, and Vikas Mittal, "Gender Jeopardy in Financial Risk-Taking," *Journal of Marketing Research*, August 2008, 414–424.

31. Anil Mathur, George Moschis, and Euehun Lee, "A Longitudinal Study of the Effects of Life Style Status Changes on Changes in Consumer Preferences," *Journal of the Academy of Marketing Sciences*, Summer 2008, 234–246.

32. "Study: Snacking Has Become the Fourth Meal of the Day," *Brandweek*, September 29, 2008, 8.

33. Ibid.

34. Loretta Chao and Betsy McKay, "Pepsi Steps into Coke Realm," *The Wall Street Journal*, September 12, 2007.

35. **www.ampacet.com**, December 28, 2007.

36. Laura Petrecca, "Axe Ads Turn Up the Promise of Sex Appeal," *USA Today*, April 17, 2007.

37. Joshua Rosenbaum, "Guitar Maker Looks for a New Key," *The Wall Street Journal*, February 11, 1998, B1, B5.

38. Elizabeth J. Wilson, "Using the Dollar-metric Scale to Establish the Just Meaningful Difference in Price," in *1987 AMA Educators' Proceedings*, ed. Susan Douglas et al. (Chicago: American Marketing Association, 1987), 107.

39. Kenneth Hein, "Teens Schizophrenic About Their Brands: Millennials Have Complex Feelings About Brands Unless, of Course, It's Apple," *Brandweek*, June 18, 2007.

40. International Chamber of Commerce's new initiative: BASCAP—Business Action to Stop Counterfeiting and Piracy **www.icc-ccs.co.uk/bascap/digest/Cases.htm**, September 11, 2007; Global Brand Protection Directory: **www.iccwbo.org/bascap/id12418/index.html**, September 11, 2007.

41. Press release: "GE Announces Advancement in Incandescent Technology; New High-Efficiency Lamps Targeted for Market by 2010," February 23, 2007; Lloyd Alter, "GE Announces High Efficiency Incandescent Light Bulbs. Why?" *Design & Architecture*, February 24, 2007, accessed online at **www.treehugger.com/files/2007/02/ge_announces_hi.php**, May 29, 2008.

42. Stephanie Thompson, "Cole Haan Fashions an Effort for Women," *Advertising Age*, August 25, 2003, 6.

43. **www.Cadillac.com**, accessed October 25, 2008.

44. Jyothi Datta, "Aspartame: Bitter Truth in Artificial Sweeteners?" Mumbai, Oct. 3, **www.thehindubusinessline.com/2005/10/04/stories/2005100404220300.htm**, accessed September 14, 2007.

45. Amy Chozick and Timothy Martin, "A Place for Cocoa Nuts?" *The Wall Street Journal*, July 15, 2005, B1, B3; **www.ethelschocolate.com**; "Ethel's Launches First-Ever Approachable, Everyday Gourmet Chocolate and Chocolate Lounges; Opens First Two Stores in Chicago, Expected to Expand to Six by End of Summer," PR Newswire, June 6, 2005; Karen Hawkins, "Chocolate Lounges' Present Themselves as Sweet Alternatives to Coffee Shops, Bars," Associated Press, February 13, 2006; Melinda Murphy, "Trend Report: Chocolate Is Hot," CBS News Online, **www.cbsnews.com/stories/2006/02/07/earlyshow/contributors/melindamurphy/main1289922.shtml**.

CHAPTER 7

1. "2008 Marketing Priorities and Plans," *BtoB Magazine*, July 15, 2008, 25.

2. Michael D. Hutt and Thomas W. Speh, *Business Marketing Management: B2B, 9e*. (Cincinnati: Thomson, 2007), 4.

3. Patricia Riedman, "BtoB's Best Brands," *BtoB Magazine*, Special Issue, 2008, 21–25.

4. Hutt and Speh, 315.

5. Ibid.

6. Mary E. Morrison, "Industrial Buyers Shopping Online," *BtoB Magazine*, October 13, 2008, 19.

7. Karen J. Bannan, "10 Great Web Sites: Overview," *BtoB Magazine*, online, September 15, 2008.

8. "Survey Says! Recent BtoB Webcast Audience Poll Results," *BtoB Magazine*, November 10, 2008, 8.

9. NetGenesis, E-Metrics: Business Metrics for the New Economy, **www.spss.com**.

10. Morrison, 19.

11. "RSS," Wikipedia, the Free Encyclopedia, accessed online at **http://en.wikipedia.org/wiki/**.

12. "B2B Marketers Missing Out on Influencing Buyers Online," *Marketing Matters Newsletter*, Chicago: American Marketing Association, online, October 28, 2008.

13. "Grainger Introduces SupplyLink Site," *BtoB Magazine*, online, July 24, 2008.

14. "Disintermediation," Wikipedia, the Free Encyclopedia, accessed online at **http://en.wikipedia.org/wiki/**.

15. Ibid.

16. Kate Maddox, "Marketers Look to Boost Customer Retention," *BtoB Magazine*, online, May 5, 2008.

17. Ibid. Reprinted with permission of Crane Communications.

18. "Office Depot Forms Alliance With Netbizz in Singapore," *BtoB Magazine*, online, August 13, 2008.

19. Steven Reinberg, "The Issue: DHL Turns to Rival UPS," *BusinessWeek*, June 11, 2008, online.

20. Erin White, "A Cheaper Alternative to Outsourcing: Choice Hotels and 1-800-Flowers Swap Call-Center Employees," *The Wall Street Journal*, April 10, 2006, B3.

21. Robert M. Morgan and Shelby D. Hunt, "The Commitment-Trust Theory of Relationship Marketing," *Journal of Marketing*, 58, no. 3 (1994): 23.

22. Ibid.

23. Gordon Fairclough, "GM's Chinese Partner Looms as a New Rival," *The Wall Street Journal*, April 20, 2007, A1.

24. U.S. Census Bureau, "North American Industry Classification System (NAICS) – United States," accessed online at **www.census.gov/epcd/www/naics.html**, January 12, 2009.

25. Steve Butler, "B2B Exchanges Transaction Activity," *eMarketer*, online.

26. J. Lynn Lunsford, "Boeing Delays Dreamliner Delivery Again," *The Wall Street Journal*, April 10, 2008, B3.

27. Marshall Lager, "Listen Up," *Customer Relationship Management*, March 2007, 24–27.

28. Kate Maddox, "Relevant Content Connects with C-suite," *BtoB Magazine*, October 13, 2008, 37–38.

29. Ibid.

30. Setting the Standard: Code of Ethics and Business Conduct. Office of Ethics and Business Conduct, Lockheed Martin Corporation, Bethesda, MD, October 2008.

31. "Right Channeling: Making Sure Your Best Customers Get Your Best Service," Right Now Technologies, online at **www.rightnow.com**, June 3, 2008.

32. This application exercise is based on the contribution of Gregory B. Turner (College of Charleston) to *Great Ideas in Teaching Marketing*, a teaching supplement that accompanies Lamb, Hair, and McDaniel's *Marketing*. Professor Turner's entry titled "Student Ethics versus Practitioner Ethics" received an Honorable Mention in the "Best of the Great Ideas in Teaching Marketing" contest held in conjunction with the publication of the eighth edition of *Marketing*.

33. Jonathan Karp, "How Bikers' Water Backpack Became Soldiers' Essential," *The Wall Street Journal*, July 19, 2005, B1, B2; "CamelBak Introduces New Line of Strength/Stealth Technology Responding to Law Enforcement and Military Needs; R&D Innovations Protect Against Infrared Detection, Provide Strongest Hydration Reservoir Available," *PR Newswire*, January 27, 2005; Mark Riedy, "The Birth of CamelBak," *Mountain Bike*, Summer 2004, 104; "CamelBak

Announces Chem-Bio Hydration Reservoir for Military, Law Enforcement and First Responders; New Reservoir Is World's Only Hands-Free Hydration System That Withstands Exposure to Chemical and Biological Agents to Provide Safe Drinking Water in All Combat Environments 24/7/365." *PR Newswire*, August 26, 2004.

CHAPTER 8

1. Jena McGregor, "At Best Buy, Marketing Goes Micro," *BusinessWeek*, May 26, 2008, 52, 53.
2. Vanessa O'Connell, "Park Avenue Classic or Soho Trendy?" *The Wall Street Journal*, April 20, 2007, B1, B2.
3. Vanessa O'Connell, "Reversing Field, Macy's Goes Local," *The Wall Street Journal*, April 21, 2008, B1, B8.
4. Evan Bailyn, "Keeping It Simple: Marketing to Tweens on a Shoestring," **www.mediapost.com**, December 2, 2008.
5. Emily Steel and Vishesh Kumar, "Targeted Ads Raise Privacy Concerns," *The Wall Street Journal*, July 8, 2008, B1; Jessica Tsai, "Oh, Behave!," *Customer Relationship Management*, January 2008, 25–29; "The Aim of Behavioral Targeting," **www.eMarketer.com**, August 5, 2008; "Behavioral Targeting and Privacy," **www.eMarketer.com**, July 29, 2008.
6. Khanh T. L. Tran, "Retailing's Sweet Spot: Stores Look to Lure Millennial Generation," **www.wwd.com**, July 2, 2008.
7. Kenneth Hein, "How to Reach Teens? It's All about the Brand," online, **www.brandweek.com**, June 18, 2007.
8. Sarah Mahoney, "Study: Gen Y Shoppers Drawn to Greener Marketers," online, **www.mediapostpublications.com**, September 21, 2007.
9. "The Issue: How P&G Brought Back Herbal Essences," *BusinessWeek*, June 17, 2008, online.
10. Jessica Sebor, "Y me," *Customer Relationship Management*, November 2006, 24–35.
11. Toni Whitt, "Boomers Rewrite Rules for Marketing," **www.heraldtribune.com**, June 25, 2007.
12. Jennifer Mann, "Advertising and Marketing: 50-year-olds Not Dead Yet," **star-telegram.com**, August 10, 2008.
13. Ylan Q. Mui, "Retailers Redesign as Boomers Hit 60," **www.washingtonpost.com**, January 17, 2006, D01.
14. Sebor, "Y me."
15. Emily Fromm, "Marketing to Women," *Brandweek*, October 4, 2004, 21–28.
16. Ross Kenneth Urken, "EA Sports' Ads Feature New Stars: John (and Jane) Q. Public," *The Wall Street Journal*, July 25, 2008, online.
17. Jennifer Waters, "Home Depot Woos Women With Concept Store Exuding 'Romance'," *The Wall Street Journal*, October 9, 2007, online.
18. Rupa Ranganananthan, "Resort Spa Uncovers Cultural Anthropology to Cultivate Male Clients," *RetailWire*, June 30, 2005, online.
19. "CoolStuffForDads.com, an Online Store Dedicated to Gifts for Dads, Continues to Add Great Products for Men," **www.biz.yahoo.com**, September 22, 2008.
20. Tom Ryan, "Targeting Male Grocery Shoppers," **www.retailwire.com**, June 4, 2007.

21. Francine Kizner, "Where the Rich Shop," **www.entrepreneur.com**, February 16, 2007.
22. "Luxury Brands: Marketing the Upscale during a Downturn," **http://knowledge.wharton.upenn.edu**, November 13, 2008.
23. Constantine von Hoffman, "For Some Marketers, Low Income Is Hot," *Brandweek*, September 11, 2006, 6.
24. "The New Mainstream: How the Buying Habits of Ethnic Groups Are Creating a New American Identity," **http://knowledge.wharton.upenn.edu/article.cfm?articleid=1270**, November 15, 2005; accessed June 9, 2008.
25. Laura Klepacki, "Ethnic Products Now Front and Center," **www.retailwire.com**, June 11, 2007.
26. "What's 'Online Marketing' in Spanish?" *RetailWire*, November 5, 2007.
27. Dan Raftery, "R&FF Retailer: Hispanic Foods Move Beyond Hot & Spicy," **www.retailwire.com**, June 4, 2007.
28. Ann Zimmerman and Miguel Bustillo, "Home Depot's New Web Site Opens Door to Hispanics," *The Wall Street Journal*, November 17, 2008, B1, B9.
29. "Amazon Launches New Software en Español Store as the Software Shopping Destination for Hispanic Consumers," **www.biz.yahoo.com**, August 12, 2008.
30. David Morse, "Brain Trust Query: Do African Americans Require a Targeted Marketing Approach?" **www.retailwire.com**, July 30, 2008.
31. Deborah L. Vence, "Mix It Up—Segmentation, Unique Events Key to Targeting Blacks," *Marketing News*, October 15, 2006, 19, 22.
32. Andrew Pierce, "Multiculti Markets Demand Multilayered Marketing," *Marketing News*, May 1, 2008, 21.
33. Ibid.
34. Alison Damast, "Love Can Hurt—Your Bank Account," *BusinessWeek*, February 7, 2008, online.
35. Stuart Elliott, "To Reach Mothers, Wal-Mart Signs Deal with an NBC Unit," **www.nytimes.com**, July 14, 2008.
36. "Baby Boomer Segmentation: Kids/No Kids," **www.retailwire.com**, February 2, 2007, online.
37. Dianne Hales, "What Your Car Says About You," *Parade*, May 15, 2005, 8.
38. Joseph Pereira, "New Exercise Targets Less-Than-Fit," *The Wall Street Journal*, February 1, 2007, B1, B9.
39. Deborah L. Vence, "Divide and Conquer," *Marketing News*, July 15, 2007, 15, 18.
40. Ann Zimmerman, "Home Depot Learns to Go Local," *The Wall Street Journal*, October 7, 2008, B1.
41. **www.claritas.com**, December 15, 2008.
42. George Stalk, Jr., "In Praise of the Heavy Spender," **www.reportonbusiness.com**, May 21, 2007, online.
43. Ellen Byron, "Aiming to Clean Up, P&G Courts Business Customers," *The Wall Street Journal*, January 26, 2007, B1, B2.
44. Juliet Chung, "Cooking Like the Stars?" *The Wall Street Journal*, June 20, 2008.
45. Jennifer Saranow and Vanessa O'Connell, "Concierge Services and Mismatched Socks," *The Wall Street Journal*, June 5, 2008.
46. Barry Silverstein, "Trader Joe's: Quirky Mart," **www.brandchannel.com**, December 13,

2008; Christopher Palmeri, "Trader Joe's Recipe for Success," *BusinessWeek* February 21, 2008, online; "A Unique Grocery Store," **http://eastontowncenter.com**, December 13, 2008.
47. "Targeting Wal-Mart's Core Customer Segments," **www.retailwire.com**, April 2, 2008.
48. "How Teen E-retailer Tripled Revenue by Allowing Consumers to Select What Email Content They Really Want," **www.marketingsherpa.com**, June 28, 2007.
49. Dianna Dilworth, "AT&T's New Multichannel Work Targets Young, On-the-Go Crowd," **www.dmnews.com**, September 18, 2007.
50. Chuck Stogel, "Callaway Gets 'Personal' With $30M Campaign," *Brandweek*, February 12, 2007, 14.
51. Ellen Byron, "Can a Re-Engineered Kleenex Cure a Brand's Sniffles?" *The Wall Street Journal*, January 22, 2007, B1.
52. Sonia Reyes, "Can Frozen Treats Sell Outside the Freezer Aisle?" *Brandweek*, March 26, 2007, 16.
53. Sandra Jones, "Sears Steps Back in Time to Go Forward," **www.chicagotribune.com**, March 12, 2007.
54. Geoff Colvin, "Selling P&G," *Fortune*, September 17, 2007, 163–169.
55. Jenny McTaggart, "Taking a Bite Out of Baggers," *Brandweek*, June 27, 2005, 42–45.
56. Ibid.
57. Gary McWilliams, "Not Copying Wal-Mart Pays Off for Grocers," *The Wall Street Journal*, June 6, 2007, B1, B5.
58. This application exercise is based on the contribution of Kim McKeage (University of Maine) to *Great Ideas in Teaching Marketing*, a teaching supplement that accompanies Lamb, Hair, and McDaniel's *Marketing*. Professor McKeage's entry, titled "Students Practice Making Market/Product Grids on Themselves," received an Honorable Mention in the "Best of the Great Ideas in Teaching Marketing" contest held in conjunction with the publication of the eighth edition of *Marketing*.
59. Case Study: Jerry Adler, "Attack of the Diet Cokes," *Newsweek*, May 14, 2007; "Coke's New 'Coke Zero' Faces Tough Going" *UPI NewsTrack*, June 13, 2005; Duane D. Stanford, "0: That's Zero. As in No Calories," *The Atlanta Journal-Constitution*, March 20, 2007; "Coca-Cola Co.," *MMR*, October 30, 2006; **www.cocacolazero.com**.

CHAPTER 9

1. Joseph Rydholm, "A Natural Extension," *Quirk's Marketing Research Review*, May 2002, 22–23, 69–70.
2. "Oscar Mayer Prepares a Better Bacon Package," *Brandweek*, June 11, 2007, 11.
3. "Why Some Customers Are More Equal Than Others," *Fortune*, September 19, 1994, 215–224.
4. Sunil Gupta, Donald Lehmann, and Jennifer Ames Stuart, "Valuing Customers," *Journal of Marketing Research*, February 2004, 7–18.
5. Janet Adamy, "Dunkin Donuts Tries to Go Upscale, But Not Too Far," *The Wall Street Journal*, April 8–9, 2006, A1, A7.
6. "Roll Out the Blue Carpet," *Business 2.0*, May 2007, 53–54.

7. Scott Pimley, "Looking to Increase Their (s) Miles Per Gallon," *Quirk's Marketing Research Review*, August 2008, 32–38.

8. Michael Fielding, "A Clean Slate," *Marketing News*, May 1, 2007, 9–10.

9. Ibid.

10. "Respondents Lie and Good Ideas Die," *Quirk's Marketing Research Review*, May 2007, 48–54.

11. D. Randall Brandt, "Improve the Customer Service," *Quirk's Marketing Research Review*, January 2006, 68.

12. "Watch and Learn," *Marketing News*, February 1, 2006, 60.

13. "The Science of Desire," *BusinessWeek*, June 5, 2006, 104.

14. Ibid.

15. Ibid.

16. Raymond R. Burke, "Virtual Shopping: Breakthrough in Marketing Research," *Harvard Business Review*, March/April 1996, 120–131.

17. Ellen Byron, "A Virtual View of the Store Aisle," *The Wall Street Journal*, October 3, 2007, B1, B12.

18. Ibid.

19. Ibid.

20. Ibid.

21. Karl Feld, "Do You Know Where Your Data Came From?" *Quirk's Marketing Research Review*, November 2007, 24–31.

22. Kira Signer and Andy Korman, "One Billion and Growing," *Quirk's Marketing Research Review*, July/August 2006, 62–67.

23. Ibid.

24. Conversation with Craig Stevens, Senior VP E-Rewards, based upon company research (November 2, 2007); also see "Market Research," *Marketing News*, September 15, 2007, 16.

25. Ibid.

26. Tim Macer and Sheila Wilson, "Online Makes More Inroads," *Quirk's Marketing Research Review*, February 2007, 50–58.

27. Based on the author's conversation with Jerry Thomas, CEO Decision Analyst, Inc. This firm has one of the largest Internet panels in the world.

28. **www.ChannelM2.com**, (accessed October 31, 2008).

29. Gregory S. Heist, "Beyond Brand Building," *Quirk's Marketing Research Review*, July/August 2007, 62–67.

30. Ibid.

31. Ibid.

32. "CGM Overview, **www.nielsenbuzzmetrics.com**, August 27, 2007.

33. Pete Blackshaw, "The Pocket Guide to Consumer Generated Media," **www.clickz.com**, August 28, 2005; Paul Verna, "User-Generated Content: More Popular than Profitable," **www.emarketer.com**, January 2009, accessed February 13, 2009.

34. "BrandPulse Insights," **www.nielsenbuzzmetrics.com**, August 28, 2007.

35. "Behavioral Issues," *Brandweek*, October 20, 2008, 21–25.

36. Ibid.

37. Ibid.

38. Emily Steel, "How Marketers Hone Their Aim," *The Wall Street Journal*, June 19, 2007, B6.

39. "Online Ads Mature," *Marketing Management*, July/August 2007, 5.

40. Carl McDaniel and Roger Gates, *Marketing Research*, 7th ed. (Hoboken: John Wiley & Sons, 2007).

CHAPTER 10

1. Valarie A. Zeithaml, Mary Jo Bitner, and Dwayne Gremler, *Services Marketing* (New York: McGraw-Hill, 2009).

2. "Employment Outlook: 2006–2016," November 2007, **www.bls.gov.**

3. Bridget Finn, "Luring 'Em In," *Business 2.0*, March 2005, 44–46.

4. "Coke, Pepsi to Sell Drinks with Stevia," *The Atlantic Journal-Constitution*, online, December 18, 2008.

5. Todd Wasserman, "P&G Seeks Right Ingredient to Wash Out Laundry Woes," *Brandweek*, August 8, 2005, 5.

6. "Kool-Aid Announces New Products and Better-For-You Brand Direction," *Yahoo! Finance*, May 27, 2008.

7. Vanessa L. Facenda, "Procter Dishes Out 3-Tiered Dawn Attack," *Brandweek*, September 24, 2007, 4.

8. Vanessa L. Facenda, "In Search of More Growth, P&G's Febreze Hits the Road," *Brandweek*, August 6, 2007, 6.

9. Julie Jargon, "Campbell's Chief Looks for Splash of Innovation," *The Wall Street Journal*, May 30, 2008, B8.

10. Al Ries, "The Pitfalls of Megabranding," *Advertising Age Online*, August 4, 2008.

11. David Kiley, "Best Global Brands," *BusinessWeek*, August 6, 2007, 56–64.

12. Nirmalya Kumar and Jan-Benedict E. M. Steenkamp, "Premium Store Brands: The Hottest Trend in Retailing," **www.marketingprofs.com**, March 20, 2007.

13. "Costco Buying Power Makes Dent in Private-Label Wine Market," **http://seattle.bizjournals.com**, April 2, 2007.

14. Elaine Wong, "Retailers Rally Behind Their 'Captive Brands'," **www.Brandweek.com**, September 29, 2008.

15. Elaine Wong, "Mr. Clean Finds Fresh Smell by Teaming with Febreze," *Brandweek*, August 11, 2008, 14.

16. Douglas Quenqua, "A Way to Save and Still Have Crisp Clothes," *The New York Times*, online, October 10, 2008.

17. "World of Coca-Cola," **www.worldofcoca-cola.com** (accessed January 11, 2009); "World of Coca-Cola," **http://en.wikipedia.org/wiki/World_of_Coca-Cola** (accessed February 21, 2009).

18. Jim Edwards, "Brand Defense," *Brandweek*, August 25–September 1, 2008, S1, S2.

19. Ibid.

20. Steve Miller, "Pennzoil Fires on all Cylinders for Overhaul," *Brandweek*, February 18, 2008, 13.

21. Deborah Ball, "The Perils of Packaging: Nestlé Aims for Easier Openings," *The Wall Street Journal*, November 17, 2005, B1.

22. "Environmentally Responsible Packaging: Convenience vs. Conscience," **www.retailwire.com**, April 30, 2008.

23. Alissa Walker, "Spin the Bottle," *Fast Company*, June 2008, 54.

24. "Dell Expands 'Green' Packaging Initiative," *Austin American Statesman*, online, December 16, 2008.

25. Ted Mininni, "Packaging That Works For the Planet," *Brandweek*, April 23, 2007, 20.

26. George Anderson, "Consumers Want More/Different Info on Labels," **www.retailwire.com**, July 17, 2008.

27. "Greenwash," **http://en.wikipedia.org/wiki/Greenwash**, January 11, 2009; David Roberts, "Another Inconvenient Truth," *Fast Company*, March 2008, 70; "The Six Sins of Greenwashing," TerraChoice Environmental Marketing Inc., November 2007.

28. Jack Neff, "When the Worm Poop Hits the Fan, Market It," *Advertising Age*, April 23, 2007; Adam Aston, "Now That's Really a Turf War," *BusinessWeek*, April 23, 2007; Angus Loten, "After a Good Fight, David Forced to Settle with Goliath," **www.Inc.com**, September 24, 2007.

CHAPTER 11

1. Reena Jana, "In Data," *BusinessWeek*, September 22, 2008, 48.

2. Jana McGregor, "In Focus," *BusinessWeek*, April 28, 2008, 61–72.

3. Reena Jana, "In Data."

4. "The Value of New Product Time to Market," **www.retailwire.com**, November 21, 2006.

5. Michael E. Porter, "Why America Needs an Economic Strategy," *BusinessWeek*, November 10, 2008, 39–42.

6. "Changing the World," *Entrepreneur*, October 2003, 30.

7. Vanessa L. Facenda, "Oh Boy! Disney Sees Market for Pre-Teen Fragrances," *Brandweek*, July 23, 2007, 5.

8. Melanie Warner, "P&G's Chemistry Test," *Fast Company*, July/August 2008, 71.

9. Renee Hopkins Callahan, Gwen Ishmael, and Leyla Nomiranian, "The Case for In-the-Box Innovation," Innovation Brochure (Arlington, TX: Decision Analysts, 2005.)

10. Melanie Warner, "P&G's Chemistry Test."

11. Geoff Colvin, "Here It Is. Now, You Design It!" *Fortune*, May 26, 2008, 34.

12. Jeff Jarvis, "The Buzz From Starbucks Customers," *BusinessWeek*, April 28, 2008, 42, 44.

13. Ibid.

14. Salvatore Parise, Patricia J. Guinan, and Bruce Weinberg, "The Secrets of Marketing In a Web 2.0 World," *The Wall Street Journal*, December 15, 2008, R4, 11. Used by permission.

15. Chris Pentilla, "Big Ideas," *Entrepreneur*, March 2007, 62.

16. Allison Enright, "P&G Looks Outside for Innovative Solutions," *Marketing News*, March 1, 2007, 20–21.

17. Tom Ryan, "Finding Sources of Innovation," *RetailWire*, July 18, 2008, online.

18. Ibid.

19. John Karolefski, "CPG Matters: P&G Changes Rules for Product Development," *RetailWire*, February 19, 2008, online.

20. Joseph L. Weber, Stanley Holmes, and Christopher Palmeri, "Mosh Pits of Creativity," *BusinessWeek*, November 7, 2005, 98–100.

21. Andrew Marton, "2006: A Face Odyssey," *Fort Worth Star-Telegram*, February 16, 2006, E1, E8.

22. Chuck Salter, "The Faces and Voices of the World's Most Innovative Company," *Fast Company*, March 2008, 74–96.

23. George Anderson, "New Products Fail to Make Impression," *RetailWire*, November 20, 2008, online.

24. Eyal Biyalogorsky, William Boulding, and Richard Staelin, "Stuck in the Past: Why Managers Persist with New Product Failures," *Journal of Marketing*, 70 (April 2006), 108–121.

25. Ibid.

26. Jena McGregor, "How Failure Breeds Success," *BusinessWeek*, July 10, 2006, 42–52.

27. Jenny Mero, "John Deere's Farm Team," *Fortune*, April 14, 2008, 121, 126. Reprinted with permission.

28. Norihiko Shirouzu and Stephen Power, "Unthrilling but Inexpensive, the Logan Boosts Renault in Emerging Markets," *The Wall Street Journal*, October 9, 2006, B1.

29. Michael Fielding, "Driving Into the Global Market," *Marketing News*, November 1, 2008, 14–17.

30. Jena McGregor, "GE Reinventing Tech For The Emerging World," *BusinessWeek*, April 28, 2008, 68.

31. Gordon Fairclough, "GM's Partner in China Plans Competing Car," *The Wall Street Journal*, April 5, 2006, B1.

32. Robert Scoble, "PassionPlay," *Fast Company*, November 2008, 90.

33. Daniel B. Honigman, "Who's on First?" *Marketing News*, November 1, 2007, 16.

34. "Colleges Perfect for Word of Mouth," *eMarketer*, August 23, 2007, online.

35. Todd Wasserman, "Word Games," *Brandweek*, April 14, 2006, 24–28.

36. Ibid.

37. Daniel B. Honigman, "Who's on First?"

38. "Internet Key to Influencing the Influencers," *Marketing Matters Newsletter*, January 12, 2007, 1.

39. "Looking for Ways to Replace CD Sales in a Flash," *Retailing Today*, February 11, 2008, online.

40. This application exercise is based on the contribution of Karen Stewart (Richard Stockton College of New Jersey) to *Great Ideas in Teaching Marketing*, a teaching supplement that accompanies Lamb, Hair, and McDaniel's *Marketing*. Professor Stewart's entry titled "New-product Development" was a winner in the "Best of the Great Ideas in Teaching Marketing" contest held in conjunction with the publication of the eighth edition of *Marketing*.

41. Chris Pereira, "Wii Play is the Best Selling Game of 2008," *1UP.com*, January 15, 2009, **www.1up.com/do/newsStory?cId=3172314** (accessed January 16, 2009); Chris Pereira, "December NPDs: Wii and DS Combine for OVER 5 Million" *1UP.com*, January 15, 2009, **www.1up.com/do/newsStory?cId=3172307** (accessed January 16, 2009); Steve Watts, "NPD Group Suggests Recession is Hurting Games Growth," *1UP.com*, January 15, 2009, **www.1up.com/do/newsStory?cId=3172306** (accessed January 16, 2009); Kathy Shwiff, "New Sony Game Nears Breaking Even," *The Wall Street Journal*, 30 December 2008, **www.wsj.com** (accessed January 16, 2009); Daisuke Wakabayashi, "Hope Fades for PS3 as a Comeback Player," *The Wall Street Journal*, December 29, 2009, **www.wsj.com** (accessed January 16, 2009); Jonathan V. Last, "Playing the Fool," *The Wall Street Journal*, December 30, 2009, **http://online.wsj.com/article/SB123069467545545011.html** (accessed January

16, 2009); Christopher Lawton and Yukari Iwatani Kane, "Game Makers Push 'Family' Fare," *The Wall Street Journal*, October 29, 2009, **www.wjs.com** (accessed December 8, 2008); Yukari Iwatani Kane, "Nintendo's Wii Music Waits for Fans," *The Wall Street Journal*, December 15, 2008, **http://online.wsj.com/article/SB122930373918205685.html** (accessed January 16, 2009); Yukari Iwatani Kane, "Interview Excerpts: Shigeru Miyamoto," *The Wall Street Journal*, December 15, 2008, **http://online.wsj.com/article/SB122834417100677251.html** (accessed January 16, 2009).

CHAPTER 12

1. **www.papajohns.com**, January 2009; Mike Sachoff, "Papa John's Launches Text-Message Ordering," **www.webpronews.com** feature article, November 15, 2007; Emily Steel and Suzanne Vranica, "Papa John's Gets Finger Friendlier," *The Wall Street Journal*, November 13, 2007, B4; **www.qsrmagazine.com**, January 2009, "Papa John's Introduces Text Ordering."

2. **www.pumpbiz.com**, January 2006.

3. **www.l-textile.com**, August 2009.

4. **www.meridiankiosks.com**, January 2006.

5. "Pepsi, Supermarkets Teaming Up," *Supermarket News*, October 31, 1994, 31; included in Starbucks Annual Report 2006.

6. **www.cisco.com**, January 2006.

7. J. Lynn Lunsford and Paul Glader, "Boeing's Nuts and Bolts Problem," *The Wall Street Journal*, June 19, 2007, A8.

8. **www.dod.mil** and **www.cmcusa.org** (accessed February 2006).

9. **www.dollartree.com**, January 2006.

10. **www.sysco.com**, January 2006.

11. Dean Foust, "Harry Potter and the Logistical Nightmare," *BusinessWeek*, August 6, 2007, 9.

12. Shelly Branch, "P&G Buys Iams: Will Pet Food Fight Follow?" *The Wall Street Journal*, August 12, 1999. Reprinted at **www.pg.com**, January 2006.

13. Eric Newman, "Red Bull, Meet Black Bunny," *Brandweek*, February 25, 2008 (accessed online July 22, 2008).

14. Lynnley Browning, "Do-it-Yourself Logos for Proud Scion Owners," *The New York Times*, March 24, 2008 (accessed online March 24, 2008).

15. Brian Nadel, "Supply and Global Demand," *Fortune*, July 9, 2007, S1–S6.

16. Evan West, "These Robots Play Fetch," *Fast Company*, July/August 2007, 49–50.

17. Ben Worthen, "Weak Links in the (Supply) Chain," *The Wall Street Journal*, June 24, 2008, B5.

18. **knowledge.wharton.upenn.edu** (accessed June 2, 2008).

19. Monica Isbell and Chris Norek, "How Global Trade and Transportation Trends Impact America's Transportation Infrastructure," *CSCMP Explores*, Spring 2008, 3.

20. John J. Fialka, "Fuel Rules Soak Soap Makers," *The Wall Street Journal*, July 10, 2007, A6.

21. George Anderson, "Best Buy Focusing RFID Efforts at Front of Store," **www.retailwire.com** (accessed June 6, 2006).

22. Faye Brookman, "RFID and Retailers: Will It Ever Be Perfect Together?" **www.retailwire.com** (accessed April 2, 2007).

23. **www.yrc.com**; **http://www.inboundlogistics.com** (accessed August 2006).

24. Anonymous, "Leveraged Procurement," **www.outsourcing-supply-chain-management.com** and **www.avendra.com** and **www.ford.com** (accessed August 2009).

25. **www.appleinsider.com** (accessed February 2006).

26. **www.iphonetoolbox.com** (accessed August 14, 2009).

27. Russ Banham, "Keeping the Links Together," *The Wall Street Journal*, June 5, 2007, A17.

28. **www.greenbiz.com/news/2008/09/25/green-supply-chain-thinking-outside-cardboardbox** (accessed January 14, 2009).

29. **http://logistics.about.com** (accessed January 14, 2009).

30. Tamara Audi, "Ailing Sheraton Shoots for a Room Upgrade," *The Wall Street Journal*, March 25, 2008, A1.

31. J. Bander, "Losing Focus: As Kodak Eyes Digital Future, a Big Partner Starts to Fade," *The Wall Street Journal*, January 23, 2004, p. A1.

32. Amy Schatz and Sarah McBride, "Hollywood Studios Seek Control over Deliveries," *The Wall Street Journal*, June 12, 2008, B6.

33. Michael Freedman, "Out of Africa," *Forbes*, November 27, 2006, 45.

34. Mei Fong, "IKEA Hits Home in China," *The Wall Street Journal*, March 3, 2006, B1.

35. Ellen Byron, "P&G's Global Target: Shelves of Tiny Stores," *The Wall Street Journal*, July 16, 2007, A1.

36. This application exercise is based on the contribution of John Beisel (University of Pittsburgh) to *Great Ideas in Teaching Marketing*, a teaching supplement that accompanies Lamb, Hair, and McDaniel's *Marketing*. The entry by Professor Beisel was a runner-up in the "Best of the Great Ideas in Teaching Marketing" contest held in conjunction with the publication of the 8th Edition of *Marketing*.

37. Meg James, "Viacom, Time Warner Cable settle contract dispute," *The LA Times*, January 2, 2009; L. Gordon Crovitz, "Consumer Choice Saves 'Dora the Explorer'" *The Wall Street Journal*, January 5, 2009; Bill Carter, "Time Warner and Viacom Reach Agreement on Cable Shows," *The New York Times*, January 1, 2009; Melissa Block, Robert Siegel, and Meg James, "Dora Roped into Viacom-Time Warner Fee Spat," *All Things Considered*, NPR, December 31, 2009, **www.npr.org/templates/story/story.php?storyId=98912395** (accessed January 15, 2009).

CHAPTER 13

1. *Retail Industry Indicators 2007*, National Retail Federation, online at **www.nrf.com** (accessed December 27, 2007).

2. Bureau of Labor Statistics, "Industry at a Glance: NAICS 42–45, Wholesale and Retail Trade," online at **www.bls.gov**, May 4, 2007.

3. Ibid.

4. U.S. Census Bureau, *Monthly Retail Trade Report*, 2006, online at **www.census.gov/mrts/www/mrts.html** (accessed December 28, 2007).

5. Alan Breznick, "Specialty Shops: What's Your Value Proposition?" *Consumer Electronics Vision Magazine*, online at **www.ce.org**, January/February 2007.

6. "Tweeter CE Playground Store," Best of Boston 2007 Electronics, *Boston Magazine*, online at **www.bostonmagazine.com**.

7. *Food CPI, Prices and Expenditures: Food Expenditure Tables*, U.S. Dept of Agriculture, **www.ers.usda.gov** (accessed December 28, 2007).

8. **www.pigglywiggly.com**; Michael Garry, "Loyalty Program Cuts Defections," *Supermarket News*, January 22, 2007.

9. Ibid.

10. **www.exxonmobil.com** (accessed June 19, 2008).

11. "Wal-Mart to Open its 3,000th International Store," online at **www.walmartfacts.com**, November 14, 2007.

12. "Supercenter Industry," HHC Publishing, online at **www.warehousclubfocus.com** (accessed December 28, 2007).

13. **www.tescopoly.org** (accessed June 19, 2008).

14. **www.familydollar.com** and **www.dollargeneral.com**.

15. "Restaurant Industry Facts," National Restaurant Association, online at **www.restaurant.org/research/ind_glance.cfm**, December 31, 2007.

16. Gene Marcial, "Vending Machines are Learning to Love Plastic," *BusinessWeek*, August 13, 2007.

17. Alli McConnon, "The Va Va Vooming of Vending Machines," BusinessWeek, January 3, 2008.

18. **www.usatech.com** (accessed June 19, 2008).

19. **www.meetmark.com** (accessed June 19, 2008).

20. **www.the-dma.org** accessed October 30, 2007.

21. "Overall Spending on Direct Mail to Reach $73.6 Billion by 2009," a white paper presented by the Winterberry Group, online at **www.winterberrygroup.com** (accessed October 30, 2007).

22. **www.dell.com**, December 2007.

23. **www.qvc.com**, February 2006.

24. **www.emarketer.com**, September 2008.

25. Ken Magill, "Great Expectations," *Multichannel Merchant*, December 1, 2007.

26. Abbey Klaassen, "Buy It from Radio Ads at the Push of a Button," *Advertising Age*, February 21, 2006, online.

27. **www.vans.com**, January 2006.

28. Alexander Peers and Nick Wingfield, "Sotheby's, eBay Team Up to Sell Fine Art Online," *The Wall Street Journal*, January 31, 2002, B8; **http://search.sothebys.com**, **www.ebay.com**, January 2006.

29. McDonald's Corporation, Inside the U.S. Franchising Fact Sheet, **www.mcdonalds.com/corp/franchise**; **www.entrepreneur.com/franchises/mcdonalds/282570-0.html** (accessed December 27, 2007).

30. International Franchise Association Web site, **www.franchise.org**, December 2007.

31. Kentucky Fried Chicken corporate Web site, **www.kfc.com/about**, December 2007.

32. **www.bluefly.com**; **www.internetretailer.com/top500/**. Vince Veneziani, "Top Online Clothing Stores," *Digital Trends*, online at **http://reviews.digitaltrends.com/guide49.html** (accessed December 28, 2007).

33. Ann Zimmerman, "Target's New Eco-Apparel Line to Debut at Barneys New York," *The Wall Street Journal*, January 2008.

34. Dean Foust, "Just Making an Honest Buck?" *BusinessWeek*, September 19, 2005; Matt Zwolinski, "The Ethics of Price Gouging," *Business Ethics Quarterly*, 18, no. 3 (2008), 347–378.

35. Janet Adamy, "Why Wendy's Finds Vanilla So Exciting," *The Wall Street Journal*, April 6, 2007, B1, B2.

36. David Moin, "High-End Opportunity for Outlets," *Women's Wear Daily*, April 14, 2008.

37. **www.rivertowncrossings.com/html/index4.asp**, February 2006.

38. Calmetta Y. Coleman, "Kohl's Retail Racetrack," *The Wall Street Journal*, March 13, 2001, B1; **www.kohls.com**.

39. "Highland Village: A Supercenter with a View," *Retailing Today*, December 10, 2007.

40. Nick Wingfield, "How Apple's Store Strategy Beat the Odds," *The Wall Street Journal*, May 17, 2006, B1.

41. Sara Silver, "Motorola's New Devices Target Retailers," *The Wall Street Journal*, January 14, 2008, B4.

42. Ann Zimmerman, "Latest Luxury: The Store Concierge," *The Wall Street Journal*, December 20, 2007, B1.

43. **www.fye.com**; **www.myspace.com/fyeevents** (accessed June 19, 2008).

44. "USA Technologies Expands into $4B Office Coffee Industry," **www.usatech.com**, February 18, 2009; **www.verisign.com/verisign-inc/news-and-events/news-archive/us-news-2006/page_039937.html** (accessed October 30, 2007).

45. Samantha Murphy, "Getting iReady: M-Commerce to Pick-Up Steam in United States," *Chain Store Age*, August 2007.

46. Leslie Price, "'Tis the Season for Holiday Pop-Up Shops," **www.racked.com**, November 14, 2007.

47. "New Pop-Up Stores: Wired, illy, Mishka, Toys 'R' Us," **www.newyorkology.com**, November 14, 2007.

48. Ibid.

49. Vanessa O'Connell, "Macy's Plans to Open FAO Schwarz Toy Boutiques in its Stores," *The Wall Street Journal*, May 16, 2008, B1; Khanh T.L. Tran, "Levi's Pops Up at American Rag," *Women's Wear Daily*, April 22, 2008, 18; Bryan Chaffin, "HP to Open Store-Within-a-Store, and It's Good For Apple," **www.themacobserver.com**, August 2003; Sharon Edelson, "Bloomingdale's, Chef Charlie Palmer Join Forces," *Women's Wear Daily*, May 27, 2008.

50. **www.levenger.com**; Peter Sayer, "Apple Opens Largest European Store-in-Store in Paris," *PC World*, June 29, 2007, **http://pcworld.about.com/od/companynews/Apple-opens-largest-European-s.htm**; "Kolo Opens First Manhattan Store-Within-a-Store at Kate's Paperie in Soho," *PRNewswire*, May 30, 2007; Paul Nunes and Brian Johnson, *Mass Affluence: Seven New Rules of Marketing to Today's Consumer* (Cambridge: Harvard Business School Press, 2004) 182.

51. This application exercise is based on the contribution of Amy Hubbert (University of Nebraska at Omaha) to *Great Ideas in Teaching Marketing*, a teaching supplement that accompanies Lamb, Hair, and McDaniel's *Marketing*. Professor Hubbert's entry titled "Discovery of Strategic Retailing Factors" was a winner in the "Best of the Great Ideas in Teaching Marketing" contest conducted in conjunction with the publication of the eighth edition of *Marketing*.

52. Monica Soto Ouchi, "Sharper Focus Helps Nordstrom," *Seattle Times*, February 27, 2007; "Sticking with the Family Formula," *WWD*, May 22, 2006; Dave DeWitte, "Nordstrom Leader Says Retail Business Is Changing," *The Gazette*, October 12, 2006; Monica Soto Ouchi, "Nordstrom Sees a Fashion-Forward Future," *Seattle Times*, May 23, 2007; Alexandra DeFelice, "A Century of Customer Love," *CRM Magazine*, June 1, 2005.

CHAPTER 14

1. Stuart Elliot, "Subway's New Campaign," *New York Times*, February 22, 2003, online; Emily Bryson York, "Subway Can't Stop Jonesing for Jared," **www.adage.com**, February 18, 2008.

2. Matthew Creamer, "Barack Obama and the Audacity of Marketing," *Advertising Age*, November 10, 2008, **www.adage.com** (accessed February 2009); Chris Dannen, "How Obama Won It on the Web," *Fast Company*, November 4, 2008, **www.fastcompany.com** (accessed February 2009); Michael Learmonth, "One Way Media Lost the Election as Cable, Interactive Dominated," *Advertising Age*, November 10, 2008, **www.adage.com** (accessed February 2009); Daniel Lyons and Daniel Stone "President 2.0," *Newsweek*, December 1, 2008, **www.newsweek.com** (accessed February 2009); Al Ries, "What Marketers Can Learn from Obama's Campaign," *Advertising Age*, November 5, 2008, **www.adage.com** (accessed February 2009); Jose Antonio Vargas, "Obama Raised Half a Billion Online," *The Washington Post*, November 20, 2008, **www.washingtonpost.com** (accessed February 2009).

3. Julie Jargon, "Kiwi Goes Beyond Shine in Effort to Step up Sales," *The Wall Street Journal*, December 20, 2007, pB1.

4. Andrew McMains, "'Absolut World' Debuts," ADWEEK, April 27, 2007, pNA, **www.adweek.com**; Jeremy Mullman, "Breaking with Bottle Fires up Absolut Sales," *Advertising Age*, February 18, 2008.

5. Ibid.

6. **www.absolut.com/iaaw/** (accessed June 23, 2008).

7. Mullman, "Breaking with Bottle Fires up Absolut Sales."

8. Stuart Elliott, "In an 'Absolut World,' a Vodka Could Use the Same Ads for More Than 25 Years," *The New York Times*, April 27, 2007.

9. State of the Blogosphere 2008, **http://technorati.com** (accessed February 2009).

10. Jason Fry, "Blog Epitaphs? Get Me Rewrite!" *The Wall Street Journal*, February 27, 2006, online, **www.technorati.com/weblog/2006/02/81.html**.

11. Tania Ralli, "Brand Blogs Capture the Attention of Some Companies," *New York Times*, October 24, 2005, C6.

12. "Blogs Can Offer a Big Advantage to Brands—If They're Honest," *New Age Media*, March 23, 2006,

13. Peter Sanders, "Starwood's Web Log Caters to Loyalty," *The Wall Street Journal,* April 12, 2006, B3.

14. www.philips.com.

15. Ibid.

16. Kim Hart, "A Flashy Facebook Page at a Cost to Privacy," *The Washington Post,* June 12, 2008, www.washingtonpost.com (accessed February 2008); www.allfacebook .com/2009/facebook-privacy (accessed February 2009); Ralph Gross and Alessandro Acquisti, "Information Revelation and Privacy in Online Social Networks (The Facebook Case)," *ACM Workshop on Privacy in the Electronic Society,* November 7, 2007.

17. The AIDA concept is based on the classic research of E. K. Strong, Jr., as theorized in *The Psychology of Selling and Advertising* (New York: McGraw-Hill, 1925) and "Theories of Selling," *Journal of Applied Psychology* 9 (1925), 75–86.

18. Apple Quarterly Sales, www.apple. com; Bob Keefe, "During the Holiday Quarter, Apple Sold 14 Million iPods, Which Equates to More Than 100 a Minute," *Atlanta Journal Constitution,* January 11 2006, C-1, and www .appleinsider.com (accessed January 2006); www.apple.com/pr/library/2008/02/26itunes. html (accessed February 26, 2008).

19. Thomas E. Barry and Daniel J. Howard, "A Review and Critique of the Hierarchy of Effects in Advertising," *International Journal of Advertising* 9 (1990), 121–135.

20. http://www.imdb.com/title/tt0382625/.

21. Louise Kramer, "In a Battle of Toothpastes, It's Information vs. Emotion," *The New York Times,* January 17, 2007, C6.

22. www.freestuffonline.com.

23. Bradley Johnson, "Global Marketers," Datacenter: www.adage.com, December 8, 2008.

24. Industry Series Reports, Professional, Scientific, and Technical Services, Advertising and Related Services, NAICS code 5184, www.census.gov.

25. Bradley Johnson, "Global Marketers," Ad Industry Jobs: Advertising Age Data Center www.adage.com (accessed February 2009); Bradley Johnson, "New Source: Media Work Force Sinks to 15-Year Low," www.adage.com February 18, 2008.

26. Bradley Johnson, "Global Marketers."

27. Michael R. Solomon, *Consumer Behavior,* 6th ed. (Upper Saddle River, NJ: Prentice Hall, 2004), 275.

28. Mark Levit, "Humor in Advertising," www.xomreviews.com/marketingsource.com (accessed March 3, 2008).

29. www.scion.com.

30. Natalie Zmuda, "What Went into the Updated Pepsi Logo" *Advertising Age,* October 27, 2008, www.adage.com (accessed February 2009); Natalie Zmuda, "Pepsi, Coke Try to Outdo Each Other with Rays of Sunshine," *Advertising Age,* January 19, 2009, www .adage.com (accessed February 2009); Jim Edwards, "Pepsi's New $1 Million Logo Looks Like Old Diet Pepsi Logo," *BNET Industries,* October 27, 2008, http://industry.bnet.com/ advertising/1000270.

31. Saul Hansell, "The Loneliness of Being AOL," *The New York Times,* February 11, 2008, C8.

32. www.bp.com; www.chevron.com (accessed February 2009).

33. www.philipmorrisusa.com and www.altria.com (accessed January 2006).

34. Alex Berenson, "Drug Approved. Is Disease Real?" *The New York Times,* January 14, 2008, A1.

35. Sean Callahan, "Nextel Wins the Race to Sponsor NASCAR," *BtoB* online, July 14, 2003; Rich Thomaselli, "Nextel Link Takes Nascar to New Level," *Advertising Age,* October 27, 2003, S-7.

36. Emily Bryson York, "Brand vs. Brand: Attacks Ads on the Rise" *Advertising Age* October 27, 2008, www.adage.com (accessed February 2009).

37. Press release, "FTC Sues Sellers of Weight-Loss Pills for False Advertising," online at www.ftc.gov/opa/2008/02/zyladex.shtm, February 8, 2008.

38. Press release, "HP Gets Personal with Super Bowl Ad, Extends PC Marketing Campaign," www.hp.com, February 2, 2007; Neal Leavitt, "HP Goes Wide to Get Personal," *iMedia Connection,* June 2006, www.imediaconnection .com/content/10070.asp.

39. Tabasco advertisement, *Advertising Age,* October 13, 2003, 8.

40. "SoBe Lizards Take Manhattan by Storm: Unleashing SoBe Life Water Thrillicious Movement in Times Square," *PR Newswire,* February 27, 2008.

41. Vanessa L. Facenda, "Kellogg Injects Some New Energy into Frosted Flakes," www.brandweek.com, February 4, 2008.

42. www.us.powerade.com.

43. Laura Q. Hughes and Wendy Davis, "Revival of the Fittest," *Advertising Age,* March 12, 2001, 18–19; www.hersheys.com/choco-lateworld/ (accessed January 2006).

44. "What the Heck Were These People Thinking?" www.tribe.net, May 17, 2007.

45. www.adweek.com/aw/national/ article_display.jsp?vnu_content_id=1000475212 and www.leoburnett.com/ideas/altoids.asp (accessed January 2006).

46. Press release, Clio Awards, http://www .clioawards.com/winners/image_pop .cfm?medium_id=4&media_ directory=billboard&website_entry_ id=200729270&is_c=0&image_no=1

47. Geoffrey A. Fowler, "For P&G in China, It's Wash, Rinse, Don't Repeat," *The Wall Street Journal,* April 7, 2006.

48. Pamela Paul, "Sell It to the Psyche," *Time,* September 29, 2003.

49. Press release, "TNS Media Intelligence Forecasts 4.2 percent Increase in U.S. Advertising Spending for 2008," www.tns-mi .com/news/01072008 (accessed February 20, 2008); http://www.adage.com.

50. Ibid.

51. Brian Steinberg, "Philips and Time Agree to Keep It Simple," *The Wall Street Journal,* April 21, 2006, B3.

52. Steven Levingston, "Spots on Traditional TV Still the Biggest Show on Super Bowl Sunday," *Washington Post,* Saturday, January 14, 2006.

53. www.neilsen.com (accessed February 2009).

54. Matthew Boyle, "Superbucks," *Fortune,* February 4, 2008.

55. Gergana Koleva, "Don't Buy It," *MarketWatch,* January 24, 2008, online.

56. Suzanne Vranica, "TV-Ad Test to Show If Less Is More; NBC Universal's Trial Run Will Measure Effectiveness of Fewer Commercials," *The Wall Street Journal,* April 5, 2006, B3; Maria Aspan, "TiVo Shifts to Help Companies It Once Threatened," *The New York Times,* December 10, 2007.

57. Erin White, "In-Your-Face Marketing: Ad Agency Rents Foreheads," *The Wall Street Journal,* February 11, 2003, B2; www.commer-cialalert.org.

58. Mike Esterl, "Going Outside, Beyond the Billboard," *The Wall Street Journal,* July 21, 2005, B3.

59. Press release, "Virgin Atlantic Airways Takes Off with New Marketing Campaign," *PR Newswire,* February 11, 2008.

60. Ryan Woo, "Adidas Wows Japan with Vertical Soccer Field," *The Wall Street Journal,* September 22, 2003, B1.

61. Virgin Atlantic Airways, www.theloerieawards.co.za/winners/ search/?show=1 (accessed January 2006).

62. TNS Media Intelligence Forecast, January 7, 2008, online at www.tns-mi.com/ news/01072008.htm#; Internet Advertising Bureau, www.iab.com (accessed February 2009).

63. Brian Morrissey, "Web Ad Spend to Diversify," www.adweek.com, October 11, 2007.

64. David Ho, "Advertisers Ditch Pop-Ups for New Tricks," *Atlanta Journal-Constitution,* December 4, 2005, C-3.

65. Carol Krol, "ComScore: Yellow Book, Google, Facebook are Internet winners of '07," *BtoB* magazine, January 31, 2008.

66. Ibid.

67. Mike Shields, "Google Leads Search Party," www.adweek.com, February 18, 2008.

68. Michael McCarthy, "Disney Plans to Mix Ads, Video Games to Target Kids, Teens," *USA Today,* January 15, 2005, B-1.

69. John Gaudiosi, "Mountain Dew Makes MMO More Than Just a Game," *Advertising Age,* January 28, 2008, 21.

70. Social Media Marketing Hits & Misses, www.oneupweb.com/search-marketing-library/ Oneupweb.07HolidayStudy.Followup.pdf.

71. Ibid.

72. www.rss-specifications.com/what-is-rss.htm.

73. Stuart Elliott, "Science Blogs as a Vehicle for Upscale Ads," *New York Times,* January 10, 2006, C2.

74. Ibid.

75. Mark Glaser, "MediaShift: Your Guide to Podcasts," www.pbs.org/mediashift/2007/02/ digging_deeperyour_guide_to_po.html.

76. Press release, "Microsoft Bringing Ads to Shopping Carts," www.cnn.com/2008/ TECH/01/14/microsoft.shoppingcart.ap/index .html.

77. www.bmwusa.com/Standard/Content/ Uniquely/TVAndNewMedia/BMWFilms.aspx (accessed March 6, 2008).

78. Tobi Elkin, "Coca-Cola's First TiVo Advertainment Airs Today," www.adage.com, October 9, 2003.

79. Jack Neff, "Floors in Stores Start Moving," *Advertising Age,* August 20, 2001, 15.

80. www.altterrain.com/light_projection_ advertising.htm; "BroadSign Works with Zoom

Media & Marketing Digital Signage Network to Manage Advertainment Screens in Popular Nightlife Venues Nationwide," *Internet Wire*, January 22, 2008.

81. Christopher Lawton, "Videogame Ads Attempt Next Level," *The Wall Street Journal*, July 25, 2005, B6; "Video Game Advertising Gets a Boost," *USA Today*, December 16, 2004, B-1; Derek Sooman, "World's First Video Game Advertising Network," October 20, 2004, **www.techspot.com**; **www.massiveincorporated.com** (accessed January 2006); **www.microsoft.com/presspass/press/2006/may06/05-04-MassiveIncPR.mspx** (accessed May 20, 2006).

82. Digital Fact Pact 2007, *Advertising Age*, **www.adage.com** (accessed February 2009).

83. Paul Korzeniowski, "Cell Phones Emerge as New Advertising Medium," *TechNewsWorld*, November 16, 2005, online at **www.tech-newsworld.com/story/46630.html** (accessed June 23, 2008); Philip John, "Going Mobile: Cell Phone Advertising Leaps Forward by Moving Sideways," *Mediaweek, September 17, 2007*, **www.mediaweek.com** (accessed June 23, 2008).

84. Juan Sanchez, "The Water Horse: Legend of the Deep" *CultureBuzz*, **www.culturebuzz.com/a_live_advertising_monster_japan_article_1566.html** (accessed February 12, 2008).

85. Sally Beatty, "Ogilvy's TV-Ad Study Stresses 'Holding Power' Instead of Ratings," *The Wall Street Journal*, June 4, 1999, B2, **www.ogilvy.com/viewpoint** (accessed January 2006).

86. Barbara Kiviat, "Chasing the Desi Dollars" *Time*, July 6, 2005, **www.time.com** (accessed February 2009); Coeli Carr, "Ring, Ring, Bollywood Calling," *Time*, February 5, 2009, **www.time.com** (accessed February 2009); Alexandra Alter, "A Passage to Hollywood," *Wall Street Journal*, February 6, 2009, **www.online.wsj.com** accessed February 2009.

87. This application exercise is based on the contribution of Lyn R. Godwin (University of St. Thomas) to *Great Ideas in Teaching Marketing*, a teaching supplement that accompanies Lamb, Hair, and McDaniel's *Marketing*. Professor Godwin's entry titled "Taboo or Not Taboo: That Is the Question" was a runner-up in the "Best of the Great Ideas in Teaching Marketing" contest held in conjunction with the publication of the eighth edition of *Marketing*.

88. This application exercise is based on the contribution of David M. Blanchette (Rhode Island College) to *Great Ideas in Teaching Marketing*, a teaching supplement that accompanies Lamb, Hair, and McDaniel's *Marketing*. Professor Blanchette's entry titled "Applying Semiotics in Promotion" was a runner-up in the "Best of the Great Ideas in Teaching Marketing" contest held in conjunction with the publication of the eighth edition of *Marketing*.

89. Sam Schechner, "Winfrey Firm to Produce HBO Shows," *The Wall Street Journal*, December 17, 2008; Guy Brighton, "Campfire's True Blood Campaign," *The New York Times* (accessed February 19, 2009); Lynette Rice, "Ad Campaign for HBO's True Blood' confuses thirsty consumers," *Entertainment Weekly*, July 22, 2008, online at **www.ew.com** (accessed February 23, 2009); **www.bloodcopy.com**; **www.hbo.com/events/trueblood/**; Douglas Quenqua, "The Vampires Are Coming, but Only

After Months of Warnings," *The New York Times*, July 15, 2008; Jeff Beer, "Campfire Sinks its Creative Teeth into True Blood," online at **http://creativity-online.com/?action=news:article&newsId=130134&sectionName=behind_the_work** (accessed February 19, 2009).

CHAPTER 15

1. **http://prweek.com/news/news_story.cfm?ID =239635&site=3** (accessed January 2006).

2. "Satellite Cured Radio Star," **http://news.yahoo.com/**, and "Oprah Signs Three-Year Deal with XM Satellite Radio," **www.philly.com/mld/belleville/business/13837515.htm?source=rss&channel=belleville_business** (accessed February 2006).

3. Adam Bluestein, "Prime-Time Exposure: How Companies Can Make a Splash in the Big-Money World of TV Product Placement—Without Spending a Dime," *Inc.*, March 2008, 66 (accessed online on June 23, 2008); **www.sourcewatch.org/index.php?title= Product_placement**; Kris Oser, "How a Product Placement Strategy Worked for Yahoo," *AdAge.com*, January 31, 2005, **http://adage.com/latestnews**; **http:// money.howstuffworks.com/product-placement.htm**; "Product Placement Spending in Media 2005," **www.pqmedia.com** (accessed January 2006).

4. Ibid.

5. Sponsorship Spending, IEG sponsorship, **www.sponsorship.com** (accessed February 2009).

6. **www.sponsorship.com**, **www.dominos.com**, **www.hiltonworldwide.com**, and **www.anheuser-busch.com** (accessed January 2006).

7. IEG sponsorship, **www.sponsorship.com**.

8. **www.stjude.org/corporate/0,2516,410_2034_16782,00.html**, **www.thinkbeforeyoupink.org/Pages/InfoMktgCampaigns.html**, and **www.bitc.org.uk/resources/research/research_publications/corp_survey_3.html** (accessed January 2006).

9. **www.goredforwomen.org/our_partners.aspx** (accessed February 17, 2009).

10. **www.stjude.org/corporate/0,2516,410_2034_16782,00.html**, **www.thinkbeforeyoupink.org/Pages/InfoMktgCampaigns.html**, and **www.bitc.org.uk/resources/research/research_publications/corp_survey_3.html** (accessed January 2006).

11. **www.playstation.com** (accessed February 2009).

12. Gavin O'Malley, "CBS Puts *CSI Miami* Twist Online," November 16, 2005, **publications.mediapost.com**, and **www.adverblog.com/archives/cat_integrated_marketing.htm** (accessed January 2006).

13. Ann Zimmerman, "Wal-Mart Enlists Bloggers to Combat Negative News," *The Wall Street Journal*, March 7, 2006, D7.

14. Ibid.

15. "Blogs Can Offer a Big Advantage to Brands—If They're Honest," *New Age Media*, March 23, 2006, 15.

16. Janet Adamy and Richard Gibson, "McDonald's Isn't Slow to React to 'Fast-Food Nation' this Time," *The Wall Street Journal*, April 12, 2006, B3.

17. Zimmerman, "Wal-Mart Enlists Bloggers to Combat Negative News."

18. Annual Report: Industry Report, October 2008, *PROMO Magazine*, **promomagazine.com** (accessed February 2009).

19. Ibid.

20. Robert Passikoff, "Why Starbucks Has Ground to a Halt," *Brandweek*, November 10, 2008, **www.brandweek.com** (accessed February 2009); Andy Serwer, "Howard Schultz Spills the Beans on His Plans to Save the Company He Founded," **www.cnnmoney.com** (accessed February 2009); Emily Bryson York, "Consumers Skip Starbucks for Plain Ole Joe," *Advertising Age*, January 19, 2009 (accessed February 2009); Howard Schultz Transformation Agenda #1, **www.starbucks.com** (accessed February 2009).

21. **www.cms.inmar.com/newsandevents**; Find/SVP, "Cut It Out: Coupons Are on an Upswing," **www.forbes.com** (accessed January 2006).

22. Annual Report: Industry Report October 2008, *PROMO Magazine*, **www.promomagazine.com** (accessed February 2009).

23. **www.kroger.com**; Internet Coupons link at **gs2.coolsavings.com/kroger/index.aspx**.

24. "Papa John's Pushes Dark Knight with Pizza," *PROMO Magazine*, **www.promomagazine.com** (accessed February 2009).

25. Suzanne Vita Palazzo, "Countdown to Kickoff," *Grocery Headquarters*, December 2005, 43.

26. **www.businessweek.com/bwdaily/dnflash/nov2005/nf20051123_4158_db016.htm** (accessed February 2008).

27. Patricia Odell, "Shrek Premiums Drive Big Sales for Kellogg's," *PROMO Magazine*, November 1, 2008, **www.promomgazine.com** (accessed February 2009).

28. **www.tequilaaficionado.com/article.php?sid=336** (accessed February 2008).

29. **www.ecommercetimes.com** accessed January 2008; Industry Report, *PROMO Magazine*, **www.promomagazine.com** (accessed January 2009).

30. **www.crmtrends.com/loyalty.html**, (accessed February 200)8; Matthew Haeberle, "Loyalty Is Dead: Great Experiences, Not Price, Will Create Loyal Customers," *Chain Store Age*, January 2004, 17.

31. **www.creditcards.com/New-Starbucks-Duetto-Visa-Credit-Card.php**; **www.askmrcreditcard.com/starbucksduettovisa.html** (accessed February 2008).

32. **www.crmtrends.com/loyalty.html** (accessed February 2009).

33. **www.verizonwireless.com** (accessed June 25, 2008).

34. "Grocers' Use of E-Mail Growing," *Promo P&I*, August 2005, **www.promomagazine.com** (accessed February 2009).

35. Peter Sanders, "Starwood's Web Log Caters to Loyalty," *The Wall Street Journal*, April 12, 2006, B3; **www.starwoodhotels.com/corporate/company_info.html** (accessed February 2009).

36. "The Inside Story on Company Blogs: Corporate America May Fear Critical Comments in Public Blogs, but It Isn't Ignoring the Medium's Potential for Improving Internal Communications," *BusinessWeek Online*, February 15, 2006.

37. Patricia Odell, "Dole Uses Blogs and Parties to Promote Fruit Parfaits, January 1, 2009,

PROMO Magazine, **www.promomagazine.com** (accessed February 2009).

38. www.hgtv.com/hgtv/pac_ctnt_988/text/0,,HGTV_22056_38648,00.html (accessed February 2009).

39. **www.marketresearch.com/product/display.asp?productid=1278351&g=1**, bloggybiz.com/business-news/use-product-samples-to-boost-your-business-in-2008/ (accessed February 2009). Tim Parry, "Sampling—Teaching Tools," *PROMO Magazine*, **www.promomagazine.com** (accessed January 2008).

40. Industry Report October 2008, PROMO Magazine, **www.promomagazine.com** (accessed February 2009).

41. "Domino's Customers Get Free Coca-Cola Zero," *PROMO Xtra*, December 22, 2005, **www.promomagazine.com** (accessed January 2008).

42. Stephanie Thompson, "Dove Targets the Chocoholic," *Advertising Age*, September 15, 2003, 45.

43. Patricia Odell, "Brands Test Sampling at Meal Assembly Kitchens," *PROMO Magazine*, December 1, 2008, **www.promomagazine.com** (accessed February 2009).

44. Patricia Odell, "Sampling Reigns as Key Method to Drive In-Store Sales," *PROMO Magazine*, online at **www.promomagazine.com** (accessed December 2008); "Dunkin' Donuts Targets Health Clubs with Sampling Program," *PROMO Xtra*, December 28, 2005, **www.promomagazine.com** (accessed February 2009).

45. "Industry report October 2008 *PROMO Magazine*, **www.promomagazine.com** (accessed February 2009).

46. "Point-of-Purchase: $17 Billion," *PROMO Magazine*, October 29, 2001, 3; "In Praise of Promotion," *PROMO Xtra*, **www.promomagazine.com** (accessed January 2009).

47. Stephanie Thompson, "Hershey Sets $30M Push," *Advertising Age*, September 15, 2003, 3, 45.

48. Mickey Khan, "Heinekin Hoaxes Are Real Deal for Building E-mail Names," *DM News Online*, October 7, 2003, **www.heineken.com** (accessed February 2009).

49. **www.marketingsherpa.com/article.html?ident=29788** (accessed February 2009).

50. **www.couponinfonow.com/Couponing/2007trendsoverview.cfm** (accessed February 2009).

51. Patricia Odell, "Lucky Brand Debuts Consumer-Generated Coupon," *PROMO Magazine*, December 10, 2008, **www.promomagazine.com** (accessed February 2009).

52. Roger O. Crocket, "Penny-Pinchers' Paradise," *BusinessWeek*, January 22, 2001, EB12.

53. **www.trade-show-advisor.com/trade-show-survey.html** (accessed February 2008).

54. Michael Beverland, "Contextual Influences and the Adoption and Practice of Relationship Selling in a Business-to-Business Setting: An Exploratory Study," *Journal of Personal Selling & Sales Management*, Summer 2001, 207.

55. Richard Morrison, "The Business Process of Customer Retention and Loyalty," *Customer Interaction Solutions*, October 2001, 4.

56. "The Right Questions and Attitudes Can Beef Up Your Sales, Improve Customer Retention," *Selling*, June 2001, 3.

57. Larry Rigs, "Hit 'Em Where They Work," *Direct*, October 15, 2003, **www.directmag.com**; **www.dmreview.com** (accessed January 2008); "Webcast Essentials," supplement to *CRM Magazine*, 2005.

58. Jean Halliday, "Chrysler Web Offerings Draw Sales Leads," *Automotive News*, December 5, 2005, 22.

59. Alf Nucifora, "Need Leads? Try a Networking Group," *Business News New Jersey*, November 14, 2000, 22; Catherine Seda, "The Meet Market," *Entrepreneur*, August 2004, 68; Jim Dickie, "Is Social Networking an Overhyped Fad or a Useful Tool?" *Destination CRM*, January 21, 2005; Kristina Dell, "What Are Friends For?" *Time*, September 21, 2004.

60. B. Weitz, S. Castleberry, and J. Tanner, *Selling* (Burr Ridge, IL: McGraw-Hill/Irwin, 2007), 196–197.

61. **www.bicworld.com**; **www.BIClink.com**.

62. **www.presentations.com**.

63. **www.chanimal.com**, "Chatrooms" link at the "Overcoming Objections" Web page (link to **www.chanimal.com/html/objections.html**).

64. Troy Korsgaden, "Fine-Tuning Your Agency's Office Systems," **www.roughnotes.com/rnmagazine/2000/june00/06p116.htm**.

65. **www.collegerecruiter.com** (accessed January 2009).

66. This application exercise is based on the contribution of John Ronchetto (University of San Diego) to *Great Ideas in Teaching Marketing*, a teaching supplement that accompanies Lamb, Hair, and McDaniel's *Marketing*. Professor Ronchetto's entry titled "Sales and Customer Service Experiential Journal and Paper" was a winner in the "Best of the Great Ideas in Teaching Marketing" contest held in conjunction with the publication of the eighth edition of *Marketing*.

67. "Ron Popeil, He of the Pocket Fisherman and Spray-On Hair, Has Perfected His Formula for Success: Invent, Market, and Sell with a Passion," *BusinessWeek Online*, October 3, 2005; Brent Hopkins, "How Ron Popeil Invented Himself," *Knight-Ridder/Tribune Business News*, August 31, 2005; Matt Myerhoff, "Infomercial King Sells Company, Ronco Goes Public for Expansion," *Los Angeles Business Journal*, July 29, 2005, 1; **snltranscripts.jt.org/75/75qbassamatic.phtml**.

CHAPTER 16

1. Franziska Volckner, "The Dual Role of Price: Decomposing Consumers' Reactions to Price," *Journal of the Academy of Marketing Science*, Fall 2008, 359–377.

2. Ibid.

3. Roland Rust, Christine Moorman, and Peter R. Dickson, "Getting Return on Quality: Revenue Expansion, Cost Reduction, or Both?" *Journal of Marketing*, October 2002, 7–24.

4. "DaimlerChrysler's Freightliner Puts New Chief at the Wheel," *The Wall Street Journal*, May 29, 2001, B4.

5. "AMD Once Again Hits the Roaring 20s," **www.clnetnews.com**, January 24, 2006; Tom Krazit, "Intel Gained Back Some Chip Market Share on the Heels of Advanced Micro Devices' Abysmal First Quarter," ZDNet News (accessed online April 24, 2007).

6. Tammo H. A. Bijmolt, Harald J. van Heerde, and Rik G. M. Pieters, "New Empirical Generalizations on the Determinants of Price Elasticity," *Journal of Marketing Research*, May 2005, 141–156; Christian Homburg, Wayne Hoyer, and Nicole Koschate, "Customers' Reactions to Price Increases: Do Customer Satisfaction and Perceived Motive Fairness Matter?" *Journal of the Academy of Marketing Science*, Winter 2005, 35–49; Gadi Fibich, Arieh Gavious, and Oded Lowengart, "The Dynamics of Price Elasticity of Demand in the Presence of Reference Price Effects," *Journal of the Academy of Marketing Science*, Winter 2005, 66–78.

7. "Summer Concerts Try New Tactics to Fill Seats," *The Wall Street Journal*, May 19, 2005, D1.

8. "In a Tech Backwater, a Profit Fortress Rises," *The Wall Street Journal*, July 10, 2007, A1. Reprinted with permission of *The Wall Street Journal*, © Dow Jones & Company, Inc. All Rights Reserved Worldwide.

9. "Seeking Perfect Prices, CEO Tears up the Rules," *The Wall Street Journal*, March 27, 2007, A1, A16.

10. Michael Mendano, "Priced to Perfection," **www.business2.com**, March 6, 2001, 40–41.

11. "The Power of Optimal Pricing," *Business 2.0*, September 2002, 68–70.

12. "What the Traffic Will Bear," *Forbes*, July 3, 2008, 69.

13. Ibid.

14. Anne Kadet, "Buyer Beware," *Smart Money*, May 2006, 90–95.

15. Ibid.

16. "Behave," *Marketing News*, September 15, 2008, 13–15.

17. Ibid.

18. Raymund Flandez, "Voluntary Pricing Lets Small Eateries Give—and Get Back," *The Wall Street Journal*, August 28, 2007, B8.

19. "Wal-Mart Launches Toy Price War," *The Wall Street Journal*, October 9, 2008, B1; also see: Harald J. VanHeerde, Els Gijsbrechts, and Koen Pauwels, "Winners and Losers in a Major Price War," *Journal of Marketing Research*, October 2008, 499–518.

20. See Joseph Cannon and Christian Homburg, "Buyer-Supplier Relationships and Customer Firm Costs," *Journal of Marketing*, January 2001, 29–43.

21. "How Shopping Bots Really Work," *MSN-Money*, July 11, 2005, **http://moneycentral.msn.com**.

22. Florian Zettelmeyer, Fiona Scott Morton, and Jorge Silva-Risso, "How the Internet Lowers Prices: Evidence from Matched Survey and Auto Transaction Data," *Journal of Marketing Research*, May 2006, 168–181.

23. *2007 Internet Crime Report* (Washington, DC: FBI) 1–17.

24. Sridhar Moorthy and Xubing Zhang, "Price Matching by Vertically Differentiated Retailers: Theory and Evidence," *Journal of Marketing Research*, May 2006, 156–167.

25. Monika Kukar-Kinney, Rockney Walters, and Scott MacKenzie, "Consumer Responses to Characteristics of Price-Matching Guarantees: The Moderating Role of Price Consciousness," *Journal of Retailing*, April 2007, 211–221.

26. "Wal-Mart Puts the Squeeze on Food Costs," *Fortune*, June 9, 2008, 16.

27. Ibid.

28. Ibid.

29. R. Chandrashekaran, "The Implications of Individual Differences in Reference to Price Utilization for Designing Effective Price Communications," *Journal of Business Research*, August 2001, 85–92.

30. Katherine Lemon and Stephen Nowlis, "Developing Synergies between Promotions and Brands in Different Price-Quality Tiers," *Journal of Marketing Research*, May 2002, 171–185. Also see Valerie Taylor and William Bearden, "The Effects of Price on Brand Extension Evaluations: The Moderating Role of Extension Similarity," *Journal of the Academy of Marketing Science,* Spring 2002, 131–140; and Raj Sethuraman and V. Srinivasan, "The Asymmetric Share Effect: An Empirical Generalization on Cross-Price Effects," *Journal of Marketing Research*, August 2002, 379–386.

31. Merrie Brucks, Valarie Zeithaml, and Gillian Naylor, "Price and Brand Name as Indicators of Quality Dimensions for Consumer Durables," *Journal of the Academy of Marketing Science*, Summer 2000, 359–374; Wilford Amaldoss and Sanjay Jain, "Pricing of Conspicuous Goods: A Competitive Analysis of Social Effects," *Journal of Marketing Research*, February 2005, 30–42; and also see Margaret Campbell, "Says Who?! How the Source of Price Information and Affect Influence Perceived Price (UN)fairness," *Journal of Marketing Research*, May 2007, 261–271.

32. Volckner, "The Dual Role of Price."

33. Ibid.

34. Christina Passariello, "Beauty Fix: Behind L'Oreal's Makeover in India: Going Upscale . . . When Cheap Shampoo Didn't Sell, Company Tapped the Rising Class," *The Wall Street Journal*, July 13, 2007, A1, A8.

35. Keith Chrzan, "An Overview of Pricing Research," *Quirk's Marketing Research Review*, July/August 2006, 24–29.

36. Kent Monroe and Jennifer Cox, "Pricing Practices That Endanger Profits," *Marketing Management*, September/October 2001, 42–46.

37. Thomas T. Nagle and George Cressman, "Don't Just Set Prices, Manage Them," *Marketing Management*, November/December 2002, 29–33; Jay Klompmaker, William H. Rogers, and Anthony Nygren, "Value, Not Volume," *Marketing Management*, June 2003, 45–48; Alison Wellner, "Boost Your Bottom Line by Taking the Guesswork Out of Pricing," *Inc.*, June 2005, 72–82.

38. George Cressman, "Reaping What You Sow," *Marketing Management*, March/April 2004, 34–40.

39. "Why P&G's Smile Is So Bright," *BusinessWeek*, August 12, 2002, 58–60.

40. "Out-Discounting the Discounter," *BusinessWeek*, May 10, 2004, 78–79. An interesting article on shoppers who use penetration pricing to their advantage is Edward J. Fox and Stephen J. Hoch, "Cherry-Picking," *Journal of Marketing*, January 2005, 46–62.

41. "One Store's Old Food Is Other's Bread and Butter," *The Wall Street Journal*, February 22, 2008, B1–B2.

42. "The Irrationalities of Product Pricing," *The Wall Street Journal*, September 22, 2008, R2.

43. "As China's Trade Clout Grows, So Do Price-Fixing Accusations," *The Wall Street Journal*, February 10, 2006, A1, A16.

44. "Ex-British Air Manager Sentenced to Jail," *The Wall Street Journal*, October 1, 2008, B2.

45. Ibid.

46. "Fresh Del Monte Settles Banana Price-Fixing Suits for More than $3 Million," *Palm Beach Daily Business Review*, June 28, 2007.

47. "Doctor Group Settle Charges," *San Diego Union-Tribune*, May 31, 2003, C-3.

48. "How Driving Prices Lower Can Violate Antitrust Statutes," *The Wall Street Journal*, January 24, 2004, A1, A11.

49. "Price-Fixing Makes Comeback After Supreme Court Ruling," *The Wall Street Journal*, August 18, 2008, A1, A12.

50. Ibid.

51. Ibid.

52. "Antitrust Trade and Practice; Predatory Bidding Mirrors Predatory Pricing," *New York Law Journal*, March 20, 2007, 3.

53. Ibid.; Alison Lo, John Lynch, and Richard Staelin, "How to Attract Consumers by Giving Them the Short End of the Stick," *Journal of Marketing Research*, February 2007, 128–141.

54. This application exercise is based on the contribution of Vaughn C. Judd (Auburn University, Montgomery) to Great Ideas in Teaching Marketing, a teaching supplement and accompanies Lamb, Hair, and McDaniel's *Marketing*. Professor Judd's entry, titled "Analyzing the Price-Quality Relationship," was a winner in the "Best of the Great Ideas in Teaching Marketing" contest held in conjunction with the publication of the eighth edition of *Marketing*.

55. Steven Levy, "How Apple's iPhone Ate the New iPods," *Newsweek*, September 17, 2007; Chris Nuttall, "Apple Apologizes to Early Buyers of iPhone After New Discounts," *The Financial Times*, September 7, 2007; Eric Benderoff, "Apple Credits iPhone Buyers," *Chicago Tribune*, September 7, 2007; Chris Churchill, "Few Hang-Ups in Wake of iPhone Price Cut," *Times Union*, September 7, 2007; John Markoff, "Apple Cuts iPhone Price Ahead of Holidays," *The New York Times*, September 6, 2007; Lev Grossman, "Apple's New Calling: the iPhone," *Time*, January 9, 2007.

NAME, COMPANY, AND BRAND INDEX

I

Note: Locators followed by "ex"
indicate exhibits.
1-800-Flowers.com, 236, 451
1-800-Tequila, 534
3Com, 542
3 Doors Down, 527
3M, 4, 126 ex4.3, 149,
162, 371
Post-It Notes, 365
7-Eleven Inc., 178, 276, 341, 448
ex13.3
Blue Vanilla Laffy Taffy Rope,
366
Candy Gulp, 366
7-Up, 343
24 Hour Fitness, 221
2006 Customer Loyalty
Engagement Index, 532
2006 FIFA World Cup, 499

A

A. C. Nielsen Company,
320, 563
Aarkstore.com, 299
AARP, 265, 267, 275
ABB Asea Brown Boveri, 148
ABC, 56
Dancing with the Stars, 504
Grey's Anatomy, 504
Lost, 504
ABC News, 507
ABC Radio Network, 118
ABC Television, 504
Abercrombie & Fitch, 54–55, 110
Abercrombie Kids, 264, 454
Hollister, 208, 218
Ruehl No. 925, 208, 273
Aberdeen Group, 103
Absolut Vodka, 473–475,
512, 583
Accenture, 398
AC/DC, 21

Ace Hardware Corporation, 397,
448 ex13.3
Acid+All, 601
Adelphia Communication
Corporation, 82
Adidas, 106, 417, 500, 506
Adobe, 232 ex7.1
Adolph Coors Company, 44, 202,
277, 310
Coors beer, 394
Coors Light, 394
Zima, 44
Advanced Micro Devices
(AMD), 563
Advil, 499 ex 14.8
Aeon, 90 ex3.7
Aeropostale
Jimmy'Z, 274
Agassi, Andre, 500 ex14.9
Airbus
A350, 133, 543
Air France, 591
AIR-serv, 458
AirTran Airways (ValuJet), 38, 192
Airwick
Carpet Fresh, 366
A.J. Wright, 132
Akers, John, 23
Alberto-Culver, 117
Albertsons, 454
Alcoa, 83 ex3.5, 399, 562
All-China Federation of Trade
Unions in Beijing, 153
Alloy.com, 376, 380
Allstate Insurance, 117, 266, 319,
422, 570, 594
Alphagraphics Printshops, 447
AltaVista, 365
Amazon.com, 5, 8, 126 ex4.3,
217, 267, 413, 446, 451,
457, 506, 577
American Airlines, 212, 277, 535

American Association of
Advertising Agencies
(AAAA), 74
American Association of
Franchisees & Dealers, 449
ex13.4
American Booksellers Association,
417
American Cancer Society, 95, 209
American Eagle Outfitters,
218, 264
American Express, 5, 95, 114,
219, 231, 319, 343, 535
American Franchisee Association,
449 ex13.4
American Girl, 458
American Heart Association,
209, 528
American Idol, 118, 488
American Manufacturers
Association, 74
American Marketing Association
(AMA), 3, 6, 24, 73, 298
ex9.2
American Medical Association,
73
American Rag Cie Denim
Bar, 459
America Online (AOL), 93, 210,
275, 414, 493, 506
America's Top Model, 376, 380
Ameriprise, 114
Ameritrade Brokerage, 506
Ampacet, 216
AMR Research Inc., 154
Amway, 443
Anderson Corporation, 249
Anheuser-Busch, 118, 277,
504, 506
Bud Bowl, 527
Bud Light, 273, 495
Bud Light Lime, 371

Anheuser-Busch (*Continued*)
    Budweiser, 281, 379
    Eagle brand, 273
    Michelob Light, 273
Ann Taylor Loft, 343
Anthony, Marc, 568
Anthony, Michael, 51
Applebee's, 103
Apple Inc., 21, 100, 105, 126
    ex4.3, 191, 241, 340, 361,
    456, 459, 460
    iPhone, 589, 591
    iPhone Apps, 415
    iPod, 191, 216, 218, 264,
        417, 442, 482, 483, 484,
        512, 599
    iPod Classic, 600
    iPod Nano, 483, 600
    iPod Shuffle, 217, 483
    iPod Touch, 371, 600
    iTunes, 21, 414, 483, 508
    Lisa, 371
    MacBook Air, 371
    Macintosh, 495
Applica, Inc., 412
Apprentice, The, 527
APV, 148
Aquilera, Christina, 568
Arby's, 448 ex13.3
Architectural Digest, 509
Ariel detergent, 350
Ariely, Dan, 589
Aristotle, 76
Arkin, Ronald, 127
Armani, 111, 417
Art of War, The, 358
Arussy, Lior, 466
Ashanti, 507
Ashtech, 143
Association of Attorneys
    General, 580
Atag Holdings NV, 159
Athlete's Foot, 447
AT Kearney Inc., 583
Atlas Corporation, 272
AT&T, 74, 231, 280, 414, 490,
    542
Audi of America, 507
Aupperle, Tammy, 91
Aur, 168
Autobytel.com, 579
Avanzi, Philippe, 172
Avaya, 95
Avendra, 414
Avon Products, 155, 397,
    442, 528
    Avon Beauty Center, 443

Avon Salon & Spa, 397
    mark, 443
Axe, The, 20
Axe deodorant, 216, 218
Aykroyd, Dan, 556

B

Babies "R" Us, 35
Babson College, 555
BabyAge.com, 591
Baby Phat, 218
Bacardi Martini India, 49
Backpacker, 578
Baden-Powell, Rosa, 221
Banana Republic, 270, 277,
    340, 446
Banderas, Antonio, 164
Bank of America, 231, 266
Banks, Doug, 118
Baret, Alex, 151
Barf, 349
Barnes and Noble, 73, 417
Barneys New York, 457
Barq's root beer, 476
Baskin-Robbins USA Co., 448
    ex13.3
Bass Pro Shops, 43, 51, 336
Bath and Body Works, 397
Batman Begins, 522
Bauer, Jack, 527
Bayer
    Aspirin, 115, 220, 334, 499
        ex14.8, 582
Bayne, Katie, 287
Beckham, David, 183
Bed Bath & Beyond, 440, 453
Bell Helicopter, 246
Bellini, Alessandra, 151
Benetton, 476
Ben & Jerry's, 38
Berger, Shoshana, 229
Berman, Sara, 104
Best Buy, 111, 174, 261, 314,
    391, 413, 435, 440, 453,
    539, 571, 591
BET, 117, 429
Better Business Bureau (BBB), 74
Betty Crocker, 122, 499 ex14.8
    Tuna Helper, 367
Beverage Institute for Health and
    Wellness, 525
Bhagwati, Jagdish, 145
Bharti Enterprises, 167
BIC
    BIClink.com, 547
    BIC Pen, 23
Bich, Bruno, 23

Bidz.com, 579
Big Bertha, 420
BIGresearch, 192
bioInfusion, 342–343
Bisquick, 46
Bizmate.com, 579
BJ's Wholesale Club, 440
Black & Decker, 305, 395
*Black Enterprise African American
    Travel Guide, The*, 117
BlackPlanet, 472
Blair, 5
Blair Witch Project, The, 521
Blake, Frank, 3
Blige, Mary J., 507
Blimpie, 438
Blinder, Alan, 145
Blockbuster Entertainment Ltd., 528
Blockbuster Video, 522
Block Drug Company, 42
BlogPulse, 485
Bloomingdale Home, 454
Bloomingdale's, 456
BLS Consumer Expenditure Surveys,
    298 ex9.2
Bluefly.com, 449, 457
Blumenthal, Richard, 93
BMW, 41, 107, 113, 126 ex4.3,
    173, 209, 219, 507, 527, 528
Boeing Aircraft Company, 41,
    133, 242, 245, 361, 366,
    368, 395, 399, 543
Boisset Family Estates, 347
Bon Appétit, 106
Bonnaroo Music and Arts Festival,
    528
Bono, 99–100
BookFinder.com, 579
Booz, Allen Hamilton, 363, 366
Bordeaux's First Growth, 167
Borders, 417
BorgWarner, 243
Bose, 335, 567
Boston Consulting Group, 361
Boston-Power, 146
Bottega Veneta, 105
Brady, Tom, 184
BrandPulse Insight, 318
Bravo, 445
    Bravo.com, 445
    Project Runway, 445
Breguet, 275, 282
Brides, 509
Bridgestone, 405
Briggs & Stratton Corporation, 248
Brinkley, Christie, 114
Bristol-Myers Squibb (BMS), 322

Britannica, 12
British Airways, 591
British Petroleum (BP), 494
British Sky Broadcasting, 169
Brooks Brothers, 107
Brookstone, Inc., 51
Bryant, Kobe, 183
Bryson, E. Brent, 80
BtoB Magazine, 232
B to B Marketing, 231
Buckle, 453
Buddy Freddy's, 42
Budget Rent-A-Car, 507
Buffy the Vampire Slayer, 499
    ex14.8
Bugle Boy, 580
Bugs Bunny, 445
Buick
    Enclave, 274, 558
    Lucerne sedan, 274
Build-A-Bear, 458
Burger King, 303, 379, 447, 478,
    498, 513, 527
    Apple Fries, 371
Business Insight Journal Report,
    589
Business Objects, 147–148
Business Periodicals Index (BPI), 24
BusinessWeek, 5, 10, 28,
    118, 361
Busta Rhymes, 118

C

Cadillac, 221, 269, 343
    Escalade Hybrid, 222
California Closets, 536
California State University,
    Northridge, 556
Callaway Golf, 280
Calloway, 586
Calvin Klein, 216, 441
CamelBak
    Low Infrared Reflective (LIRR) sys-
        tem, 255
    WaterBeast, 255
Campbell's Soup, 171, 199, 347,
    371
    Creamy Chicken soup, 337
    Red Kettle Soups, 44
    Select Harvest soups, 495
    Swanson Broth, 340
Campfire Media, 521, 522
Canada Dry, 295
Canadian Breast Cancer
    Foundation, 95
Candid Camera, 510
Cannondale, 535

Canon, 500 ex14.9
Carb Solutions High Protein
    Bars, 270
Caress soap, 217
Carl's Jr., 278
Carnegie Mellon, 480
Cars, 55, 56
Cartier, 454
Casual Male, 266
Caterpillar Tractor, 42, 105, 164,
    244, 586, 587
    CAT gear, 164
Cathay Pacific Airways, 591
CBS, 504, 528
    60 Minutes, 504
    CSI, 504, 510
    CSI: Miami, 528
CDPriceShop.com, 579
Celebrity pots and pans, 276
Center for Digital Democracy, 480
Center for Science in the Public
    Interest, 525
Central Corporation, 291
Centrum Silver, 114
CenturyTel, Inc., 263
Cerreta, Denise, 574
Chanel, 586
Chang, Gary, 104
Chang, Horace, 165
Charles Schwab, 213
Charming Shoppes Inc., 276
Charter Communications, 263
Cheerios, 588
Cheetos, 143
Chevrolet, 341
    Chevy Tahoe, 405
Chevron Texaco, 494
Cheyney University, 398
Chicago's East Bank Club, 219
Chico's, 261
Chief Marketing Officer
    Council, 235
Children's Place, The, 436
Chili's Grill & Bar, 394
Chipotle, 306
Chiquita, 90, 92–93
Chiquita Brands, 591
Cho, Dana, 307
Chocolate Marketing, 228
Chocolate Turtle Chex Mix, 537
Choice Hotels, 236
ChoicePoint, 132
Chris-Craft, 404
Christian Dior, 420
Chronicle of Philanthropy, The, 100
Chrysler, 23, 220, 544, 550
C&H Sugar, 347

Chuck E. Cheese, 110, 270
Cinergy, 217
Cingular, 74
Circle K, 448 ex13.3
Circuit City, 506
Cisco Systems, 231, 232 ex7.1,
    398
CitiCard
    Citi AAdvantage Card, 277
    Diamond Preferred Rewards
        Card, 277
    Platinum Select Card, 277
    Upromise Card, 277
Claritas PRIZM Lifestyle software,
    269
Clif Bars, 270
Clorox Company, 220
    Brita water filtration, 44
    Clorox 2, 44
    Fresh Step, 44
    Glad products, 44
    K. C. Masterpiece barbecue
        sauce, 44
    Kingsford Charcoal, 44
    Scoop Away, 44
Close-Up, 217
Cloverfield, 521, 522
CMS, 538
CNBC
    Mad Money, 504
CNET.com, 579
CNN, 507
CNN International, 169
Cnooc Ltd., 148
Coach, 111, 345
Coca-Cola Company, 6, 10, 11,
    44, 51, 111, 116, 118, 149,
    151, 154, 167, 169, 174,
    178, 194, 203, 216, 217,
    220, 222, 238, 260, 274,
    275, 308, 334, 339, 341
    ex10.3, 345, 349, 373, 379,
    442, 447, 452, 458, 476,
    478, 492, 512, 527, 529, 536
    Beverage Institute for Health and
        Wellness, 525
    Blak, 287
    Classic, 287
    Coca-Cola Light, 171, 350
    Coca-Cola Zero, 536
    Coke Zero, 286, 287
    Dasani, 260
    Diet Coke, 222, 286–288,
        338, 350
    Diet Coke Plus, 287
    Fruitopia, 260
    Full Throttle Blue Demon, 287

Coca-Cola Company (*Continued*)
Intelligent Vending, 442
Kin, 350
My Coke Rewards, 535
New Coke, 371
POWERade, 208, 260, 497, 498, 509
Sound Check, 507
Sprite, 208, 350
Tab, 279
Cocker, Joe, 499 ex14.8
Cocoa Puffs, 581
Coelho, Paulo, 496
Cole Haan, 221
Colgate-Palmolive, 149, 175, 303, 371
Gum Protection Formula, 143
La Croix Plus, 149
College Placement Annual, 24, 25
CollegeRecruiter.com, 549, 550
Colombia University, 145
Comedy Central, 429, 507
Comic-Con, 522
comida y familia, 116
Commerce Business Daily, 238
Common Knowledge, 314
Complex, 212
CompUSA, 459
ConocoPhillips, 154
Consumer Digest, 578
Consumer Reports, 191, 578
Contac cold medicine, 511
Container Store, The, 16
Continental Airlines, 343
Converse, 100
Cookie Crisp cereal, 222
Cooper, Frank, 492
Coopers & Lybrand, 586
Cooper Tire & Rubber, 245
Copilevitz, Todd, 477
Copperton sunscreen lotion, 511
Cordua, Julia, 100
Coremetrics, 570
Costco, 80, 105, 124, 266, 434 ex13.1, 440, 591
Kirkland brand, 342
Kirkland Signature, 342
Cost Cutter, 578
Council of Supply Chain Management Professionals, 400
Cover Girl, 114, 277
Covisint, 236
Crate & Barrel, 113, 441
Creative Technology, 191
Crested Butte Ski Resort, 580
Crisco, 455
Cross pens, 345

CSTV Network, 504
Cuisinart, 586
Culinary Institute of Tuscany, 329
Cullen, Shawn, 255
Cummins Engine Company, 241–242
Curves for Women, 221
Cutler, Sandy, 83 ex3.5
CVS Caremark, 434 ex13.1
Cyber Dialogue, 317
Cycle dog food, 366, 367

D

D3 Systems Incorporated, 311
DaimlerChrysler/Mitsubishi, 167, 236, 242
Dairy Queen, 448 ex13.3
Danone (Dannon), 167, 171
Activia, 270
Dansk, 441
Dark Knight, The, 521, 522
Datamonitor, 228
Datril, 42
Da Vinci Code, The, 484, 485, 512
Da Wei Sun, 139
Days Inn Worldwide, 448 ex13.3
DC Comics, 533
DealTime.com, 579
DeBeers, 92, 93
Decision Analyst, 314
Deep Purple, 20
Deere & Co., 372
Delhomme, Jake, 184
Delivery Agent, 445
Dell, Inc., 9, 90 ex3.7, 234, 302, 341, 343, 347, 396, 399, 407, 444, 460
IdeaStorm.com, 365
OptiPlex system, 410
Dell, Michael, 499 ex14.8
Del Monte
Fruit Chillers, 281
Delta Air Lines, 11, 41, 341
DemandTec, 570
Denny's inc., 448 ex13.3
Dentyne Ice, 334
Desperate Housewives, 488
Details, 212
Dew Action Sports Tour, 528
DHL, 52, 134, 177, 236
Dick's, 440
Digital Entertainment Network, 7
Dilbert, 48
Dillard's, 436, 441, 450
Dion, Celine, 164
Direct Marketing Association, 443

DirecTV, 504
Dish Network, 504
Disney, 55–56, 217, 341 ex10.3, 507
Disney Channel, 55, 56, 430
Disney Consumer Products
Buzz Lightyear fragrance, 362
Pirates of the Caribbean fragrance, 362
Disney Princesses, 55
Disney's California Adventure, 55
DKNY, 403
DMReview, 542
Doing Business with the General Services Administration, 239
Dole, 94
Sweet Retreat contest, 536
Dole Food, 591
Dollar General, 121, 439, 453, 587, 588
Dollar Tree, 402, 422, 454, 588
Domino's Pizza, 165, 447, 527, 536
Dom Pérignon, 440
Dong, Jonathan, 153
Donna Karan, 417
Donso, 146
Doritos, 115
Dorward, Alastair, 57, 140–141, 185
DoubleClick, 159, 319, 376
Dove soap, 115, 169, 220
Dow Chemical, 125, 232, 238
XLA, 125
Dr. J, 500 ex14.9
Drucker, Peter, 379
Duane Reade, 570
Ducati, 476, 477
Ducks Unlimited, 73
Dun & Bradstreet, 24, 25, 364, 546
Duncan Hines, 123
Dunkin' Donuts, 294, 495, 532, 537
Latte Lite, 537, 550
DuPont, 40, 231, 255, 368, 562
Duracell, 345
DustBuster, 366
Dutch Boy, 347
Dylan, Bob, 21, 526
Dyson, James, 134
Dyson vacuum cleaners, 495

E

E4X, Inc., 177
Eason, Yla, 117
EA Sports, 265

Eastman Kodak, 217, 342, 358–359, 385, 412, 422
  KodakGallery.com, 417
Easton Town Center, 454
Eastwood, Clint, 500 ex14.9
Eaton Corporation, 83 ex3.5
eBay.com, 8, 220, 402, 446, 571, 579
Ebbers, Bernard, 78
Eckert, Bob, 192
Eckhart, Aaron, 522
EcoLogo, 348
Economist, The, 118
Eddie Bauer, 306
Edmondson, David, 73
edmunds.com, 579
Egozy, Eran, 20
Eisner, Michael, 56
Eldson, Michael, 255
ell, 395
eMarketer, 375
e-motion software, 63
Empire Pencil, 238
Emporio Armani, 100
Encyclopaedia Britannica, 12
Energizer Bunny, 499 ex 14.8
Energy Brands, 394
Enova, 373
Enron, 74, 82
Entergy, 217
Enterline, Zach, 521
Enterprise Rent-A-Car, 276, 281
Eon, 472
Epcot Center, 20
Equifax, 132
ER, 510
e-Rewards, 314, 315
Ericsson's, 413
Ernst & Young (E&Y), 82
eS-Books, 178
ESPN, 56, 415, 430, 509
  Mobile Web, 415
  Podcenter, 415
ESPN the Magazine, 503
Essence, 117
Ethan Allen, 113, 398
Ethel's Chocolate Lounges, 227–228
  Truffles and Tea for Two, 228
Ethisphere, 82
Ethos Water, 95
E-Trade, 504
Eurasia restaurant, 296
Evrard, Alain, 583
Excedrin, 499 ex 14.8
Excite, 217
Exostar, 242, 251

Expedia.com, 397
"Experience Aloha: Hawaii on Tour," 528
ExxonMobil Corporation, 147, 154, 447, 562
  Exxon On the Run, 438
E-Z pass, 337, 412

F

Facebook, 110, 112, 210, 218, 264, 364, 472, 476, 480
Fairmont Hotels & Resorts, 5, 414
  Princess Resort, 265
Falzon, George, 124
Family Dollar, 439, 588
FAO Schwarz, 459
Farmers Insurance, 549
Fast Food Nation (Schlosser), 529
Federal Bureau of Investigation (FBI), 580, 591
Federal Trade Commission (FTC), 449 ex13.4, 495, 571, 580
Federated Department Stores, Inc., 436
Federer, Roger, 183
FedEx Corp., 11, 16, 52, 105, 134, 177, 231, 234, 235, 247, 344
  FedEx Kinko's, 542
  FedEx Office, 344
Feld, Karl, 311
Ferguson, Sarah, 213
Fila, 264
FIND/SVP, 298 ex9.2
Finn Johnson, Elizabeth, 286–287
Firm, The, 527
Fisher-Price, 203, 217
  Play Laboratory, 305
Fitness by Nautilus, 113
FNAC, 178
Focalyst, 265
FocusVision, 303
Fogle, Jared, 472
Food and Drug Administration (FDA), 525
Foot Locker, 436
Forbes, 184
Ford, Henry, 12, 13, 274
Ford Motor Company, 17, 41, 236, 396, 414, 527
  Expedition, 527
  Lincoln, 414
  Model T, 274
  Mustang, 399
Formway Furniture, 232 ex7.1
Forrester Research, 535
Fort Howard Corporation, 275

Fort James Corporation
  Dixie Rinse & Reuse, 499 ex14.8
Fortune, 3
For Your Entertainment, 458
Fossil, 570
Four Seasons hotels, 11
Fox Network, 504
  American Idol, 504
  House, 504
  O'Reilly Factor, 504
FPL, 90 ex3.7
Freeplay Energy Group, 173
Freightliner, 563, 594
French Rabbit, 347
Frescobaldi famil, 167
Fresh Del Monte Produce, 591
Friedman, Milton, 88
Frigidaire, 345
Frito-Lay, 37, 44, 143
  Rumbles, 44
  Sabritas, 171, 308, 350, 534
  Stuffers, 44
  Toppels, 44
Fritzsche, Peggy, 104
Fruit of the Loom, 342
Fuji, 417
Fujitsu, 235
Fuld & Co., 366

G

Gadzooks, 436
GameStop, 435
Gap, Inc., 95, 99–100, 264, 434, 441, 454, 458, 535
  babyGap, 112, 277
  Banana Republic, 277
  GapBody, 277
  GapKids, 277, 454
  Gap Outlet, 277
  Old Navy, 277
Garden Botanika, 113
Garner, Jennifer, 209
Gartner Research, 9, 535
Gateway, 168
Gatorade, 218, 402
Gatorade G2, 371
Gatorade Xtremo, 115
GE Healthcare
  MAC 400, 373
GEICO, 421, 422
Gellar, Sarah Michelle, 499 ex14.8
General Electric (GE), 10, 35, 41, 89, 94, 105, 125–126, 159, 174, 221, 231, 334, 336, 341 ex10.3, 490 ex14.6

General Electric (GE) Broadcasting Company, 345
General Foods
  International Coffees, 369
General Mills, 46, 81 ex3.3, 143, 199, 308, 370, 537
General Motors (GM), 13, 162, 217, 231, 236, 237, 243, 245, 338, 341, 366, 373, 412, 447, 490, 506, 536, 562
  Hummer, 528
  Nova, 202
General Motors/Toyota, 167
General Tire Company, 177
Genzyme
  Ceredase, 586
George clothing, 342
Gibson Guitar Corporation, 217
Gillette, 117, 143, 265
  Atra, 368
  Fusion, 368
  Mach3, 368, 380
  Sensor, 368
  Sientel, 350
  Silkience, 350
  Soyance, 350
  TracII, 368
Giorgio Armani, 417
GlaxoSmithKline, 90 ex3.7, 261
Global Ecolabelling Network, 348
Global Fund, The, 100
gloss.com, 451
GNC Franchising Inc., 448 ex13.3
Godiva chocolate, 47, 228, 402
Goodyear, 171, 308
Goody's Cool Orange, 299
Google, Inc., 112, 113, 126 ex4.3, 159, 218, 231, 341 ex10.3, 368, 391, 480, 484, 485, 506, 512, 574
Gordon, James, 500 ex14.9
"Go Red for Women," 528
Gourmet, 106
GQ, 212
Grand Theft Auto 4, 385
Green, Len, 555
Greenfield Online, 314
Green Giant, 150
  Jolly Green Giant, 150
Green Mountain Coffee Roasters, 438
Gross, Barbara, 556
Grossman, Lev, 599
Gucci, 111, 219, 402, 445, 454

Guess, 216
Guinness, 476
Guitar Hero, 20–21
Gymboree, 454

H

H. J. Heinz Co., 44, 90–92, 90–93, 143, 343, 398, 537
  EZ Squirt ketchup, 293
  ketchup, 199, 293
  Weight Watchers, 44, 311, 345
Häagen-Dazs
  dulce de leche, 373
Habitat for Humanity, 494
Haier Group, 152, 153
Hallmark Cards, 299, 501, 513
  Crown Media, 264
  Hallmark Channel, 264
  Shoebox greeting cards, 299, 323
Hamburger Helper, 581
Hamilton, Michael, 82
Hampton Inn/Hampton Inn & Suites, 448 ex13.3
Ha Nam supermarkets, 120
Hannah Montana, 55, 56
Hardee's, 278, 448 ex13.3
Harley-Davidson Inc., 108, 154, 173, 174, 194, 236
Harmonix, 20
HarperCollins, 586
Harris, Charlaine, 521
Harris Interactive, 315
Hartford Financial Services Group, 265
Hasbro, 117
  Scrabble, 345
Haugh, John, 228
Hawthorne, Grace, 229
Hayashi, Alden M., 589
Hayden, Diana, 583
HBO, 521–522
  Sopranos, The, 527
  True Blood, 521, 522
HealthScreen America, 218
HealthSouth Corporation, 78
Healthy Choice, 347
Heart Check America, 218
H-E-B Grocery Company, 269, 281
Heeling Sports Ltd.
  Heelys, 403
Heineken USA
  Holiday Headline Hoax, 538
Heinz, Henry, 90
Heinz Co. Foundation (HCF), 91
Helen Keller International, 91

Hellmann's, 169
Henderson, Jim, 372
Hershey Company, 11, 199, 527
  Almond Joy, 537
  Hershey Bars, 537
  Kit Kat bar, 498
  Reese's, 537
  Swoops, 537
Hertz rental car, 281
Hewlett-Packard, 3, 82, 90 ex3.7, 397, 496
  HP Pavilion, 496
Hidalgo, Antonio, 8
High School Musical, 55, 56
Hill's Pet Nutrition, 404
Hilton Hotels
  Hilton Family Skating & Gymnastics Spectacular, 527
Hindustan Lever, 175
Hintze, Jim, 235
Holiday Inn Select, 113, 305
Hollister, 208, 218
Hollywood Records, 56
Home Depot, 3, 6, 9, 107, 265, 267, 268, 272, 293, 357, 413, 434 ex13.1, 435, 440
Homefair, 122
Home & Garden Television Network
  Dream Home Giveaway, 536
HomeGoods, 105, 132, 440
Home Retail Group, 90 ex3.7
Home Shopping Network, 444
Honda, 112, 420, 476
  Odyssey, 270
Honda Motor Co., 126 ex4.3, 373
Honest Tea, 112, 394
Honeywell, 159
Hoover, 134, 495
Hopper, Robin, 535
Hormel, 120
  Spam, 120, 340
Hot Wheels, 577
Hotwire, 580
Hoyer, Christie, 293
H&R Block, 345
HSBC, 476
Hsieh, Tony, 196
Hundekari, Neelesh, 583
Hunter, Chuck, 255
Hurricane Katrina, 74, 452
Hustler, 201

Hutton, E. F., 500 ex14.9
Hyatt Corporation, 447
Hyatt Hotels, 414
Hyperion, 56

I

Iacocca, Lee, 23
Ibanez, 217
IBM Corp., 23, 80, 125, 126
    ex4.3, 153, 168, 231, 246,
    272, 319, 341 ex10.3, 389
IceRocket, 485
IDEO Inc., 307
Iger, Bob, 55, 56, 126 ex4.3
IHOP, 306
IKEA, 190–191, 420, 440, 560
illy, 459
    Hyper Espresso System,
    459
Immelt, Jeff, 126 ex4.3
Inbound Logistics, 413
    Trucking Decision Support
    Tool, 413
Inc. magazine, 357
Indiana Jones and the Kingdom of
    the Crystal Skull, 513
Industrial Strength Marketing,
    233
InFocus Corp., 232 ex7.1
Infopoll, 314
Information Resources, Inc., 320,
    369, 371, 563
    BehaviorScan, 320
    InfoScan, 321, 323
Information Technologies Toolbox,
    232 ex7.1
InnoCentive, Inc., 368, 380
Inquisite, 314
Instant Tax Service, 448 ex13.3
Intel Corp., 80, 126 ex4.3, 247,
    341 ex10.3, 343, 344,
    345, 563
    Centrino, 344
InterContinental Hotels Group,
    414, 448 ex13.3
International Federation of the
    Phonographic Industry, 379
International Franchise Association,
    447, 449 ex13.4
International Monetary Fund,
    145
International Paper Company,
    591
International Society for
    Environmental Ethics, 127
Internet Crime Complaint
    Center, 580

Intuit, Inc, 414
    TurboTax, 414
IPSOS, 302
Iridium, 587
Isaac Mizrahi domestics, 404
It Chick clothing, 110
iTextiles.com, 397
iUpload, 535
Ivory soap, 511

J

J. Crew, 441
J. P. Morgan Chase & Co., 528
Jacobsen, Arne, 172
Jackson, Gary, 457
Jaguar, 269
Jamaican Tourism Board, 489
James, LeBron, 183, 208, 222
Jani-King, 447, 448 ex13.3
Jannini, Michael E., 307
Jan-Pro Franchising International
    Inc., 448 ex13.3
Japan Airlines, 591
Jarritos, 116
Jay-Z, 115, 496
JCPenney, 111, 117, 395, 396,
    397, 402, 436, 453, 459,
    571, 581, 589
J.D. Powers & Associates,
    10, 295
Jeep, 345
Jeld-Win, 536
Jell-O, 220, 339
Jenkins, James R., 83 ex3.5
Jergens Natural Glow Daily
    Moisturizer, 491
Jet, 118
Jiffy Lube International, Inc, 448
    ex13.3
Jimmy'Z, 274
Jobs, Steve, 340, 456,
    599, 600
Joe Camel, 128
John Deere, 83 ex3.5
Johns Manville, 232 ex7.1
Johnson Controls, 562
Johnson & Johnson, 490
    Neutrogena, 491
Jonas Brothers, 55, 56
Jones Soda, 394
Jordan, Michael, 183, 500
    ex14.9
Jose Cuervo Tequila, 527
Joyner, Tom, 118
Juanes, 115, 116
Juicy Juice, 537
Juniper Research, 458

JVC, 391, 578
JWT Worldwide, 375

K

Kagome, 398
Kahlúa, 281
Kahn, Oliver, 500
Kalathur, Raj, 372
Kantor, Rich, 293
Karan, Donna, 417
Karaoki Revolution, 20
Karmaloop, 278
Kashi Frozen Pizza, 478
Kate's Paperie, 460
Kayla Beverly Hills, 118
Kedl, Kent D., 140
Keebler Sweet Spots, 294
Kellogg's, 11, 199, 222, 242,
    513, 534
    Breakfast Mates, 371
    Corn Pops, 534
    Eggo, 534
    Froot Loops, 534
    Frosted Flakes Gold, 497
    Pop-Tarts, 534
    Raisin Bran, 242
    Rice Krispies, 534
Kenmore, 334
Kenwood, 191
Kenya Airlines, 174
Keohane, Scott, 63
Kernaghan, Charles, 100
KFC. See Yum! Brands
Killian's Red, 394
Kimberly-Clark, 123, 133, 194
    Huggies, 194, 495
    Huggies Natural Fit, 308
    Kleenex Facial Tissues, 133,
    280, 455, 536
Kinko's, 344
KitchenAid, 277
Klint, Doug, 80
KLM Royal Dutch Airlines,
    174, 591
Klum, Heidi, 451
Kmart, 107, 455
Koch Industries Dixie paper prod-
    ucts, 222
Kohl's, 111, 455
Kohn, Pamela, 581
Kojima, 174
Kolo Boutique, 460
Kool-Aid, 339
Korean Air Lines, 591
Kraft Foods, 35, 38, 44, 116,
    173, 238, 267, 419
    Bagel-fuls, 371

Kraft Foods (*Continued*)
    Chocolate Creme Oreos, 339
    Chocolate Fudge Sundae Creme Oreos, 339
    Country Time lemonade, 576
    DiGiorno, 478
    Double Delight Mint Creme Oreos, 339
    Double Delight Peanut Butter Oreos, 339
    Honey Bunches of Oats, 201
    Macaroni & Cheese, 442
    Mac & Cheese Crackers, 371
    Maxwell House Coffee, 44
    Nabisco, 340
    Oreo Cookies, 173, 339
    Uh-Oh Oreos, 339
Kramer Beverage Company, 394
Kroger, 434 ex13.1, 533, 573, 577, 578
    Plus Shopper cards, 533
Kumon Math & Reading Centers, 448 ex13.3
KY Yours + Mine Couples Lubricant, 361

L

Ladders, The, 545
Lafley, A. G., 126 ex4.3
Lands' End, 177, 278, 397, 398, 408, 458, 496
    LandEnd.com, 457
Las Vegas's Fashion Show Mall, 453
La-Z-Boy, 342
Lea & Perrins, 339
Ledger, Heath, 522
Legacy Town Center, 454
LEGO Group, 368, 513
Lenovo Group, 168
Levenger, 460
Lever Brothers, 46
    Lifebuoy Soap, 46
    Sunlight dishwashing liquid, 475
Levi Strauss & Company, 41, 149, 150, 345, 373, 402, 459, 527
    Dockers, 580
    Levi's 501 jeans, 149–150
Levitt, Ted, 148
Levy, Ira J., 358
Levy, Steven, 599
Lexus, 5, 8, 42, 173, 249, 345, 527
    450LX, 558
LG Electronics Primian refrigerator, 173
Libby's Fruit Float, 367
Liberty Tax Service, 448 ex13.3

Lifestyle Family Fitness, 221
Lightspeed Research, 532
Limited Brands
    Express, 397
    The Limited, 397
Linear Technology Corp., 569
LinkedIn, 480, 545
LinoColor Picture Perfect Rewards, 539
Lippincott, Phil, 23
Lipton Iced Tea, 537
Liz Claiborne, 41, 342
L.L. Bean, 5, 249, 443, 445
Lockheed Martin, 82, 242, 249, 250, 251, 255
Loctite Corporation Super Glue, 247
Lodrup, Kim, 328–330
Logitech International, 148
Lok, Su, 358
Longs Drug Stores, 570
L'Oréal SA, 169, 176, 220, 490
    Elvive, 13
    Excellence Crème, 583
    Garnier Nutrisse, 583
    L'Oréal Paris, 583
    Vichy, 583
Los Angeles Times, The, 429, 509
Louis Vuitton, 219, 345, 417
Lowe's Home Improvement Warehouse, 107, 265, 434 ex13.1, 440
Lowry, Adam, 21, 101, 140–141
Lowry, Eric, 57
Lucasfilm Ltd., 513
Lucky, 503, 509
Lucky Brand Jeans
    Lucky Buck Off, 538
Lumber Liquidators, 536
Luna Bars, 270

M

Mackey, John, 73
Macy's, Inc., 263, 436, 454, 459, 460
Maeda, John, 104
Magness, Aaron, 196
Mahindra & Mahindra, 372
Malcolm Baldrige National Quality Award, 295
Mall of America, 454
Management Decisions, 366
Manning, Peyton, 184
Manson, Marshall, 529, 530
Maoz, Michael, 9
MapQuest, 125

March of Dimes, 35
Marketing News, 503
Marks & Spencer, 90 ex3.7
Marlboro cigarettes, 85
Marlboro Man, 128
Marriott International, 307, 344, 414
    Courtyard by Marriott, 343
    Fairfield Inn, 343
    Renaissance Hotels, 307
    Residence Inn, 343
Mars, 308
    Mars Bars, 193
    M&M's, 513
Mars, Ethel, 228
Mars, Frank, 228
Marshalls, 105, 132, 440, 456
Martha Steward Omnimedia, 445
Martinari, 591
Martinez, Zarela, 116
Marx, Michael, 476
Mary Kay Cosmetics, 338, 442, 443
Maslow, Abraham, 218, 219
Massive, Inc., 508
MasterCard, 303
Masterfoods Dove "Promises," 537
Matsushita Electric, 90 ex3.7
Mattel Inc., 192
    Barbie, 352, 577
    My Scene Barbie, 445
Maxim, 538
Maybelline, 117, 277, 499 ex14.8
Mayo Clinic, 366
Maytag, 42, 498
Mazda/Ford, 167
McCain, John, 472
McCarthy, Patrick, 466
McCormick, 123
McDonald's, 35, 39, 44, 47, 120, 149, 171, 172, 175, 199, 203, 249, 306, 337, 341 ex10.3, 345, 369, 379, 406, 446, 447, 448 ex13.3, 449, 457, 478, 499 ex14.8, 525, 529, 532, 535
    Big Mac, 172, 337
    Big Mac Challenge, 527
    Big Tasty, 172
    Chicken McNuggets, 172
    Double Cheeseburgers, 172
    Egg McMuffin, 218
    Happy Meals, 44, 47, 172, 534
    Innovation Center, 365, 380
    Maharaja Mac, 172
    McFlurry, 508

Southern Style Chicken Biscuit and Sandwich, 371
Vegetable Burgers, 447
Vegetable McNuggets, 447
McIlhenny Company
Garlic Pepper Sauce, 496
Tabasco Hot Sauce, 496, 537
McKinsey & Co., 586
McLauglin, Dave, 93
Media Metrix, 476
Medved, Michael, 100
Mercedes-Benz, 7, 173, 217, 219, 269, 341, 395
Maybach 62, 204
Merrill Lynch & Company, 267
Method, 21, 57, 101, 140–141, 185
MGM, 345
Miami Dolphins, 184
Michelin, 405, 447
Michigan Economic Development Corporation (MEDC), 242
Michigan State University, 127
Mickelson, Phil, 183
Microsoft Corporation, 12, 125, 126 ex4.3, 159, 191, 203, 231, 341 ex10.3, 345, 361, 414
Most Valuable Professional (MVP) program, 376
MSN, 506
MSN games, 508
Windows XP, 219
Xbox 360, 21, 220, 385
Xbox Live, 508
Migros, 42
Milwaukee Summerfest, 528
Mimeo.com, 234
Mindbranch.com, 299
Minis, Perry, 83 ex3.5
Minoli, Enrico, 477
Mintel International, 371
Minute Rice, 368, 380
MIT Sloan Management Review, 589
Mitsubishi Motors Pajero, 151
Miyamoto, Shigeru, 385
M&M Johnson, 117
M&M/Mars, 396
Mobissimo.com, 580
Modern Manners, 201
Modern Maturity, 509
Moen, 113, 264
Molnar, Stephanie, 108
Mondavi, 167
Monday Night Football, 508
Monster.com, 506
Montblanc, 219

Moody's, 546
Morris Sussex Pet Supply Wellness Chicken Super5Mix, 592
Mossimo, 404
Motorola Corp., 100, 247, 457, 486
Moto City, 366
Razr phone, 366
Mouton-Rothschild, 167
MSNBC, 507
MSN Music, 528
MTV Networks, 116, 169, 210, 218, 264, 429, 430, 507, 509
MyBarakObama.com, 472
My Little Pony, 110
mySimon.com, 579
MySpace, 110, 112, 210, 218, 458, 472, 480, 521

N

Nakamura, Jun, 151
Napster, 528
NASA, 193
NASCAR, 495, 513, 527
National Collegiate Tailgate Tour, 496
National Food Laboratory (NFL), 293
National Football League (NFL), 183–185, 184
National Geographic, 217
National Labor Committee for Worker and Human Rights, 100
National Restaurant Association, 441
National Retail Federation, 5, 433
National Society for the Prevention of Cruelty to Children (NSPCC), 208
Nautilus, 11
Navistar, 562
NBC Universal, 267, 445, 504, 505, 511, 527
iVillage Web site, 268
The Office, 504
Sunday Night Football, 504
Today show, 268
Neale-May, Donovan, 235
Neiman Marcus, 42, 219, 281, 417, 453, 454, 586
Last Call, 441, 454
Neosporin Neo to Go!, 371
Nestlé, 133, 173
Kit Kat bars, 173
Purina, 342
Purina's Pro Plan, 404
Wonka Division, 366

Netbizz Office Supplies, 235
Netflix.com, 506
NetGenesis, 233
Neutrogena, 209
New Balance, 165
New England Patriots, 184
New Orleans Saints, 184
NewStar Young & Tender, 293
Newsweek, 118, 508, 599
New York Giants, 184
New York Times, The, 118, 192, 429, 476, 508
NFL Network, 504
NFL Team Shop, 445
Nickelodeon, 430, 506, 507
Dora the Explorer, 429
SpongeBob SquarePants, 429
Nielsen, 266, 505
BuzzMetrics, 318
Nielsen BuzzMetrics
BlogPulse, 318
BrandPulse, 318
BrandPulse Insight, 318
Nielsen Co., 522
Nielsen Entertainment, Inc., 508
Nielsen/NetRatings, 298 ex9.2
Nike, 41, 42, 74, 208, 222, 265, 281, 338, 345, 373, 417, 435, 499 ex14.8, 500, 505
Nike Plus, 535
Nintendo Corporation, 361
DS, 385
Mario Kart Wii, 385
Super Smash Bros. Brawl, 385
Wii, 362, 384–386, 459
Wii Fit, 371
Wii Play, 385
Nissan Motor Company, 160, 236, 267, 373
Altima, 267
Quest minivan, 214
Nokia, 113, 126 ex4.3, 341 ex10.3, 361, 476, 486
Noorany, Heidi, 296, 297
Nordstrom, 9, 42, 111, 436, 454, 466–467
Rack, 441
Nordstrom, Eric, 467
Nordstrom, Jamie, 467
Nordstrom Way, The (Spector), 466
North American Securities Administrators Association, 449 ex13.4
Northwest Airlines, 9
Novamex, 116
Novo Nordisk, 90 ex3.7
NPD Group/Crest, 532

NPD Research, 302
NPR, 507

O

Obama, Barack, 118, 157, 472, 492
Ober, Richard, Jr., 358
Office Depot, 48, 235, 440, 457
Ogilvy & Mather, 303
Old Mother Hubbard Dog Food Company, 592
Old Navy, 277
Olive Garden, 306
    Culinary Institute of Tuscany, 329
Olmec Corporation, 117
Olsen, Mary-Kate, 459
Omega, 588
O'Neal, Shaquille, 498, 500 ex14.9
Oneida, 395, 441
One World Café, 584
OnStar, 274, 343
On the Run Café, 438
Operation Bidder Beware, 580
OPI, 537
OptiPlex system, 410
Opus One, 167
Oracle E-Business Suite, 63
Orange County Choppers, 496
Orville Reddenbacher, 311
Orvis Company, 42
Oscar Mayer Center Cut Bacon, 293
OshKosh B'Gosh, Inc., 276
Ostermann, Ken, 108
Outside, 578
Overstock.com, 5, 506, 570
OXO Good Grips, 264

P

Packard, David, 3, 140
Palm Centro, 459
Palmer, Stacy, 100
Pampered Chef, The, 442
Panasonic, 408
Papa John's International, Inc, 448 ex13.3
Papa John's Pizza, 390, 533
Parker Hannifin Corporation, 569
Patek Philippe, 275
PBS, 507
PC World, 578
Peaches & Cream Spa, 110
Pei Liang, 140
Pemberton, John, 344
Pemberton Place, 344
Penny, Gareth, 92

Pennzoil, 347
People, 28, 488, 510
Pepperidge Farm, 305
PepsiCo, 51, 118, 143, 169, 177, 203, 216, 220, 222, 339, 379, 398, 442, 458, 478, 504, 527, 563
    Aquafina Alive, 269, 319
    Crystal Pepsi, 279
    Diet Pepsi, 46, 222, 492
    Ice Cucumber, 171
    Mountain Dew, 345, 507
    Mountain Dew Code Red, 115
    Pepsi Cola, 269, 275, 492, 534
    Pepsi Red, 171
Perdue, David, 598
Peretz, Ervin, 574
Perrier, 169
Perseus, 314
Persil Tablets, 191
Petco, 571
Petersen, Donald E., 17
Pets-Hotel, 42
PetSmart, 42, 435
Pettibone, 404
Peugeot, 160
Pfizer Lyrica, 494
Philip Morris, 17, 494
    Miller beer, 379, 479
    Miller Lite, 495
Philips Electronics, 90 ex3.7, 104, 503
    Magnavox, 478
Piaggio, 113
Piczo, 208
Pierre Cardin, 177
Piggly Wiggly, 437
Pillsbury, 143, 214, 299
    Doughboy, 143–144, 178
    Hungry Jack pancake mix, 390, 391
    Milk Break Bars, 369
Pillsbury, John S., 81 ex3.3
Pimpeando, 116
Pirates of the Caribbean, 55, 56
Pixar, 55, 56, 126 ex4.3
Plato, 76
Playboy Energy, 404
Polaroid Colorpack camera, 368
Polident, 42
Poligrip, 42
Polo, Marco, 295
polo.com, 451
Polo Ralph Lauren, 395
Popeil, Ron "Ronco," 555–556
Pop Rite, 311
Popular Mechanics, 509

Porsche, 475, 512, 578, 586
Porter, Paul, 385
Post cereals, 35
Post-It Notes, 4, 126 ex4.3
Pottery Barn, 113, 441
PowerBar Protein Plus, 270
Prada, 219, 420
Predictably Irrational: The Hidden Forces That Shape Our Decisions (Ariely), 589
Prevish, Leslie, 108
pricegrabber.com, 579
Priceline, 8
PriceSCAN.com, 579
Private Manufacturers' Label Association, 342
Pro Beach Volleyball tour, 527
Procter & Gamble (P&G), 8, 38, 46, 114, 123, 124, 126 ex4.3, 133, 149, 151, 169, 174, 191, 202, 214, 238, 246, 264, 266, 267, 272, 279, 282, 308, 338, 364, 365, 366, 370, 380, 402, 404, 413, 418, 420, 460, 490, 504, 506, 527, 563
    Bold, 343
    Bounce, 339, 343
    Bounty Basic, 266
    Bounty paper towels, 511
    Camay, 149
    Charmin Basic, 266
    Charmin toilet tissue, 511
    Cheer, 343
    Cincaprin, 46
    Connect-and-Develop Model, 368
    Crest, 149, 340, 368, 479
    Crest Pro-Health, 489, 512
    Crest SpinBrush, 587
    Dash, 343
    Dawn liquid detergent, 340
    Dawn Plus, 340
    Downy, 339, 343, 348
    Downy Fabric Softener, 8
    Downy Single Rinse (DSR), 8
    Downy Total Care, 343
    Dreft, 343
    Encaprin, 321
    Era, 343
    Febreeze, 339, 340, 343
    Folgers Instant Coffee, 321, 369
    Gain, 123, 343
    Head and Shoulders, 149, 169, 276, 340, 500–501
    Herbal Essences, 264
    Ivory Snow, 343

Mr. Clean Disinfecting Wipes with Febreeze Freshness, 343
Olay, 281
Olay Regenerist Eye Derma Pods, 368
Pampers, 149, 281, 495
Pampers Phases, 372
Pringles, 46
Puffs Plus, 133
Swiffer Wet mop, 151
Tide, 343, 451, 479
Tide.com, 342
Tide detergent, 199, 511, 512 with Downy, 339
Tide Stain Detective, 342
Tide Total Care, 343
Tide with Downy, 339
[Product] RED, 99–100
Progressive, 422
Progresso soups, 495
ProLine, 117
Pronto Markets, 276
Prophet, 365
Prudential, 345
Puck, Wolfgang, 345
Purina, 39
Puss 'n' Boots, 534

Q

Quaker Oats, 370
Chewy Granola Bars, 321, 369
Granola Dipps, 369
Rice-A-Roni, 347
Quantas, 591
Quieno Mis Quinces, 116
Quiznos, 434
QVC (Quality, Value, Convenience) Network, 444, 445, 460

R

Rack Room Shoes, 435
Raddohl, Tara, 581
RadioShack, 73, 174
Raikkonen, Kimi, 183
Rainforest Alliance, 93
Ralph Lauren, 44
Ramada Inns, 343
Ramones, the, 20
Random House, 586
Rani Pharmaceuticals, 18
Raytheon, 73
RCA, 191, 391
Reader's Digest, 488
ReadyMade, 229, 256, 288, 330
Recipe Connection, 116
RED Blogs service, 210
Red Bull, 404, 498

RedEnvelope.com, 279, 571
Red Lobster, 328–330
Red Octane, 20
RED products, 99–100
Red Stripe, 527
Reebok, 174, 265, 266, 345
REI sporting goods, 455
Reliant Resources, 217
Renault SA, 90 ex3.7, 160, 236
Dacia Logan, 373
Resorts' "W," 9
Restaurants & Institutions New American Diner study, 211
Revlon, 117
ColorStay Liquid Lip, 499 ex14.8
Rexall drugstores, 447
Rhetoric of Western Thought (Gordon), 500 ex14.9
Right Guard, 334
Rigopulos, Alex, 20
Rite Aid, 453
Ritz-Carlton hotels, 11, 294, 295
RiverTown Crossings, 454
RJR Nabisco, 340, 373
Roadway Express, 413
Robert Mondavi Wineries, 167, 488
Twin Oaks wine, 339
Rocawear, 115
Roche, 90 ex3.7
Rock Band, 20, 371
Rock Band 2, 21
Rogaine, 265
Rolaids, 601
Rolex, 42, 275, 335, 345, 558, 588
Rolling Stones, The, 568, 594
Rolls-Royce, 133, 335, 345, 404
Ronaldinho, 183
Ronco, 555, 556
Mr. Microphone, 555
Veg-O-Matic, 555
Rossi, Valentino, 183
Ross-Simmons Hardwood Lumber Company, 594
Ross Stores, 440
Rothschild, Baron Philippe de, 167
Royal Ahold, 460
Royal Bank of Canada, 7
RSS (Really Simple Syndication), 100, 507
Rubbermaid, 171, 371, 562
Sidekick, 365
Ruben, David, 216
Ruehl, 208
Ruffles, 143
Ruiz, Nancy, 592
Runner magazine, 107

Ryan, Eric, 21, 101, 140–141, 185
Ryanair, 594
Ryder, 412
Ryze, 545
Ryz shoes, 368

S

Safeway, 437, 583
Lifestyle markets, 281
Saks Fifth Avenue, 263, 269, 280 ex8.7, 417, 453, 454, 456
Off Fifth, 441
Sales & Marketing Management, 347
Sam's Club, 266, 437, 440, 460
Samsonite, 150
Samsung Electronics, 126 ex4.3, 486
San Diego Chargers, 184
Sandoz Pharmaceuticals, 133
San Francisco Giants, 527
Sangha, Jang, 372
Sanyo Electric Company, 151
Sara Lee Corp., 44, 321
Consolidated Foods Kitchen, 369
Hillshire Farm Salad Entrees, 44
Kiwi shoe polish, 473, 512
SAS, 247, 591
Saturday Night Live, 556
Saucony, 417
Sawtooth CiW, 314
Schiffer, Claudia, 583
Schlosser, Eric, 529
Schneider Associates, 371
Scholastic Books, 402, 513
Harry Potter and the Deathly Hallows, 403, 422
Harry Potter series, 402, 403
Schultz, Howard, 139, 140, 532
Schwan Food Company, 444
Impromptu Gourmet, 444
Red Baron, 478
SC Johnson, 35, 174
RAID, 527
Shout Color Catchers, 35
Scott, Lee, 89
Scott Paper, 23
Scotts Miracle-Gro, 357, 358
Scrabulous, 345
Scrushy, Richard, 78
Seagram's, 303, 343
ginger ale, 295
Sears, 11, 111, 117, 281, 348, 402, 436, 453
Craftsman, 450, 451, 578
DieHard, 217, 450, 451
Kenmore, 450, 451

Sears Holding, 434 ex13.1
Sears Holdings Corporation, 490 ex14.6
Second Life, 364
Seed, 507
Seed Media, 507
Seiko, 578
Selling to the Military, 239
Selling to the U.S. Air Force, 239
Sensodyne toothpaste, 42
Sephora, 430–431, 459, 467–468
Servpro, 448 ex13.3
Sethi, Jaya, 583
Setta, Salli, 329
Setting the Standard (Lockheed Martin), 250
Shanghai Automotive Corporation, 167, 236
Shanghai Automotive Industry Corp., 373
Shapes, 221
Sharp, Isadore, 11
Sheraton Hotel, 416
Sherwin-Williams, 395, 536
SheSpeaks.com, 537
Showtime Rotisserie BBQ, 556
Shrek, 534
Shriners, 73
Shriver, Bobby, 100
Sierra Club, 88
Silpada, 442–443
Simpson, O.J., 78
Sirius XM, 525
Six Sigma, 10
"Six Sins of Greenwashing," 348
Slumdog Millionaire, 510
Smart Alliance (Taylor), 92
Smart Money, 74
Smith, Renee, 291
Smith, Rick, 80
Smith, Tamsin, 100
SmithKline Beecham, 322
Smithsonian Institution, 555
Smyth, Ted, 90
SnackWell's, 347
Snap Fitness Inc., 448 ex13.3
Snapple a Day, 281
Snickers, 499 ex14.8
Snoop Dogg, 527
SoBe Life Water, 497
Soft Sheen, 117
Solomon, Robert C., 76
Soloway, Elaine, 600
Sonia Kashuk makeup, 404
SonicBlue, 191
    Rio MP3 Player, 216

Sonic Drive-In Restaurants, 306, 447, 448 ex13.3
Sony Ericsson, 44, 90 ex3.7, 113, 126 ex4.3, 133, 343, 391, 445, 486, 535
    Betamax, 371
    Columbia Pictures, 44
    F.E.A.R. 2: Project Origin, 528
    Frontline Web, 380
    Killzone 2, 528
    MLB 09, 528
    Playstation 3, 21
    Playstation 3 (PS3), 385, 528
    "Sony Ericsson Da Vinci Code Trail," 485, 512
    Street Fighter IV, 528
    Surround Sound Systems, 539
    Wii Fit, 385
    Wii Music, 385
    Wii Play, 385
Sotheby's, 446, 579
Soto, James, 233
Soule, Eric, 569
Source, The, 503
South Bend Chocolate, 228
Southwest Airlines, 7, 11, 37, 38, 41, 42
Sovereign Bank, 267
Space Adventures, 535
Spam Museum, 120
Sparks, John, 23
Special Olympics, 95
Specific Media, 263
Spector, Robert, 466
SpectraLink, 542
Spike TV, 212, 429
Splenda No Calorie Sweetener, 490
SpongeBob SquarePants, 164
Sporting Goods Business, 43
Sporting News, The, 538
Sports Authority, The, 453
Sports Illustrated, 28
Sprint, 116
Sprint Power Vision phone, 116
SPSS Quanquest, 314
Spurlock, Morgan, 529
St. Jude Children's Research Hospital, 528
Standard & Poor's, 24, 546
Stanford University, 21
Staples, 410, 440
    Staples.com, 538
Starbucks, 8, 39, 80, 95, 126 ex4.3, 139–140, 169, 179, 203, 228, 264, 294, 306, 341, 379, 434, 437, 453, 495, 532

DoubleShot, 398
Duetto Card, 535
Frappuccino, 398
Hear Music Cafés, 456
I'm In program, 538
MyStarbucksIdea.com, 365
RTD coffee, 398
StarKist Seafood, 303
    Charlie the Tuna, 499 ex14.8
Starlight Children's Foundation, 528
StarTek, Inc., 414
Starwood Hotels
    Starwood Preferred Guest program, 535
    "W" chain, 9, 95, 476, 535
State of the Blogosphere (Technorati), 476
Stengel, James, 202
Stern, Howard, 525
Steuer, Joan, 228
Stevens, Robert J., 250
Stewart, Calvin
    A.P.O. Jeans, 204
Stick-Up room deodorizers, 366
Sting, 507
Stolichnaya vodka, 177
Stone, Lewis, 303
Stonyfield Farm, 191
Stove Top Stuffing, 539
Strategic Resource Group, 281
StrawberryFrog, 404
Streamline.com, 7
Street, Picabo, 499 ex14.8
Subaru, 269
Subway, 434, 438, 447, 448 ex13.3, 472, 533
Suni Imaging, 232 ex7.1
Super 8, 448 ex13.3
Super Bowl, 488, 504
Super Bowl XI, 534
Supercuts, 447, 448 ex13.3
Super Size Me (Spurlock), 529
SUPERVALU, 434 ex13.1
SurveyMonkey, 314
SurveyPro, 314
Survey Sampling, 314
Survey Spot, 323
Susan G. Komen Breast Cancer Foundation, 95, 528
Sustainable Packaging Coalition, 347
Suzuki, 269, 420
Suzuki/GM, 167
Swanson, Robert, 569
Swanson, William, 73

Swanson's Unwritten Rules of Management (Swanson), 73
Swatch, 559
Sylvan Learning Systems, 447
Synovate, 302
Szaky, Tom, 357

T

Tacoda, 319
Talbots, 453
Tampa Bay Buccaneers, 184
Tandem Computers, 280
Target Corp., 83, 126 ex4.3, 217, 281, 308, 357, 396, 397, 401, 403, 404, 408, 413, 434 ex13.1, 435, 450, 451, 452, 454, 564, 577, 590, 592
    SuperTarget, 439, 460
    Take Charge of Education card, 535
Taser International Inc., 80
Tata Motors Ltd., 151
    Tata Nano, 373
Taylor, J. Gary, 92
TDAmeritrade, 319
Team Obama, 472
Technorati, 476, 485, 512
TechSmith Corp., 232 ex7.1
Terra Bite Lounge, 574
TerraChoice Environmental Marketing, 348
TerraCycle Plant Food, 357
Tesco, 278, 439, 528
TetraPak, 347
T.G.I. Friday's, 306
ThomasNet, 232 ex7.1
Thomas O'Brien domestics, 404
Thompson, Paul, 127
Threadless, 368
Tiffany, 454, 586
Timbuk2, 499, 500
Time Warner, 490 ex14.6, 493
    America Online (AOL), 493
    Business 2.0, 503
    Fortune, 503
    People, 503
    Time, 488, 503, 508
Time Warner Cable, 429, 430
Time Warner Center, 459
TiVo, 9, 504, 505, 589
T.J. Maxx, 105, 132, 440, 452, 454, 456
TJX Companies, 105, 132
T-Mobile, 344, 345
TNS, 571
Todd Oldham home furnishings, 404

Tombstone pizza, 442
Tomlinson, LaDainian, 184
Tommy Hilfiger, 583
Tony the Tiger, 497
Topol toothpaste, 46
Toronto International Film Festival, 522
Toshiba, 90 ex3.7, 174, 391, 539
Tower Records, 459
Towle, Andrew, 91
Toyota Group keiretsu, 251
Toyota Industrial Equipment, 401
Toyota Motor Corp., 90 ex3.7, 112, 126 ex4.3, 144
    MR2, 151, 160, 168, 176, 236, 246, 341 ex10.3, 373
    Camry Hybrid, 199
    Prius, 536
    Scion, 404, 492
Toys "R" Us, 35, 83, 435, 440, 459, 577
Trader Joe's, 5, 105, 112, 276
Transformers, 522
Travelers Insurance Company, 336
Travelocity.com, 571
Trend Micro, 147
Trivial Pursuit, 171
TruBlood, 521
True Religion Jeans, 105
TRUSTe, 571
Tuesday Morning, 440
Tums, 452, 601
Twain, Shania, 499 ex 14.8
Tweeter, 436
Twentymile Mine, 124
Twitter, 196
Tyco, 82
Tylenol, 42
Tyson Foods, 7, 175
Ty's Teeny Beanie Babies, 44

U

UB Group, 49
    Kingfisher beer, 49
    Royal Challenge whiskey, 49
Underwriters Laboratories, 191
Unilever Ltd., 151, 172, 175, 191, 407, 490, 583
Union Carbide, 562
United Artist Theaters, 442
United States Postal Service (USPS), 52
Universal McCann, 476
Universal Sportswear, 574–576
Univision Radio, 222
Unocal Corp., 148, 447
UPN, 375–376

UPS, 6, 52, 125, 134, 175, 177, 231, 236, 407, 414
UPS Store, Mail Boxes Etc., The, 448 ex13.3
UPS Worldwide Logistics Group, 414
Urban Box Office, 7
Urban Outfitters, 455
U.S. Army, 127, 219, 507
U.S. Bureau of Labor Statistics, 22
U.S. Census Bureau, 298 ex9.2
U.S. Commercial Service, 162
U.S. Department of Agriculture, 162, 436, 437
U.S. Department of Commerce, 162, 177
U.S. Food and Drug Administration, 349
U.S. Government, 298 ex9.2
U.S. Justice Department, 591, 594
U.S. Marine Corps, 407
U.S. Navy, 219
U.S. Patent and Trademark Office, 345
U.S. Senate Commerce, Science, and Transportation Committee, 263
U.S. Supreme Court, 592, 594
USAA, 5, 10
USADATA.com, 298 ex9.2, 299
Usborne Books, 442
USPS, 232 ex7.1

V

Valero Energy, 88
Value Line, 24
Van Doren, Steve, 556–557
Vanity Fair, 270
Vans, 218, 446, 522–523, 556–557
Vaseline, 172
Vegpro Kenya, 174, 175
Velveeta cheese, 199
Verizon, 490, 506, 542
Verizon Wireless, 535
Vermont Dairy, 38
Vespa, 113
VH-1, 429
Viacom, 20, 429, 430
Viagra, 420
Vick, Michael, 74
Victoria's Secret, 397, 444, 451
Viking, 587
Virgin Airlines, 249
Virgin Atlantic Airways, 505, 506
Virgin Group, 126 ex4.3

Viviendo, 116
Volkswagen AG, 90 ex3.7, 373
   Jetta, 499 ex14.8
   Passat, 236
Volvo, 341
Vonage, 506
Vuitton, Louis, 417

W

Wahaha, 167
Walgreens, 334, 343, 397, 417, 422, 434 ex13.1, 453
Wall Street Journal, The, 24, 28, 118, 192, 206, 364, 488
Wal-Mart Stores, Inc., 6, 35, 41, 74, 82, 83, 89, 96, 105, 107, 116, 126 ex4.3, 147, 153, 167, 168, 234, 267, 268, 276, 277, 281, 308, 334, 357, 396, 401, 402, 404, 407, 408, 412, 413, 433, 434 ex13.1, 435, 437, 438, 439, 440, 450, 452, 453, 454, 455, 483, 528, 529, 530, 564, 573, 577, 581, 588, 590, 591, 592
   EverActive, 451
   EverStart, 451
   George clothing, 342
   Ol' Roy dog food, 342, 451
   Sam's American Choice, 451
   Sam's Choice, 581
   Spring Valley, 451
   White Cloud paper products, 451
Walt Disney Co., 126 ex4.3, 490 ex14.6
Walt Disney World, 11
Waltrip, Michael, 527
Wang, Vera, 496
Wang Jinlong, 139
Wang Ying, 153
Ward, Anne Sempowski, 118
Warner, Kurt, 184
Warner Bros. Home Entertainment, 533
Washburn, Cadwallader C., 81 ex3.3
Washkiewicz, Donald, 569
Waste Management, 94
Water Horse: Legend of the Deep, The, 508

WD-40 Co., 296, 341
   Foaming Bathroom Cleaner, 297
   Trigger Bathroom Cleaner, 297
   X-14, 296
   X-14 Foaming Bathroom Cleaner, 297
Web 2.0, 364, 475
Web Survent, 314
WebSurveyor, 314
Wegmans Food Markets, 3
Weirick, Rick, 74
Weiss, Jacob, 592
Welch's x, 346
Wendy's, 47, 379, 447, 453
Western Union, 5
Westin Hotels & Resorts, 344
Weston Group, 366
West Point Pepperell, 395, 441
Weyerhaeuser, 594
Whirlpool, 23, 264, 334, 414, 580
   Ideale, 171
White, Shaun, 496
Whole Foods Market, 73, 112
Wide Open West, 263
Wikipedia, 364
Wildlife Habitat Council, 94
Wild Oats Markets, 73
Willbros Petroleum, 418
Williams, Mona, 528
Williams-Sonoma, 113, 436, 446, 458
William Wrigley Jr. Company, 366, 403
   Altoids, 143, 500
   Life Savers, 143
   Wrigley's Spearmint, 143
Winfrey, Oprah, 99–100, 526
Winn-Dixie, 454
Wintergreen Research, 299, 323
Wipro, 148
Wolfe, Brad, 372
Wolfgang Puck, 113, 455
Wolfgang's Steakhouse, 345
Wolverine World Wide, 164
Woods, Tiger, 183, 498
Woolworth's, 555
WorkPlace Media, 108
World Bank, 145, 152, 153, 154
World Book Encyclopedia, 442
WorldCom, 74, 78, 82

World of Coca-Cola Museum, 344
   Inside the Happiness Factory: A Documentary, 344
World of Warcraft, 507
WorldOpinion, 298 ex9.2
World Trade Organization, 140, 145, 412
Worldwide Retail Exchange, 397, 422
World Wildlife Federation, 88
Wulf, William, 127
W.W. Grainger Inc., 233
Wyndam Hotels and Resorts Women On Their Way, 212

X

Xanga, 210
Xerox, 239, 345, 368, 412
Xerox Corp., 247

Y

Yahoo!, 217, 391, 484, 506
   MyYahoo.com, 279
   Yahoo! Music Unlimited, 528
Yahoo! Japan, 178
Yamaha, 217, 420
Yamaha Razz scooter, 46
Yankelovich, Inc., 113
YMCA, 341
Yoplait, 95
   Fiber One, 371
   Yogurt, 528
"You Are So Beautiful," 499 ex14.8
YouTube, 218
Yum! Brands
   KFC Corp., 337, 341, 447, 448 ex13.3, 460
   Pizza Hut, 337, 341, 438, 448 ex13.3
   Taco Bell Corp., 111, 303, 341, 438, 448 ex13.3, 492

Z

Zale Corporation, 281
   Gordon's, 281
Zanga, 110
Zappos.com, 5, 196
Zenith, 391
Ziglar, Zig, 547
Zlotkin, Stanley, 91
Zoom Store, 442
Zulueta, Manny, 82
Zweiner, Wolfgang, 345

Note: Locators followed by "ex" indicate exhibits.

9/11, 201, 218, 45
80/20 principle, 271

A

Accessibility, 262
Accessory equipment, 244
Act utilitarianism, 76
Adopters, 373
Adoption rate, 375
Advergaming, 506–507
Advertainment, 507–508
Advertising, 151, 479, 490
    advocacy, 493–494
    appeals, 497–498
    campaigns, 496
    careers, 22
    comparative, 495–496
    competitive, 494–495
    consumers and, 491–492
    cooperative, 502–503
    creative decisions in, 496–501
    developing and evaluating
        appeals, 497–498
    effects of, 490–493
    executing message, 498–501
    executional styles, 499 ex14.8
    humor in, 499–500
    identifying product benefits, 497
    institutional, 493–494
    major types of, 493–496
    market share and, 491
    media decisions in, 501–512
    objectives, 496
    pioneering, 494
    post-campaign evaluation, 501
    product, 493, 494–496
    response function, 491
Advocacy advertising, 493–494
Aesthetics, 350
African Americans, 117–118,
    201, 266, 267
Age, 212–213
Age segmentation, 264–265

Agent/broker channels, 395–396
Agents, 392
AIDA (attention, interest, desire,
    and action) concept, 482–484,
    497, 498
Amae, 236
American culture, 200 ex6.4
American values, 105–106,
    202 ex6.5
Anchor stores, 453
Ansoff's strategic opportunity
    matrix, 43, 44 ex2.4
Applications, 281
Applied research, 125
"Arm's-length" relationships, 405
Asian Americans, 118–120, 219,
    266, 267
Aspirational reference groups, 207
Atmosphere, 455
Attitudes, 220
Attributes, 280
Audience selectivity, 509
Automatic replenishment
    programs, 409
Automatic vending, 442
"Average" customers, 12–13
Average total cost (ATC), 571
Average variable costs
    (AVC), 571

B

Baby boomers, 113–115, 264
Bar codes. See Universal product
    codes (UPCs)
Barter, 560
Basic research, 125
Behavioral targeting (BT), 263,
    318, 319, 570–571
BehaviorScan, 320
Beliefs, 220
Benefit segmentation, 270
Bidding, 238–239
Blogs, 209–210, 476, 507, 5
    28–529, 535
Bodegas, 116
"Bohemian Mix" cluster, 270

Boston Consulting Group (BCG)
    portfolio matrix, 44–45, 51
Boycotts, 154
Brainstorming, 366
Brand aspirationals, 277
Brand equity, 341
Brand extensions, 194
Brand loyalty, 341
Brand marks, 341
Brand names, 341
Brand theft, 165–166
Branding, 220
    benefits of, 341–342
    global issues in, 349–350
    strategies, 342–345
Brands, 341
Break-even pricing, 574–576
Bribery, 418
Brokers, 392
Business analysis, 367
Business buying behavior,
    246–251
Business customers
    categories of, 237–239
    governments, 238–239
    institutions, 239
    producers, 237
    resellers, 237–238
Business development, 367–368
Business ethics, 78–79, 249
Business firms
    focus of, 7–12
    nature of, 11–12
    perception of customer, 12–13
    primary goals of, 13–14
    tools used by, 14
Business format franchising, 447
Business markets and marketing
    buying processes, 272
    company characteristics,
        271–272
    versus consumer markets,
        241–244
    defined, 231
    Internet and, 232–234
    segmentation bases, 271–272

Business missions, 58
Business products (industrial products), 244–246, 333
Business services, 246
Business-to-business (B2B) auctions, 579–580
Business-to-business electronic commerce (B-to-B or B2B ecommerce), 232
  trends in, 233–234
Business-to-business online exchange, 242
Buyers, 242, 436
Buyers for export, 164
Buying, 242–243
Buying centers, 246–248
Buying influences, 243
Buying processes, 272
Buying situations, 248–249

C

California's Notice of Security Breach Law, 132
Cannibalization, 277–278
CAN_SPAM act, 131
Capital-intensive technology, 148
Captive brands, 342
Car buying, 223
Careers in marketing, 22–32
Cash cows, 45
Casio, 378
Casuist ethical theory, 76
Catalog sales, 444
Category killers, 440
Cause-related marketing, 94–96, 528
Cell phones, 508
Celler-Kefauver Antimerger Act, 128
Central America Free Trade Agreement (CAFTA), 157–158
Central-location telephone (CLT) facility, 301
Certified Purchasing Manager (CPM), 243
Chain stores, 434, 435
Channel captains, 416
Channel conflict, 416
Channel control, 416
Channel cooperation, 418–419
Channel intermediaries, 392–394
  facilitation function of, 394
  functions performed by, 393–394
  transactional functions of, 394
Channel leaders, 416
Channel M2, 316–317

Channel members, 389
Channel partnering, 418–419
Channel power, 416
Channel relationships, 405–406
  arm's length relationships, 405
  cooperative, 406
  integrated, 405–406
  management of, 416–419
Channel strategy decisions, 401–404
  factors affecting, 401–402
  levels of distribution intensity, 402–404
  market factors, 401–402
  producer factors, 402
  product factors, 402
Channel structures, 395–398
  alternatives, 397
  business and industrial products, 396–397
  for consumer products, 395–396
Channels
  global distribution decisions and, 419–420
  services distribution decisions, 421–422
Channels, message, 474
Channels of distribution. See Marketing channels
Chief customer officers (CCOs), 11
Children, 211
Civil society, 73–74
Clayton Act, 128
Climate, 350
Closed-ended questions, 303
Closing, 548
Cobranding, 343–345, 535
Codes of ethics, 80, 250
Cognitive dissonance, 195
College placement offices, 24
Colors, 350, 456
Commercialization, 370–371
Communication
  direct, 376
  interpersonal, 473
  mass, 473
  process of, 473–475
  promotion and, 472–477, 481–482
  word-of-mouth, 375
Community shopping centers, 453
Comparative advertising, 495–496
Compatibility, 375
Competition
  global, 133–134

market share and profits, 133
  meeting the, 589
  pricing and, 577
Competitive advantage, 40–41, 472
Competitive intelligence (CI), 321–323
Competitors, 281
Complementary branding, 343
Complexity, 375
Component lifestyles, 106–107
Component parts, 244–245
Computer-assisted personal interviewing, 301
Computer-assisted self-interviewing, 301
Concentrated targeting strategies, 275–277
Concept tests, 366
Conceptual learning, 219
Conformity, 106
Connect-and-Develop Model, 368
Consideration sets (evoked sets), 193
Consultative selling. See Relationship selling (consultative selling)
Consumer behavior, 189, 195–196, 207–211
Consumer buying decisions
  consumer involvement in, 197–199
  cultural influences and, 200–206
  factors in, 199–200
  individual influences on, 211–215
  psychological influences, 215–222
Consumer decision making
  alternatives evaluation and purchase, 193–195
  information search, 191–193
  need recognition, 190–191
  process of, 189–195
Consumer education, 527
Consumer generated media (CGM), 318
Consumer income, 121–122
Consumer involvement, 197–199, 198, 199
Consumer markets, 241–244
Consumer privacy, 130–132, 263
Consumer Product Safety Act of 1972, 368
Consumer Product Safety Commission (CPSC), 130

Consumer products, 333–335
Consumer protection laws, 129
Consumer sales promotions. *See also* Sales promotions; Trade sales promotions
   loyalty marketing programs, 534–536
   point-of-purchase promotion (P-O-P), 537
   contests and sweepstakes, 536
   coupons and rebates, 532–534
   online, 537–538
   premiums, 534
   sampling, 536–537
Consumers, 210
Contact efficiency, 391–392
Contests, 536
Context in ethics, 82
Continuous media schedule, 510
Contract logistics. *See* Outsourcing logistics (contract logistics)
Contract manufacturing, 165–166
Control, 49–50
Convenience products, 334
Convenience samples, 310
Convenience stores, 438
Conventional morality, 79
Cookies, 263
Cooperative advertising, 502–503
Cooperative branding, 343
Cooperative relationships, 406
Corporate blogs, 476
Corporate communication, 526
Corporate social responsibility (CSR), 86–94
   arguments against, 88
   arguments for, 88–89
   cause-related marketing, 94–96
   cost of ignoring, 93
   green marketing, 94
   growth of, 89–93
   proactive social responsibility, 90–93
   pyramid of, 88
   stakeholders and, 87–88
Cost competitive advantage, 40–41
Cost per contact, 508
Costs, 571–573
Counterfeit products, 165–166, 420
Countertrade, 177
Coupons, 532–533
Cover letters, 26 ex4
Credence qualities, 336
Crisis management, 526, 529–530

Cross-tabulation, 310, 311
Cultural diversity, 121
Culture
   color and, 350
   consumer buying decisions and, 200–206
   differences in, 202–203
   global marketing and, 150–152
   relationship marketing and, 236
   research and, 311
   value and, 200–202
Customer profiles, 546
Customer relationship management (CRM) systems, 235
Customer retention, 235
Customer satisfaction, 9, 10, 341
Customer service, 196, 249–251, 456–458
Customer value, 7–9
Customer-oriented personnel, 10–11
Customers, 12–13, 242

D

DAGMAR approach (Defining Advertising Goals for Measured Advertising Results), 497
Data collection and analysis, 310–311
Data mining, 450
Database marketing, 292
Deciders, 247
Decision makers, 210
Decision making, 293–294
Decision support systems (DSS), 291
Decline stage of product life cycle, 379, 487, 577
Decoding, 475
Demand, 241–242, 564–569
Demographic segmentation, 263–268
Demography, 109–115, 160–161
Deontological theory, 75–76
Department stores, 436
Depression Generation, 265
Depth, 451
Derived demand, 241
Desi subculture, 511
Destination stores, 453
Developing countries, 85–86
Development, 367–368
Diamond trade, 92
Diffusion, 373
Digital media, 472
Direct channels, 395

Direct communication, 376
Direct feedback channels, 477
Direct foreign investment, 167–168
Direct mail, 443–444
Direct marketing, 443–444
Direct retailing, 442–443
Direct-response marketing, 443–444
Discount stores, 438–441
Discrepancies of quantity, 390
Discrepancy of assortment, 391
Disintermediation, 234
Distribution and pricing, 577–578
Distribution intensity, 402–404
Distribution resource planning (DRP), 408
Distribution structure, 242
Diversification, 44
Divesting, 46
Dogs, 45
Doha Round, 156
Drugstores, 437–438
Dual distribution (multiple distribution), 397
Dumping, 176

E

Economic environment, 121–124
Efficient consumer response, 408
Elastic demand, 566, 567
Elasticity of demand, 566, 567–568
Electronic data interchange (EDI), 408
Electronic distribution, 414–415
Electronic retailing, 444–446
E-motion software marketing plan, 63–71
Emotions, 281
Employee and investor relations, 526
Employee type and density, 455–456
Employment agencies, 24
Empowerment, 11
Encoding, 474
Environmental management, 105
Environmental scanning, 39, 103–104
Errors, types of, 310
E-tailing, 445
Ethical behavior, 18, 49, 54–55, 73, 74–77
   in business, 78–86
   culture and, 84
   decision making, 79–80
   definition of, 75

Ethical behavior (*Continued*)
dilemmas in developing countries, 85–86
guidelines and training, 80–84
product costs and, 84
technology and, 127
Ethical theories, 75–77
casuist, 76
deontology, 75–76
moral relativism, 76–77
utilitarianism, 76
virtue ethics, 77
Ethnic diversity, 121
Ethnic markets, 115–121
Ethnic segmentation, 266–267
Ethnographic research, 306–307
European Commission, 159
European Data Protection Directive, 131
European Union (EU), 154, 155, 158–160, 419
Evaluation, 49
Evaluative criteria, 248
Evaluators, 247
Everyday low pricing (EDLP), 454
Evoked sets (consideration sets), 193
Exchange, 3
Exchange controls, 154
Exchange policies, 466
Exchange rates, 176
Exclusive distribution, 404
Executive interviews, 302
Experience curves, 41
Experience quality, 336
Experiential learning, 219
Experiments, 308
Export agents, 164
Export brokers, 164
Export-Import Bank, 162
Exporting, 162–164
Express warranties, 350
Extensive decision making, 197
External information search, 191–193, 192
External marketing environment, 103–105
competitive factors, 133–134
demographic factors, 109–115
economics, 121–124
environmental management, 105
ethnic markets, 115–121
federal legislation, 128–129
multiculturalism, 121
political and legal factors, 127–132

regulatory agencies, 130
social factors, 105–109
state laws, 129
technological factors, 124–127
External opportunities and threats, 59
External stimuli, 190
Extreme-value retailers, 439

F

Facilitating, 394
Facility loss, 145–146
Factory outlets, 440–441
Families, 107, 210–211
Family brands, 343
Family life cycle (FLC), 267–268
Family life cycle (FLC) segmentation, 267–268
Family life-cycle stages, 212–214
Feature-advantage-benefit (FAB) matrix, 23
Federal legislation, 128–129
Federal Trade Commission Act, 128, 590, 594
Federal Trade Commission (FTC), 130, 131 ex4.6
Feedback, 475
Field of Dreams marketing orientation, 4
Field service firms, 310
Fixed costs, 571
Fixtures, 456
Flexibility, 509
Flighted media schedules, 511
Floating exchange rates, 176
Flooranimation, 507
Fluctuating demand, 241–242
Focus groups, 302–303
Follow-up, 548–549
Food and Drug Administration (FDA), 130
Foreign Corrupt Practices Act (FCPA), 84, 418
Foreign investment, 148
Four Ps (product, place, promotion, and price), 47–48, 450
Frame errors, 310
Franchisees, 446
Franchises, 434, 435
Franchising, 164–165, 446–449
Franchisor, 446
Free merchandise, 539
Free-standing inserts (FSIs), 533
Freestanding stores, 453
Frequency, 233, 509
Frequent buyer programs, 531, 534–535

Frugal engineering, 372
FTC Improvement Act of 1980, 130
Full-line discount stores, 438–439
Fully planned purchases, 195

G

Gatekeepers, 247
Gender, 212
Gender segmentation, 265–266
General Agreement on Tariffs and Trade (GATT), 156
Generation X, 112–113, 264
Generation Y, 111–112, 264
Generator stores, 453
Generic product names, 345
Geodemographic segmentation, 269
Geographic segmentation, 262–263
G.I. Generation, 265
Global brands, 341
Global competition, 133–134
Global innovation, 125–126
Global marketing
China and India, 152–153
contract manufacturing, 165–166
countertrade, 177
definition of, 143
demographics, 160–161
developing channels for, 419–420
direct foreign investment, 167–168
dumping, 176
economic and technological development, 152
exchange rates, 176
external environment and, 150–161
impact on workers, 145
individual firms and, 161–168
Internet impact, 177–178
joint ventures, 166–167
legal considerations in, 154–155
licensing and franchising, 164–165
natural resources, 161
place (distribution), 174–175
political structure and actions, 153–154
pricing, 175–176
product adaptation, 172–173
product invention, 171
promotion adaptation, 173–174

rewards of, 143–146
standardization of, 148–150
U.S. importance of, 144
Global marketing mix, 168–177
one product, one message,
169–171
product and promotion, 169
Global research, 311
Global vision, 143
Globalization
benefits of, 146
facility loss and, 145–146
fear of trade and, 145–146
new product development and,
372–373
Going rate pricing, 589
Golden Generation, 265
Government contracts, 238–239
Government subsidies, 41
Governments
federal, 238–239
state, county, and city, 239
Gramm-Leach-Bliley Act (Financial
Services Modernization
Act), 132
"Gray" marketing, 420
"Greed through love," 466
Green marketing, 94
Green supply chain management,
415–416
Greenwashing, 348
Grocery stores, 461
Gross margin, 435
Gross ratings points (GRP), 509
Group dynamics, 302–303
Growth stage of product life cycle,
378, 487, 576
Guaranteed price matching,
580–581
Guerrilla marketing, 357–358

H

Harcelement publicitaire (harass-
ment by advertising), 151
Hart-Scott-Rodino Act, 128
Harvesting, 46
Health Insurance Portability and
Accountability Act
(HIPAA), 132
Heterogeneity, 337
Heterogeneous shopping
products, 334
Hidden job market, 24
Hispanic Americans, 115–116,
266–267
Hoaxes, 538
Holding power, 510

Home shopping networks,
444–445
Homogeneous shopping
products, 334
Horizontal conflict, 417
Horizontal price fixing, 591–592
Humor, 499–500
Hybrid cars, 295

I

Idea screening, 366–367
Ideal self-image, 214
Identity theft, 132
Identity Theft and Assumption
Deterrence Act, 132
Implementation, 48–49
Implied warranties, 351
Inbound telemarketing, 444
Income, 121–122
Income segmentation, 266
Indentifiability and
measurability, 261
Independent retailers, 434, 435
Indirect feedback channels, 477
Individual branding, 343
Industrial distributors, 396–397
Industrial products. See Business
products (industrial products)
Inelastic demand, 241, 566, 567
Inflation, 122–123
Influencers, 210, 247
Infomercials, 504, 555
Information search, 191–193
Informational labeling, 348
Informative promotion, 478–479
InfoScan, 321
Ingredient branding, 343
In-home personal
interviews, 300
Initiatiors, 210
Initiators, 247
Innovations, 373
Innovative companies, 126 ex4.3
Inseparability, 336–337
Installations. See Major equipment
(installations)
Institutional advertising, 493–494
In-store coupons, 533
Intangibility, 336
Integrated marketing communica-
tions (IMC), 472,
484–485, 513
Integrated relationships, 405–406
Intensive distribution, 403
Interactivity, 458
Intermediaries, 389
Internal information search, 191

Internal stimuli, 190
Internal strengths and
weaknesses, 58
International Federation
of International Trade
Associations, 164
International Monetary Fund
(IMF), 160
Internet, 24, 177–178, 375,
503 ex14.11
alternative media marketing,
506–508
as alternative service
channel, 422
auctions, 579–580
business marketing and,
232–234
direct sales, 443
electronic retailing, 444–446
fraud, 579
impact on pricing, 578–580
other market research
uses, 320
secondary data and, 298
shopping, 444
shopping bots, 578–579
test marketing, 370
Web 2.0, 475–477
web sites, 528–529
Internet spam, 131
Internet surveys, 313–314
Interpersonal
communication, 473
Interviews, 27–31
Introductory stage of product life
cycle, 377–378, 486, 576
Inventory control systems, 408
Inventory replenishment, 409
ex12.7
Involvement, 197
Islam, 203

J

Job hunting, 23–31
approaching prospective
employers, 26
expenses, 24
gimmicks, 26
preapproach, 24–26
selling yourself, 26–31
Job outsourcing, 145
Joint demand, 241
Joint ventures, 166–167

K

Keiretsu, 236, 251
Keystoning, 573

"Kids and Cul-de-Sacs"
  cluster, 270
Kiosks, 446
Knockoffs, 166

L

Labeling, 347–349, 350
Labor costs, 41
Land ownership, 151
Language, 120, 151, 174
Lanham Act, 128
Laws, 73
Lead generation
  (prospecting), 544
Lead qualification, 545
Learning, 219–220
Leasing, 243
Licensing, 164–165
Life events, 213–214
Life span, 509
Lifestyle centers, 454
Lifestyle clusters, 269–270
Lifestyle segmentation, 214–215
Lifestyles, 214, 215, 269
Limited decision making, 197
Lobbying, 526
Location, 452–453
Logistics, 394
Logistics information systems, 407
Lower class, 205
Loyalty marketing programs, 437,
  534–536

M

Magazines, 503, 503 ex14.11
Magnuson-Moss Warranty-Federal
  Trade Commission Improvement
  Act of 1975, 351
Mail intercept interviews, 301
Mail order, 444
Mail surveys, 301–302
Maintenance, repair, or operating
  (MRO) supplies, 245–246
Major equipment
  (installations), 244
Management decision
  problems, 297
Manufacturer's brand, 342, 343
Maquiladoras, 86
Marginal cost (MC), 571
Marginal revenue (MR), 573
Market development, 44
Market grouping, 155
Market niche, 275
Market opportunity analysis
  (MOA), 46–47
Market orientation, 5, 7–14

Market penetration, 44
Market plans, 59–62
Market research
  customer retention and, 294
  Internet impact on, 313–320
Market segmentation, 259
  criteria for, 261–262
  importance of, 260–261
  segmentation bases and,
    262–271
  steps in, 272–273
Market segments, 259
Market share, 491, 562
Market-basket analysis, 455
Marketing, 3, 14–16
Marketing audits, 50
Marketing channels, 389–392,
  421–422, 423
Marketing communication
  integrated, 484–485
  promotion and, 472–477
  Web 2.0 and, 475–477
Marketing concept, 5
Marketing decision support
  systems, 291–292
Marketing information, 291
Marketing management careers, 22
Marketing mix, 47–48, 60–62,
  168–177
Marketing myopia, 37
Marketing objectives, 39–40
Marketing philosophies, 4–7
Marketing plans and planning, 19,
  36–37
  business mission, 58
  evaluation, 49
  evaluation and control, 49–50
  implementation, 48–49
  situation (SWOT) analysis,
    58–59
Marketing research
  aggregators, 299–312
  careers, 22
  following up, 312
  management uses of, 292–294
  objectives, 297
  problem, 297
  problem tracing, 294
  project steps, 296–298
  quality of decisions, 293–294
  reports, 312
  role of, 292–294
Marketing strategies, 46, 59–62,
  449–458
Marketing yourself, 23–31
Marketing-controlled information
  source, 192

Marketplace, 295–296
Markets, 259
Markup pricing, 573
Maslow's hierarchy of needs, 218
Mass communication, 473
Mass merchandising, 438
Materials management, 408
Materials requirement planning
  (MRP), 408
Materials-handling systems,
  409–410
Maturity stage of product life cycle,
  378–379, 487, 576–577
M-commerce (mobile e-commerce),
  458–459
Measurement error, 310
Media, 74, 502–508
  flexibility, 509
  fragmentation, 510
  life span, 509
  mix, 508
  planning, 501
  schedules, 510
Medium, 501
Meeting the competition, 589
Merchandise
  mix, 450–451
  type and density, 456
Merchant wholesalers, 392
Mercosur, 154, 155
Message transmission, 474
Metro Goldwyn Mayer
  (MGM), 346
Middle class, 204–205, 206
Middlemen, 389
Millennial generation, 218, 264
Mission statements, 37
Modified rebuy, 249
Moral character development, 79
Moral relativism, 76–77
Morality, 78–79
Morals, 78
Most favored nation (MFN)
  status, 155
Motivation, 218–219
Motives, 218, 269
MRO. See Maintenance, repair,
  or operating (MRO) supplies
Multiculturalism, 121
Multinational corporations,
  147–150, 148, 152–153,
  179
Multiple channels, 397
Multiplier effect (accelerator
  principle), 241–242
Multisegment targeting strategies,
  276, 277–278

Multitasking, 107–109
Music, 456
Music video games, 20–21
Muslims, 203
Mystery shoppers, 305–306

N

NAICS. *See* North American Industry Classification System (NAICS)
Natural disasters, 452
Natural resources, 161
Need recognition, 190–191
Needs assessment, 546
Negotiations, 243, 548
Networking, 545
New buy, 248
New products
    business analysis, 367
    categories of, 361–363
    development, 367–368
    development process, 363–370
    global issues in development, 372–373
    idea generation, 365–366
    idea screening, 366–367
    importance of, 361–363
    spread of, 373–376
    success and failure of, 370–371
    test marketing, 368–370
New-product publicity, 526
New-product strategies, 364
Newspapers, 502–503, 503 ex14.11
Niche, 275
Niche competitive advantage, 42
No-frills good and services, 41
Noise, 474
Noise level, 509
Nonaspirational reference group, 208
Noncorporate blogs, 476
Nonmarketing-controlled information source, 191
Nonprobability samples, 309
Nonstore retailing, 442
Nontraditional channels, 397–398
Norms, 207
North American Free Trade Agreement (NAFTA), 156–157, 239, 419
North American Industry Classification System (NAICS), 238, 239–240, 251, 433

Nutritional Labeling and Educational Act of 1990, 349

O

Observability, 375
Observation research, 305–306
Odors, 456
Off-price retailers, 440
One-to-one marketing, 278–279
Online coupons, 533
Online focus groups, 315–317
Online panel providers, 314–315
Online sales promotions, 537–538
Online success, 233
Online test marketing, 370
Open-ended questions, 303
Opinion leaders, 208–210
Optimizers, 272
Order processing systems, 407–408
Organizational focus, 7–11
Original equipment manufacturers (OEMs), 237
Outbound telemarketing, 444
Outdoor media, 503 ex14.11, 505–506
Outsourcing, 145
Outsourcing logistics (contract logistics), 413–414
Ownership types, 434

P

Packaging
    decisions, 352
    functions of, 346–347
    global issues in, 350
    labeling, 347–349
    universal product codes (UPCs), 349
Partially planned purchases, 195
"Pay what it's worth," 574
Penetration pricing, 587–589
"Per se" rule, 592
Perception, 215–218
    marketing implications of, 216–218
    subliminal, 217
    threshold level of, 217
Perceptual mapping, 280, 281
Perishability, 337
Personal interviewing, 300–301
Personal selling, 480–481, 540–541
Personality, 214, 269
Personality traits, 106
Personnel, 456–458
Persuasive labeling, 348

Persuasive promotion, 478–479
Physiological needs, 218
Pioneering advertising, 494
Place (distribution) strategies, 48
Planned obsolescence, 339
Planning, 36
Podcasts, 507
Point-of-purchase promotion (P-O-P), 537
Population, 109–110
Pop-up shops, 459–460
Portfolio matrices, 44–46, 45
Position, 279
Positioning, 279–282, 433, 434–435
Positioning bases, 280–281
Postconventional morality, 79
Post-interview letter, 30
Power sources/voltage, 172–173
Preapproach, 546
Preconventional morality, 79
Predatory pricing, 593–594
Premiums, 534
Press relations, 526
Prestige pricing, 582
Price discrimination, 592–593
Price equilibrium, 564, 565
Price fixing, 590–592
Price gouging, 452
Price setting
    demand, costs, and profits, 594
    goals of, 583–585
    penetration pricing, 587–589
    skimming, 586–587
    status quo pricing, 589–590
Price skimming, 586–587
Price strategies, 585–590
Price-sensitive affluents, 277
Pricing, 175–176, 248, 281, 435
    break even, 574–576
    competition and, 577
    cost determinant of, 571–576
    customers and, 589
    decisions, 589
    demand determinant of, 564–569
    demands of large customers, 581
    discrimination, 592–593
    distribution strategy and, 577–578
    going rate, 589
    guaranteed price matching, 580–581
    importance of, 560
    information effect of, 559

Pricing (*Continued*)
   legality and ethics, 590–594
   markup, 573
   other determinants of, 576–584
   power, 569
   predatory, 593–594
   price fixing, 590–592
   product life cycle and, 576–577
   profit maximization, 561–562,
     573–574
   profit oriented objectives,
     561–562
   promotion strategies and, 580
   quality and, 581–582, 583
   resale price maintenance,
     591–592
   return on investment (ROI), 562
   sacrifice effect of, 559
   sales-oriented objectives,
     562–564
   status quo objectives, 564
   strategies, 48
   unfair trade practice acts, 590
   value and perception, 559–560
Primary data, 299–300
Primary membership groups, 207
Privacy, 263, 480
Private brands, 342, 343, 451
Probability samples, 309
Problem children, 45
Processed materials, 245
Producers, 237
Product adaptation, 172–173
Product adoption, 375–376
Product advertising, 493,
   494–496, 494–497
Product and trade name
   franchising, 447
Product assortment, 435, 450–451
Product categories, 377
Product classes, 281
Product design, 41
Product development, 44, 366, 367
Product differentiation, 220, 280
Product identification, 341
Product invention, 171
Product items, 337
Product life cycles (PLCs),
   376–380, 379, 486–487
   decline stage, 379
   growth stage, 378
   introductory stage, 377–378
   maturity stage, 378–379
   pricing and, 576–577
   promotional mix and, 476–477
   of VCR, 381
Product line contraction, 340–341

Product line depth, 338
Product line tension, 340
Product lines, 338
Product management careers, 23
Product mix width, 338
Product mixes, 338
Product modification, 339, 366
Product offering, 450–451
Product placement, 526–527
Product publicity, 526
Product quality, 106
Product strategies, 47–48
Product users, 281
Production innovations, 41
Production orientation, 4
Products, 333
   items, lines, and mixes,
     337–341
   types of, 333–335
   warranties, 350–351
Product/service differentiation
   competitive advantage, 41–42
Profit, 560
Profit maximization, 573–574
Promotion, 471
   adaptation, 173–174
   goals of, 478–479
   marketing communication and,
     472–477, 481–482
   role of, 471–472
   strategies, 48, 451–452, 580
Promotional goals, 482–484
Promotional methods, 244
Promotional mix
   advertising, 479
   buying decision types, 488
   communication process and,
     481–482
   factors in, 485–490
   money and, 488
   personal selling, 480–481
   product characteristics, 486
   product life cycle, 486–487
   public relations, 480
   push and pull strategies,
     489–490
   sales promotion, 481
   target market characteristics,
     487–488
Promotional strategies, 471–472
Promotions, 31–32
Prospecting. *See* Lead generation
   (prospecting)
Psychographic segmentation,
   269–270
Psychographics, 214–215
Psychological influences, 218–222

Public affairs, 526
Public relations, 480, 525–530
Public relations careers, 22
Publicity, 525
Pull strategy, 488, 489
Pulsing media schedules, 511
Purchase volume, 242
Purchasers, 210, 247
Purchasing power, 122
Pure research, 125
Push money, 538, 539
Push strategy, 488, 489
Pyramid of corporate social
   responsibility, 88

Q

Quality, 10, 248, 281, 336,
   581–582, 583
Question marks. *See* Problem
   children
Questionnaire design,
   303–305, 311
Quotas, 154

R

Radio, 503 ex14.11, 504
Random errors, 310
Random samples, 309
Raw materials, 244
Reach, 508–509
Real self-image, 214
Real-time online focus groups, 316
Rebates, 532–534, 533–534
Receivers, 475
Recency, 233
Recency planning, 512
Recession, 123–124
Reciprocity, 243
Reengineering, 41
Referrals, 545
Reference groups, 207–208
Regional malls, 453
Regional stereotypes, 106
Regulatory agencies, 130
Reinforcement, 219
Reintermediation, 234
Relationship building, 9–11
Relationship commitment, 236
Relationship marketing, 10,
   234–236
Relationship selling (consultative
   selling), 542–543, 546
Relative advantage, 375
Relative market share, 45
Reminder promotion, 479
Repeat sales, 341
Repetition, 219–220

Repositioning, 281–282, 339–340
Resale price maintenance,
    591–592
Research, 125
    designs, 299
    follow-up, 312
    reports, 312
Resellers, 237–238, 389
Responsiveness, 262
Restaurants, 441
Resume, 24–26
Retail careers, 22
Retail entertainment, 43
Retail marketing strategies,
    449–458, 450–451
Retail operations
    classification of, 433–435
    franchising, 446–449
    level of service, 435
    major types of, 435–441
    marketing strategies, 449–458
    new developments in, 458–460
    nonstore models, 442–446
    ownership, 434
    prices, 435
    product assortment, 435
    role of, 433
Retail prices, 454
Retail stores, presentation of,
    454–455
Retailers, 392
Retailing, 433
    automatic vending, 442
    direct, 442–443
    electronic, 444–446
    nonstore, 442–446
Retailing mix, 450
Retention, 235
Return on investment (ROI), 562
Revenue, 560
Reverse engineering, 41
RFID tags, 413
Robinson-Patman Act of 1936,
    128, 592–593
Routine response behavior, 197
RSS (Real Simple Syndication)
    feeds, 233–234, 507
"Rule of reason," 592
Rule utilitarianism, 76
Rules, 78–79

S

Safety needs, 218
Sales careers, 22
Sales cycle. See Sales process
    (sales cycle)
Sales maximization, 563–564

Sales orientation, 4–5, 7–14
Sales presentations, 547
Sales process (sales cycle), 543–550
    approaching customers, 546
    closing the sale, 548
    developing and proposing
        solutions, 546–547
    follow-up, 548–550
    handling objections, 547–548
    lead generation (prospecting),
        544–545
    lead qualification, 545–546
Sales promotions. See also
    Consumer sales promotions;
    Trade sales promotions, 481
    consumer types, 531
    objectives of, 530–531
Sales proposals, 546
Samples, 308–309
Sampling, 536–537
Sampling errors, 310
Sampling procedures, 308–310
Satisficers, 272
Scaled-response questions, 303
Scanner-based research, 320–321
Scrambled merchandising, 437
Screening, 366
Search engine advertising, 506
Search engine optimization, 472
Search quality, 336
Seasonal media schedules, 511
Secondary data, 297–298
Secondary membership
    groups, 207
Segmentation bases
    (variables), 262
Selective distortion, 216
Selective distribution, 403–404
Selective exposure, 215–216
Selective retention, 216
Self regulation, 74
Self-actualization, 219
Self-analysis, 23
Self-concept, 214
Self-esteem, 219
Self-sufficiency, 105
Selling against the brand, 578
Senders, 473
Service, 196, 248, 249–251, 334
    delivery methods, 41
    levels, 435
    marks, 344
Services
    channels and distribution
        decisions for, 421–422
    goods versus, 336–337
    importance of, 335–336

Sherman Antitrust Act, 128,
    590, 594
Shop-at-home networks,
    444–445
Shopping bots, 578–579
Shopping centers, 453–454
Shopping products, 334
Simulated (laboratory) market
    testing, 369–370
Simultaneous product
    development, 368
Situation analysis. See SWOT
    analysis
Six Ps (product, place, promotion,
    price, presentation, and person-
    nel), 450
Six Sigma, 10
Smells, 456
Social class, 204–206
Social needs, 218
Social networks, 480
Social responsibility. See Corporate
    social responsibility (CSR)
Socialization process, 210
Societal marketing orientation, 6–7
Sound, 456
Sourcing and procurement, 407
Spatial discrepancies, 391
Specialty discount stores, 439–440
Specialty products, 334, 335
Specialty stores, 436
Spirituality, 201
Sponsorships, 527–528
Stakeholder theory, 87–88
Standard industrial classification
    (SIC) system, 239
Stars, 45
State laws, 129
Status quo pricing, 563, 589–590
Stealth marketing, 508
Stickiness, 233
Stimuli, 190
Stimulus discrimination, 220
Stimulus generalization, 220
Store demonstrations, 539
Store layout, 455, 461
Store-in-a-store model, 460
Straight rebuy, 249
Strategic alliances, 162, 234–236
Strategic alternatives, 43–46
Strategic business unit (SBU), 38,
    44–45
Strategic channel alliances, 398
Strategic partnership. See Strategic
    alliances
Strategic planning, 35–37, 50–51
Strip centers, 453

Subculture, 202, 203–204
Subliminal perception, 217
Substantiality, 261
Supercenters, 439
Supermarkets, 436–437
Supplies, 245–246
Supply, 564–569
Supply chain management, 399, 411–416
  advanced computer technology, 412–413
  benefits of, 401
  electronic distribution, 414–415
  globalization and, 412
  green supply chain management, 415–416
  inventory management and control, 408–409
  logistics function in, 406–411
  order processing systems, 407–408
  outsourcing logistic functions, 413–414
  security, 415
  sourcing and procurement, 407
  transportation, 410–411
  trends in, 411–416
  warehousing and materials handling, 409–410
Supply chain team, 407
Supply chains, 399–401
Surrogate ads, 49
Survey design, 314
Survey research, 300–303
Sustainability, 86–87
Sustainable competitive advantage, 42–43
Sweepstakes, 536
SWOT analysis, 38–39, 52

T

Taking title, 392
Target market strategy, 59–60
Target markets, 103, 274–278, 449–450
Tariffs, 154
Teamwork, 11
Technology, 124–127, 599–600
Teens, 110–111, 208, 210, 211, 218, 264
Telemarketing, 444
Telephone interviews, 301

Television, 503 ex14.11, 504–505
Temporal discrepancies, 391
Test marketing, 368–370
Third shifts, 166
Threshold level of perception, 217
Time, lack of, 107–109
Time-extended online focus groups, 316
TiVo, 505
Tobacco industry, 85–86
Trade agreements, 155
Trade allowances, 538, 539
Trade promotions, 540
Trade sales promotions. See also Consumer sales promotions; Sales promotions, 530, 539–540
Trade shows, 539
Trademarks, 345–346
Training, 11, 539
Transactional functions, 394
Transportation, 410–411
Trialability, 375
Trust, 236
Tweens, 110, 210, 264

U

UN Global Compact, 89–90, 91 ex3.8
Undifferentiated targeting strategies, 274–275
Unethical practices, 79 ex3.2
Unfair trade practice acts, 590
Unfavorable publicity, 529–530
Uniform Commercial Code, 351
Unique selling proposition, 498
Unitary elasticity, 566
Universal product codes (UPCs), 349
Universe (population), 309
Unplanned purchases, 195
Unsought products, 334, 335
Upper class, 206
Upward mobility, 106
Uruguay Round, 154, 155–156
U.S. Commercial Service to Exporters, 163 ex5.4
U.S. Customs Service, 420
U.S. Patent and Trademark Office, 345
U.S. Securities and Exchange Commission, 418

U.S. Trade Representative (USTR), 157
Usage-rate segmentation, 271
Use or application, 281
Users, 247
Utilitarian ethical theory, 76

V

Value-price shoppers, 277
Values, 105, 200–202
Variable costs, 571
Variables. See Segmentation bases (variables)
Vending machines, 442
Vertical conflict, 417
Video game advertising, 508
Viral marketing, 521–522
Virtual shopping, 307–308
Virtue ethics, 77
Virtues, 77 ex3.1
Visor, 378
Visual factors, 456
Voluntary payments, 574

W

Wants, 190
War Generation, 265
Warehouse membership clubs, 440
Warehousing, 409–410
Warranties, 350–351
Web 2.0, 364, 475–477
Web community research, 317
Web survey systems, 314
Webinars, 542
Wheeler-Lea Act, 128
Wholesaler channels, 396
Width, 451
Women, 107, 108, 265–266
Word-of-mouth communication, 375, 466
Work ethics, 106
Working class, 205, 206
Working conditions, 31
Working women, 107
World Bank, 160
World Trade Organization (WTO), 156
Wow factor, 454

Y

Yield management systems (YMS), 569–570

22 Social Media and Marketing

Learning Outcomes

LO 1 Describe social media, how it is used, and its relation to integrated marketing communications 351–354

LO 2 Explain how to create a social media campaign 354–356

LO 3 Evaluate the various methods of measurement for social media 356–357

LO 4 Explain consumer behavior on social media 357–358

LO 5 Describe the social media tools in a marketer's toolbox and how they are useful 358–363

LO 6 Describe the impact of mobile technology on social media 363–366

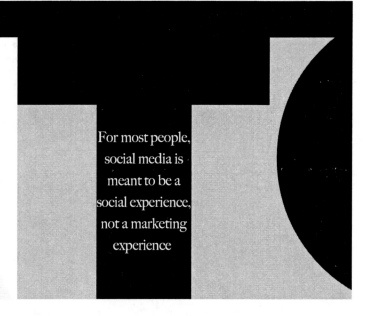

For most people, social media is meant to be a social experience, not a marketing experience

LO 1 What Is Social Media?

AFTER YOU FINISH THIS CHAPTER, GO TO PAGE 366 FOR STUDY TOOLS

The most exciting thing to happen to marketing and promotion is the increasing use of online technology to promote brands, particularly social media. Social media has changed the way that marketers can communicate with their brands—from mass messages to intimate conversations. As marketing moves into social media, marketers must remember that for most people, social media is meant to be a social experience, not a marketing experience. In fact, social media is many things to different people, though most people think of it as digital technology. Brian Solis, of FutureWorks, defines **social media** as "any tool or service that uses the Internet to facilitate conversations."[1] However, social media can also be defined relative to traditional advertising like television and magazines in that traditional marketing media offers a mass media method of interacting with consumers, while social media offers more one-to-one ways to meet consumers. Social media also has more sophisticated methods of measuring how marketers meet and interact with consumers than traditional advertising. Currently, social media includes tools and platforms like social networks, blogs, microblogs, and media sharing sites, which can be accessed through a growing number of devices such as computers, laptops, Smartphones, e-readers, tablets, and netbooks. This technology changes daily, offering consumers

social media any tool or service that uses the Internet to facilitate conversations

What do you think?

Marketers are adept at using social media as a marketing tool.

1 2 3 4 5 6 7
STRONGLY DISAGREE   STRONGLY AGREE

Find out what others think at the CourseMate for MKTG. Log in at cengagebrain.com.

351

new ways to experience social media platforms, which must constantly innovate to keep up with consumer demands.

At the basic level, social media consumers want to exchange information, collaborate with others, and have conversations. Social media has changed how and where conversations take place, making human interaction global through popular technology. Research shows that more than 73 percent of active online users have read a blog and more than half belong to at least one social network. Marketing consultant John Haydon said, "The real value of social media is that it exponentially leverages word-of-mouth."[2] Clearly, conversations are happening online; it is up to the marketer to decide if engaging in those conversations will be profitable and to find the most effective method of entering the conversation.

Marketers are interested in online communications because it is wildly popular; brands, companies, individuals, and celebrities promote their messages online. Today, Lady Gaga reigns as the queen of social media: She holds the record for the living person with the most Facebook fans; on Twitter she directly inter-

acts with her millions of followers; the music video for the song "Bad Romance" holds the title of most viewed video ever on YouTube. Lady Gaga's celebrity is due in large part to being a highly effective brand—her messages resonate with audiences worldwide, and she makes her brand easily accessible through popular social media platforms. Her carefully crafted social media strategy has translated into real money; Lady Gaga recently debuted on the Forbes Celebrity 100 Power List for 2010 at number 4, earning more than $62 million (including her corporate sponsorships and endorsements) in the past 12 months.[3] As far as brands go, very few marketers have leveraged social media to drive sales of core products better than Lady Gaga.[4]

How Consumers Use Social Media

Hoping to replicate some of Lady Gaga's social media success, many marketers are looking to get their message on the fastest-growing social media platform—Facebook. Facebook originated as a community for college students that opened to the general public as its popularity grew. There are hundreds of millions of users on Facebook: If Facebook were a country, it would be the third largest in the world. The largest area of growth in new profiles is the baby boomer segment, who use it as a way to connect with old friends and keep up with family. Other social networks, like MySpace and Bebo, offer alternative networks to other demographics. MySpace has a large music-oriented following, and many bands and musicians preview albums and music videos on MySpace pages. Videos are one of the most popular tools by which marketers reach consumers, and YouTube is by far the largest online video repository—it has more content than any major television network. Due to its connection with Google, YouTube offers a powerful search tool as well.[5] Flickr is a popular photo sharing site, where millions of people upload new photos daily. Twitter boasts hundreds of millions of registered users who average billions of tweets daily (just check out the Web site GigaTweet to see a running total). Technorati tracks hundreds of millions of blogs and indexes an estimated two million new blog posts per day.[6] More than half of Technorati's active users have uploaded photos, and almost a quarter have uploaded videos. The bottom line, according to Universal McCann's Comparative Study on Social Media Trends, is that "if you are online, you are using social media."[7]

Increased usage of alternative platforms like Smartphones and tablet computers has further contributed to the proliferation of social media usage. In the United States, 90 percent of 18- to 29-year-olds own a mobile phone. Among this group, 95 percent have sent a text message, 65 percent have accessed the Internet, and at least 23 percent have accessed a social networking site using their phones.[8] In April 2010, Apple released the much anticipated iPad tablet computer. More than 8,500 native iPad apps (many of which connect to social networks) are available for download, and within the first two months of the tablet's release, 35 million downloads had already been recorded.[9] The overall impact of tablet computing on social media (and thus the discipline of marketing) is yet to be seen, but given the incredible impact that the Smartphone has had in its short life span, tablets could prove to be game changing.

Social Commerce A new area of growth in social media is **social commerce**, which combines social media with the basics of e-commerce. Social commerce is a subset of e-commerce that involves the interaction and user contribution aspects of social online media to assist online buying and selling of products and services.[10] Basically, social commerce relies on user-generated content on Web sites to assist consumers with purchases. On Polyvore.com, members create collages of photographs of clothing items that create a fashionable look. Photographs come from various retailers and include accessories, clothes, shoes, and makeup. Once the look is complete, other members view the looks and can click on the individual items to see price and retailers. Social commerce sites often include ratings and recommendations (like Amazon) and social shopping tools (like Groupon). In general, social commerce sites are designed to help consumers make more informed decisions on purchases or services.

Social Media and Integrated Marketing Communications

While marketers typically employ a social media strategy alongside traditional channels like print and broadcast, many budget pendulums are swinging toward social media. In the U.S. Interactive Marketing Forecast, 2009–2014, Forrester Research predicts that mobile marketing, social media, e-mail marketing, display advertising, and search marketing will grow from 13 percent of advertising spending in 2010 to more than 21 percent of spending by

2014. The bulk of this budget will still go to search marketing (almost doubling in 2014), but substantial investments will also be made in mobile marketing and social media.[11]

A unique consequence of social media is the widespread shift from one-to-many communication to many-to-many communication. Instead of simply putting a brand advertisement on television with no means for feedback, social media allows marketers to have conversations with consumers, forge deeper relationships, and build brand loyalty. Social media also allows consumers to connect with each other, share opinions, and collaborate on new ideas according to their interests. In 2009, Grey Goose Vodka created an online community exclusively for bartenders. This community enabled mixologists to chat with each other and share ideas and anecdotes about their common trade. The Grey Goose online community was intended not so much to advertise the brand but to create a shared space and provide genuine value to bartenders. The brand advocacy then came naturally.[12] With social media, the audience is often in control of the message, the medium, the response, or all three. This distribution of control is often difficult for companies to adjust to, but the focus of social marketing is unavoidably on the audience, and the brand must adapt to succeed. The interaction between producer and consumer becomes less about entertaining and more about listening, influencing, and engaging.

In 2009, Hewlett-Packard used social media to avert a public relations (PR) crisis after a video claiming that HP was racist garnered two million views on YouTube. Because it was aware of its customers' social dialogues, HP learned about the groundswell early on and was able to quell the story before it gained too much momentum.[13] Mountain Dew's marketing team tested the limits of consumer control and the power of social media by moving the brand's advertising almost entirely online. The team tapped into the brand's core consumer demographic—18- to 39-year-old males with strong Facebook, MySpace, and YouTube presences—to build line extensions and help choose a marketing partner.

Using consumers to develop and market product is called **crowdsourcing**. Crowdsourcing describes how the input of

social commerce
a subset of e-commerce that involves the interaction and user contribution aspects of social online media to assist online buying and selling of products and services

crowdsourcing
using consumers to develop and market product

many people can be leveraged to make decisions that used to be based on the input of only a few people.[14] Companies get feedback on marketing campaigns, new product ideas, and other marketing decisions by asking customers to weigh in. After major retailer Gap launched a redesigned logo that received negative response, it opted to crowdsource a consumer-approved logo. Gap asked its customers to design an updated logo to replace the new, unpopular logo. After more than 1,000 people posted negative comments about the effort on its Facebook page, Gap elected to revert back to the old logo.[15] Crowdsourcing offers a way for companies to engage heavy users of a brand and receive input, which in turn increases those users' brand advocacy and lessens the likelihood that a change will be disliked enough to drive away loyal customers.

LO 2 Creating and Leveraging a Social Media Campaign

Social media is an exciting new field, and its potential for expanding a brand's impact is enormous. Because its costs are often minimal and its learning curve is relatively low, some organizations are tempted to dive headfirst into social media. However, as with any marketing campaign, it is always important to start with a strategy. For most organizations, this means starting with a marketing or communications plan, as covered in Chapter 2.

The new communication paradigm created by a shift to social media marketing raises questions about categorization. In light of the convergence of traditional and digital media, researchers have explored different ways that interactive marketers can categorize media types. One such researcher, Sean Corcoran of Forrester Research, devised a distinction between owned, earned, and paid media. **Owned media** is online content that an organization creates and controls. Owned media includes blogs, Web sites, Facebook pages, and other social media presences. The purpose of owned media is to develop deeper relationships with customers. **Earned media** is a PR term connoting free media such as mainstream media coverage. In an interactive space, media is earned through word

of mouth or online buzz about something the brand is doing. Earned media includes viral videos, retweets, comments on blogs, and other forms of customer feedback resulting from a social media presence. **Paid media** is content paid for by the company to be placed online. Paid media is similar to marketing efforts that utilize traditional media, like newspaper, magazine, and television advertisements. In an interactive space, paid media includes display advertising, paid search words, and other types of direct online advertising.[16]

To leverage all three types of media, marketers must follow a few key guidelines. First, they must maximize owned media by reaching out beyond their existing Web sites to create portfolios of digital touch points. This is especially true for brands with tight budgets, as the organization may not be able to afford much paid media. Second, marketers must recognize that aptitude at public and media relations no longer translates into earned media. Instead, markets must learn how to listen and respond to stakeholders. This

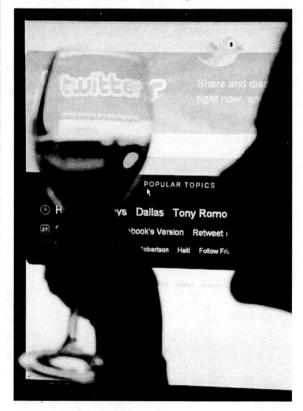

A young woman holds a glass of red wine during an online wine tasting. People from all parts of Germany regularly meet online to taste wine and exchange opinions via Twitter, generating earned media buzz for the winery whose wine they are drinking.

© Z1031/JAN WOITAS/DPA/CORBIS

will stimulate word of mouth. Finally, marketers must understand that paid media is not dead but should serve as a catalyst to drive customer engagement.[17] If balanced correctly, all three types of media can be powerful tools for interactive marketers.

The Listening System

The first action a marketing team should take when initiating a social media campaign is simple—it should just listen. Developing an effective listening system is necessary to both understanding and engaging an online audience. Marketers must not only hear what is being said about the brand, the industry, the compe-

tition, and the customer—they must pay attention to who is saying what. The specific ways that customers and noncustomers rate, rank, critique, praise, deride, recommend, snub, and generally discuss brands are all important. Negative comments and complaints are of particular importance, both because they can illuminate unknown brand flaws and because they are the comments that tend to go viral. Online tools such as Google Alerts, Google Blog Search, Twitter Search, SiteVolume, Social Mention and Socialcast are extremely helpful in the development of efficient, effective listening. In Exhibit 22.1, social media strategist Jeremiah Owyang outlines eight stages of effective

EXHIBIT 22.1
Eight Stages of Effective Listening

Stage	Description	Resources Required	Purpose
Stage 1: Without Objective	The organization has established a listening system but has no goals.	Social media notification tools (Google Alerts)	Keep up with brand and competitor information.
Stage 2: Tracking brand mentions	The organization tracks mentions in social space but has no guidance on next steps.	A listening platform with key word report capabilities (Radian6)	Track discussions, understand sentiment, and identify influencers to improve overall marketing strategy.
Stage 3: Identifying market risks and opportunities	The organization seeks discussions online that may result in identification of problems and opportunities.	A listening platform with a large staff dedicated to the client (Converseon)	Staff seeks out discussions and reports to other teams, like product development and sales. These teams then engage the customers directly or conduct further research.
Stage 4: Improving campaign efficiency	The organization uses tools to get real-time data on marketing efficiency.	Web analytics software (Google Analytics)	See a wealth of information about consumers' behavior on their Web sites (and social media).
Stage 5: Measuring customer satisfaction	The organization collects information about satisfaction, including measures of sentiment.	Insight platforms that offer online focus group solutions	Measure impact of satisfaction or frustration during interaction.
Stage 6: Responding to customer inquiry	The organization identifies customers where they are (e.g., Twitter).	A customer service team is allowed to make real-time responses	Generate high sense of satisfaction for customer but generates public complaints.
Stage 7: Better understanding of customers	The organization adds social information to demographics and psychographics to gain a better profile.	Social customer relationship management (CRM) systems to sync data	Social CRM marries database and social media to create a powerful analytical tool. (See Chapter 21 for more on CRM.)
Stage 8: Being proactive and anticipating customer demands	The organization examines previous patterns of data and social behavior to anticipate needs.	Advanced customer database with predictive application (yet to be created)	Modify social media strategy to preempt consumer behavior modifications based on trends.

SOURCES: Jeremiah Owyang, "Web Strategy Matrix: The Eight Stages of Listening," Web Strategy, November 10, 2009, www.web-strategist.com/blog/2009/11/10/evolution-the-eight-stages-of-listening/; Jim Sterne, *Social Media Metrics* (Hoboken, NJ: John Wiley & Sons, 2010).

listening. Listening to customers communicate about one's own brand can be very revealing, but social media is also a great way to monitor competitors' online presences, fans, and followers. Paying attention to the ways that competing brands attract and engage with their customers can be particularly enlightening for both small businesses and global brands.

Social Media Objectives

After establishing a listening platform, the organization should develop a list of objectives for its social media team to accomplish. These objectives must be developed with a clear understanding of how social media changes the communication dynamic with and for customers. Remember—attempting to reach a mass audience with a static message will never be as successful as influencing people through conversation. Marketing managers must set objectives that reflect this reality. Here are some practical ideas that marketing managers should consider when setting social media objectives:

▸▸ *Listen and learn.* Monitor what is being said about the brand and competitors, and glean insights about audiences. Use online tools and do research to implement the best social media practices. If you have established a listening strategy, this objective should already be accomplished.

▸▸ *Build relationships and awareness.* Open dialogues with stakeholders by giving them compelling content across a variety of media. Engage in conversations, and answer customers' questions candidly. This will both increase Web traffic and boost your search engine ranking.

▸▸ *Promote products and services.* The clearest path to increasing the bottom line using social media is to get customers talking about products and services, which ultimately translates into sales.

▸▸ *Manage your reputation.* Develop and improve the brand's reputation by responding to comments and criticism that appear on blogs and forums. Additionally, organizations can position themselves as helpful and benevolent by participating in other forums and discussions.

▸▸ *Improve customer service.* Customer comments about products and services will not always be positive. Use social media to search out displeased customers and engage them directly in order to solve their service issues.

LO 3 Evaluation and Measurement of Social Media

Social media has the potential to revolutionize the way organizations communicate with stakeholders.

BUILDING TRUST ONLINE

In order to succeed with any marketing campaign, customers' trust must be earned. Angie's List is a great example of a Web site that consumers trust to guide them to reliable service providers. Here are some guidelines for earning customer trust:

- Online content must be up to date, easy to understand, and valuable. Be the translator for your customers as they wade through message after message.

- Make sure that your Web site is easy to navigate and gives customers quick access to the information and media they came for.

- Make your social space fun and interactive. Interactivity is all about forging relationships. Treat customers like people, not data, and they will treat you as a person, not junk mail.

- Follow contemporary design trends. Your audience will inevitably judge your book by its cover.[18]

Angie's List

Angie's List is a word-of-mouth network for consumers where homeowners share real-life experiences with local service companies. With more than 500,000 members across 70 cities and growing, the online list is a way to find trustworthy companies that perform high-quality work.

	Cities on Angie's List	Major markets added	Total subscribers in all markets
2003	16	△	119,000
2004	24	▢	148,000
2005	27	○	245,000
2006	68	●▪	Nearly 500,000

Seattle ○
Portland ○
San Francisco
San Jose ● Sacramento
Fresno ● Las Vegas
○ Los Angeles
San Diego ▢ ● Phoenix
Denver
Fort Worth ▢▢ Dallas
Houston ▢
Kansas City
St. Louis
Detroit
Pittsburgh ▢ ● New York
Washington ▢ Philadelphia
Baltimore
△ Atlanta

Angie's List has yet to open in some of these markets.

© 2006 MCT
Source: Angie's List
Graphic: San Jose Mercury News

© KRT/NEWSCOM

Given the relative ease and efficiency with which organizations can use social media, a positive return on investment (ROI) is likely for many—if not most—organizations. A Forrester Research report found that 95 percent of marketers planned to increase or maintain their investments in social media. However, though they understand that it is a worthwhile investment, most marketers have not been able to figure out how to measure the benefits of social media. As social media evolves, so do the measurements and metrics that track it.[19] Yet, as with traditional advertising, marketers lack hard evidence as to the relative effectiveness of these tools. Some marketers accept this unknown variable and focus on the fact that social media is less about ROI than about deepening relationships with customers; others work tirelessly to better understand the measurement of social media's effectiveness. While literally hundreds of metrics have been developed to measure social media's value, these metrics are meaningless unless they are tied to key performance indicators.[20] For example, a local coffee shop manager may measure the success of her social media presence by the raw number of friends on Facebook and followers on Twitter she has accumulated. But these numbers depend entirely on context. The rate of accumulation, investment per fan and follower, and comparison to similarly sized coffee shops are all important variables to consider. Without context, measurements are meaningless.

THREE AREAS OF MEASUREMENT:

» *Social media measurement:* Ever-changing metrics that are used to determine the ROI of each tool. Social media measurement determines, for example, the conversion rate of a Facebook friend. Tools include Google Analytics, Social Mention, Twinfluence, Twitalyzer, and Klout, among others.[21]

» *Public relations measurement:* Since many modern PR campaigns entail social media, PR measurement exists to calculate the impact of social media on press coverage and other elements of PR. Tools include DIY Dashboard, Tealium, and Vocus, which quantizes information such as share of voice relative to competitors, stories by location, and a sentiment analysis for each press hit.

» *Social media monitoring:* Tools that are used less for campaign metrics and more for customer service improvement, brand management, and prospecting. Tools include BlogPulse, Technorati, Trendrr, Google Trends, Tweetdeck, Visible Technologies, and Trackur. Google News Alerts, a free online tool, leverages Google's search technology to report relevant news stories and blog posts about any topic or organization.

LO 4 Social Behavior of Consumers

Once objectives have been determined and measurement tools have been implemented, it is important to identify the consumer. Who is using social media? What types of social media do they use? Does Facebook attract younger users? Do Twitter users retweet viral videos? These types of questions must be considered because they determine not only which tools will be most effective but also, more importantly, whether launching a social media campaign even makes sense for a particular organization.

Understanding an audience necessitates understanding how that audience uses social media. In *Groundswell*, Charlene Li and Josh Bernoff of Forrester Research identify six categories of social media users, which are listed below.

> *Creators:* Those who produce and share online content like blogs, Web sites, articles, and videos

Facebook CEO Mark Zuckerberg introduces new features for Facebook during a one-day developer conference sponsored by Facebook. Behind him, you can see myriad ways social networking sites could interact.

2 *Critics:* Those who post comments, ratings, and reviews of products and services on blogs and forums

3 *Collectors:* Those who use RSS feeds to collect information and vote for Web sites online

4 *Joiners:* Those who maintain a social networking profile and visit other sites

5 *Spectators:* Those who read blogs, listen to podcasts, watch videos, and generally consume media

6 *Inactives:* Those who do none of these things[22]

A 2009 study determined that 24 percent of social media users functioned as creators, 37 percent functioned as critics, 21 percent functioned as collectors, 51 percent functioned as joiners, and 73 percent functioned as spectators. While participation in each of these categories trended upward, inactives decreased from 44 percent in 2007 to only 18 percent in 2009.[23] However, recent Forrester research shows that the number of people who contribute content is slowing down. Participation in most categories fell slightly, prompting analysts to recommend that marketers re-examine how they are engaging with their customers online. Despite the apparent slowdown, research also shows that more social networking "rookies" are classified as joiners. Another bright spot is a new category, "conversationalists," or people who post status updates on social networking sites and microblogging services such as Twitter. Conversationalists represent 31 percent of users.[24]

LO 5 Social Media Tools: Consumer- and Corporate-Generated Content

A number of tools and platforms can be employed as part of an organization's social media strategy. Blogs, microblogs, social networks, media creation and sharing sites, social news sites, location-based social networking sites, review sites, and virtual worlds and online gaming all have their place in a company's social marketing plan. These are all tools in a market-

ing manager's toolbox, available when applicable to the marketing plan but not necessarily to be used all at once. Because of the breakneck pace at which technology changes, this list of resources will surely look markedly different five years from now. More tools emerge every day, and branding strategies must keep up with the ever-changing world of technology. For now, the resources highlighted in this section remain a marketer's strongest set of platforms for conversing and strengthening relationships with customers.

Blogs

Blogs have become staples in many social media strategies and are often a brand's social media centerpiece. A **blog** is a publicly accessible Web page that functions as an interactive journal, whereby readers can post comments on the author's entries. Some experts believe that every company should have a blog that speaks to current and potential customers, not as consumers, but as people.[25] Blogs allows marketers to create content in the form of posts, which ideally build trust and a sense of authenticity in customers. Once posts are made, audience members can provide feedback through comments. Because it opens a dialogue and gives customers a voice, the comments section of a blog post is one of the most important avenues of conversation between brands and consumers.

Blogs can be divided into two broad categories: corporate and professional blogs, and noncorporate blogs such as personal blogs. **Corporate blogs** are sponsored by a company or one of its brands and are maintained by one or more of the company's employees. They disseminate marketing-controlled information and are effective platforms for developing thought leadership, fostering better relationships with stakeholders, maximizing search engine optimization, attracting new customers, endearing the organization with anecdotes and stories about brands, and providing an active forum for testing new ideas. Because blogs are designed to be updated daily, corporate blogs are dynamic and highly flexible, giving marketers the opportunity to adapt their messages more frequently than any other communication channel.

Several brands use blogs effectively. GM's FastLane Blog is considered a corporate best. It is packed with audio, video, and photos and is organized into categories that offer something for everyone. One of FastLane Blog's biggest draws is its high-quality writing. Each reader comment is answered in a fun and pithy tone, encouraging participation and continued readership (http://fastlane.gmblogs.com). Vans Girls

Blog, the official blog for Vans Shoes, is another corporate success. By posting fashion photos, organizing events, and highlighting style and celebrity news, Vans Girls Blog captivates its dedicated audience with content that is both interesting and relevant to the Vans brand. This blog is a great example of à corporate blog aimed at a singular audience (http://offthewall vansgirls.wordpress.com). Southwest Airlines (Nuts about Southwest, www.blogsouthwest.com) and Dell (which has created a hub for several blogs) also produce successful corporate blogs.

In contrast, **noncorporate blogs** are independent and not associated with the marketing efforts of any particular company or brand. Because these blogs contain information not controlled by marketers, they are perceived to be more authentic than corporate blogs. Mommy bloggers, women who review children's products and discuss family related topics on their personal blogs, use noncorporate blogs. The goal of mommy blogs is to share parenting tips and experiences and become part of a community. Because of the popularity of these and other types of blogs, many bloggers receive products and/or money from companies in exchange for a review. Many bloggers disclose where they received the product or if they were paid, but an affiliation is not always clear. Because of this, bloggers must disclose any financial relationship with a company per Federal Trade Commission rules. It is important for marketing managers to understand the rules behind complimentary products to bloggers as well as the high potential for social buzz; four out of five noncorporate bloggers post brand or product reviews. Even if a company does not have a formal social media strategy, chances are the brand is still out in the blogosphere, whether or not a marketing manager approached a blogger.

noncorporate blogs independent blogs that are not associated with the marketing efforts of any particular company or brand
microblogs blogs with strict post length limits

Sean Combs, aka P. Diddy, shows off his Twitter page. Combs uses Twitter as a blog to keep fans updated on his activities.

Microblogs

Microblogs are blogs with strict post length limits. Twitter, the most popular microblogging platform, requires that posts be no more than 140 characters in length. However, there are several other platforms, including Jaiku, Tumblr, Plurk, and, of course, Facebook's status updates. Originally designed as a short messaging system used for internal communication, Twitter has gained global popularity and is now used as a communication and research tool by individuals and brands around the world. A large part of Twitter's success stems from the fact that the platform is extremely versatile: Posts and private messages can be sent and received via text messages, Smartphone apps, desktop clients, external Web sites, tablet computers, and e-mail, among others. Twitter posts, commonly called tweets, can be amended with photos, videos, and external links. Recently, Twitter has changed its interface to include visuals like video and photos and has added new products to try to monetize the site. It has also developed promoted tweets, which are ads that appear in search results and user feeds both on Twitter.com and third-party clients that access the service, such as TweetDeck, twhirl, TwitterBerry and Tweetie.

Despite its strict character limit, Twitter has proven effective for disseminating breaking news, promoting longer blog posts and campaigns, sharing links, announcing events, and promoting sales. By following, retweeting, responding to potential customers' tweets, and by tweeting content that inspires customers to engage the brand, corporate Twitter users can lay a foundation for meaningful two-way

social networking sites Web sites that allow individuals to connect—or network—with friends, peers, and business associates

conversation quickly and effectively. Research has found that when operated correctly, corporate Twitter accounts are well respected and well received. Twitter can be used to build communities; aid in customer service; gain prospects; increase awareness; and, in the case of nonprofits, raise funds.

The ways a business can use Twitter to successfully engage with customers are almost limitless. The Kogi Korean BBQ truck provides gourmet tacos to Los Angeles residents throughout the night. Because traffic, construction, and other issues prevent the truck from parking at the same location every night, owner Mark Manguera uses Twitter to inform his late-night customers of where the truck will be located each evening. Because its tweets are informative, useful, and relevant to the business, Kogi Korean BBQ has built a Twitter following of tens of thousands.[26]

Social Networks

Social networking sites allow individuals to connect—or network—with friends, peers, and business associates. Connections may be made around shared interests, shared environments, or personal relationships. Depending on the site, connected individuals may be able to send each other messages, track each other's activity, see each other's personal information, share multimedia, or comment on each other's blog and microblog posts. Depending on its goals, there are several social networks that a marketing team might engage as part of its social media strategy: Facebook is the largest and fastest-growing network; MySpace caters to younger audiences; LinkedIn is geared toward professionals and businesses who use it to recruit professionals; and niche networks like Bebo, Last.fm, WeAreTeachers, BlackPlanet, and Match.com cater to specialized markets. There is a niche social network for just about every demographic and interest. Beyond those already established, an organization may decide to develop a brand-specific social network or community. While all social networking sites are different, some marketing goals can be accomplished on any such site. Given the right strategy, increasing awareness, targeting audiences, promoting products, forging relationships, highlighting expertise and leadership, attracting event participants, performing research, and generating new business are attainable marketing goals on any social network.

Facebook is by far the largest social networking site. While individual Facebook users create profiles,

brands, organizations, and nonprofit causes operate as pages. As opposed to individual profiles, all pages are public and are thus subject to search engine indexing. By maintaining a popular Facebook page, a brand not only increases its social media presence, it also helps to optimize search engine results. Pages often include photo and video albums, brand information, and links to external sites. The most useful page feature, however, is the Wall. The Wall allows a brand to communicate directly with fans via status updates, which enables marketers to build databases of interested stakeholders. When an individual becomes a fan of your organization or posts on your Wall, that information is shared with the individual's friends, creating a mini viral marketing campaign. Other Facebook marketing tools include groups, applications, and ads. Facebook is an extremely important platform for social marketers.

Facebook has proved to be fertile ground for new marketing ideas and campaigns. By creating a Facebook application called Real or Fake, Adobe used the

EXHIBIT 22.2
Facebook Lingo

Non-Individual (Usually Corporate)	Individual
Page	Profile
Fan of a page, tells fan's friends that the user is a fan, creates mini viral campaign	Friend a person, send private messages, write on the Wall, see friend-only content
Public, searchable	Privacy options, not searchable unless user enabled

© CENGAGE LEARNING 2011

© SAEED KHAN/AFP/GETTY IMAGES

social network's built-in software platform to advertise student editions of the Photoshop photo editing software to college students. When users installed the Real or Fake application, they gained access to weekly images, which they were challenged to distinguish as authentic or digitally manipulated. After they took the challenge, users were directed to tutorials that demonstrated how the altered photos were manipulated using Photoshop. By the end of the campaign, Adobe had earned additional Facebook fans and had witnessed an increase in page views from 5,057 to 53,000 per week. More than 6 percent of Real or Fake users actually purchased the Photoshop software. Through this campaign, Adobe did not just establish a social media presence but also created a novel way to engage its fans.[27] Coca-Cola's Facebook Page, boasting five million fans, was developed by two individuals in California. Rather than assuming its management, Coca-Cola decided to work with fans to maintain the page. Again, to succeed in social media, organizations must learn to share control with the customer.

LinkedIn features many of the same services as Facebook (profiles, status updates, private messages, company pages, and groups) but is oriented around business and professional connections. Unlike Facebook, LinkedIn features a question-and-answer forum, where users can ask for advice and share expertise in specific fields, and a file hosting service, where users can upload intellectual property like slides, presentations, and other shared documents.[28] LinkedIn is used primarily by professionals who wish to build their personal brands online and businesses who are recruiting employees and freelancers.

These images were used as part of Adobe's Real or Fake game on Facebook. Can you tell which is real and which is fake? The chameleon is fake (those are goat horns imposed on its head), and the road is real (it's in Morocco).

Media Sharing Sites

Media sharing sites allow users to upload and distribute multimedia content like videos and photos. Sites such as YouTube and Flickr are particularly useful to brands' social marketing strategies because they add a vibrant interactive channel on which to disseminate content. The distribution of user-generated content has changed markedly over the past few years. Today, organizations can tell compelling brand stories through videos, photos, and audio.

Photo sharing sites allow users to archive and share photos. Flickr, Picasa, TwitPic, Photobucket, Facebook, and Imgur all offer free photo hosting services that can be utilized by individuals and businesses alike. For example, to strengthen its image of transparency and its relationship with potential donors, the American Red Cross maintained hundreds of Hurricane Katrina disaster photos and tracked sentiments about Red Cross services on Flickr throughout the crisis.[29]

Video creation and distribution have also gained popularity among marketers because of video's rich ability to tell stories. YouTube, the highest-trafficked video-based Web site and the sixth highest-trafficked site overall, allows users to upload and stream their videos to an enthusiastic and active community.[30] YouTube is not only large (in terms of visitors), it attracts a diverse base of users: Age and gender demographics are remarkably balanced.

Many entertainment companies and movie marketers have used YouTube as a showcase for new products, specials, and movie trailers. For example, Lions Gate Entertainment purchased ad space on the YouTube home page in 15 countries to promote the *Avatar* movie trailer. Some teen clothing brands like Forever 21 and JCPenney build followings on YouTube by posting hauls—videos made by teens that focus on fashion. Clearly, user-generated content can be a powerful tool for brands that can use it effectively.

A podcast, another type of user-generated media, is a digital audio or video file that is distributed serially for other people to listen to or watch. Podcasts can be streamed online, played on a computer, uploaded to a portable media player (like an iPod), or downloaded onto a Smartphone (like HTC's Droid Incredible). Podcasts are like radio shows that are distributed

© KENNETH JOW/© ISTOCKPHOTO.COM/ERIC ISSELÉE

media sharing sites Web sites that allow users to upload and distribute multimedia content like videos and photos through various means and not linked to a scheduled time slot. While they have not experienced the exponential growth rates of other digital platforms, podcasts have amassed a steadily growing number of loyal devotees. A good example of effective use of the medium is Fidelity Investments' Podcast Series, which offers clients and nonclients alike free information about stock market investment.[31]

Social News Sites

Social news sites allow users to decide which content is promoted on a given Web site by voting that content up or down. Users post news stories and multimedia for the community to vote on crowd-sourced communities such as Reddit, Digg, and Yahoo! Buzz. The more interest from readers, the higher the story or video is ranked. Marketers have found that these sites are useful for promoting campaigns, creating conversations around related issues, and building Web site traffic.[32] If it is voted up, discussed, and shared enough to be listed among the most popular topics of the day, content posted to a crowd sourced site can go viral across other sites and, eventually, the entire Web. Social bookmarking sites such as Del.ici.ous and StumbleUpon are similar to social news sites but the objective of their users is to collect, save, and share interesting and valuable links. On these sites, users categorize links with short, descriptive tags. Users can search the site's database of links by specific tags or can add their own tags to others' links. In this way, tags serve as the foundation for information gathering and sharing on social bookmarking sites.[33]

Location-Based Social Networking Sites

Considered by many to be the next big thing in social marketing, location sites like GoWalla and Loopt should be on every marketer's radar. Essentially, **location-based social networking sites** combine the fun of social networking with the utility of location-based GPS technology. Foursquare, one of the most popular location sites, treats location-based micronetworking as a game: Users earn badges and special statuses based on their number of visits to particular locations. Users can write and read short reviews and tips about businesses, organize meet-ups, and see which Foursquare-using friends are nearby. Foursquare updates can also

be posted to linked Twitter and Facebook accounts for followers and friends to see. Location sites such as Foursquare are particularly useful social marketing tools for local businesses, especially when combined with sales promotions like coupons, special offers, contests, and events. Location sites can be harnessed to forge lasting relationships with and deeply engrained loyalty in customers.[34] For example, a local restaurant can allow consumers to check in on Foursquare using their Smartphone and receive a coupon for that day's purchases. Since the location site technology is relatively new, many brands are still figuring out how best to utilize Foursquare. Facebook added Places to capitalize on this location-based technology, which allows people to "check in" and share their location with their online friends. It will be interesting to see how use of this technology grows over time.

Review Sites

Individuals tend to trust other people's opinions when it comes to purchasing. According to Nielsen Media Research, more than 70 percent of consumers said that they trusted online consumer opinions. This percentage is much higher than that of consumers who trust traditional advertising. Based on the early work of Amazon and eBay to integrate user opinions into product and seller pages, countless Web sites allowing users to voice their opinions have sprung up across every segment of the Internet market. **Review sites** allow consumers to post, read, rate, and comment on

© HANDOUT/MCT/NEWSCOM

opinions regarding all kinds of products and services. For example, Yelp, the most active local review directory on the Web, combines customer critiques of local businesses with business information and elements of social networking to create an engaging, informative experience. On Yelp, users scrutinize local restaurants, fitness centers, tattoo parlors, and other businesses, each of which has a detailed profile page. Business owners and representatives can edit their organizations' pages and respond to Yelp reviews both privately and publicly.[35] By giving marketers the opportunity to respond to their customers directly and put their businesses in a positive light, review sites certainly serve as useful tools for local and national businesses.

Virtual Worlds and Online Gaming

Virtual worlds and online gaming present additional opportunities for marketers to engage with consumers. These include massive multiplayer online games (MMOGs) such as *World of Warcraft* and *The Sims Online* as well as online communities (or virtual worlds) such as Second Life, Poptropica, and Habbo Hotel. Consultancy firm KZero Worldwide reported that almost 800 million people participated in some sort of virtual world experience, and the sector's annual revenue approached $1 billion. Much of this revenue has come from in-game advertising—virtual world environments are often fertile grounds for branded content. Several businesses, such as IBM and consultancy firm Crayon, have developed profitable trade presences in Second Life. IBM has used its Second Life space to hold virtual conferences with more than 200 participants, while Crayon has held a number of virtual networking events and meet and greets in the virtual world.[36] Other organizations, such as the Centers for Disease Control and Prevention and the American Cancer Society, have held their own virtual events in Second Life. While unfamiliar to and even intimidating for many traditional marketers, the field of virtual worlds is an important, viable, and growing consideration for social media marketing.

One area of growth is social gaming. Nearly 25 percent of people play games within social networking sites like Facebook and MySpace. The typical player is a 43-year-old woman with a full-time job and college education. Women are most likely to play with real-world friends or relatives as opposed to strangers. Most play multiple times per week and more than 30 percent play daily. Facebook is by far the largest social network for gaming. The top five games on Facebook are Farmville, Bejeweled Blitz, Texas Hold'em Poker, Café World, and Mafia Wars. Because of the popularity of gaming with friends and relatives through these sites, marketers have to integrate their message based on the social network platforms and the demographic participating in social gaming.[37]

Another popular type of online gaming targets a different group—MMOGs target the 18- to 34-year-old males. In these environments, thousands of people play simultaneously, and the games have revenues of more than $400 billion annually. Regardless of the type of experience, brands must be creative in how they integrate into games. Social and real-world–like titles are the most appropriate for marketing and advertising (as opposed to fantasy games), and promotions typically include special events, competitions, and sweepstakes. In some games (like *Sims*), having ads increases the authenticity. For example, Nike offers shoes in *Sims Online* that allow the player to run faster.

LO 6 Social Media and Mobile Technology

While much of the excitement in social media has been based on Web sites and new technology uses, much of the growth lies in new platforms. These platforms include the multitude of Smartphones like iPhones and BlackBerrys as well as netbooks and iPads. The major implications of new platforms mean consumers can access popular Web sites like Facebook, Mashable, Twitter, and Foursquare from their various platforms.

Mobile and Smartphone Technology

More than 25 percent of the world's population— and more than 75 percent of the U.S. population— owns a mobile phone.[38] It is no surprise then that the mobile platform is such an effective marketing tool— especially when targeting a younger audience. In the 2008 presidential campaign, Barack Obama's staff utilized text messaging to raise funds and organize support from college students, while grassroots organizations such as DoSomething.org used messaging to alert young people to volunteering opportunities. Smartphones up the ante by allowing individuals to do nearly everything they can do with a computer— from anywhere. With a Smartphone in hand, reading a blog, writing an e-mail, scheduling a meeting, posting to Facebook, playing a multiplayer game, watching a video, taking a picture, using GPS, and surfing the Internet might all occur during one ten-minute car ride. Smartphone technology, often considered the crowning achievement in digital convergence and social media integration, has opened the door to modern mobile advertising as a viable marketing strategy.

According to an eMarketer survey, U.S. mobile marketing spending reached nearly $593 million in 2010 and is expected to grow. There are several reasons for the recent popularity of mobile marketing. First, an effort to standardize mobile platforms has resulted in a low barrier to entry. Second, especially given younger audiences, there are more consumers than ever acclimating to once-worrisome privacy and pricing policies. Third, because most consumers carry their Smartphones

One example of mobile technology is scanning bar codes off a mobile screen—a convenient and eco-friendly way to add value to customers.

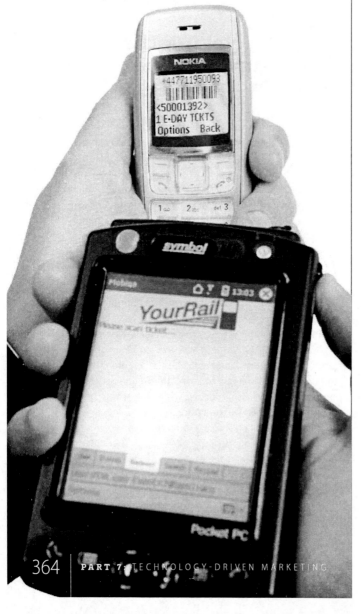

with them at all times, mobile marketing is uniquely effective at garnering consumer attention in real time. Fourth, mobile marketing is measurable: Metrics and usage statistics make it an effective tool for gaining insight into consumer behavior. Finally, mobile marketing's response rate is higher than that of traditional media types like print and broadcast advertisement. Some common mobile marketing tools include:

▸▸ *SMS (short message service):* 160-character text messages sent to and from cell phones. SMS is typically integrated with other tools.

▸▸ *MMS (multimedia messaging service):* Similar to SMS but allows the attachment of images, videos, ringtones, and other multimedia to text messages.

▸▸ *Mobile Web sites (MOBI and WAP Web sites):* Web sites designed specifically for viewing and navigation on mobile devices.

▸▸ *Mobile ads:* Visual advertisements integrated into text messages, applications, and mobile Web sites. Mobile ads are often sold on a cost-per-click basis.

▸▸ *Bluetooth marketing:* A signal is sent to Bluetooth-enabled devices, which allows marketers to send targeted messages to users based on their geographic locations.

▸▸ *Smartphone apps:* Software designed specifically for mobile and tablet devices. These apps include software to turn phones into scanners for various types of barcodes—including QR codes like those found at the ends of Chapters 1 and 2.

Rémy Martin, maker of high-end champagne cognac, used SMS, e-mail, and Web site promotions to advertise VIP events held concurrently in six U.S. cities. To ensure younger generations' interest in the events, Rémy Martin also developed a WAP Web site called Rémy's Chill Zone, where after opting in, users could gain additional information and engage with the brand on a deeper level. As a result, all six events sold out, and Rémy Martin began dialogues with younger customers who had never before experienced its product. As this example illustrates, mobile marketing is a great way to engage Generations X and Y.[39]

Applications and Widgets

Given the widespread adoption of Apple's iPhone, RIM's BlackBerry line, Android-based phones, and other Smartphones, it's no surprise that millions of applications have been developed for the mobile market. Dozens of new and unique apps that harness mobile technology are added to mobile marketplaces every day. While many apps perform platform-specific tasks, others convert existing content into a mobile-ready format. Whether offering new or existing con-

HUMANITARIAN TEXTING

After the massive flooding in Pakistan displaced more than 14 million people, the Disasters Emergency Committee set up a texting donation service similar to that used in Haiti. It is promoted here by the Boxer Amir Khan.

In January 2010, a 7.0 earthquake struck Port-au-Prince, Haiti, and the surrounding areas. By the time the dust settled, 230,000 people had died and 1.9 million more had been left homeless. Among the organizations that pledged aid, the American Red Cross's text message-based donation campaign proved to be the true breakthrough story of this crisis. By simply texting "HAITI" to 90999, individuals could make a $10 donation to the American Red Cross that was charged to the donator's monthly mobile phone bill. More than three million individuals raised more than $32 million for American Red Cross relief work throughout Haiti—simply by sending text messages.

A number of factors made the campaign successful. The major disaster inspired long-term news coverage, and the ease of texting a donation gave many people a way to help after being exposed to the tragedy. A televised public service announcement by First Lady Michelle Obama prompted a significant spike in donations, as did an NFL play-off game segment during which commentators discussed the Red Cross campaign.[40]

tent, when an app is well branded and integrated into a company's overall marketing strategy, it can create buzz and generate customer engagement.

One organization that used its Smartphone apps effectively was when Volkswagen Group of America introduced the 2010 GTI sedan in an app called VW Real Racing GTI, which it promoted through Facebook, Twitter, YouTube, and other traditional channels. VW Real Racing GTI is a racing game that allows players to enjoy competitive racing on their mobile devices. VW Real Racing GTI connected with players—it is one of the most talked about Apps from the Apple store, with nearly five million downloads.[41] Benjamin Moore Paint focused on the fact that utility can be as effective a selling point as connectivity when it developed Color Capture, an app that allows iPhone users to match colors in photos to shades in the Benjamin Moore color collection. Users can also save their favorite colors and chip names for future use.[42]

Web widgets, also known as gadgets and badges, are software applications that run entirely within existing online platforms. Essentially, a Web widget allows a developer to embed a simple application such as a

weather forecast, horoscope, or stock market ticker into a Web site, even if the developer did not write (or does not understand) the application's source code. From a marketing perspective, widgets allow customers to display company information (such as current promotions, coupons, or news) on their own Web sites. Widgets are often cheaper than apps to develop, can extend an organization's reach beyond existing platforms, will broaden the listening system, and can make an organization easier to find.[43]

Allowing customers to promote up-to-date marketing material on their own blogs and Web sites is very appealing, but before investing in a marketing-oriented widget, a number of questions should be considered:

» Does my organization regularly publish compelling content, such as news, daily specials, or coupons, on its Web site or blog?

» Does my content engage individuals or appeal to their needs as customers?

» Is my content likely to inspire conversations with the company or with other customers? Will customers want to share my content with others?

If you can answer yes to these questions, a widget may be an effective tool for your organization.

The Changing World of Social Media

As you read through the chapter, some of the trends that are noted may already seem ancient to you. The rate of change in social media is astounding—usage statistics change daily for sites like Facebook and Twitter. Some things that are in the rumor mill as we write this may have exploded in popularity; others may have fizzled out without even appearing on your radar. In Exhibit 22.3, we've listed some of the items that seem to be on the brink of exploding on to the social media scene. Take a moment to fill in the current state of each. Have you heard of it? Has it come and gone? Maybe it is still rumored, or maybe it has petered out. This exercise highlights not only the speed with which social media changes but also the importance of keeping tabs on rumors. Doing so may result in a competitive advantage by being able to understand and invest in the next big social media site.

EXHIBIT 22.3
Social Media Trends

Site	Change	Where Is It Now?
Facebook	Threaded commenting, up/down voting comments.	
Twitter	Promoted tweets.	
Facebook/Bing	Linked searching in Bing. Search results include similar items liked by Facebook friends, and people searches pull information from your profile to find the correct person.	
Facebook Places/ Foursquare	Facebook Places is just introduced; Foursquare is gaining popularity away from major cities.	
Apple's Ping social music service	Released with iTunes 10, Ping allows users to like music, follow music stars and friends, post songs and albums, and find users with similar music tastes.	

© CENGAGE LEARNING 2011

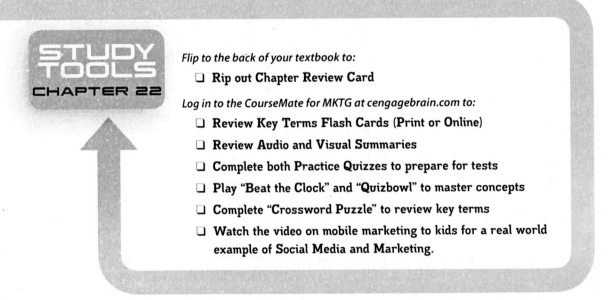

STUDY TOOLS
CHAPTER 22

Flip to the back of your textbook to:

❑ **Rip out Chapter Review Card**

Log in to the CourseMate for MKTG at cengagebrain.com to:

❑ **Review Key Terms Flash Cards (Print or Online)**

❑ **Review Audio and Visual Summaries**

❑ **Complete both Practice Quizzes to prepare for tests**

❑ **Play "Beat the Clock" and "Quizbowl" to master concepts**

❑ **Complete "Crossword Puzzle" to review key terms**

❑ **Watch the video on mobile marketing to kids for a real world example of Social Media and Marketing.**